MONEY WALKS

(PART II)

会走路的钱

(下)

Money Walks (Part II)
会走路的钱 （下）

A true story of an average income family that has made ten million dollars in ten years through investments...

普通家庭十年一千万美元理财实录

Bayfamily

贝版

旧金山，加利福尼亚州，美国

San Francisco, California, USA

2020

Money walks: A true story of an average income family that has made ten million dollars in ten years through investments...

First Printing: Jan 2020

ISBN 9798833982495

Total number of Chinese characters: 161,978 (Part II)

Chinese Proofread and Editing: Hong Hong, Amy Bai, Henry Ma

English Translation: Ching Ying Wong, Bayfamily, Gao Dan, XiaoYing

English Proofread: Ching Ying Wong

Publisher is identified as the owner of the email address bayfamily2020@gmail.com

San Francisco, California, USA

The author and the owner of this book can be reached at

bayfamily2020@gmail.com

Author's blog: https://blog.wenxuecity.com/myoverview/23244/

Author's WeChat ID: key-east

Author's WeChat Public Channel: WXC-Bayfamily

Special discounts are available on quantity purchases by corporations, associations, educators, and others. For details, contact the publisher at the above-listed address.

献给我的家人

To my family

目录 Content

钱是会走路的，即使你把钱压在箱子里，抱在被窝里，换成金银股票放在保险柜里，都挡不住钱会像长脚一样走来走去。投资理财，就是要专找那些别人看不见，正在走路的钱。

BAYFAMILY（贝版）曾是北美文学城投资理财论坛的版主，从 2006 年开始陆陆续续发表投资理财的博客文章，累计阅读人数超过数百万。贝版 2006 年因为提出"普通家庭十年一千万美元理财计划"而引发热议，该计划 2018 年最终实现。本书用纪实的方式记录了贝版实现该投资计划的每一步细节，涵盖他对市场趋势的判断，积累资本的方式，和每一笔投资交易的细节与心态历程，当然也包括众多失败的经验教训。全文按照 0-1 万，1 万-10 万，10 万-100 万，100 万-1000 万美元四个数量级的增长历程，把他投资的经历原汁原味地呈现给读者。

贝版记录了美国老中代代传下来的五条理财真经：提高信用分数、避免超前消费、开二手车、亲自维修、不打官司多运动。这本书现身说法证明你总是可以存三分之一的收入的，因为那些比你少挣三分之一的人的生活质量不比你差很多。这世上，没有人可能比你自己对自己的钱更加上心，不要指望任何人能够管好你的钱。

2007-2018 年投资理财贝版做了三件事：投资中国房地产，次贷危机湾区抄底，持有比特币。贝版投资的核心理念就是"会走路的钱"。在充分效率的市场，用懒人投资法；在非充分效率的市场，用勤快人投资法。投资要跟着屌丝年轻人走，你只需要比新钱抢先一步，永远不要和旧钱拼体力。

本书为全文的下册。记录了从 1,000,000 美元到 10,000,000 美元财富的成长历史，以及投资心得。

The author, Bayfamily, was the forum moderator of Investment BBS on Wenxuecity.com, a popular Chinese American social website. Since 2005, he has published a series of blogs on investment and personal finance, and he has attracted millions of page viewers. In 2006, he posted a blog on this investment forum about his goal to make ten million dollars in ten years by investing. He named his plan "Ten Million in Ten Years Investment Plan for an Average Income Family." Since then, he has published his investment activities and financial records every year for 11 years, and eventually, he achieved his goal and made ten million in 2018; a total of eleven and a half years, which is a bit longer than the planned 10 years. This book is a memoir and a record of his efforts to fulfill his ten-million-dollar goal. The book includes details of all of his investment activities, how he prepared himself, how he accumulated capital, how he found investment opportunities, and most importantly, the failures and hard lessons learned throughout the process.

Bayfamily came to the U.S. in 1997 with only 200 dollars in his pocket as a Ph.D. student in engineering. With his student stipend and interning income, he saved up ten thousand dollars in two years. Afterwards, he moved to the San Francisco Bay Area where he and his family only earned an average income. However, they made their first one hundred thousand in two years, and one million dollars in six years, all through saving and investing. This book is organized into four sections to describe this investment history: from zero to ten thousand dollars, ten thousand to a hundred thousand dollars, a hundred thousand to a million dollars, and finally, from a million to ten million dollars. The wealth accumulated in each section is one level of magnate higher than before.

After the 2008 financial crisis, Bayfamily graduated from a top MBA program in the U.S. and worked in a famous investment bank. During the last ten years, most of his wealth was accumulated through three investment activities: investing in the real estate market in China, purchasing Bay Area real estate during the market downturn in 2010, and holding Bitcoin since 2016.

Under his "Money Walks" theory, a good investor should understand their own personality first before investing, whether they are a "lazy man" or a "diligent man." In an efficient competitive market, investors should use the "lazy man" investment strategy; in an inefficient competitive market, they should use the "diligent man" investment strategy. In terms of saving, Bayfamily believes diligent work and a simple life are virtues. An extravagant and exorbitant lifestyle is wasteful. People can always save one-third of their money, no matter what their income level is. This is simply because those who earn one-third less than you are still living with a similar quality of life.

On his first day in the U.S., he was taught five simple rules on personal finance, which were passed down for generations by new Chinese Americans immigrates. The rules of saving money are: keep a good credit score, avoid loans and excessive consumption, avoid legal disputes, fix and repair stuff yourself, and stay fit and healthy. This book "Money Walks" uses the author's own life experiences as an example to describe all these rules and principles.

第九章 投资不是为了退休

Chapter 9 Investing Is Not For Retirement

01 为退休而投资是令人丧气的

01 Investing for Retirement Is Frustrating

在美国绝大多数时候投资理财通常和退休挂在一起。我在美国第一次接触到投资的入门读物，也是教你怎么投资退休的。然而我觉得为退休而投资，这是一个最无聊、最无趣、最让人丧气、最让人失去奋斗精神的理由。

In the U.S., investing is associated with retirement most of the time. When I was first exposed to beginner books on investing in the U.S., they were teaching their readers how to plan for retirement. However, I believe that investing for retirement is the dullest, most boring, frustrating, and discouraging goal.

为退休而理财就好比中国旧社会常说的"人活着一辈子就是为了攒棺材板钱"一样。你在年轻的时候存一些钱，这样你死了之后可以给自己买一个金丝楠木的好棺材。如果你没钱，可能就是草席子卷一卷就被埋掉了。

Investing for retirement is analogous to what Chinese old society referred to as "The purpose of your entire life is to earn money to buy your own coffin." If you save some money when you are still young, this means that you can afford to buy a gold coffin after you kick the bucket. If you do not have money, your body may be wrapped in a straw mat and then buried.

全世界几乎没有哪个地方像美国这样对着年轻人天天宣传退休的思想了。20多岁的中国年轻人，几乎都没有像美国人这样想着退休。当美国年轻人每个月忙着数自己401K 的 nest egg（金蛋）有多大的时候，太平洋对面的中国人在四处盘算着哪里去开个公司，怎样赚钱，商业模式是什么。美国社会把提早退休作为梦想的宣传，让整个国家失去了锐气。

There is no other place in the world than the U.S. that is constantly bombarding youngsters with "plan for your retirement" propaganda. Unlike their U.S. counterparts, China's young people in their 20s have barely thought about retirement. When American young people are busy counting how big their nest egg in their 401k has grown, their Chinese peers across the Pacific Ocean are occupied with finding a place to kickstart their business, how the business can earn money, and what is the best business model. The U.S. society is promoting "retire early" as a dream. As a result, the country loses its vigor.

年轻人很难接受为退休而理财这样的想法，这样的想法也很容易被"活在当下"这样的口号所推翻。退休都七老八十了，走也走不动，跑也跑不动，要那么多钱干什么？因为舆论宣传上把退休和投资挂钩在一起，所以很多年轻人压根不想着投资的事情，吃光用尽再说。

Young people may find it difficult to accept the idea of investing for retirement. Such an idea may be overthrown by slogans such as "carpe diem!" Retirees in their 70s or 80s can barely walk or run, so what good will money do for them? However, as the mainstream media and propaganda often link retirement with investing, a majority of the younger generation is not thinking about investing at all. Rather, they are "living life to the fullest" by spending all their money and indulging in consumption.

如果你赘述人类历史，甚至不用回到古代的人类历史，看一看其他国家的文化，一般都没有人是为了退休攒钱去投资的。农业社会养老问题是通过家庭内部解决的。中国叫作养儿防老。也就是说多生一些子女，为了自己养老做准备。等你老了，孩子会照顾你。

If you are reviewing mankind's history, you do not even need to go back to ancient times. Just take a look at the culture in other countries. Generally speaking, no one invests for retirement. In an agricultural society, the problem of planning for retirement is solved through the internal structure of families. In China, we refer to this solution as "raise a child for one's retirement." In other words, Chinese have children to prepare for their retirement. When they grow old, they expect their adult children to take care of them financially.

其实为了退休你不需要多少资产。因为退休之后通常你有 social security（社保），或者有 pension（年金）。更主要的是你的开支降了下来，你不再抚养孩子，你的房子也基本付清了；你身材走样了，你对衣服和穿戴失去了兴趣；你甚至对这个世界失去了探索的兴趣，不再热衷于旅行。你的生活没有那么多的开支，因为你也不必生活在物价高昂的城市中心或者是学区房里，可以选择住在廉价的远郊。

Actually, retirement does not require a lot of assets. This is because usually you will be entitled to social security or pension after retirement. More importantly, your expenses will be reduced because now you do not need to support your children financially and your house mortgage has been paid off. Similarly, if you are out of shape, you will lose your interest in fashion and accessories; if you are no longer passionate about exploring the world, you will not be enthusiastic about traveling. After retirement, you do not have so many expenses because you no longer need to live in city centers with a high cost of living or in a good school district. Instead, you can choose to live in more affordable countryside areas.

很多人梦想着六十几岁刚退休的时候，就去周游世界。但是旅行很快就会变得索然无味。因为旅行的意义是时空变幻。就像你在房间里待久了，要出去走走透透气一样。但是如果让你一直长时间地生活在户外，大部分人是受不了的。老了之后的长期旅行也是一样，会让人觉得又无聊，又不适应。走遍千山万水，还是自己的家好。等你过了 70 岁手脚不灵便的时候，大部分人选择不再出门旅行。

The dream retirement life of many people is to travel around the world in the early years of retirement, when they are in their 60s. However, traveling will soon become dull because the meaning of traveling is about creating a simple change in your environment and your perception of time. An analogy is that if you stay in a room for too long, you will feel the need to step out and breathe in some fresh air. Similarly, taking frequent trips after one gets advanced in years will render him or her bored and unable to adapt to the environment of the foreign destination. Most people will realize that, after visiting different corners of the world, nothing compares to their home. For people who are over 70 and less agile physically, most of them will choose not to go traveling.

你可能说如果我不旅行，我有钱可以吃好穿好住好吧？　其实年纪大的人，真是无法吃好，无法穿好。自己不能像年轻的时候那样随意地放纵自己，大口吃肉，大碗喝酒，你需要顾及自己身体的健康和饮食的平衡。穿好就更是一个笑话，因为你身体渐渐走形，地心引力把你连皮带肉一起往下拉，你会觉得穿什么样的衣服都不得劲儿。最后的选择都是以宽松为主的松紧带衣服。住好也是一句空话。因为老人无法管理好太大面积的房子。而一些适合老人休闲疗养的地方，总的来说要比市中心好学区住房要便宜一些。

You may then point out that, "Even though I do not go traveling, money can still do me much good by allowing me to enjoy delicacies and high-end clothes." In fact, senior citizens cannot really enjoy these delicacies or designer clothes. This is because they cannot indulge themselves in meat and wine as if they were still young. You need to take care of your physical health and make sure you have a balanced diet. Dressing up is even more of a joke because your body shape changes naturally as you age. Gravity will pull your muscles and skin down so you will not feel the same power, confidence, and energy, no matter what outfit you are dressed in. Your ultimate go-to outfit as a retiree will be loose-fitting clothes with an adjustable elastic waistband. Living in a good house is also empty words. This is because it is challenging for senior citizens to manage a big house. Furthermore, those neighborhoods which are more tranquil and suitable for senior citizens to relax and recuperate are, generally speaking, cheaper than good school districts in the city center.

如果你理性地想想，只要你保持和退休前近似的生活方式，退休的时候，你需要的金钱其实并不多。大部分退休前攒了很多钱的人，他们最终都没有能力把自己的钱花完。而老人最需要的亲情、亲人的陪伴和子孙同堂的快乐，往往又是和金钱的多少没有太大关系的。

If you think about it rationally, as long as you maintain a lifestyle similar to your pre-retirement one, you do not need that much money as a retiree. A majority of retirees who have earned lots of money before their retirement often fail to spend it all in the end. In contrast, what the elderly need the most is filial piety[1], the company of their family, and the joy of being a grandparent, which have little to do with how much money they have.

年轻人如果是抱着为退休而投资这样的想法，往往容易失去对投资的热情。他们经常想这些钱也许已经够养老了，养老的钱已经够了，我又何必努力存钱和投资呢？

If young people are harboring such an intention of investing for retirement, they will often lose their passion for investing. They may well think that their money is sufficient for their retirement life. If this is the case, why work so hard in saving money and investing?

但是为什么偏偏美国把投资和退休两件事情绑定在一起呢？你问问所有的人，打开所有的财经杂志，都是说你退休之后的金蛋有多少，你攒够了吗？

But why does the U.S. often bundle investing with retirement? Feel free to ask those around you and flip through all the financial magazines and you will realize that they are all talking about how big your nest egg will be after retirement. Have you met your retirement goal?

---

[1] Filial piety is a central concept and important virtue in Chinese culture. In general terms, it means taking good care of one's parents, showing love, respect and support, and caring for your family members and relatives.

我觉得主要原因还是来自税法和华尔街的原因。退休基金 401K 和华尔街的利益有非常密切的关系。是华尔街推动了税法改革，生出了 401K 这样的怪胎，逼着大家把辛辛苦苦挣来的钱给华尔街管理，让他们挣钱。

In my opinion, the primary reasons are tax law and Wall Street. 401K retirement plan and the interests of Wall Street are inextricably intertwined. It is Wall Street that pushed forward the tax reforms, giving birth to such a freak as 401K, forcing everyone to hand over their hard-earned money for Wall Street to manage, and generating profitable opportunities for Wall Street.

既然投资不是为了退休，那年轻的时候你好好地工作，我们为什么要去投资呢？为什么不能保持吃光用尽的状态，有一天过一天呢？

Given that investing is not for retirement and we have a paying job while young, why should we bother to invest? Why shouldn't we maintain our paycheque-to-paycheque lifestyle and live the you-only-live-once lifestyle to the fullest?

其实投资理财有远远比退休更加高尚和激动人心的理由。那个理由就是为我们拥有更多的财富而投资，为我们的自由而投资，为我们能有更多选择而投资。

Actually, there is a much more noble and exciting reason for investing and managing your wealth than retirement planning. Instead of investing for retirement, you should invest to achieve the goal of accumulating more wealth, for your freedom, and for having more options in life.

02 为自由而投资

02 Investing for Freedom

钱不是万能的，但没有钱的的确确会寸步难行。在职场上竞争非常激烈，当你年轻的时候，你只需要出卖自己的劳动力就可以了。我说的劳动力不仅仅是体力，也可以是智力和脑力。但是随着你年龄一点点的地上涨，等到中年的时候，你会发现你在这个世界上的竞争力会渐渐下降。

Chapter 9 Investing Is Not For Retirement

It is true that money cannot buy you everything. However, it is equally true that without money you will be bogged down. The job market is fiercely competitive. When you are still young, you can earn a living by selling your labor-power. What I mean by labor-power not only refers to your physical strength, but it can also mean your intellectual and brainpower. However, as you age, you will realize that your competitiveness in the world is gradually decreasing when you approach middle age.

无论是你从事体力工作的，还是从事智力工作的，无论你是蓝领阶层还是白领阶层，甚至不论你是前台的秘书，还是一个算法工程师程序员，你会发现所有的雇主都喜欢年轻人，因为年轻人学习新知识速度快，负担和牢骚少，而且没有那么多坏习惯。

Whether you are a physical worker or an office worker, ranging from a blue-collar to a white-collar worker, and from a secretary at the front desk to a computer engineer/ programmer, you will realize that all employers prefer to hire young people. This is because young workers are more adept at acquiring new knowledge, have less financial burden, complain less, and have fewer bad habits.

我自己也做过雇主。对于雇主而言，最喜欢雇佣的人是工作了 3~5 年的人。这样的人有一些经验，你不需要从头训练。对于雇主而言，大部分应聘者工作经验在 5 年以上的，就没有太大区别。但是有 10 年工作经验的人的工资要大大超过有 5 年工作经验的人。

I was once an employer myself, so I know how to think from an employer's perspective. For employers, their favorite candidates are those who have worked for 3-5 years. These people possess some experience so you do not need to train them from scratch. For employers, the difference among candidates with five years or more experience is usually very small. However, workers with ten years of work experience have a much higher salary than workers with five years of experience.

这点是我 90 年代还在中国的时候就观察到的现象。在中国以前的国企从来都是论资排辈的，你年龄越大资历越高，收入也就越高。所以让每个人都觉得自己只要在一个企业一年年地熬下去，生活就会越来越好，越来越有奔头。

This is an observation I made while I was still in China in the 1990s. Back then, the ranking of employees in Chinese state-owned enterprises was based on years of seniority. The older you were, the more qualified and experienced you were taken to be, which meant higher salaries. Therefore, everyone was thinking that as long as they could survive in an enterprise year after year, their quality of life would improve and a bright future would ensue.

改革开放之后，外企进入中国，颠覆了很多人在这方面的思考。我们大学毕业之后，有的同学直接去了外企，过了几年他们被提升为项目经理或者是部门一个小小的主管。他们有的时候手下会管一些年龄比他们大的人。而当这些小小的主管在聘用新人的时候，他们基本上的一个原则就是不会雇佣比他们年龄再大的人，或者比他们经验更丰富的人。

After China's economic reform, foreign enterprises entered the Chinese market, disrupting the old beliefs of many Chinese workers. After we graduated from university, some of my classmates directly joined a foreign enterprise. After several years, they were promoted to the position of project manager or junor manager of a department. Sometimes they would supervise team members who were older than them. In addition, when these junior managers were hiring new members, a basic principle guiding their decisions was to avoid hiring someone older or more experienced than them.

我们换位思考一下，如果你是一个 30 岁的主管，你愿意雇 30 岁以下的人呢，还是 30 岁以上的人？除非有一些特别技能的需求，你肯定愿意雇佣比你更年轻的人，因为你指挥得动他们。哪怕他们年轻经验少，你也更愿意花钱培训他们，而不愿意去雇佣那些有可能在你面前倚老卖老的人，比你年纪更大的人。

Let's try to put ourselves into the shoes of recruiters. If you are a 30-year-old manager, will you be willing to hire someone under or above the age of 30? Unless the position requires the candidate to possess special skills, there is no doubt that you would rather hire someone younger than you because you can better mobilize these young workers. Despite their lack of experience, you will be more willing to spend money on setting up training programs for them rather than hire someone who is older and may have a patronizing attitude toward other team members because of their years of seniority.

总的来说随着年龄的增长，雇员在市场上的竞争力是逐步下降的。你可能说我在公司勤奋努力，我独当一面，做个经理当个主管，这样总可以了吧。也许我的脑力和我的体力不如年轻人，但是我有丰富的管理经验，我懂得如何和人相处，我还知道如何管理一个项目的进度，对公司内部流程熟悉，知道如何调配各方面的资源，按时准确地完成一项任务。

Generally speaking, as worker ages, his or her competitiveness is gradually decreasing in the job market. You may well say that, "What about I work hard in my company, manage myself well, and climb the ladder to become a manager or supervisor? Won't this work out? Even though I cannot compete with young people in terms of brainpower and physical endurance, I am a seasoned manager with years of experience and I know how to get along well with people. On top of that, I also know how to manage the progress of a project, am familiar with the internal operation of the company, and know how to coordinate resources from different channels so as to finish a project with precision while strictly adhering to the deadlines."

非常可惜地告诉你，在一个企业里，即使你一层层地升了上去，但是随着你的职务越高，你的竞争优势也是同步在下降的。并不是你的管理能力变差，而是需要的职位变得越来越少。

I regret to tell you that even though you may have been promoted along the corporate ladder in a certain enterprise, your competitive advantage is still diminishing as your job title gets higher up in the corporate ladder. The reason is not that your managerial ability is deteriorating, but that there are fewer positions that need you.

一个公司可能需要 10 个入门级别的工作、2 个中层、一个更高级的主管。那么这 10 个入门级别工作的人，最终他们都去哪儿了呢？因为主管只有一个，那剩下的 9 个人随着时间的推移，都去哪里了？

A company may need to have 10 entry-level positions, 2 mid-level positions, and a more senior supervisor. What will eventually happen to those 10 entry-level employees? As there is only one available managerial position, where do the remaining 9 people go as time progresses?

当然整个社会经济在发展，公司在增多。但是人口总量其实没有什么太多的变化。那 10 个入门级别的职位的人，有 9 个其实被淘汰掉了。大部分公司选择的方案都是 5 年内，你或者升职上去或者被淘汰掉。

Of course, when the social economy is developing, the number of companies increases. However, the total population does not change much. Among the ten entry-level employees, nine of them have actually been eliminated. The HR planning adopted by most companies is to either promote or terminate someone after 5 years.

被淘汰掉的，往往是离开这个公司，继续做入门级别的工作。或者他们继续做那些本质上是入门级别的工作，但是为了好看前面加了一个 senior（高级）标签的。那随着时间推移，他们一天天地变老，在这个层次上的竞争力就会越来越差。当你过了四十几岁的时候，你就会惶惶不可终日，即使你还能保住最底层的工作，你也会发现你的重要性越来越低，学习能力越来越差，一有风吹草动，你就浑身紧张。

Those who are eliminated will usually leave that company and continue to find an entry-level job. Or they may find a job position that starts with "senior" despite the entry-level nature of their daily tasks to save face. As time goes by, they are getting older every day and the competitiveness at this level decreases. When you are past 40s, you will live your life in constant fear and worry. Even though you may still be able to keep your lowest-level job, you will realize your importance within the company is diminishing and your learning ability is deteriorating. Whenever there are some changes in the company, you cannot help but feel that every cell of your body is feeling anxious.

竞争可能是来自公司内部的，也可能是来自公司外部的。毕竟谁也不想永远做最底层的工作，谁都有生存的压力。即使你在一个公司里表现出色，升了主管，并且常年政治正确，跟对了领导，甚至还需要团队一起努力保住自己主管的饭碗。但是当公司整合或者公司被出售的时候，整个团队就不一定能够保住了。而这一切又完全不是你和你的工友通过努力就能够把握的事情。

Competition may stem from the internal structure or outside of the company. After all, no one is willing to work at the bottom of the company forever. Everyone faces the stress of surviving in the company. You will still need to work hard with your team members to retain your job position as a manager even though your performance may be superb in the company, you have already been promoted to a managerial position and you are always politically correct. However, when the company is being consolidated and acquired, your whole team may not be able to keep your job. This is not something that you and your team members can control by working harder.

一个失业的中年主管，除非是他主动跳槽，如果是被动裁员，其实很难一下子找到另外一个主管的职务。因为每一个主管的职务都被很多入门级别的人虎视眈眈地盯着。为了保证自己能够在职场位于不败之地，于是每个人只能拼命地混圈子。Networking（混圈子）对于有些人可能容易，但是对于大部分美国的老中是一个痛苦的事情。你总有一种要凑上去，人家又不带你玩儿的感觉。在硅谷你经常会听见老中嫉妒老印管理层爬得快，其实是我们老中在美国不擅长混圈子。

It is very difficult for an unemployed middle-aged supervisor who is passively laid off by the company to find another managerial position within a short time unless he or she voluntarily leaves that company for a better prospect at another company. This is because many entry-level employees are eagerly staring at these positions like how tigers will stare at their prey. In order to ensure that you will not be defeated in the job market, everyone has no choice but to make desperate networking efforts. Networking may be a piece of cake for some people, but for most Chinese Americans, it is an ordeal. Chinese Americans will often feel that however hard they try to get closer to a social circle, other people keep excluding them. In Silicon Valley, you will often hear that Chinese Americans are jealous of Indian managers who make their way to the top of the corporate ladder fast. This is because Chinese Americans are not good at networking.

03 不堪的中年人

03 The Miserable Middle-aged Man

我博士毕业后的第一份工作才干了几个月，就活生生看到一个案例，结结实实地给我上了一课。我刚刚到湾区不久，互联网泡沫的经济危机风暴就如期而至。一开始还只是股市剧烈下跌人心惶惶，但是就业市场还好，并没有出现大规模的裁员潮。

A few months into working at my first job after my Ph.D. graduation, I witnessed a real example that offered me valuable insights. At that time, I had just settled in the Bay Area. The financial crisis caused by the dot-com bubble had arrived. At first, it was only the stock market crash that was causing widespread fears. The employment market was not that bad as it had not witnessed large waves of layoffs yet.

大约过了一年之后，就业市场开始变得特别地糟糕。911 之后就业市场简直是到了冰点。有一次，我对面办公室来了一个客人。说他是客人，其实是我们同一个单位的同事，只是另外一个部门的。他当时应该有 50 多岁，也是一个中国人，虽然我们平时很少说话，但是我知道他是从大陆来的中国人。

After about a year, the performance of the labor market was getting abysmal. After 9/11, it reached its trough. One time, a guest came to the office opposite to my seat. Actually he was not my colleague, but he worked in a different department in my company. He was probably in his 50s at that time. Even though he was also Chinese, we barely talked to each other. But I knew that he also came from Mainland China.

这个老兄不知道为什么对中国带着特别的仇恨，大概是因为父辈在当年"文革"反右时代受到过迫害。他性格也不是特别的合群，很少跟我们老中交往，也从来不和我们说中文，张嘴都是英文和我们交流。在美国生活久了，你经常会碰到这样一批人，他们出于各种原因，好像恨不得要忘记身上中国的一切，断绝和中国的一切关系，要把中国在他们身上的痕迹都抹掉。

For some unknown reason, he harbored a hatred for China. This was probably because his father and other relatives were persecuted during the Chinese Cultural Revolution and the anti-rightist era. Besides, he was not a team player either. He seldom talked to other Chinese Americans. He did not even speak to us in Chinese. Whenever he needed to interact with us, his fellow Chinese Americans, he was using English. When you have lived in the U.S. for a long time, you will always encounter these people who, for various reasons, cannot wait to forget everything about China, cut every tie with China, and erase every trait of China from their life.

不过没有关系，每个人有自己的世界观，有自己的想法，我还是很尊重他的。经常还和他一起吃饭聊天。听他说说办公室里的八卦故事。

But none of this really mattered. I understand that everyone has his or her own values and beliefs. I still had much respect for him. I always had lunch with him and listened to office gossips he shared with me.

但是那天，他与我对面的主管几乎用一种哀求的方式在说话。他工作的那个部门因为经费的原因被砍掉了，他需要在企业内部找到一份工作，否则只能被裁员回家。

However, one day, he was talking to my supervisor in an almost begging manner. His department had been cut because of budget reasons, so he needed to find a job within the company. Otherwise, he would be laid off and could only go home.

我们部门还好，最近刚刚接到一个比较大的项目，需要一些人手。而坐在我对面的就是我这个部门的主管。他还相对年轻，那个时候还处在事业的上升期。

Our department was still doing fine because we had just received a relatively big project that required some personnel. The person sitting opposite me was the supervisor of my department. He was still young and was rapidly rising in his career.

这位不说中文的老中开始自我介绍。说明他们部门的不幸以及为何他原有的主管推荐他到这里来碰碰运气，看看有没有工作机会的来龙去脉。接着他就开始述说自己的工作能力，他的编程能力以及他做过的很多项目。

This Chinese American who did not speak Chinese started to introduce himself, explaining the misfortune that happened to his department, and why his former supervisor recommended him to try his luck by looking for a job opportunity here. Then he started to elaborate on his abilities, programming skills, and many of the projects he had worked on.

我没有参与他们的讨论，只是在远处静静地听着。一个已经在职场上混了二十多年的中年人面对一个比他年轻将近十多岁人，低声下气地说话请求他的帮助，那感觉就像是沿街吆喝着出卖体力的下岗工人。当年中国有大量工人下岗的时候，不少人在街上举个牌子写着"泥瓦工"、"电工"之类的招牌找工作。当然最惨的就是那些举着"力工"招牌的人。也就是他有力气，其他什么技能也没有。或者是他有各种技能，但是他对工作也不挑，只要给口饭吃他就干。

I did not join their discussion but was patiently listening from far away. The scene of someone in his middle age who had more than 20 years of experience in the field asking for help from another person who was more than 10 years younger than him in a begging manner was similar to how laid-off workers from state-owned enterprises were shouting along the street in the hope of finding a laborer's job to exploit their physical labor. Back then, in China, there were a lot of laid-off workers who were hanging a sign with "bricklayer" and "electrician" written on it. The poorest were those who were holding a "laborer" sign. These people did not possess other skills, so they could only exploit their physical labor. Or it might also be the case that these people possessed other skills but were not picky about jobs. As long as the job could allow them to feed themselves, they were willing to take it.

一开始这位老兄说得还没有那么惨，只是介绍一下自己，当然脸上带着讨好的口气。但是那个主管似乎不知道什么原因对他的自我介绍不是很感冒，或者主管在忙着其他什么事情，无暇顾及这个事情。主管回答的言语里闪烁着一些犹豫。大概意思是他会认真思考一下，过几天之后再给我们这个老中一个准确的答复。当然明眼人都知道，这是一种婉拒。就像在商店里购买东西的时候，你对售货员说你再看看一样。多半你是不会再回头的。

At first, this Chinese American was not telling the supervisor how miserable he was. He was just introducing himself in a friendly tone of voice as if he were trying to please the supervisor. However, for some unknown reason, it seemed that the supervisor was not very impressed with his self-introduction. Or it might be that the supervisor was occupied with other tasks, so his attention was not on their conversation. The supervisor replied to the Chinese American in a tone characterized by some elements of hesitation. The gist of his response was that he needed some time to ponder on his decision and would give the Chinese American a confirmed response in a couple of days. Of course, a smart person would know that this was a more indirect and polite rejection. This was similar to what happened in the end when you told the salesperson that you needed some time to think about your decisions. In most cases, you would not go back to the store.

我们这位老中可能是吃过类似委婉的闭门羹。他离开主管的办公室，在走廊里走了十几步之后，又重新回到那个主管的门前。这次简直是用哀求的口气在和他说话。

This Chinese American might have received a similar euphemistic rejection before. After he left the supervisor's office and paced up and down in the corridor in more than 10 steps, he went back to the supervisor's office. This time, he was talking to the supervisor in an almost begging manner.

他说他有两个孩子，都已经在上大学，所以他的 situation（处境）变得非常的 critical （严峻）。只要再熬过这两三年，孩子大学毕业就好了。眼下这份收入对他和他的家庭很重要。虽然他说话的时候总体上还是有尊严和体面的。但我也能感到他硬着头皮说话，难过得快要哭出来一样。像我小时候申请减免学费一样的尴尬。

He was telling the supervisor that he had two children who were both attending college, so his situation was very critical. All he needed to do was to survive these 2 to 3 years, after which his children would graduate from college. Therefore, the income that he earned was very important to him and his family. Even though, generally speaking, he was speaking with respect and dignity, I felt that he was biting the bullet and about to burst into tears. It was an embarrassing scene that was similar to the situation of how I applied for a reduction in tuition fees when I was young.

后来我望着他远去的背影，发了一会儿呆，仿佛可以想象自己的未来。如果我和他一样，这样稀里糊涂地混到中年，每天过着吃光用尽的日子，有点风吹草动，也免不了要找人摇尾乞怜。我坚定地给自己下了决心，这样的日子我可不要过。

Later, I was staring blankly at his back as he walked away. I was lost in my own thinking because it was as if I could see my future. If he and I shared the same fate, this would mean I would spend my days at this company and feel confused until I reached my middle age, living a paycheque-to-paycheque lifestyle. When there was a straw in the wind, I might also need to beg someone for help. Therefore, I was determined to avoid such a miserable existence.

04 财富会给你带来自由

04 Wealth Will Bring You Freedom

另外一个给我上一课的人是一个香港同胞。我们单位的宣传部门里有一个香港移民负责做各种海报和网站的美工。他比较早就到美国来，应该是 70 年代的移民。他经常和我一起吃中午饭。他的普通话说得不是很好，他用半生不熟的普通话和夹着英语的中文，和我闲聊一些私人的话题。

Another person who offered me a valuable lesson is someone from Hong Kong. In the marketing department of my company, there was this immigrant from Hong Kong who was responsible for the art and design of various posters and websites. He came to the U.S. early in the 1970s. We always had lunch together. His Mandarin was not very fluent, but he always talked to me using his limited Mandarin skills mixed with some English words. We often chatted casually about some personal issues.

当时我刚刚工作不久，一次他语重心长地对我说，买房子千万不要申请 30 年的贷款，而是要申请 15 年的贷款，最好是 10 年的。我不是特别明白，因为在我的投资理念里，低息贷款总是时间越长越好，这样通货膨胀可以抵消掉一部分本金。我就问他为什么？

At that time, I had just started working. But one day, he told me in sincere words and wishes that I should never apply for a 30-year house mortgage. His advice was that I should apply for a 15-year mortgage instead, or preferably a 10-year one. I was baffled because according to my investment principles, the longer the term of low-interest loan, the better. In this way, inflation would offset some of the principal. Therefore, I asked him why.

他说 30 年太长了，你很难有一个 30 年稳定的工作。年轻的时候咬咬牙，15 年也就付清了。而 15 年贷款比 30 年贷款每个月并不是多付一倍，只高 30% 的样子。这些钱如果你不用来付贷款，稀里糊涂也就花掉了。咬咬牙十五年付清了，就不用为每天的工作提心吊胆的。

He said that 30 years was too long because it was very difficult to find a job that would remain stable for 30 years. "When you are young, you should work harder. Time flies and you will be able to repay your mortgage in 15 years with some hard work. Besides, the monthly payment of a 15-year mortgage is not double that of a 30-year mortgage. The difference is only about 30%. If you do not use the extra 30% to repay your mortgage, you will have splurged it anyway. If you work hard in these 15 years and repay your mortgage, you don't need to feel worried and anxious about your job every day," he continued.

后来我才知道他工作得不开心，他和他的上司、同事相处得并不愉快。但是他一直选择忍让。他忍的一个原因，就是因为他的房贷还没有还清。如果他选择不忍，和同事与上级直接爆发冲突，有可能他就需要辞职或者离职。失去工作，没了收入，延误了贷款，银行就会收回他的房子，把他清扫到大街上去。他的忍让可不是一天两天，他在这个岗位差不多工作了将近 20 年，也就是说他可能也忍了这么多年。我在工作单位几乎就没见到他笑过一次，他总是没精打采地哀叹着，各种抱怨。随着时间的消逝，越来越没有勇气辞职到外面的世界去看一看。

Later, I found out that he was miserable at his job. He did not get along well with his supervisor and colleagues, but he chose to bear with it. One of the main reasons for his tolerant attitude was he had not paid off his mortgage yet. If he chose not to tolerate his miserable life and had arguments or conflicts with his colleagues and supervisor, he might need to resign or be fired. Without a job and income, he could not keep up with the monthly payments, so the bank might foreclose his house and force him to be a member of the homeless. He was not just tolerating for one day or two. He had worked at his position for about 20 years, which meant that he had been tolerating the misery for so many years. I had never seen a smile on his face before. He was always out of spirits, sighing, moaning, and complaining. As time went by, he had less and less courage to quit his job to explore the outside world.

所以他反复说，他最后悔的事情，就是年轻的时候没有对自己稍微狠一点。稍微节省一些，贷款做成15年的，而不是30年的，也许他现在房子就付清了。在美国一线城市里，房子付清了他就可以实现财务自由了，不用再看上下级的脸色行事。

This is why he was reiterating that his biggest regret was that he had not pushed himself harder when he was young. If he had been more frugal and applied for a 15-year mortgage instead of a 30-year one, he might have already paid off his mortgage now. Living in tier-1 cities in the U.S., paying off his mortgage would mean financial freedom. Financial freedom would mean that he did not need to be constantly at the disposal of his colleagues and supervisor.

"自由"。是的，就是这两个字。早日拥有选择自己生活的自由，其实才是投资理财的第一目标。

"Freedom." Yes, this is the keyword. The freedom to choose your own lifestyle when you are still young is actually the prime goal of investing and managing your wealth.

哪个人不渴望自由呢？无论是中国还是美国。美国人民热爱自由，而中国人民又何尝不是呢。美国宣传自己是世界自由的明灯，而中国天天宣传的核心价值观里也赫然写着"自由"两个大字。

Who doesn't long for freedom? Whether you are Chinese or American does not make a difference. American people love freedom, and so do Chinese. The U.S. prides itself as "freedom's lighthouse" of the world, and every day China is promoting its core socialist values which include "freedom."

政治自由跟普通人其实没有特别大的关系。但是不知道怎么的，人们像着了魔一样为之付出巨大的热情。其实和你真正息息相关的是你自己的财务自由，生活选择的自由。这个比喻就好比钓鱼岛跟你没有什么特别大的关系一样，因为那是一个远在天涯海角的海岛，改革开放之前大部分中国人都不知道有这个地方。而你自己的住房有多大，工资有多高，这才是和你息息相关的东西。可惜人们不为自己的住房去游行示威。一被鼓动，大家会为了和他们没太大关系的钓鱼岛满腔热情，操碎了心。

Political freedom has little to do with the lives of ordinary citizens. Despite this truth, it seems that people are so obsessed with pursuing political freedom that they pour their whole heart in it. In fact, what is indeed closely related to your life is your financial freedom and the freedom to choose your own lifestyle. An analogy is that Diaoyudao Islands have little impact on your life because they are located in the remotest corners of the world. Before China's economic reform, most Chinese did not even know such islands existed. Instead, it was the size of their home and the amount of wages that were closely related to their life. Regrettably, people would not participate in demonstrations and protests in a bid to improve their living conditions. Once they were instigated, people were so concerned about the future of Diaoyudao Islands which had little to do with their lives.

投资理财对我来说最大的动力就是自由。拥有财务的自由，才会拥有生活的自由。拥有生活的自由，才会拥有选择的自由，拥有选择的自由，才会拥有思想的自由。

For me, the biggest motivation behind investing and managing my wealth is freedom. Only when one possesses financial freedom can he or she have freedom in life. Only when one possesses freedom in life can he or she have freedom of choice. Only when one possesses freedom of choice can he or she have freedom of thought.

我不必去看别人的眼色行事。我工作不开心了，我可以直接和我的上司顶撞，不用担心失去这份工作。我不用特别担心这个季度或者下个季度的业绩，我也不用担心自己是不是在公司里负责核心业务，更不用钩心斗角抢任务，以避免在公司里被边缘化。我可以凭着自己的喜好而不是外在的压力工作。我拿一份工资，所以我9点钟来，下午5点走。我可以更好地平衡自己的生活和工作。社会大的经济环境有变化，经济危机来的时候，我也不用夹着尾巴做人，浑身紧张。

Then I do not need to be always at someone's disposal. If I am miserable at my job, I can directly air my grievances to my supervisor without worrying about losing my job. I do not need to be worried about the sales performance in this quarter or next quarter. Neither do I need to worry about whether I am responsible for the core business of the company, plot against each other to compete for more tasks and projects, or work hard to avoid being isolated. Instead of being forced by external pressure to take on certain projects, I can work on those that I feel passionate about. Since I am just earning a salary each month, I can come at 9 am and leave at 5 pm. I can have a better work-life balance. When there are changes in the social and economic environment and an economic crisis hits, I do not need to tuck my tail between my legs and feel that every cell in my body is filled with tension.

没有一定的物质财富，人要活得憋屈一些。这些还是次要的，大丈夫能屈能伸，一时的委屈，一时的忍让也算不了什么。更关键的是心灵的自由和思想的自由。

Without the support of a certain level of material wealth, one will lead a life filled with more constraints. This is only a secondary consideration because a man among men should know when to lie low and when to walk tall. Facing some temporary obstacles and making some concessions should not be a big deal. What is more important are spiritual freedom and freedom of thought.

我们每个人来到这个世界上，并不是为了朝九晚五每天坐在办公室里，也不是为了参加冗长、低效、无趣的会议的。生命只有一次，你的每一分钟逝去之后，就再也没有了。我们最渴望的就是做自己喜欢做的事情。也许你喜欢读书，喜欢写书；也许你喜欢绘画，喜欢舞蹈；也许你喜欢鼓捣发明创造，喜欢创业。

The purpose of our journey on Earth is not to work a 9-5 job and sit in the office every day; it is not to join dull, inefficient, and boring meetings either. Everyone only gets one chance at life. After this minute of your life passes, you can never have it back. Our deepest desire is to engage ourselves in projects that we are truly passionate about. Perhaps you are a book lover and love writing; perhaps you are enthusiastic about painting and dancing; perhaps your mind is filled with creative ideas and you take pleasure in coming up with inventions, expressing your creativity, and starting your own business.

总的来说，在你实现财务自由之前，大部分情况下，这些兴趣业余爱好都只能是业余的。你没有办法全身心地做你真正想做的事情。所以你也没有办法探索自己内心的渴望。到底那些梦想是不是自己最想做的事情，还是只是因为得不到而形成的短暂好奇。

Overall, under most circumstances, your interests and hobbies are at best amateur pursuits before you achieve financial freedom. This is because you cannot fully devote yourself to these pursuits in which your are genuinely interested. Therefore, there is no way for you to explore what your true desires are. You cannot tell whether these dreams are your true calling in life or temporary curiosity that stems from your inability to achieve them.

比如，也许你觉得你有绘画的天赋，但是因为你不可能全职地投入去进行绘画，所以你永远不知道，会不会成为下一个梵高。再比如你想做一个职业的旅行者，做一个伟大的探险家，像日本探险家植村直己一样勇敢地去漂流亚马逊河，写下伟大的游记。可是因为你还要养家糊口，你有很多责任，所以你做不到像他一样去探险。那些你儿时的美梦，就只能永远地停留在你的梦想里。

For example, perhaps you feel that you are a gifted painter, but it is impossible for you to devote all your time to becoming a professional painter. Therefore, you will never know whether you can become the next Van Gogh. Or perhaps you would like to become a professional traveler or a great adventurer, someone like Japanese explorer Naomi Uemura, who courageously rafted the Amazon alone and wrote spectacular diary entries of his adventures. However, because, as the breadwinner of the family, you shoulder so many responsibilities, you cannot just leave your life behind and embark on your adventures like Uemura. Your childhood dream will remain a dream forever.

我们每个人生下来都和所有人不同，即使我们是同卵孪生。我们也不希望和别人过一模一样的生活。生命只有一次，我们内心深处都渴望这一次生命过得与众不同，过得光辉璀璨。没人喜欢被金钱奴役和驱使着做单调无聊的重复工作。

We are all born with our unique characteristics and strengths. This is true for identical twins. We are not longing for a life that is identical to others'. Everyone only gets one chance at life. Deep inside us, we desperately hope that our life will be special and splendid. No one likes to be enslaved by money and forced to finish repetitive, boring, and monotonous tasks.

我想相当一部分的中年人可能都听说过，或者读过那部以画家高更为原型的小说《月亮与六便士》。很多人都可以理解那种对自由的渴望，但是大部分人做不到那个画家那样的决绝，抛弃一切的物质生活去追求自己的理想，追求自己的自由。做不到的原因，还是因为他们没有实现物质上的自由。

I think a certain portion of the middle-aged population may have already heard of or read The Moon and Sixpence, a novel based on the life of the French artist Paul Gauguin. While many readers can understand that kind of desire for freedom, most people will not be able to be as determined and heartless as the painter in giving up all material life in pursuit of one's dreams and personal freedom. The reason why most people cannot do this is that they have not achieved financial freedom yet.

有了一定的物质基础，我们就可以按照自己的喜好选择自己的职业。我们可以去做那些我们认为有乐趣、有意义、但是收入不高的工作。当然重要的前提条件是你必须在你还年轻的时候就要做到有一定的物质基础。等到你都七老八十了，快退休了才有一定的物质基础，那个时候什么都晚了。你的一辈子都过去了。所以关键是不但要有钱，而且还要在还年轻的时候有钱。

With some financial foundation, we can follow our passion in choosing our career. We can choose jobs that are, albeit low-paid, fun and meaningful. Of course, the most important prerequisite is that you need to build a sufficiently strong financial foundation when you are still young. If you wait until you are in your 70s or 80s, even though you may have built a strong financial foundation at that time, it will be too late. Your life has almost passed. Therefore, the key is not just that you need to have money, but that you need to have money when you are still young.

就像那些搞物理的人，不但要拿诺贝尔奖。而且要在年轻的时候拿诺贝尔奖，不然荣誉的光环照耀不了你几天。

Similarly, for those expert physicists, their goal is not just to win the Nobel Prize but to win the Nobel Prize when they are still young. Otherwise, the number of days in which they can enjoy their honor will be very limited.

你可能会说，我这个行业是越老越吃香的，我也特别喜欢我这个行业，我热爱我的工作，我的事业蒸蒸日上，所以没有必要投资理财。我可以举个例子来反驳你：越老越吃香，工作稳定的职业之一就是拿到终身教职的大学教授们。大学教授们和中医老先生一样，越老在学术圈的地位越高，在行业的影响力越大。圈子里有自己教过的学生，有曾经的同事，门徒等等，越老的老教授在学术界的地位越高，他们也就越光芒四射。

You may well say that your career field is different because it is one in which the more experienced you become, the more advantages you will have over other candidates in the job market. In addition, it is a job that you feel passionate about. You love your job and are steadily climbing the corporate ladder, so there is no need for you to invest and manage your wealth. I can rebut this line of argument by raising a concrete example. One of the occupations in which older, more experienced candidates will have an edge is university professors with a lifetime tenure. These university professors are similar to old, experienced traditional Chinese medicine practitioners: the older they are, the more reputation and respect they enjoy in academia and the more influential they will be. Their circles are filled with their students, ex-colleagues, and protégés. More senior professors enjoy a high level of reputation in the academia. Therefore, the older they are, the more charismatic they become.

可是就算这样的职业，当你获得财务自由之后，你能够做的事情也会多得多。我认识一个从麻省理工学院退休下来的教授。其实他还没到退休年龄，完全可以再干几年，很多学校都抢着聘他干下去。但是他选择了退休，是因为他不必烦恼学校的各种约束，比如发表一定数量的论文，争取一定的科研项目经费。

However, even for such an occupation as a university professor, after you have achieved financial freedom, your professional obligations will multiply. An acquaintance of mine is a retired professor at MIT. He has not reached the age of mandatory requirement yet, so he might well continue to work for another couple of years. In fact, many schools were competing to hire him but he chose to retire for more freedom. After retirement, he is no longer worried about the limitations imposed on him by his school, for example, the need to publish a certain number of papers, and solicit research funding for research projects.

这位麻省的教授选择退下来，是因为他有一个做得比较成功的公司，赚了一笔钱。所以他退休出来，不再需要花时间申请项目经费，写灌水文章，而是自己花钱来做科研。这样他可以把自己生命中有限的余下的还有创造力的十几年用在真正解决问题上。

This MIT professor chose to retire because he has a successful business that has made him some money. When he chose to retire, he no longer needs to spend his time on applying for projects funding and writing articles that are written for the sole purpose of meeting deadlines and contain little substance. Instead, he can now spend his money on research. In this way, he can devote his remaining energy, creativity, and remaining time of 20 years or so in life to solving real problems.

财务自由给人带来的好处不是在沙滩上无聊地闲荡。财务自由对你的事业也是有帮助的。你可以一门心思做自己最想做的事情。财务自由对每一个人都很重要，无论你是蓝领、白领，用体力劳动的还是用智力劳动的。钱把社会的各个部分联系在一起，这样可以实现大规模的合作。我不否认这个贡献。很多时候人是有惰性的，在没有金钱的压力的时候，很多人可能选择懒惰。可是金钱的压力也的确让人失去心灵的自由和创造力。

The benefits of financial freedom are not only limited to allowing you to wander aimlessly on the beach. Financial freedom is conducive to your career development too because it enables you to focus all your attention on the things that you are most passionate about. Financial freedom is crucial for everyone, ranging from blue-collar to white-collar workers, and from laborers and office workers. Money links different parts of society together so as to render large-scale cooperation possible. I will not dismiss this contribution made by money. But most of the time, Sapiens are lazy. Without the pressure of money, most will choose the path of least resistance, that is to slack off at work. However, it is also true that the pressure of money will make people lose their creativity and spiritual freedom.

我觉得我自己不是一个特别懒惰的人，我不会因为有钱就躺在沙发上，每天看看电视。混吃等死的日子无聊透顶。我有我自己的梦想，无论是在自己的事业上还是自己的生活中。人们的这些梦想，这些计划统统可以归结为一句就是自我实现。

I do not consider myself to be a particularly lazy person. I will not simply spend my days lying on the couch and watching TV after getting rich. The life of a couch potato is suffocatingly boring. I have my own dreams, in my professional career and personal life. People's dreams and plans can all be categorized as "self-realization."

马斯洛（Abraham Maslow）的人的需求理论，可能你也听说过。人的需求分几个层级，最下面的是食物温暖，中间是安全，人和人之间的感情，再上面是权力等等，最上面一层的就是自我实现。

You may have heard of the theory of the hierarchy of needs by Abraham Maslow. The theory, which is often illustrated as a pyramid, states that humans have several categories of needs in hierarchical levels: the bottom are physiological needs; the middle rank is about safety needs and the different kinds of emotional connections between people; a level further up is power, etc; and the top level is about self-actualization.

这个金字塔很容易理解。它是把各类需要按照金字塔形状来描述。上级的实现必须依赖下一级的实现。如果你没有满足安全的需求，有再多的钱，也没有幸福感可言。比如你是黑社会的老大，靠贩毒挣了很多钱，但是因为你随时会被追杀，你并不会因为拥有这些钱而拥有比常人更多的幸福感。

This pyramid is easy to understand. It describes the different categories of needs in a pyramidal shape: higher needs begin to emerge only when people feel they have sufficiently satisfied the previous need at the lower level of the pyramid. If you have not satisfied your safety needs, you will not feel happy no matter how much money you have. Let's pretend that you are a mafia boss who has made lots of money in drug trafficking. But since you may be assassinated any time, you will not feel more happiness than ordinary citizens, even though you own all this money.

如果你在缺乏最基本的物质保障，缺乏财务自由的时候，就去追求自我实现，你也一样没有幸福感。因为你会担心如果自我实现没有成功，就会从金字塔的上头一路跌落下来。

If you try to seek self-actualization when you are still lacking the most basic guarantee of your physiological needs and financial freedom, you will not feel happiness either. This is because you will be worried about falling all the way from the top of the pyramid lest your pursuit of self-realization fails.

人的一生可能唯一有意义的事情就是自我快乐。古希腊人伊壁鸠鲁在数千年前就想明白了这个道理。对于不信宗教的人来说，人既没有来生，也没有来世。我们只是世界上的一些原子出于偶然原因结合在一起。当生命逝去的时候，这些原子也会重新分散在大自然中去集合下一个生命。在这个短暂的集合中，我们唯一能获取的就是快乐。

The only meaning of life is probably self-happiness. The ancient Greek philosopher Epicurus had this realization thousands of years ago. Those with no religious affiliation believe that we do not have a next life or afterlife. Our existence is because of some random combinations of atoms in the world. When our life is gone, these atoms will reorganize themselves so as to form another new life in nature. In our brief existence, the only thing we can achieve is happiness.

快乐的最高等级就是自我实现。一个例子就是各种政治大人物，他们每天忙碌的主要目的其实是自我实现。他已经不愁吃，不愁穿，但是为什么还要每天忙国家大事呢？因为人们内心深处渴望自我实现。

The highest level of happiness lies in self-actualization. An example is all the big political names. The main reason why they are so busy every day is to achieve self-actualization. Their basic needs of food and clothing are already guaranteed, but why do they choose to occupy themselves with national affairs? This is because people long for self-actualization deep down.

其中一个例子就是特朗普总统，虽然我和很多人一样不喜欢他。他本可以过着逍遥的日子，挎着模特嫩妻，在庄园别墅里闲逛。但为什么要吃力不讨好地去竞选这个总统，然后每天被人骂呢？因为他要自我实现。

One of the examples is President Trump (though I, like many people, do not really like him). He might well have chosen to live a carefree life by walking around in his manor and villa with his young ex-model wife. Why did he decide to run for president, a tough job that would attract him all sorts of criticisms and attacks? This is because he needed to achieve self-actualization.

比较一下你会发现历史上的中国政治人物基本上都是在安全、以及基本的财务自由没有实现的时候，就去追求自我实现。那个自我实现是不靠谱的幻影。随时他都有可能因为政治失败而变得一无所有，轰隆隆地掉到金字塔的最下层。

In contrast, all political figures in Chinese history were basically trying to pursue self-actualization when they had not yet satisfied their safety needs and basic financial freedom. Therefore, their pursuit of self-actualization was unreasonable, or a shadowy image at best. He might well have lost everything because of his political failure at any time, and "bang!" there he fell to the bottom of the pyramid.

而特朗普则不一样，他即使自我实现失败了，也许没有连任总统，也许在总统期间被弹劾了，但是他依旧可以退而求其次，回到金字塔的中间过着富足无忧的生活。

Yet, Trump is different. Even if he fails to achieve self-actualization, loses the re-election, or is impeached during his presidency, he can still settle for the second-best by going back to the middle of the pyramid to enjoy his comfortable and affluent life.

大家觉得美国的政治系统总体而言比世界其他国家的专制制度稍好一些，或者说人们在选择政客的时候，更愿意选择那些已经有了财务自由的政客。因为财务实现自由的人，从政的目的可能相对更单纯一些，或者是为了证明自己的理论是对的，或者是为了实现某一种理念，或者仅仅出于单纯地想帮助他人。而一个不名一文的人成为政客，选民对他会天然地感到警惕。

Most people will think that the U.S. political system is, generally speaking, slightly better than the authoritarian system of other countries in the world. Or we should say that when people are electing politicians, they are more willing to give their vote to those who have already achieved financial freedom. This is because people who have achieved financial freedom may have a purer motivation behind their running for office. Their motivation may be to prove their theories are correct, to realize a certain belief, or out of a desire to help others. Yet, if a destitute person has become a politician, voters will naturally keep a watchful eye on him.

05 财富的负面影响
05 The Negative Effects of Wealth

李敖说过一句话我印象很深，而且我觉得他说的也很有道理。他说一个人如果想做一点事情的话，是需要有点小钱的。他劝每一个要从政和打算追逐自己理想的人，先赚点钱再说。

There is a saying by Li Ao that left me with a strong impression. I think he has made a brilliant point. He said, "If a person wants to achieve something, he or she needs to first have some money." He was encouraging anyone who is interested in a career in politics and pursuing one's dream to make some money first.

李敖说人一天都不可能撇开物质上的需求。哪怕你没有物质的需求，甚至你可以撇开你的伴侣，你的父母，但是绝大多数人是无法撇开对孩子的责任的。所以哪怕你想出家做和尚，你也需要有些小钱，这样可以安置好自己的亲人。

Li Ao was saying that it was impossible for us to give up our physiological needs. Even though you may have no material needs or can even leave aside the needs of your significant other and your parents, a great majority of people are unable to ignore the responsibility they owe to their children. Therefore, even if you want to leave everything behind to become a monk, you will still need some money to take care of your family first.

大部分工作、大部分职业一旦变成了挣钱的工具，就会变得特别无聊而且无趣。在我看来，最主要的原因是因为大部分挣钱的职业都要求从业者有比较高的综合素质。你不但要聪明，而且要情商高。不但会说，而且还要会写。不但要学会管理自己的情绪，还要去学会引导别人的情绪。

Once most occupations and careers are reduced to just a means of earning money, they will become particularly boring and dull. In my opinion, the main reason is that most high-earning jobs demand that the candidates have a relatively high level of overall attributes. Not only do you need to be smart, but you also need to have a high level of emotional intelligence. In addition to being eloquent, you have to be a superb writer. On top of that, you have to learn how to manage your own emotions and guide other people's emotions too.

比如，如果你是一个非常聪明的人，当你事业稍稍有成的时候，你多多少少需要做些管理工作。而管理工作就不免要和各种各样的人打交道。智商发达的人往往情商会偏差一点，很多烦恼都是在与人打交道中生成的。反过来，如果你是一个特别喜欢跟人打交道的人，你的情商很高，但是你的智商往往有限。这样的情况下，你又难于胜任非常具体的工作。

For example, if you are a highly intelligent person, you will need to at least take on some management tasks after you have made some achievements in your career. These management tasks involve networking with people from all walks of life. As high-IQ individuals usually have a lower EQ, most of their troubles are formed in their interactions with other people. Vice versa, if you are a person who enjoys socializing with other people, this means you have a high EQ. However, it also often means that your IQ is limited. In this situation, it is difficult for you to excel in very specific jobs.

所以一个十全十美的工作，一个自己非常热爱的、又有稳定回报的又非常符合自己性格特点的工作，简直和老印开中餐馆一样稀少。理论上成立，现实中很少。至少我可以说大部分人找不到。我看到的是更多的中年人在小心谨慎地熬日子，工作只为挣钱。

Therefore, the probability of finding a perfect job that you are very passionate about, yields a stable return, and suits your personalities is as rare as finding a Chinese restaurant owned and operated by Indians. Theoretically speaking, this is possible. However, such jobs are very rare in reality. It is at least safe to say that most people will not be able to find such a job. A more common phenomenon I have observed is that more middle-aged men are carefully trying to survive every day and they work just for the money.

当然，人的欲望是无穷的。对于钱的欲望也是无穷无尽的。最好的办法还是控制自己的欲望。对金钱没有休止的欲望也是会毁掉一个人的幸福和快乐的。最好的状况还是有一点钱，享受财富给你带来的自由状态。太多的钱不会给人带来更多的快乐，反而会成为你生活和生命中的负担。

Of course, human desires are unlimited. Our desire for money is also unlimited. The best way is to control our desires. An endless desire for money will eventually destroy a person's happiness and bliss. The most ideal situation is to have some money and enjoy the freedom brought by your wealth. Too much money will not bring people more happiness. Instead, too much wealth will become a burden in life.

比如，没有人会喜欢与比他们高一个财富等级或者社会等级的人交往。大家总体上是喜欢跟他们同一个社会阶层的人来往。你最真心最亲密的朋友也往往来自同一个社会阶层。

For example, no one enjoys socializing with someone who is one level higher in terms of wealth or social status. Generally speaking, people prefer to socialize with those of the same social class. Your dearest and closest friends often come from the same social class as you.

所以当你有钱之后，你就会发现你比普通人可能要更加孤独一些。不是说你认识的人少，你认识的人可能还多了，或者更多的人认识你了。但是你能记住的人就那么多，当你变得有钱之后，能够和你或者你能够跟他无所不谈的人，会渐渐变得稀少。因为世界上还是穷人多。

Therefore, when you become rich, you will realize that you may be even lonelier than ordinary folks. This is not because your social circle narrows. In fact, the list of people that you know may expand or more people will know you. However, the number of people that you can remember is limited because of the limited memory capacity of your brain. When you become rich, the number of people with whom you talk about everything will get smaller and smaller. This is because, after all, poor people constitute the majority of the population in the world.

有钱之后，你自己的心态也会发生改变。尤其是你知道"别人知道你有钱"之后。如果只是你自己知道你有钱，问题还没有那么复杂。别人知道你有钱之后，而且是你知道"别人知道你有钱"之后，你就会忍不住猜疑和防范着别人。这是一个很复杂而且绕口的逻辑。但是似乎千百年来，很多富人都明白这个逻辑。大部分富人选择低调和隐藏，也是出于同样的考虑。

After getting rich, your attitude and mindset will also change, especially when you realize that "now other people know I am rich." If the situation is that you are the only one who knows you are rich, it is less complicated. When other people know you are rich and you also know "other people know you are rich," you cannot help suspecting their intentions and starting to protect yourself. This is a very complicated and tongue-twisting logic. However, it seemed that in thousands of years, many rich people understood this logic. Consequently, a majority of them chose to stay low and hide their wealth.

太多的金钱，会让本来比较亲密的朋友变得疏远。会让你对每个陌生人带着格外的戒心。钱能够给人带来便利，因为你通过钱可以控制更多的资源。但是管理钱本身也是一个麻烦的事情。比如，你能够看到有钱的家族，他们花很多的精力在财产的分配上。亲人之间会因为遗产和公司的控制权弄得不愉快。中国古代有句老话叫作皇帝之家无父子。财富和权力类似，都会侵蚀人心，让亲人为了继承或者管理权打得不可开交。

Too much money will distance you and your close friends, and make you particularly alert to every stranger. Money can bring people convenience because you can control more resources through your wealth. However, managing wealth is a troublesome matter. For example, you can see that wealthy families spend a lot of energy on allocating their wealth. Their relatives and descendants may fight over inheritance and control of the company. To borrow an old Chinese saying, "there is no father and son in a royal family." Wealth and power are similar. They will both erode the heart, tempting family members to feud over inheritance and management rights.

也许我受中庸之道的影响，我感觉如果你想获得钱给你最大的快乐，应该是小富即安的状态。常言道，能力有多大责任就有多大。当你拥有更多的财富的时候，你就会忍不住去承担更多的社会责任。当然这没有什么不好的，本来富人就应该承担更多的社会责任。比如比尔·盖茨先生把他绝大部分的时间花在各种慈善计划上，把他手中的钱花出去，为社会谋取更大的福利。所以如果你想成为钱的主人而不是钱的奴隶的话，最好不要拥有太多的钱。

Perhaps it is because I am greatly influenced by the Doctrine of the Mean, aka Zhongyong in Chinese[2] that I feel the greatest happiness money can bring us is a state of "modestly wealthy and content." As the saying often goes, with great power comes great responsibility. When you own more wealth, you cannot help but shoulder more social responsibilities. Of course, there is nothing wrong with this as rich people should bear more social responsibilities in the first place. Take Mr. Bill Gates as an example. He devotes most of his time to various philanthropy projects. He is spending his money for the greater good of society. If you want to own your money instead of being its slave, you should not have too much money.

2006 年的时候，我综合考量了这些问题。觉得给自己定一个不大不小的目标更加合适一点。但是具体定多少为目标呢？我又怎样能激励自己的斗志去实现这个目标呢？这个时候，我不得不搬出"理想"这个魔幻工具了。

In 2006, after careful consideration of all these questions, I came to the conclusion that I should set a moderate goal for myself that was not over or under ambitious. But how should I set out my goal in a specific number? How should I motivate myself to achieve this goal? At this point, I had no choice but to resort to the magical tool of "aspirations."

---

[2] The Doctrine of the Mean or Zhongyong is a doctrine of Confucianism. The central idea is to maintain balance and harmony by striking a constant equilibrium. We should avoid extremes in our life.

第十章 为追求财富正名

Chapter 10 Defending and Justifying the Pursuit of Wealth

01 **理想是提高执行力的灵丹妙药**

01 Aspirations Are the Panacea for Increasing Execution Effectiveness

为什么要投资？因为我要有钱。为什么要有钱？因为那是我的理想！

Why invest? Because I want to get rich. Why do I want to get rich? Because this is my aspiration!

理想和信念的力量是巨大的。树立理想和信念最好的办法就是说服自己。说服自己，才能说服整个世界。如果一个人真心想做成什么事，上帝都会跑过来帮助你。人世间有些人能够做成一些事情，有些人做不成一些事情。很大的一个因素就是你是否真心地说服自己，让自己充满热情和决心去做成这件事。

The power of aspirations and beliefs is incredible. The best way to find your aspirations and establish your beliefs is to convince yourself. Only after you convince yourself can you convince the whole world. As the famous saying from the Alchemist goes, "When you want something, all the universe conspires in helping you to achieve it." In this world, some people can successfully realize their dreams and some fail. The key lies in whether you can truly convince yourself so that you can be full of passion and determination in executing your plan.

你管这个说服自己的过程叫作洗脑也好，叫作树立志向也好，这些都不重要，最主要的是给自己形成一个明确的决心和目标。

Whether you call this process of convincing yourself "brainwashing" or "finding your aspirations" does not matter. What is important is that you need to form a clear goal and find determination for yourself.

那些有宗教情节的人，往往可以做成更大的事情。那些为理想而奋斗的人，最终他们的目标往往都可以奋斗成功。没有理想，没有目标，没有坚定意志的人，很容易一时兴起，三天打鱼，两天晒网。过了几天，碰到一些困难，他们就会给自己找出很多理由。

Those who subscribe to religious principles can often accomplish bigger goals. Those who fight for their aspirations often successfully achieve their goals. People without aspirations, goals, or determination often have difficulty adhering to their goals because they embark on their new endeavor on a whim. After several days, when they encounter some difficulties, they will find excuses to quit it.

当大自然剥夺人类爬行能力的时候，又给了他一个行走的拐杖，那个拐杖就是理想。没有理想的人就像一艘无舵的孤舟，终将被大海吞没。不肯为理想奋斗的人，就像黑夜里的流星，不知会陨落何方。

When Mother Nature deprives mankind of their ability to crawl, she gives them the walking stick. This walking stick is mankind's aspirations. People without aspirations are like a lone boat without a helm: they will be inundated by the sea. Those who are reluctant to work hard for their aspirations are like meteors under dark skies: they will fall and crash into an unknown place.

投资理财也是一样，一类是有理想的人知道自己为什么要投资理财，为什么不是过一天算一天收支平衡即可。另外一类人只是简单地喜欢财富带来的快乐，财富能让他们消费更多的东西。他们并没有认真地把投资理财变成自己的理想。他们只是为了更好的生活，或者是退休的时候拥有更多的钱。

The same is true when it comes to investing and wealth management. There are two categories of investors. One group of them is the ambitious who know their motivation behind investing and managing their wealth and why life is not just about making ends meet. The other group is those who enjoy the simple happiness brought by wealth. Wealth enables them to consume more. They never seriously consider turning investing and wealth management into their aspirations. They are merely doing it for a better life or more money after retirement.

然而，如果投资理财只是为了吃吃喝喝，为了获得更多的财富从而享受更好的生活。那么无论是你在存钱的过程中，还是在投资过程中当面对困难的时候，你就会不断地给自己打退堂鼓。你会对自己说我又何必呢，我投资也好，赚钱也好，不就是为了更好的生活吗？那么我又何必让自己现在这么焦虑呢，不如现在不用想那些烦人的操心事了。

However, if investing and wealth management are merely for better food and wine and procurement of more wealth is to enjoy a more lavish lifestyle, you will more likely give up your goal in the face of difficulties that you encounter in the stage of saving up your money or investing process. You will ask yourself, "Why do I have to push myself to endure all this pain? The reason for investing and making money in the first place is a better quality of life. Why am I making myself so anxious now? I should not bother myself with this hassle."

就投资理财而言，真正肉体上的痛苦很少，大部分是精神上的负担造成的痛苦。当年做出投资决定的时候，需要你用精明的头脑判断出未来的风险。但是当面临风险的时候，人们总是害怕，因为风险给人带来很多不愉快。比如你出 100 万美元去买一个商铺，那时你就会心里忐忑不安。如果只是为了贪图财富和享乐而进行投资，你很快就会质疑自己是不是一个正确的决定。为什么要让自己这样心惊肉跳呢？为什么不太太平平地过日子，过好每一天活在当下每一天呢？

Investing and wealth management involve minimal physical pain. Most of the pain comes from psychological burden. At the time when you are making your investment decisions, you need to use your intelligent mind to make a judgment on future risks. However, in the face of risks, people are always scared because risks bring people many negative feelings. For example, let's say you are now using US$1 million to purchase a commercial property. When making the decision, you may feel uneasy. If the purpose of your investment is for better enjoyment of wealth and having fun in life, you will soon doubt whether you are making the correct decision. Why do I make myself shudder with fear? Why don't I just live a peaceful life and seize the day?

"活在当下"这是一句特别流行的话。人们的大脑大部分时候并不理性的思考，而是被语言中的一些修辞所左右。修辞能够影响我们的情感，可是修辞并不会给我们带来最大的收益。

"Carpe diem" is a very popular saying. Most of the time, our brain is not thinking rationally but influenced by some linguistic and rhetorical devices, which are able to affect our emotions. However, rhetorics will not bring us the greatest benefits.

我自己的感受是这些类似"活在当下"的心灵鸡汤、口号、修辞是用于宽慰我们的，但是不能用来指导我们的行为。行为是需要用理性逻辑指导的。鸡汤和口号是当我们遇到不顺，我们心灵不愉快的时候，可以用这些话来舒缓一下自己的。这些口号只是安慰剂。未来固然有很多不确定性，但是如果你现在压根不计划，光想着这一分钟、这一秒钟的感受，然后高呼口号"活在当下,"那是不智的。

My own feeling is that chicken soup for the soul, slogans, and rhetorical devices such as "carpe diem" are for comforting ourselves but not for guiding our behaviors. Behaviors need to be guided by rationality and logic. Chicken soup and slogans are for occasions when we encounter some obstacles. When we feel unhappy, we can use these words to lessen our feelings of unhappiness. These slogans are merely a placebo. Of course, the future is full of uncertainty. However, if you do not make a plan at all and you only focus on how you are feeling in this minute or second and hail "carpe diem," that will be unwise.

投资理财领域，如果有什么口号能激励我们斗志的话。那就是"人生如逆水行舟，不进则退，人无远虑，必有近忧"。

In the field of investing and wealth management, if there is one slogan that can inspire and motivate us, it will be "Life is like sailing against the current; either you keep forging ahead or you lag behind. If a man takes no thought about what is distant, he will find sorrow near at hand."

02 消除负罪感

02 Eliminating the Feeling of Guilt

有人对拥有财富有一些本能的负罪感。与人为善的本能几乎是与生俱来的。损人利己的事情，很难长期激发人的热情。钱多有负罪感是不对的。你拥有的财富越多，你对社会的贡献也就越大。只要你这笔财富不是靠坑蒙拐骗用暴力获得的，或者用非法手段获得的。你每创造一块钱，每拥有一块钱，就为社会创造了远大于一块钱的财富。

Some individuals harbor some instinctive feelings of guilt toward possessing wealth. Almost everyone is born with an instinct to be kind to others. Enriching oneself at the expense of others cannot arouse people's enthusiasm in the long term. Feeling guilty because of one's wealth is not right. The more wealth you possess, the bigger your contributions to society. This is true as long as you do not obtain your wealth through violence, some deceptive schemes, or illegal means. For every dollar you have created and owned, you have created wealth far exceeding $1 for society.

社会并不是一个零和游戏，并不是说你拥有一块钱，别人就少了一块钱。但是无论是东方还是西方，无论是古代还是现在，无论是宗教还是现代的人文道理，大家经常给普通民众灌输的一个思想，就是获得更多的财富是一个邪恶的事情。

Society is not a zero-sum game, in which someone loses one dollar for every one dollar you own. However, the general public, be it in the West or East, or in ancient times or modern times, are often instilled with the belief that procuring more wealth is evil in religious and modern humanity teachings.

他们看到了事情的一面，感觉这个世界财富就是从一个人口袋到另外一个人口袋的过程。我多了，其他人就少了。但是没意识到每一个获得财富的人其实都在创造财富，哪怕你获得这个财富的过程并不是现实的生产实物。

They only see one side of the story and feel that world wealth is simply the process of transferring money from one person's pocket to another's. The fact that I have more money means that some other people have less money. But people do not realize that every single individual who is procuring wealth is also creating wealth, even though your process of procuring wealth is not a result of tangible production in reality.

实物生产固然重要，但是非实物生产也是在整个流通过程中创造了财富。比如商人在商品交易的过程中实现了财富的增长。投资人购买股票，把资金直接交给公司的生产者，当公司生产出商品，发放工资的时候，购买股票的人也获得了财富。

Of course, tangible production is important. However, it is also true that intangible production creates wealth in the process of circulation. For instance, merchants achieve wealth growth in the process of selling and buying goods. Another example is when investors purchase shares in a company, they are directly handing capital to the producers in the company. When a company sells its goods and pays salaries, those who purchase its shares will also procure wealth.

并不是只有在工厂或者在农田里干活的人在创造财富。华尔街也可以创造财富。你炒股赢了的时候，说明你协助了社会资源的合理分配。你赢的这部分是促成社会资源合理分配，创造出来的财富的一部分。你买卖股票亏了的时候，你就是在为社会消灭一笔财富，因为你把社会资源与资本引到了它们不应该去的地方，浪费了资源。所以一个人如果获得了更多的财富，只要是合法合理的，不隐含着任何欺骗，无论你是投机行为，还是商品交换，其实都是在为社会创造财富。

It is not only those individuals working in a factory or farming a plot of land who are creating wealth. Wall Street is also creating wealth. When you make a profit in the stock market, this means you have assisted in the reasonable allocation of social resources. The profit that you have made has facilitated the reasonable allocation of resources in society and represents the wealth created in such a process. When you lose money in the stock market, you are eliminating some wealth in society because you have allocated social resources and capital to sources to which they should not have been allocated. Therefore, if a person has obtained more wealth in speculative activities or exchanging products and services, he or she is actually creating wealth for society provided that he or she does so in a legitimate and legal way without any deception.

人们经常把投机和投资这两个概念分开。经常说这些人是投机者，而另外一些人是投资者。比如他们会说巴菲特是一个投资家而不是一个投机家。其实投资和投机本质上并没有什么区别。从行为上来看，他们都是某个时间买入某个投资品，过了一段时间再把这个投资品试图以更高的价格卖出，无论他们这个努力是否成功。

People often separate the concepts of speculating and investing. They often say that certain people are speculators and others are investors. For example, they will say that Warren Buffett is an investor and not a speculator. In fact, the nature of speculating and investing is the same. In terms of behaviors, they both refer to buying an investment product at a certain time and then attempting to sell that investment product at a higher price after a while, regardless of whether their attempts are successful.

人们用贬义和褒义词来描述投资和投机，就像战争中胜者为王一样。打胜的人或者投资成功的，他们就把这个行为叫作投资。而那些可怜的失败者，他们通通被归为投机分子。然后再非常鄙视地对他们说，要投资而不要投机，偷鸡不成蚀把米。

People use positive and derogatory language to describe investing and speculating respectively. Similar to how winners are the king and make the rules, those who have won the battle or are successful in their investing/ speculating activities regard their behaviors as investing. And those pitiful losers are categorized as speculators, who are often looked down at. People will despise these losers and tell them that they should invest not speculate. The speculators go out for wool and come home shorn.

其实这些评价往往是事后诸葛亮，事前的时候哪里分得清谁是投资，谁是投机？只不过是同样一个行为的褒义描述和贬义描述而已。就像英雄和野心家只在修辞上有区别一样，哪个英雄没有野心呢？

Actually, these comments are often made in hindsight. Before the outcome, who can tell which activities are investing and which are speculating? These terms are merely positive descriptions and derogatory descriptions of the same behavior. An analogy is that the only difference between "heroes" and "ambitionists" is the language used[3]. What kinds of heroes are not ambitious?

如果硬要区分的话，也许有人会用投资时间的长短来区别投资和投机。比如长期的价值持有者是投资，而每天买进卖出 day trader 是投机。其实投资和投机无论长线还是短线，对社会的贡献都是一样的。没有短线的投机者市场，哪来的流动性？投资者又如何能够顺利地买进以及变现自己的投资资产呢？

If we have to distinguish between speculating and investing, perhaps some people will use the time frame of investments to determine whether an activity is speculating or investing. For example, disciples of long-term value investing are investors, and day traders who buy and sell stocks every day are speculators. In fact, whether it is long-term investing or short-term speculating, they make the same contribution to society. A market without short-term day speculators does not have liquidity. How can investors then successfully buy and sell their investment assets?

---

[3] In Chinese, "ambitionist" denotes a negative meaning. When Chinese politicians or leaders remark that a person is an ambitionist, this means that person should not be promoted or should even be dismissed.

投资和投机，长线和短线并没有道德上的高低贵贱之分，如果说有什么区别的话就是关键你要赢，要赚钱。如果你赚了钱，总的来说你就是为社会创造财富，就是好的。比如短线投机者，如果赚了钱，那多半是因为你填补了某一个市场缺乏流动性效率的地方。投资者如果赚了钱，那多半是因为你把大众的资金正确地引导到了某个产业方向。

There is no difference between investing and speculating in terms of moral principles. If we have to tell them apart, the key is that you have to win and make money. If you make a profit, this means that you are creating wealth for society, which is good. If short-term speculators make money in the stock market, this is probably because they supply capital to a certain market that lacks efficient liquidity. If investors make money, this is probably because they correctly guide the general public's capital to the right direction of a certain industry.

就拿我们最近大家都熟悉的特斯拉股票作例子。特斯拉的公司股票上涨了，你投资的钱创造了这个产业，带动了电动汽车和清洁能源的发展。但是如果特斯拉公司最后破产了，你的投资打了水漂，那就说明你误导了社会资源。这些社会资源本应该投资在更有价值的产业方向或者管理团队身上。

Take Tesla stock, with which everyone is very familiar lately, as an example. When Tesla stock rises, the money you have invested in it creates this industry, driving the development of electric cars and clean energy. However, if Tesla goes bankrupt and you lose all your money, this means you have incorrectly guided social resources. The social capital should have been invested in a more valuable industry or management teams.

而短线投机特斯拉股票的人，他们的贡献就是让特斯拉的股票不至于暴涨暴跌。还有就是当长期投资人无法兑现的时候，或者无法正确判断股票价格的时候，投机者会给市场增加一定的流动性，判断其应有的价格。

For short-term speculators in Tesla stock, their contribution is that they stabilize the price of Tesla shares so that it will not fluctuate drastically. Furthermore, when long-term investors cannot cash in their shares or correctly judge the prices, speculators increase the liquidity of the market and make a judgment on its proper price.

股票的道理也许大家都懂，房子的道理有的时候大家就会有些糊涂，好像投资购买房子，收取房租的"寓工"们都是犯了什么邪恶的贪婪者。比如我说的要跟着年轻人去买房子，在前一章我介绍了一个又一个这样的案例，你会觉得我岂不是在剥削未来的年轻人吗？

Perhaps everyone is familiar with the principles of trading stocks. However, sometimes people will be confused about the principles of real estate investing. For example, they will dismiss real estate investors and landlords as evil and greedy. In previous chapters, I am saying that we need to follow the younger generation in buying investment properties and have listed several real cases of the application of this principle. Will you think that I am exploiting the young generation's future?

其实不是，正是因为有我们这样的投资人提前买入了房子，促进了开发商在那里盖更多的房子。开发商盖了更多的房子，未来年轻的人搬入的时候，房价才不至于出现更大幅的暴涨。

That is not the case. It is because of investors like us who have purchased those properties in advance that property developers are encouraged to build more houses in that area. As property developers build more houses, property prices in that area will not witness a greater surge when young people move in in the future.

投机者或者是投资者，无论你给投资人什么样的称谓，他们最大的贡献就是对市场价格进行引导，让市场提前看到未来哪里的价格会上涨。然后把社会的各种生产要素，无论是土地、承包商、混凝土还是砖头，都调集在最需要生产的地方。

No matter how you label individuals engaged in investing, be it speculators or investors, their biggest contribution lies in guiding market prices so that the market can observe in advance where the prices will go up in the future. Then, the market can optimize the allocation of important production factors, for example, land, contractors, concrete, and bricks, to places where they are needed the most.

别忘了大部分房地产投资者，哪怕是为大家最鄙视的短线 house flipper，他们买进的房子最终都是要卖出的。因为买进的房子要卖出，他们对市场的总体供需并没有什么影响。他们做的一切只是让价格变得更加平稳。

Do not forget that most real estate investors, including short-term house flippers, who are most despised, will have to sell their investment property in the end. As the houses they have purchased will have to be sold in the end, their impact on the aggregate demand and supply of the market is minimal. Their activities will only make the prices more stable.

因为大部分人对投资房地产的投资者，炒房的人有一些偏见，我专门写了一篇文章来论述这个观点，为投资理财的人正名。

Since most people have prejudices against real estate investors and speculators, I specifically wrote an article to illustrate this point of view and defend those investors.

投机倒把的伟大意义 (2007 年 5 月 19 日)

The Great Meaning of Speculation (May 19, 2007)

by Bayfamily

古今中外的圣贤们共同特点是重道德、重农耕、轻商业，一个比一个视金钱如粪土。无论是亚里士多德还是孔老圣人的门徒们都认为商人把货物从甲地搬到乙地，不劳不作，凭空吃差价是件很不道德的事情。论语曰："君子喻於义，小人喻於利"。

The common characteristic of virtuous men, in the West and the East, and in ancient times and modern times, is that they attach much emphasis to morality and agriculture but look down on commerce. They all consider money worthless like dirt. Aristotle and the protégés of Confucius all believe that a merchant who moves merchandise from Place A to Place B and makes a profit because of the price difference is immoral because he does not participate in meaningful economic production. As the

Analects (Li Ren 16) go, "The mind of the superior man is conversant with righteousness; the mind of the mean man is conversant with gain."

亚里士多德说："他宁愿捐弃世人所争夺的金钱荣誉和一切财物，只求自己的高尚"。圣人们认为生产实物的和关心理想道德的人才是高尚的人，只有小人们天天想着如何把别人的钱财搬到自己腰包里。

As Aristotle once said, "I would give up money, honors and all goods, which others contend for, to secure to myself what is honorable." These saints believe that only those who engage in the production of tangible goods and services and care about aspirations and morality are honorable. They also contend that only mean men will think about how to move other's money and wealth to their own pocket.

撇开他们伪君子的一面不谈，但就思路方式而言，圣贤们目光短浅，全凭直觉，没有看到商人在商品交换时、优化社会资源带来的价值。这种目光短浅的思维方式，在东西方都持续了很长时间，在中国尤盛，时至今日，大家普遍还是对炒房炒股的人，感到他们不务正业。投机倒把、囤积居奇、卖空买空更是大逆不道，天人公愤。

Let's ignore their hypocrisy for a moment. In terms of their thinking and reasoning, these saints are short-sighted. Their arguments are all based on their instincts only, and they fail to see the value created for society when merchants exchange goods and optimize the allocation of social resources. This kind of short-sighted way of thinking has persisted for a very long time in both eastern and western history and is particularly common in China. Even until now, people commonly believe that speculators in real estate and the stock market are not engaging in meaningful production and that speculation, hoarding, and short-selling are monstrous crimes and should be hated by both men and God.

第一个突破直觉思维的是亚当斯密，古今最伟大的经济学家。伟大的亚当斯密先生，突破直觉思维提出，每个人在追求个人财富的时候，社会整体通过无形的手，就达到了最优化。农民种地、面包师烤面包、商人买卖。每个人为获取自身最大利润作出的努力，会导致社会财富的最大化。每个人应该干自己最擅长的事，而不是给别人添乱。

The first thinker who jumped out of the restraints of an instinctive-thinking model is Adam Smith, the greatest economist of all time. In breaking through the instinctive mode of thinking, the great Mr. Adam Smith suggests that when everyone is pursuing personal wealth, society as a whole is optimized through numerous invisible hands. Farmers farm land, bakers bake bread, and merchants buy and sell goods. Everyone is working hard to maximize their own profits, leading to maximization of social wealth. Everyone should be focused on their areas of strength instead of creating troubles for others.

多么石破惊天的理论啊，多么貌似简单，有创造力的论断啊。和圣贤们多么不一样啊。别忘了，直到 80 年代，中国还在学雷锋，坐火车要帮列车员倒水，周末不好好歇着，硬要去工地上帮民工搬砖头。更早时的知青上山下乡、后来的小学生种蓖麻、做好人好事，都是对社会资源的极大浪费，都是圣贤们阴魂不散的结果。

What a striking theory! Despite being seemingly simple, it is a very innovative thesis. The central idea is strikingly different from the beliefs held by those saints. Do not forget that until the 1980s, China was still imitating Lei Feng[4] and advocating that people should help train attendants prepare drinks for other passengers and help laborers move their bricks on construction sites on weekends. Back then, the Chinese government was encouraging educated young people to go to villages so that they could be educated by peasants and farmers alike and farm land. Later, even primary school students were encouraged to plant ricinus and do other "good deeds." All these were a tremendous waste of social resources and a result of the lingering influence of the ideas and beliefs proposed by those saints.

---

[4] Lei Feng is a heroic figure in modern China. After his death, he was characterized as a selfless and modest hero. He later became the subject of a national campaign, the slogan of which was "Follow the examples of Comrade Lei Fung."

你也许会问，商人的价值我懂，把货物从甲地搬到乙地，付出劳动，提高了资源配置，创造了价值。甚至炒股对社会的贡献我也懂，因为炒股增加了市场的流动性。可炒房，投机倒把、坐地涨价到底为社会创造了什么价值？ 连柏拉图老前辈都认为，秋天买稻米，春天原地加价卖出的行为根本就是 Sin （罪恶）.

Perhaps you may be wondering, "I can understand the value created by merchants. In moving goods from Place A to Place B, these merchants put in manual labor, improve the allocation of resources and create value. I also understand the value created for society by day traders in the stock market because they increase the liquidity of the market through their frequent trading. However, how do real estate speculators create value for society by engaging in speculation and price gouging behaviors? Even Plato, one of the most influential philosophers, considers the behavior of buying rice in fall and selling them at an inflated price in spring is a sin.

我先讲几个例子，让你明白投机倒把、倒买倒卖的伟大意义。

Let me give you a few examples to illustrate the great meaning of speculation and buying and selling for the mere purpose of making a profit.

中国古代常常发生天灾引发的饥荒，每每有易子而食、析骸而炊的惨剧。每到这时总有灾民抢吃大户，囤积居奇的商人被大家一抢而空。政府往往也是严厉打击乱涨价的商人，甚至逼他们卖粮赈灾。道理很简单，别人都快饿死了，你怎么能乘人之危，大发国难财呢？天天读圣贤书的父母官是不会"坐视不管"的。

In ancient China, famine caused by natural disasters was commonplace. Tragedies of people trading their children for food and eating dead bodies were not uncommon during such times. Victims of the famine would often rob the more well-off households and merchants who hoarded goods. Also, the government often cracked down on price-gouging merchants or even forced them to sell their food to alleviate the famine. The moral principle behind all this is simple: when everyone is starving to death, how can you take advantage of these victims and profit off a national misfortune? Ancient

Chinese officials who often prided themselves as the parents of ordinary citizens and followers of virtuous principles would not turn a blind eye to the behaviors of these merchants.

可现代的经济学家表明，正是这些读圣贤书的父母官和抢吃大户的灾民害了老百姓。如果在灾荒年，可以维持自由、自愿的市场，保证商人的利益的话，就会有很多人事先囤积粮食，灾荒年的时候粮食的供应不但不会短缺，价格也不会有大的起伏。

However, according to modern economists, these officials with seemingly good intentions and victims of the famine who robbed the wealthier families caused tragic outcomes. If a free and voluntary market could be maintained during periods of famine and the interests of merchants could be guaranteed, many people would try to hoard as much food as possible in advance. Then during periods of famine, there would not be a food shortage or great surge in food prices.

比如，三年前，第二次海湾战争打响前，很多人预测石油供应会受到影响，开始囤积原油，战争打响后，原油的价格不但没有急剧攀升，反而因为存货太多下跌。由于投机商的存在，保证了原油的平稳供应和世界经济的平稳运营。

For instance, three years ago, before the second Gulf War began, many people predicted that the supply of petroleum would be affected so they started to hoard crude oil. After the second Gulf War took place, crude oil prices did not drastically climb but had dropped instead because of excessive stocks of oil. The presence of speculators guaranteed the stable supply of crude oil and the smooth running of the world economy.

再比如，由于美国农产品期货市场存在，农民便可以把所有的风险转嫁给别人，保证农场的平稳经营。农产品期货市场的投机商和当年中国的囤积居奇的商人一样，获利的同时，为社会承担了巨大风险。只有判断正确的投机商可以获利，判断错误的当然是血本无归。在自由的市场经济条件下，优胜劣汰，社会整体对市场判断会越来越正确，保证了价格和市场的平稳。

Another example is the existence of the U.S. agricultural futures market, which enables farmers to transfer all their risks to others, ensuring the smooth running of farms. Speculators in the agricultural futures market are no different from hoarding merchants in China back in the days. Even though they were making a profit, they were bearing huge risks for society at the same time. Only speculators who make correct judgments can make money, and those who make wrong judgments will lose every single penny. Under the conditions of a free market economy, it is about the survival of the fittest. When society as a whole makes more correct judgments about the market, this stabilizes prices and the market.

对于炒房而言，炒房长期来看不会造成房价的上升。因为炒房者买的房子，最终是要卖的，炒房不会对市场的长期供求有任何影响。从短期来看，炒房增加市场的交易量和流动性，便于大家买卖房子。另一方面，长期来看，由于炒房人的存在，反而让有房子需求的人可以住上更便宜的房子。

When it comes to real estate speculation, this kind of behavior will not cause property prices to go up in the long term. Since real estate speculators will have to sell the properties in the end, speculating activities will not have any impact on the long-term demand and supply in the market. On one hand, when we focus on the short-term impacts, real estate speculation increases the number of transactions and liquidity of the market, making it easier for everyone to sell and buy houses. On the other hand, in the long term, because of the existence of real estate speculators, people with housing needs can now live in cheaper houses.

美国 20 年代，是个铁路泡沫的年代，随着经济的发展，铁路运费开始上升。很多人投机铁路，铁路大亨们造了大量铁路以图获利。但后来，发现铁路造的太多了，导致运费的急剧下跌。投机铁路的人血本无归，但运费却降下来了，需要铁路运输的人反而捡了个便宜。

The 1920s in the U.S. is an era of a railway bubble. As the economy grew, railway prices started to increase. Many people speculated on railway projects. Railway tycoons built a lot of railroad lines in a bid to make a profit. However, they realized that they had built too many railways, which caused the freight charges to plummet. Railway speculators lost everything, but, thanks to the lowered freight charges, those who needed railway transportation benefitted from the bubble.

我刚到美国的时候，往中国打电话一美元一分钟，后来赶上网络泡沫和网络的扩张，现在往中国打电话，一分钱一分钟。整整降了一百倍。

When I first arrived in the U.S., long-distance calls to China cost US$1 per minute. Thanks to the internet bubble and expansion of networks, a call to China only costs 1 cent per minute now, which is a 100-fold decrease.

事实证明，投机商蜂拥到一个行业，加大了那个行业的投入。形成泡沫，泡沫崩溃后，会留下廉价的实物资产造福社会。

The reality has proved that when business opportunities are concentrated in a single industry, the input into that industry will be increased. This forms a bubble. After the bursting of the bubble, society benefits from cheap tangible asset prices.

炒房的也不例外，炒房的人短期内提高了市场价格，把未来的市场需求提前表现在价格上，对社会的资源的投入形成提前导向。比如，美国的佛罗里达，由于预测到 baby boomer （婴儿潮族）在未来会大量涌入，2000 年后，大量的投机分子涌入，哄抬房价。房价急剧上升，带动了开发商，最近一年，开发建造了大量房屋。随着供应加大，投机分子们撤离，房价下滑，为将来 baby boomer 们留下了廉价的房屋。试想，如果没有这些投机分子，baby boomer 们怕是退休了更买不到房子了，如同灾荒年的中国农民们彻底没粮吃一样。

Real estate speculation is no exception. When real estate speculators drive up the market prices in the short term, the future market demand will be reflected in the current prices, guiding the input of social resources in advance. For example, in Florida, U.S.A., because of a prediction that there would be a large influx of baby boomers in the future, many speculators flocked to the real estate market after 2000, driving up property prices. The surge in property prices motivated land developers. In about a year's time, land developers built a lot of houses. With an increase in supply, speculators fled the scene, and property prices dropped, leaving cheap houses for baby boomers in the future. Imagine what would happen without these speculators? I am afraid that baby boomers would not be able to buy a house until they were retired, just like how Chinese farmers did not have any food during years of famine.

Flip   房子（炒楼花）的人更是意义重大，因为他们为开发商分担了风险， 让开发商可以专心盖房子，不用担心卖不出去和未来价格的波动。和期货市场对农民的意义一样。

Those who flip pre-construction houses also make meaningful contributions because they help property developers share risks so that the latter can focus on finishing the project without worrying about not being able to sell the houses or future price fluctuations. This is similar to how the agricultural futures market benefits farmers.

事实上所有的投机行为，囤积居奇，倒买倒卖，只要没有垄断行为，都是对社会有重大贡献。它们起到了经济向导的作用，为社会创造了价值。它们合理地调配了社会资源，预测了市场走向，降低了实业风险。

In fact, all speculative behaviors, for example, hoarding and buying and selling for the sole purpose of making a profit, are making significant contributions to society as long as they are not anti-competition. They serve to guide the economy, creating value for society. They facilitate the reasonable allocation of social resources, predict the market trend, and lower business risks.

但为什么社会总是视投机行为为不耻呢？总认为他们是社会的吸血鬼呢？ 我看一是"圣贤书"读的太多，流毒犹在。二是凭直觉思维，没有看到生产实物以外的价值。三是红眼病。常见的论调是，人人都炒房，社会怎么办？不会人人都炒房，就像不会人人是和尚，人人是农民，人人当兵一样，社会分工而已。只有对经济走向有敏感嗅觉，和正确判断的人，才会在投机活动中长期立于不败之地。他们对社会资源的引导作用，比计划经济委员会的老爷们喝茶拍脑袋的判断可要灵光的多。

But why does society despise speculative behaviors? Why does society always think that speculators are vampires in society who feed on the blood of others? In my opinion, the first reason is that they have read too many "virtuous books and principles" and fallen prey to the limited beliefs of those "virtuous mindsets." The second reason is that they are only using their instinctive thinking and fail to see the value created by intangible production. The third reason is jealousy. The most common criticism is that, "If everyone is a real estate speculator, what will happen to our society?" This is a non-argument. It will certainly not be the case that everyone is speculating on real estate. An analogy is that it is impossible for everyone in society to be a monk, everyone to be a farmer, or everyone to be a soldier. Society has its own division of labor. Only those who are sensitive about future economic trends and possess correct judgments can have an edge in speculative activities. These speculators facilitate the allocation of social resources, and their judgments are more accurate than those made by grandpas in the Planned Economy Committee.

"君子喻于义，小人喻于利"。圣贤们以钱为耻，视谋财获利为大逆不道。可惜君子实在对社会没啥贡献，反而小人们在谋利的过程中推动了社会的发展。君子小人之争，今天还在。君不见多少人对炒房、炒股嗤之以鼻，诅咒他们明天就赔个精光。

"The mind of the superior man is conversant with righteousness; the mind of the mean man is conversant with gain." Virtuous men such as Confucius were ashamed of making money and viewed profit maximization and pursuit of wealth as monstrous crimes. It is a pity that while these "superior men" did not make many contributions to society, mean men drove the development of society in the process of profit maximization. The debate of "superior men versus mean men" still exists today. Don't you see that so many people still treat speculation in the real estate market and stock market with contempt and wish that speculators would lose all their money tomorrow?

投资理财、投机倒把的同志们，你们是背负小人之名，行伟人之业，我在这里为你们摇旗呐喊。

To all the investors and speculators out there: you have been looked down upon and labeled as "mean men" while in fact, you are making great contributions to society. I would like to give a shoutout to all of you.

投资理财、投机倒把是件利国、利民、利己的伟大事业！

Investing, wealth management, and speculative behaviors are conducive to the development of one's country, the quality of life of other citizens, and your own personal development.

这篇文章写过之后将近 10 年，到了 2017 年的时候，中国出台了一个口号，那就是"房子不是用来炒的，而是用来住的"。这个说法会导致了更高的房价。所以我又写了一篇文章来说明这个口号背后的经济规律。

In the 10 years after I wrote this article, which was around 2017, the Chinese government promoted a slogan that was "Houses are not for investing or speculating but for living in." This saying pushed the property prices higher, so I also wrote an article to explain the economic pattern behind this slogan.

其实中国自从 2000 年后房价开始飙升，很多都是因为出台一系列的不尊重市场规律的错误政策导致的。只有我们对这些政策的经济后果做出相对正确的判断，我们才能够实现比较好的投资回报。

In fact, the reason why China's property prices started to skyrocket after 2000 was that the government introduced a series of wrong policies that did not respect the market pattern. It is only after we make a correct judgment about the economic consequences of these policies can we achieve a better investment return.

从炒房者的社会贡献说起 (2016 年前后)
Starting From the Social Contributions Made By Real Estate Speculators (Written in Around 2016)
by Bayfamily

"房子是用来住的，不是用来炒的"。这一句话让炒房者几乎一夜之间陷入过街老鼠人人喊打的境地。现代经济学认为所有的交易都是好的，只要是自愿的，并且不涉及暴力和欺骗。因为每个交易，交易的双方如果出于自愿，都是由于能够增加自己的收益才会交易。炒房过程中，买卖都是自愿的，炒房的行为应该属于亚当·斯密所说的"每个人都为自己的利益而努力，全社会因此整体而获益"。为什么从经济学理论上看起来一个好的行为反倒成为一个过街老鼠了呢？

The saying that "houses are for living in, not speculating or investing" has put real estate speculators in a situation in which they become a public enemy. Modern economists believe that all transactions are good as long as they are voluntary and do not involve violence or deception. This is because, in every transaction, the parties are looking to increase their own benefits, assuming that they are voluntary players in the market. In real estate speculation, both the selling and buying are voluntary acts. Therefore, real estate speculation should be categorized as what Adam Smith describes as "When everyone is working hard for their own interests, society as a whole will benefit too." Why does a behavior that is highly regarded in economic theories become a public enemy?

我们先看几个例子，来正确理解炒房者的社会价值。

Let's examine a few examples to better understand the social value of real estate speculators.

商人从江西 100 元一斤买入茶叶，运到辽宁 200 元一斤卖出，获利 100 元。中国传统是个重农轻商的社会。根据儒家传统思想，认为商人没有创造价值。因为茶叶是农民种的，凭什么你一转手就谋取暴利。大家只看到了生产实物者对社会的贡献，却没有看到流通和贸易对社会财富的贡献。

There is a merchant who buys a pound of tea leaves in Jiangxi, China, at CN¥100 and transports these tea leaves to Liaoning, China, for sale at CN¥200 per pound. During this process, his profit is CN¥100. The traditional Chinese society emphasized agriculture but neglected commerce. According to traditional Confucian thinking, merchants do not create any value. Since the tea leaves are planted and harvested by farmers, what entitles merchants to reap unfair and tremendous profits? Everyone is only able to see the contributions made by producers of tangible products and services but fail to notice the contributions made by the circulation and trading of goods to social wealth.

现代社会对经济学有些了解的人，就不会这样认为。商人实际上创造了200 元的价值。因为如果没有商人的协助，江西的那一斤茶叶没有需求，是生产不出来的，或者因为没有商人的购买，江西的茶叶根本就卖不到 100 元的价格。如果没有商人的工作，农民的收入就少了 100 元。社会的总财富就少了 200 元。农民、商人、消费者是在协作基础上的非零和博弈，共同创造了200 元的价值。

Modern citizens who have some understanding of economics will think otherwise. As a matter of fact, the merchant has created a value of CN¥200. This is because that pound of Jiangxi tea leaves will not have been produced in the first place without the merchant's assistance in creating a market demand for it. Or the Jiangxi tea leaves cannot be sold at CN¥100 per pound without the merchant's purchase. Therefore, the income of farmers will be reduced by CN¥100 if the merchant does not do his job, which means the aggregate wealth in society will be reduced by CN¥200. The coordination between farmers, merchants, and consumers is not a zero-sum game, and they have collaboratively created a value of CN¥200.

下面看第二个例子。商人在春天，100 元一斤买入茶叶，原地不动，到了秋冬加价到 200 元卖出。获利 100 元。这在中国的传统思维里，叫作囤积居奇。大家认为这样的行为基本是社会的寄生虫。凭什么不劳不作，凭空获得100 元

Let's look at a second example below. This time, a merchant buys a pound of tea leaves at CN¥100 in spring. Instead of transporting the tea leaves to another destination for sale, he chooses to sell them at CN¥200 in the fall and winter months, making a profit of CN¥100. According to traditional Chinese beliefs, this is hoarding and price gouging. Almost everyone will categorize this kind of behavior as parasitic on society.

What entitles them to gain a profit of CN¥100 out of thin air without any physical labor and effort?

了解现代经济学的人会知道其实即使不涉及搬运货品，商人创造的价值也是 100 元。因为如果没有商人春天收购茶叶，囤积起来，到了秋天大家会沦落到无茶可喝的地步。或者到了秋天茶叶由于供需不平衡涨到天价，大家都喝不起。但是秋天买茶的人通常不会这么想，他们会觉得奸商凭空让茶叶涨了一倍，从自己的口袋里硬生生地抢走了 100 元。或者是从心理层次，总觉得付出辛苦努力的人创造了价值，倒买倒卖的人没有。他们没有看到倒买倒卖的人的资金成本、对价格趋势的判断，和最重要的——对春天茶叶增产的贡献。

Those who understand modern economics will know that even though the above behavior does not involve the transporting of goods, the value created by the merchant is also CN¥100. The reason is that without the merchant purchasing tea leaves in spring and storing them, everyone will have no tea to drink in fall. Or the price of tea leaves will skyrocket to an unreasonable high in fall because of an imbalance in demand and supply, at which point no one can afford tea anymore. However, those who buy tea in fall will think otherwise. They will feel that they have been robbed CN¥100 by those unscrupulous businessmen who double the price of tea leaves for no legitimate reasons. Or from a psychological level, these people feel that those who work hard create value but those who hoard and engage in price gouging do not. They fail to see the capital cost incurred by these hoarding merchants in purchasing and selling the goods, their judgments about the price trend, and most importantly, their contributions in encouraging farmers to increase their production of tea leaves in spring.

价格是由供需平衡决定的。商人春天买入茶叶秋冬卖出茶叶，买卖平衡，没有增加整体的茶叶总需求量。对茶叶整体价格的影响其实是零。在春天由于商人的收购，反而增加了茶叶的生产，其实对茶叶的价格降低做出了贡献。如果没有商人，茶叶的全年整体价格应该更高。

The market price is determined by demand and supply. When the merchant buys tea leaves in spring and sells them in fall and winter, this does not increase the overall demand for tea leaves, having zero impact on the overall price of tea leaves. Thanks to the merchant's purchase of tea leaves in spring, its production has increased, which in turn contributes to lowering the price of tea leaves. In the absence of the merchant's activities, the overall price of tea leaves will have been higher in that year.

第三个例子就是大家所熟悉的，把第二个例子中的茶叶变成房子。茶叶是可用可不用的消费品，一到房子，一旦和自身利益息息相关，一旦涉及大的数字，大家就情绪激昂，脑子也开始变得不理性。炒房者100 万买入一个房子，一年后200万卖出。获利100万。

The third example is one with which everyone is familiar. Let's substitute tea leaves in the second example with houses. Tea is not a necessity in life, but houses are closely related to one's own interests. Whenever it involves big numbers, everyone will become excited, overcome by emotion, and lose their rational thinking. Real estate speculators buy a house at \$1 million and sell it at \$2 million after a year, making a profit of \$1 million.

如果你明白经济学基本原理，炒房者对社会的贡献和买卖茶叶的商人没有任何区别。房子和茶叶本质没有任何区别，都涉及各种生产要素，比如土地、劳动力、技术等。如何把这些生产要素有效地组织起来，最有效的就是价格指引。买卖过股票的人都会知道，市场在任何一个价格点上，永远是供需平衡的。就是一半人看跌，一半人看涨。如果没有炒房的人，开发商在100万这个价格位置上就会担心卖不出去，降低自己的开发量。炒房人对社会房子的总需求也是没有任何改变，因为炒房买进来的房子，最终都是要卖出去重新回到市场上去的。打击炒房者，只会让房子的建设量变得更小，人为造成短缺。

If you understand the basic theories of economics, the social contributions made by real estate speculators are no different from those by tea merchants. Houses and tea are essentially the same. They both involve various production factors, for example, land, labor, and skills. On the issue of how to effectively organize these production factors, the most effective way is price indications. Anyone who has bought and/or sold stocks will know that at any price point in the market, the demand and supply are in balance. This means that half of the people are expecting an increase in price and half a decrease. In the absence of real estate speculators in the market, at the price level of $1 million, property developers will be worried about not being able to sell the houses, so they will reduce their overall development effort. Real estate speculators do not affect the aggregate demand for houses in society at all because they will have to sell the houses they have purchased at some point, putting these houses back to the market. Clamping down on real estate speculation will only discourage the construction of houses, causing a man-made shortage.

这也是越限购房价越涨的道理。因为越限购，开发商越是看不清未来的市场销售前景，盖出来的房子自然就少了。越是打击炒房者，市场越是没有人接盘，越是会导致后期的房产短缺。你可能会认为房子和茶叶不一样，茶叶是可有可无的东西，房子是刚需，炒房者在我前面抢先一步，不劳而获就赚了一倍，凭什么？

This is also why the more strictly the government limits the purchase of houses, the faster the property prices surge. Because of stricter limits, property developers cannot see clearly the future prospect of the market and their sale, so they build fewer homes. The more the government discourages real estate speculators, the smaller the number of people who are willing to purchase houses in the market, which in turn causes a shortage of houses later. You may well think that houses are different from tea. While tea is not a daily necessity, houses have a rigid demand. What entitles real estate speculators to make a 100% profit from buying a house one step ahead?

首先在一个自由买卖的市场，炒房者是不可能长期获得高额利润的。如果把风险因素考虑进去的话，炒房者实际的获利空间不会大于这段时间的资金成本。对于未来市场的判断都已经反映在当前价格上了。炒房者谁有资金都可以进入市场，按照微观经济学市场充分竞争的理论，获利不会大于资本成本。换句话说，你光看见吃肉的了，却没看见挨打的。

Firstly, in a free trade market, it is impossible for real estate speculators to persistently achieve high profits in the long term. If we take into account risk factors, the actual potential for profit will not be greater than the cost of capital in that period. Any predictions about the future market have already been reflected in current prices. Any real estate speculators who have the capital can enter the market. According to the theory of perfect competition in microeconomics, the profit will exceed the cost of capital. In other words, you only see the profits but fail to see the costs.

对于炒房而言，长期来看并不会造成房价的上升。因为炒房者买的房子，最终是要卖的，炒房不会对市场的长期供求有任何影响。即使不卖也是要出租的，通过租房市场减轻买房需求和压力。

Real estate speculation will not cause property prices to increase in the long term. This is because the houses bought by real estate speculators will have to be sold in the end. Therefore, real estate speculation will not affect the long-term demand and supply in the market at all. Even though some real estate speculators will not choose to sell their houses at this point, they will need to rent them out, reducing the rigid demand for houses and pressure through the rental market.

从短期来看，炒房增加了市场的交易量和流动性，便于大家买卖房子。长期来看，由于炒房人的存在，反而让有住房需求的人可以住上更便宜的房子。2007 年的时候，在美国的佛罗里达州，曾经房价也被炒房者抬高了好几倍。开发商争相开发建设，遍地都是楼盘。但是到了金融危机，炒房者血本无归。可是给佛罗里达留下了大量的空置楼盘，从纽约州来的真正要退休的人低价搬入。如果没有这些炒房者抬高房价，刺激生产，恐怕这些退休者最后住不到这些便宜的房子。

In the short term, real estate speculation increases market transactions and liquidity, making it more convenient for everyone to buy and sell houses. In the long term, the presence of real estate speculators guarantees that those with housing needs can live in more affordable houses. In 2007, in Florida, U.S.A., the property prices increased manifold because of real estate speculation. Property developers were all in a race to build more homes. Construction sites were ubiquitous. However, during the financial crisis, real estate speculators lost every penny they had. But this left Florida with scores of empty homes, benefitting retirees from New York State who could now move in at a low price. If these real estate speculators had not driven up the property prices and encouraged production, these retirees would probably never have been able to live in such cheap houses.

我们社会的很多问题看似是分配不均导致的，其实很多问题的来源是错误的观念导致错误的政策。圣人们认为生产实物的和关心理想道德的人才是高尚的人，只有小人们天天想着如何把别人的钱财搬到自己腰包里。当我们碰到某种社会问题的时候，本能地喜欢把社会问题归结到某一类特定人群上。套用零和博弈的思路，似乎所有的问题都是这些人的贪婪所致，是他们抢了我口袋里的钱包，所以才导致我今天的问题。

Even though it seems that many of our social problems are caused by unfair distribution, their root is wrong policies induced by mistaken beliefs. Those saints believe that only those who engage in the production of tangible goods and services and care about aspirations and morality are honorable and that only mean men will think about how to move other's money and wealth to their own pocket. When we encounter certain social issues, our instinct is to blame those social problems on a particular group of people. Adopting the zero-sum game mindset, it seems that all problems are caused by people's greed: these people rob money from my pocket which causes the problems that I face today.

二战期间德国的犹太人，苏联、中国当年的地主都曾经背过这样的黑锅。比如当年的中国，曾经认为农民之所以穷，都是地主剥削导致的。这表面看起来很有道理，农民辛辛苦苦劳作一年，凭什么要把收成的一部分交给不干活的地主？其实地主和农民不是零和博弈关系，而是非零和博弈关系。地主在挑选佃农、管理土地、市场预测方面的努力被大家忽视。地主和农民共同工作，才能创造出更大的价值。土地公有化，地主消失后的苏联和我国都经历过粮食减产、食品短缺和饥荒的惨剧。

During the Second World War, Jewish people in Germany and landlords in the Soviet Union and China bore similar blame. For instance, in China back in the days, people used to think that the reason why farmers were so poor was because of exploitation by landlords. This saying seemed to make sense: Why did the farmers have to hand in part of their harvest to landlords who never worked? In fact, the relationship between landlords and farmers was not a zero-sum game. It was a non-zero-sum game in which mutual benefit was possible. The landlords' contributions in selecting farmers, managing the land, and predicting the market had been ignored by everyone. It was only when landlords and farmers collaborated could immense value be created. After the disappearance of landlords and the adoption of public ownership of land in the Soviet Union and China, both countries faced the tragedies of reduced food production, food shortage, and famine.

面对炒房者，人们的本能也是一样的，首先各种贬义词倾泻到炒房者的身上，诸如炒房团、奸商、投机商等等，甚至动用法律手段进行打击。炒房的"炒"字也是抹黑他人的办法，给人不务正业的感觉。其实炒房和投资房地产是一样的。你可以说特朗普是炒房的，也可以说他是地产大亨。名称只会让你困惑。如果没有看到炒房者创造的价值，恐怕也只会让供应不足，房价一路继续攀升，最终受苦的还是真正的购房者。

People's instincts are the same when facing real estate speculators. They first use different derogatory terms to label these real estate speculators, for example, hit-and-run artists, hot money handlers, drive-by dealers, parasites, and sandwichers. Sometimes they even resort to legal action to clamp down on them. A literal translation of the Chinese term for real estate speculation is "pan-frying houses." Combining the word "pan-frying" with "houses" is also a way to badmouth other people because this phrase implies that real estate speculators spend time in an activity that does not have a real purpose. In fact, real estate speculation and investing are the same. You can say that

Trump is a real estate speculator or a tycoon. The name will only confuse you. If a person fails to see the value created by real estate speculators, this will probably cause an insufficient supply of homes and skyrocketing property prices. The real losers, in the end, are bona fide home purchasers.

限购貌似可以短期抑制需求，但是经验告诉我们某种商品限购一定会导致这个商品价格奇高。限购和限产本是孪生，不可分割，往往同时出现。这边限购那边严控土地供应。改革开放前，曾经在中国肉、蛋、油限购，同期这类商品常年短缺。不熟悉中国这段历史的人可以想想发达国家的毒品，毒品在美国也是政府严重限购的对象，最终结果也是本来生产成本不贵的毒品价格奇高，是生产价格成本的上千倍。大麻不限购的墨西哥，大麻和香烟的价格没有什么区别。常年限购的中国房地产价格也在远远脱离生产成本，常年保持在不可思议的高度。

Though it seems that limiting purchase can curb demand in the short term, experience tells us that limiting the purchase of a certain commodity will definitely lead to unreasonably high prices of that commodity. Limiting purchase and production are two sides of the same coin: they cannot be separated and occur together. For example, purchase limits go hand in hand with restricting land supply. Before China's economic reform, the government limited purchases of meat, eggs, and oil, causing a persistent shortage of these commodities in the same period. For those who are not familiar with this era in Chinese history, another obvious example is drugs in developed countries. It goes without saying that the U.S. government stringently limits the purchase of drugs. The end result is that the prices of drugs, which have low manufacturing costs, reach an unreasonably high level, a thousand-fold increase compared to its manufacturing costs. In Mexico, where the purchase of marijuana is not limited, the prices of marijuana and cigarettes are almost the same. In China, where the purchase of homes is limited, the property prices derail from the manufacturing cost and stand at an unreasonably high level.

03 挣钱要理直气壮

03 Pursuing Wealth Unapologetically

中国是一个社会主义国家，我们可以理解出台抑制资本获利的政策。共产主义在意识形态上总体而言是不鼓励个人拥有更多财富的，而强调共同富裕。但是资本主义国家的美国，似乎人们也越来越变得像社会主义国家。

Since China is a socialist country, we can understand why it launches policies to control activities of making a profit from the capital. Generally speaking, the ideology of communism does not encourage individuals to possess more wealth but stresses collective wealth. However, in the U.S., which is a capitalist society, it seems that people are becoming more and more socialist.

美国四年一度的大选就是这样情绪的宣泄。每次不断有政客跳出来，他们会主张瓜分富人口袋里的钱，然后把这些钱给穷人。这些政客的特点就是特别喜欢花别人的钱，为自己买荣誉。就是花张三的钱给李四买东西，然后给自己冠个好名声。我从来不见他们把自己的钱都捐了再说。想当年中国共产主义运动的时候，很多革命者还是把自己家地分了，把自己家房子烧了，然后投身革命的。至少这说明他们自己真信。而美国主张高福利的总统，一个个都是卸任之后，自己大捞特捞。你看看克林顿家族和奥巴马家当总统前后的财富增长情况就明白了。

The U.S.'s presidential election held every four years is an occasion for venting such sentiments. Every time, there are these politicians who jump out and propose that we should take money from the rich and give it to the poor. The characteristic of these politicians is that they like using other people's money to buy honors for themselves. In other words, they are using a person A's money to buy things for person B. In this process, they can earn a good reputation. I have never seen any such politicians donate their own money to the needy. In contrast, during the Chinese Communist Revolution, many revolutionists divided their own land and shared it with other peasants, burned their houses down, and devoted themselves to the revolution. These behaviors at least demonstrated that they genuinely believed in the ideology and the slogans they were promoting. Yet the U.S. presidents who advocated high welfare levels during their presidency were turning their political fame into a huge fortune after stepping down from office. Take a look at the increase in the net worth of the Clintons and Obamas before and after their presidency.

我不是说国家不需要有基本的福利，这些是需要的。国家需要给一些残疾的人、丧失劳动能力的人或者老人，一个最基本的社会保障。但是如果消灭了创造财富的激情，那么社会总体财富会变得越来越少。无论那些超级富豪拥有多少钱，其实他们拥有的钱并不是从别人口袋里挖来的，而是因为他们创造了更多的财富。他们拥有的财富只是他们创造了的更多的财富中的一个部分，甚至很多时候只是一小部分。

I am not saying that a country should not guarantee basic welfares of citizens. These are necessary. The government needs to provide the handicapped, senior citizens, and people who have lost their ability to earn money with some basic social guarantees. However, if the passion to create wealth is extinguished, the total wealth in society will gradually decrease. No matter how much wealth those super-billionaires own, they do not steal their money from other people's pockets. Instead, their wealth comes from their ability to create wealth. The wealth that they own personally only represents a fraction, if not a tiny fraction, of the wealth they have created.

比如没有比尔·盖茨就不会有微软。没有乔布斯就不会有苹果。比尔·盖茨个人财富虽然在全世界排名前三，可是他拥有的财富只占微软公司股票总市值的很小的一部分。

For example, we would not have Microsoft without Bill Gates and Apple without Steve Jobs. Even though Bill Gates' has the third-highest net worth in the world, the wealth that he personally owns only represents a tiny fraction of Microsoft's market cap.

会走路的钱
Money Walks

普通民众容易觉得财富是个零和的游戏。有人多了一分钱，我就少了一分钱。所以社会多多少少都有一些仇富的心态。仇富的心态在中国更严重一些，因为他们觉得那些一夜暴富的人多多少少都有一些非法行为。或者是官商勾结，或者是利用改革开放之初，法制不完备，市场规律不清晰的时候，狠赚了一笔。也许他们说的有一定的道理。但是他们忘了，如果没有和官商勾结，很多事情根本做不成。官商勾结之后，做成的那些事情，可是实实在在给社会带来了社会财富。不然你看看中国那些高楼大厦的建设哪一个离得开政府支持呢？要是没有那些商人搞官商勾结，土地批不下来，恐怕上海和北京到今天还是一片平房呢。

Ordinary citizens may easily succumb to the belief that wealth is a zero-sum game: when someone has one more dollar, I have less money. Therefore, people in different societies feel some resentment toward the rich. This resentment of the rich mindset is more prevalent in China. Chinese people often think that those who become rich overnight have more or less engaged in illegal activities, for example, collusion between government and business, and exploiting a loophole in the legal system and unclear regulatory rules in the early stage of the economic reform. Perhaps they have some basis to support their claims. However, they are oblivious to the fact that without some form of collaboration, or collusion, between the government and business, many projects would not have come to fruition. After the collusion, these projects were approved and finished, which generated wealth for our society. The construction of all skyscrapers in China was backed by government support. Without the government's collusion with business, the land would not have been approved and Shanghai and Beijing would probably be a sea of low-rise buildings.

美国也有仇富心态，这种仇富心态并不像中国那样赤裸裸且暴力，而是隐藏在人们内心背后的。总体而言，英美文化中的人们对钱这件事情保持高度的隐私，不愿意和别人分享。

Resentment of the rich can be found in the U.S. society too, but this kind of attitude is not as naked and violent as that in China. Rather, Americans hide their resentful sentiments. Overall, in Western culture, people prefer to be private about money. They are reluctant to share any information related to money and wealth with others.

表现出来就是很多基督徒内心深处是觉得作为个体，不应该拥有太多钱。对拥有更多钱的人，他们多多少少会搞一些道德绑架，对他们提出更高的要求。当然一个原因也是一部分富人总是喜欢用豪宅、名车、漂亮媳妇、奢侈的生活方式这样的事情来刺激老百姓。

The manifestation of this kind of mindset among many Christians is that they believe that as an individual, they should not own too much money. These Christians more or less exert moral coercion on rich people by setting higher moral standards for them. Of course, one of the reasons is that some rich people show off their extravagant lifestyle characterized by mansions, luxury cars, and gorgeous wives, which may stir up bitter feelings among ordinary citizens.

可能你会认同一个人合法赚的每一分钱都是创造了社会的财富。但是你会质疑富人花掉的每一分钱，特别是那些奢侈的享乐，是不是对社会资源的浪费？

Perhaps you will agree that every single penny earned by a person in a legal manner has indeed created wealth for society. However, you will also suspect, is every single penny spent by the rich, especially their splurges on luxuries, a waste of social resources?

其实富人能够消费的财富并不多。一个大富豪能够消费掉的财富无非是一日三餐，可能外加几个普通人没有的管家、佣人、秘书、司机等。比尔·盖茨也好，巴菲特也好，他们一生花掉的钱，真实的消费不见得比你我高多少。因为那些房子、珠宝首饰、艺术品本质上都是投资品。他们可能比你我实际的消费高出 10 倍、100 倍，但绝对达不到 10 万倍或者上亿倍的程度。

In fact, the amount of wealth that can be consumed or spent by the rich is not a very significant sum. The spending items of a billionaire are his or her three meals of the day, plus some items and services which are not accessible to ordinary citizens, such as a butler, some servants, a secretary, a driver, etc. The actual money spent by billionaires, be it Bill Gates or Warren Buffett, may not be much higher than the amount consumed by you and me because those houses, jewelry, and art pieces are essentially investments. Their actual spending may be ten-times, or even 100-times higher than yours and mine. However, it is impossible that they spend 100,000-fold or 100-million-fold more than ordinary citizens.

因为一个人的肚子只有那么大，一天只有 24 小时。我在美国生活了这么多年，我看到实实在在的，真正是富人把社会资源浪费掉的例子只有一起。那就是闹得沸沸扬扬，著名高尔夫球手泰格伍兹的前妻把泰格伍兹送她的豪宅，用推土机推掉这件事情。

This is because everyone only has a limited appetite and 24 hours in a day. Based on my own experience of living in the U.S. for so many years, I have only observed one real instance in which rich people wasted social resources. It was in the tabloid headlines that the famous golfer Tiger Woods's ex-wife bulldozed a mansion that Woods gifted her.

由于感情上的一些不愉快，这个女子属于泄愤，把一幢价值几百万美元的房子用推土机直接推掉了。虽然站在法律上这是合法的，但是这真是一件人神共愤的事情。因为那个房子里面凝结了很多工人的劳动时间。如果你不喜欢，你可以把房子卖掉，甚至把它捐赠出去都可以。一己之怒把它用推土机消灭掉，是对社会财富的破坏，也引起了美国人的愤怒。除这类现象，我很少能找到富人浪费了大量社会财富的例子。

Because of some relationship problems, this woman was trying to vent her anger by demolishing a mansion that was worth millions of dollars. Though her behavior is totally legal, it is a monstrous act. This is because that mansion represented the labor of many workers. If she did not like the house, she could well sell it or even donate it to charity. Tearing it down out of anger is undoubtedly an act of destroying social wealth, arousing public anger in the U.S. Other than this observation, I can rarely find other examples of the rich wasting tremendous social wealth.

04 葛朗台是个好同志
04 Eugénie Grandet Is a Good Guy

有钱人不可避免地把一部分钱存在银行里。拥有大额存款有时也会让人觉得富人们为富不仁。好像你把钱存在银行里，就是把社会上的财富锁了起来一样。

Rich people inevitably put some of their money in banks. Their possessing large amounts of saving deposits makes people think that they are rich but unrighteous, because they lock up social wealth.

很多人有这样一个偏见，那就是只有消费才是一件利国利民的事情，因为每一笔消费都促进了社会的生产。存钱是有罪的，因为每一笔存款都抑制了消费。社会的财富似乎应该在流动中才能被大家所掌握，才能生产出更多的财富，而把钱存在银行里，似乎只是吝啬鬼和葛朗台才会做的事情。

Many people harbor a prejudicial view that the only way to make contributions to society and country is through consumption as every single transaction facilitates production in society. Saving money is highly reprehensible because every deposit curbs consumption. It seems that social wealth can only be made good use of and facilitate the creation of more wealth when it is circulating. It seems that saving money in the bank is something that only misers and Eugénie Grandet will do.

其实不是。这个观点就像我们曾经拥抱生产鄙视消费一样的不靠谱。存款其实是促进社会生产最好的方法。你把钱存在银行里，银行是不会让这些钱在保险箱里睡大觉的。银行会把钱投入生产环节，因为银行的钱需要贷出去。这些存款如果不投入生产环节，它也会通过消费贷款被投入到更需要的消费环节。因为那些是人们愿意支付更高利息的消费，说明有比你更急迫的消费需求。

The truth says otherwise. The above point of view is as unreasonable as how we used to embrace production but despise consumption. Saving money is indeed the best way to facilitate production activities in society. When you deposit some money into the banking system, these financial institutions will not let all this money sit in the drawer. Banks will redirect all this money to production activities because banks' money has to be loaned out. If these deposits are not reinvested in production activities, they will be allocated to consumption activities, which may have an even greater need for money, through consumption loans. In taking out a consumption loan, borrowers are willing to pay for a higher interest to finance their consumption, which means they have much more urgent consumption needs.

对社会最大的浪费，其实是那些不会给你带来快乐和没有意义的消费。比如酗酒或者吸毒，因为这些消费最终给你带来的是病痛，也不会让社会上的总体财富更加多起来。或者当你消费在一些没有价值的奢侈品、纪念品上，也会误导了一定的社会资源。

In fact, the biggest waste to society is those meaningless consumptions that bring you feelings of pleasure, for example, heavy drinking and taking drugs, because these consumptions will eventually bring you pain and diseases and fail to increase aggregate wealth in society. Or when you spend your money on some valueless luxury goods and souvenirs, you are misguiding social resources to a certain extent.

相比之下，存钱、投资是和生产与消费一样对社会有促进作用的事情。但是为什么大家总觉得像葛朗台这个守财奴一样的存款行为是可耻的呢？

In comparison, saving money and investing are as productive to society as production and consumption. But why does everyone think that Grandet's parsimonious habit of saving his money is despicable?

总体来说还是漫长的文化影响。人类进入资本主义时代的时间并不长，人和人通过和平合作的方式共同生产、创造出更多的社会财富的时间经历也不长。在早期暴力掠夺的时代，你拥有的更多财富，多半是从穷人那里抢掠而来的。所以我们自古各个民族各个文化都有鄙视富人的传统。而富人总是在不停地存款、放债。莎士比亚有威尼斯商人，法国有葛朗台。在中东的一些宗教文化里，甚至不允许收取利息。他们觉得利息是最不公正的，放债的人什么也没有做，凭什么就白白挣了钱呢？

Generally speaking, we are influenced by our history and culture. The time since mankind entered the capitalist era is not very long. Our experience with peaceful cooperation between a very large number of strangers in coordinating production and creating more social wealth is limited. In the early days of violent plundering, the wealth owned by a person was probably a result of robbing the poor. This is why many cultures and races have an ancient tradition of despising the rich. Yet the rich are always saving their money and extending credit. Shakespeare created the Merchant of Venice, and France had Grandet. In some religions in the Middle East, charging an interest on loans is prohibited, because they believe that interests are the most unrighteous: What entitles the lenders to earn interests when they have done nothing?

今天我们知道利息的本质是期权(option)。就是我们股票交易中经常说的期权。因为放债人把钱借出之后，他就失去了一个 option。在没有把钱借出去之前，他的钱可以今天花也可以明天花。钱借出去了，那他只能明天花，所以他就丢掉了自己今天花钱这个选择的自由。因为少了这个 option，所以他必须获得一定量的补偿。

Now we know that the nature of interests is an option, a term which is also commonly referred to in stock trading. When a lender extends credit, he loses an option. Before lending out the money, he can choose to spend his money today or tomorrow. After lending out the money, he can only choose to spend it tomorrow, so he loses the freedom to choose to spend the money today. Because of the loss of such an option, he has to be compensated to a corresponding extent.

这个人并没有坐在这里不劳而获。因为他失去了这个 option，导致他可以把自己的财富投入到更需要的生产过程中。这样会使整个社会的生态要素效率更高。只要你明白一些数学和基本的经济学常识，你都知道那些传统的道德绑架，其实很多时候是站不住脚的。无论葛朗台还是夏洛克都为这个社会创造了大量的财富。

Therefore, this person does not simply sit there and reap without sowing. At the same time when he loses an option, he has reinvested his wealth into other production processes that are in more desperate need of money. This whole process of saving money and extending credit improves the efficiency of the entire economic ecosystem and other production factors in society. As long as you understand some basic mathematics and economics, you will know that all this traditional moral coercion is often unfounded. Both Grandet and Charlotte have created enormous wealth for society.

我说这些抽象的经济学概念就是想说明，挣钱是光荣的，存钱是光荣的，获得财富和拥有财富也是光荣的。大家没有必要为追求财富、炒房子、炒股票、倒买倒卖这些事情而感到心虚和自卑。

The reason why I explain these abstract economic concepts is to illustrate that earning money is laudable, that saving money is laudable, and that procuring and possessing wealth is also laudable. There is no need for us to doubt or feel ashamed of our pursuits of wealth, real estate speculation, trading stocks, or the behavior of buying and selling for the mere purpose of making a profit.

中国在改革开放之前，曾经很长时间以贫困为荣。大家渐渐发现计划经济没有办法指导社会的生态要素到最需要的地方去。反而是"让一部分人先富起来"这样的口号，让市场决定社会资源的分配和合作方式才让国家富裕起来。想象一下，在一群为共产主义奋斗终生抛头颅和洒热血的 70 多岁的老革命中，邓小平能提出"致富光荣，让一部分人先富起来"的口号，这是一个多么否定自己，思想解放的事情。

Before China's economic reform, there was a long period during which Chinese people were proud of being impoverished. However, people started to realize that a planned economy failed to guide production factors in society to the places that needed them the most. On the other hand, it is slogans such as "Let some people become rich first," under which the market determines the allocation of social resources and cooperation, that lets the country become rich. We can only imagine how brave and insightful Deng Xiaopeng was in proposing the slogan of "Getting rich is honorable, and let us let some people become rich first" when he was facing a bunch of old revolutionists in their 70s, who devoted their entire life to building a communist utopia. Deng Xiaopeng was negating himself and also liberating his own thinking.

然而美国没有经历过这样思想解放的过程。美国人虽然一直是资本主义，但是也许是受清教徒宗教的影响，文化上还是多多少少鄙视敛财的。圣经上说："富人进天堂比骆驼穿过针眼还难"。因为有些为富不仁的事情，总是让有钱人灰头土脸的，必须低调。而那些没有钱的人反而可以理直气壮地伸手要福利。很多人不敢把追求财富作为自己的理想，至少不敢堂而皇之地公开讲。我在美国听孩子们的演讲，有将来想成为总统的，将来想成为发明家的，将来想成为一个律师的，或者将来成为一个义务工作者，帮助贫困人们的。但是我很少听见哪个小孩能够理直气壮地说我将来的理想就是成为商人，就是要去倒买倒卖，追求财富，变得有钱的。

Yet the U.S. has not gone through such a process of liberation of thinking. Even though Americans are capitalist, culturally speaking, they more or less despise the pursuits of wealth, perhaps because of the influence of Puritans. The Bible says, "It is easier for a camel to pass through the eye of a needle than for a rich man to enter into the kingdom of God." Because of the common belief that it is unrighteous to be rich, rich people keep their heads down. But those without any money feel justified in demanding welfare benefits. Many people do not dare set the pursuit of wealth as their aspirations. At least, they do not dare talk about it openly. When I was in the U.S. listening to children's speech on their dreams, they aspired to become a president, an inventor, a lawyer, or a volunteer to help the underprivileged in the future. But I have seldom met a child who says in a confident manner that his aspiration is to become a businessman, to buy and sell for the purpose of making a profit, to pursue wealth, and to become rich.

也许大家心里会这么想，但是没有人敢像喊口号一样地把这句话说出来。事实上你会发现人过了青春期之后，当步入社会步入现实的生活中，大部分人的生活目标就是想拥有更多的财富。既然是这么想的，为什么要做伪君子呢？为什么不能大声地喊出来呢？

Perhaps everyone is thinking about these pursuits, but no one dares shout it out loud like a slogan. In fact, you will realize that after puberty, when you enter society and reality, the life goal of most people is to own more wealth. If they are thinking about money, why do they become a hypocrite? Why don't they shout it out loud?

背后的原因还是我上面说的文化的原因。我把这些讨论专门整理为一章就是想破除这些虚伪的面罩。想挣钱的人可以理直气壮地站起来，大声宣布自己的挣钱理想。

The reason behind has to do with the cultural contexts I have mentioned above. Now that I have organized all the arguments raised on the issue of pursuing wealth to reveal their hypocrisy, those who aspire to earn more money can stand up and shout their goal out loud without feeling sorry or ashamed.

有了理想，才有目标。有了具体的目标，为了这个目标，我就会制定出详细的周密的计划，一步步地实现这个目标。我在 2006 年公开发表了自己的博客，大声喊出了我的目标就是"十年一千万"。

With my aspirations, I am able to come up with specific goals. In order to achieve these goals, I will formulate detailed and thorough plans to help me achieve these goals step by step. In 2006, I published a public blog post in which I exclaimed that, "My goal is to accumulate \$10 million in 10 years."

第十一章 普通家庭十年一千万投资理财计划

Chapter 11: An Average Family's $10-million-in-10-year Investment and Wealth Management Plan

　　除了说服自己，我还需要一个外界的压力，为此我 2006 年 12 月圣诞节放假的时候，写了一篇"臭名昭著"的"普通家庭十年一千万投资理财计划"。我用"臭名昭著"这个词来形容是因为大家就这个话题在投资理财论坛上几乎整整讨论了十年，这篇文章的累计阅读量在 10 万次左右。

After convincing myself, I decided that I needed some external pressure to motivate me too. In a bid to exert some external pressure on myself, I wrote a notorious article titled "An Average Family's $10-million-in-10-year Investment and Wealth Management Plan" during the Christmas holiday in December 2006. I used "notorious" to describe this article because it has become a popular discussion topic for users on the investment and wealth management forum for almost a decade. This article accumulated about 100,000 views.

普通家庭十年一千万的理财计划 (2006 年 12 月 25 日)

An Average Family's 10-million-in-10-year Wealth Management Plan (December 25, 2006)

by Bayfamily

　　我的投资理财目标不大，有一千万就可以了。钱财多了有害无益。但适量的富足可以给人带来安全、自由、舒适、和小小的成就感。我的计划是

500 万的时候，太太不工作，可以全心照顾刚上小学的孩子们，一千万的时候我退休。和 va-landlord 的目标一样。退休不是什么都不干了，而是不为衣食工作，彻底实现 financial freedom（财务自由）。计划看起来好像太遥远，但我觉得再有十年时间，运气不太坏的话，在我们 45 岁以前是可以实现的。

My investment goal does not involve a big number as my goal is to accumulate $10 million. The shortcomings of having more money outweigh its benefits. But a suitable level of wealth can bring people security, freedom, comfort, and some sense of achievement. My plan is for my wife to quit her job when our wealth reaches $5 million so that she can take good care of our children who will be starting primary school then. I will retire when I have $10 million. Similar to forum user *va-landlord*'s goal, being retired does not mean idling. Instead, it means "being able not to work for the sole purpose of earning a living." Though this plan looks distant, I think that we will be able to achieve our goals in a decade, before the age of 45, if our luck is not too bad.

我们家是湾区再普通不过的家庭了。家庭税前年收入 20 万不到一点点，Bonus（年终奖）多的时候可以达到 22 万。六年前我们一文不名地来到湾区的时候，那时年收入只有 14 万，看着湾区的天价房价，感觉生活毫无希望。那时经过密密麻麻的住宅区的时候，老是叹息何时才能有自己的家啊。那时个别同事家房价已达 800k，在我当时看来如天上的银河一样可望不可及。

My family is the typical, average family in the Bay Area. My family income before tax is slightly less than $200,000. If my wife and I have a big year-end bonus, our family income can exceed $220,000. Six years ago, we arrived in the Bay Area basically penniless. As we only had an annual salary of $140,000 at the time, we felt that life was hopeless when we looked at the exorbitant property prices in the Bay Area. At the time, when we were driving past those densely-populated residential areas, we sighed and wondered, when could we have our own home? Meanwhile, the home of one of my colleagues was worth $800,000, and I thought that this was a distant reality, just like how I could see the galaxy but could never reach it.

　　通过和湾区前辈的接触，明白投资理财的道理后，才渐渐明白发家致富的渠道。只怪刚到美国时，中西部的城市信息太闭塞，读书就开始注重投资的话，资产应是现在的一倍。五年前，我对太太说，五年后我们会有一百万。我太太说我做梦，就是不吃不喝，不交税，把工资全存下也不会有一百万。我说不是这样算的。过去六年里，每年年终我都会计算一下家庭的账目，下表过去六年的总结（万美元）。

	2001	2002	2003	2004	2005	2006	2007
现金	0.5	0.0	3.0	2.0	5.0	1.0	2.0
股票	0.5	2.5	2.0	2.0	0.0	0.0	0.0
退休金	3.0	6.0	9.0	12.0	16.3	21.1	29.2
房屋净值	0.0	8.0	12.0	23.0	45.0	64.8	89.0
总和	4.0	16.5	26.0	39.0	66.3	86.8	120.2
增长率		313%	58%	50%	70%	31%	38%
债务							84.0

After some interactions with my seniors and more experienced investors in the Bay Area, I had a more in-depth understanding of the principles of investing and wealth managing. I began to understand what the ways to become wealthy were. However, I was regretting that if only I had started paying attention to investing when I embarked on my Ph.D. studies, my asset would have doubled now. Regrettably, when I first arrived in the U.S., the information in Middle West cities was highly untransparent. Five years ago, I was telling my wife that we would have $1 million in five years, and my wife told me that I was daydreaming. "Even if we do not drink, eat and pay tax and save all our salaries, we will not have $1 million in five years," she explained. "This is how you should do the calculations," I replied. In the last six years, I calculated the net worth of my family at the end of every year. Please refer to the table below for a summary of the performance of my family's investments in the last six years (the unit is US$10,000).

	2001	2002	2003	2004	2005	2006	2007
Cash	0.5	0.0	3.0	2.0	5.0	1.0	2.0
Stock	0.5	2.5	2.0	2.0	0.0	0.0	0.0
Retirement	3.0	6.0	9.0	12.0	16.3	21.1	29.2
House Equity	0.0	8.0	12.0	23.0	45.0	64.8	89.0
Total	4.0	16.5	26.0	39.0	66.3	86.8	120.2
Growth Rate		313%	58%	50%	70%	31%	38%
Debt							84.0

六年以后果然有了 120 万。买房时间分别是 2002, 2003, 2005, 2006。地点是湾区和中国轮着来。这样的数据大家可能都看腻了，同样的故事在湾区千千万万的中国人家庭里同样地上演着。

Six years later, we did manage to have $1.2 million. We bought a house in 2002, 2003, 2005, and 2006 in the Bay Area and China. Perhaps you are bored with such data because the same story happens in tens of thousands of Chinese families in the Bay Area.

我想说的是，如何从 120 万，再用十年左右的时间里，达到一千万。首先看 growth rate（增长率）。头几年的增长率比较高，在 50%~60% 左右，因为还没有什么资产，最近几年下滑到 30%～40%。主要原因是盘面大了，每年固定的现金进账相对减小。我估算了一下，未来三年里 growth rate 会下降到 15%，主要原因有两个：leverage 用光了。我的投资策略还是保守的，每次至少 10% 的首付。现在总的贷款是八十万，是我们收入的四倍。如加上其他的房租收入，贷款只有三倍。 Debt/Asset ratio（债务资产比）也控制在 50% 左右，就是说美国中国房价明天一起跌去一半，也不要紧。但 leverage 确实是用光了，第一不能 refinance 了，因为我们现在的利率很好。第二，大房子收益很差，小房子太辛苦了，担心管不过来。未来几年的行情很难说，盘面大了，保本最重要。也就是说，我们家遇到了谷米家遇到的同样问题，增长的瓶颈问题。如果不开拓新的投资渠道的话，十年后的我们家的资产将只有 250 万左右，离一千万还很远。也许太太十五年后可退休，我可还得再奋斗 20 年，才会有一千万,那时也是五十多了，没什么意义。

I want to talk about how to use 10 years to grow $1.2 million to $10 million. The first thing we need to look at is the growth rate. My growth rate in the first few years is quite high, at around 50-60%. This is because we did not have many assets. In recent years, the growth rate dropped to 30-40% because our asset base is larger now, which means the fixed annual cash inflow is relatively reduced. Based on my calculations, the growth rate will drop to 15% in the next three years. There are two main reasons. Firstly, there is no leverage. My investment strategies are rather conservative because I pay a down payment of at least 10% every time. Now our total loan is $800,000, which is four times our income. Adding rental income, the amount of loan is three times our income. Our debt/asset ratio is controlled at around 50%, which means even if property prices in both the U.S. and China drop by 50% tomorrow, my family will not be affected much. However, we did use up our leverage. Therefore, the first reason is that we cannot refinance as we enjoy an excellent interest rate now. Secondly, the return generated by big houses is bad, but managing smaller houses is exhausting. We are worried that we might not be able to manage so many smaller houses. It is difficult to ascertain the market trend in the next few years. When one has a big portfolio, preserving the capital is of paramount importance. In other words, my family has encountered the predicaments faced by forum user Gumi's family too, that is the growth plateau problem. If I do not try to explore new investment channels, my family will have $2.5 million of assets only, which is far below the goal of $10 million. Perhaps my wife will be able to retire in 15 years, but I will have to work hard for 20 years more in order to accumulate $10 million, at which point I will be in my mid-50s, which defeats the purpose of my goal.

春节时候，我用各种模型反复比较，除非是用特别大的 leverage，比如零首付，凭着 20 万的收入，是很难达到一千万的，要想用稳健的方式，10％的首付，固定的现金流以备不测的话，按历史平均回报，最多可以达到

500 万。这和我在湾区的观察非常一致。在这里生活 20 年，头脑清醒善于经营的家庭最多也就 400 万～500 万了。

During Chinese New Year, I used various models to carry out different calculations and comparisons. Unless I am using an unusually high level of leverage, such as zero down payment, it is very difficult for me to achieve my goal of $10 million when we are earning $200,000 annually. If I adopt a safer investment strategy that I pay a 10% down payment and maintain a fixed cash flow in case of uncertainties, I can only accumulate $5 million at most, according to average historical return. This calculation is in line with my observations made in living in the Bay Area: those families who have lived in the Bay Area for 20 years have $4-5 million at most.

过去六年里，我的现金总是很低。要想达到 1000 万，又要规避过度风险，只有一个办法，就是增加自己固定的现金流。我家每年现金净存款是 5 万。过去，我们每年基本上可以用它 leverage 30 万的 Asset，如果每年现金净存款可以提高到 20 万的话，每年的就可以 leverage 120 万的 Asset，十年 1200 万。如果十年房价回报是 80％到 100％的话. 加上现有的 120 万，十年以后应该可以赚到 1000 万。

In the last six years, I had very little cash. The only way to achieve $10 million while avoiding excessive risks is to increase one's fixed cash flow. My family's annual net cash deposit is about $50,000. In the past, we could basically use it to leverage $300,000 of assets. If we can increase our annual net cash deposit to $200,000, we can leverage $1.2 million of assets, which will grow to $12 million ten years from now. If the annual return from real estate is between 80-100% in the next decade, we can make a profit of $10 million using the $1.2 million we now have.

账算好了，几个问题要一一解决。

Now that I have figured out the numbers, I need to solve a few problems.

1）如何把每年的净存款提高到 20 万。没什么好办法，趁自己还年轻，改行做金融　　，两年前改行的兄弟们，现在一年的收入已经到 20 万～30 万

了。争取趁这两年房市平稳，赶紧改行。三年后争取把净存款提高到每年
15 万~20 万。

1) How to raise my family's annual savings to $200,000? Well, the options are
limited. Some of my friends who changed their career path two years ago to become a
finance worker have an annual income of $200,000 to $300,000 now. I may as well
hurry up and change my profession in these two years during which the real estate
market is relatively stable and try my best to increase the amount of annual net savings
to $150,000-$200,000.

2）房子多了的管理问题，我觉得湾区最大的优势就是房子贵。房子
贵，所以 2000 万的 Asset 也就是 30～40 套公寓。在其他地方，上百套公寓肯
定管不过来。公寓数超过五个的时候，我就成立自己的管理公司，雇人来
管。湾区的另一个优势是有便宜的 labor（劳动力），不会英语的中国人管管
房子，1500/month 就可以请到。房子吗，我只租给中国人，所以语言不会有
问题。

2) How to manage multiple properties? The biggest advantage of the Bay Area is
that its property prices are expensive. As houses are expensive, having $20 million
worth of assets means owning 30-40 apartments. In other places, that number stands at
hundreds of apartments. If I own more than five apartments, I will set up my own
management company and hire people to help me manage them. Another advantage of
the Bay Area is that it has cheap labor. I can hire Chinese whose English skills are
limited to manage my properties for me. These Chinese are only asking for a monthly
salary of $1,500. As for renting out my properties, I will only target Chinese tenants, so
language will not be an issue.

3）入市时机。我打算房价涨起来以后再开始买。房子要么不涨，一旦
开涨，会持续很多年。错过头里的 10% 的涨幅根本无所谓。现在的首要任务
是积累现金。手上有现金，未来又有大笔的固定的现金流作保证的话，就可
以 leverage 很大的 Asset。过去六年，扩张太快，现金一直在一二万的样子。
这几年停一下，三年以后，我手上的现金应该在 20 万~25 万左右。

3) When should I enter the market? I have decided that I will enter the market when property prices start to increase. Once property prices begin to increase, this trend will last for many years, so missing the early 10% price increase does not really matter. Therefore, my top priority now is to accumulate cash. When I have cash and a large amount of fixed cash flow as a guarantee in the future, this will enable me to leverage a large number of assets too. In the past six years, I expanded my portfolio too fast and maintained my cash at $10,000-$20,000 only. I should stop in the next few years to make sure that I will have around $200,000-$250,000 of cash three years from now.

4）Cash flow。很多人抱怨湾区找不到正现金流的房子。那要看你怎么算了。如果是 interest only 的话，不是不可能。头几年会 slight negative cash flow（微负现金流），35 万的公寓可以租 1200～1500/month，在 Rent control（租控）　　　　　的区域，25 万的公寓可以租 1200/month。我不怕 rent control，因为我只租中国人，他们过几年就自己买房了。在中国，interest only（只付利息）的话，很多地方现在就可以做到 positive cash flow（正现金流）。不过中国的房子不敢多买，有两三套就够了。未来三年 cash flow 的状况会有所显著改善，rent 会上调 15～20％左右。

4) The cash-flow problem. Many people complain that they cannot find a positive cash flow house in the Bay Area. Well, this depends on how they do their calculations. If the mortgage is interest only, finding positive cash flow is not impossible. In the first few years, they may experience slight negative cash flow. An apartment worth $350,000 can be rented for $1,200 to $1,500 per month. In regions where rent control is in place, a $250,000 apartment can be rented out for $1,200 per month. I am not scared of rent control because I only rent my properties to Chinese, who will buy their own home in a few years. In China, the properties in many places have a positive cash flow if the mortgage is interest only. However, I do not dare buy too many houses in China, and 2-3 properties will suffice. In the next three years, the cash-flow situation will significantly improve, and rent will increase by around 15-20%.

5）风险。如果房价不涨，持续下滑，我压根没有风险，因为我不会入市。十年后的资产在 300 万到 400 万之间。如果房价涨了一年又连跌十年，诱我入市，也没关系，因为有强大的现金流保证，我就长期持有，等待下一个革命高潮。事实上，房价下滑两年涨了一年又连跌十年，这种事情在任何一个国家从未发生过。我担心的是，房价今年又开始一路猛涨，那我的计划就落空了。只能持币寻找其他的机会了。

5) Risks. If property prices do not increase and are consistently decreasing instead, I do not have any risks at all because I will not enter the market. Ten years from now, my assets will be worth around $3-4 million. If property prices rise for one year and then fall for ten years, I may be tempted to enter the market. But this does not really matter, because I have a strong cash flow backup, which allows me to hold my investments and wait for the next revolutionary peak. In fact, no country has ever witnessed a pattern of property prices going down for two years, then increasing for one year, and eventually declining for ten years. What I am worried about is that my plan will not work out if property prices start to soar this year, in which case I can only hold my cash and wait for other opportunities.

6）如果像很多人预计的那样，房价这两三年持平，未来看好，房价重复加州过去的四次 cycle 的话。我可就发了。因为我的全部计划就是按这个准备的。下一个 cycle 结束的时候，我 45 岁前资产肯定会超过 1000 万。那时是我就把他们逐步全卖了，买个 S&P Index，慢慢用。人生花不了那么多钱，再多也是无意义。

6) If, like how others have predicted, property prices remain stagnant in the next 2-3 years and the market is bullish about the future, which means California will repeat its last four cycles in history, my profits will be extremely handsome. This is because I have prepared all of my plans based on these patterns. When the next cycle ends, my total assets will definitely exceed $10 million before I turn 45. Then, I will gradually sell all my investments, invest the proceeds in an S&P index, and enjoy my wealth. The

amount of money one can spend in his or her lifetime is limited, so having more money beyond a certain goal may simply be meaningless.

如意算盘打了一圈，各位见笑了。是不是有点像大跃进时，毛主席说"粮食太多吃不完，怎么办？"的口气？这里的大师很多，千万资产的就好几个。欢迎砸砖，也请前辈多赐教。人生要做的事情很多，不光是发财。但理财是人生要做的诸多事中必不可少的一件，如同娶妻生子一样。相对埋头苦干而言，理财劳神不多，回报丰厚。

Please excuse all my meticulous calculations. Isn't this similar to Chairman Mao's tone when he said, "We have more food than we can consume. What should we do now?" There are many investment experts and professionals here; several forum users have a net worth in the tens of millions. Therefore, everyone's opinion and advice are welcomed and highly appreciated. Life is about many different responsibilities and goals, and getting rich is just one of them. However, managing your wealth is essential in life, similar to getting married and having children. Compared to working hard at one's job, investing and managing your wealth does not demand much laborious work, but their returns are lucrative.

博客文章和正式文章不一样，可以嬉笑怒骂，可以夸张不正经。为了保持原味，我不作修改的发表在这里，以图历史真实。

Blog articles are different than formal articles. In writing the former, I can make jokes and exaggerate my tone. In order to keep everything original, I have not edited my past blog articles when including them in this book to preserve the real historical picture.

文章发表之后，网友的评论不一而足，有叫好的，也有嘲笑的。我想可能内心深处大部的人是嘲笑的。只是有些人出于礼貌没有当众嘲笑而已。大部分人都觉得是天方夜谭。少部分人得到了启发，让他们敢想从前不敢想的事情，感觉眼前一亮。

After publishing this blog article, I received different kinds of comments from netizens. Some people applauded it, and some teased about the ideas. I guess most people are laughing at me behind my back. It is just that they do not do so publicly out of courtesy. Most people think my plans are mere fantasy. A few are inspired by my words to dream the impossible dream, and they feel enlightened.

别人嘲笑不要紧。我一辈子都是喜欢特立独行的。成吉思汗有名言，"人生至乐，就是打败曾经压迫过、蔑视过、欺辱过你的敌人，然后占有他的一切，看其终日以泪洗面。"我当然没有成吉思汗那么邪恶，我只是喜欢他的强人思维。我一向认为，世界上最缺的就是看你笑话的人，最不缺的就是附和你的人。

I do not really care when others make fun of me because I have been a contrarian my entire life. To borrow a saying by Genghis Khan, "The greatest happiness is to vanquish your enemies, to chase them before you, to rob them of their wealth, to see those dear to them bathed in tears, to clasp to your bosom their wives and daughters." Of course, I am not as evil as Genghis Khan. What I appreciate about him is his strong will. I have always thought that there are few people who are making fun of you but, those who blindly agree with you abound.

现在回顾起来，我这个投资计划其实是很不成熟的。主要的缺点有下面几个：

In retrospect, my investment plan was actually an immature one. Its major deficiencies are as follows:

一、过度依赖曾经有的经验，过去 6 年我实现了 10 万到 100 万的成功增长，但是未来是不是会出现一样的市场机会不好说。事实上后来出现了我在 2006 年完全想不到的市场机会，比如中本聪要 3 年后才发明比特币。

1. My plan was overly dependent on past experiences. In the last six years, I successfully achieved an increase from $100,000 to $1 million. However, it was uncertain whether the same opportunities would be present in the market in the

future. In reality, some market opportunities that I did not foresee in 2006 appeared; for example, Satoshi Nakamoto developed bitcoin three years later.

二、对提高自己挣钱能力过于乐观。我当时是调侃的口气说话。其实当时没有决定去从事金融行业的想法。我只是觉得自己未来收入会变高一些。事实上，后来收入没有变高，反而更低了，因为我转身去搞创业去了，常年低收入。

2. I was overly optimistic about my earning ability. I was joking at the time when I was making my plan: I had not decided to work in the finance industry. I was only thinking that I should increase my future income. In fact, my income did not rise but decreased because I was trying to start my business, which resulted in low income every year.

三、Rental control（租控）地方的房子是不可以买的。那个时候我没有经验，完全没有涉足过管理租控的房子。想象得过于乐观了。房子超过 5 个也要自己亲力亲为管，忘记考虑自己的时间成本了。

3. I should not have bought houses in areas where rental control was in place. At the time, I did not have any experience in managing properties that were subject to rental control law. I was overly optimistic about the situation that I insisted on managing more than five properties myself and forgot about my own time cost.

四、对未来的计算也有些问题。后来湾区的的确确像我预言的那样，重复了之前的四个涨跌循环。但是光靠这一个涨跌我也没有办法挣满 1000 万美元。

4. My calculations about the future are problematic. Later, the market in the Bay Area did repeat its previous four cycles of ups and downs. However, it was impossible for me to make $10 million simply by relying on this cycle.

不过，过了这么多年现在回首，当时这篇文章大面上的预测没有错。最重要的是这篇文章给自己树立了一个灯塔，一个目标，让自己可以去追寻。我当时也知道不可能对未来的每一个细节都能计划的那么周全。人生的关键是有目标，就像唐僧取经一样，知道往西走就好了。再弱小，再遥不可及的事情，有了目标都一点点会变成现实。西天路上自然会有孙悟空这样的人来帮你降妖除魔。没有目标的人，就像美国在中东，纵有天大的本事，一身的武艺，花了再多的人力物力，也是苍蝇乱飞，一事无成。

Nonetheless, looking back, my overall predictions detailed in that blog post were correct. Most importantly, my blog post served as a lamppost for me; it was a goal that I could pursue. Back then, I knew that it was impossible for me to plan out every detail about the future. The key in life is that we need to have a goal. This is just like how, in the Journey to the West, the main character Tang Sanzang knew that he needed to keep walking to the West. Even the most seemingly impossible dream will become reality step by step as long as you have goals. During your own Journey to the West, I am sure that Sun Wukong, the Monkey King who assisted Tang Sanzang, and others will appear and help you clear your obstacles. People without any goals are analogous to "the U.S. in the Middle East": No matter how many resources they put in and how powerful they are, they will not achieve anything.

当然也有人平心静气的和我讨论我的目标。最主要的质疑就是为什么要那么多钱。为什么要 1000 万美元。不是几百万美元就可以退休了吗。为此我写了一篇博客文章，叫作为什么要拥有 1000 万？和大家解释为什么我要制定这个目标。

Of course, there are also those who calmly and rationally discuss my goals with me. Their biggest question is why I need so much money. Why US$10 million? Won't a few million be sufficient for retirement? To answer these questions, I specifically wrote a blog article titled "Why '$10 million in 10 years?'" to explain why I set this goal.

为什么要"十年一千万" (2007 年 6 月 1 日)
Why "$10 million in 10 years"? (June 1, 2007)
by Bayfamily

我是这个坛子上第一个宣布投资理财的计划是"十年一千万"的。为此挨了不少砖头。有网友有着同样的理想，先我在这里小声嘀咕一下，但没大声宣布。阿毛今天问道："为什么要一千万，这一千万，是安心呢，还是为子孙后代？"

I was the first person to announce my "10-million-in-10-years" investment and wealth management plan on this forum, and I received some negative feedback on this. Some netizens share the same aspiration. I was just mumbling before but did not announce my goal out loud. *A-Mao* asked me today, "Why 10 million? Is your goal of 10 million for a sense of security or for your children and grandchildren, and so on?"

当然都不是。没钱我也蛮安心的。财富对后代有害无益。我是一文也不想留给他们的。我在"投机倒把的伟大意义"中说得很明白。赚一千万是我对社会最好的贡献。亚当斯密先生说的好。每个人追求获得最大的利润，做自己擅长的事，就是对社会最好的贡献。

The correct answer is none of the above. I feel a sense of security even without money, and wealth will do more harm than good for my offspring. My plan is to not leave any money to my children. I have made it clear in a previous article titled "The Great Meaning of Speculation" that making $10 million is the best contribution I can make to society. Mr. Adam Smith has done an excellent job in theorizing that "By pursuing his own interests, he frequently promotes that of the society more effectually than when he really intends to promote it." When everyone is focused on their areas of strength, this is the best contribution to society.

一个赚一千万的面包师比一个濒于破产的面包师，对社会的贡献要大得多，一个能赚一千万的投机倒把分子，比一个亏钱的投资商对社会的贡献要大得多。巴菲特先生，比你我对社会的贡献要大得多，即使他一文也不捐给社会。因为他正确地引导了投资，提高了社会效率。没有他，成千上亿的财富就会被浪费在低效的项目里。所以，对于每一个投资人来说，你赚得越多。对社会的贡献就越大。只要你不犯法，不搞垄断。

Chapter 11: An Average Family's $10-million-in-10-year Investment Plan

A baker who earns $10 million makes a more significant contribution to society than a baker who is on the edge of bankruptcy. Similarly, a speculator who makes $10 million makes a much more significant contribution to society than an investor who is incurring a loss. The contributions made by Mr. Buffett are much bigger than those by you and me, even if he does not donate a single penny to society. This is because he has correctly guided investments and increased social efficiency. Without him, millions or even billions of wealth would be wasted in projects with low efficiency. Therefore, for every single investor, the more money he or she earns, the greater his or her contribution to society, as long as he or she does not break the law or engage in anti-competitive behavior.

一千万是我的目标。因为有生之年，我只想做这么多劳动了。 好比雷锋同志，只在周末推砖头，他也知道劳逸休闲，晚上没去搬砖头。 我一生短暂，只想奉献十年、通过赚一千万来贡献社会。 当然，雷锋是添乱、浪费社会资源。 我是在赚钱、炒房、炒股的过程中，为社会创造财富。两者不可同日而语。

My goal is to have $10 million. This is because, in my lifetime, I only want to do a certain amount of work. Just like how Comrade Lei Feng helped construction workers move the bricks on weekends and took a break at night. My life is short, and I only want to devote 10 years of my life to making a contribution to society by earning $10 million. Of course, Lei Feng was merely creating troubles for others and wasting social resources, but I am earning money and creating wealth for society in the process of investing in real estate and stocks. Therefore, his behaviors cannot be compared to mine.

另一方面，我不是圣人。赚一千万也有私心。1） "生命诚可贵，爱情价更高。要为自由故，二者皆可抛。"

On the other hand, I am not a saint. I have my own selfish motives behind earning $10 million.

1) "Life is dear, and love is dearer. Both can be given up for freedom."

拥有一千万，可以换取财务自由。这样我的人生会更有趣。因为我可以领略更多不同的生活。 人生短暂，我可不想一辈子朝九晚五地坐在隔间里。李敖同志讲过"人要做点事，是要有点小钱的"。我要想放心大胆地做自己想要的事，也是要没有后顾之忧的。小钱可以给我一点安全感，一点自由。

Having $10 million gives me financial freedom and makes my life more fun. This is because I can now experience different lifestyles. Life is short, and I do not want to spend my entire life sitting in a cubicle from 9 to 5. As Comrade Li Ao once said, "If a person wants to achieve something, he or she needs to first have some money." If I want to pursue my passion without worries, having some money gives me a sense of security and freedom.

当然，你也可以说，财务自由纯粹取决于自己的舒适度，出家当和尚，立刻财务自由。我的财务自由的要求，比和尚要求高一点，但并不需要一千万，房子付清，孩子上大学，有两百万足矣。一千万是为了上面更崇高的理想。

Of course, you may also say that financial freedom depends on one's own comfort level. For example, a person may feel comfortable with giving up everything in life to become a monk now. This person can immediately achieve financial freedom. My own standard of financial freedom is higher than being a monk, but it does not require $10 million: pay off my mortgage, pay for my children's college education, and $2 million. Having $10 million is for achieving my higher aspirations.

2）我想我爱的人更快乐一点。我不想看到太太，长期为 pay check 工作，不能和孩子在一起，不能随意地干她喜欢的事情。我不想让我的孩子们，在有能力的时候，无法受到最好的教育。男子汉，大丈夫，做人就是要让自己快乐，同时让周围的人快乐。

2) I want my loved ones to lead a happier life. I do not want to see my wife to always work for a paycheck and not be able to spend more time with our children and pursue her interests. I do not want to see that my children are not able to receive the best

education when they have the ability to do so because of money concerns. As a man, my life motto is to bring happiness to myself and others around me.

3）太多的财富是累赘。 君不见亿万富翁，个个要保镖，担心被绑架。达赖喇嘛曾经讲过，有钱人是很难有真正的朋友。 因为钱越多，人与人之间的关系，越虚伪。要是我能赚一亿的话，对社会贡献更大。 我只是说如果。没有吹牛的意思。

3) Too much wealth is a burden. Don't you see that all those billionaires have bodyguards surrounding them because they are worried that they may be kidnapped? As Dalai Lama once said, "Someone may be rich and powerful, but without trusted friends, they will never be happy." The more money one has, the less likely it is for him or her to have trusted relationships. If I can earn $100 million, my contribution to society will be even greater. I use "if" here, and I hope that I do not appear boastful.

可是，我想自己的日子好一点，朋友多一点，不用花太多的精力想怎样花掉那笔钱的话，我就不能有超过一千万。 比尔盖茨刚刚辞去总裁职务，现在沦落到要全职工作去花掉他的钱。 过了一千万，财富有害无益，即使我再想贡献社会，也不想搞成那个样子。牛皮吹上天，满纸荒唐言。但句句属实，信不信由你。

However, if I want to have a better quality of life and more genuine friends and prefer to spend less time thinking about how to spend my money, my net worth cannot exceed $10 million. As of the time of writing this blog post, Bill Gates has just stepped down from the position of CEO, and now spending his money is his full-time job. Having more than $10 million of wealth will do more harm than good. However much I would like to contribute to society, I do not dare put myself in that predicament. Even though I may sound boastful and this article seems to be full of ridiculous claims, every sentence holds much truth. It is up to you to decide whether you believe my words.

当时我写这篇文章的时候，带着一些轻浮的语气。有的时候在网上说话太认真会吃亏，因为网上一方面是交流，更多的时候是打口水战，寻开心。

用调侃的口气反而进退自如。当时并没有对很多问题有成体系的思考，更多的理论是在我今天回顾的时候把它们整理了出来。

When I was writing this blog article, I used a frivolous tone. Sometimes, being too serious on the internet will do you more harm than good. This is because, on one hand, the internet is about interacting with others. But more often, it is a lighthearted version of a war of words: Everyone is arguing but deriving immense happiness from it. Therefore, using a frivolous tone gives me more flexibility in this war of words. At the time, when I was thinking through all those issues, I did not use a systematic approach. When I am now reviewing my past blog posts, I am reviewing and organizing all the theories proposed.

如果有什么新的补充思考的话，就是我感觉一个人作为社会的载体，应该是丰富而全面的。钱只是我们生活中的一部分，当然我这本书因为写的都是关于钱的故事，所以在这里重点讨论钱的问题。

If I can add something to my previous analysis, I will say that since individuals are the forming blocks of society, our life should be colorful and multifaceted. Money is only a part of our life. But since this book is devoted to stories about money, I will focus my discussion here on money.

无论你是信仰宗教的还是不信仰宗教的，你总希望自己的生命过得更加的有趣，更加的丰富多彩。我们多多少少都有一些精神上的追求。而那些精神上的追求，总是需要在满足了一些物质需求的基础之后去实现。

Whether you have religious beliefs or not, you always hope that your life is more interesting and colorful. Everyone has at least some spiritual needs, but the fulfillment of these needs often requires satisfying some materials needs and securing a more solid material foundation.

思考这些问题的时候，不可避免地就会涉及生死之说。虽然这本书不是一本哲学的书，但是因为投资理财涉及理想，而理想又涉及人生信仰等哲学问题，所以我后来又不得不再写一篇博客。那就是"人为什么活着"，试图理性地探讨这些问题。这个话题很大，我只是很粗浅地论述了一下，每个人都需要建立起自己对生命的认知系统，我也不能例外。

When we are pondering on these questions, it is inevitable to think about life and death. Even though this is not a philosophy book, I have included a blog post on the meaning of life here. As investing and wealth management involves aspirations, which involve philosophical questions such as life and beliefs, this blog article titled "What is the meaning of life?" is my attempt to start a rational discussion on these questions. This is a vast subject that warrants much discussion, so my article only outlines the main arguments. Everyone needs to construct their own understanding of life, and I am no exception.

我们为什么活着(2013 年 12 月 7 日)

What Is the Meaning of Life? (December 7, 2013)

by Bayfamily

少年贪玩，青年贪情，中年贪名，老年贪生。

Teens are hungry for excitement; young adults are hungry for romantic love; the middle-aged are hungry for fame, and the elderly are hungry for longevity.

这几乎是最精辟的人生总结了。作为中年的我，可以对这四句话比青年的时候更有体会。 贪心很正常，不要让欲望的魔鬼把你吞噬掉就好了。碌碌无为的人往往做得很好，天才和精英们往往因为自己的能力比较强，陷入不可自拔的地步。君不见多少青春男女为爱情整日以泪洗面，君不见多少英雄豪杰没有过得了名利两关。打开新闻，几乎都是四个贪字惹的祸。从失恋毁容跳楼，到苍井空风靡神州，到薄熙来阶下做囚。从古代秦始皇求长生不老，到今天的刘晓庆追求逆生长，人生的故事在不同的时代，以不同的方式一遍遍演绎着这四个贪字的故事。

This saying is perhaps the most accurate summary of life. As a middle-aged man, I have even deeper reflections on this saying than when I was a young adult. Desires are normal, but do not let them enslave you. A person with average or below-average skills often do pretty well in life. However, geniuses and elites are often susceptible to obsessive pursuits because of their intellectual giftedness. Don't you see that multitudes of young men and women get their hearts broken when looking for romantic love? Don't you see that so many heroes and great people fall prey to the temptation of fame and money? Flip through the news and you will see that a pang of hunger for the abovementioned desires underlie all the headlines and stories, from breakups and disfigured face to jumping off a high building; and from the sweeping popularity of Sola Aoi, a Japanese pornstar, to the imprisonment of Bo Xilai, a former high-ranking Chinese official. As for the pursuit of longevity, the first emperor, Qin Shi Huang, sent officials on quests seeking an elixir of immortality around 210 BC. Today, a famous Chinese actress, Liu Xiaoqing, is eagerly looking for ways to reverse time and "grow young." Even though these stories happened in different eras, they are all demonstrating mankind's pursuits of excitement, romantic love, fame, and longevity.

第一次接触弗洛依德的时候，听到他说，人类一切行为的原动力都是性，一切都是性。看见他的话，有皇帝的新装的感觉。感觉这样简单的道理，被一个率真而聪明的人一语道破。而其他芸芸众生都是在街上看皇帝新装的懵懂的狂欢者。攻击他的人，不过是因为弗洛依德扫了他们的自欺欺人的好心情。

When I first came across Freud's theories, he propounded that all human behaviors are driven by sexual instincts. Studying Freudian theories is like reading the story of the Emperor's New Clothes. Such a simple principle is identified and expressed by a forthright and intelligent person, and the other spectators are indulging themselves in viewing the emperor's new clothes. Freud's critics are attacking him because he forced them to wake up from their dreams and face the unpleasant truth.

难道不是么？年轻的时候，我们所做的一切都是在为获得异性做准备。无论是更好的成绩，更高的收入，更健康的体魄。我们陷入的不过是一个漫长的征服异性的争战。一开始是直接的征服异性，后来是征服同性来获得异性。于是有甄嬛传女人后宫内斗，有潘金莲和李瓶儿死去活来。于是有毛爷爷的与天斗其乐无穷，与人斗其乐无穷。可是与人斗，男人和男人相斗，女人和女人斗，本质还是为了获得异性。

Isn't this the truth? When we are young, everything we do is to prepare ourselves for finding a mate. Better academic performance, a higher income, and a healthier body are all parts of our long quest to conquer the opposite sex. At first, we attempt to conquer the opposite sex directly. Later, we try to appeal to our potential mate by conquering people of the same gender as us. This is why stories of women plotting against each other abound, for example, the main plot in Empresses in the Palace, a popular Chinese television series, and how in the Golden Lotus, protagonist Pan Jinlian vowed to remove Li Pinger by indirectly murdering her son. This is also why Mao derived great pleasure from rebelling against the universe and attacking other people. However, the nature of attacking other people, in particular, men attacking men, and women attacking women, is to procure a mate.

我们关心下一代的教育，婚姻，做虎爸虎妈。希望给下一代留下一个好的基础。这一切的本质动力，都是性。似乎身体里面的DNA无时无刻的发挥它的能力。我们自以为的理性，理想，都是这些DNA希望疯狂复制自己的幻影。

We care about the education of our children and marriage and become a tiger father or mother in the hopes of leaving a good foundation for our offspring. The driving force behind all these behaviors is sex. It seems that our DNA is influencing us 24/7. Our rational thinking and aspirations are actually a product of our DNA's desire to make as many copies of themselves as possible.

非常佩服弗洛依德先生。有幸去过他维也纳的寓所，一个不起眼的小博物馆，一个小小的人物发出石破天惊的呐喊。看见他的手稿，他的照片，深深地表达敬意。

I greatly admire Mr. Freud, and I had the pleasure of visiting his home in Vienna, an oft-neglected small museum, where a small potato tried to shout his ground-breaking theories out loud. Looking at his manuscripts and photos, I could not help but feel much respect for Freud.

不过，进入中年以后，发现性的能量似乎没有那么巨大。似乎很难解释为何有人会不惜牺牲，杀身成仁。很难解释，已经是亿万富翁了，为何还要再获取更多的财富。很难解释为何毛爷爷 70 岁还会发动文化大革命，为何邓小平会 70 岁搞改革开放。他们早就过了可以传递自己 DNA 的年龄。

However, after entering middle-age, I realized that the power of sex is not as immense as I imagined. Relying on this theory alone cannot explain why some people are willing to sacrifice themselves for the better good of our species. And there are those who are already billionaires, and they are trying to procure even more wealth. It is also difficult to explain why Mao launched the Chinese Cultural Revolution at the age of 70 and why Deng Xiaopeng led China through a series of economic reforms in his 70s. They were well past the age when they could pass on their DNA.

除了性的力量，还有一个神奇的力量支配和主导着我们。那就是死亡。

Other than our sexual instincts, there is another mystical force guiding and dominating us, which is death.

我们活着的一切活动的目的，是为了更好地迎接死亡。在逻辑上有些荒谬，但是我们的确千百年来在重复同样荒谬的事情。

The purpose of all activities during our lifetime is to prepare ourselves to better embrace death. Even though this may sound logically absurd, we have been repeating the same absurdity for thousands of years.

表面上似乎我们很少会想到自己会死，至少对于年轻的人来说。死亡似乎是遥远的事情。但是死亡的恐惧，像是终点站上一个矮矮的树丛，在夕阳西下的时候，会投射出很长很长的影子。

On the surface, it seems that we rarely think about our death. This is at least true for young people, to whom death seems to be distant. However, the fear of death is like a shrub. Though it looks small in size, its shadow looms large during dusk.

是的，我们所做的一切的第二源动力，就是更好地迎接死亡。死亡是一定的，每个正常智力的少年到老年人都清楚地知道这点。这样的恐惧是无时无刻的。 千百年来，这些恐惧改变了我们的社会，我们的文化，也改变了我们每个人的行为。

Yes indeed, the second primary force behind everything we do is to prepare ourselves to embrace death. Nothing is as certain as death, and every adult of normal intelligence should know clearly about this. The fear of death is ever-present. In mankind's thousands of years of history, such fear has changed our society, our culture, and our individual behaviors.

最近看了一下他人的总结，人类对付死亡恐惧，自欺欺人地编出了四种方法。不同民族，不同时段，这些方法会以不同的面目出现。不过似乎我们人类已经黔驴技穷，再也编造不出超越这四个方法的新内容了。

Looking at mankind's responses to the fear of death, I have extracted the four main coping mechanisms that humans have devised here. These methods manifested themselves in different formats depending on the specific cultural context and times. However, it seems that we have run out of ideas and fail to come up with new content other than the following four methods.

1. 不死。无论是秦始皇的长生不老药，刘晓庆的逆生长，还是今天全民吃保健品，研究长寿村的秘密。都是不死的折射。也就是开篇所说的老年贪生。

1. Immortality. Whether it is Qin Shi Huang's elixir of immortality, Liu Xiaoqing's growing young, the trend of everyone taking supplements today, and investigating the secret of "longevity village," they are all reflections of human's eager pursuits of immortality and examples of the abovementioned saying that "the elderly are hungry for longevity."

2. 灵魂。用各种办法让自己相信，除了肉体之躯之外，还有灵魂的存在。灵魂可以离开腐朽的肉体，灵魂可以上天堂，在天堂可以永远地活下去。这里常见的各种方法就是各种的宗教。因为有死亡，才会有宗教。

2. Soul. People use all sorts of reasons to convince themselves that other than their physical body, they have a soul that leaves the body and goes on to live a perpetual existence in heaven. The most common ways are various religions. It is only because of death that religions exist.

3. 转世。典型例子就是藏传佛教的转世灵童，转世在佛教印度教盛行的地方流传很久。但是不是始作俑者，古埃及人修建金字塔，秦始皇修建兵马俑，都是转世的期盼。

3. Reincarnation. A typical example is a common practice of finding the reincarnated soul boy in Tibetan Buddhism after the spiritual leader passed away. The construction of the pyramids by ancient Egyptians and the Terracotta army by Qin Shi Huang are reflections of mankind's hopes about reincarnation, despite uncertainty on who actually built them.

4. 传奇。传奇是四种自欺欺人的抗拒死亡恐惧的方法中最理性的做法了。因为通过观察，理性的人们发现，肉体会腐烂，转世不靠谱，灵魂似有似无，通灵无法证明。传奇大约是看得见摸得着的。传奇有很多种，可以是王朝帝国，可以是微软苹果，可以是爱因斯坦牛顿，可以是举着炸药包的董存瑞，也可以是大学校园里捐赠的一把椅子。

4. Legends. Legends are the most rational to resist the fear of death among the all four self-deceiving methods because, after some observations, rational people realize that body will decay after death, that reincarnation does not make sense, that the concept of an immortal soul is dubious, and that it is impossible to prove the existence of an afterlife. However, legends are more tangible. There are different kinds of legends. Some of them are about building a business empire, for example, Microsoft and Apple. In some stories, the protagonists are scientists, for instance, Einstein and Newton. In other cases, a war hero such as Dong Cunrui, who carried explosives to destroy his enemies, leaves a legend to be praised by generations. Some trivial objects, such as a chair donated to a university, can be a legend.

瞧，为什么我们活着，一半的原因是因为我们身体的 DNA 需要复制，一半原因是因为我们会死掉。我们之所以活着，之所以是用今天这样的方式活着，是因为我们会死掉。话有些绕口，逻辑上有些荒谬。但是如果你细细地品味，就会明白的确是这样的。

See, half of the explanation of why we are alive is because our DNA needs to copy themselves. The other half is that we will die. The reason why we are alive or why we are living our present lifestyle is that we will die. It seems that ridiculous logic underlies this tongue-twisting saying. But if you think about it more deeply, this saying embodies the truth.

生命本没有意义，追求意义的行为都是怕死的表现。我们只是亿万年前从宇宙深处飘来的一片 DNA 复制品，生命的源动力只是这片 DNA 有着神奇的驱动力。它渴望最大限度地被复制。我们追求伟大光辉，是因为这片 DNA 的载体最终要死亡。

Life is meaningless in itself. Any behaviors with an attempt to pursue meaning are a sign of the fear of death. All of us are merely a copy of DNA that originates somewhere in the universe and has been passed down for billions of years. The driving force of life is the deep desire of our DNA to be copied and passed down. We pursue glorious legends because the carrier of this piece of DNA will eventually die.

说的有些凄凉，真相冷酷但是并不代表就悲催。我觉得生命最美好的事情就是快乐。开始和结尾都不重要，如果你一定要说点什么人生的意义的话，那就是过程的快乐。做个快乐的人吧，给自己快乐，给自己身边的人快乐。我们不在意我们为什么活着，只在意怎样快乐地活着。

This may seem bleak, but a cruel reality does not mean life is hopeless. In my opinion, the best thing in life is happiness. The beginning and the ending do not matter. If you insist that I should give you an answer on the meaning of life, I will say the greatest happiness is derived from the journey or the process. We should strive to be a happy person who brings happiness to ourselves and those around us. Instead of fixating on why we are here, we should focus on how to live happily.

生死问题古往今来无数仁人志士，先知思想家已经想破脑袋了。我们能做的就是在那些厚厚的经典里面，寻找一点能够支撑自己信念的东西。说到这个，总是不可避免地讨论人生意义。空谈人生意义是没有用的，就像空谈赚那么多钱是为了什么也是没有意义的。最终我们是需要落实到很具体的目标上。而只有那些具体落地的理想和目标，才是点燃我们生命真正的火焰，照耀我们前进。

The great question of life and death has baffled many philosophers and great thinkers. What we can do, as ordinary people, is to find something from all those thick classical writings that can support our own beliefs. When it comes to a discussion on life and death, it is inevitable to also explore the meaning of life. Empty talk on the meaning of life will not do us any good. Equally futile is empty talk on why we should earn so much money. What is of utmost importance is that we should focus our attention on actually progressing toward more specific and actionable aspirations and goals. Only with these goals and aspirations will we be able to spark a flame that shines upon us, illuminates our way, and guides our future.

除了投资理财，我的人生就有三大理想。如果都能够实现，我就会相对比较满足。我也不知道这些理想是怎么样稀里糊涂地钻进了我的大脑。久而久之，这些理想成为我人生选择的指明灯。这些理想能否实现也就成为我能否快乐的标尺。

Other than investing and wealth management, I only have three aspirations in life. If I can realize all of them, I will be relatively satisfied with my life. I have no idea how these aspirations pop up in my mind out of nowhere. But what I am sure is that as time goes by, they have become a compass guiding me through life decisions. Whether I can achieve these aspirations has become a yardstick for measuring whether I am happy.

第一个理想就是我感觉我生活在这个世界上，从小到大，有人种地，有人生产粮食，有人生产家具，有人盖房子。我享受了这个世界上大量的物质财富，我有足够多的义务去生产相当量的物质财富，回馈社会。

Firstly, I feel that I have benefitted from the fruits of other people's labor all my life. Some people farm, some produce food, some manufacture furniture, and some build houses. I have enjoyed a tremendous amount of wealth, so I have sufficient obligation to produce at least an equivalent amount of material wealth to pay back society.

也就是说我需要尽可能多创造物质财富。这些物质财富可以是具体有形的，比如一棵树，比如一样工具，比如你组织大家一起办的一个企业。也可以是无形的，比如你帮助了社会提高了商品的交换的效率，你让社会更安全，你让人民思想更自由。总之我感觉社会对我不薄，我有必要反哺。这既是我的责任，也是令我愉快的事情。

In other words, I need to make my best endeavors to create as much material wealth as possible. All this material wealth may be either tangible or intangible. They can take such a particular form as a tree, a tool, or an enterprise in which I mobilize others to participate. I can also make some intangible contributions, for instance, increasing the efficiency of the circulation of goods in society, making our society safer, and liberating the mind of citizens. Overall, I feel that society has been good to me, and I have a responsibility to pay back. Contributing to society also brings me happiness.

我的第二大理想在思想领域。今天能够有幸福的生活，是受益于古代前辈们在思想上和知识上的贡献。我能够伸手打电话，出门坐飞机，生病有药吃，要感谢那些伟大的科学家和思想家。那些伟大的科学家和发明家在知识和思想上的突破让我受益。是他们发现了新的自然科学定律，发现了人类社会更好的协作方式，发现了宪政政府抑制王权的重要性。总之是因为有一些先贤，他们把新的思想、新的知识、新的信息带到了这个世界。

My second aspiration pertains to making contributions in the form of ideas and theories. The reason why I can enjoy a high quality of living is that I have benefitted from the contributions made by my predecessors in terms of thinking and knowledge. Thanks to these great scientists and thinkers, I can now take out my phone from my pocket and stay in touch with my friends, hop on a plane to travel to other destinations, pop some pills when sick. They discover new natural scientific theories, how humans can better coordinate with one another in society, and the importance of constitutional monarchy, which keeps the power of the head of state in check. Overall, these influential historical figures brought new ideas, knowledge, and information to the world.

而我是这些思想者的受益者。所以我感觉我也需要生产足够多的思想和知识来反馈给社会。也许是我写一本书，也许是我有创造发明，也许是我发现的一个新的知识理论，也许是我写的某一首诗，写过的某一篇散文，或者说我写的那些博客。因为我生产出了有用的信息，反哺给社会。无论是在自然科学还是人文科学，只要我在从事这样的知识生产工作，我就是快乐的。当然，如果生产的东西越多，我自然会更加快乐一些。这个理想也是我多年坚持写博客以及写这本书的一些最原始的动力。

Since I am a beneficiary of these thinkers, I feel that I should generate sufficient ideas and knowledge to pay back to society. Perhaps I can write a book, create or invent something, discover a new theory or some new knowledge, compose a poem, or write an article and blog posts. As long as I am working to share and generate knowledge, be it in science or humanity field, I am happy because I am able to generate useful information to pay back society. Of course, the more ideas I generate, the greater my happiness. This aspiration is also part of the motivation behind my persistent publication of blog articles and writing this book.

我的第三个理想就是来自亲人和爱。人如果拥有绝对多的物质和精神上的财富，但是没有爱没有亲人，孤独一世，那也是可悲和可怜的。我能有幸福的生活，是因为周围的人给了我爱。我的母亲，我的爱人，我的朋友，我的亲人。所以我也有必要把更多的爱生产出来反哺给他们。在我的博客里我写的就是快乐自己，幸福他人。我拿这句话作为我写博客的座右铭。

My third aspiration is inspired by my family and loved ones. If a person does not have any love or a family in his or her life, he or she will live a miserable and lonely life no matter how much material and spiritual wealth he or she possesses. The reason why I have a happy life is that those around me give me love: my mother, my wife, my friends, and my family. Therefore, I deem it necessary that I should generate more love to pay back their love. In my blog, I put down the saying, "Bring happiness to myself and others" in the description box. This is a motto that inspires me to write more blog posts.

当然这些爱不见得一定要给我认识的人。我也可以给我不认识的人。比如有的时候当读过博客的网友给我回信表达感谢的时候，我就会很快乐而满足。因为我知道给这个世界生产出了更多的温情，更多的温暖。就像当你行走在陌生的异国他乡，给路边的一个陌生人微笑；或者当你在下雪天，给一个雪地里打滑的陌生汽车推一把力一样。一个小小的帮助会生产出格外的温暖。我并不期待得到什么回报。只是我想给这世界生产出来更多的爱。希望这些爱和温情能够被更多的人传播到更广阔的世界里去。

Of course, I can also give more love to other people who are beyond my existing social circle. For example, sometimes, when netizens who have read my blog expressed their gratitude to me in their comments, I felt immensely content and happy. This is because I know that the world is now a better place with more warmth, kindness, and love because of my presence. This is similar to how you smile at strangers when you are a traveler in a foreign destination, or how you push a broken car to help strangers in snow. A simple act of kindness goes a long way and generates much warmth. I do not expect any returns. I only hope that I can generate more love for this world and that all the love and kindness can spread to an even wider world through the interactions between people.

当然我相信读者不一定和我有一样的理想和目标。每个人的世界观不一样。大体而言，人过中年，总是有他精神层面的一些追求。不然生活就会变得行尸走肉般灰暗起来。仿佛每天都在混吃等死。

Granted, my readers may not necessarily share the same aspirations and goals as me because of differing worldviews. But generally speaking, when a person enters middle age, he or she should have some non-material pursuits. Otherwise, life will become gloomy and he or she will become a walking corpse. It will be as if his or her life were only about sustaining his or her physical body and waiting for death.

对于我个人而言，实现这些理想的一部分就是我这个财富目标的实现。因为在这个过程里，三个部分都有了。在我的认知世界里，赚钱本身就是创造财富，赚钱过程中积累的经验就是知识，获得财富之后给亲人的都是爱与温暖。2006 年我几乎用了一年的时间在思考这些问题，当一切都想好了，于是我就开启了我的"普通家庭十年一千万理财计划"的旅程。

As for me, achieving my investment and wealth management goals is part of a grander mission of realizing my aspirations. This is because the process of creating wealth takes care of the abovementioned aspirations. In my own belief system, earning money is equated with creating wealth. And the experiences I have accumulated in this process will become part of my knowledge bank. With more wealth, I can better protect and care for my loved ones. In 2006, I spent about a year reflecting on these questions. After sorting through all these questions, I embarked on my "An Average Family's 10-million-in-10-year Investing and Wealth Management" journey.

这个投资的旅程一共分四部分。一部分是知识储备，其他三部分是实战。从华尔街到香港，从上海到湾区，从实物到虚拟。有意想不到的转折，有惊喜，有绝望，有突如其来的机会。我像一个在探险乐园里面的旅行者，时而被惊吓，时而乐得开怀大笑。你坐好小板凳，我把我后面旅途中看到的一路的风景，一段一段的故事慢慢继续讲给你听。

My investment journey can be divided into four components. The first part is about theories or my knowledge bank. The other three components are my real experiences, from Wall Street to Hong Kong, from Shanghai to the Bay Area, and from tangible to virtual investments. I encountered some unexpected ups and downs in my journey; some of them are happy surprises, some of them are despair, and some are unforeseen opportunities. I was like a traveler in an adventure park: I was sometimes startled and sometimes burst into laughter. My readers, please now sit back, relax, and enjoy this journey with me. I will depict the details of the sceneries I saw in it and share with you some intriguing stories.

第十二章 从 MBA 到投行

Chapter 12: From MBA to Investment Banking

01 为什么搞金融的收入高

01 Why Finance Workers Have A High Income

我的十年投资理财计划的第一步并不是去赚钱，而是去知识充电，我选择了先读一个在职的 MBA。很多人在走向衰老，开始回首往事时，可能都有同样的感触，那就是年轻的时候应该尽可能地接触更多的事情和更多的人。每一种经验、每一次经历以及和不同背景的人打交道对自己总是有好处的。

The first step in my 10-year investment and wealth management plan is not to make money but to ramp up my knowledge. I chose to study a part-time MBA first. When many people are aging, they start to look back on their lives and realize that they should have tried their best to participate in as many events and projects and met as many people as possible. Every experience, adventure, and encounter with people from all walks of life is highly beneficial to personal development.

我读 MBA 的灵感也是来自我的一个朋友。这个朋友性格有些内向，说话有些结巴，口齿不是特别好，猛一看不是那种能够事业有成的样子。但是他当时比我有钱多了，因为他在帮他的导师经营一个基金。

I was inspired to get an MBA because of a friend of mine. You will not think of him as highly successful in his career because he is an introverted person, stammers when he speaks, and is not particularly eloquent. However, he was much wealthier than me at the time because he was running a fund for his teacher.

用他导师的原话就是："他值得变富有""You deserve to be rich"。我想每个人可能都希望读书的时候能够遇到这样的导师，能够说出这样振奋人心的话。那位导师是某个大学金融系的教授，自己成立了一个投资基金。而我认识的这个朋友，就是帮他管理投资基金的对冲计算模型。

To borrow the original words from his teacher, "You deserve to be rich." I guess everyone will hope that we can encounter such inspiring and encouraging teachers in our learning journey. That teacher is a professor in the Faculty of Finance at a university. He founded an investment fund. This friend of mine managed the calculation model on hedging strategies for him.

年轻人总是争强好胜，我觉得我自己并不比我这个朋友笨，甚至还觉得自己各方面能力比他更强一些，无论是数学还是和人沟通的能力。难道仅仅是因为一些机缘巧合，他做金融行业而我做理工，就让我们的生活有这么大的差距么？

Young people are always aggressive and competitive. I did not think that I am less intelligent than this friend of mine. In fact, I considered myself as possessing more superior skills than he did in certain aspects, such as mathematics and communication. Isn't it merely because of some coincidences that he is a finance worker and I am an engineer, which resulted in such a vast income gap and differences in our standards of living?

那时候我一直想不明白的一个道理就是为什么从事金融行业的人工资或待遇远远超过其他行业的从业者。为什么同样智力水平的大学毕业生，从事金融行业的获得的工资就比其他人要高很多？

At the time, I was bewildered by the phenomenon that the income of finance workers far exceeds that of professionals in other industries. Why do university graduates who enter the financial industry earn a much higher salary than their peers who are of the same level of intelligence?

在中国早期从事金融行业的大多是文科生。而在我们那个时代，文科生多半都是班级里比较笨的，是因为他们读理科有困难，所以转而学文科，搞一些死记硬背的东西。所以理科生内心里是有一些看不起文科生的，总觉得我们比他们更聪明一些。

In the early days in China, a vast majority of the finance workers had an educational background in liberal arts. In my generation, most art students were less competent. These students were dropouts from the science stream.[5] As they found studying science difficult, they decided to give up and choose some subjects that could be handled by rote learning. Therefore, science students often looked down on liberal arts students because the former felt that they were more intelligent than the latter.

然而我们这些自以为比他们更聪明一些的人，后来挣的钱却比他们少。这个事实让很多人心里愤愤不平，难道人生就是因为偶然而阴差阳错？行业的差异为什么会这么大？

Yet, it turned out that our generation of science students who felt more superior than the art students earned less money than them. This reality arouses bitter feelings among science students: Why is it that success in life seems to be the product of a series of random events and coincidences? Why are there such huge discrepancies between different industries?

90 年代我们国家还没有金融产业。我的另一个朋友到美国之后注意到这个现象，他的解释是因为搞金融的，他们的产品就是钱。既然他们的产品就是钱，常在河边走，哪有不湿鞋？近水楼台先得月，所以金融行业的人挣的钱就会多一些。

In the 1990s, China did not have a financial industry. Another friend of mine has also noticed this phenomenon after he settled in the U.S. He attempted to explain this by suggesting that the products marketed and sold by finance workers are money. Since their products are money, they benefit from being closer to

---

[5] In the Chinese education system, high school students are required to choose either the science stream or liberal arts stream.

money. As they handle money every day, how can they not be good at making it? Therefore, finance workers earn more money than others.

这样的道理其实经不住推敲。建筑工人从事建筑行业，然而建筑工人只能住比较差的住房，而金融大亨们却住在各种豪宅里头。按照这个近水楼台先得月的道理，岂不是建筑工人的住房条件应该最好吗？

In fact, this explanation is unfounded. Construction workers work in the construction industry, but they can only live in relatively poor housing. Yet, finance tycoons live in all sorts of mansions. If this "proximity theory" is valid, shouldn't it be the construction workers who have the best housing environment?

还有一些人认为是金融行业的人特别聪明，他们从名校毕业，受教育的成本比较高。所以需要获得更多的收入来补偿他们教育的投入。

There are also those who opine that finance workers are more intelligent. Also, since they graduate from a prestigious school and their education costs are higher, they need more income to compensate for their investment in education.

如果是医生这个道理也许说得过去。医生的教育过程很漫长，所以医生获得的收入会稍微高一些。这是对他们的教育投入进行补偿。而金融行业不是这样的，你经常会看到很多非常年轻的金融行业从业者，刚刚大学毕业就可以挣很多钱。

If the subject of our discussion is medical practitioners, this theory has some truth. Medical education is a continuous, lifelong journey, so doctors' income is slightly higher. This is because they need to be compensated for their time and money spent on their education. The same cannot apply to the financial industry because you will often see that many young finance workers are making lots of money even though they are fresh graduates.

还有一种说法，他们从事的工作非常重要，因为要管理动辄成百上亿的资金，所以他们从中挣一些钱也是可以理解的。

There is a third theory proposed: Their work is of utmost importance because they are managing millions, if not billions, of money. It is understandable that they make some money from it.

这个说法其实也站不住脚，因为从事重要的工作，不见得能多挣钱。举个例子，从事核武器发射的人掌握着地球上的亿万生命，但是他们挣的钱并不多，只能挣普通军人的一份基本工资。没有什么比生命更重要的，同样是治病救人的医生，在中国和美国他们的工资待遇也有很大不同。

This claim is unwarranted either. The importance of the task is not necessarily directly proportional to the income. For instance, workers who control the launching of nuclear weapons have trillions of lives in their hands, but they do not earn a lot of money. They are only paid a basic salary as an average military officer. Nothing is more important than lives. The same can also be said of doctors who cure patients and save lives. Doctors in China and the U.S. have diametrically different rewards. For example, according to a survey conducted in China in 2015, the average doctor's annual income is CN¥77,000 (which is approximately US$11,000).

还有一种说法，就是从事金融行业的人特别聪明，工作格外努力，他们能够解决别人解决不了的问题。其实不是的，金融行业的大部分就业者，他们做的只是很机械重复的工作，并不比其他行业的人需要格外的智商，真正需要智商的行业也许是基础物理和数学。普通的投行里肯定不需要绝顶聪明的人，而往往需要像销售员一样的情商高的人。

Another explanation suggested is that finance workers are more intelligent and hardworking so they can solve problems that baffle others. This is not true. Most finance workers are doing highly repetitive and robotic tasks that do not require a high level of IQ. Perhaps working in the basic physics and mathematics fields demands a higher IQ, but investment bankers are not necessarily the brightest. Instead, they possess a high EQ as their job nature is similar to that of a salesperson.

金融行业的从业者收入，无论在中国还是美国，在日本还是欧洲都是偏高的。按理说，如果这是一个市场充分竞争的劳动力市场，应该有更多的人去从事金融行业，直到金融行业的工资降下来才对。但是我们始终没有看到这个现象。我们看到是这个行业入门难，大家都打破头想进到顶级投行里面去。

Generally speaking, the income of finance workers, be it in China, the U.S., Japan, or Europe, are higher than other workers. Basic economic theories will dictate that if the financial industry has a fully competitive labor market, more people will choose to enter the field until the income drops. However, we have not witnessed this phenomenon yet. What we can see now is that there are entry barriers to this industry and that everyone is leaving no stone unturned in trying to secure a job with investment banks.

金融行业挣钱比其他行业要高一些，我觉得可能有以下几个方面的原因。

I attribute the fact that finance workers earn more money than workers in other industries to the following reasons.

一、货币垄断。垄断包括几个方面的原因：一是国家对于货币的垄断以及像华尔街这些金融机构所形成的行业垄断。国家对货币的垄断导致了货币的发行必须通过一些固定的渠道。那么离这些渠道越近的人，他们就可以优先获利。

1. A monopoly of the currency. Monopoly entails different aspects, which include the state's monopoly of the currency and the monopoly of the industry by financial institutions on Wall Street. The state's monopoly of the currency means that the issuance of currency needs to go through certain channels. People who are closer to these channels can make a profit before everyone else does.

举一个例子，美元总共的货币发行量大约是 16 万亿美元，而这 16 万亿美元都是凭空印出来的。而比其他人优先一步获得这些货币的人，就能先挣钱。中国的货币发行总量是 200 多万亿人民币，这些钱也都是凭空制造出来的。既然是凭空制造出来的，自然有人凭空受益。

For instance, the total amount of U.S. dollars issued is around $16 trillion. All this $16 trillion is printed out of thin air. Those who can get ahead of others in obtaining this money can make a profit. The total amount of Chinese Yuan issued is more than CN¥200 trillion. Of course, all this money is printed out of thin air too. Since the money is created out of thin air, it must be the case that someone will make profits out of thin air.

二、行业垄断。搜索引擎 Google 的员工非常能挣钱，是因为 Google 垄断了搜索引擎这个行业。华尔街和屈指可数的大金融机构垄断了金融行业，无论是公司的股票发行，还是债券发行都要找这几个大公司才可以。比如一个美国公司要上市，只能去华尔街，只能去纽交所或者 Nasdaq。有垄断的地方自然就有暴利。我们小的时候，副食店的售货员阿姨是个令人羡慕的职业，也是同样的道理。

2. A monopoly of the industry. Google's employees make lots of money because Google enjoys a monopoly on search engines. Wall Street and the few large financial institutions monopolize the financial industry. Whether it is issuing new company shares or bonds, businesses turn to these big names. For example, when a U.S. company is considering an IPO, it has to go to Wall Street, the New York Stock Exchange or Nasdaq. A monopoly entails staggering profits. This is also why being a salesperson at a snack store was an enviable job when I was a child.

三、人们的消费行为心理。前面两个原因还是无法解释，即使是黄金作为货币的时候，为什么开钱庄的人挣的钱也比普通行业的要多一些。

3. Consumer habits and psychology. The first two reasons are still unable to explain why in the days when gold was the currency, owners and employees of banks earned more money than workers in other industries.

我觉得最主要的原因还是人们的消费心理，比如说当你去菜市场买菜的时候。明明只有几美元的差价，但是你不惜花上十分钟跟小贩们讨价还价。小贩在你身上多花了十分钟，也就多挣了一美元。

I think the main reason is consumer habits and psychology. For example, when you buy your grocery in the farmers' market, you will not hesitate to haggle with the vendors for a discount. For every ten minutes the vendor spends on bargaining with you, he earns one more dollar.

然而你在从事一亿美元交易的时候。你同样花十分钟讨价还价，来去的金钱数量就是上百万美元的。同样一个人拥有同样的情商，付出的劳动也是一样，一个劳动产生的价值是另外一个劳动的几百万倍。

Yet, when you are working on a $100 million transaction, spending 10 minutes on bargaining means that the amount that can be earned or saved is millions of dollars. So even though two people may have the same EQ and make the same effort in their work, the value of their fruits of labor may differ by a factor of millions.

你购买了一个 100 美元的咖啡机，如果你发现在网上能便宜 10 美元，你并不介意开车去把这 100 美元的咖啡炉退掉，再到网上去买一模一样 90 美元的商品。然而你花 1 万美元买一只钻石戒指的时候，你不会因为这个戒指多收了你 10 块钱而再回去找商家理论。因为你心里的总价值已经被调高了，人们都是在用百分比做自己行为的计算。

Let's say you have now bought a coffee maker at a store. If you discover that you can save $10 by buying it online, you will not mind driving to the store to return it and then buying an identical one online at $90. Yet, when you buy a $10,000 diamond ring, you will not bother to bargain with the seller even if he has accidentally charged you $10 more despite a higher total cost of acquiring the diamond ring. This is because you calculate your actions based on percentages.

你在餐馆里吃饭花了 50 美元，服务员对你毕恭毕敬，提供周到的服务，你心情一好就给了他 10 美元作为小费。你在投资银行工作，如果你能够让一个一亿美元的交易过程顺利和令人愉快，那这个时候客户就实在不好意思只掏出 10 美元给你做小费了，而是拿出 100 万美元来给你。

When you have a $50-dollar meal at a restaurant and you are satisfied with the waiter's service, you leave a tip of $10. Let's say now you work at an investment bank. If you can make a transaction that is worth $100 million smooth and pleasant, your client will be embarrassed to give you $10 as tips. Instead, your client will reward you with $1 million.

在机器和人工智能取代人做金融交易之前，恐怕金融行业的收入会一直偏高。这些道理在我决定去 MBA 的时候还没能想得特别明白。只是后来在投行工作了一段时间，才明白为什么金融行业挣钱。

Unless and until machines and artificial intelligence replace finance workers, they will continue to have a relatively high income. Actually, I had not figured this out when I decided to get my MBA. It was only after I worked with an investment bank for a while that I understood why the financial industry is a lucrative business.

比如说一个 1000 人的企业，员工辛辛苦苦工作了一年，获得了 10%的利润。为了简单计算，先说这相当于 10 万美元的利润。这个公司要上市了，这个时候上市，企业估值可能是利润的 20 倍，200 万美元。而这 200 万的估值中要拿出 5%给投行作为佣金。这样算下来，这 1000 个人辛苦了一年的收入，也就相当于投资银行 2-3 个人几个月的工作量。

Let me further illustrate this by doing some simple calculations. Take a hypothetical corporation with 1,000 employees. As a result of the diligent work of the employees throughout the year, the company makes a profit of $100,000. It is looking to launch its IPO. At the time of its IPO, the business is valued at 20 times the annual profit, which is $2 million, 5% of which is the commission fee payable to the investment bank. Therefore, the revenues generated as a result of the hard work of 1,000 staff members are equivalent to a few months' work by 2-3 investment bankers.

你可能会问，那上市公司为什么不愿意付更小的佣金呢？既然市场是充分竞争的，为何上市公司不是只支付千分之一或者是万分之一的佣金? 为什么愿意付 5%的佣金给投资银行作为上市的费用呢？

You may ask, "Why are listed companies willing to pay such a large amount of commission? Why don't these organizations pay a 0.1% or 0.001% fee instead? Why are they willing to pay investment banks a 5% commission for their IPO?"

因为股票每天的价格波动就不止 5%，在这样大笔的钱剧烈波动的时候，人们不介意付出更多的钱获得更好的服务。然而你说投资银行确实给社会创造了 5%，或者是相当于那 1000 个人一年工作的价值吗？我看没有。社会的确给金融行业的人支付了偏高的酬劳。

The reason is that the extent of daily fluctuation in stock prices is greater than 5%. Coupled with a large amount of money involved in the transactions, people do not mind paying more fees for better services. Yet, you may still be wondering, "Do investment banks create value equivalent to the 5% fee charged or the fruit of the labor of those 1,000 workers?" My answer is in the negative. Society does pay finance workers an income that is higher than the value they have created.

02 求学若渴

02 A Constant Thirst for Knowledge

我去读 MBA 一方面的确是受到了金融行业的诱惑。因为我想既然我对钱有兴趣，为什么不进一步看看自己的这个兴趣能走多远呢。另外一方面的动力还是想彻底搞明白金融和财务的一系列问题。我感觉自己所有的金融知识都是零零星星学来的。既然提出了"十年一千万"的口号，那还是认真系统地学习一下相关知识为好。

There are two main motivations behind my studying MBA. On the one hand, I have to admit I was tempted by the perks of working in the financial industry. I was thinking to myself, "As I was interested in finance and money, why not take a further step and see how far I can go in this field?" On the other hand, I wanted to find an answer to a series of questions on finance. I felt that I gained all my financial knowledge piecemeal. Having suggested the slogan of "10 million in 10 years," I should as well acquire the relevant knowledge in a serious, systematic manner.

MBA 的课程学了十几门，从必修到选修，学到的知识很多。知识分两类，有用的和无用的。大部分无用的知识，随着时间的流逝，自然会从你记忆中被淡忘。就像我们中学大学学到的大部分数理化知识一样。淡忘并不要紧，很多知识是在记忆深处默默地做着储备。

I finished more than a dozen courses in my MBA, from electives to compulsory courses, and acquired much valuable knowledge. There are two types of knowledge, namely "useful" and "useless." Most useless knowledge will naturally fall into oblivion as time goes by. This is like how we forgot most of the mathematics and science concepts we learned in high school and university. Being forgetful is not a big issue because much knowledge you learned is preparing you for your success in your subconscious mind. To borrow a saying from Ralph Waldo Emerson, "I cannot remember the books I've read any more than the meals I have eaten; even so, they have made me."

学习的很大一个目的并不是立刻把这些知识用到什么具体的用途上，而是因为有某方面的知识储备，让你对某一些领域的问题不再害怕了。等问题来临的时候，你知道上哪里去寻找相关的资料。

One of the most important goals of learning is not how to immediately apply all this knowledge for a specific purpose but how to build a reserve of knowledge about a particular field so that you will not be intimidated by some questions or difficulties pertaining to that field. When you encounter these obstacles, you will know where to find relevant information and solutions.

我自己是理工科背景的，所以对于这一点有着深刻的感受。比如我们大学一年级时候都学过复杂的高等数学，但是我敢说大部分人 95% 以上再也没用过。可是这并不等于高等数学没用，最大的用处就是当你看到微分和积分符号方程的时候，你不再害怕了。

Because of my background in science, I can deeply relate to this reflection. For example, even though my classmates and I all studied complicated, advanced mathematics in my freshman year, I feel confident to say that 95% of my classmates have never applied them since. However, this does not mean that those advanced mathematical skills are useless. The greatest benefit is that I am no longer intimidated by all those symbols and equations in calculus.

现在回忆起来，MBA 的课程和知识点是对我的投资理财经历非常有帮助的。我简单整理一下供读者参考。

In retrospect, all the concepts and knowledge in the MBA's curriculum prove to be highly conducive to my investment and wealth management journey. Below is my attempt to organize and outline some of the useful concepts for my readers.

一个是微观经济学，这是经济学的基础科目。它让我明白了价格是和成本没有关系的，价格完全取决于供求的平衡。在我这一代美国华人中，曾经受到过很多片面和错误的教育。很多观点不仅是书本上错误的公式，在现实生活中，也害了很多人。

I have found many concepts in microeconomics, which is a foundational subject in economics, to be tremendously useful. Firstly, it taught me that prices have nothing to do with costs. Market prices are determined by the law of demand and supply. The education received by my generation of Chinese Americans was often misleading and one-sided. Not only did these points of view manifest themselves as wrong formulas in textbooks, but they also ruined the lives of many people in reality.

比如我们一向认为一个商品的价格是围绕着它的生产成本进行周期的波动。当市场价格超过它生产成本的时候，就会有更多生产者涌入。当价格低于它生产成本的时候，就会有卖家退出，这个动态的过程中实现了价格围绕着成本的上下波动。

For example, we often thought that the price of a product revolved around changes in its manufacturing costs. When the market price exceeded its manufacturing costs, more producers would enter the market. When the price was lower than its manufacturing costs, sellers would quit the market. In this dynamic process, the market price fluctuated correspondingly with the changes in the manufacturing costs.

这个理论听上去不错，但是在实际生活中其实是一个到处碰壁的理论。2005 年以后，当中国的房地产价格开始飙升的时候。有人用同样的理论去预测未来的房价。比如当时上海一栋楼的土建成本只有 2000 元每平米，而当时的地价大概是 5000 元每平米。那么售价怎么可能长期保持在 2 万元每平米以上呢？

Though seemingly logical, it is a problematic theory if applied to our daily lives. When China's property prices start to soar after 2005, some people attempted to predict future property prices by applying this theory. For example, the construction cost was CN¥2,000 per square meter in Shanghai at the time and the land price was CN¥5,000 per square meter. The question is, "How is it possible that property prices remain steady at more than CN¥20,000 per square meter?"

根据马克思的理论，应该是大量开发商投入生产，商品房的价格下跌到 7000 每平米以下才是合理的。所以有人根据这个理论就是坚持不买房。更有甚者是把自己唯一的住房卖掉，期待房价下跌之后用更低的价格买入。

According to Marxism, the reasonable outcome is that a multitude of land developers would increase their production, driving property prices down to CN¥7,000 per square meter. Therefore, relying on this theory, some people insisted on not buying real estate. Some even sold their only home, expecting to buy it back at a lower price in the future.

然而现实不断在给这些梦想着房子会降价的人打脸。房价非但没有低于 7000 人民币每平米，而且持续高于 2 万每平米。然后上升到 3 万 4 万，一路涨到今天的 10 万元每平米。在整个过程中从来没有跌落到生产成本价格以下。

Yet, the reality is cruel to those who dream that property prices will plummet. Not only did property prices remain stable above CN¥7,000 per square meter, but they also stood at CN¥20,000 per square meter for a long time and then gradually increased to CN¥30,000-40,000. Today, the price is CN¥100,000 per square meter. During this whole process, property prices never dropped below the construction costs.

系统地学习微观经济学的知识才让我知道一个商品的价格和它的成本是没有关系的，市场价格取决于纳什均衡点，是买卖双方按照他们各自是否有其他更好的选择(Alternative best choice)，而互相博弈的结果。既然是这样的博弈，房价自然可能是长期远远高于生产成本的。

Studying microeconomics in a systematic manner makes me realize that the price of a commodity has nothing to do with its manufacturing costs. Instead, market prices are determined by the Nash equilibrium, which is a result of a non-cooperative game between the seller and buyer who make their moves based on whether they have an alternative best choice. Even this is the case, it makes sense that property prices are persistently higher than construction costs.

明白这个道理可以帮助我们讨价还价。比如我们去旅行的时候，经常到自由市场上和小贩讨价还价买工艺品。小贩们总是喜欢开出一个很高的价格，然后等你杀价。我为此发明了一套讨价还价的方法，屡试不爽，每次都可以保证几乎最低价成交。我在这个讨价还价的过程中，其实就是在寻找那个平衡点。因为这些摊子上的很多商品雷同，我从来不关心小贩们开价是多少。我讨价还价购买商品的方法就是先给对方一个不可能卖给我的基价，注意这个价格一定要低到对方不卖给你才行。

Understanding this theory can help us improve our bargaining skills. For example, when I traveled to a new destination, I enjoyed visiting the flea market to buy some art. The sellers always asked for a high price, leaving plenty of room for buyers to bargain with them. I have specifically formulated an invincible bargaining strategy that guarantees that I can buy the item at the lowest price in every transaction. My strategy revolves around finding the equilibrium. As the products sold by different vendors are very similar or even identical, I do not care about the price the stall owners initially offered. The key is to make a counteroffer of a price that is so unreasonably low that the vendor will not accept. This counteroffer serves as a base price in your negotiation.

然后我换一个小贩，在这个价格上往上加 10%试试。然后再换一个小贩，再加 10%，直到有一个小贩愿意卖给我。我用这样的办法买东西，在世界各国的旅行中很少吃亏。当然缺点就是免不了受很多小贩的白眼，因为我一开始开的价格总是低到他们愤怒地想打我。

I will then try to make an offer to another vendor by adding 10% to that base price, the third seller by adding 10% again, and so on until a seller is willing to accept my offer. By using this strategy as a shopper, I am always the winning party in the negotiation. Of course, a big shortcoming is that many vendors looked down on me because my initial offer was so low that they were so angry that they wanted to punch me.

微观经济学中另外一个对我有用的知识点就是市场效率理论。这个理论让我认识到各行各业，除非你拥有长期的垄断权，不然是无法实现长期高利润的。用通俗的话概括就是，马路上你不会随随便便看到一张真钞票，但是如果你看到的话，要赶紧把它抓在口袋里，因为你再也没有这样的机会了。用到房地产投资上，那就是好学区永远不会有正现金流的房子。如果有，那一定是转瞬即逝的机会，你要赶紧抓住它。

Another useful concept in microeconomics is the efficient-market hypothesis. This theory makes me realize that in every industry unless you have a long-term monopoly right, you cannot persistently achieve high profits. A more casual way of saying this is that it is not a usual occurrence that you find a real banknote on the street. But if you do, you need to grasp the chance and put it in your pocket because you will not find such an opportunity in the future. Applying this to real estate investing will suggest that there will never be a house with positive cash flow in a good school district; if it does, it will be a fleeting opportunity and you need to seize it as soon as possible.

沉没成本和边际成本也是微观经济学的两个重要概念。沉没成本的概念对于买卖股票其实是非常有帮助的。人们在买卖股票的时候，因为出于期待盈利的心理，总是经常给自己设置一些错误的规定。比如很多人死守底线，不愿意以低于自己买入价格的成本去卖出股票。其实卖股票你最需要关心的是如何按照可能的最高价卖出，你的买入价格已经全部变成沉没成本了，压根不需要考虑。

Sunk cost and marginal cost are two fundamental concepts in microeconomics. The concept of sunk cost is highly useful in stock trading. When people are buying or selling stocks, they always lay down some wrong rules for themselves. For example, many people are reluctant to sell their stocks at a price lower than their initial buying price. The sunk cost theory will suggest that what you need to focus on is selling your stocks at the highest price possible because your initial buying price has become sunk costs that you should completely disregard.

我们人的一生中，曾经过去的所有事情都是沉没成本。你投入的时间、金钱、情感都已经沉没了。想明白沉没成本的概念，会让我们更好地放眼于未来。边际成本是另一个给我深刻印象的概念。当你购买一样东西的时候，如果卖家的价格高于它的边际成本，他就有一万个理由愿意卖给你。即使这个价格，远低于他的平均总成本。比如小贩卖东西的时候，进货价是边际成本，而房租则是总成本的一部分。这对我们讨价还价的时候，摸清对手的底线很有帮助。

In our lives, everything in the past is sunk costs. The time, money, and love you devoted to them have already sunk. Understanding the concept of sunk cost prompts us to focus on the future. Marginal cost is another memorable concept. When you purchase a certain thing, the seller has a thousand reasons to sell it to you if the price is higher than the marginal cost, even though the price is lower than his average total costs. For example, when a vendor tries to sell something, his or her marginal cost is the cost of inventory, and the rental is part of the total cost. Knowledge of the cost relationship can help us figure out the bottom line in our negotiation with the seller.

不过学习一些经济学的知识也让我对美国的一些深层次的社会问题有了更深刻的理解。比如很多已经是板上钉钉的经典经济学理论，为什么在现实生活中执行起来那么困难？每一个学过经济学的人都会告诉你，房租控制是毁掉一个城市最好的手段。可是并不耽误加州出台一个又一个的房租控制法令。所有的经典理论都会告诉你，工人罢工、工会集体议价最后伤害的是工人自己。可是这并不耽误工会的存在，并几乎把整个底特律的美国汽车产业弄破产。

Meanwhile, because of my studies in economics, I now have a deeper understanding of some underlying social issues in the U.S. For instance, why is the execution of so many well-established classic economic theories so difficult in real life? Everyone who has a background in economics will tell you that rent control is the best way to ruin a city. However, this has not discouraged California from passing one rent control bill after another. Furthermore, almost all classic theories will tell you that strikes and collective bargaining by labor unions hurt the workers the most, but all this does not inhibit unionization. In fact, the American automotive industry in Detroit almost went bankrupt because of this.

这好比是说今天已经有了现代医学，有了数理化学，但是并不耽误大家去相信巫术，或者用星座相亲是一个道理。

This is analogous to how everyone believes in witchcraft or uses horoscope to find a significant other despite the advent of modern medicine, mathematics, and science.

且不说那些不读书的人。世上有太多的人，他们在读书的时候，很少把书上的内容和自己的生活实践联系在一起。书上的内容对于他们来说，就像是看动画片里哪吒闹海一样，虽然看着很热闹，但是和他们的生活没半点关系。他们不会把书上的知识运用到生活实践中。另外一方面，国家与社会，特别是民主的社会，在权衡社会利益的时候，往往对短期利益的关注远远超过长期利益。短期利益是自己的，长期利益天知道是谁的。

Multitudes of high-educated people, let alone those with a lesser education background or who do not read, fail to apply their knowledge learned at school or from books to their daily lives. To these people, studying the concepts in the books is similar to watching how Nezha conquers the Dragon King in Chinese cartoons: They enjoy the experience of studying or watching but think that it has nothing to do with their lives. To put it simply, they fail to apply the knowledge and ideas in real-world settings. In addition, the government and society, especially a democratic one, often attach much more emphasis to short-term interests than long-term ones. This is because long-term interests are simply too remote and uncertain. Their priority is to secure certain short-term interests for themselves.

所以你经常可以看到那些拥有高学历的博士生们，那些系统学习过统计学理论的人，津津乐道星座与人的性格特征之间的关系。商学院的毕业生大肆鼓吹租控公共政策。

This is why you can often see that Ph.D. holders and those who have studied statistics in a systematic manner are passionate about exploring the relationship between personality and horoscope and that graduates from business schools are advocating public policies on rent control.

微观经济学还会告诉你垄断的力量。虽然之前我明白垄断的威力，但是我从来没有用图表用供需曲线去精确地描绘垄断对商品价格的影响到底是多少，并不知道如何量化和计算这部分。学习了微观经济学，我可以精确地算出来，当一个国家或一个政府对土地的供应发生垄断的时候，对价格会产生多么大的扭曲影响。这些问题用文字说明往往不容易清楚理解，但在供求曲线上描绘时，一切就变得一目了然。

Microeconomics can also tell you about the power of monopoly. Even though I knew the power of monopoly before taking my MBA, I had never used graphs and demand and supply curves to accurately portray the influence of monopoly on market prices. Neither did I know how to quantify and calculate this part. After studying microeconomics, I can now accurately calculate how prices are skewed when a country or government monopolizes land supply. A picture is worth a thousand words. It is often difficult to understand and illustrate these problems through a mere verbal description. But when we plot demand and supply curves on a graph, everything becomes crystal clear.

微观经济学还会告诉你，海关税收和抵制某一国家的货物到底伤害的是谁？比如当年我上这门课的时候，中国正好发生抵制日货。我今天在写这本书的时候，美国和中国在打贸易战。学习经济学可以让大家对这些问题看得更加清楚。所有税收最终都是消费者买单。抵制某国的商品导致的结果也是两败俱伤，而是让第三国受益。

Microeconomics will also give you the answer to the question of "Who is the loser when a country boycotts imports from another country?" When I was taking this course back then, China was boycotting Japanese products. As of the time of writing, China and the U.S. are in the midst of a trade war. Learning about economics can facilitate a better understanding of these issues. All tariffs imposed will come out of the pocket of consumers. Boycotting imports from another country will only be a lose-lose for both the boycotter and the boycotted country, benefitting a third-party country.

03 知识储备

03 A Reserve of Knowledge

对于宏观经济学，我自己感觉最有用的就是搞清楚了利率、GDP、货币政策、贸易政策等等这些每天报纸上看到的指标之间的相互关系，明白了背后的原理。这个时候你就可以看清楚报刊媒体新闻背后的故事，不会轻易被别人忽悠。

When it comes to macroeconomics, my biggest takeaway is that I have now sorted out the relationships between such indicators as interest rates, GDP, monetary policies, and trade that are frequently mentioned in newspapers and the principles behind. Such knowledge empowers me to be a critical reader who is able to perceive hidden agendas in mainstream media and will not be easily fooled.

比如宏观经济学解释什么是钱，钱的本质是什么？这对我后来投资比特币有非常大的影响。宏观经济学也揭示了 GDP 以及一个国家的财富构成到底是什么？让我更能看清楚中美之间 GDP 之间的差异。也能够看得清楚财富正在朝哪个国家转。

For example, macroeconomics explains what money is and its nature. This knowledge has greatly influenced my strategies of investing in bitcoin. Macroeconomics also reveals what GDP is and the composition of a nation's country. I am able to see more clearly the differences between China's GDP and that of the U.S. and which countries are creating more wealth.

如果回到 100 年前，有人告诉你，香港有一天人均 GDP 将是英国的两倍，估计你会笑他们发疯了。然而这样的事情实实在在地发生了，而曾经辉煌的英国，人均 GDP 在今天只能排到美国最落后的几个州里面，仅仅是加州的一半。明白这些道理才能看清楚世界的财富往哪里转。

If we went back in time to a century ago and somebody told you that Hong Kong's GDP per capita would be two times that of the U.K. one day, perhaps you would think that he was a lunatic. Yet, this claim has indeed become a reality. The GDP per capita of Britain, which was once a superpower, is only half of that of California, falling behind that of a majority of states in the U.S.

对 GDP 的理解可以让我们大概明白哪些是舆论宣传，哪些是忽悠。比如经常有媒体说中国的 GDP 做假。这样的报道我在过去几十年里不知道看过多少次。另外一方面还有人认为美国的 GDP 水分很高。因为据说美国 6% 的 GDP 都是法律服务，20% 的美国 GDP 都是医疗保健。有人认为这是垃圾 GDP。此外永远不断有政治人物出来批评不能以 GDP 为论，要考虑幸福感。这些貌似有道理的宣传，如果你仔细学过宏观经济学，就会自己分析和判断，而不再受到他们的蛊惑。

Our understanding of GDP helps us tell nonsense and propaganda apart from facts. For example, some mainstream media often say that China's GDP data is fake. I have encountered numerous such articles in the last several decades. At the same time, some people also claim that the U.S. GDP statistics were also inflated. This is because it was said that 6% of U.S. GDP comes from the legal services sector and 20% from the healthcare industry. Some think that all this is "garbage GDP." In addition to these claims of inaccurate statistics, there are almost bound to be politicians who are saying that we cannot make our evaluation based on GDP but should consider GNP- "gross national happiness." In the face of all these seemingly logical and reasonable claims, you will not be fooled if you have studied macroeconomics in detail, which will enable you to become an independent and critical thinker.

GDP 是测量一个地区和国家发展再精确不过的指标了。尤其是名义 GDP。当你到世界各地去旅行的时候，你几乎从一个国家的人均 GDP 就可以判断一个国家的市容和干净程度。读者有机会去看一看，比较一下西欧、东欧、中东、南亚、东南亚的各个国家。看看人均 GDP 能不能代表一个国家的发展水平。

GDP, especially nominal GDP, is perhaps the most accurate indicator of a country or region's development. When you are traveling around the world, you can have a rough idea of the atmosphere and cleanliness of that country by simply knowing its GDP per capita. If you have the chance, you can try to test this rule by comparing the countries in Western Europe, Eastern Europe, the Middle East, South Asia, and Southeast Asia. Judge for yourself whether the GDP per capita can represent a country's development level.

宏观经济学让我们更好地理解通货膨胀。之前我对通货膨胀的大部分理解都来自自学的结果。你经常会看到一些神奇的文章，比如输入型通货膨胀、农产品型通货膨胀。因为某些外界因素，导致某一类商品的价格上涨而引发通货膨胀。学完通货膨胀的理论，你大概知道通货膨胀就是钱发多了，其他都是掩饰的借口。你也知道对付通货膨胀的办法并不是拥有某一类不再增发的商品，因为世上没有永远保值的东西。

Macroeconomics can help us better understand inflation. Before studying MBA, most of my understanding of inflation was a result of self-learning. You can often stumble across some magical articles mentioning terms such as "imported inflation" and "agricultural commodity inflation." Because of some external factors, the price of a certain category of commodity increases, leading to inflation. After studying theories of inflation, you will know that inflation is essentially due to the printing of too much money and that all other proposed explanations are excuses to cover up the truth. You will also know that the best way to tackle inflation is not to own a certain category of commodities whose supply is fixed and limited because nothing in the world can retain its value forever.

其实这些课对我最主要的用处是对于平时听到的一些基本概念有了更明确的认识。比如失业率并不表示没有工作的人的比例。而是那些努力找工作，但是找不到工作的人的比例。明白这个道理就可以知道特朗普竞选时候打出美国失业率高的悲情牌是多么不靠谱。宏观经济学关于增长的理论，让我明白人口是决定的因素。一切增长背后的本质是靠人、技术和资本。而人工的增长是永远敌不过资本的增长的。

The greatest takeaway from these courses is that I have clarified my understanding of some basic concepts. For example, the unemployment rate does not represent the proportion of people without a job but those who are unemployed despite their efforts in finding a job. Understanding this principle helps one understand that how unreasonable Trump was when he was trying to win the election by highlighting a high unemployment rate in the U.S. All those macroeconomic theories on growth make me see that population is a key factor. Growth is essentially spurred by people, skills, and capital. And an increase in wages can never outpace an increase in capital.

我这里不想把我学到的关键知识点都罗列出来。微观和宏观经济学让我学会了用经济学的思路思考现象，理清了大量基本概念。

I do not intend to list all the relevant knowledge and concepts I have learned in my MBA. It suffices to say that microeconomic and macroeconomic theories equip me with an economist's way of thinking for examining a certain phenomenon and help me clarify a lot of basic concepts.

我学完微观经济学和宏观经济学之后的感受就是，这些课程的基本知识与我们的生活那么的贴近，也许都应该放到中小学阶段进行学习。就像基本的物理数学常识应该是每个现代人都应该掌握的知识

My most profound reflection after studying microeconomics and macroeconomics is that the basic concepts in these courses are so closely related to our daily lives and should be part of the curriculum in elementary and secondary schools. They are like basic physics and mathematics knowledge that every modern sapiens should grasp.

还有一些专业的课程对我也很有帮助，比如说会计（Accounting）和企业财务（Corporate Finance）这两门课。学习 MBA 之前，我是看不懂一个公司的财务报表的，也看不懂复式记账法，我也不知道如何对一个公司进行有效的估价。学习了这两门课，我大约可以从上市公司的财务报表中大体看明白一个公司的基本情况。投资这门课，更是让我知道怎样手把手地从最底层去给公司做一个估价。

There are some other professional courses that are eminently useful too. Take accounting and corporate finance. Before studying an MBA, I had no idea how to read a company's financial statements; nor did I have any clue about double-entry bookkeeping. After taking these two courses, I can now briefly assess the situation of a listed company by reading its financial statements. In addition, the course on investing taught me how to evaluate a company step by step from ground zero.

金融衍生品交易的课，是一门对数学要求很强的课程。那些复杂的公式，那些复杂的交易策略（trading strategy），渐渐在我的脑海里都被忘掉

了。可是这些知识在研究如何购买比特币的时候又重新冒了出来。我用到了相关的知识，毫无风险地获得了比特币。这点我在第十七章还会仔细介绍。如果我当时没有上这些课程，那么可能就没有这样的知识储备，等这个问题来临的时候，我也想不到这样的好方法去投资。

Trading of Derivatives is a course that requires strong mathematical skills. To be honest, I have forgotten about most of those complicated formulas and trading strategies. However, all this knowledge popped up again in mind when I was looking to buy bitcoins. I applied the relevant knowledge and procured bitcoins risk-free. I will elaborate on this in more detail in Chapter 17. If I had not taken these courses, I would not have had this reserve of knowledge; all this knowledge empowers me to come up with good investing strategies in the face of setbacks.

市场学（Marketing）这门课也很有意思。学习这门课之后，你会知道，市面上大部分商品的价格跟他们的生产成本没有关系，而完全取决于商家忽悠消费者的能力。人们的购买习惯是非常复杂的，不是简单的比对性能和价格，而是受很多心理因素的影响。人们在掏钱的时候，觉得自己是上帝。任何人一旦傲慢，智商也就自然直线下落。B2C 市场大量的消费品销售价格长年远远高于生产成本，比如 LV 包。

Marketing is a fascinating course that tells you that the prices of most products in the market have nothing to do with their manufacturing costs. The pricing depends on the ability of the sellers to fool their customers. Consumer's buying habits are intensely complicated. They do not simply compare the functions and prices of products, but they are influenced by a myriad of psychological factors. When people are paying money, they feel that they are God. When a person begins to be full of themselves, their IQ also plummets. In the B2C market, the prices of a lot of consumer products are much higher than the manufacturing costs, for example, LV handbags.

读书期间的另外一件乐事就是阅读了大量的案例(case)。这些 case 大部分都可以当历史书来看。比如洛克菲勒经营房地产的历史，我就写了一篇文章，来看看地主是怎么分家的？

Another enjoyable part of my MBA studies is that I read a plethora of cases. Most of these cases are historical stories, for instance, the story of how the Rockefellers ran their real estate business. I specifically wrote an article on how such a big landowner as Rockefeller Sr. divided his assets among his heirs.

洛克菲勒中心分家的故事 (2008 年 2 月 14 日)
The Story of Dividing the Rockefeller Center (February 14, 2008)

by Bayfamily

大家都知道纽约有个赫赫有名的洛克菲勒中心。洛克菲勒家族从 1932 年到 1952 年的时间里，在纽约的 mid town（中城）先后盖了十二栋楼。占地 12 个 acres（英亩），总面积 6.5M 平方尺。一度是纽约人以及美国人的骄傲。虽然我每次去都特别不以为然，可纽约人把它当成个宝，尤其是那个小溜冰场。我实在看不出有什么特别的地方。洛克菲勒家当年盖这个房子暗箱操作的事情可没少干。从地皮到特许经营权。在这房子上洛克菲勒家族可是赚嗨了。哗啦哗啦猛收了三十几年的租子。

Rockefeller Center is a well-renowned landmark in New York City. From 1932 to 1952, the Rockefeller family constructed twelve buildings in mid-town New York City, spanning twelve acres of land with a total floor area of 6.5 million square feet. These buildings were once the pride of New Yorkers and Americans. Though I could not see anything special about those buildings, New Yorkers were very proud of them, especially the ice-skating rink. In developing the building complex, the Rockefellers were involved in a significant amount of under-the-table dealings. From procuring the land to franchise rights, the Rockefellers made big bucks. They had received handsome rental income for more than three decades.

会走路的钱
Money Walks

事情到了 1985 年，问题来了。首先是家族根深叶茂，子子孙孙，要分家产。不是每个人都对房地产那么有兴趣。房子不像股票，可以分得很细。当然过去中国人分家是另外一回事，老大东厢房，老二西厢房。你看，前些日子中国的李连杰，在上海浦东最好的地段盖了个房子，然后向媒体宣布，打算东边这栋留给大女儿，西边这栋留给二女儿。整个还是一个土财主的脑子。老外分家要分个干净，何况这帮子孙们不再满足收租子过日子。最好是把房子卖掉，大家一分，然后该干什么干什么去。

However, problems arose in 1985. Firstly, the Rockefeller family had grown to include many descendants of John Rockefeller Sr. Therefore, these family members wanted the family property to be divided among them. However, not everyone was interested in real estate which, unlike stocks, could not be divided into smaller units. Of course, dividing family property in China is a different matter. Chinese parents often reserve the east-wing of the family home for their elder child and west-wing for the younger child. Take Jet Li, a Chinese film actor. He has earlier built a house in the best location in Pudong, Shanghai, and announced to the media that he reserved the east-wing for his elder daughter and the west-wing for his second daughter. He is the epitome of an old landlord's thinking. In contrast, westerners prefer to divide their family property completely, i.e., treating each family member as an independent individual. This is not to mention that Rockefeller's descendants were not content with simply sitting there and collecting rents. Therefore, the best way was to sell the real properties and divide the proceeds among heirs who could then use the money for whatever pursuits they desired.

要卖房子，麻烦可来了。第一是税。到了 1985 年，房子的市场估价是 1.6Billion。可在账本上由于长年的 depreciation write off（折旧抵扣），房子的价值已经几乎是零了。这真是投资房地产的好处，明明是天价的房子。Sam 大叔的账面上却过瘾地把它的价格当成零。 以前 claim depreciation（申报折旧）是不错，可现在一下子要交 1.6Billion 的 capital gain（增值）的税，洛克菲勒家可实在不甘心。

However, selling those real properties was fraught with other obstacles. The first is tax. In 1985, the market valuation of the Rockefellers' real properties was $1.6 billion. However, because of decades of depreciation write-off, the book value of these real properties was close to zero. This is indeed an advantage of investing in real estate: real properties that are worth an astronomical sum was valued at zero on accounting books by Uncle Sam. It was a clever maneuver to claim depreciation; however, now this would mean that the Rockefeller family needed to pay a capital gain tax of $1.6 billion.

第二是名声。洛克菲勒家的老一辈革命家对房子有深厚的感情，希望永远掌控房子的实际经营权，要把洛克菲勒的名字永远继承下去。要是随便把房子卖掉，明天被人改成李嘉诚大厦，岂不是很伤家族的面子。

The second problem is their family reputation. The older generation in the Rockefeller family had a deep emotional connection with their real properties, and they hoped that they could control the operating rights of these properties forever so that they could continue the legacy of their family name. What if the buyer of these buildings changed the name to Lee Ka Shing Center? The family would lose face.

第三是房子的总值太高。一下子出卖，也没有哪个买家能买得起。如果弄个 exchange（互换）来延税，也找不到类似的房子和买主。

The final obstacle is that the total value of the real properties was too high. No buyers could afford to buy the entire building complex in one go. Even if the Rockefellers structured the transaction as an exchange to delay tax payments, they could not find similar properties and buyers.

怎么办？说来简单，refinance。

What should they do? The solution is simple, that is through refinancing.

首先是先化整为零，弄一个占 80% 股份的 REIT (real estate investment trust)。在 REIT 的名下，出售 750M 的股权。等于是扩招新股，股本进来的钱总不用交税吧。接着是发行 500M 的债券，发行的是 convertible 的 bond（可转债）。若干年以后，可以转成股份。发行债券不但不交税，反而可以用利息来减税。后来日本人在 89 年买了 1.3billion 中大部分股份，当冤大头的故事，大家都知道，我就不说了。

They first divided the interests into smaller units by establishing a REIT which has an 80% share component. REIT stands for real estate investment trust. They sold 750 million shares of the REIT. This act was equivalent to raising new capital, so the inflow of capital was not taxable. The Rockefeller family then issued 500 million convertible bonds that could be converted into shares after a certain period of time. The issuance of bonds is not taxable either. In fact, the interest payable on these bonds could be deducted from tax. In 1989, some Japanese bought most of the 1.3 billion shares. I will not go into detail the story of how the Japanese took a hit in this deal.

你看看，这样一来，洛克菲勒家占了 20%的股份。其他 80%的股份分散在其他千千万万的投资人手里，洛克菲勒家族保持房子的实际经营权。同时大量的现金进账，一分钱税也没有交。子孙们吃喝玩乐，分散投资。

As you can now see, after all these maneuvers, the Rockefeller family now owns a 20% stake, with the other 80% held by millions of investors. The Rockefeller family maintained actual control of the building complex, obtained much cash, and did not pay any tax. The descendants can now enjoy their lives and invest their time and money on other projects.

好了，洛克菲勒的故事讲完了。很简单，是个大地主分家产和逃税的故事。从中我们可以学到什么呢？

So that is the end of the story of the Rockefeller family. It is a story of how a big landowner divided his property among his heirs and avoided tax. What can we learn from this story?

首先是要知道，在美国投资房地产是几乎不用交税的。无论是大地主还是小地主，我很少听说有人交过 capital gain 的税。穷人有 500K 的免税，可以 exchange, 富人有无数的漏洞可以钻。不但不交税，depreciation 和 interest 还可以到处抵税。相比之下，401K 的延税和 Roth 的免税实在不算什么。在中国投资也是同样的道理。洛克菲勒家把钱取出来和我们做

refinance 没什么区别。 在中国买卖房子的税费很高，最好的办法就是长期持有，要钱的时候，cash out 贷款提现出来。

We have to first understand that investing in U.S. real properties involves very little tax. I have seldom heard that a landowner, be it a big or small one, has paid capital gain tax. Not only does it involve very little tax, but its depreciation and interest incurred can also be deducted from tax payments. When compared to real estate investing, 401K's delayed tax payments and Roth's tax exemptions are not that attractive. The same is true for investing in China. The Rockefellers' turning their stakes into cash is no different from how we, ordinary people, refinance. Selling and buying real properties in China has a high tax rate, so the best way is to hold them long-term. When you need money, cash out on your real properties by taking out a loan.

第二个是洛克菲勒中心当年估价用的数据非常有意思。在 1985 年，当时的估价是鉴于未来 20 年里，每年 7% 的房租增长，6% 的成本增长和二十年后 8% 的 Cap rate 作出的。后来实际的 rent 没有涨那么多，成本倒是呼呼猛涨。也是后来日本人退出，中心濒于破产的原因之一。俗话说，买的没有卖的精。新手买出租房，老房主常常是玩了几十年了的老江湖。信息是不对称的。对于未来的房租估计不能太乐观。切记这点。

Equally noteworthy are the valuation statistics of Rockefeller center back then. In 1985, the valuation was based on a 7% growth rate in rental income, a 6% growth rate in cost, and an 8% cap rate in the next 20 years. But it later turned out that the actual increase in rents was less than 7% and the cost skyrocketed. This is also why the Japanese left the scene and why the Rockefeller Center was on the verge of bankruptcy. There is a common saying that goes, "The buyers are not as savvy as the sellers." When a new real estate investor is buying a rental property, the vendor often has decades of experience. The information is asymmetric. Therefore, we must bear in mind that we should not be overly optimistic about future rental income that could be generated by that property.

其他的比较精彩的 case，给我留下深刻印象的还有几个。一个就是为什么计算机上会贴 Intel 标签的？ FedEx 是怎么创业成功的？当然可口可乐和百事可乐的故事永远是经典。他们两家互相争斗的历史也可以反映消费者的弱点。那就是消费者是盲目的，他们根本不知道自己在买什么。而卖家永远在利用人性的弱点获取高额利润。如果你仔细想一下我们生活中的细节，不单限于奢侈品，甚至是一个纽扣、一袋大米、一块肥皂，它们都不会无缘无故地跑到你家里来。这些商品之所以跑到你家里来，你之所以买了这些商品而没有买另外一些商品，都是因为在成千上万个渠道和环节上被别人精心算计过。

There are several other intriguing cases that left me with a strong impression. Why do computers have an "Intel" sticker? How does FedEx become so successful? Of course, the stories of Coca-Cola and PepsiCo are classics. The history of their battle for dominance reflects consumer's weakness, which is they are blind; they have no idea what they are buying. Sellers are always leveraging human's weaknesses to maximize their profits. If you think about the details of our lives, from luxury goods to even a button on your shirt, and from a bag of rice to a piece of soap, they do not just appear at your home out of thin air. The reason why all these products appear at your home is that you chose to buy them instead of other products. Your buying decisions are a result of some careful calculations in numerous channels and processes by those businesses.

04 次贷危机爆发
04 The Outbreak of the Sub-prime Crisis

在美国给人的感觉就是你是自由的，你可以做任何你想做的事情，我感觉自己既然对金钱和投资这么感兴趣，那也许应该去金融业去尝试一下，人做自己感兴趣的事情总是对的。读过 MBA 的人都知道，学习知识只是 MBA 教学中很小的一部分。

The U.S. is said to be the land of the free where you can do whatever you desire. Personally, as I felt that I was interested in money and investing, I thought I should give working in the financial industry a go. Pursuing one's passion is always right. Anyone who has studied MBA will know that acquiring knowledge is just a small component of the MBA experience.

更大的一部分是 networking，和各种各样的人打交道，其实就混圈子。我读的商学院是全美排名前 15 名的商学院，大部分同学毕业之后都去了金融领域工作。我也给各个投资银行的工作人员打电话，与他们套近乎，争取寻找工作实习的机会。

A more significant part of the learning experience is building a rapport with people from all walks of life, that is networking. My business school is one of the top 15 business schools in the U.S. Most classmates worked in the financial industry after graduation. I also tried to look for internship opportunities by calling different investment banks and developing a relationship with their staff members.

但是 networking 实在不是我特别擅长做的一件事情。我擅长于思考和观察，不属于能说会道的人。在美国更是这样，作为少数族裔，总有一种你努力挤进别人圈子里的感觉。这也有可能是我过于敏感。有的人和别人共事的时候，很自然就能成为这个团体里的领袖，而我不是，我更喜欢像一个局外人一样静静地观察。既然性格里不是领袖，那就不用勉强自己去做个领袖。

However, I am not adept at networking. My strengths are thinking, analyzing, and observing. I am not a particularly expressive person, especially when I am in the U.S. As an ethnic minority, I always feel that I am trying so hard to squeeze into other people's social circles. Perhaps it is because I am overly sensitive. For some people, they will naturally become a leader in a group setting; but I am not one of them. I prefer to quietly observe other teammates as an outsider. As I do not have a leader's personality, I will not force myself to take on such a role.

我 10 年投资理财计划的成功要点取决于自己现金流的提高。所以我很自然地就会想到去从事金融行业。而当我积极努力地联系各个投行公司，看看能否谋到一份工作的时候，又一个想不到的事情发生了，那就是次贷危机。

The key to the success of my investing and wealth management plan lies in increasing my cash flow, so it was natural for me to try to work in the financial industry. Just when I was diligently contacting different investment banks to find a job, something unexpected happened, which was the sub-prime crisis.

如同 911 灾难发生的时候一样，次贷危机发生那一天的每一幕我也是一样印象深刻。次贷危机当然是有一个渐渐演化的过程。我印象中，从 2007 年一开始便是山雨欲来风满楼。做贷款的公司 Countrywide Financial 要破产的时候，我正在上投资学(Investment)这门课，老师解释了 Countrywide 是如何把房地产债券分成几段，然后合并起来打包出售。课堂上拿出了这个公司的财务报表，让我们看看能否分析出这个公司要破产。

Just like how people can remember with great clarity what they were doing on 911, I can still vividly remember every single detail about the day of the sub-prime crisis. Of course, the sub-prime crisis was not built in one day and unfolded itself in different stages. In my recollection, the turbulent wind preceded the storm: we could see some signs from the beginning of 2007. When Countrywide Financial, a mortgage lender, filed for bankruptcy, I was in the middle of a lecture on Investment. My professor explained how Countrywide repackaged mortgages and resell them to investors. The financial statements of Countrywide Financial were discussed in the lecture. Our task was to analyze whether the company was on the verge of failing.

从财务报表上根本看不出这个公司有任何破产的迹象。不但我们看不出，连专业人士也看不出。因为很快美国银行(Bank of America)就花了几十亿美元买了这个公司。哪里知道其实是买了有毒资产，后来差点把 Bank   of America 拖破产。财务报表只能是后知后觉，很难先知先觉。

From the financial statements, there were no signs that the company was on the brink of bankruptcy. We, MBA students, failed to perceive the real picture, but so did professionals. Soon, the Bank of America was spending more than billions to acquire Countrywide Financial. They had no idea that they were buying toxic assets that almost dragged the Bank of America into bankruptcy too. Financial statements only tell us those red flags in hindsight but not in advance of a catastrophe.

这是我对次贷危机的第一次理性认识。但是整个次贷危机的高潮点是美国政府宣布不救助雷曼兄弟而让其破产的那一天。之前美国联储局救了 Bear Stearns，把该公司用两美元一股的价格转给了 JP Morgan。我当时看到这个消息的时候还想，怎么美国跟中国一样，也搞大国企并购。到了 9 月份，雷曼兄弟不行了。联储局、财务部长和华尔街所有的银行大佬在一起开会，决定救还是不救雷曼兄弟。

This is also the first time I had a rational and scientific understanding of the sub-prime crisis. But the climax of the entire sub-prime crisis was the day when the U.S. government announced that they would not bail out Lehman Brothers, which caused the latter to file for bankruptcy. Earlier the Fed saved Bear Stearns and sold its stake in the company at $2 per share to JP Morgan. When I was reading the news, I was wondering, "Since when did the U.S. join China in acquiring a private company and turning it into a state-owned enterprise?" In September, Lehman Brothers was on the brink of death. The Fed, the Secretary of the Treasury, and all other big bankers on Wall Street were having a meeting to decide whether they should save Lehman Brothers.

那天是 September 13, 2008，如果我没有记错的话是一个周六，我正在上一堂课。当时手机已经普及了，大家一边听着老师讲课，一边都在等着当天下午的新闻。每个美国人都在关心那个会议的结果。

It was September 13, 2008. If I remember it correctly, it was a Saturday. I was sitting in a class. At the time, cell phones were already popular. Everyone was paying attention in class and waiting for the news. Every American was concerned about the outcome of that meeting.

课上到一半的时候，有一个同学举起了手，老师问他有什么事。那个同学对老师说，我只是想跟老师和同学们说一下，联邦政府和华尔街的银行们决定不救助雷曼兄弟。

In the middle of the class, a classmate raised his hand and said, "I just want to share with the class that the federal government and banks on Wall Street decided not to bail Lehman Brothers out."

教室里发出"轰"的一声，大家交头接耳的议论着。以前的各种金融危机，普通老百姓都是吃瓜群众，看热闹不嫌事大。但是那年是我们临近毕业的时候，大家从吃瓜群众变成了群众演员，金融市场的好坏直接关系到我们的工作与就业。

Then the classroom erupted, and everyone was chatting and discussing with one another. In the past, all those financial crises were none of our business because we were just ordinary citizens. However, this time, as MBA graduates, everyone was no longer a spectator but an actor in the scene. The success and failure of the financial market were directly related to our job prospects.

老师在台上让他把新闻头条读一下，然后沉思了一会儿，静静地说，这非常有趣，咱们看看会发生啥"That will be interesting. Let's see what happens."。我能感觉到教室里沉重的气氛，很多人脸色铁青。因为读 MBA 都交付了很高的学费，有些人背负了比较重的贷款，这个时候大家最需要的就是一份高薪的工作。而经济危机的到来，尤其是直接由金融行业爆发的经济危机，让每个人的未来都变得前途暗淡。

The teacher asked that classmate to read the news headlines aloud. The teacher paused for a while and said, "That will be interesting. Let's see what happens." I could also feel the tension in the classroom. Many people had a long face because they paid high tuition for their MBA, and some of them had heavy student loans. At the time, what everyone needed the most was a high-paying job. With the advent of the financial crisis, especially one that was triggered by the financial industry, everyone's future seemed bleak.

这场灾难现在回想起来仍然历历在目，和我回忆 911 那个早晨简直是一模一样。因为美国政府宣布不救助雷曼公司，第二天爆发了总危机。市场上大家谁也不相信谁，因为大家不知道下一个倒闭的公司是谁。很快联储局不得不到国会申请要求 7000 亿美元的救助计划，而且还说即使给了 7000 亿美元，也不清楚能不能救活金融市场。但是如果不救的话，一切都将陷入彻底崩溃。显然当初那个不救雷曼兄弟的决定是错误的，金融市场一切的秘密就是信心，如果大家都没有信心的话，系统就会发生崩塌。

Looking back, I can still recall that disaster with vivid details, just like how I was able to remember with great clarify what I was doing on 911 morning. The big crisis broke out the next day after the U.S. government announced that they would not bail out Lehman Brothers. Market players lost their trust in one another because no one knew which company would fall down next. Soon, the Fed had no other means but to apply for a US$700 billion relief program from the Congress, and made clear that even if the request was granted, they had no idea whether it could revive the financial market. But if the Fed failed, everything would collapse. Obviously, the decision not to save Lehman Brothers was a mistake. The foundation of everything in the financial market is trust. If everyone has lost their trust, the system will collapse.

我就是在这样混乱的背景下，去投行找我的实习机会。

Under such a chaotic backdrop, I began my hunt for internships with investment banks.

05 投资银行

05 Investment Banks

尽管我不是很喜欢 networking，但是我对华尔街和投行到底是怎么工作的却有着很浓厚的兴趣。所以我也加入了 networking 的洪流，不停地和投行校友们打电话，说一些言不由衷的话语，重复聊着一些快能背出来的话题。电话 networking 主要是介绍自己，然后顺便让对方感觉到，我对这个投行的工作付出了极大的热情。这样的招聘方式其实是非常荒唐的，但是不知道为什么这些年来投行一直保持这样的惯例。这也是我开始感觉到金融行业根本不是我原来想象的一样。那段时间可能是我一生中说过言不由衷的话语最多的时候。

Even though I do not particularly enjoy networking, I am earnestly interested in understanding how Wall Street and investment banks operate. Therefore, I also jump on the bandwagon of networking by phoning alumni working at investment banks, saying something that does not come from my heart, and discussing the same topics repeatedly. Phone networking is mostly about introducing myself and making the other person feel that I am highly passionate about working in investment banks. To be honest, such a recruitment process is ridiculous, but I have no idea why this is the norm. This is also the moment when I started to realize that working in the financial industry was different from what I expected. This stage of my life is one in which I did not speak from my heart most of the time.

不过我的运气不错，在市场最糟糕的时候，我居然在世界前十名的投资银行，找到了一个实习机会，让我可以有机会在一线了解金融公司是怎么运作的。投行的收入虽然非常高，但是每天做的工作却不用费什么脑子。根本不需要一个聪明人从事金融行业，每个人就像一个大机器上的螺丝钉，只要把自己的那部分工作做好就可以了。

But I was quite lucky. Amidst the worst market conditions, I was able to secure an internship with a top 10 investment bank in the world. This job opportunity helped me understand how a top-tier financial institution operates. Even though investment bankers earn a high income, their daily tasks are not very intellectually challenging. One does not need a high IQ to be a finance worker. In fact, everyone is like a screw in the machine: working at investment banks is about focusing on one's own duties.

说白了投行就是一个中介业务，和普通的房地产中介没有什么区别，只是投行做的是买卖公司的中介业务而已。比如投行的大部分工作是做上市和并购。整个过程和买卖房屋的中介代理也没有什么区别。主要是和一个快要上市的公司领导套近乎，争取把业务揽到。谈好委托代理协议，然后帮着公司做估值，就像给房子做估值一样，然后再按照流程办理上市手续。

In essence, investment banks are an intermediary, the role of which is similar to that of an average real estate agent, but the former is involved in the selling and buying of a company. For example, most of the projects at investment banks are about IPO and M&A. There is not much difference between the processes at investment banks and the selling and buying of a house by a real estate agent. The main difference is that investment banks work closely with senior decision-makers at listed companies to solicit business from them. After the signing of an agency agreement, the investment bank will evaluate the listed company, just like how a house is evaluated, and then work on the IPO procedures.

这个过程其实很简单，难点就是你是否能做好人际关系，需要的基本技能就是讨人喜欢，做好对人的服务工作。而作为基层的分析员，其实做的工作也没有智商挑战，只是把一些 PPT 和财务表格整理得漂漂亮亮的，不要有错误。

It is a simple process, but the difficulty lies in whether you can manage interpersonal relationships well. Strong interpersonal and communication skills are required. You need to become a people magnet because your job is about working with people. But as an analyst in the bottom of the company's organizational structure, the daily tasks are not particularly challenging. They are about organizing some PowerPoint slides and financial tables and making sure there are no mistakes.

既然是个"拼缝"的买卖，社交就成了最重要的环节。我在那里工作的两个月中去了无数多的派对。即使次贷危机后金融市场已经糟糕到那个样子，大家还是忙于派对。差不多每周都有两个以上的派对。在派对上大家觥筹交错，谈论着各种很大的数字和经济形势，喝得有些上头之后再回到办公室通宵熬夜地赶各种 PPT。

Socializing is of utmost importance in the financial industry because success is determined by whether you can solicit deals from big clients. In the two months I spent with the firm, I attended numerous parties. Even though the financial market was in abysmal conditions after the sub-prime crisis, everyone was busy with partying. There were, on average, two or more parties every week. In these parties, people were toasting each other with wine and discussing all sorts of big numbers and economic trends. After getting a bit drunk, everyone would then head back to their office to burn the midnight oil, making various PowerPoint slides.

社交不是我擅长的，我自己的个性是擅长观察和冷静的思考，最不擅长的就是和人面对面打交道。有些人天生具有亲和感和号召力，我却没有这个天然的能力。我话不多，经常冷场。

Socializing is not my strength, but I am observant and a rational thinker. Actually, socializing with people is my weakness. Some people are born with charisma that attracts other people, but I am not gifted with these traits. I am not a talkative person, and sometimes I run out of topics in my conversations.

我总体的感觉是金融行业的人并没有为这个社会创造出那么多的价值，金融公司和投行获取的高额利润并不因为他们提供多么复杂的服务，而在于他们做的是高额的金融交易。社会出于各种原因，分配了太多的蛋糕给他们。

My overall feeling is that finance workers do not create such an enormous amount of value for society. The reason why financial institutions and investment banks are able to make big profits is not that they provide complicated services but that they handle astronomical financial deals. For all sorts of reasons, our society gives them too big a share of the cake.

我当时做了一个市值大约 10 个亿的上市案子，市盈率大约是 25 倍。我们几个人忙了几个月，拿到的服务费在 2000 万左右。也就是说投行基本上拿走了一个企业半年的纯利润，等同于 2000 个企业员工拼死拼活干了半年。这还是能够上市的公司，几千家公司里面才能出一家上市企业，大部分公司的利润率根本没有这么高。

At the time, I was working on an IPO project that was worth $1 billion with a P/E ratio of about 25. After working on the deal for a few months, our team of fewer than 10 members took home a service fee of around $20 million. In other words, investment banks took away almost half of the company's annual profit. The service fee charged by investment banks is equivalent to the fruits of the labor of 2,000 employees who have worked for 6 months diligently. And I am talking about a company that can be listed in the stock exchange. You can only find such a company in thousands of others. Most businesses do not even have such a high profit.

所以投行的收入高，是因为我们几个月就拿走了几千人半年产生的利润。但是你说投行这些服务有多大的价值，或者难度有多高，却实在看不出来。无非就是整理一下财务报表，规范了一下法律流程。连财务审计和尽职调查（due diligence）这些事也通通是外包的。

The reason why investment bankers have a high income is that a few finance workers can take away the profit made by a few thousand employees in other industries in a 6-month period. But I do not think that the services provided by investment banks have added much value for society or involve particularly difficult tasks. All they do are organizing the financial statements and preparing for the legal procedures. Other tasks, such as financial auditing and due diligence, are outsourced.

分配的不合理，导致很多人对金融行业趋之若鹜。可是金融行业的文化总是和我格格不入。我不知道该用什么词来描述，找不到一个描述这种感觉的词汇，也许就是浮夸和 Snobbish。在金融行业工作的顺利与否很大程度取决于他人对你的信心和信任。所以大家对外仕的东西都非常关心。穿衣服要穿名牌，东西要用最好的，业余生活就是关心哪里去弄一个好的跑车，哪里去住一个豪华的酒店，哪里去弄个飞机。说起话来要口若悬河夸夸其谈。

As a consequence of such an unreasonable allocation, many people think highly of the financial industry. However, I do not fit in with the culture in the financial industry. I cannot find the exact wording to describe the culture, but "boastful" and "snobbish" are pretty close. Whether you are successful in the financial industry depends to a large extent on whether others have faith in and trust you. Therefore, everyone is very concerned about their physical appearance. They wear designer clothes and use the best of everything. In their personal lives, they care about what sports car brand they should buy, which luxury hotels they should visit, and how they can get a private plane. They sound boastful when they talk.

虽然很多人受过良好的教育，都是著名的高校毕业生，可是他们特别看重那些虚无缥缈的东西，搞各种攀比和浮夸的人生观。

Even though many of them have a good education, they attach much emphasis to all these illusory belongings. Many of them are graduates of elite universities, but they are motivated by vanity and busy winning the race of "who drives the most exclusive sports car?" and "whose handbag is more expensive?"

可是另外一方面，因为投行的收入比较高，当然公司也会提高行业准入门槛。门槛之一就是特别长的工作小时。投行的工作小时数经常会超过100小时每周，每个人累得像死狗一样。让人感觉投行里面的人都像是金钱和欲望的奴隶，没有自由。每个人心里算计的都是年终的分红有多少，内心并没有什么快乐。

Meanwhile, because of the attractive remuneration package, investment banks are raising the entry requirements. One of them is long working hours. A typical investment banking associate or analyst can routinely expect to work more than 100 hours per week. Everyone is exhausted. The overall atmosphere at investment banks makes me feel that the people there are deprived of their freedom and enslaved by their desires and money. Though they are calculating how much year-end bonus they will have, they do not feel happy inside.

相比之下，做我理工科的老本行，虽然金钱收入没有那么多，但是我很快乐，而且很自由。我不需要花那么长的时间做一些在我看来特别无趣和假大空的事情。所以我最后选择不去金融行业而是继续做我的老本行。因为我觉得金钱给予人的最大好处是自由，我可不愿意在以后 10 年或者 20 年的时间里，度过那么多通宵达旦加班的生活。

In contrast, even though the income of an engineer is less than that of an investment banker, I will feel happier and have more freedom as an engineer. There is no need for me to spend so much time on something that I deem boring and superficial. Therefore, I chose not to work in the financial industry but go back to my previous occupation as an engineer. Furthermore, I think that the biggest benefit brought by money is freedom. I am not willing to work the investment banking hours for the next 10 or even 20 years of my life.

06 资产分析师
06 Asset Analysts

金融系统里的另外一个高薪的工作就是 Equity analyst。这是一个需要冷静思考的职业。你需要观察一个公司的运转情况，然后估算出它们到底值多少钱，未来是否有增值空间。可是近距离接触后，我发现这些分析师大部分的工作基本上是盲人摸象。他们写出厚厚的分析报告，说得头头是道，可是那些头头是道的预测他们自己都未必相信。

Another high-paying job in the financial ecosystem is equity analyst. This is a position that requires independent and critical thinking. An equity analyst needs to observe the operation of a company and evaluate its fair value and whether there is potential for growth. However, after some first-hand observation and experience, I realized that these analysts are analogous to the blind men and company to the elephant in the parable of the Blind Men and Elephant. Even though these analysts write detailed reports that seem quite plausible, they do not necessarily believe in their own forecast themselves.

我当时要做一个可再生能源公司的并购买卖，所以专门拿了一份花旗银行的分析报告来阅读。这个报告是由当时在这个行业里非常著名的分析师写的。他分析了光伏产业的未来前景，比对了众多公司，最后得出的结论是光伏行业未来几年看好，而且中国无锡尚德将会一枝独秀。

Back then, I was working on an M&A of a renewable energy company, so I read an analysis report on this subject matter by Citibank. That report was written by a famous analyst in the industry. He analyzed the future prospects of the photovoltaic industry and compared a number of companies. In the end, his conclusion was that the photovoltaic industry would boom in the next few years and that Suntech, a Chinese company based in Wuxi, would stand out from the crowd.

我翻看了一下，就知道他其实是在胡说，他对可再生能源不了解，对尚德这个公司也不了解。我之所以敢说这样的话，是因为我的理工科专业领域跟尚德有很大的相关。我的技术背景让我对尚德看得更清楚，我知道尚德太阳能和其他公司无论从技术门槛和管理能力上其实没有什么太大的区别，而且整个行业面临严重的产能过剩。

Even after merely flipping through the report, I could tell that all the analysis was nonsense. He knew nothing about renewable energy or Suntech. I dare make such a bold claim because my expertise in science and engineering is closely related to the industry in which Suntech operates. My skills and background make me see through Suntech. I know that in terms of skills and managerial capabilities, Suntech is no different from all other companies and that the industry is facing excess capacity.

果不其然，过了几年之后尚德破产重组。如果你现在再把这个分析报告拿出来看看，他的预测就如同说梦话一样。我记得那个报告里的财务分析，信誓旦旦地认为尚德太阳能的股票会超过 100 美元一股。

Just as I predicted, Suntech filed for bankruptcy and restructured after a few years. If you take out that analysis report now, you will see that he was daydreaming when making those predictions. I still remember that in the financial analysis part of the report, the analyst asserted that Suntech's stocks would trade at more than US$100 per share.

到底这些资产管理的分析师对于公司有多大的理解，我一直表示怀疑态度。因为有非常多的数据，证明这些分析师给出来的报告并没有很好地指导市场投资到正确的公司上。哪些分析师有名，哪些分析师没有名，往往取决于他在圈子里的资历和人脉混得怎么样。

I have always been skeptical of how well these equity analysts understand those companies. There are plenty of statistics that suggest that these analysis reports have not guided the market to invest in the right companies. The fame of an analyst depends on his or her experience in the financial industry and personal network.

这也是印证了我一再相信的，在对市场未来的判断上，没有人是专家。大到宏观经济未来的判断，小到对一个具体公司的财务判断。我后来自己创业的经历也证明了这一点。作为公司的创始人，在我掌握了全部的财务信息和管理信息的情况下，对于公司的未来我自己都看不清楚，更不要说分析师了。

This is a piece of evidence supporting one of my core beliefs that no one is an expert when it comes to predicting the future, from judgments about the future macroeconomic conditions to judgments about a specific company's financial future. Later, my experience of starting my own business also proves this point. As the founder of my company who has all the financial information and management information available, I still have no clue about the future of my company, let alone analysts.

07 MBA 经历总结

07 A Summary of My MBA Journey

我的 MBA 经历总体是正面的。我最大的损失就是金钱上的损失，我总共付了大约 10 万多美元的学费。但是如果当时没有读 MBA，这 10 万美元会被用来投资房地产。而按照后来局势的演变，我估计损失了 100 万到 200 万美元。

Overall, my MBA experience is a positive one. The biggest loss is monetary. I paid more than US$100,000 for tuition fees. But if I had not studied an MBA, I would have invested all this money in real estate. Based on the market conditions at the time, I estimate that my opportunity cost is US$1-2 million.

MBA 学费虽然是大学学费，但是不能抵扣任何税费。我还是秉承以前的消费理念，学费贷款和其他的信用卡贷款本质上没有什么区别，都属于超前消费。所以 MBA 学费我也是自己老老实实地把它付掉了，没有申请一分钱的学生贷款。这样我在毕业的时候可以有一个比较好的状态，不用因为身上有财务的负担而不得不去选择一些挣快钱的职业。

Even though the tuition fee for my MBA is payable to a tertiary educational institution, it cannot be deducted from any tax payments. According to my spending philosophy, student loan and credit card loan are essentially the same because they both involve spending beyond one's current means. Therefore, I paid all my MBA tuition fees out of my own pocket without applying for any student loans. This gave me more freedom at graduation because I did not have to be forced by any consideration of financial burden into making fast money.

但是我并不后悔这件事情，最主要的是学习到了知识，还有让我更清楚的了解，自己是一个什么样的人，未来应该做什么样的事。

However, I do not regret it because I have acquired much knowledge and had a better understanding of who I am and what I should do in the future.

还有一点，就是在公司上市的过程中，我认识了一些企业家。在和他们的交往过程中，让我对创业有了进一步的了解。在我以前的记忆中创业的人都是一些特别八面玲珑的人，或者有资本渠道的人。后来我发现创业其实需要的是一些意志坚定的人，他们并不需要能说会道，甚至性格偏内向和冷静。

Furthermore, in assisting a company's IPO, I made a connection with some entrepreneurs. During our interaction, I had a more in-depth understanding of entrepreneurship. Prior to this experience, the entrepreneurs that I knew were all very sociable or had access to capital channels. But later, I found out that people who are strong-willed and rational are more prone to success in starting their businesses despite not being very sociable or even introverted.

投行实习快结束的时候。一个资深一点的 MD 约我一起喝咖啡。他知道我有博士学位之后，语重心长地对我说，"你还是去做实体企业更合适。我们这些人没有一个人知道怎么样像垒砖头一样，把一个公司一点一滴地建起来。你和我们不一样，我们这里只有你知道。"

Toward the end of my internship, a more senior MD and I had a coffee chat. Knowing that I had a Ph.D., he told me sincerely, "You are more suited to working with a real business entity. None of us here knew how to build a company from ground zero. You are different. You are the only person among us who knows how to achieve this."

也许是被他的真诚感染，也许是被他忽悠得我自我感觉良好。之后，我决定先尝试一段创业的生活。我的创业故事可以另外写一本厚厚的书。限于篇幅，我这里不说那里面的甜酸苦辣了。创业鲜有一帆风顺的，大部分创业公司三年就倒闭了，其余的 90% 都变成了鸡肋。我的运气就是鸡肋的那一部分。创业导致我长年低收入，远低于我找个大公司混日子的收入。现在想想要是当年不创业，我的投资理财之路，十年一千万的目标会实现得更快更加顺利一些。

Perhaps I was influenced by his genuineness or flattered by his comments. Afterward, I decided to give founding my own business a go. Stories of how I started my business can fill another book. Because of space constraints, I will not go into detail the ups and downs in the journey. Starting a business is bound to be a jumpy ride. Most startups fail within the first three years, and 90% of the survivors become mediocre. As a consequence of my decision to start a business, I had low income in the following years, much lower than my days at big corporations. In retrospect, if I had not started that business, my investing and wealth management journey toward the goal of $10 million would have been much smoother and I would have reached my goal much earlier.

1,000,000 到 10,000,000 美元
From US$1,000,000 to US$10,000,000

你的存款只是允许你上车玩游戏的门票。游戏的胜负不取决于资本的多少，而是上车和下车的时机。你能住什么样的房子，基本上也取决于你游戏玩的好坏，或者你是否参与到这个游戏当中。

Your savings only allow you to buy the entry ticket so that you can get on the car and play the game. Who will be the winners in this game is not determined by who has the most capital but the timing of entering and exiting the market. Your living conditions are determined by how good you are at playing this game, or whether you can participate in this game.

第十三章 从 100 到 1000 万（一）抢房

Chapter 13: From $100 million to $1000 million (1) Competing for Houses

01 上海购买第二套住房

01 Buying a Second Residential Property in Shanghai

当目标确定，理想定好，知识储备完毕，一切理论问题都想清楚了之后，就是开始埋头苦干奔向 1000 万的目标了。不付诸实践的，再好的道理都是空话。我在投行工作的时候，一个同行对那些媒体上经济评论人非常不屑地说："你别看他们夸夸其谈，口若悬河。明天真的给他们一百万美元让他们对赌试试做到 15% 的年收益，恐怕他们会吓得屁滚尿流，落荒而逃。"

When you have a clear goal, set your ambitions, built your knowledge reserve, and sorted out all theoretical questions, it is time for you to start working hard toward your goal of $1000 million. Even the best theories are empty words if they are not being put into practice. When I was working at an investment bank, a colleague despised those economic commentators in mainstream media and said, "These people seemed eloquent with their boastful remarks. But if you really give them $1 million as a bet on whether they can achieve an annual return of 15%, this will probably scare the pants off them. They will all be defeated and flee."

光耍嘴皮子是没有意义的。实践才是检验理论的唯一标准。这点上我一向欣赏王阳明先生。所以在后面几章里，我会尽可能的把自己制定投资目标后的十年投资历程，以实录的方式呈现出来。无论你同意还是不同意我的观点，这是我们这个时代，我们这代华人，实打实的历史纪录。

Empty talk, however eloquent and seemingly promising, is meaningless. The application of theories is the only way to test their efficacy and effectiveness. On this point, I have always admired the great Chinese philosopher, Wang Yangming. Therefore, in the following chapters, I will make my best effort to show you my 10-year investment journey after I set my investment goal in a documentary style. Whether you agree or disagree with my points of view, this is a true historical record of how our generation of Chinese made our way in the investment battlefield in this era.

现在回想起来可以把"普通人家十年一千万理财计划"的投资经历分为三个阶段。每个阶段都完成了一个重要的投资工作。当然这个划分并不是绝对的。因为很多投资都是连续的，这样划分只是让读者便于理解。

In retrospect, my investment experience of "an average income family's $10-million-in-ten-year wealth creation and accumulation plans" can be divided into three stages. At each stage, I have accomplished an important investment task. Of course, this categorization is not set in stone because many of my investments are continuous. This categorization is only to facilitate the understanding of readers.

我做了三件比较大的事情，分别是：投资中国的房地产、抄底次贷危机后的美国湾区房地产、投资比特币。这三件事情大体有一定的阶段性。就是2007-2010、2010-2016、2016-2018。

I have three main achievements, namely, investing in Chinese real estate, buying the dip in the U.S. Bay Area real estate market after the sub-prime crisis, and investing in Bitcoins. Generally speaking, these three incidents can be treated as three stages in the timeline, which are 2007-2010, 2010-2016, and 2016-2018.

当然很多投资都是连续的，我在做一个投资的同时，另外在关注着其他的市场。我这里基本上是按照具体落实的行动而划分阶段的，并不只是自己关注的对象。一个好的投资者其实是在不断地关注着周围有可能出现的投资机会的。

Of course, many of my investments are continuous. When I am making one investment, I am also keeping an eye on other markets at the same time. The categorization of stages I have listed here is according to the general timing when I executed my investment ideas and not by my areas of focus. In fact, a good investor is constantly looking for potential investment opportunities around him or her.

2007 年的时候，根据我对加州房地产形势的判断，在我制定的十年投资理财计划里，决定先不再买房，而是等一阵子再说。加州的房地产投资规律性很强，过去三十年里经历了四次涨跌起落。为了更好地执行制定的计划，我当时在投资理财的论坛上，提出的口号是"三年不买房"。并把这一个策略在网络上用博客公布出去。

In 2007, I was trying to formulate my 10-year investment and wealth management plan. At that time, based on my understanding of and judgment about the trends in the California real estate market, I decided not to purchase any real properties and chose to wait patiently. The California real estate market has a strong "investment pattern" by which I meant that in the past 30 years it underwent four cycles of ups and downs. In order to better execute my plans, I advocated a slogan of "not buying a house in three years" on the investment and wealth management forum at that time. I also disseminated this idea on my blog.

2007 年，我的十年计划的头一年里，我最关注还是在中国的房地产。由于在北京的买房计划迟迟无法落实，我把手上几乎所有的存款，在上海买入了第二个房子。

In 2007 which was the first year in my 10-year investment plan, my primary area of focus was the Chinese real estate market. Since I had been experiencing difficulties in executing my plan to purchase a property in Beijing, I used all of my savings and bought a second property in Shanghai.

当时大部分回中国大陆的购房者，只是为了满足他们老了退休的打算，或者给家人改善生活的愿望。很多人说在中国买一个房子，现在给自己的亲戚住，老了之后他们可以回国有地方住。这些打算背后的逻辑是中国比美国的物价便宜，有更多的亲情，适合养老。

At that time, a majority of those investors who went back to China to buy a house were doing so for their retirement planning or to improve the quality of life of their family members who were still in China. Many of these investors said that they bought a house in China so that their relatives could live in it now and they would also have a place to live in after they retired and returned to China. The underlying logic of these arrangements was that the cost of living in China was cheaper than that in the U.S. Furthermore, with the company of and love and care from their relatives, China is a better place for life after retirement.

换一句话就是，美国的钱好挣，中国的钱好花。所以在美国挣美元以后，按照 1：8 的汇率汇到中国花人民币。

To put it simply, it is best to earn U.S. dollars and spend your money in Chinese Yuan. Therefore, after one earns his or her living in the U.S. in dollars, he or she should wire the money back to China under an exchange rate of 1:8 and spend it in Renminbi in China.

我可不这样想。如果你看日本、香港、台湾这些亚洲四小龙的历史，你就会大体预测到再过几十年，等我们老了的时候，中国会变得异常的昂贵。中国的核心城市，根本不是普通退休美国老人可以住得起的地方。老了退休应该在美国住才对。而中国是在快速发展的阶段，所以应该现在赶紧在中国挣钱才是重要的。更为现实的模式应该是倒过来，在中国来挣钱，回美国来养老。

I was thinking otherwise. If you take a look at the history of Japan, Hong Kong and Taiwan, members of the Four Asian Tigers, you will be able to have a broad estimate that several decades from now, when we grow old, China will become an abnormally expensive place to live in. The core cities in China are not where the ordinary American retirees can afford to live in. Therefore, when we grow old and retire, we should live in the U.S. When China is in a stage of rapid economic growth, what is of paramount importance is that we should hurry and make our fortune in China. A more practicable approach should be the opposite of that advocated by some people, that is, to earn money in China and live in the U.S. after retirement.

2006 年夏天，虽然房价比起几年前已经涨了一倍多，但上海的房地产依然非常抢手。于是我利用回国探亲的机会，去落实购买第二套住房的计划。按照我自己原先想好的投资理念，打算投资上海的 2 号地铁沿线住房。2006 年夏天上海的房价已经今非昔比。2001 年的时候，我们在美国工作的白领双职工可以在上海的几乎任何地方买得起房子。2006 年只能选择内环线以外的房子了。我当时看中一个在长宁区天山路的楼盘，专门委托了一个在房地产公司工作的亲戚，让他帮忙找开发商打一下招呼。

In the summer of 2006, even though the property prices had doubled in just a few years, real properties in Shanghai were still highly sought after. In light of this, I decided to fully utilize my decision to go back to China and visit my relatives by executing my plan to purchase my second property during the stay. According to my premeditated investment principles, I intended to invest in residential properties which were located along Shanghai Metro Line 2. The property prices in the summer of 2006 were unprecedented. In 2001, those U.S. white-collar families with double income could buy a real property in almost any location in Shanghai. In 2006, these families could only choose real properties situated outside the Inner Circle Area. At that time, I had my eye on a real estate project on Tinshan Road in Changning District so I specifically asked a relative of mine who worked in a real estate company to help me contact the property developer.

那天是早上 9:00 开盘，我因为要陪母亲一起吃早饭，所以 11 点才赶到现场。我去的时候，售楼处说房子一套都没有了。真的就是这样，整个楼盘开出来，一个小时就全部卖完了。很多人拥挤到售楼处，销售对所有人都是摊着手，用扩音器喊，"楼盘已经全部销售完毕，请大家不要滞留"。 房子没有了，即使我们打了招呼，找了关系也没有用，因为全都卖完了。

The homes were available for sale at 9 am on that day. Since I needed to have breakfast with my mother, I arrived at the sales center at 11 am. Upon my arrival, the sales office told me that all the units were sold out. If this was the case, this meant that the whole project was sold out within an hour. Many people gathered at the sales office. But the sales representative told everyone with a loudspeaker that "All units are sold out. Please do not gather and stay here." There was no unit left. Even though we had previously contacted the developer and resorted to *guanxi*, our attempts were in vain because all units were sold out.

亲戚埋怨说："你为什么这么晚才到？"我哑口无言。其实现在想一想真的是怪自己，没有把买房子做为最高的优先。因为买房子毕竟是买东西，买东西的时候人总觉得自己花钱，应该被当作上帝一样服务才对。

My relative complained to me, "What took you so long? Why did you arrive so late?" and I was speechless. In retrospect, I have only myself to blame because I did not put buying a property as my top priority. At that time, my thinking was that buying a property still meant that I was a customer who should be treated as god because I was paying money.

我和很多人一样低估了中国一线城市的购买力。1990 年的时候，中国每年的建成面积是 1000 万平米。2000 年的时候，中国每年的建成面积是一亿平米，整整涨了十倍。2010 年的时候，中国每年的建成面积是 10 亿平米，又涨了十倍。即使这样也挡不住汹涌澎湃的购买力。涨了 100 倍的产能在任何一个国家早已过剩了。但是中国人口城市化汹涌澎湃，一线城市的住房永远盖不完，永远都不够。

Many people, myself included, have underestimated the purchasing power of China's tier-one cities. In the 1990s, the total construction floor area in China per year was 10 million square meters. In 2000, the total construction floor area was 100 million square meters, a tenfold increase. In 2010, that number was 1 billion square meters, another tenfold increase. The drastic increase in supply still could not balance the surging purchasing power. A 100-fold increase in any country would have resulted in an excess. However, given China's rapid urbanization and surging urban population, there is no end to the construction of residential properties in tier-one cities. There will always be a shortage of residential properties.

等人群渐渐散去了，我找到公司里的熟人询问情况。那人客客气气地说他也没办法，都是定金塞过来买房的。也许等几天会有人退出来再给你们消息。我觉得他是友好地宽慰我们。抢到篮子里的都是菜，这个楼盘是不会有人退出来的。

When the crowds dispersed and left the sales center, I managed to talk to someone who was familiar with the operation of the company. That person politely told me that there was nothing he could do for me because every potential purchaser had their deposit ready with them. He comforted me that they would contact me if, after a couple of days, someone withdrew their offer and forwent their deposit, which was not unlikely. I knew that he was just being nice because those who managed to get a unit had competed for it and no one would be willing to quit the game.

亲戚宽慰我说这个楼盘其实也有很多问题，不买也罢。首先离一个废水处理厂比较近，偶尔能闻到一些臭味，另外此地和中环高架路也比较近，比较吵。其实买房子哪里有十全十美的，十全十美的房子哪里又轮得到你。

My relative comforted me that there were many problems with that real estate project. It was not a big deal that I could not get a unit. The first problem was that it was near a wastewater treatment plant and residents would smell the revolting odor sometimes. Furthermore, its proximity to Central Ring Road meant that road noise would be an issue.

我的态度还是很坚定，我说这次回来一定要买一个房子。因为我知道这样的机会失去之后，恐怕未来几年就再也没有了。他后来想了想和我说，也许我们可以去浦东看一看。 他的另外一个朋友，在那里开发一个新的楼盘。但是那里既没有地铁也不是很繁华，而且不是 2 号线沿线，恐怕买了会出租不出去。因为那个时候，很多人担心上海的房价已经涨得太高了。报纸上到处都是类比日本当年的房地产泡沫的文章。我的这个亲戚也是有过很多年投资经验的人。他建议我不要去买太偏僻的房子，核心区的房子可能更加保值一些。

My attitude was still adamant. I told my relative that I had to buy a real property this time because I knew that once I missed this opportunity, I would not be able to find another in several years. After some thought, my relative told me that maybe we could go to Pudong and take a look. A friend of his was developing a real estate project there. However, because of the absence of a metro network in Pudong, it was not a prosperous area, let alone my criterion of situating along Metro Line 2. He was afraid that I would have difficulty renting the property out. At that time, many people were concerned that the property prices in Shanghai were too high. Newspaper articles that compared the situation to the real estate bubble in Japan were everywhere. My relative also had years of investment experience. His advice was that I should not buy a property that was in a remote area and that properties in the central area would hold their value better.

我说没有问题，因为我在美国的经验告诉我，房价涨起来的时候，是边缘地带的涨幅更加可观一些，因为世上总是穷人多。

I replied that that would not be a problem. My experience of investing in the U.S. had taught me that when property prices increased, the outskirt areas would witness an even more significant increase as poor people were the majority in this world.

就在我要离开上海的最后一天，亲戚帮我联系好了。我到那个楼盘去，我记得那天下着小雨。浦东那片地方因为有很多建设工地在建，所以一路泥泞不堪。目力所望的地方全部都是脚手架和工地，一眼望不到头的在建项目。

On the last day before I left Shanghai, my relative had helped me contact his friend. I went to that real estate project. I could still remember that it was raining on that day. There were many sites under construction in Pudong so the roads were muddy. Anywhere my sight reached was full of scaffolds and construction sites and there were endless projects under construction.

那个楼盘不是很抢手，虽然规划了两条地铁线在楼盘附近，可是规划毕竟只是规划，还没有建成。周围基本上也没有什么服务设施，到哪里都不方便。

That real estate project was not a popular one even though two metro lines close to the neighborhood were planned. After all, planning was merely planning and the metro lines had not been constructed yet. There were no amenities around the housing estate and it was not convenient to go anywhere from that estate.

尤其有些让人不安的是周围大量的在建楼盘，附近也没有什么像样的产业。当时浦东的产业都集中在张江和金桥，陆家嘴也集中了很多金融公司。我看的楼盘在联洋附近，虽然也在内环线里头，但离小陆家嘴还有一定的距离。这次我的运气很好，经理热情而且客气。因为还没有正式开盘，所以整个项目的楼盘都摆在那儿让我随意挑。

What was particularly worrying was the numerous real estate projects under construction. There was no decent industry in that area. At that time, Pudong's industry was concentrated in Zhangjiang and Jinqiao. There were a number of financial services companies concentrated in Lujiazui. The real estate project I was visiting was near Lianyang. Even though Lianyang was in the Inner Ring Area, it was quite distant from the Central Lujiazui area. But I was lucky this time. The sales manager was enthusiastic and polite. As the project was not officially for sale yet, I could choose from all of the units in the project.

这几乎也是我这辈子从未有过的经历，整个楼盘十几栋楼、几百个单元任我挑选。经理对我说"你要买哪个，你挑吧"。

This was probably an experience that I had never had in my life. The project consisted of more than 10 buildings which had several hundreds units in total from which I could choose freely. The manager told me that I could choose whatever unit I liked.

我当时被一个现在看来可能是错误的观点所引导，就是只想着 IRR 而忽视了 NPV。IRR 和 NPV 是两个投资领域经常用来评价项目好坏的指标。IRR 就是 internal rate of return,说白了就是回报率。NPV 是 net present value，大白话的说法就是赚了多少钱。

At that time, I was guided by a principle which now looking back is probably a wrong one. I was only focusing on IRR and neglected NPV. IRR and NPV are two commonly used indicators to evaluate an investment project in the investment world. IRR stands for internal rate of return or, to put it simply, the rate of return on investment. NPV represents the net present value or, in laymen's terms, how much money the investor has earned.

按照 IRR 来选择的话，要买小房子，特别要买犄角旮旯的楼层，比较差的便宜房子。这些房子的成本低，而升值的比例却要比那些大房子好楼层的房子要高一些。所以宁可买两套小房子，也不要买一套大房子。因为两套小房子的回报率要高一些。在美国也有类似的说法，就是要买同一个社区里最小的房子。大房子的价格会被小房子的价格往下拉一些，而小房子的价格会被大房子往上拉一些。而且越小的房子，越便宜的房子，越容易出售和出租，流动性也会更强一些。

If one makes his or her investment decision based on IRR, he or she should choose to buy a small real property, especially those in a remote area, or in other words, lower quality but cheap units. The cost of these houses is low but the ratio of appreciation is higher than those spacious units on the top floors. Therefore, one should buy two smaller units rather than a big unit because the return rate of the former approach is higher. There is a similar theory in the U.S. which is that when you buy the smallest house in a neighborhood, the price of the biggest house will be pulled down by the small house. Vice versa, the price of the small house will be pulled up by the big house. The smaller the house and the cheaper, the easier it is to rent it out and sell, entailing higher mobility.

但是我忘了一点，就是买房子本身是要有时间成本的，购房也是有机会成本的。同样花了一个月的时间，项目 A 的 IRR 是 20%，投资是 100 元。项目 B 的 IRR 是 10%，投资额是 1000 元。项目 B 的 IRR 比项目 A 要低，但是显然是更好的选择，因为项目 B 的 NPV 更大，挣到的钱更多。此外投资机会也是稍纵即逝的。如果机会只有一次，你应该尽可能地买最大的那个房子。

However, I had forgotten about the time cost involved in buying a real property. Purchasing a house has its own opportunity cost. Assuming that an investor uses 1 month to purchase Project A which has an IRR of 20% and an initial investment of \$100. Alternatively, the investor can also use one month to invest in Project B which has an IRR of 10% and an initial investment input of \$1000. Even though Project B has a lower IRR than Project A, it is a better choice. This is because Project B has a high NPV which means the return will be more. Besides, investment opportunities come and go in a flash. If there is only one chance, you should try your best to buy the bigger house.

这是我后来越来越少用 Excel 表计算来决定投资的一个原因。很多投资因素是在 Excel 表上没有办法体现出来的。Excel 表可以算出你的投入和产出、你的回报率以及各种情景。但是事后往往完全不是那么回事，因为有太多不确定因素，人的因素也没有办法被考虑计算。这里的一个例子就是你的时间成本和机会成本，后面我还会讲其他的例子。

This is why I gradually relied less and less on Excel spreadsheets in analyzing my investment options and making my decisions. Many investment factors cannot be shown in an Excel spreadsheet. Excel spreadsheets can calculate your input and output, your return rate and other scenarios. But what happens in reality is often not the situation portrayed in Excel because there are so many uncertainties. Human factors cannot be considered and calculated in Excel. Examples include your time cost and opportunity cost. I will talk about other examples below.

我当时选了一个 2 室 1 厅的公寓，面积 100 平米。虽然当时有房型更好的楼层，3 室 1 厅，150 平米的。

At that time, I had my eye on a 2-bedroom apartment with a floor area of 100 square meters even though there were units on other floors with a better layout of 3-bedroom and a floor area of 150 square meters.

经理对我的选择表示惊讶。因为我选的是一个两面全黑，夹在中间的一个房子。我也没有选择接近顶部尽可能高的楼层，而是选择了一个在五层楼的单元。他跟我说了这个房型的弊端，并且建议我选择建筑两端的，更大面积一点的房型。

The manager was surprised by my choice because I chose an apartment that was squeezed by two other units. I did not choose a unit on the top floor either and chose a unit on the 5th floor instead. He told me about the shortcomings of that unit and recommended I chose corner units with a bigger floor area.

我没好意思跟他解释我的"投资理念"。那些今天看来幼稚可笑的理念。只是说："两室够用了。"

I did not dare explain my "investment strategies" with him which look naïve and laughable today and I just told him that "two rooms would be enough."

他也就没有多劝我。只是说，"你看中了就好，我帮你记下来，你回去吧，等开盘的时候我告诉你，你来办手续。"

He did not try to persuade me further and merely said, "What matters most is that you like the unit. I will help you mark it down and you may leave now. I will notify you when the project is officially open for sale and then you can proceed with the administrative procedures."

我和他说我人在美国，开盘的时候可能没有办法来办手续，能否委托他帮我把手续都办了，他说没有问题。因为他自己就是开发商，负责整个项目的总经理。

I told him that I lived in the U.S. so I might not be able to handle the procedures. I asked him if I could authorize him to help me handle them. He said no problem because he himself was the developer who was responsible for the whole project as a general manager.

不过我还是吸取之前的教训，把定金付给了他一些。他说你不要给我钱，还没有正式开盘。我却无论如何让他把钱收下，连个收条我都没有要。这个房子总算买了下来，虽然不是最好的选择，我应该买最大最贵的那套房子。不过，买到总比空手要好，人生哪能十全十美。这个投资能够跑中国一次就搞定，现在看来，最主要的原因还是清晰的决心和周围人的帮助导致的。

However, I had learned my lesson from my previous experience and I paid him some deposit. He told me not to give him any money because the project was not officially for sale. I insisted that he took the money and I did not even ask for a receipt. Anyways, I had finally purchased the real property even though it was not the best choice because I should have bought the biggest and most expensive unit. But, it was still better than not being able to buy one. Life is not perfect. I was able to close that deal in one single trip to China. Looking back, I attributed my success to a clear determination and the kind assistance of those around me.

02 中国房市判断

02 Judgments About the Chinese Real Estate Market

我能这么坚定决心地继续购房，一方面是因为自己仔细研究过日本、韩国、台湾、香港在经济腾飞的时候房地产的一些变化过程，另外一方面应该感谢微观经济学的一些基本知识，这些知识让我能够自己对一些简单的经济现象做出正确的思考。

There are two reasons I was so steadfast in continuing to purchase real properties. On one hand, I have studied closely the changes in the real estate market in Japan, Korea, Taiwan, and Hong Kong during their rapid economic growth. On the other hand, I am grateful for the basic concepts in microeconomics. All this knowledge allows me to engage in a correct thinking process on some simple economic phenomenons.

当上海出现第一轮房价暴涨的时候，国家紧跟着出台了一系列的房价调控政策。当时还是温家宝在做总理的时候。这个政策开启了后面漫长的十几年房地产调控政策。几乎每次房地产价格出现暴涨，都会随之而来一些新政策出台。朝令夕改，让市场出现极度的混乱。开发商忽视工程质量，天天赶进度。

When Shanghai witnessed its first round of skyrocketing property prices, the Chinese government formulated and implemented a series of regulation policies to curb the soaring. Wen Jiabao was then the Premier. These policies marked the beginning of housing prices regulation policies that lasted for more than a decade. Every time when property prices soared, this was followed by the implementation of new policies. The government was frequently moving the goalposts which caused extreme chaos in the market. Property developers sacrificed the quality of the construction to catch up with the progress because they were trying to complete the project as soon as possible.

每一次房地产新政的出台都叫新政。后面因为不断地加新政，媒体为了区分，干脆起名"新新政"，"最新政"。可是每一次这些政策的出台，稍微有些经济学常识的人都不难看出，政策的目的并不是降低房价的，而是为了防范宏观经济的风险和产业的过度扩张。

Every time when a new real estate policy was introduced, it was referred to as a "new policy." In a later stage, the government was constantly adding new policies. In order to distinguish between them, the media titled these policies as "new new policy" or "the latest policy." However, every time when the policies were launched, it was not difficult for those with some basic knowledge of economics to see that the ultimate purpose of these policies was not to lower property prices but to prevent macroeconomic risks and the over-expansion of industries.

读者感兴趣可以自己去网上搜查一些 2003 年到 2013 年一系列的房地产调控的历史。从国八条、国五条、新国八条。政策密集到几乎每隔半年就出台一个新政。不过现在时过境迁，人们可以用冷静的头脑分析一下，看一看这些政策有可能把房价降下来吗？

For those readers who are interested, feel free to google the history of a series of measures on curbing property prices, for example, "National 8," "National 5," and "New National 8." The issuance of rules and regulations was so frequent that the Chinese government launched a new policy almost every six months. Now that the time has changed, we can analyze the situation with rationality and objectivity to see whether it was possible that these policies could lower the property prices.

经济学常识告诉我们，一个商品价格上涨是因为供需不平衡造成的。所以抑制房价的最好办法是加大供应。如果想改变人们对未来的预期的话，最好的办法就是改变人们对未来供应的预期。

Basic economics told us that the increase in price of a certain product is because of an imbalance in demand and supply. Therefore, the best way to curb the soaring of property prices is to increase the supply. If we want to change people's expectations of the future, the best way is to change people's expectations of future supply.

然而国家并没有这么做，他们出台的房地产政策全部都是打压开发商、控制土地、控制房型、减少商品房的供应、增加交易环节税费、抑制需求。所以这样的文件标题是写着控制房地产价格，也许初衷也是为了控制房价，但实施的结果只会是火上浇油，让老百姓涨价预期更加强烈，让房价像脱缰野马一样向上涨。

Yet, the government had not done so. The real estate policies they launched were all targeted at suppressing land developers, controlling land and house layouts, reducing the supply of commercial houses, increasing transaction tax, and curbing demand. The heading of these documents was that the rules were for "controlling property prices." Even though the original intention of these rules was to control property prices, the outcome was that they only worsened the problem because the general public had even higher expectations of an increase in future prices, resulting in skyrocketing property prices.

其实你有足够多的人生经历，你就会知道。这样的事情在美国的政治经济里也经常发生。任何一条法规或政策的标题，永远是符合人心、符合大众意愿的，任何政客和领袖不可能与大众的意愿为敌。

If you have sufficient life experiences, you will realize that the same phenomenon also happens frequently in U.S. politics and economics. The heading of any regulations, rules, or policies, is always in line with the public wishes and the popular consensus. It is impossible for any politicians or leaders to hold themselves out as an enemy to the public consensus.

但是魔鬼在细节里。细节里有两部分，一部分是无法落实的事情，一部分是可以落实的部分。真正可以落地的内容往往是政策制定者最真实的意愿。至少能反应政策的执行者的意愿。而那些无法落实的细节只是为了说辞。

However, the devil is in the details. There are two aspects of details, namely those policies which cannot be implemented in reality and those which can be implemented. The content of the latter represents the true intentions of the policymakers, or at least reflects the intentions of those who execute these policies. Those details which cannot be implemented are just for rhetoric purposes.

比如为了反对恐怖分子在美国搞破坏，防止911这样的事情再发生，美国政府需要在全国各地加强情报收集工作和在海外搞监听。可是民众往往对政府入侵自由和民众隐私表示警惕。所以这个法案出台的时候就不能叫作"监听法案"。如果叫"监听法案"十有八九老百姓就不乐意了。布什总统管这个法案叫作《爱国者法案》。谁能不爱国呢？特别是911之后，美国人的爱国情绪到达了顶点。所以这样的方案就很容易通过并获得老百姓广泛的支持。

Take the U.S. anti-terrorists measures as an example. In order to prevent incidents like 911 from happening, the U.S. government needs to strengthen intelligence and surveillance in local land and also overseas. However, the general public is always cautious about the government's intrusion of their freedom and privacy. Therefore, the relevant law cannot be titled "Surveillance Act." If this is the case, most citizens will not be happy about it. President Bush named it the "Patriot Act." Who is not patriotic? This is especially so after 911 when the patriotism of Americans reached a peak. Therefore, such an act could easily win the widespread support of Americans.

在 2003 年到现在的十几年里，所有的房地产调控都是中央政府在唱高调，树立爱民形象，地方政府忙着捞钱，趁机加税和推高土地价格。总体而言，政府是没有任何意愿控制房价的快速上涨的。因为控制房价对于地方政府简直就是与虎谋皮的行为。

In the period between 2003 and the present time, all real estate curbing measures are simply what the central government uses as propaganda to establish an image that they care deeply about the people. In fact, local governments are busy making money by increasing taxes and pushing up land prices. Overall, the government does not have any intentions to control the soaring of property prices. This is because the government's controlling property prices is essentially a hunter asking a tiger for its skin.

如果一个人打算找一只活蹦乱跳的老虎，商量能否借其皮一用，大部分人会觉得他是疯子。可是真的有民众相信政府会主动地降低房价？殊不知，高房价对于地方政府和老虎皮对老虎一样重要。

If a hunter is asking a healthy tiger to give up its life so that he can borrow its skin, people will think he has lost his mind. This is the story behind a Chinese idiom whose literal translation is "asking the tiger for its skin" which means it is impossible to ask someone to give up his or her own interests. Similarly, will anyone genuinely believe that the government will voluntarily lower property prices? What people do not know is that high property prices are as important to local governments as a tiger's skin to a tiger.

因为政府需要卖土地，才能获得大量的收入。所以房价越高，土地价格才能卖得越高，政府才能有更高的收入。哪个机关或者是单位会嫌自己收入多呢？特别是中国很多城市的财政收入将近40%要靠卖地挣钱。没有这些收入，政府如何给公务员发工资奖金，如何有钱搞基础设施建设和谋求产业的发展？

This is because the government needs to sell land to generate significant revenues. Therefore, the higher the property prices, the more expensive they can sell their land and the higher the government revenues. What government institution or unit will think that they have too many revenues? This is especially true when many Chinese cities have 40% of their total revenues coming from selling land. Without these revenues, how can the government pay the public servants salaries and bonuses and how will they have the money to build infrastructures and develop different industries?

治大国如烹小鲜，政府和老百姓过日子本质没有多少区别。政府要花钱的事情太多了，要扶贫、要搞人才引进、要置办医院学校养老院。哪个地方不需要钱？事实上政府缺钱的程度比我们普通老百姓还要严重。

Governing a large country is like cooking a small fish. This is a classic quote from Lao Tzu's philosophical classic "Tao Te Ching." The way a government operates is essentially the same as how the general public manages their daily lives. The government has a lot of spending. It needs to eradicate poverty, attract talents, and build hospitals and nursing homes for the elderly. All these projects need funding. In fact, the government may be in more desperate need of money than ordinary citizens.

我们老百姓一般手上有一块钱，就当一块钱花。个别如我这样省钱节俭的主，有一块钱还恨不得只花五毛存五毛。

For us, the ordinary citizens, we wish that we could spend 50 cents as one dollar. For those who are frugal like me, if I had one dollar, I wish I could spend 50 cents and save 50 cents.

174

政府则不一样。无论中国还是美国，我从来没有见过哪个政府会省钱下来给下一任政府用的。政府一般都是超前消费。因为下一任的政绩属于下一任的，我在任的政绩才属于我。为了政绩，政府往往喜欢用信贷的方式超前消费。2000 年以后很多地方政府基本上都是手上有一亿的时候，敢搞十亿的建设。

However, the way the government manages its budget is different. Whether it is the Chinese government or the U.S. government, I have never observed that a tenure will save money for the next tenure. Governments usually spend more than they can earn. This is because the political achievements of the next tenure are not the concern of those currently in position. The current officials only care about their own achievements. In order to boost their political performance, government officials spend more than the government revenues by way of credit. Starting from 2000, many local governments who only had CN¥100 million at hand dared start a CN¥1 billion infrastructure project.

大部分情况下，政府特别是地方政府对钱的渴望，就像是太平洋上海难的人对淡水的渴望一样。只要看见水就会慌不择路地赶紧往喉咙里灌。真的渴极了哪怕海水都敢喝。这个时候你要跟地方政府说，希望你们能够平抑房价，多供应土地，这样我就可以买得起房子。其实和与虎谋皮有什么区别？

Under most circumstances, the government's desire for money, especially that of local governments, is like how survivors of shipwrecks in the Pacific Ocean long for drinking water. As long as they can see water, they will immediately gulp it down their throat. They may be so thirsty to a point that they will even drink seawater. At this moment, if you ask the local government to curb the soaring of property prices and supply more land so that you can buy a house, will this be any different from asking a tiger to give up its skin?

地方政府总体上来说是把城市当作公司一样来经营。政府都希望城市做到产业兴旺，这样有税收。所以政府往往对引进和发展产业都是不遗余力的，无论这个产业是制造业工业、高科技产业还是商业。因为有产业就有税收，有税收就有钱，有钱就能摆平很多事，能摆平很多事才能有政绩。

Generally speaking, local governments regard governing a city as managing a company. Governments all hope that the city can have thriving industries so they can have tax revenues. This explains why the government leaves no stone unturned in introducing and developing industry, be it the manufacturing industry, high-tech industry or commercial industry. This is because only with a thriving industry can a local government tax revenues which means money and money can help them solve many problems. Solving these problems means that they have political achievements.

另外一方面每个城市的管理者天然地会把人都看作是负担。没有哪个城市希望这里来更多的人，因为每个人对于城市的管理者都是负担。政府需要管好他们的吃、喝、拉、撒、衣、食、住、行。来的人孩子要上中学小学，所以需要花钱去建中学小学。来的人会生病，所以需要去建设医院。好人来了，坏人也会跟着一起来，所以就要有更多的警察和建设更多的监狱。每多一个人，城市服务设施统统要跟上。而这些都是需要政府花钱的。

On the other hand, the administrators of every city will have a natural tendency to view people as burdens. This is because every city dweller is a burden to the city administrators. The government needs to take care of their daily needs, from eating to defecating, from drinking to urinating, from clothing to living, and from transportation to food. The children of the newcomers to the city need to attend primary schools and secondary schools so the government needs money to build these educational institutions. The residents may get sick so the government needs to build hospitals. The newcomers may be good citizens but bad people will come to the city too so the government needs to hire more law enforcement officers and build more detention facilities. When the population of the city increases, the services and facilities of the city need to catch up with the population growth. All this requires the government to spend money.

所以作为城市的管理者，他们永远希望的是，最好有不生病不生孩子不会老的年轻人来到这里把产业建起来。所以你可以看到一个怪现象，大部分城市都把土地优先留给产业。他们喜欢盖商业楼、商场、工厂。尽管有时候土地明明不缺，他们也不喜欢供应土地盖住宅。而且进来的人口最好是高端的没有本地户籍的人口。这样所有的社会负担统统可以扔下，养老上学的这些事统统和城市管理者无关。最好这些人的孩子都留在老家农村，以后等这些人老了，自己回原籍养老，再也不要来找我。

Therefore, as administrators of cities, what they always hope for is that there will be an influx of young people who will never get sick or old or have children and who can support the development of industries. Therefore, you can witness a strange phenomenon that most cities will reserve their land for enterprises. These cities love erecting commercial buildings, shopping malls, and factories. Even though there is no shortage of land, the governments just do not like supplying land for residential properties. Furthermore, newcomers should be high-quality individuals with no local *hukou*. In this way, the government can kiss goodbye to all of its burdens. Tasks such as taking care of the elderly and nurturing the young will have nothing to do with the city administrators. It will be the most ideal if the city dwellers all leave their children in their villages and these people will go back to their villages and spend their retirement days there so that they do not bother the city administrators.

当地方政府抱着这样的管理模式和想法，你可以想象，在中国的一线城市里房地产价格怎么可能会降下来呢？事实上可以看到每一轮出台的限制房价政策的最终结果，都是地方政府趁火打劫，顺便捞钱。比如房地产调控各个执行条例中，最容易落地的，也是地方政府最喜欢干的一件事情，就是搞户籍限制和在交易环节中加税。户籍限制不会减少需求，只会逼着没有户籍的去租房，推高租金，从而推高房价。加税不会让一件商品的价格变得更便宜，交易环节交税只会增加商品的成本。

When local governments follow this kind of management style and subscribe to these views, it is conceivable that the property prices in China's tier-one cities will never come down. In fact, you can see that the outcome of the implementation of every round of house price control policies is that the local governments "rob the owners while the house is on fire." This means that the local governments take advantage of ordinary citizens. For example, in the implementation of these rules and regulations on curbing property prices, the easier execution which is also what local governments are most fond of is to limit transactions based on *hukou* and adding transaction tax. *Hukou* limitations will not reduce the demand but only force those without a local *hukou* to rent a house, further driving up property prices. Increasing transaction tax will not make the price of a product cheaper but will only add to the costs of the product.

就像明天猪肉价格如果高涨了，你在交易环节去加税，规定猪肉每次交易都要交 20%的税费，这样只会让猪肉的价格变得更贵。一个房子买进的时候是 100 万，卖出的时候是 200 万。炒房人赚钱了，往往让人看着眼红。如果这个时候政府进来要让炒房人缴 50 万的税，那么实际上会把最终的交易价格推到 200 万~250 万中间。因为这 50 万的税是由上家和下家共同分担的。要看上家和下家谁的议价能力更强势，谁就分担的更少一些。在当年政府出台这些政策的时候，几乎所有的税费都是下家承担。结结实实地推高了房价。

An analogy is that if the price of pork surges tomorrow and you increase the transaction tax by stipulating that every transaction of pork needs to pay a 20% tax, this will only increase the price of pork. Let's say that the purchasing price of a house is CN¥1 million which can be sold for CN¥2 million now. The investor makes a profit and others are jealous. If the government now steps in and requires that investor to pay CN¥500,000 of tax, this will actually push the ultimate selling price to anywhere between CN¥2-2.5 million. This is because the tax burden of CN¥500,000 will be shared by both the seller and purchaser. The party with stronger bargaining power will bear a lesser burden. When the government implemented these policies at the time, it was almost always the buyer or those who were further down the transaction chain who bore the burden. This is how transaction tax drives up the property prices.

但似乎民众并不明白这一点，总感觉惩罚了上家，好像自己就能占到什么便宜一样。这让我想起小的时候看过的一个童话故事，一只狐狸给两只狗分一根香肠。这个香肠一开始分的左边大一点，右边小一点。两条狗就喊着说分配不均。于是狐狸做裁判，把大的那头咬掉一些。咬掉之后分配又变得不均匀，因为小的那头变大了，于是狐狸接着把大的这头再咬掉一截。这样来来回回，最后香肠都被狐狸吃走了，两条狗什么也吃不着。

But it seems that many people do not understand how this works. They think that the transaction tax punishes the seller or those who are further up the transaction chain and that they are actually benefitting from this policy. This reminds me of a childhood fable. A fox was dividing and allocating a sausage to two dogs. Originally, the left end of the sausage was bigger and the right one was smaller. The two dogs complained that it was not a fair allocation so they asked the fox to judge who bit off the bigger end. After the bite, the allocation was still not fair because the originally smaller end now became bigger. Then, the fox bit off the bigger end again. After several rounds, the fox ate the whole sausage and left nothing for the dogs.

中国的房地产调控差不多就是这个样子，政府以各种房地产调控为目的出台的各项政策，其实最后都是肥了地方政府，害了正在需要住房的人。这样的事情只有老百姓亲身经历，用真金白银去买一次二手房才会知道。因为你会发现自己居然要交那么多的税费给政府。今天在中国的一线城市买一个二手房，税费没有几十万是下不来的。一手楼盘也因为二手楼盘有这几十万的税费，所以也毫不客气地把自己的价格抬高几十万。

The curbing of property prices in China is more or less the same story. The government launched different policies to control soaring property prices but in the end, these policies only made local governments richer and harmed those who were in real need of residential properties. An ordinary citizen can only see the true picture after going through the experience by buying a second-hand property using his or her hard-earned money. Only then will you realize that you have to pay so many taxes to the government. Today, if you want to buy a second-hand real property in a tier-one city in China, the tax amounts to at least CN¥300,000 (approximately US$42,000). Knowing the enormous tax in the secondary market, the property developers also raise the price of first-hand property by the same amount.

2006 年以后在投资理财论坛上，有相当一批人认为上海、北京、深圳的房价不会像曼哈顿和香港一样狂涨。因为中国这些城市没有天然的地理屏障。曼哈顿和香港都是孤岛，所以土地紧张。而中国这些城市都是平原，可以像摊大饼一样无限扩展的。

From 2006 onwards, there have been a certain group of people who are of the opinion that the property prices in Shanghai, Beijing, and Shenzhen will not skyrocket like those in Manhattan and Hong Kong have. This is because these Chinese cities do not have a natural geographical limitation. Manhattan and Hong Kong are an isolated island with tight land supply. In contrast, these Chinese cities are plateau which can expand indefinitely like rolling out pizza dough.

他们其实忘了，地理上没有孤岛，但是政策和人心有孤岛。再宽广的平原也是可以人为地制造出稀缺的。

They are oblivious to the fact that even though there is no isolated island geographically speaking, policies and human nature have their isolated island. Even the vastest plateau may witness a man-made shortage of land supply.

因为我在中国买房，所以无论是在文学城的线上，还是生活中的线下，总有人跑过来向我请教中国买房的事情。所以我干脆把这些道理写出来和大家共同分享。写这些文章虽然我一分钱直接的好处都没有。但是就像我一直相信的那样，当你为他人做出好事的时候，冥冥之中，上天总是会有一种特殊的方式，回报你为他人做出的努力。写这些文章虽然没有人给我稿费，对我最大的帮助就是通过写作理清了自己的思路。

When I was trying to buy a house in China, many people, including netizens on Wenxuecity and real people in my daily life, liked asking me for advice on investing in China's property market. Therefore, I chose to write these principles out and share them with everyone. Even though I do not reap any direct monetary benefit from writing these articles, I believe that when you do a good deed, the universe will reward you in a special way for the efforts you put in helping others. Though no one is paying me any remuneration for writing these articles, I have also helped myself by organizing my own thoughts through writing.

此外就是在和投资理财网友的这个互动过程中，加深了我对很多问题的理解。我的印象中 2007 年的时候有两个投资理财的网友，他们的投资都比我更加激进更加大胆，所以我印象深刻。

Furthermore, my interactions with netizens on the investment and wealth management forum have deepened my understanding of many issues. If I remember it correctly, in 2007, there were two forum users who were interested in investing and had even bolder and aggressive strategies than I did, which left me with a very strong impression.

一个是当时倾其所有在深圳买房子。2007 年的时候全国各地还没有出台限购政策，深圳房价开始上涨。有人游行示威，希望政府平抑房价。这位网友在网上跟我聊他的投资经。当时他觉得自己的投资杠杆已经加到自己都不好意思说了，他把所有的美国信用卡通通都刷爆了，所有能贷的钱能借的钱都借光了，在深圳购买了三套房子。

One of them was "all in" buying real properties in Shenzhen. In 2007, when cities and counties in China still had not implemented "limiting purchases" policies, the property prices in Shenzhen began to soar. Some citizens participated in protests and demonstrations, urging the government to control the property prices. This forum user discussed his investment strategies with me. At that time, his investment leverage was so high that he was even embarrassed to tell me about it. He had maxed out all of his U.S. credit cards and borrowed every penny that he could to purchase three houses in Shenzhen.

另外一个人没有深入的交流。他只是简单地跟我说，他计划此行在上海高校附近购买 10 套老公房。最后我不知道他落实的情况怎么样。他因为在美国和加拿大都生活过，知道高校周围的小房子永远都是容易出租的。有年轻人在的地方就永远有钱可以挣。

I did not have an in-depth interaction with the other forum user. He simply told me that he had planned to purchase 10 old public housing units near colleges and universities in Shanghai. I had no idea whether and how he executed his plans. Because of his experience of having lived in both the U.S. and Canada, he knew that it was always the easiest to rent out small houses in proximity to colleges and universities. You can always make money in places where young people are concentrated.

我自己感觉我没有他们那么极端。然而现在回首往事，在你看清了市场趋势的时候，他们这些极端的做法是对的。

I felt that I was not as extreme as they were. In retrospect, when you have a clear understanding of the market trends, their extreme approaches are the right thing to do.

当然认为中国房价一定会降下来的，政府一定会把房价控制住，甚至中国会重演日本房地产泡沫的观察者也不在少数。尤其是在大众媒体上。举个例子就是当时的一个财经评论红人，谢 X 忠。

At the same time, those observers who thought that the property prices in China would come down eventually and that the government would control the property prices or even that the real estate bubble in Japan would happen in China too were not in the minority. Such views were especially ubiquitous on mainstream media. An example was a famous financial commentator, Xie Xzhong.

这位谢先生是某个国际著名的投资银行的经济顾问，号称自己预测了1997 年泰国的房地产崩盘。所以他用同样的道理预测中国的房地产崩盘，而他自己的名头又是挺唬人的，兼任这个基金那个投资公司的首席经济学家。他不断在电视媒体中露面，甚至号称暴跌就在某年某月之前必然发生。

This Mr. Xie was a famous economic consultant at an internationally well-known investment bank. He alleged that he had correctly predicted the collapse of the real estate market in Thailand in 1997 so he was using the same strategy in predicting the collapse of China's property market. At the same time, he had some pretty impressive titles. He was also the chief economist at a certain investment fund and also investment company. He was a frequent guest in various TV programs and even claimed that the steep fall would definitely come by a certain month in a certain year.

我在投资银行和金融系统工作过，所以我知道这些所谓的首席经济学家是个什么样的货色。其实他们对未来的判断能力和你我并差不了多少。但是他们喜欢口若悬河地说一些经济学名词。让听众听得似懂非懂，感觉他们是牛人。然后用讨好听众的方式说一些义愤填膺的话，利用道德绑架让听众听着舒坦。听众觉得牛人的观点和自己一致，所以会产生自己也是牛人的幸福感。

I have worked at investment banks and in the financial system before so I know the qualifications and abilities of these so-called chief economists. In fact, their ability to predict the future is almost the same as that of you and me. However, they like flaunting economic jargon so that the audience has a difficult time understanding what they are really trying to say. Thus, the audience will feel that they are giants in their fields. These economists will then try to please the audience by a passionate speech about justice so that they can "morally hijack" the audience who will then feel pleased and content listening to their speech. The audience will think that the experts hold the same points of view as they do so they will have a feeling of bliss that they are also an expert.

其实他们最关心的是如何成为网络红人，没有什么真知灼见，也不诚实，并没有能力准确地预测未来。

In fact, what these so-called experts really care about is how to become a celebrity. They do not have any valuable insights into the market. They are not honest either because they simply do not have the ability to predict the future.

那些他们用来吹牛的曾经的预测纪录，也都是经过自己粉饰过的。比如看跌的人会坚持看跌，直到市场下跌了，他就会以此作为证据说明自己多么厉害。其实他们对未来的预测能力和巫师祈雨没什么区别。你不断说明天要下雨，明天要下雨。坚持一年，终于有一天明天下雨了，然后你就说自己有先知先觉的本事。

The accurate prediction record about which these so-called specialists are boasting is a product of window dressing. For example, those who are bearish will strongly adhere to their view. When the market indeed falls, they will use this as proof that they are so brilliant. In fact, their ability to predict the future is no different from a shaman who does the rain dance. If you do the rain dance every day for an entire year and then one day it rains, you can claim that you have the ability to invoke rain and predict the future.

网络红人里大部分人都需要去弄个冠冕堂皇的头衔，比如这位谢先生。还有一些是屌丝起家的，比如当时在深圳就有个赫赫有名的网络红人，叫"牛 X"的先生。这位先生高峰的时候，粉丝上百万，每天发一篇文章论证深圳的房价为何会下跌。当现实不断打脸的时候，粉丝愤怒的时候，他们又会自圆其说地说，中国不是一个正常市场。那逻辑好比祈雨的巫师说，不是我的巫术不给力，是老天爷不遵守气象学规律一样。

A majority of internet celebrities need a seemingly impressive title. An example is this Mr. Xie. There are also those celebrities who were originally penniless. Take Mr. Niu X who was a famous internet celebrity in Shenzhen at the time. At the peak of this Mr. Niu's fame, he had millions of followers. Every single day, he published one article arguing why property prices in Shenzhen would fall.

When the reality was indicating the contrary and his followers became angry, Mr. Niu would try to justify himself by saying that China was not a normal market. The logic of this saying was similar to how the shaman who did the rain dance and blamed nature for not following the patterns of meteorology when he failed to invoke rain.

其实只要仔细分析一下，看他的背景是什么就能看穿把戏。他做过房地产开发么？他系统地理解过金融和经济的基本原理吗？其实这位牛先生什么都没有。他只是利用民众的情绪宣泄，给自己圈粉丝。

In fact, if one takes a closer look and does his or her own analysis of Mr. Niu's background, he or she will be able to see through the tricks. Had he ever developed a real estate project? Did he have a systematic understanding of the basic theories of finance and economics? In fact, Mr. Niu had nothing to support his claims. He was merely trying to invoke the general sentiment to win himself some followers.

我是喜欢从数据入手分析问题的。当时我写了这样一篇博客告诉大家房价恐怕还要再涨一阵子。

I like to approach a problem by analyzing the data. At that time, I specifically wrote an article telling others that the property prices would probably continue to rise for quite a while.

涨！涨！涨！ (2010 年 5 月 14 日)
Up! Up! Up! (May 14, 2010)

by Bayfamily

小的时候看过电影"金刚"。里面的大猩猩面对直升飞机扫射，喜欢拍胸脯。可惜终究没能保护自己。为了心中的美女一命呜呼。中国在宏观调控房价。让我感觉如同金刚一样。喜欢拍胸脯。不知道是真傻，还是假傻。效果不重要，关键能讨个老百姓的口彩就行了。倒下去了，20 年后，还是一条好汉。

会走路的钱
Money Walks

In the movie King Kong, which I watched when I was young, the enormous gorilla liked pounding its chest when the helicopter was firing bullets at it. Regrettably, he still could not protect himself and died while chasing after the beauty. How China is trying to regulate the macroeconomic property prices reminds me of that movie. Both King Kong and China like pounding the chest. I have no idea whether they are in fact so ignorant or just pretending to be so. The effect does not matter. What matters is how the ordinary citizens think. Even if the measures fail, this does not matter either. All it takes is another 20 years and he will be a good guy again.[6]

别的地方我不知道，但是单单就上海而言，目前和未来都是严重的供需不平衡。长期来看房价的涨跌绝对是一个供求平衡的问题。炒房客对房价会有推波助澜的作用。但是对于炒房客而言，买进来的房子总是要卖出去的。不会影响最基本的供求平衡。如果把过去12年的连续增长一味地归结为炒房的作用不是一个理性的思考。短期的房价变化，会受到宏观汇率，利率，信贷，这些外界因素的影响。

I am not familiar with other cities but if we are talking about Shanghai, there is a significant imbalance between the demand and supply which will persist in the future. In the long term, the rise and fall of property prices are a question of demand and supply. Real estate speculators will help drive up property prices. However, for these people, they will have to sell the houses at one point so this will not affect the basic balance between demand and supply. If one merely attributes the consecutive and persistent increase in property prices in the past 12 years to speculation activities in the real estate market, this is not a rational thinking process. The changes in property prices in the short term were affected by macroeconomic and external factors, such as exchange rates, interest rates, and the availability of credits.

---

[6] This is a famous quote from the Chinese historical novel "Sui Tang Yanyi." Chinese believe in reincarnation after death. Even though a hero may die one day, all it takes is another 18 or 20 years and he will be a good man again.

我们先看看上海最基本的供求数字。需求方面，假设投资需要为 0，基本的需要有两类，一个是新增人口的需求。上海市每年新增人口 40 万。这是官方统计，不算发廊和餐馆里面打工的外地人。按照三口之家，每家 90 平米计算。因为人口增加的需求大约是 1000 万平方米。

Let us take a look at the numbers of demand and supply in Shanghai. On the demand end, let us assume that the demand for investment properties is zero. The basic demand for properties can be divided into two categories. The first type is the demand for newcomers. The population of Shanghai grows by 400,000 every year. This is the official statistics that exclude migant workers working at hair salons and restaurants. My calculation assumes that a family of three needs a living environment of 90 square meters. Therefore, the demand for land arising from population growth is about 10 million square meters.

第二个是改善型需求，根据上海未来的远景规划，每年人均居住面积大约是增长 0.5 平米的样子，改善性面积需要为 1000 万平方米每年。这个数字基本上是靠谱的。因为和过去几年的供应数字基本一致。 2006 年到 2007 年的销售基本上在 2000 万每年。2008 到 2010 年，这个数字下降到 1700 到 1800 万平方米。留下一些欠债。供给方面。房子的建设是有周期的。过去几年里批出来的土地，是未来几年的基本供应。

The second category is what I call "a need for improvement." According to Shanghai's future strategic planning, the increase in the average living floor area per resident is about 0.5 square meter. Therefore, the demand for land because of existing residents' need for a better living environment is about 10 million square meters. This number makes sense because it is in line with the supply in the last several years. The sales from 2006-2007 were basically about 20 million square meters per year. From 2008 to 2010, this number dropped to around 17-18 million square meters. There are some loans left. In terms of the supply, the construction of houses is cyclical. The land that has been approved in the last couple of years will be the basic supply for the next few years.

会走路的钱
Money Walks

过去 5 年里，上海出让的可供应土地是 8000 万平方米，转换成 1000 万左右的供应面积。也就是说在未来的 5 年左右的时间里，供需平衡严重失调，缺口大约在 50%左右。这是宏观基本面的数字。再看看微观的数字。北京房价奥运会之后猛涨，主要原因是奥运期间建筑工地停工。到了 2009 年，市场上的供给严重短缺引起的。而上海的世博会长达半年，市区内的建设也基本停工。世博结束后，也同样面临一样的短缺。上海本月的房产库存面积已经达到历史最低点，400 万平方米。紧紧够市场两个月消化的。世博结束之后，恐怕库存会达到历史新低。进一步促进房价上扬。

In the last 5 years, the available land supply approved by the Shanghai government was 80 million square meters which could be converted into around 10 million in terms of gross area. In other words, in the next five years, there will be a serious imbalance between demand and supply. The shortage is about 50%. This is the fundamental number from a macroeconomics perspective. Let us look at the microeconomics numbers. After the 2008 Beijing Olympics, the property prices in Beijing surged. The main reason is that the construction sites paused their progress during the Olympics. In 2009, there was a serious shortage in the housing market. And the 2010 Shanghai Expo will last for about six months during which most construction projects in the city are put to a pause. After the Expo, Shanghai will face the same shortage. The housing supply in terms of floor area has reached its historical low this month with a supply of 4 million square meters which is just enough for the market to digest in two months. After the Expo, this number will probably fall to an even lower point, further driving up property prices.

我对中央的房价调控实在是不以为然。我不清楚他们是真的不懂，还是装不懂。在交易环节上做动作，只会影响市场的成交量，不会影响基本的供需平衡。打击房产开发商，降低商品房的土地拍卖量，只会减少供应，让供求平衡进一步恶化，房价更高。

I do not think very highly of the central government's attempts to control property prices. I am not sure if they indeed have no idea or pretend to have no idea about the operation of the property market. Focusing on the transactions will only affect the number of deals in the market but not the basic balance between demand and supply. Discouraging property developers and reducing the amount of available land for commercial houses in land auctions will only decrease the supply, exacerbating the imbalance between demand and supply and driving up property prices.

以上海为例，所谓的增加保障性住房完全是句空话。拿今日新闻来看，上海宣布筹建 23 个大型社区，120 万套住宅，8000 万平方米。猛地一看是猛药重拳。仔细一看，原来是个政府的碰头会，领导表示一下决心。规划部门表示，大约需要 2 年的时间，完成土地的储备工作。等到真正建成上市，恐怕猴年马月，下届政府的事情了。

Take Shanghai as an example. The so-called "increase security housing" is merely empty words. Let us take a look at the news headlines today. Shanghai has announced that it has planned to develop 23 large-scale communities, 1.2 million residential units, and 80 million square meters. At first glance, it seems that these all are highly effective measures aimed at curbing property prices. However, when one takes a closer look, he or she will realize that this was just a government briefing meeting that the leaders used to show their determination. The relevant planning departments have said that it needs around 2 years to finish its work on land reserves. It will probably take donkey's years for these units to be actually constructed and be available for sale. It will then become the agenda for the next tenure of government.

君不见，2003 年的时候，政府同样拍过胸脯建 2000 万的保障性住房。7 年过去了，后面两个零都人间蒸发了。2008 年同样拍过胸脯。两次拍胸脯都过去，今天干脆再拍 8000 万的胸脯。我看和金刚里面的大猩猩有一拼。

Don't you see that in 2003 when the government also pounded its chest and promised to build 20 million security housing units? Seven years have since passed and the last two zeros in that figure have vanished into thin air. In 2008, the government also pounded its chest. The two occasions where the government pounded its chest have already passed. Maybe the government should pound its chest and promise 80 million this time. In my opinion, this can be compared to the enormous gorilla in King Kong.

但是为了保障性住房的供应，商品房土地在严重缩减。因为住宅土地的总供应面积没有变化。北京为例，住宅土地里面，不到 30% 为商品房。如此下来几年之后，房价不涨才怪呢。

However, in order to guarantee the supply of security housing, the land supply of commercial houses is shrinking. This is because the total land supply of residential housing has not changed. Take Beijing as an example. Less than 30% of the total supply of residential housing is commercial housing. I will be baffled if the property prices do not increase in the next few years.

让人担心是这次政府这么大的决心，房价半年之后再一路狂涨，不知道政府能否面对底层社会的政治压力。进一步做出疯狂的事情来，如同那个大猩猩一路在纽约狂奔。

What is worrying is that the government has shown a huge determination this time and yet the property prices still skyrocketed six months later. I am not sure if the government can resist political pressure from the lower class. If the government further commits acts of craziness, it will be akin to how the enormous gorilla was running around in New York City.

转一篇 1989 年的人民日报社评。今日看来，忍俊不禁。从中央到地方，都有金刚的遗风。过去 20 年了，看来还是没有什么长进。

Let me repost an editorial from People's Daily in 1989. Reading this article now, one cannot help but burst into laughter. From the central government to the local government, we can still see the style of King Kong. 20 years have passed and it does not seem that the governments have improved.

1989 年人民日报新闻评论房地产泡沫，"北京最近提供两万多平方米的住房，每平米 1600—1900 元。若买两居室，少说也要六万元。一名大学生从参加工作起就日日节衣缩食，每月存款 50 元已是极致，100 年才能买上两居室"（人民日报 1989 年 2 月 20 日第 2 版）。

The editorial in People's Daily in 1989 was commenting on real estate bubbles. "Beijing has recently provided residential housing of more than 20,000 square meters at a price of CN¥1600-1900 per square meter. If one buys a two-bedroom unit, he or she needs at least CN¥60,000. Let us assume that a university graduate diligently saves his income from the day of joining the workforce, the maximum amount that he or she can save is CN¥50. Therefore, it takes 100 years for this person to be able to buy a two-bedroom unit." (The Second Edition of People's Daily dated February 20, 1989)

2005，上海东方网 "两个一千万，可降房价 15%"，"东方网 3 月 31 日消息："两个一千万工程"刚被提出，已经成为上海市民耳熟能详的关注焦点，在央行和上海市政府轮番推出的调控政策中，这一增加中低价房源供应的保障性举措无疑是最亮眼和最有力的。专家认为，市政府提出"年内新开工配套商品房 1000 万平方米、中低价商品住房 1000 万平方米，争取可预售 2000 万平方米"的目标，在为上海增加大量老百姓买得起的商品房同时，也寄予了以此调控房价的厚望。能使上海住宅的均价降低 15%。"

In 2005, the headline of the website of Shanghai's Eastday News was "Two 10 million can decrease the property prices by 15%." Eastday News reported on March 31 on its website that "Two 10-million construction projects have been proposed and have become a focus and hot topic among Shanghai citizens. Among the controlling measures by the Central Bank and Shanghai Municipal Government, this measure to increase the supply of low-to-mid-price-range housing is undoubtedly the most eye-catching and effective. Experts are of the view that the target proposed by the municipal government to increase supply of commercial housing by 10 million square meters and supply of low-to-mid-price-range housing by 10 million square meters which are 20 million square meters in total can help significantly increase the supply of commercial housing that ordinary citizens can afford and also show the government's ambition in controlling property prices. This proposal will bring down residential property prices in Shanghai by 15%."

会走路的钱
Money Walks

在中国过去十几年的房地产暴涨过程中，由于舆论的管控，大部分明白人都选择不作声。当时敢于说实话的只有任 X 强先生。他是坚定地看涨，屡次警告年轻人，赶紧买，不买还涨。实话听起来难听，可是你要理解后面的道理，而不要用动机猜测他人意图。任 X 强因为自己亲自参与房地产开发，他自己是房产公司的老总，所以他知道是怎么回事。他知道政府的心态是怎么样的，他也明白地方和中央是怎么互相博弈的。他就老老实实地说了一些真话，结果挨了无数多的砖头。良药苦口利于病，忠言逆耳利于行，这话不但是对皇帝适用，对老百姓也适用。

In the last decade or so during which China's property prices skyrocketed, most people who understand what is going on in the market chose not to say anything because of the government's censorship. At that time, the only one who dared speak the truth was Mr. Ren Xqiang. He held a bullish view adamantly and warned the young people that they should purchase their property as soon as possible. If they did not take action now, the property prices would continue to rise. Sometimes the truth is hard to swallow but you have to try to understand the reasons behind and do not wildly guess others' intentions based on motives. Mr. Xqiang was himself a property developer and a chairman of a real estate company so he knew clearly what was going on. He also understood well how the government thought and how the central government and local government behaved in this game. He was telling the truth but received many criticisms. The Chinese old saying that "A bitter medicine cures the disease; honest advice may be unpleasant to hear but it is best for your life" which was originally for Chinese emperors is also useful for ordinary citizens.

其实大部分老百姓和昏君并没有什么区别。这不但对于中国适用，对美国也适用。你可以看到当无数政客在上台演讲的时候，他们从来都是没有底线拍老百姓的马屁。老百姓怎么可能没有错误呢？老百姓经常性地显示出乌合之众的很多特质。只是因为你手里多一张选票，难道你就真的变成上帝永远正确了吗？

In fact, most ordinary citizens are no different from fatuous and self-indulgent emperors. This saying not only applies to the situation in China but also to the U.S. You can see that many politicians do not have their own sets of principles and are just trying to please the general public. How can the general public be so perfect and make no mistakes? Ordinary citizens often display the many qualities of the crowd who are without any discipline or order. Just because you now have a vote in your hand, does this mean that you have become God and is always correct?

除了经济网络红人，即使到了 2009 年，上海本地人看空房地产的人当然也不在少数。当时有几个上海本地的名人在媒体上说，上海的房子要跌。他们算了一下，自己的孩子不缺房子，因为自己有房子一套，爷爷奶奶有房子一套，外公外婆有房子一套。由于独生子女政策，大部分上海的孩子最终都有三套房子，至少能继承的房子就有三套。所以未来的房子肯定过剩，房价要跌。

Other than Internet "economist" celebrities, local Shanghainese who is bearish on the real estate market is not in the minority. At that time, several local Shanghai celebrities were saying on different media that the property prices in Shanghai were going to fall. They made a calculation that their own kids did not need to buy a house because the parents had already owned one, the maternal grandparents owned one, and the fraternal grandparents also owned one. Because of the one-child policy, most children in Shanghai would end up with at least 3 properties by way of succession. Therefore, there would be a surplus of houses in the future and the property prices would fall as a consequence.

这样的思考方式最主要的问题就是只看到了自己认识的周围人的小圈子。用小圈子的数据采样来替代整体。他们没有意识到支撑上海房价的不是本地人。本地人在计划生育的影响下的确是人口越来越少。但是每年那么多新毕业的大学生，那么多带着梦想到一线城市打拼的年轻人。他们才是撑起房价的顶梁柱。

The problem of this way of thinking is that these people based their observations on a very small circle of people that they know. They were over-generalizing by using the limited data collected from the small circle. What they did not realize was that what supported the soaring property prices was not the local population. Because of the influence of the one-child policy, the local population was decreasing. However, there are so many university graduates every year who come to tier-one cities with their ambitions to make a name for themselves in these cities. They are the supporting pillars of increasing property prices.

03 上海卖房
03 Selling Houses in Shanghai

2006 年我上海的第二个投资房买入之后，就是一路蹭蹭蹭的暴涨。两年不到的 2008 年 2 月份，房子交给付给我的时候，房价已经从我买入时候的 100 万涨到了 230 万。也就是说房子我还一天还没有用过，房价已经涨了一倍多。

After I bought my second investment property in Shanghai in 2006, the property prices soared. In February 2008, which was shy of two years from the date the house was delivered to me, the price had increased from CN¥1 million, the price that I paid, to CN¥2.3 million. In other words, even though I had not lived in that property for one single day, the price had more than doubled.

因为房价上升，我这个房子的贷款杠杆率自然也就下降了。根据我的勤快人理财法，需要不断保持房地产杠杆率才可以。另外一方面虽然我每个月在负担着贷款，但是未来有多少房租收入还很难说，因为那个地方房子不是很好出租。

A natural outcome of the price increasing was that the leverage of this investment property decreased. According to my "Investment Strategies for Diligent People," I need to maintain my leverage used in real estate investments. On the other hand, even though I was still paying my mortgage every month, it was difficult to ascertain how much rental income that property would generate in the future because it was not that easy to rent out houses in that neighborhood.

中国的房地产没有再融资贷款(refinance)之说，所以很难从房子里拿出钱来。我找了几个银行咨询，他们告诉我的消息都是最多可以用房产抵押做一年或者三年的贷款，没有长期贷款。这么短期的贷款对我没有什么意义。既然房地产投资的秘密就在于杠杆，当杠杆消失了之后，房地产投资的回报就不如股票了，所以我要想办法加大杠杆。

There is no refinancing in China's real estate market so it is difficult to cash out on a real property. I turned to several banks for a consultation. They all told me that I could use the investment property as collateral to apply for a one-year or three-year loan and long-term loans were not available to me. But these short-term loans were of little use to me. The secret of successful real estate investing lies in leverage. When the leverage disappears, the return from real estate investing is not as good as return from stocks. Therefore, I needed to increase my leverage.

另外一方面 2008 年的经济危机已经开始爆发，美国股市一路狂跌。美国的房地产市场在 2008 年的时候并没有出现急速下挫，基本上是持稳稍稍有一些回落，这里面很大一部分原因是联储局一路降息硬撑着房地产市场。

Another relevant factor was that the 2008 financial crisis had already begun and the U.S. stock market plummeted. The U.S. real estate market did not witness a crash in 2008 but remained steady with some slight dips. The main reason for this was that the Federal Reserve supported the real estate market by lowering the interest rate.

可是在我看来，当时美国的房地产下跌已经是不可逆转的事情了。只是没人知道下跌会持续多久，也不知道会下跌到什么程度。我感觉抄底的机会在一步步朝我走来。市场的变化基本上是按照我之前的预期。如果这次和前四次加州房地产市场一样出现下跌和反转，那我投资计划的外部条件就基本形成了。

However, I held the view that a real estate market crash was irreversible but it was just that no one knew for how long the market would continue to drop or the extent of the plummet. I was feeling that the chances to buy the dips were approaching me. The changes in the market were basically in line with my previous expectations. If the market showed the same pattern of decrease and reversal, the external conditions of my investment plan would be basically present.

问题是根据我这个投资计划，市场最低点的时候我手上需要有现金，不然抄底机会来的时候现金没有也是一场空。

The problem was that according to my investment plan, I needed to have cash when the market dropped to its low. Otherwise, I would not be able to buy the dips even when such chances presented themselves.

综合以上各个方面的因素考量，我需要把中国的第二个房子卖掉。这三个原因就是：房子可能租不出去，杠杆需要增加，需要准备美国抄底资金了。

Taking into account all of the above considerations and factors, I needed to sell my second investment property in China. In summary, the three reasons were: I might not be able to rent that house out; I needed to increase my leverage, and I was preparing my capital for buying the dips in the U.S.

所以我委托一个同学把房子简单装修了一下，总共花了 5 万元人民币，然后放到市场上。一方面是看看有没有机会把它出租出去，另外一方面也同时挂牌在销售，如果能卖掉干脆就卖掉吧。

Therefore, I entrusted a classmate of mine to help me carry out the simple decoration of the house which cost a total of CN¥50,000, after which that house was put in the market. The house was listed for rent and also for sale. But if someone was interested in buying the house, this was exactly what I wanted.

为了计算可能出现的局面和权衡各种投资回报，我做了一个复杂的 Excel 表格，几乎和投行做投资的表格一样尽善尽美。很多指标都列出来，各种情景分析弄得明明白白。无论我怎么计算，Excel 的结果都是支持我卖出这个房子。两年不到涨了一倍，后续市场风雨飘摇，现在还不赶紧卖了套现更待何时？

In order to calculate the possible scenarios and the various investment returns, I compiled a complicated Excel spreadsheet that was as perfect as the tables made by investment banks. I listed out various indicators and detailed analysis of a myriad of scenarios. No matter how I did my calculations, the result shown in Excel was that I should sell the house which had doubled in less than 2 years' time and the market was full of uncertainties. What could be a better time than now to sell the house for cash?

然而今天看来，这个 Excel 表格完全是我一厢情愿的想法。或者夸张地说，我还没有一次投资决定正确是因为 Excel 表的数据提供了有用的帮助。大部分时候是自己辛辛苦苦整理出来的计算结果反而误导了自己。主要原因就是一个投资过程的影响因素太多，不可知因素太多。迷恋 Excel 表的计算让我忘了很多公式以外无法计算的内容。这个教训很深刻。本次房子的卖出就是一个例子。后面还有其他的例子我再和读者分享。

However, now that I look back at my investment decision, the Excel spreadsheet was an embodiment of my own wishful thinking. To be candid, there was not a single time in my investment history in which I made a correct decision because of the assistance of the statistics and calculations presented in an Excel spreadsheet. Most of the time, I was misled by my own diligent calculations. The main reason for this was that the investment process was influenced by a plethora of factors that included so many unknowns. An obsession with doing calculations in Excel spreadsheets made me oblivious to the fact that investment involved content that was beyond the scope of different formulas. This was an unforgettable lesson that I learned that the hard way. The house that I sold this time was such an example. I have many other examples to share with my readers in the later parts of this book.

会走路的钱
Money Walks

2008 年的夏天，美国在一片风声鹤唳之中。但恐慌的情绪还没有传递到中国。中国普通民众还都是看热闹，一副吃瓜群众事不关己的态度。电视里都是经济学家做科普，解释为什么会有次贷危机？老百姓听的云里来雾里去的，感觉很新鲜。作为亲历者，当时既买卖了房子，也经历了投行破产。我认为其实直到今天，都没有一本中文的书籍把次贷危机到底是怎么回事说清楚的。

In the summer of 2008, the U.S. was in "facing the sound of the wind and the cry of the cranes." This is a literal translation of a Chinese idiom which refers to the great fear of routed soldiers in that situation. But the fear of the U.S. investors had not yet spread to China. The general public in China was rubbernecking and thought that they would not be affected. Economists were educating the general public on TV shows. They were explaining why there was a sub-prime crisis. The ordinary citizens in China were confused but they thought it was a novel topic. As someone who has the first-hand experience of the crisis and who purchased and sold houses during that time and also witnessed the bankruptcy of investment banks, I think that even up to today no Chinese books have offered a clear explanation of the sub-prime crisis.

2008 年中国正在准备奥运会。坊间的流言是奥运会的时候中国的房价是不会下跌的。我觉得这几乎是玩笑话。奥运会跟全国的房价一点点关系都没有。不知道为什么很多人会把这两个事情扯在一起，即使有关系的话，可能也是局限于某些特定地区。比如，因为工地停工的关系，奥运会对北京房价可能会有一些影响。

In 2008, China was preparing for the Beijing Olympics. Rumors had it that during the Olympics, China's property prices would not drop. I dismissed this claim as a joke. The Olympics game had nothing to do with the property prices. I was baffled why so many people linked these two incidents. Even if a certain relationship existed between them, it was probably limited to certain specific areas.

For example, because of the suspension of construction sites, the Olympics might affect the property prices in Beijing to some extent.

无论怎样。我清晰地记得 2008 年夏天的时候，中国的房价并没有发生大幅的下跌，虽然所有人都看到金融风暴已经形成。这就是我一再说的房地市场具有很强的粘性。房地产市场效率不像股票市场效率那么高。金融市场上的一些动荡并没有办法立刻反映到房价上，而是有几个月的滞后时间。

Anyway, I can still remember vividly that in the summer of 2008, even though property prices in China did not witness a significant decrease, everyone could see clearly that a financial storm had already formed. This is also why I have reiterated that the real estate market has a high level of viscosity. The efficiency of the real estate market is not as high as that of the stock market. Any fluctuations in the financial market will not be immediately reflected in the house prices but there will be a delay of several months.

如果你是一个勤快人，就可以利用这几个月的时间，来把握市场的脉搏，Timing 市场。在房地产投资上，我就是一个超级勤快的人。至少在那几年的时候，精力充沛，斗智高昂，每次回中国出差和探亲，我都会利用这些机会做房地产投资的功课。

If you are a diligent person, you can make good use of this delayed period of several months to understand the trends in the market and the timing. When it comes to real estate investing, I am a super diligent person. This is at least true during those years when I was always energetic and ambitious. Every time when I went back to China on a business trip or to visit my relatives, I would utilize these opportunities to do my research on real estate investing.

我房子挂出去不久，很快就有一个买家来买，是在浦东一个大银行工作的一对年轻夫妻。我对此印象深刻，是因为当时银行坐班管理严格，他们很难工作日请假出来签合同。而我又是只能在国内停留几天就跑的人。这对年轻的夫妻是解决自己的刚需住房。虽然我那个小区周围各种服务设施还没有上来，但是对口的中小学是浦东比较好的学校，且和我的房子只隔着一条马路。他们刚刚生了孩子不久，所以想把我的房子买下来。

Not long after I listed that property, a young couple who both worked at a large bank in Pudong was interested in buying it. The reason why they left me with a strong impression was that banks had very strict requirements of work shifts at that time. It was very difficult for them to take a day off on weekdays to sign the contract. Meanwhile, I was only able to stay in China for a few days. This couple was looking to solve their own need for a residential property. Even though there were not many amenities in the neighborhood of my investment property, the house was situated next to a great primary school and secondary school in Pudong, which were separated by a road. They had just welcomed their first child so they would like to buy my house.

由于政府不断出台的调控法规，当时让房地产交割已经变得有些复杂。主要是转移贷款的手续非常麻烦。每付一笔钱都要办一些手续。买卖双方都需要有比较好的信誉和诚意才能顺利成交。中间有人变卦，都不知道该怎么收场。当时是我第一次在中国卖房子，我感觉比在美国卖房子复杂多了。为此我由衷地感谢美国的那些律师们和游戏规则的制定者，让老百姓生活中少了太多不必要的烦恼。大部分美国人不比较不知道，没有意识到自己享受到的便利，也不太知道珍惜。

Because of the government's frequent introduction of rules and regulations on controlling real properties, the closing of a real estate transaction had become pretty complicated at that time. The main source of trouble was the transactions involved in applying for and transferring loans. There were procedures involved every time a sum of money was paid or received and both the seller and buyer needed good credits and good faith for the transaction to successfully close. If in the middle of the whole process, a party changed his or her mind, no one would know how to handle the mess. That was the first time I had sold a house in China which was a lot more complicated than in the U.S. On that note, I would like to express my sincere gratitude to the lawyers and rule-makers in the U.S. who have helped the public reduce much unnecessary trouble. Most Americans have no idea how lucky they are because they have never done a comparison before. They have not realized the convenient life they have so they do not know to be grateful or cherish it.

等我收到了最后一笔钱，整个交割过程结束之后，我忽然对这两个年轻的夫妻不知道怎么心里出现了一种深深的同情。230 万人民币在当时还是一笔很大的钱的。即使是银行工作，2008 年的时候，收入也不是很高。所以这对年轻的夫妻需要承担很多年的债务，慢慢偿还。

When I received the last sum of money and closed the deal, it suddenly dawned on me that for some unknown reasons I was feeling sympathetic toward this young couple. CN¥2.3 million was a very significant sum of money at that time even for those who worked at a bank. In 2008, the salaries were not very high which meant that this couple needed to bear years of loan obligations and repay the loan gradually.

我当时非常确信房价过几个月会下跌。下跌之后，他们夫妻之间会吵架，会因为白白损失的几十万弄得不愉快，也许会互相埋怨对方。不知道他们是不是能够平静地度过这段令人折磨的时间。另外他们还有一个刚出生不久的宝宝。我非常为他们即将到来的家庭风暴而感到担心。

I was very confident that the property prices would drop in a few months. After the decline, the couple would have an argument over the fact that they had lost hundreds of thousands of money. They might even blame each other. I was wondering if they could peacefully get through this torturing time. On top of that, they had a newborn baby. I was very worried about the family storm that was coming on their way.

而这一切可能只是因为我比他们拥有的信息更多一些。大家都是普普通通的老百姓，虽然一切都是自愿的，可是我内心总有些占了便宜的忐忑不安。房地产交易和股票交易不同，股票交易你是看不见你的对手的。房产交易，站在你对面的是有血有肉的大活人。在办几次来来回回的交割手续过程中，让我感觉他们是很好的人。当然现在再想一想当年的担心其实也是多余的。房地产投资真的不知道谁是杨白劳，谁是黄世仁。也许他们当时会有一些摩擦，但是这么多年过去之后，还真的不知道到底谁应该感谢谁。因为现在那套房子涨到了 1000 万人民币左右。比我卖出的价格差不多涨了四倍多。谁笑到最后还不一定呢？

The reason for all this was probably because I had more information than they did. We are all ordinary citizens. Even though the transaction was an entirely voluntary one, I was feeling uneasy because I thought that I had taken advantage of them. Real estate transactions are different from stock transactions. In the latter, you cannot see your opponents. In real estate transactions, those standing before you are people of flesh and blood. In the several rounds of back-and-forth procedures in closing the transaction, I could tell that they were very nice people. Of course, now looking back, I know that the worries that I had at that time were totally unnecessary. In real estate investing, you will never know who is Yang Bailao and who is Huang Shiren.[7]

04 融化的冰棍
04 A Melting Popsicle

扣除贷款，我手上拿到了将近 180 万人民币的现金。我实际的投入是 40 万人民币左右，两年回报四倍。数钱的快乐大约只持续了一天，我就一下子又慌乱了起来。

After deducting the loan, I received about CN¥1.8 million in cash. My actual input was around CN¥400,000 so my money quadrupled in two years. The happiness of counting the money only lasted for one day and I was panicking again.

---

[7] Yang Bailao and Huang Shiren are the protagonists in "The White Haired Girl," a Chinese opera. In the story, Yang Bailao had a sad ending and Huang Shiren had a happy ending.

我决定卖房的时候。我的一个上海的亲戚就问我，你拿到钱打算干什么呢？我也不好明确告诉他我要干什么。我那么复杂的投资理财计划，我的会走路的钱理论，我的懒人和勤快人理财法也不是三言两语说得明白的。但是我知道当时大多数人没有选择卖出，是因为国内没有什么其他的好的投资渠道。手上的现金除了房产，别无去处。

When I decided to sell my house, a relative of mine who was in Shanghai asked me what I was going to do with the money. I did not tell him exactly what my next action would be because my investment and wealth management plans were pretty complicated. My money walks theory, "Investment Strategies for Diligent People," and "Investment Strategies for Lazy People" could not be explained in simple words in a short amount of time. But I knew that at that time many people did not choose to sell their properties because there were no better investment options than real estate which was the only outlet for people's cash.

2008 年年底次贷危机爆发几个月之后，美国的房子就像雪崩一样的下跌了。我印象中 2009 年元旦那天我去看一个湾区的二手房。中介开玩笑地说，他等了几个小时，只等到我一个人。上海的房价下跌要比美国的房子下跌再晚几个月。但是到 2009 年春节的时候也是一片哀鸿遍野。我卖出的那个房子，房价大约下跌了 20%左右。

Several months after the sub-prime crisis occurred at the end of 2008, U.S. property prices were sliding like an avalanche. From my memory, on New Year's Day in 2009, I was touring a second-hand property in the Bay Area. The real estate agent told me in a joking manner that I was the only one who appeared after he had waited for several hours for a potential buyer. The decline in Shanghai's property prices occurred several months after the decline in the U.S. market. But in Chinese New Year in 2009, the Chinese property market was filled with sighs and mourning in distress. The house that I had just sold had dropped by 20%.

那个开发商总经理跟我亲戚夸赞我的投资本事大。他说他们境外的人士肯定是掌握了什么特殊的信息，能够这么准在最高点把房子卖掉。以后他要多请教我一下。我听了这样的夸赞，心情却一点也高兴不起来。也许是我天生有很强的共情倾向，我会忍不住想象一下买我房子的那对小夫妻不知道正在受着什么样的煎熬。

The general manager of the land developer was singing my praises in front of my relative. He said that I had a very astute investment acumen. He reckoned that as a foreigner, I must have had some special information which explained why I was able to sell my house at the exact peak level. He would also like to ask me for advice in the future. After hearing such compliments, I was not feeling any happiness at all. This is probably because I am an empath. I could not help but think that the couple who bought my house was suffering greatly.

这是一方面，另外一方面我为自己手上这 180 万现金如何快速投出去也是煞费了苦心。现金就像冰棍一样的，当你把冰棍从冰箱里拿出来攥在手里，它就会融化掉。这个道理我懂。可是即使我明白这个道理，在执行层面上，我依然没有办法 100% 的做到冰棍不融化。不动产的好处就是"不动"两个字，因为不动的原因，所以资产就容易被保留住，冰棍就不会融化掉。

That was one reason. Another reason was that I was racking my brain into coming up with a strategy to invest the CN¥1.8 million of cash that I had at hand as soon as possible. Cash is like a popsicle. When you take the popsicle out from the freezer and hold it in your hand, it will melt. Even though I knew this theory well, I had difficulty executing it. I still could not find a way to make sure that my popsicle would not melt at all. One of the benefits of holding immovable property is that it is immovable. It is precisely because of this feature that it is easy to preserve your assets and make sure your popsicle does not melt.

那个时候中国还没有今天这么严格的外汇资本管控。2009 年 3 月的时候，我看到美国的一个好学区核心区的房子，开出来了之前一个不可想象的低价。美国市场上好的机会渐渐多了起来。于是我把这 180 万人民币中的 50 万人民币汇回了美国，打算用这笔钱来抄底。

At that time, China did not have as strict control on capital outflow as today. In March 2009, I saw that a house located in a core area and a great school district in the U.S. was for sale at an unbelievably low price. Good investment opportunities began to abound in the U.S. market. In light of this, I wired CN¥500,000 from the CN¥1.8 million to the U.S. and was planning to buy the dips using this sum of money.

50 万人民币换成美元，差不多是 7 万美元的样子，分两笔汇回了美国。不过冰棍融化事件还是控制不住地发生了。我之前开的车被撞了，要换一辆车。当你手上有钱的时候，特别是刚刚赚了一笔钱的时候，你本能地想犒劳自己。去买一个价格比较高的车。一般人们购买大宗商品时，比如自住房，汽车的时候，往往是奔着自己能力上限去的。同样一个汽车销售员（Dealer）在给你洗脑做工作，你手上有钱和没钱的时候效果是不一样的。有钱往往就管不住自己，抵挡不了销售员的甜言蜜语。

CN¥500,000 was converted into around US$70,000. I wired this sum in two transactions back to the U.S. but I still could not prevent the popsicle from melting. My old car crashed and I needed to buy a new one. When you had much money at hand, especially just after making a huge profit, your intuition was to reward yourself and buy a more expensive car. When people are purchasing an expensive commodity, for example, one's own residential home and cars, they have a tendency to max out their ability. Similarly, when a car dealer is trying to brainwash you, the effect of the brainwashing is different between times when you have money and do not have money with you. When you have money, you cannot resist the picture painted by the salesperson.

因为人的内心深处多多少少都是想对自己好一些，特别是当你衣食无忧的时候。于是汇过来的这 7 万美元并没有全部用来抄底买房子。而是当场融化了一大块，去买了一个好车。显然当时车不是这笔钱最应该去的地方。同样一笔钱如果当时按照我的计划用在投资上，几年之后就会变成十辆车。当然你也可以反过来说，如果这笔钱用于投资，事实的结果是锁在不动产里，我可能一直都享受不到一辆好一点的车。

This is because deep inside each of us, we would like to treat ourselves better, especially during times when you do not have to worry about the expenses of your daily necessities. Therefore, I did not use the entire sum of the US$70,000 that I wired from China to buy the dips in the real estate market. A big part of my popsicle melted because I used the money to buy a nice car. Obviously, buying a car was not the most ideal place to which my money should go because if I had used that amount of money for investing, it would have bought me ten cars in a few years' time. Of course, you can also say that the opposite is true too because if I had indeed used that sum of money for investing, what would actually have happened was that the money was locked in immovable property and I could not have enjoyed driving a nice car.

汇回美国的现金在融化，留在中国的现金也在融化之中。一个亲戚找我们借钱，因为他想买一个房子。当一个人借钱，最直接能够想到的就是最近刚卖了房子的人，因为他们手上有大量现金。

The money I wired back to the U.S. was also melting and the money that remained in China was melting too. A relative of mine who was looking to buy a house contacted me and would like to borrow some money from me. When a person is trying to borrow money, the most obvious candidate of lender is those who have recently sold their house because these people will have a large amount of cash at hand.

虽然我明明知道我是有本事把这借出的这40万人民币几年就变成400万人民币。但是亲情很多时候是不讲道理也是没有办法拒绝的。人活在世上，各种情感关系交织在一起，不是所有属于你的钱你都可以完全做到100%控制的。至少家庭的财务需要夫妻双方共同决定。该借出的钱还是要借。借出了40万人民币，我的冰棍又少了一大块。剩下的钱已经不多了。

Although it was very clear to me that I was able to turn the CN¥400,000 that I lent to my relative to CN¥4 million in a few years' time but family is not all about rational decision-making and I find it very difficult to say no to my family. Our life journeys on Earth are intertwined with different emotions, feelings, and relationships. It is not possible to exercise 100% control over all your money. This is at least true for those who have a family of their own who need to make joint decisions on household budget and finance with their significant other. Therefore, this CN¥400,000 was a sum that I should lend to my relative. After this, another big part of my popsicle melted and I did not have much money left.

读者这个时候可能会意识到，这些冰棍的融化现象在你的 Excel 表上是永远无法显示出来的。人并不是机器，没有办法冰冷地可以按照公式计算去完成计划。

You may have realized at this point that the changes in how your popsicle melts cannot be shown in an Excel spreadsheet. This is because humans are not machines. Our lives cannot be fully captured or planned by formulas and calculations.

05 一个变四个

05 Turning One into Four

像每个焦虑的孩子需要尽快吃光阳光下的冰棍一样。2009 年底的时候，我无论如何要把这些钱投出去。当时我在上海看中的是浦东陆家嘴世纪大道一带的老公房。就是以前在 80 年代，上海市为了急切解决住房短缺，大批量用预制板建造了面积比较小的公寓楼。

Just like how every anxious kid was trying to finish his or her popsicle under the sun, I was determined to invest my money at all costs at the end of 2009. At that time, I was interested in buying those old public housing units along Century Avenue in Luijiazui in Pudong. These houses were built in the 1980s when the municipal government was trying to solve the housing shortage by mass building small-area apartments using precast concrete slabs.

2009 年的时候，浦西传统的好学区已经开始被浦东的好学区超越。道理很简单，浦东来的是全国各地最聪明、最能折腾的一些人。作为新移民，他们的后代，勤劳而有压力，所以学习成绩自然比浦西的那些传统的上海人要好。就像美国最有成就的人往往是第二代或者第 1.5 代移民一样。

In 2009, the traditional elite school district in Puxi was being outperformed by a great school district in Pudong. The reason behind this was simple. Pudong was home to the most intelligent and hardworking people in China. As the offspring of new immigrants, the students were under great pressure to study well and be diligent, so the academic performance of these students outshone that of local Shanghainese. The same is true in the U.S. that the most successful people are often the second or 1.5 generation of immigrants.

当时那一带的房子一套大概是 60 万元人民币左右。单价是每平米 2 万元人民币。这些老公房面积狭小，一般是 30 平米。小户型的房子比较抢手，因为大家买这些房子的主要目的是挂靠上学指标。这样的小户型房子流动性比较强，变现快，容易出租。我算了一下手上尚未融化的冰棍，利用贷款，剩下的钱做首付可以一下子买四套这样的房子。

At that time, the average price of a residential unit in that neighborhood was around CN¥600,000. The price per square meter was CN¥20,000. These old public housing units had a small floor area of around 30 square meters. Small houses were very popular in the market because people bought this house to enroll their children in good schools. The mobility of these small houses was relatively high and it was easy to rent them out and sell. I made a calculation of the popsicle that had not melted yet. If I used the remaining money as a down payment and applied for loans, I could buy four old public housing units.

购买四套总价 300 万左右。这样可以把我的杠杆水平重新提升回 60% 以上。另外租金和房贷基本打平。当时上海按照户籍指标的限购政策还没有出台。你可以一下子登记拥有多少套住房都没有问题。但是贷款审查已经开始变得严格，银行不太会批准你四个房屋贷款。

The total price of buying four units was around CN¥3 million. In this way, I could increase my leverage back to above 60%. Furthermore, the total rental income would be more or less equal to the mortgage payments. At that time, the government had not yet restricted the purchasing of houses based on *hukou*. You could register and own as many houses as you desired. However, the credit approval process had become stricter and it was unlikely that the bank would approve all four mortgages.

所以我找了中介咨询。他说唯一的办法就是你四套一起买。不同的银行同时收到四个贷款，它们之间是彼此不通气的。一起做贷款可以绕开银行审批的问题。于是这就成了我的计划，一次买四套。我把这一个任务委托给了我的好同学，然后我自己就赶着回美国了。我每次去中国只能是出差，经常只有 1-2 天的时间，没有办法长时间的逗留。

Therefore, I reached out to an agent for a consultation. He told me that the only way was to buy all four units in one go. When several banks received four mortgage applications at the same time, they would not exchange their information with each other. In this way, making four applications at the same time could help me get around the approval requirement. This was how I decided on my investment plan to purchase four units. I delegated this task to a classmate of mine and then I rushed back to the U.S. Every time when I went to China, I was on a business trip that I only had 1-2 days so I could not stay there for too long.

我的同学过几天给我打电话，说你要买的房子没有那么多，目前只找到 2 个合适的。于是这个事情就耽搁了下来。因为永远都没有办法凑足四套一起买，不知不觉就又拖了大半年过去。拖来拖去的另外一个原因是我自己在犹豫。当时我手上有的钱是 100 多万，我在北京也看中了顺义的一套联排别墅，手上的钱也够买下。但是出于各种原因也是没有买。期间我还看中了一套将近 200 平米的上海人民广场的公寓。我可以买下是因为当时中国的外资银行给外籍人士有特别优厚的贷款条件，只是手续很复杂。

My classmate called me several days after, telling me that there were not enough units available for sale and he could only find 2 suitable units. This was how I started to procrastinate this investment plan. Since I was never able to find four suitable units in one go, I procrastinated executing my plan for six months. The other reason for my procrastination was that I was indecisive. At that time, I had more than CN¥1 million cash at hand and I had my eye on a townhouse in Shunyi in Beijing. I could buy it with the money I had but because of different reasons, I did not do so in the end. During this process, I was also interested in a condominium unit of around 200 square meters in People's Square in Shanghai. The reason why I could buy it was that foreign banks in China offered attractive conditions of loans for foreigners but these loans involved complicated procedures.

可是机会就在我的权衡、等待、凑足四套房子一起买中悄悄地溜走。当时我对后市的市场走向也看不清。我总感觉下跌可能要持续一阵子，所以内心深处可能也是犹犹豫豫的。时间在流逝，冰棍也在融化。我依然没有办法把手上的钱花出去。

However, opportunities slipped away when I was meditating, waiting, and looking for four suitable units. At that time, I was not sure about the imminent market trend. I was feeling that the decline might last for a while so I was indecisive deep inside. Even though the clock was ticking and my popsicle was melting, I still could not find a suitable outlet for my money.

到了 2009 年 9 月份。也许是上帝厌烦了我的犹豫。只听见"轰"的一声巨响，中国政府 4 万亿刺激计划就来了。巨响之后，中国房价开始暴涨了。

In September 2009, perhaps God could not tolerate my indecisiveness anymore. Bang! The Chinese government had introduced a stimulus plan of CN¥4 trillion. After this big bang, China's property prices have begun to soar.

06 抢房

06 Competing for Houses

2009 年，随着金融危机的加深，全世界都开始量化宽松政策，各国纷纷出台各种刺激计划。美国的量化宽松政策似乎对市场的影响很缓慢。中国作为计划经济强势政府的国家，刺激政策是迅猛、有效和立竿见影的。

In 2009, as the financial crisis escalated, governments around the world had started their quantitative easing policy and introduced various stimulus programs. But it seemed that the quantitative easing policy by the U.S. government had slow effects on the market. As an aggressive government that believed in a planned economy, the stimulus policy of the Chinese government was the most immediate, effective, and efficient.

2009 年 9 月份，中央一不做二不休来了一个 4 万亿的刺激计划。各级当地政府纷纷跟进，中央政府敞开印钱，地方政府敞开花钱。这样的好事哪个官员不愿意干呢，梦里都会笑醒。2009 年底据说各种平台机构累计合在一起的刺激经济资金达到了三十几万亿。

How did the Chinese central government react to the financial crisis in September 2009? In for a penny, in for a pound. It introduced a stimulus plan of CN¥4 trillion. Different levels of local governments were all joining the game: the central government was busy printing money and the local governments were busy spending money. What kind of government officials would not be willing to participate in such a good deal? I bet that the officials would laugh in their sleep. It was said that the aggregate of capital that was used to stimulate the economy on all platforms and by all organizations exceeded CN¥30 trillion.

量化宽松其实就是信贷敞开了发钱。在通货膨胀下，最直接的受益者就是离钱比较近的那些人。通货膨胀本身并不会消灭财富。通货膨胀的主要后果就是把 A 的钱神不知鬼不觉地掠夺到 B 的口袋里。离新发货币最远的就是 A，最先拿到新发货币的就是 B。第一个拿到钱的人，在物价没有涨的时候，他们有足够多的机会买进廉价资产。最后一个拿到新发货币的人，等待钱流通到他手里，资产价格已经上涨完毕，他原来的钱就缩水了。

To put it simply, quantitative easing is an expansion of credits and issuing money. In times of inflation, the most direct beneficiaries are those closer to money. Inflation by itself will not destroy wealth. The main consequence of inflation is that A's money will be robbed and moved to B's pockets without anyone realizing it. A is farthest to the newly issued money and B is the closest. The person who gets the money first has more than enough chances to purchase cheap assets before the price level increases. After the newly-issued money circulates to the last person who receives it, the prices of different assets have already increased, meaning that this last person's wealth has diminished.

那年中国房价的上涨就是符合这样一个趋势，我印象中 2009 年那一轮的房价开始上涨是来自于北京，因为那里离刺激计划新发货币最近。四万亿之后，北京几乎在 1-2 个月的时间里房价蹭地一下，涨了 50%左右。

The increase in China's property prices in that year is in line with this trend. In my memory, property prices first started increasing in Beijing in 2009. This was because Beijing was the closest to the stimulus plan and newly-issued currency. After the CN¥4 trillion, Beijing's property prices surged by 50% in 1-2 months' time.

我在北京的亲戚告诉我，他说你看到的所有房子都没有了。房价一下子涨了很多。我问哪里涨了？是城里还是外围？他说都涨了，所有的地方都涨了，所有的房子也都没有了。

A relative of mine who was based in Beijing told me that the houses I was interested in were all gone now and the property prices had skyrocketed in a short period of time. I asked him about the locations that witnessed the growth. Did the property prices of the city center grow or those on the city's outskirts. He replied me that the property prices of all neighborhoods were up. Everywhere in Beijing was more expensive now and all houses were gone.

北京著名的房产开发商潘 XX，在一个采访中，描述了他当时看到的一幅惊人的画面。就是一个楼盘在开盘的时候因为有太多人过来买房子，不但是挤坏了门，而且半个小时全部卖光。有人因为买不到房子，在售楼处现场哭泣。不是简单的哭泣，而是号啕大哭。

During an interview, a famous Beijing land developer, Mr. Pang, had described a shocking scene that he witnessed. When a development project was open for sale, the scene was crowded with people who squeezed the doors and bought all the units in half an hour. Some people did not get a unit so they burst into tears. This was not just "the usual crying" but they were crying their eyes out.

潘 XX 观察了一下那几个号啕大哭的妇女，让他感到惊讶的那些人穿着和言谈，一点都不像底层低收入阶层，甚至有的人是开着豪车而来。显然她们不是因为刚需满足不了，没法结婚或者没地方居住而号啕大哭。他感觉这些人大哭最大的原因是她们觉得自己错过了千载难逢的上车机会，是因为错过了赚钱的机会而哭泣。

Mr. Pang made an observation of the women who were crying their eyes out. What made him feel shocked was that judging from the demeanor and appearances of these people, it did not seem that they belonged to the lower class with a low income. Some of them drove a luxury car to the sales center. Therefore, they did not cry because they could not satisfy their craving for marriage or a place to live in. Mr. Pang felt that the main reason why people were crying their eyes out was that they thought they missed a once-in-a-blue-moon opportunity to buy real property and to make a fortune.

我看到这个新闻吓了我一身汗。根据过去的经验上海和北京是此起彼伏的。这次上海比北京稍微慢一点。但是疯狂的热情很快就会传递到上海。读者感兴趣研究历史的话可以看看深圳、上海、北京三地的房价每次暴涨的特征。全国性暴涨每次都是某一个一线城市率先发难，半年一年后传播到其他两个城市。2004 年领涨的是上海，2009 年是北京，2016 年是深圳。你只需要关注新闻，就能够比其他当地人抢得先机。

Hearing this news, I was so shocked that I was soaked in cold sweats. Based on my past experience, Shanghai and Beijing have synced markets even though the market reaction in Shanghai is slower. But the craze would spread to Shanghai soon. For those of you who are interested in studying history, you can take a look at the pattern in Shenzhen, Shanghai, and Beijing when the property prices skyrocketed. Every time when there was a national surge, it was triggered by a certain tier-one city. After six months to one year, the surge would spread to the other two cities. In 2004, Shanghai led the surge; in 2009, Beijing; in 2016, Shenzhen. All you need to do is to follow the news and you will be able to find good investment opportunities before other locals.

我连夜打电话给我同学了解上海的房价。他回答不是很清楚。大部分人不会每天盯着中介问房价。当时中国房地产有很多论坛，人们还可以基本畅所欲言。我晚上也经常去那些论坛上逛一逛，看一看市场的行情。

I immediately phoned my classmate to ask him about property prices in Shanghai that night. He told me that he was not very sure about the recent trend. Most people would not ask the real estate agent about property prices every single day. At that time, there were many forums on China's real estate market on the internet on which people could freely express their opinions. At night, I was a frequent visitor to these forums to take a look at the market trend.

不看不知道，一看不得了。市场的行情就是我卖掉的那个房子已经涨回了我卖出的价格，而且比我卖出的价格还要再稍微高一点。这是一个令人恐怖的消息，就是你以为你聪明摸到了最高点，占了便宜，结果发现自己一脚踏空。

I would not know what was happening in the market if I had not visited these forums. But when I did take a closer look, I was flabbergasted. The market trend was that the house that I had previously sold soared to the price at which I sold it and slightly exceeded it. This was a piece of terrifying news. Just when you are thinking that you are smart and have made a profit by selling your house at the highest point, you realize you completely missed it.

不单是一脚踏空，我的那根取出来的冰棍还融化了一半。

Not only did I completely miss it, but half of the popsicle that I took out from the freezer had also melted.

所以我没有什么选择，我像热锅上的蚂蚁一样，需要尽快地把手上的现金变成房子。在美国的钱我已经无能为力了，因为美国的市场可能还需要再跌一段时间。中国那边已经很明显触底反弹了。正好出于公务我来到上海。我来到浦东那个我原先计划买入四套的小区，毫不犹豫地把市面上的每一个房子都给了一个 offer。

Therefore, I did not have many choices. I was like ants on a hot griddle. I needed to hurry and convert my cash at hand into houses. There was nothing I could really do with my money in the U.S. because it would take a while before the U.S. market reached its bottom. In contrast, the Chinese market was obviously bouncing from its bottom. At that time, I was on a business trip in Shanghai. I went to the neighborhood where I was planning to purchase four houses. I did not hesitate and I gave an offer to every single listing in the market.

那位中介小哥看到我这么豪爽高兴坏了。他觉得我是一个土大款，怎么一下子要买这么多房子。我懒得和他废话，就说这里可能要拆迁了，我想多买点。他听了认真地对店铺里的其他客户大声喊"大家赶紧买，这里要拆迁了。"

The real estate agent was thrilled by my generosity. He was thinking that I was a tycoon who needed to buy so many houses in one go. I did not even bother to tell him much about my investment plan. Instead, I was telling him that that neighborhood might soon be appropriated by the government and I wanted to stock up.[8] After listening to my explanation, he told all the other customers in the store in a very serious tone that they should hurry because the land would soon be appropriated.

---

[8] In China, whenever a piece of land is being appropriated, the landowners often receive a very attractive compensation offer.

其实我哪里有什么拆迁的小道消息。不过是当时人困马乏随口的搪塞。不过我后来想想，那些人听到我这样的恫吓也许能帮他们下决心买房，也算是帮了他们一把。对于我来说，赚钱和吃饭一样，一个人赚钱不如看到更多人一起赚钱更有意思。看见其他人挣钱我也开心。这大约也是我这么多年一直在投资理财论坛上笔耕不断的一部分动力吧。

In fact, I knew nothing about the government's land appropriation plan. It was just an excuse. But in retrospect, my intimidating claim might have helped other customers make up their mind and nudged them in the right direction of buying a house. As for me, making money is like having dinner. The more people joining the feast, the merrier. I am happy to see others making a profit. This is probably another motivating factor behind my diligent posting on the investment and wealth management forum.

我的出价没有人接受，因为大家都在抢房子。后来我跟中介说我只有钱买一个或者是两个。那边有两种主流户型。三十平米的 A 户型和七十平米的 B 户型。如果是 A 户型我可以买两个。如果是 B 户型，我的钱只能买一个。中介小哥知道我不是土豪大款热情瞬间掉了一半。

No one was willing to accept my offer because everyone was competing for houses. Later, I told the real estate agent that I could only afford to buy one or two houses. There were two main layouts in that housing estate, Type A and Type B. Type A was about 30 square meters and Type B 70 square meters. For Type A, I could buy two units. However, I could only afford one Type B unit. After knowing that I was not some tycoon, the real estate agent was much less enthusiastic.

不久，有人同意卖给我一个 A 户型的房子。我毫不犹豫地就签了合同付了一万元定金。可是还没高兴一分钟，付完定金我马上就后悔了。

Not long after that, someone was willing to sell me a Type A unit. Without any hesitation, I signed the agreement and paid CN¥10,000 as a deposit. I was overwhelmed with joy the minute I signed the contract and then I was feeling remorse.

因为我又陷入了两难的境地，到底是买还是不买呢？如果不买可能会错过。如果买，又没有办法凑两套或者更多一起去办贷款。因为需要一起买才行。只买这一套 A 户型的小房子会变得可惜，上海当时已经出台了贷款的限购政策。市面上已经出现了"房票"这样的新鲜词汇。房票就像曾经的计划经济时期的副食品卷一样。"房票"用了就没了。

I was feeling remorse because I realized I was caught in a dilemma: should I proceed and close the deal? On the one hand, if I did not buy this unit, I might miss the opportunity. On the other hand, if I bought this unit, there was no way for me to gather two more units for my loan applications. The reason for this was, as mentioned earlier, the stricter loan requirement. But if I could only buy one Type A unit, this would be a pity because the Shanghai government had already introduced a policy to limit the number of properties an individual could buy on loans. New phrases such as "house ticket" had already emerged in the market. House tickets were like ration coupons back in the days of a planned economy. Once you used your tickets, you could not get any more.

卖家催的急，因为等不到第二套房子成交，这个 A 户型的房子在我付了定金之后，只能硬生生地退了回去。 这是我这么多年的唯一一次定金损失。又等了几日，终于有一个 B 户型的房子出来了。几经周折终于把它买了下来。这次虽然有一个小的损失，但不管怎么说，我还是买回了这里的房子。

The seller was pressing me to proceed with the transaction. However, I was still looking for a second unit. As a result, even though I had already paid a deposit for the Type A unit, I withdrew my offer and forwent the deposit. This is the only time I lost my deposit. After a few days of waiting, I finally found a Type B unit listing. After all the trouble, I finally purchased a Type B unit. Even though I did incur a minor loss in the process, I accomplished my goal of buying a house in that neighborhood.

读者读我这些故事的时候，可能因为年代的原因，对当时的财富和价格没有直觉的感受，会质疑我，觉得我这么辛辛苦苦地折腾到底值得么？

Those of you who are reading this may have vague ideas about the wealth level and price level at that time. Therefore, you may be doubting my decisions. Was it worth all my hard work?

我可以简单告诉大家一下一些价格的比对。被我卖掉的那个房子，我买入的时候差不多是 10,000 一平米，总价 100 万人民币。我卖出的时候是 23,000 一平米，总价 230 万人民币。我写这本书的时候，现在那个小区是 10 万一平米，总价 1000 万人民币。如果当时不进行置换，我在这个房子拥有的净值差不多是 1000 万人民币的样子。按照中国的年薪 20 万人民币计算，差不多相当于 50 年的全部工资，一个大学教育程度的工程师一辈子的收入。即使按照美国一个毕业生 6 万美元的税后收入，这个房子的净值也差不多将是美国大学教育程度工作人员 25 年的全部税后收入。

I would like to give you a brief idea of the comparisons of prices. In relation to the second investment property that I bought in China, I purchased it at about CN¥10,000 per square meter at a total price of CN¥1 million. I later sold it at CN¥23,000 per square meter at a total price of CN¥2.3 million. As of the time I am writing this book, that house can be sold for CN¥100,000 per square meter at a total price of CN¥10 million. If I had not changed my holding of properties, my net equity of owning this house would have been about CN¥10 million which is a Chinese worker's 50 years of salaries. This is the total income a university-educated engineer can earn over his or her entire working life in China. Even if we adopt the U.S. standard that a graduate has an after-tax income of US$60,000, the equity of this house will be equal to the total income of a university-educated worker earns in 25 years.

你瞧我根据我的勤快人理财法，按照 Excel 表格的计算执行投资计划，弄的一圈儿落得什么好了？原本 100 平米的房子被我变成了 70 平米的房子。本来不用折腾就是 1000 万人民币的资产，被我辛辛苦苦一下之后变成了 700 万人民币。

As you can see, I was trying to implement my Investment Strategies for Diligent People based on the calculations I had done in my Excel spreadsheet. What was the outcome? I had converted a 100-square-meter house into a 70-square-meter one. I could have just sat there and had an asset worth CN¥10 million in China. The irony is that despite my hard work, my asset is now worth CN¥7 million only.

这个教训很深刻，不动产不动产恒心一条就是要不动。买卖过程越少越好。你在 Excel 表上很多因素难以考虑。你能考虑到有人会来找你借钱吗？你能考虑到朝令夕改的限购政策么？你能考虑外汇突然被管制了吗？你能考虑到你内心软弱，没顶住销售员的三寸不烂之舌么？

I have learned this lesson the hard way. The rule of thumb in real estate investing is that you should not move your immovable property. The fewer the transactions, the better. An Excel spreadsheet cannot help you take into account any external factors. Are you able to consider that someone may borrow money from you? Are you able to consider that the government will frequently introduce different policies to limit property purchases? Are you able to consider that there will be restrictions on foreign exchange? Are you able to consider that you may be easily swayed by the salesperson's speech?

根据我后来的经验，勤快人理财法最好的办法还是再融资贷款。想办法把钱借出来，最好不要买卖，每次买卖都是伤害。

Based on my subsequent experiences, the best way to apply Investment Strategies for Diligent People is through refinancing. You have to try your best to borrow money and avoid selling and buying. A transaction may damage your portfolio.

买完那个 70 平米的房子，我手上还有 20 几万人民币。连个最小的房子也买不起了。正当我犯愁的时候。一个同学介绍我参与了当时的另外一个房产投资。这是一个游走在金融管理灰色地带的房地产集资项目。按照规定开发商在建筑封顶之前，是不可以卖房子的。这个开发商胆子大，他用集资的方式来把图纸上的房子先卖掉。然后用集资款再去盖房子。按理说这是违法行为，风险比较大。但是我觉得房价飙升的时候，开发商跑路的可能性很小。于是把剩下的钱都投了进去。果不其然，开发商信守承诺，准时交房。

After buying that 70-square-meter unit, I only had around CN¥200,000 left so I could not even afford the smallest house. When I was worried about this, a classmate of mine introduced me to another real estate development project. This project was a fundraising project that lay in the gray area of financial regulations. According to regulations, land developers shall not sell the units before the construction was completed. But this land developer was bold in that he was trying to sell the houses that were on the architectural drawings by way of fundraising and then began the construction after getting the funds. Strictly speaking, this was not legal and the risk involved was relatively high. However, I was of the view that during times of skyrocketing property prices, the likelihood of land developers defaulting was very small so I invested my remaining money into this project. As predicted, the land developer adhered to its contractual obligations and delivered the houses in time.

这一轮下来，我的一个房子变四个房子的勤快人理财计划没有实现。建筑平米数略有提高，差不多是一个房子变成了 1.5 个房子的样子。

After this round of investing, I failed to achieve my "turning one house into four" goal in my Investment Strategies for Diligent People. But I was successful in increasing the total floor areas of my investments and I turned one house into 1.5 houses.

07 持续高涨的房市
07 A Long Bull Market in Real Estate

这个阶段我一方面在中国市场上交易，一方面整理自己的思路，写了一些博客。2009 年秋天，中国市场价格暴涨的时候。我连续写了三篇题为"上海房价朝不可思议的高度奔去"的博客。

At this stage, while I was trading in the Chinese market, I was also organizing my thoughts and writing some blog posts. In the fall of 2009, when the Chinese market soared, I wrote three articles titled "The Sky's the Limit for Shanghai's Soaring Property Prices."

上海房价朝不可思议的高度奔去(2009 年 9 月 17 日)

The Sky's the Limit for Shanghai's Soaring Property Prices (September 17, 2009)

by Bayfamily

如果一个人祖上没有什么财产继承，赚的钱从来都是你的零头，一没西门庆的本事，二没副业。但是有一天你突然发现他比你有钱。你相信吗？

Let's say there is this person who does not inherit any assets from his or her ancestors who is not Ximeng Qing[9] and does not own any business himself or herself and he or she is earning one-tenth or even only 1% of your income. But what if one day you realize that he or she is much wealthier than you are? Will you believe it?

你可能觉得奇怪。如同我们公司的领导突然发现唯命是从的女秘书比他还有钱。但我相信，因为财富不是加减法。财富是会走路的。而且这是真真实实发生的。

Your first reaction may well be that you are bewildered. An analogy is that a high-ranking officer at our company has suddenly discovered that his obedient female secretary is richer than him. But I believe that the accumulation of wealth is not about addition and subtraction. Money walks. This is what is happening in reality.

本轮的政府刺激计划结束后。中国的房价几乎让所有人跌破眼镜（包括我自己），转身回头，涨幅凶猛。

---

[9] Ximeng Qing is a fictional Chinese Song dynasty merchant. He is a successful businessman but is portrayed as a lascivious and immoral man.

After this round of the government's economic stimulus plan, China's property prices were completely out of everyone's expectations, myself included. The property prices had a sharp reversal and were surging in leaps and bounds.

在上海，不但是豪宅屡创新高。比如众目昭彰的浦东星河湾。6 万元一平方米的高价。一个上午立刻被席卷而空。普通住宅也一样。上海即使最最远郊的地方，几乎再也找不到 1 万元一平米以下的楼盘了。

In Shanghai, the prices of both luxurious housing and affordable residential properties were hitting record highs. For example, even though the high-profile Chateau Star River in Pudong was selling at a high price of CN¥60,000 per square meter, all units were sold out in one morning. The same was also true of other more affordable housing estates. You would not be able to find any houses that were selling at below CN¥10,000 even in the most remote area of Shanghai's countryside.

本轮调整结束后。我们看看中国对美国的房产财富总价水平。

After this round of adjustments, let us take a look at the aggregate price level of wealth represented by real estate in China versus that in the U.S.

上海：住宅总面积大约在 4—5 亿平方米之间。按照统计数据，目前上海均价为 1 万五一平米。我初步估算了一下。当前上海住宅地产的总价大约是 1 万亿美元。

Shanghai: The total floor area of residential housing is around 400 to 500 million square meters. According to statistics, the current average price is CN¥15,000 per square meter in Shanghai. Based on my rough calculations, the aggregate value of residential properties in Shanghai is worth around US$1 trillion.

加州：加州的住宅总价格大约也是 1 万亿美元左右。上海的房地产总价已经和加州相当。尽管加州的人口比上海多出将近一千万，尽管加州的人均 GDP 是上海的 4 倍。

California: The total price of residential properties in California is also around US$1 trillion which is equal to that in Shanghai even though California's population is 10 million more than Shanghai's and its GDP per capita is four times that of Shanghai.

222

中国：根据国家统计局的数据显示，2008 年底城市住宅的总建筑面积约为 175.14 亿平方米。再来看目前的房价水平，今年以来，住房累计销售额 2.35 万亿元，除以今年累计销售面积 4.94 亿平方米，全国平均房价约为 4754 元/平米。2008 年全年，全国商品房销售面积 6.21 亿平方米，销售金额为 2.4 亿元，销售单价 3870 元。按年头和年尾的均值计算，全国住宅每平米价格为 4312 元。结合前面所计算出来的城市住宅总建筑面积 175.14 亿平方米，可以得出全国城市住房总价值约为 75.5 万亿元。

China: According to the statistics released by the National Bureau of Statistics of China, the aggregate construction floor area of residential properties of cities was approximately 17.514 billion square meters at the end of 2008. If we look at the current level of house prices, the accumulated sales this year as of September is CN¥2.35 trillion. Dividing this number by 494 million square meters which are the accumulated sales in terms of floor area, the country's average price level is around CN¥4,754 per square meter. Multiplying CN¥4,754 by the aggregate construction floor of residential cities of 17.514 billion square meters, we can know that the aggregate value of residential properties in China is worth around CN¥75.5 billion.

美国：全美的住房总价在 11 万亿美元左右。按照可比汇率推算，和中国相当。美国 2009 年的 GDP 是中国的 4 倍不到一点。

The U.S.: The aggregate value of residential properties in the U.S. is around US$11 billion which is equal to that in China after applying the exchange rate. In 2009, the U.S. GDP was shy of four times that of China.

比完了总价，再比人均。全国的人均没有意义，人人都知道美国比中国富裕。但就上海而言，如果按照全市 500 万家庭计算，平均家庭净资产大约是 20 万美元左右。这里面可不只是所谓的精英阶层，包括了下岗工人，保姆，和流动的民工人口。即使这样，上海的平均家庭净资产恐怕一点都不输给美国的华人。美国人家庭净中位数资产是 15 万美元左右。华人稍稍高一些，但是应该没有超过 20 万美元。你瞧瞧，当年富裕象征的美籍华人们，和中国上海的普通人家已经没有什么区别了。这剧烈的变化，几乎就是在最近十年内完成的。

After comparing the total price, let us do a per capita comparison. A national per capita comparison is meaningless because it is common knowledge that the U.S. is more affluent than China. However, if we examine the situation in Shanghai which has a total of 5 million households, the net worth of the average household is around US$200,000. The calculation of this number does not only include the elites in society but also includes laid-off workers, nannies, and mobile migrant workers. Even so, the net worth of the average household in Shanghai is not outshone by their Chinese American counterparts. The median net worth of the average U.S. household is around US$150,000. Even though Chinese American households have a slightly higher net worth than this number, the number is still below US$200,000. As you can see, Chinese Americans who used to be the epitome of affluence are no different from ordinary families in Shanghai. This drastic change took place in the last decade or so.

上海的房价，无论从哪一个指标上来看，都是有泡沫的迹象。比如，租售比，房子的总价和每月的房租比，在很多地方已经超过了 500:1。即使是老公房，租售比也达到了 300:1 左右。如果是投资股票，好比是 PE ratio 已经达到了 25 倍到 40 倍之间。按照发达国家的经验，租价比的畸形高位，最终会把房价拉下来。

No matter which indicator is used, it is clear that the real estate market in Shanghai at its current price level shows signs of a bubble. An example of such an indicator is the gross rental yield which is the annual rent as a percentage of the purchase price or value of a property.

是不是可以得出一个简单的结论说，上海和中国的房价过高了，有待调整，泡沫马上会崩溃呢？

Does this mean that we can then jump to a simple conclusion that the property prices in Shanghai and China are too high, in need of price adjustments and so the bubble will soon burst?

上海房价朝不可思议的高度奔去（2）（2009 年 9 月 22 日）

The Sky's the Limit for Shanghai's Soaring Property Prices (2) (September 22, 2009)

by Bayfamily

认为上海和中国的房价过高了已是严重泡沫，马上会崩溃的理论从来都是屡见不鲜。2002 年，赫赫有名的谢 X 忠先生就持这样的观点，看空楼市。今天回头看看非常可笑，这样的结论会害死很多人。

Claims that the property prices in Shanghai and China are so high that a colossal asset bubble has already formed and that the real estate market will soon crash are ubiquitous. In 2002, the famous Mr. Xie Xzhong also held these points of view. He was bearish on the property market. In retrospect, these conclusions were ridiculous and they would harm many people.

我记得八年前，上海的房价刚刚起步的时候。美国的时代周刊撰文，说房价在几个月的时间里面上涨 50％，极其不正常，泡沫马上要破灭。当时有无数的主流经济评论人员持同样的观点。可惜只有温州这些不信邪，没读多少书的家伙，勇敢买进，连炒十年，今天成了大的赢家。

I remember that eight years ago, Shanghai's property prices were just beginning to rise. An article in Time Magazine argued that it was highly unusual that the property prices had surged 50% in a few months so the bubble was about to burst. Numerous mainstream economic commentators subscribed to the same point of view. However, some contrarians in Wenzhou, China who, albeit not very educated, are bold enough to keep buying in these ten years and have become the biggest winners today.

过去十年上海的房价一路高歌猛进。中间虽有小的调整，但几乎是笔直向上的。浦东的老公房涨幅最大，几乎涨了 10-15 倍以上。高档楼盘稍差，但是 5－8 倍也是有的。十年前，湾区的双职工，老公房可以在上海头十套，豪宅除了老洋房以外，几乎都可以头得起，今天，渐渐的一套都舍不得头不起了。豪宅，渐渐的只是富人的游戏。美国的工薪阶层，看着里面的零，恐怕都数不清。

Over the past decade, Shanghai's property prices have been surging. Despite some minor adjustments during the process, it is almost a straight upward curve. Old public housing units in Pudong saw the biggest rise with a 10-fold to 15-fold increase. The performance of high-end properties was slightly worse but still had a 5-fold to 8-fold increase. A decade ago, a double-income family in the Bay Area could afford to buy any other luxurious properties except old villa or ten public housing units in Shanghai. Today, they cannot afford to buy even one house in Shanghai. Luxurious properties are becoming a rich person's game. The U.S. wage earners cannot even count the zeros in this game.

上海的房价，按照通常的房地产理论都是有泡沫的迹象。但是泡沫不见得就会破，泡沫会持续很长一段时间，甚至会被吹到不可思议的程度再破。这中间的过程有可能是几年，也可能是十几年。

That Shanghai's property prices are showing signs of a bubble according to the usual real estate theories does not mean that the bubble will soon burst. In fact, the bubble may well persist for a very long time or even burst at an unbelievably high level. It may take several years or more than a decade for the bubble to eventually burst.

我认为上海房价短期内还会继续上升的理由有这么几个：

The reasons why I think Shanghai's property prices will continue to rise in the short term are as follows:

普通的租售比理论不成立。在中国，老百姓几乎是被逼着买房子的。自己的房子和租来的房子在功能是不可同日而语的。比如，没有房子，没有办法落户口。没有办法落户口，集体户口的年轻人，不能生孩子，孩子无法正常上学。没有户口本，生活中到处都是不便。豪宅也许可以靠租售比计算房地产的合理价格。穷人家的刚性需求是硬碰硬的，就是房价涨到天上，老百姓也要买。

The usual theory of gross rental yield cannot be established on the facts. In China, almost every citizen is forced to buy a house. The functions of a self-owned house and a house you rent cannot be compared. For example, without a self-owned house, one cannot register an individual *hukou* in China. Without an individual *hukou*, those young people with a collective *hukou* account will not be able to have children.[10] Their children cannot attend schools. Without an individual *hukou*, life is very difficult. Perhaps one can still use the gross rental yield to calculate the reasonable price range of luxurious properties. However, the less well-off families have a rigid or more inelastic demand for commercial housing. Even if the house prices have touched the sky, ordinary citizens will still be willing to buy a house.

长期的低利率。中国现行的利率政策很像 2001 年美国格林斯潘时期的政策。长期的低利率会刺激地产价格恶性膨胀。目前上海外国人购房的商业贷款只有 3-4% 的利息。上海的房价相对全国而言，并不是很高。而且目前为止，全国和上海北京房价的联动性很强。要涨大家涨，要跌大家跌。显示了宏观基本面是涨跌的控制因素，而不是某个城市的地域特征。

Another factor is a persistently low-interest rate environment. China's current interest rate policy is similar to that of the U.S. in its Greenspan's era in 2001. A persistently low-interest rate environment will lead to hyperinflation in property prices. The current interest rate of commercial loans for foreign house buyers in Shanghai is around 3-4%. Shanghai's property prices are not very high when compared to other regions in the country. Furthermore, the property prices in the entire country, Beijing, and Shanghai are highly-linked in that they all rise and drop simultaneously. This shows that fundamental factors and macroeconomics instead of certain geographical characteristics of a city are the controlling factors of whether property prices will go up or down.

---

[10] In China, pregnant women need to apply for a "Birth Approval Certificate" without which they cannot give birth to their baby in a hospital. The prerequisite for applying for this certificate is a *hukou*.

中长期的风险有这么几个：如果光看土地的供应和新房盖的速度。上海和北京一样是没有天然的地理限制的，城市可以无限扩张。房价最终会下来才是。可是目前为止人口的增长总是比房子的供应要高一步。但是人口红利最终会被消耗掉。如果单看上海，人口红利今年正好消耗完（附件）。由于外地人口的涌入，人口红利可能还会持续一段时间。但总会有结束的那一天。

There are several medium- to long-term risks. If we merely focus on land supply and the speed of construction of new houses, both Shanghai and Beijing have no natural geographical limitations. These two cities can expand limitlessly. Along this line of reasoning, the conclusion should be that property prices will eventually go down. However, reality shows otherwise. This is because the growth in population has been continuously higher than the increase in land supply. Demographic dividend will eventually come to an end. If we look at Shanghai, the demographic dividend will disappear this year (please refer to the Appendix for more details). Because of the influx of newcomers, demographic dividend may persist for a while but it will have to come to an end one day.

通货膨胀。通货膨胀总是会来临的。现在票子已经发出去了。总有一天会显示在商品价格上。等到通货膨胀来临的时刻，房地产不是大家想象的那样会水涨船高。央行会调整利率控制通货膨胀，房价会因为银根收紧和利率调高，应声而落。利率如果是15%，有几个人能买得起上千万的房子。

Inflation is an important factor to help us understand changes in property prices. There will always be inflation. Now that more money has been printed and issued, the new supply of money will be reflected in commodity prices one day. However, when inflation eventually comes, the extent and pattern of increase in property prices will be different from what we have imagined. The central bank will adjust the interest rate to control inflation. Property prices will drop when credit is tightened and interest rates are higher. If the interest rate is 15%, how many people will be able to afford a CN¥10 million house?

所有的理论分析都挡不住一个最重要的因素。人气。你可以把所有的宏观因素做成最完美的数学模型。但是无法计算人心和投机心理下的冲动。在中国和亚洲，因为价值取向的单一，炒作某种商品的时候，都会一直到不可思议的高度才罢休。当年的君子兰、猴年邮票。最近的 6000 点股票，都是很好的例子。上海的房价现在是高于基本面的支撑。但是还远远没有到达不可思议的高度。现在已经无人相信房价会跌。上海的房价正以不可阻挡的势头，朝那个光辉的顶点奔去。

All these theories may be defeated by one paramount factor: popularity. You can build a perfect mathematical model with all the macroeconomic factors but you will not be able to calculate people's attitudes and their impulsive behaviors driven by a speculative mindset. In China and Asia, because of monotonous value orientation, when people who participate in a certain market are guided by speculation, they will not quit until the price level reaches an unbelievably high level. Past examples included Chinese traders' obsession with a plant called "clivia" and postage stamps in the Year of the Monkey. Recently, the stock market has hit 6000 points. This is another good example. Shanghai's property prices are at a level beyond the support by the fundamental factors but they have not reached an unbelievably high level yet. Right now, no one believes that property prices will drop. The increase in Shanghai's property prices is unstoppable and the sky is the limit.

上海房价朝不可思议的高度奔去 （3）（2009 年 9 月 23 日）

The Sky's the Limit for Shanghai's Soaring Property Prices (3) (September 23, 2009)

by Bayfamily

无论怎么看，仿佛是宿命一样。中国和上海的房价会像当年的香港和日本一样，是一条道跑到黑，总有崩溃的那一天。顶点之后的事情，其实根本就不是我们这些小人物能够操心的事情了。

No matter from which angle we examine the situation, it is almost like destiny. The property prices in China and Shanghai are just like those in Hong Kong and Japan back in the days. They are all a straight upward curve followed by a point of collapse. What happens after the peak is not the business of ordinary citizens like you and me.

我们小人物关心是如何投资获得回报。到底是现在追高还是旁边观战。长期来说，随着人们收入的增加，上海和北京核心区的房价最终会超过台北甚至是香港。但是这个过程肯定不是一帆风顺的。对于中小投资者而言，机会和风险并存。毕竟那个光辉的顶点还有些距离。只要风险控制得好，机会还是不错的。

Small potatoes like us are instead concerned about how to reap returns from investments: whether we should buy high or be a patient observer. In the long term, as people's income continues to increase, the property prices of the core areas in Beijing and Shanghai will eventually exceed those in Taipei or even Hong Kong. But this process will not be smooth sailing. For medium to small investors, opportunities co-exist with risks. After all, there is still some distance between the current price level and the peak. With good risk control, the prospect is still quite good.

今年上半年一共出手两次。一次是与人合伙直接从房产商那里直接弄得房子的购房期权。好处是未来出手不上税，没有中间交易费。缺点是靠关系，没法复制。按照当前市场价格，现金回报率(Cash on Cash)大概在80%左右。第二次是头拆迁房。未来的前途还未定，如果按照计划拆迁顺利的话，按照目前市面的赔偿价格，现金回报率（Cash on Cash）的回报应该在150%左右。这两笔交易比起最近股票市场的回报当然不算什么。但是我的风险控制很严格。即使未来拆迁不果，每月贷款和租金的差价微小，基本上没有什么可以担心的，无非是长期持有而言。

I made two investments in the first half of this year. The first investment concerns a real property purchase option. The pros are zero tax in future selling and no intermediary transaction fees. The cons are that I resorted to *guanxi* in getting access to this opportunity so my success cannot be easily replicated. According to the current market price, my cash-on-cash is around 80%. The second investment is the purchase of a "demolition and relocation house."[11] The future of this house is full of uncertainties but if the appropriation plan proceeds smoothly, my cash-on-cash should be about 150%, a calculation made based on current compensation level. These two transactions are short of extraordinary when compared to the recent returns on stocks but I have exercised very strict risk management. Even if the land appropriation plan is aborted, the difference between my mortgage payment and rental income will be minimal. I have nothing to worry about if I hold it for a long time.

在未来，我的投资策略是：

My future investment strategies are as follows:

看地段，不看房子。装修再好的房子，最终也会过时。房子是地在升值，房子本身在贬值。核心地带的老房子是规避风险的最好办法，而且没有什么物业费。

Focus on the location, not the house. Even houses with the best interior design and decorations will become outdated one day. In real estate investing, it is the piece of land underneath the house that is appreciating. Meanwhile, the house itself is depreciating. The best way to manage and avoid risks is to buy old public housing units in the core areas. Besides, these units have little, if not none, property management fees.

不买豪宅。豪宅最近几年的回报非常好。而且因为总金额大，很多人赚到满盆的银子。但是捧着豪宅如同捧着定时炸弹一样。击鼓传花的游戏不知道会停在谁的手上。

Do not buy luxurious properties. The return on luxurious properties has been very impressive in recent years. Since the total sum of investments is large, many people have made lots of money. However, holding luxurious properties is similar to holding a

---

[11] "Demolition and relocation house" is a house that is to be demolished and relocated. Because of rapid economic growth in China, houses are often being appropriated by the government or land developers. These houses are known as "demolition and relocation houses." The Chinese central government has enacted rules and regulations to ensure that house owners will receive reasonable compensation for the demolition and relocation. Oftentimes, landowners are able to receive very attractive compensation.

ticking time bomb. This is similar to the British party game of "pass the parcel" that you have no idea who will get the parcel except this time everyone is passing a ticking time bomb.

不买过时地段的房子。比如赫赫有名的淮海路。性价比失调，就业流失。只有过去的遗老遗少喜欢那里。上海真正的新人口，没有地域偏见，会集中在新崛起的地段上。

Do not buy houses in outdated locations. An example is the well-known Huahai Road in Shanghai where the price-performance ratio, or to put it more aptly, the price-value ratio, of houses is out of whack. Meanwhile, employment opportunities are diminishing. Only those who are nostalgic about the past like that location. The genuine "new population" of Shanghai who has no geographical prejudice will all focus on newly developed locations.

选择新兴的轨道交通带来的增长点，特别是多条线路交汇的地方。比如宜山，耀华，蓝村，曹杨，江苏路，虹桥交通枢纽。随着浦东的成熟和崛起以及大虹桥的修建，上海未来的发展必定的东西轴线上。轨道交通很多，让人看不过来，但是最有潜力的应该在东西轴线的两端，和3，7，9，11这些非主流轨道交通和中心城市的接轨处。

Choose "growth points" brought by newly-constructed rapid transit railway networks, especially where multiple lines intersect, for example, Yishan, Yaohua, Lancun, Caoyang, Jiangsu Road, and Hongqiao Transportation Hub. As Pudong matures and rises and the Greater Hongqiao Area is being developed, Shanghai's future development has to be along the east-west axis. The railway network consists of numerous lines but the areas with the greatest potential are the two ends of the east-west axis, the non-mainstream railway transportation of lines 3, 7, 9 and 11, and the junction locations connecting the city center to other areas.

看租金不看升值。升值难以预料。租金虽小，但是实打实的东西。稳定的租金，容易出租的地方，什么样的风浪来了，都高枕无忧。

Look at rental income, not appreciation. It is difficult to predict appreciation. Even though rental income is a small sum of money, it is a real benefit. With a house that can be easily rented out which generates a stable flow of rental income, you can sit back and relax amid any crises.

买拆迁房。了解规划，跟踪政府动态。拆迁房政府补偿通常在市价的130%以上，而且不用交税，没有中介费用。好的拆迁房，可以很快实现资金回笼。

Buy houses that are being appropriated and will likely be appropriated. Understand the government's development plans and updates. The government compensation for "demolition and relocation house" is usually 130% of the current market price. And you do not have to pay taxes or transaction fees. Good demolition and relocation houses will help you cash out your investment return in a very short amount of time.

这些策略的实施最大的困难就是时间的投入。投资上海地产已经过了傻子都能赚钱的好时候了。后面缺的是傻子去接最后的棒子。没有办法能够投入时间和一心想买了就赚的人，劝你们还是远离上海这块烫手的山芋。

The biggest difficulty in implementing these strategies is putting in time. Gone are the days when even fools could make a fortune in buying real properties in Shanghai. At this stage, the market is looking for fools who are willing to take the ticking time bomb. For those who are unable to devote the time and are looking to make money immediately after making the investment, my advice is to stay away from Shanghai, a hot potato.

不过，从我到美国的第一天起，永远有一群人坚信"中国崩溃论"。也不知道他们是基于什么的心理总是盼着中国崩溃。这些人因为盼望中国要崩溃，所以就找各种证据支持自己的观点。他们中间有的是有名的经济学家，但是更多的是普通老百姓。

However, since the day I arrived in the U.S., there has been this group of people who believe in "the collapse of China." I have no idea why they are always hoping for the collapse of China. These people are always looking for different arguments and evidence to support their own points of view. Though this group includes well-known economists, most of them are ordinary citizens.

我写这些文章的时候的一个深刻感受就是你是永远叫不醒一个装睡的人的。这些人看不到中国的巨大变化和快速的财富积累，脑子里一直还是僵化的意识形态斗争。

When I was writing these articles, the most profound feeling I had was that you cannot wake a person who is pretending to be asleep. Those people are unable to notice the drastic changes that are undergoing in China or the rapid accumulation of wealth. Their mind is still fixated upon the rigid ideological conflict.

于光远是改革开放之后中国一个比较有名的经济学家。我读他的回忆录，记得他说的一件事。1979 年，改革开放之初，当时他所在的经济研究所里一个年轻人去香港考察，回来后在所里做汇报。那个年轻人用统计数据告诉说香港有多富裕，人均工资有多高，商店里商品有多丰富。相比之下，中国大陆有多穷，比他们差很多。

Yu Guangyuan, a relatively famous economist after the Chinese economic reform, included an anecdote in his memoir. In 1979, the early stage of the reform, a young colleague of his who was a fellow researcher had a field visit to Hong Kong. After his return, he did a presentation, telling others how rich Hong Kong was, how high the average wages were, and the wide variety of products in shops. In comparison, Mainland China was a very poor country lagging far behind Hong Kong.

然后经济研究所里一个老干部就不干了。拍着桌子在那儿大声说，"香港有钱又怎么样？工资高又怎么样？商品多又怎么样？　他们能学马列主义吗？"

Upon hearing this, a more experienced senior researcher at the economic research institute was angry and annoyed. He was pounding the table and shouting,

"Hong Kong is rich, but so what? The wages are high, but so what? They have a variety of merchandise, but so what? Can they learn about Marxism and Leninism?"

这实在是一个让人哭笑不得的笑话。那个老干部认为掌握马列真理才是人生最大的幸福和意义所在。40 年后，历史老人神奇地转了 180 度面对今天的香港人、中美两地的华人。现代版的这个笑话今天也是经常可以听见。总会有人给你说"中国人有钱又怎么样？富裕了又怎么样？治安好又怎样？网购发达，生活方便又怎样？他们能投票选总统吗？"

I did not know whether to laugh or cry when I was reading this joke. The senior researcher believed that the greatest happiness and meaning of life was understanding the principles of Marxism and Leninism. 40 years later, the "Magician of History" has miraculously reversed its attitude toward Hongkongers, Chinese and Chinese Americans by 180 degrees. The modern version of this joke is everywhere today. There are always those who are saying, "Chinese have money, but so what? Chinese are rich, but so what? China is a safe country, but so what? Online shopping is booming in China, but so what? Life is convenient in China, but so what? Can Chinese vote for their president?"

第十四章 啃老是可耻的

Chapter 14 Shame on "Elderly-gnawing Young Adults"[12]

01 如何在一线城市拥有自住房

01 How to Own a House in a Tier-1 City

在中国和亚洲很多房价昂贵的城市里，都普遍存在啃老现象。最常见的就是年轻人靠父母的财力帮助购买婚房。而子女往往又对婚房提出了一些要求，比如必须是市中心的，至少是两室一厅的，俗称一步到位，不然不婚不嫁。

In many Chinese and Asian cities with exorbitant property prices, the phenomenon of "gnawing on the elderly" is prevalent. The most common situation is that young people need to rely on their parents' help to buy a "house for marriage."[13] These adult children often have certain requirements for the house. For example, it has to be in the city center with 2 bedrooms. This is known as "meeting all requirements in one go." Otherwise, they will not get married.

---

[12] "Elderly-gnawing young adults" is a literal translation of the Chinese term "啃老族." This term refers to a group of young adults who, albeit unemployed, voluntarily give up employment opportunities and rely on their elderly family members to take care of their daily expenses which may well include luxuries and other expensive purchases. They are figuratively gnawing on the elderly's savings. Similar concepts include NEET which stands for Not in Education, Employment, or Training and the boomerang generation. However, what distinguishes "elderly-gnawing young adults" from these two concepts is that the former seek to take advantage of their parents out of laziness.

[13] "A house for marriage" is probably a foreign concept to non-Chinese. In Chinese society, most people, especially women and their parents, view that stable housing, income, and some savings are the main requirements for marriage. A survey of Chinese mothers with young mothers even revealed that 80% of the respondents would object to their daughters marrying a non-homeowner.

我常常能看到这样的牢骚。比如上海北京市区这样的一套房子至少要600万人民币。普通年轻人20万一年的工资怎么可能买得起？不啃老怎么行？当然也有很多人觉得一线城市房价太高，不合理不科学。因为殷实之家的中产阶级靠工资也根本买不起房子。

I can always hear these grievances. A typical complaint goes something like this: buying a home in urban Shanghai or Beijing costs at least CN¥6 million. How can an ordinary young adult with an annual salary of CN¥200,000 afford it? What choices do they have other than gnawing on their elderly parents? Of course, many people think that house prices in tier-one cities are too high, totally unreasonable, and unscientific because even the more well-off middle-class cannot afford a home based on their income.

同样的现象发生在纽约东京这样的城市。只是这些城市的文化圈里没有啃老这个风气。但是年轻人会一样地觉得愤愤不平，抱怨房价太高，民不聊生。现在似乎华人把啃老的风气带到了美国。在洛杉矶、旧金山你经常可以看到华人给刚刚工作的孩子买房子，如果不是全款，至少也是父母负担所有的首付。

The same phenomenon also occurs in other cities such as New York City and Tokyo but it is just that the phenomenon of "gnawing on the elderly parents" is absent in the local culture of these cities. But the young generation is indignant. They are complaining that the house prices are too high and people have no way of making a living. It seems that Chinese are bringing the "gnawing on the elderly" phenomenon to the U.S. In Los Angeles and San Francisco, you can often see that Chinese parents are buying a home for their children who have just started their careers. Sometimes even though the parents may not pay the full price of the home, they are at least responsible for paying the down payment.

很多抱怨房价高的人其实没意识到收入和财富是两件事情。就像速度和位移是两件事情一样。为此我专门写了一篇博客文章解释了美国华人的亨利族现象。

Chapter 14 Shame on "Elderly-gnawing Young Adults"

Many of those who complain that property prices are too high do not realize that income and wealth are distinct concepts, just like how speed and displacement are two separate matters. I have specifically written a blog article on this to explain the HENRY phenomenon among Chinese Americans.

HENRY 族：高收入，但不富裕 (2008 年 12 月 17 日)
HENRY: High Earner Not Rich Yet (December 17, 2008)

By Bayfamily

在美国的 80 年代，甚至到 90 年代初的时候，六位数的年薪是一个很多人向往的数字。除了跨越一位数给人带来的心理感觉以外，更重要的是当年十万的年收入的确能够带来非常好的生活。年薪十万，意味着度假、大屋子和好车。

In the 1980s or even the 1990s in the U.S., a 6-figure annual income was the dream of a great many individuals. In addition to the mental excitement that came with a breakthrough from 5-figure to 6-figure, what was more important was that an annual income of US$100,000 could bring a high quality of life. This figure meant vacations, a spacious house, and a nice car.

由于通货膨胀的原因，特别是医疗和教育费用的上升，80 年的 10 万年薪，相当于今天的 24 万左右。可是在美国的中国人，特别是双薪的家庭。即使家庭收入到了 20～25 万，通常还是会一种感觉，就是收入高，但是没有富裕感。

Because of inflation, especially the increase in medical and education expenses, an annual income of US$100,000 in the 1980s is equivalent to US$240,000 today. However, for Chinese Americans, especially double-income families, even though their family income has already reached US$200,000 to US$250,000, they do not feel rich despite the high income.

一个新名词，叫做 HENRY，亨利族。我看再适合在美华人不过。亨利族指的是 High Earning Not Rich Yet。家庭税前收入达到 20 万，在美国是 Top

5%的水平。很多老中都能达到 20 万的水平。在美国这样一个富有的国家，又是 Top 5%的收入。为什么还会觉得日子过得紧巴巴呢？因为你是亨利族。对亨利族来说，再高的收入也是镜子里面的繁华，是无法切实享受到富有的。

The newly-coined term HENRY which stands for "high earner not rich yet" is, in my opinion, an apt description of Chinese Americans. Families with a pre-tax income of US$200,000 are the top 5% earners in the U.S. Many Chinese Americans are able to reach this level. In such an affluent country as the U.S., why would someone with a top 5% income feel that they are making ends meet? This is because you are a HENRY. For HENRYs, a high income or an even higher number is merely a mirage image of a prosperous world. They have no ways to actually enjoy wealth.

这里面有这么几个原因：

The reasons for this are manifold:

第一是亨利族多半是没有家底子的。财富的积累是需要时间的。刚刚高收入几年能够积累的财富和祖上传下来一笔家产是不能比的。今天的北京上海的外地人也是一样。在中国北京上海这样的大城市里很多名牌大学毕业的高收入的年轻人，为了一套房子要花上十几年的积蓄。而同样在这些城市里的当地人，往往父母就拥有好几套房子。即使学历低，收入低，富裕的感觉是不一样的。

Firstly, a majority of HENRYs does not inherit any money from their relatives or ancestors. The accumulation of wealth takes time. The savings accumulated by a high earner in the first few years of his or her career cannot be compared to inheriting a sum of money from one's family. The same also applies to non-locals in Beijing and Shanghai. In China's megacities such as Beijing and Shanghai, many young higher earners who graduate from elite schools need to save up for more than ten years to buy a home. Meanwhile, the parents of the locals already own several properties. Even though these locals may be less educated and have a lower income, the feeling of affluence is different for these two groups of people.

Chapter 14 Shame on "Elderly-gnawing Young Adults"

第二个原因是年龄，20 岁拥有 100 万和 50 岁拥有一百万是不一样的。很多老中，颠簸流离，到了美国，读完书，已经是三十好几。等到少有积蓄的时候，已经是 40 多岁的人了。美国 45 年龄的家庭，平均净财富为 64 万美元。高学历的更高。如果按照年龄排名的话，老中的财富并不突出。

The second factor is age. Having a net worth of US\$1 million at the age of 20 is totally different than at 50. Many Chinese Americans arrive in the U.S. in their 30s after they have finished their studies. When they have finally accumulated some savings, they are already in their 40s. The average net worth of U.S. families whose head of household aged 45 is US\$640,000. The higher the educational level, the higher the net worth. If we look at the ranking based on age, the wealth of Chinese Americans is not that impressive.

第三个原因是支出。赚得多，花的多，好比是在消防水龙头下面洗澡，水冲得大，流得也多。过瘾可以，但是没有积累。最后还是没留下什么。亨利族都是注重教育的，往往不惜代价送孩子去私立学校。或者为了好学区，砸锅卖铁，住在好学区的破房子里。这样一来，当然富裕感下降。

The third reason is the expenses. The more one earns, the more he or she spends. This is similar to taking a shower under a fire hydrant. A huge stream of water gushes out of the fire hydrant but an equally huge stream goes down the drain too. HENRYs satisfy their cravings but they cannot accumulate anything, leaving nothing behind in the end. HENRYs attach much emphasis on education so they send their children to private schools at all costs. Or they are willing to leave no stone unturned by spending their entire fortune to live in an old and broken house in a great school district. This is how they feel less rich.

第四个原因是收入的来源方式。同样赚 10 块钱，来源方式不同。幸福指数是不同的，如果是朝不夕保，看领导脸色的工资收入和稳定的 passive income 是不可同日而语的。税务也不同，工资收入要交 social security tax.

The fourth factor is the nature of the source of income. Earning the same \$10 from different sources imply different happiness index. The salary earned from an unstable job where you are at your supervisor's disposal cannot be compared to a stable passive income. The tax implications are also different because one needs to pay social security tax on wage income.

好了，说了半天，有什么破解之道呢？首先是认清形势，避免自己成为亨利族。《穷爸爸富爸爸》里面的穷爸爸就是典型的亨利族，再多的努力，一生也不会有富裕感。其次，是要学会理财，或者投资，或者自己创业，或者看看哪里弄些 passive income。一是减一点税，二是增加安全感。

Alright, I have spent some time explaining the phenomenon but how should we tackle the situation then? The first step is to figure out the situation so as to avoid falling into the trap of being a HENRY. In Rich Dad, Poor Dad, the poor dad is a classical example of a HENRY. However hardworking he is, he will never feel rich in his life. The second point to note is that we should learn how to manage our finance, invest, start our own business, and/or generate a source of passive income. By doing so, you can alleviate some tax burdens and increase your sense of security.

最后是调整好自己的心态，如果不幸干了一个自己特别热爱的工作，当当 Henry 族也没什么不好。毕竟富裕不是让人幸福的唯一因素。如果自己注定是亨利达人，干脆对自己好一点，该玩的玩，该花的花，及时行乐，反正也发不了财。

The final step is to change your mindset. If unfortunately, you are very passionate about your job, being a HENRY is not that bad. After all, wealth is not the only cause of happiness. If you are bound to be a HENRY, then treat yourself: you can be generous with your spending. Carpe diem! This is because at the end of the day, as a HENRY, you will not be able to get rich.

有一次我在上海和一些亲戚的孩子们一起聚餐。这些快要结婚的年轻人抱怨上海的房价太高。然后每个人都在理直气壮地算计着怎么样从父母那儿弄到一些钱帮他们支付首付。我忍不住把他们劈头盖脸地臭骂一通。啃老是年轻人最没出息的表现。父母生你养你，成年之后，应该是自己动手打拼世界，反哺父母和社会，怎么能够光想着啃老呢？

There was an occasion where I was in a gathering with some children of my relatives. These young people who were about to get married were complaining that Shanghai's property prices were too high. Then everyone felt that they were justified to devise a scheme to get some money from their parents as a down payment. I could not help but scold them. Young people gnawing on their elderly parents is the most shameful behavior. Your parents gave you life and nurtured you. Having entered adulthood, you should work hard and conquer the world by yourself, take good care of your parents, and contribute to society. How can you be so fixated on gnawing on the elderly?

他们说大道理他们也懂。但是现实问题摆在那里。他们总感觉到自己要结婚，需要婚房。结婚生子需要最小的婚房也是两室一厅。双职工上班，所以只能住在交通便利的地方。按照自己的工资，一辈子也攒不出足够多的钱买这个房子。虽然他们也知道这样不好，但是除了啃老，到父母亲爷爷奶奶那边搜刮一下，还有什么办法呢？

They replied to me that they knew these preachings by heart but the reality was grim. They always felt that they needed to get married so they needed a house for marriage. In order to start one's own family, he or she will need a house for marriage that has at least two bedrooms. For double-income families, they can only live in convenient locations. Based on their income, they will never be able to earn enough money to buy such a home. Even though they knew it was not good to gnaw on the elderly, what other choices did they have other than asking for money from their parents and grandparents?

我给他们讲一个很通俗的道理，那就是在股市里头最后拥有最多财富的人显然不是一开始资本投入最多的人。而是能正确把握市场机会，能够更准确判断股价涨跌的人。房地产市场也是一样的，拥有大房子住的人，并不是带着最多资金进场的人。你只需要能够正确的判定，房地产未来价格的涨跌起伏，在买卖过程中，你就可以最终获得最多利润，拥有最多最好的房子。

I then told them a common-sense principle which was those who end up with the most wealth in the stock market are not those who enter the market with the most investing capital but who grasp the opportunities in the market by accurately judging the trend of stock prices. The same is true of the real estate market. Those who are living in a spacious house now are not those who enter the market with the most investing capital. As long as you can make correct judgments about the patterns and changes of future house prices during the investment process, you will end up with the most profits and own the highest number of the best houses.

事实上，你只需要看看上海的历史变迁。你就可以明白。市中心的房子一直都是那些房子，可是人来来往往的。一会儿这些人住，一会儿那些人住。如果假设你自己是房子，从房子的角度来看，你就会发现原来住房问题是人和人在玩各种游戏。每个时代玩不同的游戏。比如解放前是玩一个关于钱的游戏，谁有钱，谁住大房子。抗日战争到新中国成立是玩一个跟队伍的游戏，谁的队伍跟对了，谁住大房子。文革年代是玩一个生辰八字的游戏，谁的出身好，三代贫农，谁住大房子。改革开放之后，又开始玩一个钱的游戏。所以一切的重点是你怎么玩这个游戏，能否玩好这个游戏，而不是去爹妈那边搜刮钱财。

In fact, all you need to do is to look at Shanghai's historical changes and you will understand what I mean by this. The houses in city center do not change. What is constantly changing is the people who live in these houses. People come and people go. Let us now pretend that you are a house. From your perspective as a house, you will realize that the housing problem is essentially people playing different games. The game is different for each generation. For example, before the Chinese liberation,[14] it was a game about money: those with the most money lived

---

[14] "Liberation" is a term used by the Chinese government to refer to the Chinese Communist Party started governing China.

in big houses. From the Second Sino-Japanese War and the founding of People's Republic of China, it was a game about standing in the right line: those who joined the right team could live in big houses. During the Chinese Cultural Revolution, it was a game about one's family background: those with good family background, for example, the third generation of peasants, got to live in big houses. After the Chinese economic reform, it was a game about money again. Despite the changes, a universal rule is that it is about how you play the game. Success in the game is about your own maneuvers, not plundering funds from your parents.

喜欢收藏艺术品的人都知道，最终大量古董艺术集中在古董商和鉴定师手里。不是因为他们工资高，靠省下来的工资来买这些艺术品。而是因为他们在倒买倒卖的游戏过程中，通过正确的市场价格判断而拥有了那些名贵艺术品。

Art collectors will know that most pieces, artifacts, and antiques are concentrated in the hands of antique dealers and appraisers. This is not because they have high salaries which they save to buy these pieces. The real reason why they can own these expensive pieces is that they have exercised correct judgments about the market prices in the game of selling and buying.

投资理财论坛上也有人冒出来问类似的问题。不过这次是主动被啃老，是父母们也觉得孩子在世界各地的一线城市买不起房，不啃他们啃谁呢？

Some forum users posted a similar question on the investment and wealth management forum. But this time the role was reversed: these users were voluntarily being gnawed at. These parents were also of the view that their children could not afford houses in tier-one cities around the world so their children had no option but to gnaw at their parents. Who else can these children rely on?

所以我想在这里大声地说。啃老是可耻的。年轻人啃老可耻。父母主动被啃老是一种溺爱。男儿当自强。男子汉大丈夫遇到人生困难的时候，首先是自己动脑筋想办法解决问题，而不是躲在妈妈裙子下面哭诉。没有经历这个过程的孩子是没有出息的。

Therefore I would like to shout out loud here that: gnawing on the elderly is shameful. Parents who are willing to be gnawed at are spoiling their children. A man should strengthen himself and be self-reliant. In the face of adversity, a true man should first rely on his own powers and resources to come up with solutions instead of hiding behind their mothers, sobbing, and complaining. Children who have never experienced this process of tackling problems on their own will go nowhere in life.

我可以用我自己的例子来说明，年轻人根本不需要啃老。只要你足够勤劳和聪明，在哪里都是可以自己解决住房的。

I can use my own experience to illustrate that there is no need for young adults to gnaw on the elderly. As long as you are sufficiently hardworking and smart, you can always solve your own housing problems no matter where you go.

2012 年，我因为创业公司的事情越来越多。每年有几个月的时间在中国工作，所以我需要有一个自己的住房。那个公司业务一直没有做起来，投资人把我的工资压得很低，远远低于我在湾区工作时候的正常工资。

In 2002, as my own business started to grow, I needed to spend a few months in China every year for work reasons. Therefore, I needed a place to live in. My business had not yet taken off by then so the investors had much more bargaining power in negotiating my salaries. My salaries back then were much lower than the usual amount of working in the Bay Area.

但是即使这样，我通过六年时间，从零开始，在上海也解决了自己的自住问题。这是我在上海持有的第四套房子。买这个房子，我完全没有动用其他资本，也没有动用之前买的投资房，它们还在升值中。我在上海的自住房是个很新的公寓，在离地铁站 200 米远的地方，周围学校、商场、公园设施一应俱全。现在这个房子市场价格差不多有 600 万左右。

Be that as it may, it took me six years to start from ground zero in solving my own housing problem in Shanghai. This is the fourth property I own in Shanghai. I did not use any other capital in purchasing this property. Nor did I touch the investment properties I had bought because they were still appreciating in value. My principal residence in Shanghai was a brand new condominium apartment which is about 200 meters away from the metro station and surrounded by amenities such as schools, a shopping mall, and parks. The current market price of this unit is about CN¥6 million.

我的亲戚们知道我房子多。但是我告诉他们买这套房子真正从我口袋里出来的钱只有 30 万人民币。就是我只花了 30 万，就拿到了这个 600 万的住房。他们都很惊讶问我是怎么做到的？

My relatives know that I own many properties but I told them that I only took out CN¥300,000 from my own pocket in purchasing this property. They were all surprised that I got a CN¥6 million house by paying only CN¥300,000 and asked me how I achieved that.

我说道理很简单，看清价格走势，通过几次买卖就做到了。

I replied that the principle was straightforward: with a sound judgment about the price trend, I achieved it by making several transactions.

我 2012 年用 30 万人民币首付买了一个 60 万的小公寓给自己住。那个公寓在城市的边缘，也不是什么特别好的地方，但是附近正在建轨道交通。在我搬进去住了两年之后，轨道交通就通车了。

In 2012, I bought a 60 square-meter condominium unit as my principal residence with a down payment of CN¥300,000. That unit was located on the city's outskirts. It was not a prime location but it was near a metro station under construction. Two years after I moved in, the metro station was opened.

通车之后这里的房价就出现了暴涨，三年差不多涨了一倍多的样子。到 2015 年的时候，我 150 万人民币把这个房子卖掉了，然后用卖掉的钱做首付买了一个 300 万的房子，而这个房子现在涨到了 600 万，就是这么简单。

After the opening, the property prices in that neighborhood surged. The property doubled in three years' time. In 2015, I sold this unit for CN¥1.5 million. I used the proceeds as a down payment to buy a CN¥3 million house which is now worth CN¥6 million. It is as simple as that.

熟悉国内房地产交易的人可能马上会反问，你是如何解决限购和二套贷款首付 70%的问题的？每次我那些年轻的亲戚们向我陈述这些困难的时候，我总是气不打一处来。人的大脑是用来解决复杂问题的，不是用来给自己找借口。如果作为一个成年人这样的限购问题都解决不了，那还是老老实实躲在妈妈裙子底下当巨婴吧。

Those who are familiar with real estate transactions in China may be quick to ask how I solved the issues of the purchase restrictions and 70% down payment for the second property onwards. Every time when my younger relatives told me about these difficulties, I was really mad. The human brain is for solving complex problems not finding excuses for oneself. If an adult cannot solve issues such as purchase restrictions, he or she had better be content with being his or her mother's big baby.

对于全世界一线城市的年轻人来说，要解决自己的住房问题，最好的办法不要好高骛远，不要追求一步到位。你从外地来到一个陌生的城市，难道希望这个城市里的人都把最好的房子让出来给你，然后恭恭敬敬夹道热烈欢迎么？前面的人通过几十年的努力搬进了最好的学区，最好的地段。凭什么你一来就能拥有这些呢？

For young people in tier-one cities around the world, the best way to solve their own housing problem is to avoid biting more than one can chew. Do not insist on meeting all requirements in one go. In other words, do not trap yourself by insisting that your first house has to meet all your criteria. When you come to a strange city from another place, will you expect that the residents of the city will offer you the best houses and accord you a red-carpet welcome? These people have finally moved into a great district in the best location after years, if not decades, of hard work. What makes you deserve all this as a newcomer?

文学城投资理财论坛上，很多中产阶级和稍微富裕的人迁徙到大城市经常有这样的感慨，就是一线城市房子这么贵，谁买得起？有人还专门写文章，因为自己家境不错的亲戚在北京买不起住房，质疑中国一线城市到底谁买得起。针对这个问题我写了一篇博客。

On Wenxuecity's investment and wealth management forum, many middle class and more well-off people often sigh with emotion that property prices are exorbitant in tier-one cities. Who will be able to afford them? Someone specifically wrote an article on this saying that even some more well-off relatives of his could not afford a house in Beijing so he was doubting who could afford these exorbitant houses. In response, I also wrote a blog post.

房子这么贵，谁买得起？(2016 年 7 月 30 日)
Who Can Afford These Exorbitant Houses? (July 30, 2016)

by Bayfamily

每次房价暴涨之后，这句话是我最经常听到的一句问话。这句话的潜台词就是，我都买不起，谁能买得起呢？典型的以己度人的心态，把自己观察到的世界，熟悉的圈子推广到整个市场上去。这样的心态去决定是否投资房地产其实很不正确的。

Each time after the property prices skyrocketed, this is the most common saying. This question implies a mindset of "if I cannot afford it, who else can?" of the speaker. This is typical judging and measuring others by one's own standards. What is meant by this is that the statement-maker over-generalizes the whole market based on his or her own observations of his or her own social circle and world. Adopting this mindset in determining whether to invest in real estate is highly problematic.

印象最深的一次是 2000 年的时候，一个在美国的 50 多岁的上海人和我聊起上海的房价。当时人民广场的一个楼盘是 5000 元每平米。他虽然在美国年薪 10 万美元。但是他在国内认识的亲戚朋友收入都不高，他的很多朋友当时正好赶上国企下岗。所以他认为上海房价贵得离谱，和我说，5000 元每平米，谁买得起？后面的故事我就不多说了。他只看到了他那个年龄段 50 后人们的收入，没有看到当时 60 后，70 后快速增长的收入。

What left me with the strongest impression was a conversation I had with an American Shanghainese on Shanghai's property prices in 2000. At that time, a real estate project for sale in People's Square was asking for CN¥5,000 per square meter. Even though his annual salary was US$100,000, his relatives and friends in China had low income. Many friends of his were laid off from state-owned enterprises. Therefore, he believed that Shanghai's property prices were outrageously high. "CN¥5,000 per square meter? Who can afford it?" he said. I would not go into detail about what happened next. He could only saw the income of his own generation who was born in the 1950s but he failed to notice the rapid growth of income of those who were born in the 1960s and 1970s.

同样的故事还在不断上演。今天依旧有人质疑北京上海的房价、曼哈顿旧金山的房价谁买得起。 所以我们有必要仔细分析一下到底谁买得起这个事情。

The same story is happening again and again. Even today, people are still doubting who can afford a house in Beijing, Shanghai, Manhattan, or San Francisco. Therefore, we need to take a closer look at the issue of who can actually afford the expensive houses.

我们先看全球都存在着谁买得起这个问题，如果你看看全球市场，知道汉城，孟买的房价。你会更加惊叹，到底是谁买得起。

The question of who can afford these houses can be found in all corners of the world. If you look at the global market, you will have an idea of the property prices in Seoul and Mumbai. You will be even more surprised and wonder who can afford these houses.

我们先看第一种情况。就是如果一个市场没有什么新增面积。100%都是既有面积换手。那么是否存在谁买得起的问题。

Chapter 14 Shame on "Elderly-gnawing Young Adults"

Let us examine the first scenario in which there is no newly constructed area in the market and 100% of the transactions involve changes in ownership of the existing floor area. Will the issue of who can afford the houses arise under such circumstances?

显然，无论价格多么贵，哪怕是 1 亿美元每平米，都不存在谁买得起的问题。因为只是拥有房子的人互相换手，换手价格无论多贵这个市场都是可能成立的。和当地人收入完全没有关系，而是与当地租金和收入有关系。但是如果只考虑房子的投资属性，从数学上讲，什么价格都是合理的。就像黄金和艺术品一样，任何价格都是可能存在的。是否合理那是另外一回事。这样的市场典型例子就是孟买。孟买不但是中产阶级买不起房子，就是一般的企业老板也买不起。只有已经有房子的人买得起。曼哈顿基本也是这个情况。

It is patently clear that however exorbitant the property prices, even at US$100 million per square meter, the issue of who can afford these houses will not arise. This is because all transactions in the market are in essence an exchange of ownership between those who have already owned a house. Regardless of how exorbitant the exchange prices are, this market will still exist. The existence of such a market has nothing to do with the income of the local. Instead, the relevant factors are the local rent level and income. However, if we merely consider the investing properties of real estate, mathematically speaking, any price is a reasonable price. Just like gold and art pieces, any price is possible. Whether such prices are reasonable is another matter. A typical example is the market in Mumbai, where both the middle class and even business owners cannot afford to buy a house. Only those who have already owned a house will be able to afford buying another. The same also applies to Manhattan.

那么我们再看另外一种情况，就是市场不是完全封闭的。每年有 5%的新增面积。

Let us turn to another situation in which the market is not totally closed and there is a 5% newly added area per year.

数学上讲，还是任何一个价格都是可能存在的。你会问，如果房价涨到了三倍，谁能买得起这些新增面积呢？其实很简单，因为贷款的原因，拥有房子的人，把自己的房子卖了，加大贷款额度就买得起。这样的例子在中国到处可见。就是所谓的改善型需求。原来住 50 平米的房子，卖了变成首付买 100 平米的房子。只要房价是持续上涨的，那么从数学上看这个游戏就可以一直玩下去。

Mathematically speaking, any prices are possible. You may wonder who can afford the newly constructed area if the property prices triple? The answer is very simple. Because of the availability of loans, existing homeowners can afford these exorbitant houses by selling their houses and increasing their credit limit. Such examples are everywhere in China. This is the so-called "move-up demand," "move-up buyers," or "upgraders." Existing homeowners who live in a 50-square-meter house can sell it and use the proceeds as a down payment for a 100-square meter home. As long as the property prices are increasing, mathematically speaking, this game can go on and on.

第三种情况，就是一个全新的新城。从零开始，一夜之间供应了 100% 的面积。

The third scenario is that a new city is starting from ground zero. 100% of floor area is supplied overnight.

这种情况，就需要真金白银 100% 的用新钱来购买房子。的确会出现买不起的现象。无论房价多么低，都会发生买不起。典型例子就是国内的各种新城和鬼城。鬼城的价格很低，很多价格甚至不足 4000 元每平米。但是大家还是买不起。如果你贪便宜投资进去，还是会亏得一塌糊涂。

In this scenario, one needs 100% of new money in hard cash to buy a home. Therefore, the phenomenon that people cannot afford these houses may indeed occur. No matter how low the property prices are, people cannot afford a home. Typical examples include new cities and ghost cities in China. The property prices in ghost cities are very low, many of them not exceeding CN¥4,000 per square meter, but no one can afford it. If you are solely motivated by greed and decide to invest in these cities, the losses will be abysmal.

　　谁买得起这个问题还有一个陷阱就是错误估计大的宏观数据。一般大家对宏观经济数据喜欢用多、少这些定性词汇。对定量数据没有概念。我举一个例子，大家都在说上海北京的房价高得离谱吓人。可是你们有没有算过，2015 年上海城乡储蓄存款余额已经过了 10 万亿人民币大关。北京差不多也是这个数量级。两个城市每年的新增住宅面积是 2000 万平米左右的样子。10 万亿/2000 万=50 万。你们自己可以算算 3-5 万每平米的房价到底合理不合理。到底老百姓是买得起还是买不起。

There is a trap hidden in the question of who can afford these houses that is the statement-makers have an inaccurate estimate of the macroeconomic data. Generally speaking, people prefer to use more qualitative terms such as "more" and "less" in making sense of macroeconomic data. They have no idea about quantitative data. An example is that people are saying the property prices in Shanghai and Beijing are unreasonably high. However, how many of you have calculated that the total amount of saving deposits in Shanghai's urban and rural areas has well exceeded CN¥10 trillion. The number in Beijing is similar. The newly constructed residential area of these two cities is about 20 million square meters every year. Dividing CN¥10 trillion by 20 million, we arrive at CN¥500,000 per square meter. You can do your own calculations and judge for yourself whether the current price level of CN¥30,000 to CN¥50,000 is reasonable or not and whether ordinary citizens can afford these houses.

　　结论，一个地区房价高与低，合理还是不合理，不能只看房价和收入，要看这个城市住宅市场的构成，是否有大量的新增面积，是否待在这里的人都不愿意走。如果没人愿意走，凭啥你就可以轻轻松松进去呢？要用数学思考。尤其不能只看自己熟悉的圈子的人收入。因为你的圈子可能很穷，也可能太富。

In conclusion, in determining whether the property prices of a region are high or low, reasonable or unreasonable, we cannot simply look at the property prices and income. We need to examine the composition of the residential housing market of that city: whether the number of newly constructed floor area is high and whether current residents are unwilling to move out of the city. If no one is willing to leave the city, what makes you deserve an easy entrance into the city? You have to base your thinking process on mathematical calculations. In particular, you cannot simply base your conclusion on an observation of the income of your own social circle. This is because people in your social circle may be too poor or too rich.

谁买得起？已经在那里有房子的人，再贵也买得起！

Who can afford the exorbitant houses? Existing homeowners in that region can afford them however expensive they may be.

其实大部分时候你应该感到足够的庆幸，就是当地人允许你参与到这个房地产博弈的游戏里。你要做的事就是如何早点参与到这个游戏里，然后击败别人变成赢家。香港人用的一句话叫作"上车"。你的工资只是给你攒够上车的门票。聪明的人都知道银行的钱不借白不借，利息抵消掉通胀后实际上等于白借钱给你。用自己辛辛苦苦攒下来的工资付清房屋总价的是傻瓜。

Actually, you should feel grateful most of the time because the locals allow you to participate in this real estate chess game. What you need to do is to join the game as soon as possible and defeat others to become a winner. Hongkongers refer to buying one's first home as "getting on the bus." Your salaries will only buy you an entrance ticket. Smart people will know that bank loans are real free lunch. Your interest payments will be offset by inflation so essentially your cost of borrowing is zero. Those who use their hard-earned money to pay for the home prices are fools.

在世界上的很多地方，当地人为了保护自己，压根就不让你来参加这个游戏。如果你去纽约或者孟买，那里房价高到普通工薪阶层压根儿买不起"车票"，上不了车，完全没有机会参与到这个游戏中。在上海，你如果是单身外地人，压根不允许你买房。政府说结婚才能买房，丈母娘说买房才能结婚。真的是逼得循规蹈矩的好男人只能跳楼。

In many places around the world, in order to protect themselves, the locals will not allow you to join the game. If you buy a property in New York City or Mumbai, the house prices are so high that the ordinary wage earners are simply unable to buy a ticket to get on the bus so they have zero chance of participating in the game. If you are a single non-local in Shanghai, the government does not allow you to buy a home unless you get married first. But your future mother-in-law insists "no house no marriage." This is essentially forcing rule-abiding men to jump off the building.

在一线城市，你要计算的，不是说要花多少年的时间，攒多少的钱才能买到一个称心如意的房子。因为那是不可能完成的任务。你需要的是如何省吃俭用，用工资攒足够多的资本来参与到这个游戏里。

In tier-one cities, what you need to calculate is not how many years or how much money it takes for you to buy an ideal home because this is simply mission impossible. What you need to calculate is how to save more money and accumulate enough capital using your wages so that you can participate in the game.

毕竟房地产和股票不一样，股票你可能有 100 元就可以开户。而房地产这个游戏里，在中国的一线城市，最低的起始成本至少也要有个 20 万~30 万人民币。

After all, real estate is different from stocks. In the stock market, you can open a brokerage account and play the game even if you have only $100. For the real estate game, the minimum starting capital is at least CN¥200,000 to CN¥300,000 in China's tier-one cities.

我总是碰见有人说他们错过了最好的时代，最好的机会。事实上要解决自己的住房问题，永远都不晚。只是你不要傻乎乎地复制前人做的事情，需要自己独立思考，找到解决办法。2012 年，上海的房价已经疯涨了 10 年。即使在这么晚的时候，我也只花了 30 万就解决了我的住房问题。

I always encounter those who tell me that they have missed the best timing and the best opportunities. In fact, it is never too late to solve your own housing problem as long as you do not follow blindly the strategies of your predecessors. Instead, you should have independent thinking and come up with your own solutions. In 2012, Shanghai's property prices had already been surging for 10 years. Even at this late stage, I only used CN¥300,000 in solving my own housing problem.

其实我用的这个套路和我在湾区买第一个自住房的方法一模一样。即使今天，我依旧有勇气说，在世界上的任何一个核心城市，一个聪明人都是可以靠自己的努力解决自住房问题的，根本不用"啃老"。道理很简单，任何一个城市的老人最终都会离开人世。那些房子总是要给年轻人的。至于归属于哪个年轻人，那就看谁的头脑灵活了。本钱多少不重要，最关键的是你擅不擅长玩这个游戏，你是否能够准确地判断出未来市场的变化。

In fact, the strategy that I applied is exactly the one I used in buying my first home in the Bay Area. Even today, I still have the courage to say that in any core city in the world, a smart person is able to solve his or her own housing problem by diligence. There is no need to "gnaw at the elderly." The theory is simple: the elderly in any city will eventually pass away and the houses will be left for young people. But as to which young people will get these houses, it depends on who has an agile mind. The amount of initial capital does not matter. The key lies in whether you are good at playing this game and whether you can make accurate judgments about future market trends.

如何来判断未来市场的变化，总的来说还是"会走路的钱"那几条投资原则。

How should we make a correct judgment about the future market changes? It goes back to the recurring investment principles in my "Money Walks" investment philosophy.

一个就是看这个地区是不是有更多的年轻人过来。这个地区是不是有兴旺和充满活力？是否有新的产业？是否有特别的政治原因让更多的年轻人愿意来。宏观的层面，就是看一个地区长期的人口流入和经济的繁荣。

One factor is whether that region has an influx of young people. Is that place prosperous and energetic? Does it have new economic activities or industries? Are there special political factors present which encourage young people to move to that place? The macroeconomic factors are the long-term population increase and prosperity of the economy of that region.

在微观层面上，最简单的办法是跟着一个城市基础设施的建设。你可以靠近轨道交通，可以靠近重要的产业园。而这些都是规划上画得清清楚楚的。当然规划和现实还有一些差距。但无论如何你需要做的是买在那些有变化的地方。不要在没有任何变化的老城区里打转，在那些地方转是没有希望的，只有变化才能够产生机会。

From the microeconomic perspective, the simplest way is to follow the construction of the infrastructure of a city. You can track the development of rapid transit railway networks or important industrial parks or high tech parks. These plannings are written in black and white. Of course, there will be discrepancies between the planning and reality. But what you have to do is to buy properties in areas that will certainly undergo changes. Never waste your time in old districts that have no prospect of changes because these places are hopeless. Only changes can generate opportunities.

02 关爱父母是美德
02 Loving and Caring One's Parents is a Virtue

当然我在中国的买房也有不是那么成功的。这些不成功的案例往往是牵扯到很多其他因素。2011年的时候因为母亲的住房比较老旧了，所以我决定给母亲购买一套公寓。

Of course, my real estate investing journey in China had some less successful days. Those failed cases often involved a myriad of other factors. In 2001, as the flat that my mother was living in was quite old, I decided to purchase a condominium unit for her.

当时母亲已经70多岁了，我希望她搬到新一点的公寓楼里。原先的公寓楼建设于80年代早期，已经变得破旧不堪。2011年是美国房地产入市最好的时候。我明明知道，这些钱如果投到美国，会有更多的赚钱机会。但我还是决定帮助我母亲去改善她的居住。人生有些事情可以等，有些事情不能等。对于 70 多岁的人而言，能享受到的东西越来越少了，所以不能等。

At that time, my mother was already in her 70s so I was hoping that she could move to a new condominium building. The original condominium unit my mum was living in was built in the early 1980s so it had become dilapidated. 2011 is the golden year to invest in the U.S. property market. I knew clearly that if I invested the money in the U.S. market, I would have more lucrative opportunities. However, I still decided to help my mother improve her living conditions first. Some, but not all, things in life can wait. For someone in her 70s, there were fewer things that she could enjoy so buying a house for my mother was not something that could wait.

虽然我还有兄弟姐妹。但是我知道这样的事情，如果很多人参与进来的话，稍有不慎就会弄得兄弟不和，破坏了亲情。钱不是生活中的一切。亲情、友情、爱情都能够给你提供钱不能提供的美好。所以我没有和其他兄弟姐妹商量，只是独自一个人出钱给我母亲购买了一套公寓。这是我在中国的第五套房子。

Although I have other siblings, I know that the more people involved in these kinds of matters, the messier it may get. Small mistakes might result in sibling fallouts. Money is not everything in life. Family, friendship, and romantic love can offer you happiness money cannot buy. This is why I did not consult my siblings and decided to use my own money to buy a condominium unit for our mother. This is my fifth property in China.

2011 年不是一个投资中国二线城市的好时候，基本上买完了之后，中国的房地产价格就整体低迷了几年。这笔投资如果拿到美国来，我后来算了一下差不多可以增长到 100 万美元的样子。人生就是这样的，不可能每一分钱都用到极致，很多时候就是明明不可为，可是又必须为之。

2011 is not a good time to invest in China's tier-two cities. Basically, after closing the transaction, China's property prices remained sluggish. Based on my calculations in hindsight, if I had invested that sum of money in the U.S., it could have grown to around US$1 million. But life is like that. It is impossible that you can obtain maximum return on every single penny. Sometimes, we knew that an option was perhaps not the best but it was the right thing to do.

不过亲情又是很复杂的事情。房子买好了，我母亲却坚决不住过去。说她喜欢原来的社区和周围的朋友。所以我花了钱，损失了增长 10 倍的机会，又没有帮上忙。只能等她以后搬过来，这一等就是七年。从经济上算来那次可能是我在中国最糟糕的一个投资，不过我也不后悔，就当是亲情的消费了。

However, family matters can sometimes be complicated. After I bought the new unit, my mother remained reluctant to move in. She told me that she liked the old community and her friends there. Therefore, I lost some money, missed a 10-fold growth opportunity, and was not being helpful. There was nothing I could do but wait until she changed her mind. After a seven-year wait, she finally moved into the new unit. Even though this is perhaps the worst investment I have made in China, I do not regret my decision because it is something I did for my family.

在中国或者在我后面所有的投资体验里，我自己的感觉就是买住房的时候最好只登记你一个人的名字。人们购买房子最容易犯的错误就是为了孩子着想，把孩子的名字也放进去。有的甚至把爸爸妈妈七大姑八大姨的名字通通放进去。

Based on my investing journey in China and all other fields and places, my takeaway is that it is best to only register yourself as the legal owner of the property. When people are purchasing a property, the most common mistake is that they add their children's names to the house title. Some even add their father, mother, aunties, and uncles, etc.

投资是讲究效率的事情。放一个名字，一切都会变得简单，你要出具的文件和相应的手续都会变得简单。无论是买卖还是贷款，还是未来的再贷款。

Investing is about efficiency. A sole legal owner makes everything simpler, ranging from preparing the documents and handling the relevant procedures, from selling to buying, and from loans to refinancing.

投资就是投资，亲情就是亲情。投资是逐利的。亲情是回味的。啃老是利用亲情对他人的掠夺。投资和亲情不要纠缠在一起。

Investing and family should be kept separate from each other. Investing is about profit maximization. Family is about cherishable moments. Similarly, gnawing at the elderly is robbing others in the name of family. Investing and family should not be intertwined.

03 中国投资总结

03 A Summary of My Investing Journey in China

我在中国的房地产投资，大概持续了将近十五年。因为持续的价格上涨，这十五年里其实任何时候都是买入的好机会，而且几乎在任何一个城市都是好的机会，无论你是在一线城市上海、北京、广州、深圳还是二线城市南京、成都。

My investing journey in China's real estate market has lasted for about 15 years. Since property prices were always increasing, any point in time during these 15 years was a great buying opportunity in any cities, whether you were in tier-one cities such as Shanghai, Beijing, and Guangzhou, or tier-two cities such as Nanjing and Chengdu.

我可以拿我的例子说一说这个投资的回报大概是多少。下面的计算都是现金回报比（cash on cash）。我在上海买的第一个房子，当时付出的现金是5万美元，其余是贷款。今天这个房子可以卖200万美元，现金对现金的回报差不多是40倍。

I will illustrate the investment return by using my own experience as an example. The following calculations are based on cash-on-cash returns. I paid US$50,000 in cash in buying my first property in Shanghai with the remaining financed by a mortgage. Today, this unit can be sold for US$2 million. The cash-on-cash is about 4000%.

我在上海买的第 2 个房子，如果当时没有卖出的话，大概回报率是 30 倍。因为我卖出中间做了一些置换，导致投资有所折扣，所以差不多回报率是 20 倍。我给自己买的自住房那一连串投资的回报率是 20 倍。为了照顾母亲购买的房子，到今天的回报率大约是 3 倍。

The cash-on-cash return on my second property in Shanghai, if I had not sold it out, would have been 3000%. Since I did some selling and buying in the middle of the process, the investment return was discounted. The final cash-on-cash was approximately 2000%. The series of investments I made in relation to the flat that I purchased as my principal residence in Shanghai had a cash-on-cash of 2000%. The condominium unit that I bought for my mother had a cash-on-cash of about 300%.

所以即使我投资时犯了错，错误的进行了置换。最后的效果还是不错。过去十五年是个闭着眼睛都能挣钱的年代。是一个猪都能飞到天上的时代。关键是你投资了还是没有投资。对于大部分喜欢投资的海外华人，如果你错过了这个机会，非常可惜。

Therefore, even though I did make some mistakes in my investing journey by wrongly changing my holdings, the outcome is still pretty good. In the past 15 years, it was an era where you could make a fortune even though your eyes were closed. For most overseas Chinese who are passionate about investing, it is a pity if you have missed this opportunity.

当然也有很多人是因为长期不看好中国，过去十五年里总有各种各样无数多人不断地唱衰中国。我就听过无数个版本的"中国崩溃论"。然而中国没有崩溃，反而越来越富裕。

Of course, many people are pessimistic about the long-term development of China. In the past 15 years, people from all walks of life were trying to smear China. I have heard countless versions of "The Collapse of China." Yet, China's collapse, while often predicted, did not come to fruition. Contrary to these predictions, it is getting more affluent.

中国未来的命运会怎么样一切不好说，但我自己感觉最好的投资时间已经过去了，至少在房地产投资领域，因为中国的农村已经没有什么年轻人了。不会有更多的新人从农村进入城市，所以在中国至少三四线城市会持续地萎缩，而中国的一线城市政府对人口管控越来越严格。也许中国房价还能再涨，但不会再涨到哪里去了，至少不会有过去这样十倍几十倍的暴涨。

The future of China is hard to tell but my view is that the best time for investing in China has passed. This is at least true of the real estate market. This is because the number of young people in rural areas in China is very low now. There will not be an influx of newcomers from rural areas into cities in the future. Therefore, China's tier-three and tier-four cities will continue to shrink. At the same time, China's tier-one cities are imposing stricter control over their population. Perhaps China's property prices may still rise but the extent will not be impressive. At the least, a 10-fold increase or more which was common in the past will not happen again.

我的这些故事并不是让年轻人去盲目模仿。每一个时代周围的环境都是不一样的。不可以套用细节。我希望读者从我的故事里听到一些有益的经验和教训。啃老是可耻的，人活得要有骨气，要相信自己是可以用双手改变自己的生活状态和命运。在投资理财的操作层面有这样一些建议。

My stories are not to be blindly followed by young people. The conditions facing each generation are different. The details do not matter that much. I hope that readers can benefit from hearing some experiences and the lessons that I have learned. And gnawing at the elderly is shameful. Besides having moral integrity and a strong character are essential, we also need to believe that we can change our life and destiny through our hard work. The following is some advice for those who are interested in executing investment plans.

Chapter 14 Shame on "Elderly-gnawing Young Adults"

一、选对大的局势比具体操作更重要，具体操作你可以有失误，可以不用特别完美。 比如我一而再再而三的失误，但是一样挣钱。

1. Making a correct judgment about the trend is more important than the details of execution of your investment plans. You may make some mistakes in executing your plans. You need not be perfect. For example, despite my mistakes, I have still made a profit.

二、年轻的时候，不能只关心周围一点点的小事情。而是要"胸怀祖国，放眼世界"。机会来自四面八方。眼界很重要。今天无论你是生活在中国还是在美国，尽可能地多的去了解世界上其他地方的事情，可能对你的生活有启发。

2. When you are young, do not be fixated on the trivial matters that are happening in your surroundings. Rather, you should have a vision of your country and the world. Opportunities come from all directions and places. Your vision is important. In today's world, whether you are living in China or the U.S., make your best endeavors to deepen your understanding of other places in the world. Knowledge of global issues may further inspire you.

三、房地产投资和其他所有的投资一样，没有人能够帮助你做决策。需要独立思考。不要指望别人能替你思考。不能只是从名人的嘴里寻找答案。大部分人依赖名人替他们思考其实是逃避责任。 要相信自己，要通过自己进行艰苦的分析作出判断，并勇于为这些判断负责。

3. Investing in real estate is similar to all other investments: no one can make the decision for you. Do not rely on others to do the thinking for you. Do not try to find the answer from the mouths of celebrities. Most people who rely on celebrities to think for them are shirking their responsibilities. Instead, believe in yourself. You need to conduct your own analysis, make a judgment, take responsibility, and bear the consequences of your judgments.

四、还是那就老话，"没有人比你更在乎你的钱"。而另外一方面，"啃老是可耻的"。不劳而获只会让一个人离成功更远。爱你的亲人，不要把亲人的爱当作战利品。

4. It is the old saying again: no one cares about your money more than you do. Meanwhile, "gnawing at the elderly" is shameful. Free lunches will only drive a person further away from success. Do not rob your family in the name of love.

第十五章 从 100 到 1000 万（二）抄底！抄底！

Chapter 15: From $1 million to $10 million (2) Buying the Bottom! Buying the Bottom!

01 指数房

01 The Index House

在我最初的普通人家十年一千万理财计划里，美国才是重头戏。中国的房地产投资的故事写得很长，但是其实我更多的时间是花在美国这边的。毕竟我生活在这里，每次去中国都是来去匆匆。所以在这一章里我回忆一下投资过程中的第二个重要的阶段，就是美国次贷危机之后的抄底阶段。

The U.S. is the main arena for the early stage of my "An Average Family's $10-million-in-10-year Investment and Wealth Management Plan." Even though most of my blog articles detail how I invested in China's real estate market, I actually spent more time in the U.S. After all, this is where I live. And whenever I went to China, I was in a rush. Therefore, this chapter is dedicated to a recollection of a second, important stage of my investment journey, which is buying the bottom after the U.S. sub-prime crisis.

美国房价是从 2008 年底开始一路走软的。我自己住的房子价格当然也在下跌。只要自己保持好的心态，自住房的涨跌其实是没有什么关系的。因为我每个月要付的贷款都是一样的。

The U.S. property prices started to decline in late 2008. Of course, the price of my principal residence also dropped. But as long as I maintain a good attitude, fluctuations in the price of my own principal residence do not really matter because my monthly mortgage payment remains the same despite those changes in property prices.

房价下跌对我反而有好处，因为我可以交更低的房产税。当房价大约下跌了 20%的时候，我写了一封长长的信给当地城市的税务局，陈述我的住房估价是多么的不合理，市场的房价应该比他们给的估价更低一些。在那封信里，我用 MBA 学到的知识，用各种方法给出房地产的估价，然后取了一个平均值和区间范围证明我的房子被高估了。

Instead, I actually benefitted from decreasing property prices because property tax also decreased. When property prices plummeted by about 20%, I wrote a long letter to the tax agency of my city, arguing how unreasonable their evaluation of my house was. The market value of my house should be lower than their evaluation. In that letter, I applied the knowledge I learned in my MBA by using different models to evaluate the value of my house. I calculated the average of the evaluation numbers obtained by these models and cited the range of the value of my house to prove that their evaluation was too high.

结果当然大家可想而知。税务局完全没有理我，既没有给我更低的估价，也没有回信反驳。账单上的金额一分没少。有本事你不付，政府马上来拍卖你的房子。当然我也可以去法院起诉，但我觉得这样是多此一举，有这功夫可以在其他地方挣很多钱。各国政府都是一样，仗着自己资源多，最不怕的就是和你打官司。

It was easy to guess the ending of the story: The tax agency ignored me. Neither did they use a lower evaluation nor reply to my letter to rebut my points of view. The amount payable remained the same. If I dare not pay my property tax, the government will immediately auction my house. Of course, I can also sue the government, but I think this is meaningless. If I had the time and energy to file a lawsuit, I would better invest them in other channels to create more wealth.

Governments around the world are all the same: Because of their abundant resources, they are not afraid of lawsuits.

在整个次贷危机过程中，我一直在用我在美国买的第一个房子作为价格的标杆。房价不同于股价，没有什么指标来跟踪。美国仅有的几个房价指数也是全国性的，对于某个社区和城市，没有太多意义。我 2002 年买的第一个房子，同类的房子很多，流动性也比较好。所以用它的价格作为指数比较合理。这里为了方便阅读和理解，我暂时管那个房子叫作"指数房"。

During the sub-prime crisis, I used the first house I bought in the U.S. as a yardstick to measure property prices. Property prices are different from stock prices because you cannot really use an index to track the former. The only few house-price indexes are national, so they are meaningless when applied to a specific community or city. When I bought my first house in 2002, similar properties abounded, which meant the liquidity was good. Therefore, using its price as a benchmark is quite reasonable. For the ease of reading and comprehension, I will refer to that house as "an index house."

我 2002 年买入"指数房"的价格是 43 万美元，2005 年我以 72 万美元的价格卖掉。2008 年底的时候，大约跌到 60 万美元。2009 年中的时候，大约跌到 50 万美元。跌到 60 万美元的时候，炒房者先把房子扔给银行。跌到 50 万的时候，很多实际居住的人也开始把房子扔给银行，大量的法拍屋（foreclosure)开始出来了。

I purchased my "index house" at US$430,000 in 2002 and sold it at $720,000 in 2005. In late 2008, its price plummeted to around US$600,000. In the middle of 2009, it further dropped to US$500,000. At the price point of US$600,000, real estate speculators threw their houses to the bank. At the price level of US$500,000, many homeowners also started to throw their houses to the bank. The number of foreclosure listings mushroomed.

这个道理也很简单，因为很多以 72 万美元购入的人没有付首付或者只有 10%的首付，等房价跌到 60 万美元或者是 50 万美元的时候，对于他们来说经济上更好的选择就是把房子丢给银行。

The logic behind this phenomenon is simple. For many of those who actually purchased the house at US$720,000 without any down payment or a 10% down payment, the best option was to throw the house to the bank when the property price dropped to US$600,000 or US$500,000.

而且美国的大部分地方都有一个奇葩的法律，就是这种情况下银行没有权利去追缴债务人的债务，银行最多能做的事情就是把房子接手过来，然后给债务人一个不好的信用记录。

Yet there is a bizarre law in most places in the U.S., which is that under these circumstances, banks are not entitled to follow up on the loans except taking back the house and leaving the borrowers with a bad credit record.

这个不好的信用记录，差不多需要 3~5 年才能完全抹清。大部分人觉得 3~5 年不是什么大不了的事情，相比十几万实际的现金损失是个更好的选择。所以并不是他们负担不起这个房子了，他们明明还能够负担得起，但是他们选择把房子交还给银行。

To erase this bad credit record takes about 3-5 years. Most people will think that 3-5 years is no big deal when compared to an actual loss of tens of thousands of cash. Therefore, it is not that they could not afford the mortgage payments anymore, but they chose to give the house back to the bank.

而且把房子还给银行往往他们还可以免费多住上一年。他们可以理直气壮地停止付房贷，因为银行不会一夜之间把他们赶出去。银行走法律程序需要一年左右的时间。即使在银行走完了法拍屋流程之后，甚至法拍屋的新购买人来了之后，耍无赖的房东还可以拒绝搬家，索要一笔搬家费。

Furthermore, giving the house back to the bank often means that the borrowers can live in the house for one more year. They can now unapologetically stop repaying their mortgage because the bank would not evict them overnight. It takes around a year for the bank to go through all the legal procedures. Even if the bank has completed the foreclosure step and the new buyer comes to the scene, some shameless borrowers may still refuse to move out and demand a relocation fee.

所以次贷危机很大程度上是一个人为制造的危机。并不完全是因为银行把贷款贷给了没有能力负担的人。更主要的可能是银行的执行条款和法律的执行层面也过于宽松导致的。这也是为什么在全世界除了美国都没听说过有次贷危机的。

Therefore, the sub-prime crisis is, to a large extent, a man-made one. The cause is not that banks had lent money to those who could not afford repayments. The primary reason is that the banks were too loose in enforcing the relevant laws and regulations. This is why the sub-prime crisis is generally speaking unique to the U.S.

当这些房子拿出来做法拍屋之后，引起房价的下跌。随着房价下跌会引起更多的人选择把房子扔还给银行，进入法拍屋程序。这是一个自我加强的正循环。最严重的城市社区，比如 Stockton 最后的结果几乎是大半个城市的住房统统换手一遍。

When these houses become foreclosures, the property prices will drop. With decreasing property prices, more people will choose to give their houses back to the bank by entering the foreclosure procedure. This is a self-reinforcing cycle. In the worst cities and communities, such as Stockton, the outcome was that almost more than half of the city's residential properties changed hands.

次贷危机的时候，当时法拍房分两种，一种是短售（short sale），一种是法拍屋（foreclosure)。短售指的是业主走正常的流程卖房，事先和银行商量好，并且获得银行短售许可的卖房方式。因为房子的价格已经低于贷款，所以卖多少钱就把多少钱全部给银行。选择短售说明业主还是认真负责的，对他的信用记录影响要比被法拍屋小。法拍屋就是很不负责任地把房子扔给银行，逼银行走法院拍卖的手续。一个人一旦有过法拍屋的经历，信用记录会严重受损。

In the sub-prime crisis, there were two types of foreclosure listings, namely "short sale" and "foreclosure." The former refers to when an owner goes through the normal procedure of selling his or her house with prior consent to the foreclosure from the bank. Since the house price is now lower than the mortgage, all the proceeds from the sale will go to the bank. Choosing to foreclose the house voluntarily means the owner is responsible because such an option will have lesser adverse effects on his or her credit record. In contrast, a "foreclosure" is when the homeowner irresponsibly throws his or her house to the bank, forcing the bank to conduct a foreclosure auction under the supervision of the court. Once a person has a foreclosure experience, his or her credit record will be significantly tarnished.

我的指数房要是当年没有在最高点把它卖掉的话。恐怕我也会进入法拍屋或者短售的程序。因为这个房子的价格，后来又从 50 万跌到 40 万，从 40 万美元跌到 30 万美元。我不知道我是否能够抵制住诱惑。

If I had not sold my index house at the peak level back then, I would probably have gone through the foreclosure or short sale procedure. This is because the price of the index house dropped from US$500,000 to US$400,000, and further down to US$300,000. I had no idea whether I would be able to resist the temptation.

02 抄底准备

02 Preparing to Buy the Bottom of the Market

从 70 万美元跌到 60 万美元的时候，还有很多勇敢者冲过去买。但是从 40 万跌到 30 万的时候，大家都吓傻了，没有人再敢进去。因为没有人知道市场的底部在哪里，整条大街上到处都插满了法拍屋标签。

When the price dropped from US$700,000 to US$600,000, the brave rushed to buy real properties. But when it plummeted from US$400,000 to US$300,000, everyone was terrified and no one dared enter the market because no one knew where the market bottom was. Streets were drowned in "foreclosures" signs and banners.

可是我知道一切都会逆转过来。而且越接近底部，逆转得就会更加剧烈。当时我在投资理财论坛上经常说的一句话就是"one foreclosure sold, one foreclosure less." 每卖一个法拍屋，市场上就少一个法拍屋。

But I knew that everything would be reversed. And the closer the market was to the bottom, the more drastic the reversal would be. Therefore, I was always advocating the slogan that "one foreclosure sold, one foreclosure less" on the forum. For every foreclosure house sold, there will be one less foreclosure house in the market.

我几乎每个周末都出去看房子。甚至可以说我一直在出价试图购买。但是我一直没有买到，因为我出价每次都很低，是当时法拍屋开价上再下压 30%-50%。我出的价格之低，让中介都懒得理我，觉得我完全没有诚意。事实上我也的确没有诚意。因为我手上的钱很少，当时我只有 5 万美元的现金。我就用这点钱去摸到市场的最底部，买不到也没有什么，至少我不想接那个下落的刀子。

I was basically going to open houses every weekend. In fact, I was trying to buy a house by constantly making an offer, but to no avail. I failed because I offered a very low price every time, which was at a 30%-50% discount of the original list price. As my offer was so low, the real estate agent was less than enthusiastic because he did not think that I was serious. At the time, I had very little cash, which was about US$50,000. I was trying to use this little money to enter the market at its bottom, so I did not really care if I failed to buy a house in the end. My primary concern was to avoid catching the falling knife.

我不断看房、和很多中介沟通、不断出价的目的是 get engaged (参与进去)。因为我知道光看新闻是无法判断市场底部的。而且市场真的触底时，就看谁抢得快。等触底反弹那个时候再和中介接触，建立人脉关系就来不及了。

The reason why I was always visiting houses for sale, communicating with many real estate agents, and making an offer was to get engaged in the market. I knew that I could never accurately judge when the market bottom was by simply reading the news. Furthermore, when the market indeed hits its bottom, it is a race of speed. If you try to contact a real estate agent and build your connections when the market has reached its trough, everything will be too late.

不过也有很真诚的中介建议我不要买。我记忆中当年帮我卖掉指数房的那个中介就是这样的。他说房子经常几个月租不出去，还是小心为妙。因为当经济危机来临的时候，住房的总需求也会减少，即使人口不变。租房的人也会压缩自己的生活开支，比如原来一个人住一个公寓的选择两个人合租一套公寓，失业的年轻人回到父母身边，失业的老人选择和兄弟姐妹孩子们一起居住。

However, at the time, there were some genuine real estate agents who advised against my decision to buy a house. If I remember it correctly, the following is the advice given by my real estate agent back then. He said, "Now, owners could not rent out their houses in months. Better safe than sorry. When an economic crisis hits, the total demand for housing will decrease, even though the population remains unchanged. Tenants will try to cut down on their daily expenses. For example, let's say there is this person who originally lives in an apartment by himself. He will choose to share an apartment with a roommate now. Unemployed young people will go back to their parents' house, and unemployed senior citizens will choose to live with their siblings or children."

我原来想在大学周围买房子，那里的房租比较稳定，可是大学周围的房子价格总是很坚挺。和好学区的住房一样，下跌幅度不大。尝试了几次基本上就放弃了。下跌幅度小的地方，上涨空间也有限。

Originally I was looking to buy a house that was in proximity to a university because it would then generate a more stable rental income. Yet the prices of houses near a university stood firm. Similar to houses in a good school district, the extent of the decrease in prices was not big. After several futile attempts, I gave up on this goal because neighborhoods that witnessed a smaller extent of price drop have limited potential for price growth.

在这个不断出价的过程中，我也渐渐学到了一些门道。短售和法拍屋交易中，并不是出价最高的人就能够拿到房子，经常会有些不能摆到桌面上的东西。有的时候，中介会想方设法不卖给你。

I have some takeaways from this process of constantly making an offer to buy. I have learned that in a foreclosure or short sale listing, it is not the buyer with the highest bid that got the house. In fact, success depends on other under-the-table considerations. Sometimes, the real estate agent will try every means not to sell the house to you.

比如我当时看到一个 fourplex（四单元房）在短售。这是一套四个单元的公寓房。这套房子临近一个数一数二的好小学，步行就可以走到那个小学，所以未来出租不会有问题。因为孩子上学，所以租金和房客会很稳定。我当时计算了一下，当时按照它的开价买下来就是正现金流。好学区的正现金流的房子像宝石一样的稀少，碰见了要赶紧抢。

For example, back then, I had my eye on a short sale listing of a fourplex. It was an apartment building with four units, which was in proximity to a top elementary school. As the school was within walking distance from the property, I would not have any difficulty in renting the units out in the future. I would have a stable rental income and tenants because their children would need to go to school. Based on my calculations, the real property would yield a positive cash flow if bought at the listing price. An investment property with positive cash flow in a good school strict is as scarce as desert orchid: I need to hurry and grab whenever I find one.

房东是一个犹太人，拥有这四个单元快三十年了。现在年龄大了不善管理，房子又出了几个比较大的维修责任，他就用六十万的价格把四套房子一起拿出来卖。这样的房子在市场正常的时候价格应该在 100 万-120 万美元之间。

The landowner was Jewish, and he had owned these four units for almost thirty years. As he was now getting older with less energy to manage the units which were suffering from some major maintenance issues, he was trying to sell all four units at a total of US$600,000. Such a real property would have a market value of US$1-1.2 million under normal circumstances.

我马上和对方的中介联系，中介倒是热情带我去看房子。但是用一大堆的理由跟我说这个房子有多么不好，有各种各样的问题，地基有问题，墙有问题，屋顶有问题，都是大修，简直要重盖了。我当时并没有完全听明白他的意思，我只是相信了他，表示感谢，谢谢他告诉我实情，不然一上来就演砸了。

I immediately contacted the vendor's real estate agent, who was quite enthusiastic about arranging a visit for me. However, he was trying to discourage me by listing all sorts of problems of that property, for example, its architectural base, walls, and roof. He said all these parts required a huge repair that would be equivalent to rebuilding the house. At the time, I could not perceive the real meaning behind his "advice." Instead, I believed in him and thanked him for telling me the truth. I thought I would have messed it up without his candid advice.

这么多年以后，等我有了很多管理房屋的经验之后，才明白其实那个中介是想把我吓跑。不知道当时有什么内线的买家已经谈好了，怕我出高价搅了局。现在想一想他说的那些白蚁和屋顶问题，其实都不是什么大不了的问题。只是在当时我还没有太多管理投资房的经验，所以被他说一说就吓怕了。那些问题现在看看可能也就是 5 万~10 万美元就可以全部解决。

It was only after I had years of experience in property management that I realized the purpose of his speech was to scare me off. It was perhaps the case that the real estate agent had already struck a deal with some secret buyer and that he was worried that I would outbid that buyer. In retrospect, the roof and termite problems he talked about were no big deal. However, I did not have much experience in property management back then, so I was scared off by his words. In retrospect, all those so-called problems could be solved by spending a total of US\$50,000 to US\$100,000.

这样的房子绝对是现金奶牛（cash cow)的房子。这个房子价格是 60 万美元，四个单元的租金每个月就 1 万，一年 12 万美元。Cap rate 将近 20%。如果你玩过大富翁的游戏，就知道玩房地产这个游戏的秘密之一，就是要在早期有一头现金奶牛不断地给你生产出你买房子需要的现金来。只有这样才能持续盖房买地，成为游戏的赢家。

Such a real property is, for sure, a cash cow. At the time, the asking price was US\$600,000 and the four units would bring in a monthly rental income of US\$10,000 in total, which would mean an annual rental income of US\$120,000. The cap rate was close to 20%. If you have played the board game Monopoly before, you will know that one of the secrets of the game of real estate investing is that in the early stage, you need to find a cash cow that can generate cash for your subsequent purchases. Only with the support of such a stable cash flow can you continue to buy more land and build houses and become a winner.

我在摸底的过程中还碰到过一个老中卖房子。应该说当时中国人卖掉房子的人很少，买房子的人居多。卖房子的拉丁裔和非洲裔要多一些。帮我买卖指数房的那个中介，2009 年的时候，他的生意糟糕透了。因为他之前都是做中国人的生意，次贷危机之后，一下子没人买卖了。他和我说"幸亏当时没有辞掉正式的工作，当中介只是兼职，不然现在要去街上要饭了。"

When I was trying to buy the bottom, I met a Chinese American who was trying to sell his house. Back then, there were very few Chinese home sellers, but Chinese home buyers were in the majority. Most home sellers were Latin Americans and African Americans. The real estate agent who helped me buy my index house struggled to close a deal in 2009. This is because his major source of business was Chinese clients before the sub-prime crisis. After the sub-prime crisis, no one was buying or selling houses. "Fortunately, I did not quit my full-time job and being a real estate agent is a side hustle. Otherwise, I would be a beggar now," he told me.

到了 2010 年，他的生意突然又好了起来，我问他是怎么样做到的。他说以前中介广告他都是发给自己过去的客户，大部分都是中国人，所以没有生意。因为中国人只买不卖，而且买房子不需要中介。后来他把代理短售卖房的广告专门发给拉丁和非裔的低收入人群。结果生意一下就好了起来。客观地说，在整个次贷危机过程中，走法拍程序或者短售的大部分业主也都是低收入人群，高收入人群在次贷危机过程中只是坐了一次资产账面上的过山车，并没有选择卖出，所以对他们没有实质性的影响。

In 2010, his real estate business started to bounce back. I asked him how he achieved that. He explained that in the past, he sent his own advertisements to his clients, most of whom were Chinese, so he did not have any business. Since Chinese only bought but rarely sold houses during the crisis and often closed the deal themselves without the assistance of a real estate agent, he directed his advertisements on short sale listings at Latin Americans and African Americans who have a low income. After this adjusted strategy, his business recovered rapidly. Objectively speaking, in the sub-prime crisis, most homeowners who went through the foreclosure or short sale procedure belonged to the low-income group. In contrast, higher earners were merely on a roller coaster ride in terms of the book value of their assets. Since most of them did not choose to sell the houses, the crisis had no real effects on them.

当时碰到中国人在卖一个短售房，所以我就感到很好奇。我也不好意思问他们为什么要把房子短售出去。我只能跟他们说中文套近乎，我说我的信誉良好，把我的 offer 提交给银行，肯定能够批下来。那个老中支支吾吾地回答，不是很干脆，似乎恨不得我马上人间蒸发，最好别来烦他。当然，最后我没有买到这个房子。后来一个越南中介告诉我，她说这样的情况，多半是房东压根不想卖。只是走一下流程把房子转卖给自己的亲戚朋友，这样实际的拥有人还是他们自己。但是可以借这个短售的机会抹掉一些银行的贷款。这样的短售房旁人自然是买不到的。

Back then, I found a short sale listed by a Chinese seller. Though I was curious, I did not have the courage to ask him why he was short-selling the house. I tried to break the ice by saying that I had a good credit score, so I was confident that my offer would be approved by the bank. The Chinese seller hesitated and stammered in his response. It seemed as though he wished that I should immediately disappear so that I would not bother him anymore. Not surprisingly, I did not get that house in the end. Later, a Vietnamese real estate agent told me that the Chinese seller probably did not want to sell his house to me at all, but he was merely going through the procedure so that he could short sell the house to his relatives or friends who would hold the legal interest as a trustee for him. By doing so, he could erase some bank loans. Without a doubt, all other buyers would be excluded.

我计划买的房子是独立屋。但是公寓的房价其实跌得最狠。当时我刚到湾区租的公寓也有法拍屋和短售在卖。价格已经跌到大家不可想象的程度。因为 2008 年在房价高峰的时候需要 25 万美元一套，而在 2010 年法拍屋的价格只有 5 万美元一套，而且还可以再讨价还价一下。2019 年这些公寓的价格已经涨到 40 万美元左右。2010 年，虽然我也觉得价格低的诱人，值得买入。但由于各种原因，我就是没有买到这个公寓。很多年之后，有感而发，这个故事我还专门写在下面这篇博文里。

I planned to buy a single-family detached house, but it was the prices of condos that were decreasing the most drastically. The condo building where I lived when I first settled in the Bay Area had both short sale and foreclosure listings, and the prices were unbelievably low. At the peak of the real estate market in 2008, each unit was sold for US$250,000. However, in 2010, these foreclosures were asking for US$50,000 per unit, which even had room for further bargaining. In 2019, the prices of these condo units soared to around US$400,000 per unit. Back then, in 2010, even though I also deemed the low prices very attractive and I should probably enter the market, I did not buy that unit in the end for all sorts of reasons. After many years, I was inspired by this experience and specifically wrote a blog article, which is produced below, to share this story with others.

调情的艺术(2018 年 3 月 6 日)
The Art of Flirting (March 6, 2018)
by Bayfamily

上一篇文章居然被微信管理员封杀了。正经的事情不让谈，这会只能说点不那么严肃的事情。今天换一个角度来讲投资理财的细节，调情的艺术。The Art of Flirting. Flirting 的正式翻译是调情，这个词比较反面。（此处略去1000 字）

It hit me by surprise that my last blog article was blocked by Wechat administrators. Let's put aside all those serious matters for a moment and talk about something more casual. In this blog post, I will try to examine the details of how to invest and manage one's wealth from a new perspective, which is "the art of flirting." The word "flirting" is neutral in the English language, but the Chinese translation of the word ("调情") denotes a slightly negative meaning. I will not go into detail on the differences between the English and Chinese meaning of the word here.

Flirting 是 Seduction（勾引）前奏。这个世界充满了各式各样的 seduction。有的时候你是被政客 seduced，比如 70 岁的特朗普老头不知道诱惑了多少红脖子。有时你被金钱诱惑了。有时你被男女明星诱惑了。诱惑的本质就是，诱惑者扔出一个 magic spell，让被诱惑者心甘情愿臣服于你。

Flirting is a prologue to seduction. This world is full of a wide variety of seductions. Sometimes you are seduced by politicians; sometimes you are seduced by money; and sometimes you are seduced by money or celebrities. The nature of seduction is that the seducer throws a magic spell that turns the seduced into obeying his or her every order.

你可能会问，这和投资理财有什么关系？ 投资理财需要和人打交道，无论买房，还是买车，还是购买理财产品，保险产品，都需要讨价还价。人和人沟通，有各种各样的力量。经济学的一个重要假设就是人都是理性的。可惜我们人恰恰是非常不理性的。 人有愤怒，有共情。大家不要忽视了性、暧昧、诱惑在讨价还价中的力量。要做到暧昧的力量为我所用，而不是为我所害。

You may be wondering, "What does this have to do with investing and wealth management?" The answer is investing and wealth management involves people, so people skills are vital. Whether you are trying to buy a house, a car, financial products, or insurance, you need to possess strong bargaining skills. A variety of forces are at play in our interactions with other people. A fundamental assumption in economics is that human beings are rational actors. However, the truth is that we are emotional and easily distracted beings. We feel anger and sympathy, long for sex, enjoy flirting, and seduce others or are being seduced. Therefore, leveraging the power of flirting can assist your investing and wealth management journey too. At the same time, it is equally important that we are able to see through and resist the seduction.

先举两个例子说明一下吧。

Let me explain this in greater detail by raising two examples.

一次是我在北京秀水街买包。北京秀水街都是一些浙江的小姑娘在卖包。我在一楼的某个柜台上看中了一个包，秀水街的包其实都很类似。同样的商品很多柜台都有。我讨价还价的技巧一般是第一家价格一定要砍到对方不卖的地步。然后第二家同样的商品，价格往上加 10%，他再不卖给你。你再找第三家，再加 10%。 直到有一家商家卖给你。这样你知道你是买在很接近他们成本价格的地方。

One time I was buying a bag on Xiushui Road, Beijing, where some young women from Zhejiang sell bags. I had my eye on a bag in a counter on the 1/F of a mall. The bags sold on Xiushui Road were very similar, if not identical, in style, so the same merchandise was available in many counters. My invincible bargaining tactics are that I will first make an outrageously low counteroffer to the first seller that I know will not be accepted, and then I will ask a second seller by adding 10% to my first offer; if he refuses to sell it to me, then I will find a third seller by adding 10% to my previous offer; it goes on and on until I can find a seller who takes my offer. This is an approach that helps me to buy the product at a price as close to their costs as possible.

当时和我讨价还价的是个个子不高的皮肤白皙的浙江小姑娘，说话带着南方口音，白里透红的皮肤。我一下子被她的容貌迷惑住了，按照常规，第一家无论什么价格我是坚决不买的。一定要找到一个不肯卖的价格，然后再一家家加上去。

At the time, I was bargaining with a young woman who had a petite frame and glowing skin and spoke with a Southern accent. I was immediately attracted by her beauty. My bargaining tactics would suggest that I should not give in to the first seller's counteroffer, however low the price is. Normally, I will insist on finding a price that will be rejected by the seller and then adding 10% to that price by talking to a second seller and so on.

我正要离开的时候，她柔声地对我说，"就买咱家的吧，去哪家买，不是买呢？"她就那样站着直视着眼睛对我说，吐气如兰地补上一句 "对不对？"像是小时候邻居家小妹妹找我要糖吃。

When I was about to leave, she spoke softly to me, "Won't it be great if you could buy a bag from me? Because you will have to buy a bag anyway." She was standing there looking straight in my eyes when she added, "Right?" The situation was similar to how a younger girl living next door asked me for candies when I was a child.

讨价还价的结果你可想而知。我一下子就稀里糊涂同意了。走出秀水街大厦，被长安街的冷风一吹。我就明白，我是多么傻瓜一样地上当了。居然把自己讨价还价的原则都忘了。这是我被人暧昧和 seduce 的例子。

The outcome is easily conceivable: I gave in and accepted the pretty woman's offer. When I walked out of the mall, I was awakened by the cold. It dawned on me that I got the short end of the stick in the bargaining. I could not believe that I completely ignored the principles of my bargaining tactics. This is an example of me being flirted and seduced.

再举一个我 seduce 和暧昧他人的例子。

Let me raise an example where I seduced and flirted with others.

2009 年房地产危机的时候，我在湾区开始看房子。中介是个越南裔少妇。带我看了半个月的房子，平时有说有笑的。最后我看中了一个很小的 apartment。当时银行要的价格是 5 万美元（现在价格 30-40 万）。当时市场非常低迷，根本没有人给 offer。我对中介说，我看中了这个房子，咱们给 offer 吧。当然我也表达了深深的忧虑，万一租不出去怎么办。

During the real estate crisis in 2009, I embarked on my hunt for investment properties. One time, I was assisted by a Vietnamese real estate agent who was a young married woman. She arranged different house visits for me for about two weeks, and we chatted and laughed during those visits. In the end, I had my eye on a tiny apartment, the bank valuation of which was US$50,000 (the apartment is worth US$300,000 to US$400,000 now). But back then, the market was sluggish and no one was making an offer. I told my real estate agent that I liked that apartment and that we should put down an offer. Of course, I also expressed my deep worries about not being able to rent it out.

我想这个中介可能是被我迷惑了。中介总是标榜他们是真心真意地为客户着想。也许真的最后我的中介就替我真心真意地着想了。结果我的中介来了这么一句。

"可是万一，银行接了你的 offer，怎么办？"

I guessed that the real estate agent was also seduced by me. Real estate agents often claim that they have the best interests of their clients in mind. Perhaps my real estate agent did have my best interests in mind when she responded, "What if the bank accepts your offer? What should we do then?"

我当时一下子就糊涂了。中介居然害怕 offer 被接受。堪称千古奇谈。现在回想起来其实我让中介真的产生带入感了。

Hearing this response, I was confused. A real estate agent was worried that her client's offer might be accepted. That real estate agent was worried about an offer being accepted was as rare as dragons. Now looking back, my explanation for this rare occurrence is that I was able to make the real estate agent put herself into my shoes.

当然这个暧昧害了我。于是我没有给 offer，中介可能事后也觉得自己被暧昧忽悠得糊涂了，有些不好意思，于是再也没有和我联系过。

Of course, the flirtatious atmosphere also did me some harm because I did not make an offer in the end. The real estate agent has not contacted me ever since. I guess this is because the real estate agent also realized that she was blindfolded by the flirtatious atmosphere and felt embarrassed about it.

商家是最明白如何利用性和暧昧的力量进行销售的。君不见，国内售楼处的销售员都是小姑娘。因为小姑娘忽悠大叔，一拿一个准。走街串巷卖保健品的，都是小姑娘和小鲜肉。小鲜肉逗得老奶奶乐哈哈。老爷爷从小姑娘手里一大包一大包地买保健品。 商店化妆品柜台里没有用帅哥进行推销，因为没有哪个女人想被帅哥知道她们化妆的秘密。

Sellers understand how to use the power of sex and flirting in promoting and selling their products and services better than anyone else. Don't you see that the sales agents at sales centers of real estate projects in China are all young women? This is because for these young women, talking middle-aged men into accepting their offers is a piece of cake. Another observation is that the salespeople of health supplements are all young men and women. Young men make grannies laugh, and grampies buy bags after bags of health supplements from young women. But you will also find that skincare and makeup brands rarely hire handsome guys to promote their products for them at their counters because no woman will want the cute guys to know how they do their makeup and how they look like without wearing makeup.

我自从有了秀水街的教训，凡是讨价还价的场合，碰见小姑娘转身就跑。

Since the "Xiushui Street Incident," I have learned my lesson. Now, whenever I need to bargain with someone, I will flee and find another seller when my opponents are young women.

我自己最成功的一次讨价还价是和一个印度中年油腻大叔手里买车。昏天黑地地一路讨价还价到半夜。对方头上的气味熏的我眼睛都快睁不开了，我当时就预感到，今天肯定能谈个好价钱。 如果，你是帅哥小鲜肉，尽量找大婶大妈讨价还价。 如果，你是女人，千万不要跟小姑娘费口舌，直接找他们男经理。

The most successful bargaining experience I had was when I bought a car from a middle-aged Indian man. The bargaining lasted from dusk till midnight. I could almost tell what perfume he was using because of the prolonged bargaining war. In the middle of the negotiation, I had a gut feeling that I could walk out here with a good deal. If you are a cute guy, try to bargain with middle-aged married women. If you are a woman, do not waste your time with young women and you should talk to the male manager directly.

女人购买大宗商品的时候，记得把自己打扮得漂漂亮亮的。你花那么多钱买的衣服，终于有用武之地了。对了，别忘了上一点点眼妆，一个杀人般的眼神，会让对方魂飞魄散，白花花的银子就都流到你口袋里了。

For my female readers who are trying to make big purchases, my advice is that remember to put on a nice outfit. You can finally make good use of the clothes on which you have spent a lot of money. Oh right, do not forget to apply some eye makeup too. Use your mesmerizing eyes to your advantage in the bargaining so that you can save as much money as possible.

男人购买大宗商品的时候，记得多准备点笑话。你读了那么多的书，不是只为了深夜没事思考宇宙真理的。记得几句轻松的话语，争取把对方逗得花枝乱颤。

For my male readers looking to make big purchases, my advice is that remember to prepare more jokes. The knowledge you have acquired from reading tonnes of books is not limited to an understanding of the meaning of life and the truth of the universe at midnight. Try to throw in some witty jokes here and there in your negotiation and make your opponent laugh.

人的因素是买卖房屋中最不可控的因素。读了我的博文就会明白，其实是出于一些特别荒唐的小理由，让我错过了这样的机会。

The human factor is the least controllable factor in buying and selling real properties. After reading the following story, you will see how I missed precious opportunities because of some ridiculous, trivial reasons.

2009 年的夏天，我出差去佛罗里达开会，顺便去看我的一个朋友。他住在奥兰多。老中聚会总是忍不住谈论起房子。当时的奥兰多与迪斯尼周围的很多公寓卖到不可思议的低价。

In the summer of 2009, I was on a business trip to Florida. I thought I could make good use of this opportunity to also pay a visit to a friend of mine who lived in Orlando. In Chinese Americans' gatherings, we could not help but talk about real estate. At the time, apartment units in Orlando and the Disney area were sold at unbelievably low prices.

我印象中大概一室一厅的公寓价格是 5 万美元左右。但是我那个朋友就是坚决不肯买。我说这是一个好的投资，你应该买下迪斯尼周围的公寓，以后不愁租的。因为迪斯尼会有游客来，现在经济萧条不容易租出去，以后经济好了肯定会容易租出去。

In my recollection, the price of a one-bedroom apartment was around US$500,000. But that friend of mine was adamant not to buy it even though I told him, "This is a good investment. You should buy apartment units in proximity to Disneyland. You will never have to worry about renting them out because Disneyland brings a constant, steady flow of tourists. Even though it will be difficult to find a tenant now because of the depression, it will be an easy task once the economy recovers."

但是他给我算了一笔账，他和我算了一下物业费和房地产税费。最后算下来一个月刚刚打平。他说自己忙活一场一分钱不挣，那又何必呢？所以不值得买。我说按照你这样的算法，哪怕这个房子价格跌到 0，也不值得买，白送给你也不值得买，因为即使白送给你，你也还是基本打平，或者每个月挣100-200 美元。你不能光看现在的收入来决定买不买房子，要看未来的收入和房价。另外不能只看现金流这点小钱，要看房屋价格的变动和你能利用的杠杆。

He showed me his calculations. He had calculated the amount of management fee and property tax, which was equal to the rental income. He told me that it was not worth the time and effort if he could only break-even. And I said, "According to how you calculated and evaluated the decision, even if the price dropped to zero tomorrow or someone gave you the house for free, it would still not be worth it. According to your logic, your rental income and expenses will also "just break-even" (or you will have a monthly profit of US\$100-200) regardless of the price of the unit. You cannot simply make your investment decision based on the current cash flow. You should also consider future income and property prices. Besides, you should not only focus on the cash flow but also look at the changes in property prices and leverage."

最后这个朋友似乎买了一套，好像是用全现金买的。因为贷款额太小，没找银行贷款。后来他跟我说一直不挣钱，于是他就再也没有买。最后似乎错过了这个历史大底。其实他当时借助银行的贷款杠杆，是有足够的能力，一下子买到 10 套 20 套的。现在这些公寓也就成了他的现金奶牛。

In the end, if I remember it correctly, this friend of mine did buy a unit with full payment in cash. As the amount of loan would be too small, he did not apply for a loan from the bank. Later, he told me that he did not make any profits on that investment, so he did not buy other real properties. He missed the greatest bottom of the market in history. If he had used leverage by applying for bank loans, he would have been capable of buying 10-20 apartment units, which would now become his cash cows.

03 股票与抄底时机

03 The Stock Market and the Timing of Buying the Bottoms

虽然我不炒股，但是次贷危机之后，我一直关注股票价格的动荡，因为股票价格和房地产价格有着互相紧密的影响关系。我只能凭着我的记忆回忆这段历史。有兴趣的读者可以比照一下实际的历史数据验证一下我说的对不对。

Though I rarely invest in stocks, I have been keeping an eye on the changes in stock prices since the sub-prime crisis. This is because stock prices are inextricably intertwined with real estate prices. I will try to explain this point by relying on my recollection of the sub-prime crisis. For those who are interested, feel free to compare my claims with the actual historical data.

股票市场在雷曼兄弟倒闭之后开始一路往下跌。Fannie Mae, Freddie Mac, Washington Mutual，纷纷破产或者被政府接管。一个银行接着一个银行破产倒闭。到 2009 年初的时候跌得非常惨。对于市场底部的标志性事件，记忆中我有这样几个。一个是 AIG 破产了，一个是花旗银行的股票跌破了一美元。而花旗银行一年前还是 40 多美元一股。终于大家达成共识，银行是太大了不能破产"too big to fall"。连高盛这样的公司都不敢确信自己不会破产，找巴菲特伸出援助之手。巴菲特给了一个包赚不赔的可转债券的金融援助。最后连 GM 这样以实业为主的公司也破产了，政府只能援助。2009 年初，作为美国工业经济、制造业的明珠，美国制造的标志，通用电气(GE)也摇摇欲坠要破产了。

The stock market had been plummeting since the bankruptcy of Lehman Brothers. Fannie Mae, Freddie Mac, and Washing Mutual all filed for bankruptcy or were taken over by the government. Banks were also bankrupted and closed one after another. At the beginning of 2009, stock prices declined to abysmal levels. I can recollect some of the most significant events in the market bottom. The first is the bankruptcy of AIG, and the second is the share price of Citibank dropped below US$1, which traded at more than US$40 just a year ago. Finally, the stakeholders reached a consensus that banks were "too big to fail." Amidst the crisis, even such a prestigious company as Goldman Sachs had no idea whether the company would also fall, so it turned to Warren Buffett for help. Warren Buffett offered Goldman Sachs financial assistance in the form of a purchase of its convertible bonds, which would only bring the former profits. In the end, even GM was bankrupted. As it was a company that mainly involved industrial activities, the government intervened to help. At the beginning of 2009, as a titan in the American industrial sector and a symbol of "made in the U.S.A.," General Electric (GE) was also on the verge of bankruptcy.

我当时不太信这样综合性很强、既有实业、又有品牌的 GE 会破产。所以格外关注了一下。原来 GE 有一个非常庞大的金融部门。它的商业部门运行正常，但是它的金融部门有毒资产要把整个 GE 帝国拖下水。

At the time, I did not believe that GE, a multinational conglomerate with its own brand and industrial activities, would fail, so I paid special attention to it. My research revealed that even though GE's operation and business were healthy, its gigantic finance department was a toxic asset that was dragging down the whole GE empire.

GE 开了一个非常庞大的新闻听证会来证明公司不会受到大的冲击和影响。我仔细看了一下他们那天做出来的财务分析报告。当时我还感慨一下，因为我知道那些 PPT 不知道是哪个投行里的 MBA 毕业生，用了不知道多少个不眠之夜赶出来的。

GE hosted an enormous media conference to prove that the company would not be adversely affected by the crisis. I examined the financial analysis and reports they published on that day in detail. I even sighed because I knew that some MBA graduates who worked in investment banks probably burned the midnight oil to make those PowerPoint slides.

看完报告，我忍不住玩儿一样的买了一些花旗和通用的股票。我印象中只买了 100 股花旗，100 股通用，花了不到几百美元。读了通用的分析报告，我也完全不能判断市场底部在哪里。我只想买一点股票作为一个标志，以后可以用来回忆这段历史。当时我太太和我说，我应该记一个日记，把每天发生的事件和自己的感受记录下来。这样可以当风浪过去的时候，回头看看，提高自己的抄底水平。

Having read the report, I could not resist the temptation of buying some Citibank and GM's shares for fun. I vaguely remember that I bought 100 shares of Citibank and 100 shares of GM only, which only cost me a few hundred dollars. I could not really judge where the market bottom exactly was even after reading GM's report, but I bought those shares nonetheless as a symbol that I can use to remember this historical time. At the time, my wife was telling me that I should journal the daily events in the market and my own reflections. When the crisis has passed, I can take out my journal and improve my skills in buying the bottom.

那个时候，股票震荡剧烈。道琼斯多的时候一天起伏就有 1000 多点。每天对股票指数震荡的报道，好像很是家常便饭的事情。没有人知道底部在哪里。专业人士不知道，我也不知道。但是总是有无数多的大师出来预测底部在哪里。

Back then, the stock market fluctuated drastically. On a certain day, the extent of the fluctuation of the Dow Jones index was more than 1000 points. People had become accustomed to news about fluctuating stock indexes. No one knew when the market bottom was, not even professionals or me. However, there were always dozens of "experts and masters" who openly predicted the market bottom.

我印象最深刻的是前总统克林顿都跳出来发表见解。在 2009 年初的有一天股票大跌之后，大约是 3 月份左右，他侃侃而谈，痛斥本次次贷危机的根源，然后他说他感觉市场还远远没有到底"This is still far from over"。这是他的原话，我印象深刻。他说我们犯下了很大的错误，需要漫长的时间来慢慢修正。

What left me with the strongest impression was a speech by former President Clinton. After the stock market witnessed a terrifying decline in March 2009, he

第十五章 从 100 到 1000 万（二）抄底！抄底！

Chapter 15: From $1 million to $10 million (2) Buying the Bottom!

came out to give his "insightful" speech. He blamed the culprits of the sub-prime crisis and asserted that "This is still far from over." This is a direct quote from his speech that left me with a strong impression. He also said that we were making a huge mistake and that it would take a long time for the market to recover.

大人物说出这样的话，说明市场真是已经到底了。因为市场没有更多的人看空了。

When a prominent figure makes such a speech, it means that the market has hit its bottom because no one is shorting the market anymore.

克林顿这句话说完，股票开始一路反弹。一口气不停，是个完美的 V 型反弹。在我印象里，克林顿当时的讲话基本就是股票的最低点，是整个次贷危机的历史最低点。

After Clinton's speech, the stock market bounced all the way back in a V-shaped curve. In my memory, the time when Clinton made his speech was the lowest point of the stock market and also the historical low in the entire sub-prime crisis.

所以你大概可以判断出股票的最低点和经济的形势并没有太大的关系。最低点取决是后面是否还有更多的空头。市场是否到谷底是看是否还有更多的绝望者。市场是否到顶点是看是否还有更多的乐观派。就是连前总统这样的话的人都说出绝望的话之后，实在不能再有更多的绝望了，股票市场这个时候就到了最低点。当然这样说说容易，只能用来做大趋势判断。具体的节点不确定性很大，这也是我从来不炒股的一个原因。

Therefore, you can see that the lowest point in the stock market has little to do with the economic situation. Where the lowest point is depends on whether there is more shorting activity in the market and whether there are more desperate players in the market. Whether the market has hit its peak depends on whether there are more optimistic players in the market. So, when a former president lost all hopes, this meant that there could not be any more desperate people in the market and that the market had hit its bottom. The points I have made here are simple theories that can only be used to make a judgment on the general trend, but the detailed timing and price points are full of uncertainties. This is also why I rarely trade stocks.

股票到了最低点之后一路反转上涨。是的，真的就是一路反转上涨，根本不给任何人上车的机会。一口气不停地涨了很久。我自己不炒股票，但是每天看市场的行情，我可以听到或者感觉到千千万万一脚踏空的人，发出痛苦的呐喊声。我的一个朋友就是这样。她是斯坦福大学学经济出身，但是在市场最低点的时候，竟然她也说定投的投资策略不 work。现在回想起来，她应该和克林顿一样，都是最后一批绝望者。

When the stock market hit its lowest point, it bounced back immediately and kept rising. Yes, it did show a V-shaped bounceback, leaving no room for anyone to get on the bus. It kept soaring for a very long time. Even though I rarely trade stocks, I read the market news every day. I can only imagine the sighing and moaning of those who shorted the market. A friend of mine was among such a crowd. She studied economics at Stanford. But when the market hit the bottom, she surprised me by saying that the investment strategy of dollar-cost averaging did not work. In retrospect, she was a member of the last group of desperate people in the market as Clinton.

经历过这样的 V 型反转，就会更加对股市充满敬畏之心。这也是每次经济危机到来的时候，很少有基金公司敢把股票卖掉的一个原因。金融风暴来临之前，往往大家都能看到下跌趋势，但是没人能够控制好节点。股市会随时发生反转，让你一脚踩空，追悔莫及。

When one has experienced a V-shaped stock market bottom, he or she will fear and never underestimate the stock market. This is one of the reasons why few fund managers sell their stocks when an economic crisis hits. Before a financial storm, people can often notice a downward trend, but no one can control the timing. When the stock market reverses, those who short the market will regret their decisions.

但是在房地产市场就不一样了。我每个周末都在看房子，摸着市场脉搏。2010 年，当股市大约上涨了一年左右，我给自己下的命令就是要开始买，而且一定要开始买。房地产一个循环就是十几年，一辈子没有几次这样的机会。而且为了这个机会，我已经整整准备了 5 年。从 2005 年起，我就期待着有一天房地产崩溃触底。市场崩溃我已经等到了，触底要是错过了，那就太辜负我 5 年的心血了。

However, the real estate market is different. I was visiting houses on sale every weekend, so I had an in-depth understanding of the market trend. In 2010, when the stocks had been rising for about a year, the order that I gave myself was to start buying at all costs. A market cycle in real estate lasts for more than ten years, which means we only get a few opportunities. For this opportunity, I have prepared for five years. Since 2005, I was waiting for the real estate market to collapse and hit the bottom. The market had already started to collapse. If I miss the market bottom, I will waste all my planning and effort in these five years.

因为我已经苦等了 5 年，所以我要毫不犹豫地全仓杀入。

As I have already waited patiently for five years, I am going all in this time without hesitation.

04 艰难的抄底
04 Buying the Bottom Was an Uphill Battle

抄底说说简单，全仓杀入。可是我哪来的钱呢，花钱的地方到处都是，存钱的篓子千疮百孔。因为付清了所有的 MBA 学费，买入了中国的房子，买了好车。这个时候我把美国所有的钱都汇总在一起，可以投资的钱大概也只有 8 万美元左右。

It is easy to say, "Buy the bottom and all in." However, where should I get the money? At the time, I could not save much money because I had many expenses: I paid off my MBA tuition and bought real estate in China and a nice car. My total "investable money" amounted to around US$80,000.

看着银行里的 8 万元存款。我对我太太说：“我要买 8 套房子”。

Looking at my bank savings of US$80,000, I told my wife, "I have to buy eight investment properties."

她说"你疯了吗？我们手上只有 8 万美元，你怎么买 8 套房子？我们目标小一点，我们买一套就可以了。"

She said, "Have you gone nuts? We only have US$80,000. How can you buy eight investment properties? Let's set a more realistic goal of one investment property."

我说"不行，我一定要买 8 套房子。"我斩钉截铁地说。这样的机会太少了，而且我盘算了这么久，我一定要买 8 套房子。

I was adamant and told her, "No. I have to buy eight investment properties because these opportunities happen once in a blue moon. Besides, I have made such a detailed plan and have been waiting for these opportunities for so long. I have to buy eight investment properties."

我像赴刑场就义一样的口号似乎吓到了她，她都没有理我。她倒是好奇我有什么本事变出魔术，有本事买 8 套房子。她同意我先买一两套房子。并且她说你从来没有在美国当过房东，根本不知道怎样管理出租房。还是先实际一点，买一套房子练练手再说。还可以等下一次经济危机再找机会。

My determination and slogan seemed to scare her a bit, but she ignored me. She was curious about how I could magically buy eight investment properties. She consented that I should buy 1-2 investment properties first. She also told me, "You have never bought an investment property in the U.S. before, so you have no idea how to manage it. We have to be realistic and start with one investment property. We can wait for more opportunities in the next economic crisis."

"我要买 8 套房子。"我还是那句冰冷的话。像复读机一样一字不差，像南极的石头一样冰冷而坚硬。

"I have to buy eight investment properties," I replied with this emotionless slogan. I was like a reading machine with a cold and determined tone.

她没好气地走开了，懒得理我这个神经病。

292

She walked away because she did not bother to talk to a lunatic.

我之所用这样吓人的口气说话，是因为我知道，没有坚定的意志和钢铁一样的决心，人是做不成事情的。

The reason why I used such a scary tone is that I know without a strong will and determination, one can achieve nothing.

这个时候我 2005 年 72 万美元卖出的"指数房"已经标出了一个不可思议的低价，26 万美元。比最高点跌掉了 64%！ 我看到这个价格心砰砰直跳。就像小时候抓蟋蟀一样，小心翼翼地扑向我的猎物。我知道市场底部就在眼前，每下跌一步就越接近底部。因为仅仅两个月之前"指数房"还是 32 万美元。两个月一下子又跌了 20%。一切都完美地符合经典的市场底部的特征，持续下跌一个阶段后快速探底。

At the time, the "index house" that I sold for US$720,000 in 2005 reached an unbelievably low price of US$260,000, a 64% drop from the peak. I could feel my heart begin to race. This "buying the bottom" game was like how I was trying to catch a grasshopper when I was a child: I approached my prey meticulously. I knew that the market bottom was right here in front of me. The more the property prices dropped further, the closer the market was to the bottom. This is because just two months ago, my index house was priced at US$320,000. In these two months, the price dropped by 20%. Everything fit in with the typical features of a market bottom: After a persistent decline, the market was heading toward a new bottom.

现在想起来。真的我非常感谢我买入的第一个住房。我不但从这个住房挣到了自住房的首付，而且因为和这个房子类似的房子当时市场上很多。让我有一个我熟悉的"指数房"把握市场的脉搏。

In retrospect, I was grateful for the first residential property that I bought. Not only did I earn a down payment for my own house, but it also served as a useful "index house" for me to understand the market trend because there were many similar listings on the market.

指数房跌到 26 万美元的那个月就是当年整个次贷危机湾区房价的最低点。我还记得当时的那个法拍屋里面的样子。在一开始的时候，大部分法拍屋都是干干净净整整齐齐的，后来的法拍屋越来越破。当时那个 26 万的法拍屋里面已经破烂不堪。地毯要换，墙要重新刷。厨房油腻不堪，垃圾扔了一屋子。看来是一个极度不负责的人搬走留下的。

The month in which the price of my index house dropped to US$260,000 marked the lowest point of the property prices in the Bay Area during the entire subprime crisis. I still remember how the conditions of foreclosure houses deteriorated as the market approached its bottom. In the beginning, most foreclosure houses were tidy and clean. Later, the foreclosure houses were getting more dilapidated. At the time, there was a US$260,000 foreclosure house that had an uninhabitable interior: The carpet needed replacement, the wall needed to be repainted, the kitchen was dirty and oily, and the house was drowned in garbage. Everything indicated that a highly irresponsible person moved and left all this mess behind.

就在那个 26 万美元指数房标价出售的那一周，市场似乎一下子从昏睡中醒了过来。很多买家蜂拥出现。我的 offer（出价）很快就淹没在其他 offer 的大海里了。

In the week when the index was sold for US$260,000, the market awakened from its deep sleep. Dozens of buyers flocked to the market. My offer was soon inundated in the sea of other offers.

我没有抢到这个房子。于是我开始诚心诚意地写 offer。市面上在法拍的房子非常多。一个小区里 10%的房子都在走法拍程序，总共有二三十个。但是交易过手速度非常快，成交量也非常大。

I failed to get that house, so I started to spend more time and effort on writing my offer. There were many foreclosure listings on the market. Ten percent of houses in a community, which was a total of 20-30, were going through the foreclosure procedure. The speed of transactions was very fast, and the volume of sales was huge.

我当时看中了两个社区的房子。一个离我住的地方比较远，开车 45 分钟，一个离我住的地方比较近，30 分钟。我做了非常详细的 Excel 表，根据租金、价格，利率，保险、HOA 费用、地税。我把能想到的因素都考虑进去了，包括未来可能出现的空置率和维修费用。也参考历史价格计算了未来可能出现的增值。当时按照保守计算，离我近的房子 Cash on cash 的年回报率是 15%，离我远点的房子年回报率是 20%。

At the time, I had my eye on two communities. One of them was quite far from where I lived, with a driving time of 45 minutes. Another community was closer to my home with a driving time of 30 minutes. I made very detailed Excel spreadsheets to calculate every factor that I could think of, from the usual considerations of rental income, house price, interest rates, insurance, HOA fee, and land tax to more remote considerations of future vacancy rate and repair expenses. I also calculated possible appreciation based on historical prices. According to a prudent estimate at the time, the house that was closer to my home had an annual cash-on-cash return of 15%, and the other house that was farther a 20%.

所以显然我应该买离我远一点的地方。好在我当时吃过 Excel 的亏，没有书生意气，我两边都同时给 offer. 我当时想的是买到哪个都可以，当然最好是买到回报率高的地方。这么多年过去的结果显示，那个 Excel 表计算的完全没有意义。因为最后影响空置率和维修成本的居然是距离。距离远的地方我懒得跑和管理。出现维修的事情，也懒得去维修而让客户自己去找更昂贵的维修工。最关键的是，你在房租议价上，远的地方没有近的地方那么强有力。往往是好不容易找到租客，想想跑起来太烦，能租个什么价，就租掉算了吧。

Therefore, it was obvious that I should buy the house that was farther from me. But luckily, as I had been tricked by my spreadsheet analysis before, I decided to play safe by making an offer on both houses. I was thinking that I would be happy buying either one even though I preferred a higher return rate. Time has passed since I made my analysis on Excel, and reality showed that my Excel analysis was completely meaningless. When I was making my spreadsheet, it did not occur to me that distance affected the vacancy rate and repair costs the most. I was too lazy to manage the house that was farther from me. Whenever the tenant needed to have something repaired, I was lazy and let the tenant find a more expensive repairman. But the most critical factor is that I have less bargaining power in trying to rent out a house that was farther from me. It was often the case that I did not bother to stand firmly in the bargaining when I found a tenant because of the hassle of commuting back and forth between my investment property and home.

当然当时我还没有想那么多。我思考的最主要的事情就是尽可能地买到房子。我知道抢房的时候，根本不要挑挑拣拣，哪个都可以。我根本不等上一个 offer 是否给回复，就抢着出下一个 offer。但是过了一个月，我的 offer 没有一个被接纳的。我给的基本都是要价（ask price）的 offer。我赶紧问相关的中介，到底是什么情况？

Of course, I was not thinking about all these details at the time. My main consideration was to buy as many investment properties as possible. I knew that in competing for houses, I would not have the time to choose a house. I would be content if I could get a house even though it might not be to my liking. I was so eager that I would make another offer before even receiving a response to my previous offer. However, after a month, none of my offers were accepted. Most of my offers were on an ask-price basis. I immediately talked to the real estate agents to find out what was happening.

中介跟我说，其他人都会加价，加价从 5%-10%不等。而有些短售屋的加价加得太多，超过了银行贷款。业主干脆收回去不卖了！

The real estate agent told me that other potential buyers would increase their offer for the foreclosure house by 5-10%. Some foreclosure houses witnessed an even greater increase in price that now exceeded the amount of the bank loan so owners decided not to sell the house.

我的子弹有限，不敢加价太多。8 万美元，按照 20% 的首付。我满打满算我可能可以买两个独立屋。如果运气不好只能买一个或者买一个公寓。我可不想我等了 5 年的机会就这么错过了。显然我需要去找钱，我需要大量的钱做首付。

My bullets were limited, so I did not dare increase my offer by too much. I was planning to buy two single-family detached houses with US$80,000 by paying a 20% down payment for each. If I had bad luck, I could only buy one house or an apartment. I did not want to miss the golden opportunities that I had patiently waited for five years. The solution was obvious: I needed to find more money. I needed lots of money for my down payments.

可是钱从哪里来呢？这是一个大问题，我抓破脑袋在想。

But where should I get the money? This is a big problem, and I was scratching my head about it.

05 克服千难万险也要抢
05 Leaving No Stone Unturned in Buying Investment Properties

抢房子不顺利让我渐渐回到理性。又过了两周我也学乖了，我加的价格比别人也更加多一点，终于买到了第一个法拍屋。这是一个离我比较近的一个小小的三居室独立屋。22 万成交，我的买入价比 2008 年最高点 65 万美元低了一半还多。

The bumps in my hunt for investment properties forced me to become more rational. After another two weeks, I learned my lesson: I offered more on top of the asking price than other potential buyers. This is how I finally bought my first foreclosure house, which was a three-bedroom single-family detached house that was pretty close to my home, at US$220,000, which was more than 50% lower than the peak of US$650,000 in 2008.

办完交割手续，我立刻就找贷款中介，让他给我再开一个新的贷款预批函（loan pre-approval letter）。房价每天都在涨，我一分钟也等不及。可是贷款中介几乎给了我一个晴天霹雳一样的消息。他说你买不了了，你的条件只能买一个房子。

After the closing and delivery, I immediately contacted a loan agent to ask him for a new loan pre-approval letter. Property prices were increasing every day, and I did not want to waste another minute. However, the loan agent replied to me with some bad news that I could buy one investment property only.

我说"为什么我只能买一个房子？"我没好意思说我的雄心壮志是买 8 个房子。

"Why could I buy one investment property only?" I asked. I was embarrassed to tell him that my grand aspiration was to buy eight investment properties.

他说你们的收入和自己现在有的贷款负担比例太低了。你要买下个房子也可以，但是必须把这个房子先出租出去。要有半年以上的房租收入证明，这个时候你才可以买下一个房子。如果运气不好，你可能还要一年以上的出租收入证明，才能买下一个房子。

He said, "The ration of your family income and existing loan burden ratio is too low. If you want to buy another real property, you have to rent out your first property. With proof of rental income for more than six months, then you can buy your second property. If you have bad luck, you may need to provide proof of rental income for a year before you can buy a second property."

我心里咯噔了一下。"半年以上？房价每天都在飞涨。我怎么可能等半年？"

My heart skipped a beat, "More than six months? Property prices were soaring every day. How could I wait for another six months?"

我经历过中国的抢房过程。我知道这个时候循规蹈矩是没有用的。需要八仙过海，各显神通。买一个房子可远远不是我的目标，我要买 8 个房子。我的内心对自己呐喊。虽然我不知道我怎么样才能买到 8 个房子，但我要克服千难万险去买到这 8 个房子。因为那是我的目标。是我写在投资理财博客上，给几十万个读者看过的目标。我有一万个理由要去完成这个目标。我今天在写这篇回忆录的时候，我还能够感觉到我当时激情澎湃的心脏。

I have experienced the whole "competing for houses" process in China before, so I knew that playing strictly by the rules would not help me. Instead, I needed to leave no stone unturned by trying every means possible. Buying one property was far below my goal. "I need eight," exclaimed my heart. Even though I had no idea how I could buy eight properties, I needed to overcome all obstacles in achieving this because that is my goal. I had written this goal on my investment and wealth management blog, which was read by hundreds of thousands of readers. I had a million reasons to finish this goal. Even when I am now writing a recollection of my experience, I can still feel that my heart was filled with passion and excitement.

怎么办？换贷款中介！找个不用等那么多时间的。

What should I do? Find another loan agent that will not ask me to wait for another six months.

是的，我只能一个又一个的去寻找各种各样的贷款中介，让他们帮我解决我的问题。大部分的回答都是 NO！因为我当时在创业，所以以我自己的收入属于自雇收入（self-employment income），而自雇（self-employment）需要多年的收入历史才能够证明自己有稳定的收入。

Yes, I did contact different loan agents one after another to find someone that could help me solve my problems. Most of them gave me a big "NO" because I was starting my business at the time, which meant I was self-employed. Self-employed individuals are required to submit years of income history to prove that they have a stable income.

我需要找到一个贷款中介，在这方面相对宽松一些的。

I need to find a loan agent who has some looser requirements in this respect.

贷款的问题没有解决。抢房子又总是被 overbid （他人抢价），更糟糕的是钱的问题还是没有解决。买第一个房子首付用掉了 4 万多美元。我还能最多买一个。我上哪儿弄更多的钱呢？

Just when I was still trying to solve my loan problem, I encountered another difficulty: My offer was always overbid. Worse still, money remained a big issue. As I had already paid US$40,000 as a down payment for my first house, I could only buy one more investment property at most. Where could I get more money?

我当时焦急的心态就和玩大富翁游戏里，手忙脚乱完成土地置换交易后开始盖房的人一样。那个游戏里砸锅卖铁也要想办法盖房子。但是往往不是有地就可以盖房子，你需要有现金才行。

I was anxious like someone playing the Monopoly who tried to build houses after exchanging and buying the land. In this board game, the key is to build houses. However, owning the same collection of land is not enough; you need to have cash.

更多的首付款大概有这么几个来源，一个是把中国的房子卖掉，那样可以筹措一些钱。二是从美国自住房里申请一些房屋净值贷款(home equity loan)。三就是把自己 401K 的钱取出来。

There were several possible sources that could fund my down payments. The first was to raise more money by selling my properties in China. The second was to apply for a home equity loan using my own residential home. The third is to take money out of my 401K.

中国的房子当时正在狂涨。我害怕像上次一样偷鸡不成蚀把米。自己自住房的 home equity loan 可以用，但是我尝试了几个银行最后都不行。因为房价下跌了，我自己的自住房的价格也下来了，所以我剩下的 equity 没有那么多。次贷危机后，银行吃一堑长一智，对 loan to equity value 的要求也特别高。401K 的钱取出来有很多问题，最直接的问题就是罚款。虽然我知道房子的回报会比 401K 更好，但是蒙受罚款却不是我想要的。因为罚款是真金白银，交了就没有了。

At the time, China's real estate market was skyrocketing. I was afraid that I would make the same mistake as last time. A home equity loan was a better alternative, but I was rejected by several banks. As the price of my house dropped with declining property prices, I did not have much equity left. After the sub-prime crisis, the banks learned their lessons so they had a strict requirement on loan-to-equity value. Taking out money from 401K entails many other problems, the most direct of which is a penalty. Even though I knew that real estate investing would yield a better return than 401K, I did not want to bear the penalty because I would need to pay cash upfront.

当你缺钱的时候，没有人愿意给你钱。不但是我一个人缺钱。当时投资理财论坛上抄底的各路英雄没有一个不缺钱的。我印象中有一个网友甚至开出 15% 年利率的回报，用房子做抵押，找人借钱。可是还是借不到。

When I desperately needed money, no one was willing to lend it to me. But it was not only me who desperately needed money. At the time, all the heroes on the forum who were trying to buy the bottom were all in desperate need. In my recollection, a netizen who tried to borrow money by offering a 15% interest rate per annum and using his own house as collateral at the same time also failed to solicit more funds.

我买的第一个房子空置了一个月之后，勉勉强强出租出去了。但是出租也不是一帆风顺，因为我那个区非核心地带，经济还没有复苏，来看房的都是一些稀奇古怪的人。我头一次在美国当房东，这些人是不是能交下月的房租，我心里也没有底。

After a month of vacancy of my first investment property in the U.S., I managed to rent it out. However, the process was not a smooth sail because that neighborhood was not a central district and the economy had not yet recovered. Those who were interested in renting my house were some weird people. It was the first time I had been a landlord in the U.S., so I had no idea whether these people would pay their rents next month.

我只能好声好气地伺候着，有求必应。灯泡坏了我都跑过去帮他们换一下。把房客伺候得像大爷一样。因为我知道这个时候不能有任何闪失。我想起了前一阵子在拉斯维加斯买房子的那个网友说的话。做了房东才知道，真不知道谁是杨白劳，谁是黄世仁。

But I still tried my best to please my tenants by answering to their every need. When the light bulb was out, I drove there to help them change it. I was serving them as if they were kings and queens because I knew that I needed the money. This experience reminded me of a saying by a netizen who bought real properties in Las Vagas earlier: As a landlord, you will never know who is Yang Bailao and who is Huang Shiren.

06 抢到第二个房

06 Buying My Second Investment Property Amid Fierce Competition

又过了两个月，我终于找到一个贷款中介，他可以帮我办第二个房子的贷款，不用等半年。不过利息要稍微高一些。利息高就高吧，回头 refinance 时候再说，这个时候顾不得那么多了，赶紧抢到房子是最重要的。

After another two months, I finally managed to find a loan agent who was willing to help me apply for a loan for my second investment property. I did not need to wait another six months, but he would charge me a higher interest rate. Despite a higher interest rate, I went ahead with my purchase because, at this moment, getting the property was of utmost importance. I could leave the issue of a higher interest rate later when I tried to refinance my house.

我买的第二个房子是在游轮上买到的。那个时候每周都不停地在发各种 offer。几乎所有的 offer 都全军覆没。最大的障碍就是我的银行现金太少，卖家不是很肯定我有足够的能力 close deal。发那个 offer 的时候，正好碰到我们全家去海上坐游轮度假。

I bought my second investment property in the U.S. when I was on a cruise. Back then, I was busy sending different offers every week. Almost all of them lost in the fierce competition for houses. The biggest obstacle was that I had too little cash in my bank account, so the sellers were not sure if I was capable of closing the deal. When I submitted the offer that was later accepted by the seller, I was on a cruise vacation with my family.

工作再忙，不能耽误休息。买房再忙，不能耽误度假。我的这个回忆录可能给读者一种错觉，感觉我每天都在忙房子的事情。其实不是的，大部分的精力我还是在忙我的工作，照顾孩子。买卖房子的事情，只限于周末和晚上下班。每年的度假再忙也是必不可少的。

No matter how busy I am with my work, I make sure it does not disrupt my rest. No matter how busy I am with real estate investing, it cannot interfere with my vacation. Even though readers may feel like I am always busy with real estate investing 24/7, this is not a true picture of my life. I spend most of my time and energy on my full-time job and taking care of my children. I only deal with real estate investing on weekends and weekday nights. An annual vacation is indispensable, however hectic my schedule is.

当时手机还没有这么发达，游轮上完全没有信号。整个游轮只有一个网络端口，按分钟收费。但是没有办法，我也只能一边看着墨西哥湾的落日，一边在游轮上写 offer。游轮上没有打印机。所以我只能用带着的计算机把长长的合同每一页截屏截下来，然后手描的在上面签字。写完 offer 再用邮箱发送出去。轮船在大海上航行，外面是喧闹的人群。我在游泳池边完成了这个工作。当时有种生意人做大买卖的感觉，因为电影里大富豪们都是在高尔夫球场上和游泳池边上把生意做完的。

Back then, cell phones were less technologically advanced. My phone could not receive any signal when I was on the cruise, and there was only one internet connection point on the cruise, which charged by the minute. But I had no other choices, so while I was enjoying Mexico Bay's sunset, I was writing my offer on the cruise. As the cruise did not have a printing machine, I used my laptop to take a screenshot of every page of the contract and then signed it. After writing my offer, I send it via email. The cruise was sailing, and I was surrounded by noisy crowds. I finished this task by the swimming pool. At the time, I felt like I was a businessman who secured and closed a big deal because most billionaires in the movies finished their business by the swimming pool or on the golf course.

07 不要相信媒体

07 Do Not Trust the Media

2011 年，当房价止跌回升的时候，跳出很多著名的经济评论家预测未来。这些评论家，每个人都带着吓死人的头衔，包括诺贝尔奖经济学奖获得者 Robert Shiller。他号称因为准确地预测了互联网泡沫和次贷危机而获得诺贝尔奖。我是不信这些事后诸葛亮式的吹牛把戏的，无论他有多么大的头衔。因为普通民众可能很少注意到他 2015 也预测美国股市泡沫严重，立刻会崩盘。结果被打脸。看空的人永恒看空。吹牛的把戏就是不断地试错，试对一次就无限扩大宣传，然后拿诺贝尔奖，试错了就默默无语。

In 2011, when property prices started to bounce back, many famous economic commentators jumped out to predict the future. These commentators had impressive titles and positions, including Nobel laureate in Economic Science, Robert Shiller. He claimed that he won the Nobel Prize because he accurately predicted the dot-com bubble and sub-prime crisis. Personally, I do not believe in these boastful claims that are often made in hindsight, however impressive his title is. Most ordinary citizens will fail to notice that in 2015, Shiller also predicted that the U.S. stock market was in a huge bubble that would burst soon. The reality? It entered the longest bull market in history. His strategy is to always predict that the market will go down. Despite the many wrong predictions, all it takes is one correct prediction that is widely circulated in the mainstream media for him to rise to fame and win the Nobel Prize. When he makes a mistake, he will lay low.

当时电视采访他问他觉得房价会下跌多久，他说可能会下跌 3~5 年的样子。最后又有人问他，你觉得房价什么时候会回升？什么时候会有下一个房地产泡沫？他当时的一句话是，"probably not in your life again."

In a TV interview back then, he was asked for how long the property prices would continue to drop, to which he replied the next 3-5 years. At the end of the interview, he was asked when the property prices would begin to rise. His answer was, "Probably not in your life again."

我对他后面这半句话特别不以为然，我甚至认为房价下跌 3~5 年这样的判断也是不靠谱。至少对于局部地区，湾区这样的地方不是这样的。市场反转就在眼前。说美国此生再不会有房地产泡沫更是不可能的事情，下跌之后就意味着暴涨。只要是自由市场，有跌就有涨，有涨就有跌。

In my opinion, what he said did not make any sense. For example, at least in the Bay Area, property prices would not continue to drop for the next 3-5 years. The market reversal was right here. Saying that there would never be a real estate bubble in the next 70 years or so was nonsense. A drastic decline in prices entails a drastic increase. As long as it is a free market, there will be declines and rises.

可是所有的媒体报刊杂志都不这么说，如果你有兴趣去考古看一下 2010 年 2012 年前后的所有的媒体，没有一个媒体会告诉你房地产价格在下跌之后会暴涨，反而会有大量法拍屋源源不断出来。你今天去查一下 Foreclosure second wave 这个关键词。就能看到当时汹涌澎湃的报道是多么的错误，当时很多媒体认为第二轮法拍屋浪潮马上就到。我随便节选一段 2012 年初的新闻报道。

"Foreclosures have plagued the United States for the past few years and it seems that trend is set to continue. Now even though the amount of foreclosures dropped 19% in January and another 8% in February, it's expected that a massive increase in foreclosures is on the way. Experts warn that the massive $26 billion settlement between five of the largest banks in the country will cause a major ripple when it comes to foreclosures and how they are inherently handled."（无翻译）

Yet all the mainstream media were saying otherwise. If you are interested, feel free to take a look at all the media reports and articles from 2010-2012. None of them told you that the property prices would soar after the decline and that countless foreclosure listings mushroomed. If you search "foreclosure second wave," you will see that all these reports were erroneous because many media believed that a second wave of foreclosure listings would soon arrive. Here is an excerpt from a news article at the beginning of 2012:

"Foreclosures have plagued the United States for the past few years and it seems that the trend is set to continue. Now even though the amount of foreclosures dropped by 19% in January and another 8% in February, it's expected that a massive increase in foreclosures is on the way. Experts warn that the massive $26 billion settlement between five of the largest banks in the country will cause a major ripple when it comes to foreclosures and how they are inherently handled." （重复）

没有一个著名的经济学家，没有任何的股票评论人，至少我没有看到一个公开预测 2012 年之后的房地产价格的狂飙。

My observation is that no well-known economists or stock commentators openly predicted that property prices would skyrocket after 2012.

然而在我眼里，这简直是秃子头上的虱子的事情，虽然我也不知道什么时候价格会反转上升，但我知道反转是肯定的，因为过去的历史一次一次都是这样的。而且反转不会用几年就会达到新高。

Yet in my opinion, this is just common sense. Even though I have no idea exactly when the prices would reverse and rise again, I am sure that a reversal is inevitable because this has happened every single time in history. Furthermore, it only takes a few years for the market to reach a new high.

这个现象又一次印证了我之前的一个观察和理论，就是所有的这些评论人，他们最关心的是如何讨好听众，他们并不关心自己的判断是否正确。他们也许独立思考，但是真正独立思考的人，很少敢在公共媒体上公开说。至少媒体不愿意播放和广大民众意见相悖的观点。

This phenomenon is supporting evidence for another observation and theory that I mentioned earlier, which is that the priority of these commentators is how to please their audience but not whether their judgments are correct. Perhaps they had their independent thinking, but real independent thinkers rarely talk about their views openly in mainstream media because the media is unwilling to feature viewpoints that are contrary to public opinion.

做出独立思考而采取行动的人是默默无语的。黑石 Blackstone 这样的对冲基金就在干这件事。他们突破传统思维，直接从银行手里购买法拍屋。据说前后整整买了将近 100 亿美元的法拍屋，最后发了一大笔财。他们默默买进的时候能够声张么？当然不能，恐怕还要雇经济学家在媒体上鼓吹泡沫和衰退有多么严重呢。

Those who think independently and take action often keep a low profile. Take Blackstone. They broke through the limits of traditional thinking and purchased foreclosures from banks. It was rumored that Blackstone bought at least $10 billion foreclosures in total, making a huge profit. Can they tell others about their plans when buying those real properties? Of course not. I am afraid they will even hire economists to talk about how serious the bubble and recession are in mainstream media.

08 信息不对称的房市
08 Information Asymmetry in the Real Estate Market

第一年抄底的工作结束，我在文学城博客上写了一篇新年总结的文章。我告诉大家不要迷信名人和媒体以及各种 Excel 的指标，抢到篮子里的就是菜，不要犹豫赶紧抢。

After my first year of buying the bottom, I wrote an article on my blog to summarize my job. I told people not to blindly trust celebrities, the media, and all sorts of indicators on Excel. As long as people could get their hands on an investment property, they should not hesitate to join the buying spree.

我这样是在警示大家市场底部已经形成，鼓励别人抄底。但是这些鼓励给我自己可能带来了很大的副作用，因为我在当时发现我买房子的时候，很多和我同样背景的人在和我竞争。我抢房子的时候，我发现一多半是中国人、印度人，和其他亚裔面孔居多。似乎美国普通的民众非常的少，至少在湾区是这样的。我感觉这里面可能有很大一部分程度来自信息不对称。

I was warning everyone that the market had already hit its bottom and encouraging them to buy the bottom. However, my encouraging words to others brought some side-effects for myself because I realized that my other competitors came from a similar background as me when I was buying real properties. In this fierce competition, I discovered that most of the potential buyers were Chinese, Indians, and other Asians. It seemed that the number of buyers who came from an ordinary "American background" was very small. This was at least true in the Bay Area. I think that the reason for this observation is to a large extent due to information unsymmetry.

大部分中国人和印度人在 IT 领域工作。他们在公司里已经感觉到了经济在复苏。那个时候又是中美的蜜月期，我们作为美国的华人，我们知道还有太多的中国人要到美国来。他们或者是为了子女教育，或者是厌倦了中国恶劣的空气环境，想移民到美国来。就像当年山西的煤老板赚了钱都去北京生活一样。

Most Chinese Americans and Indian Americans work in the IT field. They could already feel that the economy was recovering in their work environment. At the time, China and the U.S. were having a honeymoon period. As Chinese Americans, we knew that there would be an influx of more Chinese immigrants to the U.S. These people came here for better education for their children or because they were sick of the bad air quality in China. This is like how mine owners in Shanxi, China, moved to Beijing after they became rich.

此外还有大量的中产阶级中国人效仿 70 年代和 80 年代的台湾，把他们的孩子从高中就开始送到美国来。这些孩子过了几年大学毕业的时候，首选的工作也还是 IT 领域，最大的可能也就是落户在东西海岸人口密集的城市。我认识的聪明的中国家长那个时候已经开始为孩子将来的婚房做准备。婚姻和住房，按照我们东方人特有的习惯，都是这些家长要负责到底的事情。这些国际买家的购买力和当地人当下的就业和收入是没有关系的。

Furthermore, countless middle-class Chinese were imitating Taiwanese in the 1970s and 1980s who sent their children to study in U.S. high schools. After these children graduate from college a few years later, their priority is to work in the IT field, so they will most probably settle in densely populated cities on the East or West Coast. A few thoughtful Chinese parents that I knew were already preparing for their children's wedding house at the time. According to Asian traditions, weddings and marriage are the responsibilities of the parents. The purchasing power of these international buyers has nothing to do with the current employment situation and income of the locals.

美国人也许知道自己家里的事情，但是对于美国以外的事情不是特别了解。在旧金山房地产历史上出现过好几次这样的例子。我印象中 90 年代香港的大批移民曾经救了旧金山因为经济衰退导致的低迷的房市。

Americans are familiar with their own culture, but they are not particularly knowledgeable about international buyers and other cultures. Such examples appeared several times in the history of San Francisco's real estate market. In my recollection, an influx of Hong Kong immigrants saved the sluggish real estate market in San Francisco that was caused by an economic recession.

人们对于房市底部的判断往往过于悲观。因为人们经常用库存除以销售量来确定房市走出低谷的时间。我曾经阅读过一个 80 年代的 San Jose 地区的房地产衰退时期的报告，当时预计需要 30 年才能消化掉现有库存。可是最后只用了两年的时间，就把库存消化掉了。主要的原因是销售速度和库存本身都是变化值。人们会根据预期随时调整买入和卖出。

People's judgments about the bottom of the real estate market are often overly pessimistic because they often divide the stock or supply of houses by the sales to determine when the real estate market will recover. I once read a report on the real estate recession in the San Jose area in the 1980s. It was estimated that it took 30 years for the market to completely digest the existing supply. However, the reality was that it took 2 years only. The main reason is that the speed of sales and stock supply are variables. People adjust their buying and selling activities based on their expectations.

如果有企业在大规模的扩张，那么人就会源源不断地进来。2010 年前后像苹果，谷歌这样的公司，已经渐渐走入如日中天的阶段。他们都在湾区大举扩张的计划，购买土地，新建更多的办公楼。Facebook 这些原本创业阶段并不在湾区的，也在湾区大规模地招聘人员创建企业。当时的特斯拉已经初现规模。湾区一个本来不生产汽车的地方，未来会变成美国汽车建造的重要中心之一。湾区的风险投资在 2012 年开始活跃起来。一大批科技企业在湾区开始孵化，包括后来鼎鼎有名的 Uber 等。

A company that is rapidly expanding will keep attracting people to that place. In around 2010, companies such as Apple and Google were on their way to becoming the most powerful and successful companies. Their plans were to expand rapidly in the Bay Area by buying more land and constructing more office buildings. Startups such as Facebook that were originally not based in the Bay Area were also recruiting talents and building their business on a large scale in the Bay Area. Back then, Tesla was already showing promising signs. Risk investment in the Bay Area started to boom in 2012, and a large number of tech companies were being hatched in the Bay Area, including the well-known name Uber.

这些 IT 的产业信息以及亚洲买家的信息，普通美国民众特别是传统行业的普通民众是不知道的，也没有切身的紧迫感。IT 行业的人，印度、中国等新移民知道这些信息，我们比仅接受大众媒体影响下的普通美国人信息掌握得更多更全面一些。因为这个原因我看到了大量的亚裔背景的人在那个时候开始抄底买入大量的住房。

Information about the IT industry and Asian buyers is not available to the general public in the U.S. who work in traditional industries. The average Americans also do not feel the heat. IT workers and immigrants from India and

China have a more comprehensive assessment of the situation because of their access to all this information that cannot be obtained through the mainstream media by the average Americans. This is precisely the reason why I saw that many Asian Americans were trying to buy the bottom by purchasing lots of residential properties.

房价上涨的时候，基本规律是核心区的房价先涨，然后蔓延到外围。比如在湾区，2012 年湾区最好的学区，最核心的地段的房价已经涨过了 2008 年时的最高点。然而此时，外围的房价刚刚触底不久开始反弹。房价还没有达到 2008 年最高点的一半。

When property prices increase, the basic rhythm is that the property prices of the central district will lead the rise, slowly driving up the property prices in neighboring areas. For example, in 2012, the property prices of houses in the central district with the best schools had already exceeded their 2008 peak level. Yet meanwhile, the property prices of the neighboring areas had just hit its bottom and started to bounce back; they had not even reached half of their 2008 peak level.

用我的指数房作为例子。2012 年的时候，那个房子仅仅涨到 36 万。而同时其核心区的房子已经超过了 2008 年的最高点。房地产的区域性很明显。

Take my index house as an example. In 2012, the price of the house only grew to US$360,000, but meanwhile, the property prices in the central district had already exceeded its peak level in 2008. In the real estate market, location makes a marked difference.

然而全美的经济学家或者联储局，他们关心的是全国的经济形势。大部分人是沉浸在 Great Depression 的痛苦中。我记忆中，当时我的一个朋友委托我帮他一个朋友的孩子在美国找工作。还是刚刚从斯坦福硕士毕业。这在以前是闭着眼睛就能找到工作的，可是那个时候真的就是找不到。报刊杂志还是各种负面的消息，因为就业率依旧不高。

Yet all economists in the U.S. or even the Fed only care about the economic situation in the entire country. A great majority of people were still steeped in the pain of the Great Depression. In my memory, a friend of mine asked me to help his friend's child, who had just finished a master's at Stanford, find a job. Before the crisis, such a candidate could close his eyes and still found a job. However, he really could not find one at the time. The magazines and newspapers were filled with all kinds of negative news because the employment rate was still low.

湾区的房地产投资人群里反而是另外一种声音。就是我们是否形成一个新泡沫（Are we forming another bubble）？因为房价反弹太快了。不过在我看来，因为核心区的房子涨过了 2008 的最高点，就认为新的泡沫又在形成中是很荒唐的一个想法。我坚持的一个观点是房价才刚刚开始起步，要涨很漫长的一段时间。也许是 5 年，也许是 10 年。因为你看看过去的历史就知道，每次这样大的循环都是 5-10 年一个周期的。

Among the discussion by real estate investors in the Bay Area, I saw a different theme. They were discussing whether we were forming another bubble because the property prices were now increasing drastically. However, in my opinion, the argument that a new bubble was forming because property prices in central districts had already exceeded its highest point in 2008 was ridiculous. I insisted that property prices were just starting to recover and that the bull market would last for a very long time, perhaps 5 years or even 10 years. Just take a look at the history: Every big cycle lasts for about 5-10 years.

大众媒体很少有前瞻性思维。我这么多年对大众媒体的总体观察就是，媒体的反应总体是滞后的。因为一个事情变成热点之后，才会引发媒体关注。而引发媒体关注之后，经过采访和调查，整理成文章，再传到普通人的时候，节拍已经慢了一大步，最好的机会已经过去了。媒体擅长做的就是利用这种痛苦，最大化销售自己的杂志，或者赢得更多的点击率。

Rarely is the mainstream media forward-looking. My years of observation of the mainstream media told me that the response of the media always lags behind reality. It was only after a certain incident became a hot topic that the media would notice and report it. But after that incident attracted the attention of the media, the media would interview the relevant parties, conduct an investigation, organize everything into an article, and publish it, so the best timing has already passed for their readers. The media is particularly good at making use of this kind of pain to maximize the sale of their publications and to win more clicks and views.

当我们做一个投资决策的时候，首先要想到的就是我这个信息从哪里来的？我是不是这个信息的最后一批知道者。是否我身后还有比我更晚知道这件事情的。如果没有，那可能要深思熟虑了。

When we are making an investment decision, we have to first ask ourselves the questions of where we obtain the information, whether we are the last group of people to know this news, and whether there will be people who will receive the news later than me. If the answer to the final question is in the negative, we need to think twice.

前瞻式的信息获得只能通过亲力亲为，在一线的人手中获得。比如投资理财的论坛，2012 年就充满了各种购买法拍屋的经验帖子。从这些帖子中你能够获得的信息和知识远远超过多数主流媒体。

The only way to obtain information before anyone else is by seeking first-hand information directly from the relevant actors. For example, in 2012, the investment and wealth management forum was full of discussion threads on how to buy foreclosures in which forum users shared their experience. The information and knowledge one can obtain from these discussion threads are far more comprehensive and useful than the information published by the mainstream media.

不过，在美国的华人相当一部分人有一个大的心病。就是总是强调融入主流社会，远离中国人的社区和媒体。事实上，从主流媒体中我们能够获得的信息总是非常有限。主流英文媒体，一切似乎都是朦朦胧胧得，总是不具体，说不到关键点上。这不单单是限于投资房地产，包括孩子们的教育、升学、办理移民。你会发现最有用的信息都来自华人本身的中文社交媒体。

However, the biggest hindrance faced by Chinese Americans is that there is an over-emphasis on merging into the host society by staying away from the Chinese community and media. In fact, the information that we can obtain from the mainstream media is very limited. Everything on the mainstream English media seemed to lack a focus. The content was often not specific enough and not focused on the crux of the issue. This observation is not limited to information on real estate investing but also applies to other areas such as our children's education, colleges, and immigration. You will find that the most useful information comes from Chinese social media, the content contributors of which are Chinese immigrants.

我认为房价会陷入长期复苏的观点和当时在投资理财论台上一些勤于笔耕的人基本一致。房价上涨远远还没有到泡沫的程度，这只是一个漫长上涨的开始。随着大家工资的升高以及就业率的提高，那个时候大量的需求才会真正被释放了出来。

My point of view that the real estate market would enter a prolonged period of recovery is in line with the analysis by some diligent content contributors on the investment and wealth management forum. Despite the rapid increase, property prices were still far from forming a bubble. It was only the beginning of a long bull market. The demand for houses will rocket as wages and the employment rate increase.

09 哪里都找不到钱
09 I Could Not Find Money Anywhere

道理都明白，最后没有抄到底也是一场空。最后谁可以抄到底，其实就是执行力的问题。我自己非常清楚地知道这点，可是执行层面越来越困难。

Everyone knows that they should buy the bottom, but most of them fail to buy anything when the market indeed hits its bottom. Who can succeed in their mission to buy the bottom depends on their ability to execute plans. As for me, even though I knew the principles behind this investment strategy well, the execution part was getting more difficult.

我几乎是以历史最低点的时候买入了第一个房子。过了几个月，等我心急火燎买入第二个房子，房价已经涨了 10%-20% 左右。要买第三个房子却费了老劲了，因为所有的中介都告诉我不能贷款。要等两个房子都有比较长的出租历史才可以。

I bought the first investment property when the market was near its historical low. After several months, when I was hurrying to buy a second investment property, property prices had already increased by 10-20%. Buying my third investment property was full of seemingly insurmountable obstacles because all the agents told me that I could not apply for a loan until the first two houses had a long history of generating rental income.

我可等不到那一天。我要买 8 个房子。我自己一遍一遍给自己坚定地强调这个事情。如果你老老实实的，把自己想象成一个人肉皮球，被其他人踢来踢去，最后你就是什么也做不成。这个时候我只能找审查稍微宽松一点的贷款中介帮我出主意。他的一个办法就是把我的海外的一些咨询收入加进来。因为这些收入并不是有清晰和明确的定义的，解释的空间有很大的余地。

But I could not wait to act until that day. I had already brainwashed myself with the slogan of "I have to buy eight investment properties." You are bound to fail if you take no for an answer and allow others to reject your request as if they were kicking a ball. At the time, I had no other choices but to find a loan agent who had looser requirements for solutions. One of his suggestions was that I added some consultation fee I received from overseas projects to my application. As all this income did not have a clear definition, it left much room for me to explain my situation.

贷款解决了，可是我的首付问题依旧没有解决。买两个房子已经耗尽我手上所有的现金。一有风吹草动，恐怕要动用信用卡过日子了。机会放在这里，杠杆我也能拿到，可是我没有撬动这个杠杆的金钥匙。

Now that the loan problem was solved, I still needed to tackle the down payment issue. I had already used all my cash in buying the first two investment properties. Even anything happened, I would probably need to take out money from my credit card to take care of my daily expenses. The opportunities were right here in front of me, and I had already obtained the leverage. What was now missing was the golden key to trigger the leverage.

当时我有几个选择。一个办法是把中国我买的第一个上海中心城区的房子卖掉，那个时候中国的这个房子已经涨过了 100 万美元，如果把它卖掉，我就用这笔钱做首付，一个独立屋只需要 5 万美元。那么可以购买 20 套住房，总市价 500 万~600 万美元左右。这 20 套住房价格涨一倍，回到 2008 年的次贷危机前最高点，那么我"普通人家十年一千万"的理财目标就实现了。能够实现这样的目标该是多么令人开心的事情啊。

I had a few options at the time. The first solution was to sell the first real property that I bought in Shanghai's central area. At the time, this house was worth more than US$1 million. If I sold it, I could use the money as down payments to buy 20 investment properties because the down payment required for a single-family detached house listed at US$5-6 million was only US$50,000. Once these twenty houses doubled in price, returning to its highest point before the sub-prime crisis in 2008, I would achieve my "An Average Family's $10 million in 10 Years" goal. What brings greater happiness than accomplishing one's goal?

然而明明知道纸面上这是正确的投资决定。可是我不敢。我担心那些理论计算以外的不确定性因素，让我真正落实这件事非常困难。第一，我可能要交一些资产增值税。当时我已经持有绿卡了。这个房子我在中国按照比较低的价格买进，较高的价格卖出，我可能要补交大量的税费。交多少税，怎么交，这点我不是很明确。

Yet even though I knew that this was the right investment decision, I did not dare go ahead with it. I was worried about uncertainties that were out of the reach of my theories and calculations, which deterred me from executing my plan. Firstly, I might need to pay some capital gains tax because I had already received my Green Card. According to the low buying price and high selling price of this investment property in China, I might well need to pay a lot of tax, but I was not sure about the exact amount.

我当时咨询了一些会计师 1031 Exchange 的办法。我说可不可以把中国的房子卖出，作为 exchange 买美国的房子，这样我可以延税。会计给我的答复是否定的。他们说中美两边的房子很难说明是同类或者相似的房子。我说都是住宅啊，很相似啊。会计师依旧直摇头。当然会计师的答复都是偏保守的，他们不想承担更多的责任。但不管怎么说让我对这个问题产生了一些疑虑。

I also consulted some accountants about 1031 Exchange. I was wondering whether I could sell my house in China as an exchange for buying a house in the U.S. so that I could delay the tax payment, to which the accountants answered "No." They told me that because of the differences between China and the U.S., it was very difficult to explain that the two investment properties were similar or identical. I replied that they were both residential properties so they were highly similar, but the accountants were still shaking their heads. Though I understand that accountants tend to be more risk-averse because they do not want to bear more responsibilities, I had some doubts and worries about this issue.

还有就是这么大笔钱进入美国，会不会有其它的问题？我没有做过100 万美元以上的国际汇款。大额的美元汇入美国，可能需要向税务部门甚至 FBI 解释这个钱的来龙去脉。虽然我是守法公民，但是被别人调查的感觉非常不好。尤其是当时中国外汇管控已经变严格了。一人一年五万美元的限额。我需要找 20 个人帮我汇款才可以。问题是即使我在中国那边想办法绕过了外汇管制，我在美国这边说得清么？他们能理解我找 20 个人代我汇款这事么？我有证据么？我能说明这不是洗钱和非法交易么？调查你的税务官员，他们能明白中国那边关于外汇管制的一些措施吗？你雇佣律师和会计师说明白这些事情代价有多大？

Furthermore, will there be other problems when I transmit such a large amount of money into the U.S.? I have never wired more than $1 million from another country to the U.S. I may well need to explain the origin of the money to the tax departments or even the FBI if I transmit such a large sum of money to the States. I am certainly a law-abiding citizen, but being the subject of an investigation would bring uneasy feelings for me, especially when China now had stricter limits of foreign exchange of US$50,000 per person per annum, which meant I would need to find 20 people to help me transmit the money. Could I convince the U.S. authorities of the legality of the money? Could they understand why I found 20 people to transmit the money on my behalf? Would I have evidence to prove the legitimacy of the transactions? Would I be able to explain that this sum of money had nothing to do with money-laundering and illegal transactions? Would the tax officials who investigated my case be able to understand China's policies on control of foreign exchange? What did my lawyers and accountants say about the cost of this series of maneuvers?

很多人对美国的金融管制很反感，让你感觉普通人其实没有多少自由。当然我理解可能这些管制一开始的出发点是好的，防止有人逃税或者防止恐怖分子毒贩洗钱。但是副作用也是明显的。普通人用钱也是战战兢兢的，生怕政府把自己当成坏人。这也是我后来坚信比特币未来会有一定市场的一个原因。这部分在后面比特币的章节里我再展开讲。

Many people are critical of the U.S. financial regulations, which make them feel that ordinary citizens do not have much freedom. Of course, I understand that legislators had a good intention of curbing tax evasion behaviors and money-laundering by crime syndicates in mind when passing these laws. However, the side-effects are also obvious: Law-abiding citizens are feeling uneasy about spending their money lest the government mistakes them for criminals. This is also one of the reasons why I firmly believe that bitcoin will have a sizable market in the future. I will further elaborate on this in subsequent chapters on bitcoin.

在美国，你没有办法把几万块钱随便借给朋友。因为你担心会有政府找你要证据，找你要赠予税。所以你或你父母在中国卖掉房产的钱也不太敢拿回美国来，倒不是因为你说不清楚，而是因为被调查本身就是一个很痛苦的事情。

In the U.S., one cannot just casually borrow a few hundred grand to your friends because of the worry that the government will ask you for gift tax or proof of the legitimacy of the transfer. This is why people do not dare transfer the proceeds from selling their real properties in China back to the U.S. It is not necessarily that they cannot explain the source of the money but that being investigated already brings many trouble and uneasy feelings.

我想想这些事情都很头大。另外一方面让我担心的就是上一次在中国置换房的经验教训。当时我也是想一个换四个，但最后的结果是还不如什么都不做。我对未来的趋势能够把握得那么准么？所以我放弃了卖掉中国的房子，转钱到美国投资的想法。中美之间的投资还是各管各的吧。

All these issues gave me a headache. In addition, I still remember the painful lesson I learned when I was trying to displace investment properties in China. At the time, I was trying to sell one property in exchange for four new purchases. But it turned out that I would have been better off if I had done nothing. Was my judgment about the future trend accurate? I was not sure about this, so I gave up the thought of selling my houses in China to transfer the money for investments in the U.S. In the end, I decided to separate my investments in China from those in the U.S.

当然现在回顾往事，看看当时我的这些担心，也许是我把风险想象得太大了。因为在投资理财论坛上的确也有人把中国的房子卖掉，拿到美国来投资的，也没有什么太多的事情。比如当时就有一个投资理财的网友，咨询我在 San Jose 买 multi-family house 是不是一个好主意。她是一个 2012 年到美国的新移民。她算了一下圣荷西的回报率比上海高太多了。我告诉她在美国管理房屋跟中国是很不一样的，要负责维修。如果是一个 multi-family，甚至还要处理邻居的关系。最后她买到了没有我不知道，但我衷心祝她好运。只是我知道她的确做到了从中国汇款上百万美元到美国。

Now that I looked back on my journey, most of my then worries stemmed from my exaggerated attention to risks because there were some netizens on the forum who successfully sold their houses in China in order to solicit more funds for their investments in the U.S. For example, there was this netizen, who immigrated to the U.S. in 2012, on the forum who asked me whether buying a multi-family house in San Jose was a good idea. Her calculations suggest that the return of an investment in San Jose trumped that in Shanghai. I told her that managing properties in the U.S. was different than in China because U.S. landlords were responsible for repairs. Landlords of a multi-family house would also need to handle the interpersonal relationships between the neighbors. I had no idea whether she indeed bought that property in the end, but I wished her the best of luck. One thing I knew for sure was that she did transmit about US$1 million from China to the States.

我最终下决心不卖中国的房子，压倒骆驼的最后一根稻草其实是信誉。2011 年的时候，我把上海的第一个房子租给了一对年轻夫妻。他们带着家里的老人，一起搬了过来。因为老人的年纪比较大，所以他在搬过来的时候一再跟我确定，他希望长住这个房子，所以当时签了一个 5 年的合同。

I had finally made up my mind not to sell my properties in China. What prompted me to make this decision was my tenants' trust in me. In 2011, I rented the first investment property that I bought in Shanghai to a young couple who moved in with their parents. Because of the old age of their parents, they confirmed with me that they wanted to live in that house in the longer term, so we signed a five-year contract.

当然我也可以撕毁这个合同，撕毁合同也就是赔偿他们一个月的房租而已。可是签约的时候他们和我说得非常恳切，有明确的约定。他们说宁愿房租高一点，也希望找一个稳定的地方。因为他们的父母当时已经 70 多岁了，不想也不能再折腾。而且这个家庭从来都是准时准点付的房租，从来没有给我找过任何的麻烦。甚至房租每次都是截止日期前三天付给我。房屋的维修也都是他们自己去办理，然后征求我意见之后把账单寄给我，从房租里扣除。

Of course, I could still terminate this contract by paying them a month's rent as compensation. However, at the time of signing the contract, they were very sincere, and I made an unequivocal promise. They told me that they would rather pay higher rents for a more stable place because their parents were already in their 70s. Frequently moving homes would be inconvenient and exhausting for the elderly. Besides, this family paid me rents on time every single month and did not bring me any troubles. In fact, the tenants paid me three days in advance of the deadline. After having the house repaired with my consent, they would send me a bill, the fee of which would be deducted from the rent payment next month.

我这么多年跟房客打交道的经验是，如果你为别人着想，为房东省下了金钱和精力，最终这些好处都能反馈到你自己身上。房东可能会在房租上给你更多的优惠，可能在你搬出的时候给你更多的宽松日期。然而很多房客不明白这一点，尤其是美国的大多数房客。他们不知道房东付出的所有劳动，每一个修缮，每一个看似合理的要求，最终羊毛都出在羊身上。而房东的小时工资往往远比房客的小时工资要高很多。所以房客麻烦房东是一件很傻的事情。

Based on my years of experience in managing rental properties, a major takeaway is that if tenants put yourself into the shoes of the landlords by helping them save more money and energy, all the good karma will come back to the tenants. For example, the landlords may give more discount on the rent payment or set a flexible time when the tenants move out. Yet many tenants do not understand this simple logic, especially those in the U.S. They fail to see that all the labor and time spent by the landlord on every repair request, however reasonable, will come out of the tenants' pocket. Meanwhile, the landlords earn a much higher hourly income than the tenants, so tenants making troubles for landlords is a very silly behavior.

因为我不想违背信用，所以我没有把房子卖掉把他们赶走。这是我十几年投资的一个基本原则，就是我极其在意自己的信用。维持信用记录不仅仅是保证我有较高的信用分值，可以帮我获得贷款。另外一方面我总觉得冥冥之中，人世间一切都是环环相扣，紧密相连的。一个人如果做到又诚实又守信，上天总是会用各种方式来奖赏你。一个人如果言而无信，出尔反尔，那么也许你可以占一些小便宜，但是命运总是会想办法把这些小便宜成倍地从你身上夺走。也许是通过某种阴差阳错，也许仅仅是因为你内心的不安导致你犯错。

As I did not want to destroy the trust between us, I decided not to sell the house or evict them. Being a trustworthy person is a fundamental principle guiding years of my investment journey. A more tangible benefit of this principle is that I am able to maintain an excellent credit score, which means it is easier for me to obtain loans. On the other hand, I believe in karma. If a person is honest and trustworthy, the universe will reward him or her. But if a person breaks his or her promises, the universe will take away all those benefits derived from these dishonest behaviors. Losing the benefits in the end may be a result of coincidences or because of the subconscious mind constantly reminding the dishonest individuals of their wrongdoings.

既然这样不行，那样不行，我只有最后一个办法了。那就是从 401K 里头贷款。401K 明明是自己的存款，但是此刻只能走贷款程序，把钱取出来。你瞧政府又何必多此一举呢？让人们自己管好自己的钱不是很好么？何必养活那么多中间人。401K 里一个好处就是利息还是付给自己，所以利息再高也不是什么损失。但是 401K 的贷款金额是有限的，就是如果你换了工作，rollover 那部分是没有办法贷款的。你只能用在当下公司工作期间的 contribution 抵押做贷款。也不知道当初为什么制定这些荒唐的规矩，对于自己的钱设定那么多的管理规则。

Having ruled out the above options, I had only one solution left, which was to take out a loan from my 401K. Any money in a 401K account is essentially saving of the account holder, so why did I push myself to go through the loan procedure while taking out the money? This also brings another question: The government has set up many layers in the organizational structure of 401K, generating employment opportunities for dozens of middle-men. One of the advantages of 401K is that the interest is payable to oneself, so I will not suffer any loss no matter how high the interest rate is. However, the amount of loan that can be taken out from 401K is limited. For example, if you have changed your job, the part of rollover is not loanable and you can only use the contribution you have made while working at the current company as collateral for your loan. I am absolutely clueless about why the government set all these ridiculous rules on how people should manage their own hard-earned money.

因为这个原因，所以虽然我们当时的 401K 退休金有几十万，但是我能贷出来的钱非常少，只有 5 万多美元。但不管怎么说，这笔钱够我买第三个房子的首付了。于是我又开始不断每个周末去看房子，抄底的挖掘机继续前进。但是正当我满腔热情地疯狂递交 offer 的时候，另一个灾难又发生了。上帝总有各种办法磨炼一个人的心智。

For this reason, even though I had accumulated hundreds of thousands in our 401K, the amount loanable was very little, which was slightly more than US$50,000. But anyway, now I could use this sum of money as a down payment for my third investment property in the U.S., so I resumed visiting houses on sale every weekend. I turned on full turbo of my "buying the bottom" machine. Just when I was fanatically making offers, another disaster occurred. God tests our faith by letting hard times happen to us.

10 抢到第三个投资房
10 Buying My Third Investment Property Amid Fierce Competition

这次是我生病了。就在这个最重要的节骨眼上，我生病了，而且病得很严重。我运动的时候，一个不当心，腰椎受伤了。一开始是隐隐约约地疼痛，后来是钻心地疼痛，最后我只能躺在床上了，一动不能动。医生说只能静养，别无他方。我说需要多久能恢复？医生说他也不知道，少则几个月，多则半年一年。

I was sick. At this critical moment, I was not feeling well. In fact, I was seriously sick. When I was working out, I hurt my spine. At first, I was only feeling some intermittent pain which later deteriorated into intolerable pain that I could only lay in bed. The doctor said the only way to treat the condition was to rest. I asked him how long this would take, to which he said he had no idea either. It could be anywhere between a few months to a year.

人休息躺在床上，可是房价还在蹭蹭地上涨。我心急火燎也没有用。

So, I was lying in bed every day while property prices were soaring. No matter how much I wanted to get out of my bed and continue my plan, I was still confined to my bed.

当时房价不能一步涨到位的原因其实是银行。很多房子即使再加 10% 的价格也是卖得出去的。因为一个房子经常是十几个 offer。但是银行的贷款估价限制了房价的快速攀升。比如当时一个 40 万美元的房子，offer 从 40 到 45 万美元不等。虽然卖家希望卖到最高价 45 万美元。但是 45 万的 offer 没有办法成交，因为银行贷款评估的时候并不认可。此时银行贷款吸取次贷危机的教训，变得极其小心。他们只会根据最近几次交易的价格，也许稍稍有一点浮动来决定你这个房子的合理价格。即使合同是 45 万美元，最后也是要根据银行评估重新商量。

The reason why the property prices at the time could not rise to the corresponding level in one go was because of banks. Many sellers would still be able to sell their houses if the asking price had a 10% increase. For example, a house that was listed at US$400,000 would receive offers ranging from US$400,000 to US$450,000. Of course, the seller would want to sell the house to the highest offer, but the US$450,000 was usually not approved by the bank. After learning the lesson of the sub-prime crisis, banks were much more prudent now. They would evaluate the property based on the latest transactions and perhaps make some adjustments to determine a reasonable price of that property. Even though the consideration listed in the contract was US$450,000, it was subject to the evaluation and approval of the bank.

因为有银行贷款这一关做最后的保险，所以我后来胆子变得越来越大，给出的 offer 也越来越高。加 10%~20% 都不在话下，卖家想卖多少钱都行。签了合同再说，后面银行估价下来再慢慢谈。如果给出的价格我没有排在第一名，后面压根没有谈的机会。

Because of the safeguard offered by the bank's evaluation process, I was making bolder moves that my offering price was getting higher and higher. I was trying to get the contract signed by routinely adding 10-20% on top of the asking price or even accepting whatever counter-offer the seller was making. My approach was to sign the contract first and deal with the bank evaluation process later because I could not even have the chance to negotiate with the bank or seller if I had not outbid other buyers in the first place.

我只能躺在床上带病坚持工作。躺床上并不妨碍我给他们出 offer，躺在床上，我依旧可以打电话给中介。但是躺在床上让我没有办法去看房子，其实很多房子我也不需要看，因为通过照片和地图我大概知道这个房子的价格是多少，以及是否有更好的升值空间。

I could only work in my bed. Lying in bed did not deter me from making offers. Being confined to my bed, I could still call real estate agents. Not being able to visit the houses on sale did not really matter because I could approximately evaluate the value of a house by looking at the pictures and maps to determine the room for asset appreciation.

最大的问题是我不去看房子，卖家总觉得我没有诚意。即使我给出高价有的时候他也不愿意接受。卖家觉得我可能是胡乱试试的，房子都没有看，没有诚意。因为这样我错过了好几个 deal 我只能干着急直瞪眼，一点办法也没有。

My biggest weakness in this "competing-for-houses" game was that since I was unable to visit the house on sale, the sellers often thought that I was not serious and sincere. No matter how high my offer was, they were reluctant to accept it because they thought I was just messing around. After all, why would a buyer make such a high offer without even seeing the house in person? This was why I missed several deals. However anxious and worried I was, it seemed that there was nothing I could do.

但是只要你动脑筋。办法总是有的。办法总是比困难多。我的信用良好，分数很高。我只能用非常规的办法解决这个问题。就是每次我出 offer 的时候，附上自己的信用分数的截屏报告。中介告诉我没有人出 offer 的时候附上自己的信用报告，这样不符合常规。我说因为没人这样，所以我才一定要给。这个办法果然有效。就这样费尽周折，我也买到了第三个房子，这时候我又没有钱了。

But God always opens a window. As long as you focus all your attention on solving problems, there are more solutions than problems. I decided to leverage my excellent credit score by attaching a copy of my credit report to my offer. The real estate agent told me that no buyer would do this, so it did not fit in the norm. I said this was precisely how I could stand out from the rest of the buyers. This strategy proved to be highly effective. This was also how, after all the bumps in the road, I bought my third investment property. I ran out of money again.

那个阶段感觉自己的钱就像打游戏时候的血条。好不容易满血复活了，上去几下子就被妖怪打没了，然后心急火燎地接着等复活。

At the moment, I was feeling like I was playing a computer game. I spent so much time and effort on restoring my health bar, only to find out that it went down to zero again. And then I was anxiously trying to revive my health bar.

我像一个残疾人一样躺在床上。没有首付的钱，也不能工作。可我买 8 个房子的计划才执行了一半不到。怎么办呢？

I was lying in my bed like a handicapped person. Now I had neither the money to make a down payment nor a job, but I had not even completed half of my "eight investment properties" goal. What should I do?

好在当时我已经工作很自由，我不需要担心失去工作。因为当时我主要的工作是在创业经营一家公司。因为在创业阶段，我没钱给自己发工资，所以我大部分的收入来自做一些咨询业务。咨询业务稍微停停不要紧。这个公司因为我是老板，所以我不去，问题也不是特别大。

Luckily, my job was quite flexible at the time, so I did not need to worry about losing it. I was starting my own business. As it was still in its early stage, the business did not have money to pay me my salary. Most of my income came from some consultation projects. It would not cause a big problem if I paused my consultation side business. Meanwhile, as I was the owner of my company, I was free not to go to work every day.

病痛的打击更多是来自信心。我不知道我的脊椎能不能好。在床上整整躺了一个多月之后，我几乎还是下不了床。我不知道以后会怎么样，如果我一直像个残疾人一样，我的创业公司该怎么办？我还能不能管理投资房？

However, the physical condition was a huge blow to my own confidence because I had no idea whether I would fully recover. After lying in bed for more than a month, I still could not get out of my bed. I had no idea what the future would entail. What if I would need to lie in bed like a handicapped person for the rest of my life? What would happen to my startup? Would I still be capable of managing my investment properties?

11 抢到第四个投资房

11 Buying My Fourth Investment Property

大概又过了三个月，这个时候我可以下床活动了，可以开车到处走一走了。但是我不能站很久，只能坐着或是躺着，或者是快步行走。如果是站着不动，只要一分钟脊椎就会疼得我呲牙咧嘴。我去医院拍了核磁共振，显示的确我有一部分脊髓液外流压迫神经。医生也没有什么好的办法，告诉我唯一的办法就是尽量恢复，不要让脊椎受力。

After another three months, I was finally able to get out of my bed and drive around, but I could not stand for a long time. I could only sit or lay down or walk swiftly. If I stood still for even one minute, the pain from my spine would be unbearable. I had an MRI scan at the hospital, which showed that some leaked cerebrospinal fluid was affecting my nervous system. The doctor said the only treatment was to let the body heal itself by not applying pressure to the spinal cord.

那时候房市依旧火热，非常地抢手。有的时候中介都见不着，我觉得记忆中最夸张的一次，大概我们有五六个人同时约好了去看一栋房子，在门口等了一个多小时，中介都没露面。

The real estate market was still bullish, and the competition among buyers was fierce. Sometimes, I could not even find a real estate agent. The most unbelievable experience was that one time there were 5-6 buyers touring a house on sale. We waited at the doorstep for more than an hour, but the real estate agent did not show up.

但是我要买 8 个房子的目标还在那里，我心中的火焰还在燃烧，我还是要去实现我这个目标。虽然我没有什么首付的钱，虽然我不能站立太久，虽然我几乎无法贷款，我也要继续看房子，找机会。

But my goal of buying eight investment properties was still in my mind, and the flame of my heart was ignited. I was determined to accomplish my goal. I needed to keep touring houses even though I did not have much money left for a down payment, could not stand for too long, and might not get a loan. I was still looking for opportunities.

下一个看到的房子是一对老夫妻在卖的短售屋。这是一个在铁路边的房子，真是一个破得不能再破的地点。这里虽然离铁道不远，但是我知道附近正在规划建设一个大的研发中心。几年后可能会有几千人到这附近来工作。

The next house on sale I visited was a short sale house listed by an old couple. It was a dilapidated house situated alongside a railway. Despite its proximity to the railway, I knew that a large research center was part of the urban planning in the community, which meant that thousands of people would come to this area for work after several years.

这是一个独立单位的房子，短售标价只有 11 万美元。这对夫妻不打算要这个房子了，我当时觉得很奇怪。房子地点虽然很差，但是房子里面修缮得很好。后来了解到这对夫妻在这个房子上倾注了大量的心血，次贷危机前，他们申请了 home equity 抵押贷款，把这个房子装修一新。把卧室客厅全部重新翻修过，屋顶重新换过，厨房和厨房电器全部都是新的。

It was a single-family detached house listed at US\$110,000. Despite the bad location, the house was in good condition, so I was curious why the couple did not want the house anymore. I later found out that the couple spent a lot of time and energy on the house by applying for a home equity loan to carry out a major repair and renovation before the sub-prime crisis. The bedroom and living room were all newly-renovated. The roof, kitchen, and electrical appliances were all brand new.

他们花了两年的时间去修这个房子。光修房子就花了 15 万。但是这 15 万都是从银行来的。这个房子在 2007 年的时候估价是 45 万，当时他们因此款贷了 15 万美元去修这个房子。

They used two years to repair the house at the cost of US\$150,000, which was borrowed from the bank. In 2007, the house was valued at US\$450,000 by the bank, so they applied for a US\$150,00 loan to repair the house.

按理说他们好好地在这个房子里享受自己的生活就好了，慢慢地把贷款还掉。但是就是因为房价跌了，跌到只有十几万，他们觉得自己背着 15 万的贷款实在不合算，于是就想把这个房子短售掉。

An investor's common thinking would suggest that they should enjoy their lives in the house while slowly repaying the loan, but they felt that it did not make sense to bear a debt of US$150,000 when the house was only worth the same amount of money. They short sold the house in an attempt to get rid of the debt burden.

在其他正常的社区里，我当时感觉无力和别人抢房子。我一没钱，二行动不便。但是这个房子因为离铁路比较近，后院经常可以听到火车的轰鸣声，所以没有什么人来买。

In other better communities, I felt powerless in the "competing-for-houses" game because I did not have money and I moved with difficulty. But as this house was a stone's throw away from the railway, which meant you could often hear the noise of the train in the backyard, no one was making an offer to buy.

于是我出价把它买了下来。11 万的房子，20%的首付，我只花了 2 万多元就把它买了下来，而且没什么人和我抢。这两万元是我从各种犄角旮旯里凑出来的。包括 2008 年的时候我以 1 美元买入的 100 股花旗银行股票都卖了。又用了一个一年不付利息的信用卡刷了一些钱。好不容易凑齐了首付。

So I made an offer, which was accepted by the couple. The closing price was US$110,000, so I only paid a down payment of about US$20,000 in buying the property. And no one was competing against me. I managed to gather US$20,000 from different sources, including selling the 100 Citibank shares I bought at US$1 per share in 2008. I also withdrew some money from a credit card that waived my interest rate for one year. Finding the money for the down payment was very challenging.

房屋主人走的时候收拾得特别干净。我去接手的时候，院子里都没有一片落叶，草坪整整齐齐。仿佛可以感觉到前主人对这个房子的深情。他们对房子倾注了那么多的爱，付出了那么多的劳动，但是在最关键的时候，他们却选择了抛弃它。

When the couple moved out, the house was in excellent condition: It was very tidy and clean. When the house was delivered to me, there was not a single fallen tree leaf in the backyard. The lawn was neat. I could feel how much the former owners loved this house. Yet despite the love and their hard work, the couple decided to abandon it at the most critical moment.

房子的地点虽然很差，但是房子很好，基本上没有什么修缮工作要做。所以我很容易地就把这个房子出租出去了，房租一个月 1500 美元，不但足够还房贷，而且还有富余。

Notwithstanding the bad location, it was a nice house. There was not much repair work needed, and I easily rented the house out at US$1,500 per month, which was more than enough for me to my mortgage payment.

虽然这个房子靠近铁路边上，但是出租反倒很容易。世上总是穷人多，很多人在租房期间不在意压缩一下自己的生活质量，只求租金低。所以在后来的日子里，这个房子没有空置过一天。

Even though the house was situated alongside the railway, it was very easy to find a tenant. In this world, poor people are in the majority. Many of them will not mind lowering their quality of life for lower rent. This is why the house has not been vacant for even a single day since I bought it.

现在这个房子的价格早已突破了历史最高点，估价 55 万美元。如果认真想想，基本上这对夫妻两年的心血和银行的 15 万美元是白送给我了。对于他们，这些本来都是可以避免的，只是因为自己太过于贪婪和算计自己的利益。所以人在做事情的时候，不能光想着自己，不能只是做一个精致的利己主义者，人还是要有一些诚信和担当的。

Now the price of that house has already exceeded its previous historical high and is valued at US$550,000. If we do some calculations, we will see that the couple basically gifted me US$150,000 and the energy they spent on the house. They incurred these avoidable losses because they were too greedy and calculating. Therefore, a takeaway from this story is that we cannot only think about our own interests. We should not be so selfish. Instead, we should always strive to be a responsible person who keeps promises.

12 抢到第五、第六个投资房

12 Buying my Fifth and Sixth Investment Properties Amid Fierce Competition

我买第 4 个房子的时候，房价的趋势已经很明显，一轮一轮在上涨。半年之后，我渐渐恢复得可以自由行走了。虽然时不时有些不舒服，但是没有大碍了。但是我实在凑不出更多的钱去买后面的房子，如何实现我 8 个房子的目标呢？

The trend of the property prices was already very obvious when I bought my fourth investment property. The real estate market witnessed waves of a price increase. After six months, I had almost fully recovered that I could now walk freely despite some occasional discomfort. But I really had no idea how I could find more money to finance subsequent purchases to achieve my eight-investment-properties goal.

读者可能会觉得我为什么痴迷于这 8 个房子的目标？如果没有在文学城上写下自己十年一千万的豪言壮语，可能我也就放弃了。因为自己有这样的承诺，有这样的公开目标，内心深处给自己制造了一些压力，想看一看自己的能力极限在哪里？

For those of you reading this, you may be wondering why I was so obsessed with my goal. If I had not written the slogan of "$10 million in 10 years" on wenxuecity.com, I would have probably given it up. But as I had already made a promise that I published openly, I created some mental pressure for myself to push my own limits.

可是钱呢，钱从哪里来？每天我看着不断上涨的房价急得直搓手。人可以有各种各样的目标，但是没有钱你一点办法也没有。

But where should I get the money? I was anxiously clamping my hands. We can set any goals for ourselves, but without money, we can achieve nothing.

常言道"如果一个人真的想做什么，上帝都会被感动跑过来帮你。"

As the common saying goes, "When you want something, all the universe conspires in helping you to achieve it."

历经磨难，我的好运气终于也跟着来了。这个时候我突然接到一个特别古怪的咨询项目。这样的咨询项目，我一辈子也只做过一次。

After all the obstacles, I finally had some good luck. At the time, I was entrusted with a special consultation project. I have only done such a project once in my life.

有一个我所在行业的创业公司要去上市。他们的核心技术专利需要有人做一下技术评估，来证明他们的技术是独一无二的。上市公司的技术负责人，通过很多关系找到了我，让我帮他们做一下技术评估。因为我曾经在这个领域发表过一些期刊论文。他们觉得我比较适合做这方面的技术评估。

A startup company in my professional field was looking to launch its IPO, so it needed an expert to evaluate its technology and patents to prove that their capabilities are unique in the industry. The person responsible for developing the company's technology contacted me to ask if I was interested in writing the evaluation for the company. As I had published some journal articles in the relevant field before, he considered me to be a suitable candidate.

你会觉得奇怪，为什么这个工作是创业公司自己去找人评估而不是投行找人评估。其实不是，是投资银行要对他们的技术做尽职调查。但是投资银行的人压根也不懂这些技术，所以就让创业公司的人给他们推荐专家来做评估。

Perhaps you are now curious why it was the startup company but not the investment bank that reached out to an expert to evaluate the technologies. In this case, the investment bank was originally trying to evaluate the technologies as part of their due diligence. But as they were not familiar with the technologies, they entrusted the startup company with the task of recommending an expert to conduct the evaluation.

做这个工作不复杂，只要写一份报告，把相关的技术优点和缺点比对一下就可以。技术内容我很熟悉，差不多一个星期就可以写完。不过我知道投行是怎么回事。因为我在那里实习过，所以如果按照小时计算的话，这样一个咨询费用不过是 5000 美元左右的酬金。可是这个上市过程是一个上亿美元的交易，我就不客气地把自己的要价放大了 10 倍，给了一个 5 万美元的咨询费估价。

It was not a complicated project as I only needed to write a report to simply compare the pros and cons of the relevant technologies. I was very familiar with the relevant technologies and professional knowledge, so it would only take me a week to finish the report. But since I understood how investment bank operated thanks to my previous internship experience, I knew that they would charge me by an hourly rate of mere US$5,000 out of a transaction that was worth more than hundreds of millions of dollars. So I multiplied my usual consultation fee by a factor of 10 and quoted a total consultation fee of US$50,000.

创业公司的这位老总对我非常的客气。他主动说可能你还是要少了一点，他建议我可以再加一些。他说最关键的是能不能快一点出这份报告。反正钱也不是他出，最终都是投行买单。写报告这种事情得心应手。我写一本书也不过是几个月的事情。于是我价格又抬了抬，我说那干脆就 10 万美元了吧。

Having received my quotation, the CEO of the startup, who was a very kind and nice person, offered to pay me more if I could finish the report as soon as possible. I guess the reason for his generosity was that it was the investment bank that would pay me for the report. Writing is a piece of cake for me. It only takes me a few months to finish a book. Therefore, I raised my price to US$100,000.

他看着我呵呵笑，觉得我一副不开窍的样子。一个公司在上市的时候，眼睛里看到的都是大钱。对这些小钱完全不在乎。反正这笔钱也不是他出。我感觉他似乎呵呵的样子是说可以再加一些。在上市的交易过程中，各种财务数据报表的最后一位往往是一百万，百万以下的他们连看都不看。

He smiled at me as if I could not understand what he was saying. When a company was preparing to be listed in the stock exchange, all the expenses were astronomical figures, so they did not care about small money. After all, the company did not need to pay the money out of its own pocket. I felt that the smile on his face was implying to me that I could charge more. In an IPO, the unit used in the financial statements is often "million." It seems that any amount below that is not worth their time.

不过我没有再贪心。过了几天投行的人找我，签了合同。我开的 10 万美元的价格，他们一口就答应了，压根没有还价。但是只有一个条件，就是这个周末结束前必须把报告给他们。

But I am not a greedy person. After a few days, the investment bank contacted me, and we signed a contract. They accepted my offer of US$100,000 without any further bargaining. The only thing they asked of me was that I needed to send them the report immediately after the weekend.

于是我忙了整整一个周末，那几天几乎没有合眼，把这个报告赶好给他们，算是尽职调查的一部分。其实大部分时候公司的并购，这些尽职调查都只是走一个过程。买卖双方内心深处都很清楚，投资银行这个时候接到这个单子，难道能让这个公司不上市吗？公司努力上市，难道他会找一个人对他们的技术评估说坏话的吗？

So I barely slept during that weekend. My finished report would constitute part of the due diligence investigation. But in reality, in most M&A deals, the due diligence investigation is a procedural requirement. Both the buyer and seller know well that the investment bank will not let the deal go south. It is common sense that the company will not delegate the task to someone who disapproves of their technologies.

对于我而言，别人雇我做技术评估，难道我能评价他的技术一无是处吗？当然我也会保护自己，我不会说一些违背原则的话。创业公司能够做起来，技术只是一方面的，还靠技术以外的很多东西。独门秘籍一样的技术是不存在的。大部分的技术评估有非常大的弹性空间，我不能把黑说成了白，白说成了黑，但是灰度的颜色到底是多少，评估者的自由度很大。

As for me, will I comment that the technologies of the company who entrusted me with the task as totally worthless? Of course not. But meanwhile, I know how to protect myself by not acting contrary to my own principles. The success of a startup company hinges on various factors, and technology is just one of them. There is no technology that is unique to one particular company. But most technical analysis and evaluation leave much room for flexibility. Of course, I will not mistake black as white or vice versa, but there is some gray area. I have much flexibility in determining how gray that area is.

我自己觉得我的报告无懈可击。虽然仓促之间完成，但是也没有违背自己的职业道德。这可是雪中送炭，意外横财。我用一个周末就挣了 10 万美元。

I felt that my report was impeccable because I did not breach my professional standards despite the hurried schedule. This sum of money was totally unexpected and a great shot in the arm. I earned US$100,000 in one weekend.

这 10 万美元对于投资银行的人可能根本不算什么，对我来说其实很重要。靠着这笔钱我买入了第 5 和第 6 个房子。离目标还差两个。等我买完第6 个房子不久。我的指数房已经涨过了 45 万美元。比最低点几乎要涨了一倍。这个时候抄底的最好机会基本已经过去。我感觉房价肯定会突破新高，现在只是市场进行正常的恢复，远远没有进入到泡沫。真的市场疯狂进入泡沫的状态，需要换一批购房者。曾经经历过房地产泡沫的业主，恐怕会小心谨慎，很难再制造一个泡沫。

Perhaps US$100,000 was negligible for investment banks. It was like life-saving money for me. I bought my fifth and sixth properties with it. Two more to go. Not long after I bought my sixth investment property, the price of my index house exceeded US$450,000, which almost doubled the lowest point. Though the best timing of buying the bottom had already passed, I felt that the property prices would reach a historical high. The market was recovering itself and far from forming a bubble. For the market to enter a new bubble, a new wave of home buyers needed to enter the market. But anyone who had just experienced a real estate bubble would be much more prudent, rendering another bubble an unlikely occurrence.

13 买到第七、第八个投资房
13 Buying My Seventh and Eighth Investment Properties

这个时候房价稍微稳定了一段时间。一年后，我用平时的积蓄又凑了一些钱，买入了第七个房子。这时候我的指数房已经涨到快 55 万了，我实在没有办法再买更多的房子了。

At this point, property prices had remained stable for a while. After a year, I used some savings to buy my seventh investment property. My index house was now worth US$550,000. Even though I still had one more house to go, I could not think of ways to buy more investment properties.

这些大约就是我在整个次贷危机之后，湾区抄底过程中的真实记录。第七个房子买好之后又过了一阵子。我把第一个房子 refinance 了一下。用 cash out 的钱买入了第 8 个房子。终于了了我的心愿。

This chapter is a real record of how I bought the bottom in the real estate market in the Bay Area after the sub-prime crisis. After I bought my seventh investment property, I bought my eighth investment property by refinancing the first one, eventually accomplishing my goal.

在整个抄底过程中。房价平均涨了一倍。因为是 20%的首付，所以现金回报率(Cash on cash)是 10 倍左右。最赚钱的是那个铁路边上的小黑屋，现金回报率三年是 20 倍左右。

Throughout the entire process of buying the bottom, property prices had, on average, doubled. Because of a 20% down payment option, my cash-on-cash return is about 1000%. The most profitable investment is the house that was located alongside the railway, which brought me a cash-on-cash return of 2000%.

在整个抄底过程中，我基本上没有特别大的资金投入。当然主要原因是因为自己是普通人家，没有太多的积蓄。因为自己在创业，没有太高的收入。大部分时候家庭税前收入一年只有 15 万-20 万美元。个别时候有些额外的咨询收入，量也很少。

My entire experience of buying the bottom did not demand a high capital input. The primary reason is that my family has an average household income before tax of around US$150,000-200,000 per year. Even though sometimes I would have extra income from my consultation side hustle, the amount was negligible.

我对自己在次贷危机之后抄底的执行能力是基本满意的。如果再给我一次这样的机会的话，我几乎想象不出我怎么能比这一次做得更好了。因为我作为手边可动用的资源就这么多，我给自己的表现打 80 分吧。

I am quite satisfied with my own performance and execution of my buying the bottom plan. If I were given an opportunity to go through the experience again, I guess I could not outperform myself. Because of the limited capital I had, I would give myself 80 marks for my performance.

第十六章 在美国做房东

Chapter 16: Being a Landlord in the U.S.

01 初试房东

01 First Time Being a Landlord in the U.S.

次贷危机抄底过后。我开始了在美国当房东的日子。美国的房东有很多外号，有的时候叫地主，有的时候我们老中自嘲为"淘粪工"。淘粪工的语义来源是投资理财论坛上经常讨论房东维修房子的事情。包括马桶堵了，都需要房东亲力亲为。所以房东们自嘲自己为"淘粪工"。当你经营的出租房规模很小的时候，其实大部分时候业主都是淘粪工。经营上规模之后，可以有比较长期的工人帮你工作。

After buying the bottom in the sub-prime crisis, my life as a landlord in the States officially began. Landowners in the U.S. have other nicknames among Chinese Americans, for example, "Gong farmers." Forum users coined this nickname during a discussion on repairing the houses for the tenants. Even when the toilet is broken, the landlords will fix it themselves, so "gong farmers" is a self-deprecating joke. When the scale of real properties managed by a landlord is small, most of them are gong farmers. But when their investment portfolio grows larger, they can afford to hire repairers to do the work for them.

我一开始做房东的时候，也觉得很诡异。特别是我急需钱抄底买湾区的房子的时候。一方面自己是一个博士，创业公司再不济我也管着十来个人。另外一方面每到周末，我却经常要提着工具箱，帮别人修门锁，修开关。通马桶的事情我倒的的确确没有干过。和上下水相关的活儿我都交给了水管工 (plumbers)。抄底那几年过去之后，一般的维修我也不再亲自上手。但是有的时候，活儿太小找不到合适的工人，也只能自己亲力亲为。

When I first became a landlord in the States, I found this weird, especially when I was buying the bottom back then. On one hand, I am a Ph.D. No matter how small my business was, I managed and supervised at least ten employees. On the other hand, I was busy repairing door locks and switches for my tenants on weekends though I was lucky that I did not need to fix a toilet. I delegated all repair works of the water pipes to the plumbers. Several years after my buying the bottom, I began to entrust all repair works to repairers. But sometimes, when I cannot find a worker, I need to do it myself.

在中国当房东和美国当房东是完全不一样的。过去十年我同时体会了这两种当房东的感觉,可以分享对比一下。

Being a landlord in China is entirely different than in the States. In the last decade, I have experienced both so I can compare the two and share my experience with my readers.

在中国当房东是活脱脱的黄世仁。因为你只需要管好钱，具体的事情都不用你管。因为人工费不贵，维修的事情有物业去帮你去做。另外因为中国大部分房子是公寓楼，所以没有什么要修的，屋顶不会漏，墙不会漏，窗户不用换。如果让我写中国当房东的故事，可能一千个字就够了。

Being a landlord in China is like being the Huang Shiren, a protagonist in the Chinese opera and ballet the White-Haired Girl, who made a fortune. My only job is to manage all money matters. I do not need to worry about all other problems because the cost of labor is cheap in China, and the property management office will do the work for me. Furthermore, most residential properties in China are apartments and condominium units, so there is not much repair work required. At least, I will not have to worry about a leaking roof and wall and changing the windows. Being a landlord in China is a short story because it is an easy task.

在美国当房东，特别是小业主当房东，活脱脱的就是杨白劳，因为美国的房子大部分都是独立屋(Single   Family   House)。考虑到租金控制(rent control)和屋主委员会—物业（HOA）的管理费，我购买的大部分房子都是独立屋。因为真正升值的是土地。非独立住房 HOA 年年上涨，也会对你的利润有很大影响。

In contrast, being a landlord in the U.S., especially for beginner investors, is without a doubt like being Yang Bailao, who had a tragic life in the White-Haired Girl because most residential properties in the U.S. belong to single-family houses. With the considerations of rent control and HOA fees in mind, most of my investment properties are single-family detached houses. It is the piece of land beneath the house that appreciates. The HOA fee increases gradually every year, which will erode profits.

美国修房子的人工费很高。然而对于小业主，不单单是人工费的问题。当你房子不是很多的时候，没有稳定的维修工作量，你去找一些陌生的工人来修理，难免要被宰。

Repair costs are exorbitant in the States. Yet for beginner investors who own a smaller number of investment properties, it is not merely an issue of labor costs. A smaller number of properties means little or less frequent repair work for the repairmen. Therefore, the small landowners may well be charged much more than the usual fees.

唯一的办法就是自己去做修理。我觉得大丈夫能上能下，既然中华民族优秀的妇女同志们可以上得了厅堂，下得了厨房，我们这些油腻的大老爷们，自然也是发得了 Nature 论文，通得了马桶。四体不勤的男人没啥值得骄傲的。

The only solution is to repair your investment properties on your own. I think that being a great man means being hardworking in all aspects of life. Women take care of the family by preparing meals and organizing the household, so men should also know both how to publish a journal article on Nature and how to fix a toilet. Men should strive to be good with their hands and be diligent.

我自己家的修缮工作大部分都是自己做的。无论之前我说过的自己铺设地板还是平时空调暖气汽车的维修。我感觉给自己家修东西其实是充满了乐趣。尤其是我不忙的时候，周末在家鼓捣一些工程项目都是很有趣的。比如在后院建造一个小孩玩的秋千滑梯，在侧院搭建一个花架子。这些事情很长一段时间都是我周末最大的乐趣。我会兴致勃勃地去 Home Depot 采购原材料，自己设计，动手完成。最享受的就是每次完成之后，坐下来喝一杯清茶，细细欣赏自己的劳动成果。

I finished most of the repair work of my own house by myself, ranging from laying floor tiles to repairing the air-con system of my car. I feel that repairing my own home is full of joy. When I have a less busy schedule, I find it fun to work on some construction projects for my family, for example, building a swing in the backyard for my children and a flower rack in the side yard. For a very long time, these projects brought me the most fun on weekends. I would enthusiastically buy some materials from Home Depot, design the structure, and build it myself. The most enjoyable moment was when I sat down, sipped some tea, and looked at my creation.

给自己家干活永远都是充满了动力，当然最主要的原因是有成就感，所以你能享受其中。这就好像你给家人做一顿丰美的菜肴，然后看到家人们吃得开心的样子，你会心满意足。哪怕此刻已经累得腰都扶不起来了，你也会很开心。

I am always full of energy when improving my house. The primary reason is that it brings me a sense of achievement and enjoyment. This is similar to how people take pleasure in preparing meals for their families. They will feel hugely satisfied seeing that their family enjoys the meals even though they may be exhausted afterward.

给自己修房子和给房客修房子的差别，大概就是相当于给自己做饭和在餐厅做饭的区别。给房客修房子，你通常没有心情，只想对付了事，赶紧逃之夭夭。这对每个初期当房东的人都是考验。

Repairing one's own house and his investment properties for the tenants is analogous to cooking one's own meals and cooking for the customers at a restaurant as a chef respectively. The landlord will usually try to finish the task as soon as possible without making much effort. This is a trial for every beginner real estate investor.

02 调整心态
02 Adjusting My Mindset

我的体会是，最重要的第一条就是调整好自己的心态，控制住自己的傲慢。大部分的美国华人都受过高等教育，而且往往不可避免地鄙视体力劳动者。其实体力劳动也好，智力劳动也好，并没有什么高低贵贱之分。大部分人很多时候都是在自欺欺人地找感觉。

The greatest takeaway from my experience of being a landlord in the U.S. is that I must adjust my mindset first by reminding myself to be humble. Most Chinese Americans are well-educated and despise labor work. Actually, both intellectual and labor work are noble, so most people are simply deceiving themselves when they try to distinguish between the two in terms of superiority.

我给你算一笔账，你就会明白。比如投资银行的人是最讲究体面的，一个个西装革履的在高楼大厦里面工作。可是当投行的 Managing Director (MD)也好，副总裁(VP)也好，会见客户的时候，不是也要恭恭敬敬客客气气么？因为只有对客户恭恭敬敬客客气气，这单生意年终奖就可能提成 10-50 万美元。即使客户蛮横无理，刁钻找碴，看在钱的份上，你也忍了。

Let me do some calculations for you to understand why I made this claim. For example, investment bankers care about their being presentable the most. They all wear a suit that costs an arm and a leg. But when they meet their clients, these bankers need to treat the clients as the king, regardless of whether they are a Managing Director or Vice President at the bank. The bankers often take home a year-end bonus of about US$100,000-500,000, so they will tolerate it no matter how rude and unreasonable the clients' requests are.

我在抄底买房子的时候，仔细核算了一下。如果我可以稳住租客继续租住，房价持续涨到年底，那么这几个房子加一起我就可以挣到 50 万美元左右。我帮助修理一下房屋，通一下马桶，那又和投资银行的工作有什么区别呢？无非在投资银行，你服务的是大老板们。而当一个淘粪工，你服务的是普通民众，甚至是挣扎在温饱线上远不如你的普通民众而已。

When I was buying the bottom of the real estate market, I did some calculations on my potential return from investments. If my tenants continued to live in my properties and property prices kept increasing till the end of the year, I could make a profit of US$500,000. Therefore, the time I spent on repair work and fixing the toilet for my tenants would generate the same income as an investment banker. Besides, landlords and bankers both serve others. The only difference is that gong farmers serve ordinary citizens or the grassroots, and investment bankers serve the most senior decision-makers of big corporations.

但是毕竟都是服务，钱都是钱。老百姓更多的时候比那些刁钻的生意场上的老板容易对付多了。其实主要的问题往往还是来自你的心态。人本能地不喜欢给低于自己社会阶层的人服务。要是给比尔·盖茨家修个车库门，即使没好处，我看很多房东也会乐于跑一趟去看看富豪家怎样。

But after all, they both make a profit from providing services. In fact, it is often easier to serve ordinary citizens than experienced businessmen. My point is that one's problems often stem from his or her own mindset. Instinctively, we do not like the idea of serving someone who belongs to a lower social class than us. I guess landlords who are reluctant to repair their investment properties for the tenants will be more than happy if Bill Gates asks them to repair his garage.

我说这些道理是告诉你，同样做一件事情，有理想和没理想，有长期计划和没有长期计划是不一样的。明白了这些道理，就会让你在做这些体力劳动的时候充满了干劲。不然就会顾影自怜，抱怨人生。

The reason why I tell you about this principle is that two people who are working toward the same goal will end up with different outcomes if one of them has a long-term aspiration and planning and the other does not. Understanding this rule will help you become full of energy and complain less when you are doing labor work.

我认识一个朋友，当我的指数房价涨到 40 万左右，在我看来还有很大的上涨空间的时候，他受不了做房东之苦，把房子卖掉了。这位朋友也是博士毕业，房客老找他修这个修那个，最后他不堪其烦，毅然把房客赶走，房子卖出。我觉得他没有调整好自己的心态。他总觉得自己一个大博士，去服务于这些个没文化的，又被那些人呼来喝去地搞维修，心里多多少少有些不甘。

When the price of my index house increased to around US$400,000, which I thought still had much room for further appreciation, a friend of mine sold his property because he hated the trouble of being a landlord. This friend of mine also holds a Ph.D., and he was annoyed by his tenant's frequent requests to repair this and that. He was feeling uneasy with having to serve the less educated and the need to be at their disposal because he was a doctor.

美国房子的修理工作一点都不难，房客其实自己都可以修。只是大部分的房客没有意识到，把房东呼来喝去做这些修理之后给自己带来的后果是什么。我印象中有一个房客，家里有一只蚂蚁，他都会打电话让我去。他说这个房子出问题了，客厅里竟然有蚂蚁。要我帮他把蚂蚁清理掉。对待这种客户最好的办法就是赶紧涨房租让他们滚蛋，爱去哪里去哪里。

The repair work is not difficult at all, and most tenants will be able to do it themselves. But they do not realize the negative consequences of always bothering the landlords. Take my personal experience. I once had this tenant who would ask me to handle even the tiniest problem. One time, he called to tell me that he found it unacceptable that there was an ant in the living room and hoped that I could get rid of it. My response? I later raised the rents hoping that they would soon move out.

其实四体不勤的人，你一眼就可以判断出来。四体不勤的人的共同特征就是不考虑他人，只想着提要求。面谈的时候，会对房东提出各种各样的清洁卫生要求。你问他能修什么的时候，他们说自己什么也干不了。

In fact, you can easily tell who is lazy and not good with his or her hands. Their common characteristic is that they are wholly inconsiderate. They will often make all sorts of requests to the landlords during the negotiation. If the landlord asks them if there is anything that they can help repair, their answer will be, "I am afraid not."

很快我就找到减少自己维修工作量的办法。每次和他们签合同的时候都会附加一项专门条款。在已经谈好的房租上，我说可以帮你每个月降 50 美元，但是如下所有的小事情通通你自己来修理，材料费我来负担。这些小事情包括换灯泡、换门锁、换纱窗、杀臭虫等等，我列了长长的一个清单。

Soon, I was able to find a way to reduce my workload by adding a clause to the lease which stipulates that I can reduce the rent by US$50 every month if they are responsible for the listed items, for example, changing the light bulb, door lock, window screen, getting rid of termites with the expenses reimbursed by me.

如果房客对这些清单有质疑，或者是房客说他自己处理不了这些事情的，这样的房客还是直接拒绝了为好。事实上，大部分勤劳的房客，还是乐于接受突然降低了 50 美元房租的好处的。用这样的方法显著地降低了我的工作量。

If the tenant is reluctant to accept that clause or says that he does not know how to handle those listed items, my experience will suggest that I should not even rent my properties to them. In fact, most diligent tenants are happy to see that they can save US$50 from the monthly rent payment. Meanwhile, I am also content because my workload is significantly reduced.

03 选房客

03 Finding Good Tenants

我在美国当了 8 年的房东，同时管理着 8 个住宅。我感觉如果想让自己生活舒适一些，最主要的是要找到靠谱的房客。同样的一个房子，一个靠谱的房客和一个不靠谱的房客，给你带来的烦恼，差不多会差 10 倍的样子。而你每个月的租金收入并差不了多少。

Having been a landlord in the U.S. managing eight residential properties for eight years, my tip on how to make my life as a landlord easier is to find trustworthy and responsible tenants. For the same investment property, the troubles created for the landlords by irresponsible tenants will approximately be ten times those by responsible ones, but the rental income will be almost the same.

那么怎样通过短暂接触，了解对方是否是靠谱的房客呢？可以从以下几个基本原则挑选：

So how can landlords determine whether the tenants are responsible individuals from their short encounters? I will suggest the following considerations for landlords.

一、信用记录，几乎没有什么东西比信用分数更能预告对方是否是个麻烦制造者了。我曾经有过两个信用分数 800 分的房客，后期的麻烦都少极了。平均一年才来找我一次，一切问题都自己解决。信用分数高的人一方面为了保护自己的信用分数，不愿意跟房东发生纠纷。另外一方面信用分数高的人往往有好的习惯。这些习惯表现在富有责任心，富有同理心，会替别人着想，而不是只顾自己，言而无信。也是因为这个原因，我后来几乎很少租给 700 分以下的房客，我宁肯房子空着，也不要租给找麻烦的人。

1. The tenants' credit record. The tenant's credit score is perhaps the most useful information to help you predict whether they will be a troublemaker. In my own experience, I dealt with two tenants who had a credit score of 800, and they created very few, if no, troubles for me. They only called me for help once a year and solved all other problems by themselves. Individuals with a high credit score are often very committed to maintaining it, so they will avoid having a dispute with the landlord. In addition, their excellent credit score implies that they are sympathetic, responsible, considerate, and trustworthy. For these reasons, I have rarely rented my properties to tenants with a credit score below 700. I would rather have an empty investment property than rent it to a troublesome person.

二、当然有的时候你找不到信用记录好的房客。比如我出租的第一个房子，那个时候就业市场还一塌糊涂，根本找不到合适的房客。还有很多不错的房客，由于各种原因没有积累自己的信用分数。如果没有信用记录的时候，我就会用另外一个原则就是"语言原则"。

2. The tenants' language skills. This is a rather unusual consideration that I apply when I cannot find tenants with a good credit score. For example, when I was trying to rent out my first investment property in the U.S., the employment market was terrible, so I could not find tenants based on the first criterion alone. But there were some nice tenants who had not accumulated a good credit score for various reasons.

总的来说给你写长长的邮件的，给你发长长的短信的，打电话一口气能说上五分钟以上的，都不是好的房客。在加州湾区有来自世界各地的移民。我整体的感觉是语言能力越差的，越是好的房客。如果英语基本上不太会说，用翻译机才能和你沟通的，那基本上就是值得你优先考虑的优质房客了。语言能力越强，说得天花乱坠的，往往都是劣质房客。

A short-cut is that individuals who write you long emails and text messages and talk endlessly on the phone for at least 5 minutes are often not ideal candidates. The Bay Area is home to immigrants from different corners of the world. Generally speaking, I feel that individuals with bad language skills are often better tenants. If the tenants can barely speak English and need to Google-translate the correspondence with the landlord, they will be the best tenants that you should prioritize. Individuals with stronger language skills and fancier speech often create more troubles for the landlords.

在加州有时你会碰上不交房租的房客。他们利用法律上对自己的一些保护跟你胡搅蛮缠。这些法律条文说起来好像是保护了房客，其实是破坏了房东和房客的信任关系，变相地提升了租房成本。

In California, landlords will sometimes deal with tenants who do not pay their rents. Relying on the legal protection of tenants, these irresponsible individuals will trouble their landlords with all sorts of unreasonable requests. The relevant laws seem to offer tenants better protection, but in fact, they destroy the trust between landlords and tenants, increasing the costs of renting a house for the tenants.

在中国出租房屋的时候，你很少担心房客付不出房租。你也不用查对方的信用记录，付一个月的押金就可以了。因为如果付不出房租就被赶走，这是天经地义的事情。根本不需要法院或者警察来做什么。不交房租，你去敲敲门赶人，房客吓得屁滚尿流就走了。

Landlords in China rarely have to worry about non-payment of rent or checking the credit record of the tenants because they will often require the tenants to pay a deposit of one month's rent. Also, landlords can evict tenants for non-payment of rent by themselves without asking the court or police for help because most tenants will move out voluntarily when the landlords knock on their door.

在美国有各种法律条文对房客进行保护，本质上是害了房客。他们让那些最需要租房子的低收入人群很难租到房子。因为在美国赶走一个房客需要花很长时间，走法庭程序，走警察流程，往往一拖就是大半年。这期间的损失都要房东来负担。

In contrast, there are different laws that protect the tenants in the U.S., which only do them more harm than good because these laws make it very difficult for low-income individuals to rent a house. In the U.S., evicting a tenant is highly time-consuming thanks to all the court procedures, which often take at least six months. The landlords bear the losses incurred during this period.

我自己曾经经历过一次驱逐房客（eviction）的经历，大约让我损失了半年的房租。整个过程中不胜其扰，付出的律师费就更不用说了。原本很简单的事情，一切都要走漫长的法庭程序。而走法庭程序看起来是由房东负担的，但是长远来看，和房租加税并没有什么区别。最终所有的负担，其实羊毛出在羊身上，都是最终由全体房客来负担的。也是因为这个原因，没人敢把房子租给收入很低的人群。一个佐证就是美国的租售比，同样在人口稠密的大城市，美国要远比东亚国家高很多。这是因为房东在出租的时候不可避免的要把这些风险通通加到房租上。

I went through the eviction process in the U.S. too. During the process, I lost six months of rental income. The whole process is expensive and time-consuming because of the legal costs and tedious court procedures involved. On the surface, it seems that all the burdens are shouldered by the landlords. However, in the long term, the relevant laws are essentially imposing a tax on rents because all the financial burdens will be shifted to the tenants by the landlords. It is precisely because of this that no one is willing to rent their houses to low-income individuals. Evidence supporting this observation includes the homeowner to renter ratio, which is much higher in U.S. cities than cities in South Asian countries with a similar population density.

如果你学过微观经济学就会明白这些道理。这些貌似保护租房者的法规其实是养肥了一个大的政府机构。而养肥这些政府机构的人，并不是房东。真正的出钱者反而是社会的最底层租房子的人们。最后的结果是低收入人群真的很可怜，租不到房子。

Anyone who has studied microeconomics will understand the logic behind it. These laws that seem to protect the tenants are, in fact, only benefitting the government. The money that goes to the government does not come from the landlords' pocket but the grassroots in the society who need to rent a house. The end result is that the low-income group suffers the most because they cannot rent a house.

三、第三个选房客的原则就是不要租给急于要搬到你这儿来的人。我碰到的最糟糕的租客是当时住在汽车旅馆里找房子的人。她谎称是从外州搬来，其实是被撵得无处可住。我动了同情心，就租给了她。结果住进去后我就再也没有收到过房租。直到大半年后请警察把她驱逐出去。

3. Do not rent your investment properties to those who are hurrying to move in. The worst tenant I have ever dealt with is someone who was staying at a motel and looking to rent a residential property. Though she claimed that she came from another state, the truth is she had been evicted so many times in my state. At the time, I was sympathetic, so I rented my property to her. The end of the story is that I had never received any rent payment from her and finally had her evicted by the police after six months.

作为房东，人们都恨不得房子明天就租出去，因为空置一天就是一天的损失。但是如果有房客说他明天就可以搬进来，多半不要租给他。相反那些未雨绸缪的房客，说他们一个月之后才能搬进来，往往是更加靠谱的房客，虽然你的房子会空关一个月。

Landlords often desperately hope that they can find a tenant tomorrow because they incur a loss for every single day of an empty house. But if a tenant says that he can move in tomorrow, my advice is, "Don't rent the house to him." This is true even at the expense of your investment property being empty for one month. In contrast, tenants who can only move in at least one month from signing the lease are often better tenants because this shows that they are organized and have planned their actions.

四、总的来说家庭完整的是好的租客。如果家庭结构健全，有比较小的孩子，如果你的房子又在学校附近，那么他们通常会稳定住很多年。如果是未婚同居，或者很多朋友凑在一起，往往不稳定。有自己事业的租客，也都是好租客，因为他们关注在自己的事业上，不会跟你胡搅蛮缠。

4. Rent your house to a family. If the tenants have a stable family, preferably with younger children, they will stay in your investment property for many years,

especially when the property is in proximity to a school. But if the tenants are single, a cohabiting couple, or roommates, this implies instability of rental income. Furthermore, tenants with their careers are often better tenants because they focus most of their energy and attention on developing their careers.

五、凡事物极必反。信用分数特别高，家庭完整，收入又高的人，不见得是好的租客。他们往往是有购房能力的，经常他短暂的住一阵子之后就自己买房子搬走了。

5. Beware of extremes. Tenants with a high credit score, a family, and high income are not necessarily the best tenants. These individuals have good purchasing power, so they will often move out after a while when they purchase their own homes.

六、尽量不要租给较短历史的自我雇佣者(self-employed)。他们的收入不稳定，即使是很好的人，但是没有钱付房租也没办法。

6. Avoid renting the house to a self-employed person with a short history of income because their income is not stable. No matter how nice and kind the tenant is, he or she simply cannot afford to pay the rent if his or her business is not profiting.

我买的第三个房子就是租给一个开幼儿园的人。她是一个东欧来的移民。当时就在我买的房子边上开了一个幼儿园。她从外州过来，曾经经营了二十几年的幼儿园。她一再和我说没有任何问题，让我不用担心。她当时同时租了我的房子和我边上的一个房子开办幼儿园。把我的房子作为她的个人住址。

I rented my third investment property to an owner of a kindergarten. She was an immigrant from Eastern Europe. She was running a kindergarten next to my investment property. She came from another state and had more than twenty years of experience in operating a kindergarten. She repeatedly reassured me and told me not to worry. She rented my investment property to live in and the house next to it for running her kindergarten.

但是她的幼儿园一开张生意就不好。她是一个特别好的人，勤劳而努力，信用记录也非常好。但是幼儿园因为种种原因就是没有生意。最后她经营不下去了就开始拖欠我的房租。

However, the kindergarten was not doing great since day 1. She was a very nice, diligent, and hardworking person with an excellent credit score. But for various reasons, her business was failing. In the end, she closed the kindergarten and stopped paying rent.

我只能请她搬走。她走的时候把房子打扫得干干净净，然后说欠我的那一个月房租以后有钱了一定会还给我。当然我再也没有见到过她，她也没有还给我，我也没有去通过讨债公司去索要，给她留下不好的信用记录。我想人活在世上都有各种不测的风云，能够互相帮助的时候，还是互相帮助一下吧。

So, I could only ask her to move out. When she left, the house was in perfect condition. She even promised me that she would pay me back the outstanding one month's rent payment. Of course, I have never heard from her since, and I did not try to demand the money back through a debt-collection agency lest I would ruin her credit score. We never know what battle others are fighting in life. When we have the ability to give a helping hand, we should not hesitate to do so.

七、最后一条最重要。就是无论是谁，都需要走标准流程审查。标准流程就是你永远都要那三样东西：信用报告、银行账单、工资条。无论什么人都要去信用记录上查一下，看看有没有犯罪记录，有没有被驱逐的历史。

7. Most importantly, remember to go through the standard screening procedure, regardless of who your tenants are. The standing procedure comprises of credit reports, bank statements, and income records. Regardless of who your tenants are, remember to also check their criminal history on the credit report and whether they have been evicted.

理论成千上万，说的再多也没有用，只有你去亲身实践的时候，你才会慢慢积累经验，找到门道。我在湾区的房子基本上都买好了之后，美国的经济越来越好，失业率越来越低。原先把房子扔给银行的人，都要到市场上来租房子。有经济能力的人越来越多地开始买房子。所以房价在涨，房租也在涨，我的日子好极了，每天都看到各种上涨的好消息。每一次换房客，租金都可以上涨一大截。

There are countless theories, but they are useless without application. Only when you have experienced being a landlord can you find the tricks. After I bought all eight investment properties in the Bay Area, the U.S. economy began to recover and the unemployment rate was getting lower. Individuals who threw their houses to the bank were now looking to rent a house. Meanwhile, people whose purchasing power had increased were starting to buy a house. As a result, both property prices and rents were surging. I had a great time because property prices were increasing every day. Every time when I had new tenants, my rental income would increase.

当我想着可以好好享受一下数钱的日子的时候，又一个灾难发生了。是的，真的又是一个把我打懵的突发事件。人生就是这样，总不能让你一切顺利。有一阵子好日子，倒霉的事情就来了。持续的坏日子也不会长久，转机往往就在前面。

Just when I was going to enjoy my life by counting my cash at home, another disaster struck. It was totally unexpected. But this is how life is: full of ups and downs. After some good days, bad days came, but these bad days would not last for too long before a turning point emerged.

04 种大麻的老中

04 The Chinese American Who Grew Cannabis at Home

这次倒霉的灾难事件，是我的中华同胞给我造成的。我抄底买的第一个投资房，后来租给了一对年轻的中国夫妻。这对夫妻刚从中国来，据他们说，那个女的刚到美国三个月，男的是一个广东人，应该是通过亲属移民过来的。女的是从国内嫁过来的，当时已经怀孕。看着是一个令人羡慕的温馨家庭。

The culprits of this unfortunate, disastrous accident are my Chinese counterparts. Later, I rented my first investment property that I bought in the "buying the bottom" plan to a young Chinese married couple. They had just settled in the U.S. They told me that the wife arrived in the U.S. three months ago and the husband was from Guangdong, China, who immigrated to the U.S. through family union scheme. The wife obtained her legal status in the U.S. by marrying the guy and was pregnant when they were renting my house. Everything looked so happy and warm.

他们租我的房子三年，从来不给我找任何麻烦，没有提出过任何修理要求。偶尔有事也都自己修了。每个月房租都是按时付，正确的说每次都是提前一天付。

In the three years they rented my house, they had never brought me any troubles. Neither had they made any requests for repair. They always repaired the house themselves and paid the rent on time. To be more precise, they paid their rent one day before the deadline every single time.

我还经常心里嘀咕，感觉还是我们老中同胞靠谱。我的第五个房子买到之后，我还打电话问他们有没有什么亲戚朋友也要租房子。他居然还介绍了一个他的表妹来租我的房子。他们看我的第五个房子很满意，但是阴差阳错，其他人比他们早付了定金订走了，当时我还有些后悔。

Because of their "exemplary behaviors," I was feeling that Chinese Americans were more reliable. This is why after I bought my fifth property, I even called them to ask if they had any relatives or friends who were looking to rent a house. They recommended a cousin of the husband to me, and she was interested in renting my fifth investment property. But other tenants paid a deposit earlier than her, so I did not rent the house to her, about which I was feeling regretful at the time.

所以我对这对夫妻的印象特别好。我房子的邻居是 HOA 的主席。有一次我还写邮件问他："我那个房客怎么样?" 他说非常好，他们好像有一个小孩子经常推着车进进出出的，非常安静，从来不给大家找任何麻烦。

This married couple left me with a very good impression. One of my neighbors was the president of the HOA, so I even emailed him to ask how he thought of my tenants. He replied, "Excellent. It seemed that they had a kid because they were always using a stroller. They were very quiet and never brought any troubles for anyone."

大约三年之后，因为利率变化的原因，我那个房子需要 refinance。银行让我去约一下房客。他们需要进屋做一下评估。我给那对中国夫妻打电话，预约来做评估的时间。打过这个电话，这对夫妻就人间蒸发了，我再找不到他们了，邮件不回，电话也不回。

Three years later, because of a new interest rate, I was trying to refinance that property, so the bank asked me to contact the tenant to arrange a house tour for the bank to value it. I called the couple to make an appointment. But after this phone call, they disappeared out of thin air. I could not contact them anymore. They did not reply to my emails or answer my phone calls.

我隐隐约约地感觉到不太妙，于是跑到现场去看。房子很安静，我敲门没有回应，门锁已经换掉。我绕到后院去，所有的窗帘全都是遮蔽得严严实实的。而且是那种特别小心的严严实实的，都找不到一个缝隙看到室内。我试图从二楼的窗户看进去，但是也是一样，完全遮挡了，什么也看不见。

I had this gut feeling that something was wrong, so I drove to my investment property. The house was quiet. I knocked on the door, but no one answered. The door lock had been changed. I went to the backyard and saw that all windows were carefully covered. I could not even glimpse through the windows. I tried to look inside from the windows on the second floor, but they were also fully covered that I could not see anything inside.

我心想坏了，最近电视新闻上经常看到有人租房种大麻。会不会被我碰上了。我耳朵贴到门上听，这时候我听见房间里隐隐约约的嗡嗡的声音，像是有风扇或者是其他什么电机在转。我心里一凉，我的房子真的变成了大麻屋，被他们种上大麻了。

I knew things were very bad. News that tenants growing cannabis was frequent on the TV. Would I encounter such an unfortunate situation? I put my ears on the door and heard some intermittent buzzing sound that was probably caused by a turning electric fan or some kinds of turbos. At this moment, my heart sank because I knew that my investment property was turned into a cannabis farm.

不过我还是心存侥幸，不太相信那对看起来很正常的夫妻会种大麻。房子一旦被种上大麻会很麻烦，因为房子的结构会被他们破坏和改造，长期种大麻，高温高湿，霉菌滋生。需要更换所有的地毯、石膏板。电路系统也会出问题。

But part of me refused to accept the truth. I still could not believe that the married couple who looked so normal was cannabis growers. Once a house is turned into a cannabis farm, it will be an endless ordeal for the landlords because the structure of the house is destroyed and redesigned. On top of that, the growing of cannabis requires a high-temperature and high-humidity environment, which is a hotbed for molds, which means I will have to replace all the carpet and plasterboard. The home electrical system will also have some problems.

我犹豫了再三，只能选择报警。当然现在看看报警不是最好的选择，因为警察不会去保护房东的利益，警察只会秉公办事，按流程走。此外，在警察眼里每个人都有可能是嫌疑人。

After much hesitation, I finally decided to call the police. Of course, now looking back, I can see that calling the police was not the best option because the police's duty is not to protect the interests of the landlords. Their job is to adhere to the prescribed procedures. Furthermore, in their eyes, everyone is a possible suspect.

警察很快鸣着警笛就来了，我同时约了锁匠来。警察敲门没有人回应，于是警察命令锁匠把门打开。一开门，眼前的景象把我惊呆了。

The police officers soon arrived with their car siren on. I also called a locksmith. The police officers knocked on the door, but no one answered it. They then ordered the locksmith to open the door. I was stunned by what I saw.

全是大麻，整个房子像热带森林一样。每个房间已经分不出功能了，地上全是种大麻的水池，屋顶上各种照明设备和各种稀奇古怪的通风管道，那对中国小夫妻把房间彻底改造成了大麻屋。

It was cannabis everywhere. The house was like a tropical rainforest. I could not tell the function of each room anymore. There were buckets of water everywhere on the floor, and the roof was now full of different lighting equipment and ventilation tunnels. The Chinese couple had completely transformed my house into a cannabis farm.

警察做的第一件事不是去找犯罪分子，而是录我的口供。让我把和房客当年签的合同找出来，把房客的所有信息都给他们，包括房客的驾照、银行账号等等。当我急忙把这些东西都找给他之后，警察又说都是假的，没什么用。同时另外一批警察到房间里，先把电源切断，然后拿一个大口袋，把所有的大麻从根部剪掉，把叶子放到大麻袋里。

The first thing the police did was not to hunt down the criminals but to record a police statement with me. They asked me to find the lease and give them all the information about the tenants, including their driving license and bank account details. After I handed them the documents, they said they were all fake. Meanwhile, some more police officers had arrived in the scene. They cut the power off, cut all the cannabis from its roots, and put them into a big bag.

我问能否抓到坏人？他们说这样的案子他们一周好几起，他们会做备案。他问我房租多少？我实话实说。他说你不知道他们这些人种大麻挣了多少钱，光今天剪掉的，就能卖十几万。我问哪里可以申请赔偿么？他说你可以民事诉讼告他们，不过"I won't bet on it"（我可不指望）。这基本上就是警察的全部服务。然后警察就呼啸着警车扬长而去。走的时候还给我留下一句狠话，说以后你出租房子，需要睁大眼睛看清楚点。如果你再有大麻屋事件，你也要被当作同伙嫌疑人接受调查。

I asked them if they could catch the bad guys. They told me that they handled at least several such cases every week and that they would file a report. They then asked me how much the monthly rent was, and I told them the truth. A police officer said, "You have no idea how much these cannabis growers make. The cannabis that we cut today is worth hundreds of thousands of dollars alone." My next question was whether and how I could apply for compensation. Though they suggested a civil claim against them, they also added, "I won't bet on it." The above is all the services provided by the police. After our conversation, the police officers left. They even warned me that I should be more careful next time and that they would investigate me as an accomplice if I have another cannabis home incident.

警察撤退走了，毒贩留给我的是一个千疮百孔的房子和一屋子种大麻的设备，各种水管水盆，和数不清的通风管道。

After the police left the scene, I was left with a house that was riddled with holes and different equipment for growing cannabis, including the water pipes, buckets, and all the ventilation tunnels.

后来我读到其他人的攻略，如果发现房子里被种了大麻，更好的办法不是报警，而是跟房客商量一个协议(deal)。要求房客把我的房子复原到原来的样子，然后毒贩自己走人。否则报警。

When I was reading some sharing by other landlords, it is recommended that the best way to deal with a cannabis farm is not to call the police but to make a deal with the tenants to demand that they restore the house by threatening to call the police.

我没有这方面的经验，选择了直接报警。毒贩固然损失了十几万，但是警察拿到了相关罪证，他们什么都不会去做。好像警察对这样的事情非常司空见惯，种大麻在加州已经变成一个警察管不过来的罪行。他们压根儿也不会去费力缉拿这些犯罪分子。

I had had no prior experience before, so I chose to call the police. The criminals had lost hundreds of thousands of dollars, but the police would not do anything even after obtaining all the relevant evidence. It seems that the police are accustomed to such reports. In California, illegal cannabis cultivation was so prevalent that the police did not have the manpower and time to crack down on it. Sometimes, they would not even try to arrest the criminals.

我后悔当时自己的轻率。因为租给中国人，在情理上多一些信任，三年里都没有想着过来看一下。尤其吓人的是我甚至傻乎乎的差点把我的第五个投资房也租给他们。那个表妹应该是同他们一伙种大麻的。想一想真是有些后怕，当时如果把那个房子也租给他们，警察更有理由怀疑我是同伙了。

I regretted that I was so careless. As the couple was also Chinese, I had more trust in them emotionally speaking. In the three years they rented my property, I had not inspected it once. What is even more terrifying was that I almost also rented my fifth property to their cousin. What if the cousin was also a cannabis grower? I was terrified at this thought. If I had indeed also rented the house to them, it would give the police even more reason to suspect that I was an accomplice.

后悔归后悔，抱怨归抱怨，眼前面对的是恶梦一场，一片狼藉的摊子，总得我来收拾，承担损失。我买了那么多房子已经弹尽粮绝了，我都不知道这个房子收拾好之后该怎么办？能出租么？能卖出去么？而且我的腰伤还没有痊愈，我也不能干重体力活。这下子让我怎么办呢？

After all the regretting, moaning and complaining, I had to clean up the mess. As I had already used up all my savings in buying those eight properties, I had no idea how I could afford the loss? I was equally clueless about the future: Would I still be able to rent it out again? Could I sell it? Meanwhile, I still had not fully recovered from my spinal cord injury so I could not do heavy labor. What should I do now?

05 峰回路转

05 A Turning Point

我在房子里转了几圈，评估了一下自己的损失。折腾了一天，天色已经变暗，房子没电了，很快黑了下来。种大麻照明耗电比较高，所以他们采用了偷电的办法。为了绕过电表，他们把主电缆那片墙砸破。在电表前用一个偷电夹，夹住进户主电缆。偷电夹有一圈锋利的尖刺，可以刺破厚厚的电缆保护皮，从中偷走电。

I toured the house and estimated my loss. The sun had set, and the house was dark because it ran out of power. Since the lighting equipment required for planting cannabis consumes a lot of electricity, the young couple came up with a method to steal electricity. In order to bypass the electricity meter, they smashed the wall where the main cable was located and used a special clip around the electricity meter that pierces through the protective layer of the cable to steal electricity from other households.

因为种大麻必须要偷电，电力公司应该很容易识别哪里有人种大麻的。他们只要看到一个小区有严重的偷电现象，就可以初步判断这个地区是否有人种大麻。偷电也很容易判断，把一个片区总表用电和各家各户分表的总和比较一下就知道了。但似乎电力公司对这样的事情也是睁一只眼闭一直眼懒得管。警察经常拿着红外线视频摄影器在街道上巡逻，四处拍建筑的外立面的温度，来判断是不是有人种大麻。我那个房子是在一个大门封闭小区(Gated Community)里面，警察平时不太容易进去。所以自然也就被毒贩看中了。

As cannabis growers have to steal electricity, it is easy for electric companies to tell who are planting cannabis at home. They can make a rough estimate of whether someone is planting marijuana in that community when they notice that there is a serious problem of electricity theft there. It is also easy to identify electricity theft by adding the total usage of electricity in that community and comparing it with the total usage shown on all electricity meters. But it seems that energy companies are turning a blind eye to the problem. Police officers usually use an infrared imager at the walls of a structure to detect indoor marijuana growing operations while patrolling on the street. My investment property was situated inside a gated community, so police officers did not usually enter it. This explained why the criminals rented my property as the base for their operations.

应该说这个时候文学城的投资理财论坛还是帮助了我。我咨询了一个比较资深的大地主，问他这种情况应该怎么处理。他说他没有直接的经验，不过感觉保险公司应该负责赔偿。我问这应该属于哪一类赔偿？他说这个应该算蓄意破坏（vandalism）。

Once again, I benefitted greatly from the information on the investment and wealth management forum on wenxuecity.com. I turned to an experienced landlord who had a large portfolio of investment properties for suggestions. He told me that though he did not have a similar experience, the insurance company should compensate me for the loss. I then asked him how I should frame my claim. He said this belonged to vandalism.

真是雪中送炭的好建议。我赶紧给保险公司打电话，每年我交了这么多保险金，不能白交。保险公司第二天派了两个人来了，他们特别平静，似乎都司空见惯了，来了就拍照、画图和测量。他们告诉我这样的案例，一周他们要处理好几起。我这才算放下心来，可见加州的大麻屋已经泛滥到什么程度，而警察的放纵又是到了什么程度。他们画完图，做完测量，然后就回去了，说明天给我一个赔偿的估价。

It was a brilliant idea. I immediately called my insurance company. I have paid a large sum of insurance fees every year, and I could not let it go to waste. The insurance company sent two staff members the next day. They were very calm as if it were no big deal. They took pictures, drew some graphs, and measured my house. They also told me that they handled several similar cases every week. Their words eased my nerves and reflected how serious the problem of indoor marijuana growing activities was in California and how police were turning a blind eye to the problem. After drawing the graphs and measuring my house, they left and said they would give me a quote tomorrow.

保险公司的效率很高，第二天赔偿估价就给了我。我可以有两种选择，一种是拿钱自己修，一种是保险公司负责给我修。

Insurance companies were highly efficient that they did call me back with a quote the next day. They gave me two options: I could either take the money and do the repair work myself or entrust all repair work to the insurance company.

我看了一下赔偿的估价。保险公司给的估价其实是挺慷慨的，赔偿里包括所有的房间隔断、石膏板、电缆电线的更换。我觉得有些其实并不需要，只要换一部分就可以了。电路系统我了解，大部分是好的，不用换。大部分房东看见电路系统就害怕，我不是这样的。我唯一不确定的是大麻味道很重，不知道那个味道能否彻底散掉。

The compensation amount was quite generous. It covered all expenses involved in re-partitioning the house, replacing the plasterboard and cable, but I thought some of the items were not necessary. It would suffice if only some parts of the house were replaced. For example, based on my understanding of the home electrical system, most components were still working and needed no replacements. Most landlords are intimidated by the seemingly complicated electrical system, but I am an exception. My only worry was I was not sure whether I could erase the overbearing smell of cannabis in the room.

保险公司的人走的时候，我问了一下他，我说这一大堆种大麻的设备应该怎么处理才比较合适？那个人客气地看了我一眼，欲言又止，最后说，我如果是你的话，估计会放到租赁仓库里去。然后在 Craigslist 上登个广告，谁要来买就可以把全部设备卖给他，这样省得未来有麻烦。

When the staff members of the insurance company were about to leave, I asked him how I should handle the equipment. After some pondering, he looked at me and said, "If I were you, I would probably put all the equipment in a self-storage unit and publish an ad on Craigslist to see if anyone was interested in buying it. This way. I could prevent any future troubles."

于是我到街上找了两个墨西哥工人来，把大麻屋里的主要设备放到附近的一个租赁仓库里。然后去登广告开卖。在 Craigslist 上登广告我才发现这里头卖设备的人太多了。加州真是一个大麻泛滥的地方，你根本不用担心卖设备是否犯法。

Having heard the suggestion, I hired two Mexican repairmen, moved the equipment to a storage center nearby, and put an ad on Craigslist. I was surprised to find out that there were dozens of ads on such equipment. Cannabis was so common in California that people did not even worry about whether selling the equipment was illegal.

然后我又找了两个老墨工人，帮我一起干活儿，修理房屋。把地毯全部揭掉，把屋顶里面的一些东西拿下来，把通风管道全部拆掉，把石膏板该换的都换掉，把墙上打的很多洞全部封闭掉。然后重新油漆一遍。

Then I hired two more Mexican workmen to help me repair the house. We changed all the carpet, removed the ventilation tunnels and other equipment from the rooftop, replaced all the plasterboards, filled the holes on the wall, and painted the house.

这个工作让我前前后后大概忙了两周的时间，房子很快又焕然一新了。完全看不出种过大麻的痕迹。但是最麻烦的是电力系统的恢复。报警之后，电力公司把电完全切断了，他们需要检查电路合格之后才能恢复电力系统的供应。

It took us about two weeks to repair and renovate the house. Now people cannot find even a single trace of cannabis-growing operations. But the most difficult part was restoring the supply of electricity. After I called the police, the electric company cut off the power, saying that they would only restore the power supply after checking that the system passes the safety requirements.

因为毒贩偷电扎破了主电缆。所以电力公司要跨过一条街，把整个主电缆全都换掉才可以。其实主电缆上刺破的小孔很小，拿胶封住就可以。但是电力公司不干，换一根电缆就要花 4000 美元，前后用了将近两个月的时间。

As the drug dealers cut the main cable when they were stealing electricity, the electric company said they needed to change all the power lines across the street. But in fact, the holes on those lines were tiny, which could be handled by wrapping plastic tape. However, the electric company insisted on changing all the power lines. In the end, it cost US$4,000 to change one power line and took 2 months to finish the whole project.

电力公司和政府差不多。因为都是垄断经营，效率低下。走手续就能走到你断气。5 元能解决的问题，一定要用 4000 元去解决。主电缆更换，一个小时都不用的工作，要两个月才帮你解决。

Energy companies are like the government because they are both a monopoly that has low efficiency. Meanwhile, there are numerous layers of procedures in place. The power line problem could be solved at US$5, but the company insisted on expending US$4,000 on it. Usually changing the power lines only takes one hour at most, but they spent two months.

好在保险公司慷慨大方，电力公司的这些费用和房租损失保险公司也负责。因为房子是我自己请人修的，所以实际的费用比保险公司赔偿的要少很多。等一切都弄好了，大麻设备也卖掉了，我算了一下账，最后竟然赚了 2 万美元。忙了两周挣 2 万美元，这买卖还不错。

But fortunately, the insurance company was generous that it compensated the energy company for its expenses incurred and my loss in terms of rental income. As I organized and oversaw the repair myself, the actual repair costs were much lower than the compensation I received. After finishing the work and selling the equipment, I did some simple calculations, according to which I had actually made a profit of US$200,000 in two weeks, which was a pretty good deal.

不过这样的挣钱买卖以后也再不敢干了，警察临走时候对我的威胁我还记得。之后我所有的房客在租住房屋的时候，我都专门写上一条，特别说明我每半年需要入室来检查一下房屋的水管和屋顶。就这一条让我再也没有碰到过大麻屋。虽然我从来没有像合同上说的那样去主动检查过水管和屋顶。

That being said, I wish I would never be involved in another cannabis farm situation in the future because I can still vividly remember how the police warned me. Since this unfortunate incident, I have incorporated a clause in the contract stipulating that I will visit the investment property every six months to inspect the water pipes and rooftop. Thanks to this clause, I have never encountered any cannabis grower tenants since, even though I have never actually inspected the pipes and rooftop on my own initiative.

06 白人黑人化

06 The White Becoming Black

在美国当房东还有一件有乐趣的事情，就是让我有机会更全面的接触美国的社会。应该说之前我在读书和工作的时候只能接触美国社会很小的一面，局限于工程技术领域的人群。因为跟我打交道的大部分都是知识分子，受过良好教育的人。

Another fun part of being a landlord in the U.S. is that it gives me a chance to meet Americans from all walks of life. When I was studying and working in the States, I only had the chance to interact with a specific group of Americans who are professionals in the engineering field. Therefore, my social circle consisted of well-educated people only.

而当房东却让我接触到鱼龙混杂各行各色的人。他们来自不同的国家，来自不同的族裔背景。这些接触一方面让我感觉到美国的多样性，另一方面第一手感受到美国的各种社会问题。美国是在一片荒原上建立起来的国家。全世界各种各样的人来到美国来。因为多样性，所以才有创造力。每个人因为不同的文化背景，有人擅长做这些，有人擅长做那些。

Being a landlord gives me the chance to meet people from all walks of life and cultural backgrounds. They come from various countries with different ethnic backgrounds. In our encounters, I witness first-hand the diversity of U.S. society and also the related social issues. The U.S. was built on wasteland and is home to immigrants from all over the world. Because of its cultural diversity, the U.S. is a creative country because its people have different strengths and skills.

可是在带来各种天才的同时，也不可避免地把各种问题带到了美国。我觉得美国最伟大的地方不是民主自由，西方其他很多国家都做到了。美国最伟大的地方是让不同族裔之间，不同背景的人群和平共处。这实在太难了。族裔融合这事基本上没有什么国家能够比美国做得更好了。通过法律系统和政治正确主旋律的宣传，让各个族裔之间求同存异，和平相处，走向融合。

Just when the free land was welcoming the talents, their arrival also inevitably brought different problems to the U.S. In my opinion, the greatest thing about the U.S. is not democracy and freedom, which are also guaranteed in other western countries, but its harmonious environment where people of various ethnicities and cultural backgrounds thrive. Nurturing such an environment is an arduous task. There are no other countries that have better ethnic integration measures than the U.S. Through its legal system and education, different ethnic groups respect each other's cultural differences and share core values that bind them together, contributing to the unity and cultural richness of the American society.

我在美国还观察到另一个现象。平时报刊媒体很少讨论，但是在我眼前真正发生的现象。那就是就是白人的黑人化。

My other observation of the American society, which is rarely discussed in the mainstream media but happening in real life, is the white people becoming black.

从前白人试图帮助黑人，让更多的黑人进入中产阶级，像白人一样生活和工作。但是随着经济的发展，贫富悬殊拉大，有相当一部分比例的白人渐渐沦为低收入阶层。低收入阶层白人的生活方式越来越像黑人。他们的受教育程度、人生态度、家庭结构、子女教育、以及在社会上的竞争力，渐渐变得越来越像黑人。白人的低收入单亲家庭和黑人低收入单亲家庭似乎都越来越多。

In the past, whites tried to improve the living standards of black Americans by helping them enter the middle class to work and live like whites. But as the economy grows, the wealth gap also widens. A certain proportion of the whites are slowly falling out of the middle-class rank into the low-income group. The living standards of low-income whites are becoming more similar to those of blacks, in terms of education level, demographics, family structure, the education of their children, and competitiveness in society. It seems that the numbers of both white low-income single-parent families and black low-income single-parent families are rapidly increasing.

在中国人们经常讨论一件事，就是中国会不会掉入中等发达国家陷阱，会不会拉美化？现在看来中国可能不太会拉美化。倒是美国有可能变得拉美化。我说的这句话并不是针对拉丁裔。而是说我接触的低收入阶层，无论是黑人、白人还是拉丁裔似乎都变得越来越像。没有做房东之前，我没有意识到有那么多家庭破碎的低收入人口。收入阶层的划分渐渐取代了族裔的划分。

A common discussion topic among Chinese is whether China will fall prey to Latin America's middle-income trap? It now seems to me that while China will not fall into the trap, the U.S. may well become another Latin America. A disclaimer is that my argument is in no way targeted at Latin Americans; it is just a name for an economic phenomenon. What I am trying to say is that the low-income individuals with whom I have interacted, be it blacks, whites, or Latin Americans, are becoming more indistinguishable. Before becoming a landlord in the U.S., I had not realized that we had a large population of single-parent low-income families. Social classes in American society are no longer associated with race. Instead, income is now the defining characteristic.

在美国种族是一个特别敏感的话题，你不当心就会掉到政治不正确的陷阱里。作为外国人非常容易在这点上犯错误，特别是生长在单一种族国家的外国人。我们过去生长在中国，一直都是主流族裔，所以我们很少从少数民族的角度看社会。但是生活在中美两岸，让我既能作为社会的主体，也能作为社会的少数民族来感受两种不同的定位。

第十六章 在美国做房东
Chapter 16: Being a Landlord in the U.S.

Race is a highly sensitive topic in the U.S. You have to be very careful; otherwise, you will easily fall into the trap of political incorrectness. Newcomers to the U.S. are particularly prone to making such a mistake, especially for someone like me who was born and raised in a mono-racial society. In China, I belong to the racial majority, so I have rarely tried to look at the society from the perspective of a racial minority. However, now as someone who is living in both China and the U.S., I am both a racial majority and minority, enabling me to view social issues from a broader angle.

在美国当好房东还有一个很重要的经验，就是要有大海一样宽阔的心胸。尤其在钱方面，不要和房客斤斤计较。如前面所说，你收入的主要来源是房地产的那四大收入。即：增值、抵税、折旧、通胀。房租收入只是让你能够保持现金流打平，持续玩这个游戏。既然如此，就不要太在意房租多一点少一点。我在投资理财论坛上经常看到有人为鸡毛蒜皮的一件事情跟房客闹得不可开交。总的来说房客在经济上是弱势群体，房东是稍微强势一点。得饶人处且饶人，和气才能生财。

Another important tip on how to be a good landlord in the U.S. is that one has to be kind, accepting, and generous, especially on money matters. Do not haggle over every last dime with your tenants. As mentioned earlier, landlords have four sources of income, namely appreciation, tax reduction, depreciation, and inflation. The only function of rental income is to maintain a break-even cash flow so that the landlords can continue playing the game. Therefore, landlords should not be too fixated on the amount of rent. I can often see that some landlords on the forum said that they had a heated argument with their tenants on some trivial matters. Generally speaking, tenants are the weaker party in terms of economic power, and landlords are the stronger party, so landlords should be more forgiving, generous, and kind. There is an old Chinese saying that goes, "Harmony brings fortune."

过去十年里，有两次新闻报道过华人房东跟房客发生口角，被房客一枪打死的事情。作为旁观者，房客杀人是肯定不对的，但房东为一点房租送了性命也是不明智的。我的理想不是做一个超级大地主。 房产只是一个让我获得财富的方法，所以不值得为了那点房租那么敬业。我这篇文章里说的所有抄底的故事都是我在业余时间完成的，当房东并不是我生活和工作的全部。现在我花在房地产管理的时间，一年也就一周左右。

In the last decade, there were two news reports about Chinese American landlords being shot to death by their tenants in a quarrel. Murder can never be justified, but as a bystander, I also feel that a wise landlord should not argue with the tenants in a bid to increase their rental income. My aspiration is not to become a mega landlord. Real estate investing is one of the many ways that can help me procure more wealth, so losing one's life because of some rental income is not worth it. I executed all my "buying the bottom" plans in my spare time. Being a landlord is not all of my life and work. Now I only spend around seven days managing my real estate every year.

07 怎样滚雪球

07 How to Roll a Snowball

投资理财论坛上，2006 年曾经有个叫作石头的网友很活跃。他是网上公开的第一个实现 1000 万美元资产的人。2006 年，他所在的地区房地产价格涨了 10%，因为他有 1000 万美元的资产，所以那一年他在纸面上至少挣了 100 万美元。他当时感慨地说，"如果用工资去挣这 100 万美元，那要付出多少年辛辛苦苦的努力啊？而用资本挣资本的方式获得这 100 万多么简单啊。"他这一年什么都没有做，账户上凭空就多了 100 万美元。

On the investment and wealth management forum on wenxuecity.com, a netizen with the username "*Shitou*" was very active in 2016. He was the first forum user to have openly accumulated US$10 million of assets. In 2006, the property prices in the area where he was based increased by 10%. As he had $10 million of assets, he at least made US$1 million on the book that year. He was filled with emotion when he said, "How many years of hard work will it take for a person to earn US$1 million from his full-time job? Yet earning US$1 million from capital gains is so easy." He did not do anything in that year, but the balance in his bank account had increased by US$1 million.

我做房东的感觉就是特别像玩大富翁(Monopoly)。大富翁游戏里你的工资就是每转一圈银行给你的 200 美元。如果你没有被动收入，200 美元很快就坐吃山空了。上班族就像那个棋子，永远在奔波下去，可是并不富裕，毫无安全感。当你投资拥有一定数量的房子之后，再买更多的房子，让钱生钱，一切都变得简单了很多。

From my own experience, I feel that being a landlord in real life is very similar to playing the board game Monopoly. In the game, players collect $200 every time they pass GO. This $200 is like our salary in real life. If you do not have a passive income, you will soon use up the $200. The working class is like a game piece in Monopoly: They are always on the go but never feel rich or a sense of security. But when they have accumulated a certain number of properties, they can buy more properties using the rental income and appreciation. Making your money work for you is much easier.

用钱生钱，让自己的房产投资变成一个赚钱的列车滚滚向前，会有三种情况：

Real estate investing is all about making your money work for you. There are three ways to turn your real estate investments into a cash-making machine.

第一种情况就是在房价比较便宜的地区。比如中西部地区的房子，的的确确会给你带来正现金流的收入，然后你用这些收入投资购房，又可以让你买更多的房子。

The first situation is to buy properties in regions where the property prices are lower, for example, the Middle West region. Such real estate properties will bring you extra income from positive cash flow. Then you can use the income to buy more properties.

第二种情况，就是我的情况。对于我所在的湾区，即使我抄到了世纪大底，靠租金收入去买下一个房子也是不可能的。随着房产涨价，我每个月有了几千美元的正现金流。这个时候，需要通过不断重新抵押贷款(refinance)，套现现金（cash out）出来投资买房。当然每次买入新的房子，你的现金流又会变成持平或者轻微变负。这不要紧，你的任务是滚动出更多的房子，而不是收取租金。

The second situation, which is also my strategy, is where the cash flow of investment properties is even or slightly negative at first. I am based in the Bay Area, so it will be impossible for me to rely on rental income alone to buy my next investment property, even during the biggest market bottom in history. With increasing property prices, I will have a bigger positive cash flow of a few thousand dollars. At this point, I need to keep refinancing to cash out on my current investment properties so that I can buy new ones. But every time, when I buy a new investment property, I will have an even or slightly negative cash flow again, but this does not matter. The focus is not the rental income. The goal is to keep the snowball rolling so that we can keep buying more investment properties.

第三种情况，就是我在中国碰到的情况。现金流永远是负的。但是房价还在上涨，又不能重新抵押贷款。你就只能通过不断的买卖，来实现扩张。

The third situation is what I have encountered in China: the cash flow is always negative. But as the property prices are increasing and I cannot refinance my investment properties, I can only keep buying and selling my investment properties to expand my portfolio.

无论上面哪种情况，核心的一点其实都是保持自己的杠杆率。杠杆是房地产投资的灵魂，没了这个灵魂就失去了前进的动力。

In all three situations above, the key is to keep your leverage, which is the soul of real estate investing. Without a soul, one will lose all motivation to keep going.

08 如何还清自住房贷款

08 How to Pay Off the Mortgage of Your House

大部分正在工作的年轻人的梦想就是还掉房贷，没有房贷一身轻松。然而大部分人都是省吃俭用，用辛辛苦苦挣来的工资，一点一点地把自己的房贷付掉。

The dream of most working-class young adults is to pay off their mortgage so that they can be freed from the debt burden, so most people live a frugal life and use their hard-earned money to pay off the mortgage bit by bit.

其实我想跟他们说的是，只有傻瓜才用工资把自己的房贷付掉，聪明的人应该是把自己工资省下来的钱去投资，然后用挣来的钱把自己的房贷付掉。

But my advice to them is that only fools will use their salaries to pay off the mortgage. Smart people will save up their salaries to make investments and pay off the mortgage with the profits from investments.

我在美国自住房的房贷也有好几次机会可以把它都付清。第一次是上海的房子涨价。2006 年的时候，我买入的上海第一个房子涨了好几倍。我可以把那个房子卖掉，然后把美国的房贷都付掉。也就是说，我可以在刚到湾区 5 年的时候就把自己的自住房全部付清。

I had several chances to pay off the mortgage of my own home. The first opportunity arose when property prices in Shanghai soared. In 2006, the price of the first investment property that I bought in Shanghai had more than tripled. This meant I could sell that property to use the proceeds to pay off my mortgage in the U.S. In other words, I could pay off the mortgage of my home five years after settling in the Bay Area.

但是我没有选择那样做，因为我相信投资的回报更高。当我次贷危机抄完底，买了 8 个投资房之后，2014 年之后，我再也不用为自己的房贷而担心。因为投资房的被动收入已经足够支付我的自住房房贷。这和房贷都付掉又有什么区别呢？

But I did not choose to do that because I believed that my investments will yield a higher return. After I bought eight investment properties in the sub-prime crisis, I have not worried about my mortgage payment since 2014 because the passive income generated by my investment properties is more than enough to cover the mortgage payment of my own residence. This is no different from paying off the mortgage.

回到第十章我的那个香港同事说的话，他当时语重心长地建议我贷款做 15 年，不要做 30 年。因为一个人很难有 30 年的稳定工作，30 年一直背着房贷，工作的时候忍气吞声。

I mentioned in Chapter 10 that a then colleague of mine from Hong Kong recommended me to apply for a 15-year mortgage instead of a 30-year one because he said that a 30-year mortgage would force one to tolerate a miserable job and that it was very difficult to find a job that would remain stable for 30 years.

但事实上你通过投资抓住了一次房地产价格变化的机会，基本上就可以把你的房贷都付清。当然这些的前提是，你平时必须有能力管好自己的财务。要做到按需消费，存下该存的钱。如果你是一个花钱手松而没有毅力的人，他的建议是正确的，房贷做成 15 年的，可以强制你储蓄，早日摆脱房贷给你的精神压力。

But actually, you can basically pay off your mortgage if you make one single judgment about the price trend in the real estate market and leverage it through investing. The prerequisite to your success is that you are a disciplined individual in managing your personal finance that plans your budget based on needs, not wants and saves your money. If you cannot control your desires and lack self-discipline, you should take my colleague's advice by taking out a 15-year mortgage, which can force you to save your money because of the mental pressure caused by a debt burden.

在中国有一句官宣的话，那就是"房子是用来住的，但不是用来炒的"。这句话从经济学原理上是靠不住的。更正确的描述是，对于个体小老

百姓而言，应该是"如果你想住房子，必须要学会炒房子"。房地产市场和
股票市场一样，人生最后的赢家不是那些辛辛苦苦挣工资的人，而是对市场
趋势做出正确判断的人，能抓住机会的人。高楼总是穷人盖，忙碌了一年的
民工，工资存款可能一平方米都买不起。遍身罗绮者，不是养蚕人，穿丝绸
最多的是买卖丝绸的商人。亘古不变的道理是因为背后的经济学规律，仅仅
靠煽动仇富情绪是没有用的。

Chinese officials are promoting the saying that "houses are for living in, not
speculating or investing." This saying does not make any sense according to
economic theories. For ordinary citizens and individuals, a more accurate
description should be "if you want to live in a house, you must learn how to invest
in real estate." In both the real estate and stock market, the winners are not the
diligent working class but those who can make a correct judgment about market
trends and know how to grasp the opportunities. Skyscrapers are built by the poor.
Construction workers in China cannot even afford to buy 10 square feet of the
building they help erect. In ancient China, those who wore silk the most were not
the silk farmers but the businessmen of silk. This is a law in economics that cannot
be changed by invoking a resentful sentiment toward the rich.

在美国当房东，特别是在核心一线城市当房东，不抓住历史大机遇，靠
平时省吃俭用上车的可能性是不大的。我回顾自己能够抓住历史性的房地产
市场的大回转，最主要的原因还是来自计划。如果没有从 2006 年就开始的计
划和前期准备，我不太会近距离紧密观察房地产的动态，也就会错过 2010 年
到 2012 年的历史最低点。

It is almost impossible to buy a property in the U.S., especially in big cities, by
saving your salaries if you do not leverage the power of the market trend. In
retrospect, the main reason why I was able to jump on the historical chance in the
real estate market is that I had detailed planning. If I had not started planning for my
"buying the bottom" investments, I would not have closely monitored the changes in
the real estate market and would have missed the historical low in 2010-2012.

会走路的钱
Money Walks

09 雪球不要停

09 Do Not Let the Snowball Stop Rolling

未来我打算把这 8 个房子打造成一个自我滚动的机器。就是随着房租在涨，我就用重新贷款(refinance)方式去买下一个房子。这样我不需要有新的投入进去，实际上我第 8 个房子就是这样买的。第 8 个房子我自己没有出一分钱，都是通过重新贷款用银行的钱买的。

My original plan was to turn my eight investment properties into a self-operating machine. But as my rental income grew, I decided to purchase my next investment property through refinancing, so I do not need to invest new money into it. This is also how I bought my eighth investment property using the bank's money: I did not take one single penny out of my pocket.

我需要做的事情就是保证这台机器不要出现负现金流，一直保持稍微正一点现金流就好。这样我就不用交个人所得税。按照现在的计算差不多这个机器每年可以增长 5%~10%左右，就是每隔 1-2 年我可以增加一个房子。但是这是一个指数增长的机器，预计 10 年之后，差不多每年可以新增两个房子。

What I need to do is to make sure that my machine does not yield a negative cash flow. My goal is to maintain slightly positive cash flow so that I do not need to pay personal income tax. According to my calculations, my machine can grow by 5-10% per year, which means I can buy a new investment property every 1-2 years. But as this machine operates at an exponential growth rate, I predict that ten years from now, I can add two more investment properties to my portfolio every year.

这样一个滚雪球机器本质上是一个打折版的"勤快人理财法"。长期投资最好的办法就是启动一个自己会滚动的雪球。但是房地产和股票不同，房地产的启动雪球需要克服一开始的阻力，并且有一定的份量。不然雪球是滚不起来的。雪球一旦过了临界质量，自己就会沿着山坡往山下滚去，越来越大。这个时候，你需要做的只是控制运动的方向，并不需要你再往上面添雪和推动了。

The nature of such a snowball rolling machine is a discounted version of my "Investment Strategies for Lazy People." The best way to approach long-term investing is to form a snowball that will keep rolling. But real estate investing is different from stocks. For the former, you have to overcome certain obstacles before you can put your snowball in motion. After your snowball accumulates enough mass, it will start rolling and grow bigger even without your help. At this point, all you need to do is to control the direction of the snowball, but you do not need to keep adding snow or pushing it anymore.

大部分人在房地产领域没能形成这样一个雪球。或者是一直没有机会形成规模，或者是因为在平地上滚雪球。今天中国的大多数房地产持有者都是这样。他们只是靠历史机遇，稀里糊涂地拥有几个价格不菲的住宅。但是他们中间的大部分人忙着高兴了，无法形成滚动效应。大部分人不知道怎样形成滚动效应，也不明白保持杠杆率的奥秘。

But most real estate investors fail to form a self-rolling snowball, or they do not have the chance to increase the scale of the snowball, or they are trying to roll the snowball on flat ground. Today, the situation of most landowners in China fits into the above description. These people own some expensive residential properties because they were able to jump on some historical chances earlier. However, most of them are content with the scale of their investments that they forget to turn their snowball into a self-rolling one. In fact, most of them have no idea how not to let their snowball stop rolling and the importance of maintaining leverage.

这些年来我在美国做房东的日子越来越轻松。因为随着时间的推移，坏的房客被筛选掉，留下来的渐渐都是优质的房客。另外我把一些可能经常出问题的房子交给房地产公司去管理。这点不得不说美国这个领域的服务还比较差，不像中国有房屋管家这样的包租地产管理公司。未来随着服务业变得越来越发达，房子管理也就会变得非常省心。

In recent years, my life as a landlord in the U.S. is becoming easier. With the passage of time, I was able to filter bad tenants, so I am now only dealing with high-quality tenants. Furthermore, I have now delegated the task of managing the more time-consuming investment properties to professional management companies. My experience so far is that the U.S. companies lag behind their peers in China in the property management field. In China, property management companies provide all-inclusive services that even include butler. But I believe that as the service industry develops, managing one's properties will become easier.

完成次贷危机抄底之后，我自己不再靠攒下来的钱进行投资。生活变得非常的宽裕，我们挣的钱都花掉了。不再存钱来投资，那个铁路边上的小黑屋后来涨价涨到 55 万美元。我做了一个重新贷款，套现了一部分美元。2016 年我开始用这笔钱去做一个更大胆的投资。之所以我敢做更大胆的投资，因为这些钱都不是我的辛苦钱，都是银行的钱。即使全亏掉也不是什么事。

After my "buying the bottom" operation in the sub-prime crisis, I do not need to use my own savings to make investments anymore, so we are very comfortably well off. My wife and I spend all of our income from our job because we do not need to save it for investing. When the price of the investment property that was located on the railway increased to US$550,000, I refinanced it to take out some cash. In 2016, I used the money to make an even bolder investment. The reason why I dared make such a bold move was that I was not using my own hard-earned money but the bank's money, so I did not worry about losing it.

这个更大胆的投资，也让我在投资理财论坛上的所有网友都大跌眼镜、出乎意料。我一改之前只投资房地产的习惯，开始了一个崭新的投资，也掀开了我人生的一个新阶段——投资比特币。

Netizens on the forum were all surprised by my bolder investment move. I said goodbye to my past focus on the real estate market and embarked on a novel investment, bitcoin, marking the beginning of a new stage in my life.

第十七章 从 100 到 1000 万（三）比特币

Chapter 17: From $1 million to $10 million (3): Bitcoins

01 缘起

01 Inspiration

比特币和房地产看起来是八竿子打不着的两个事情。但是根据我的"会走路的钱"原理，它们本质上是一回事。至少在湾区、上海、深圳这样的一线城市的房子投资和比特币投资是一回事。

It seems like real estate and bitcoins are totally different. But according to my "money walks" theory, investing in real estate, at least in tier-one cities such as the Bay Area, Shanghai, and Shenzhen, and bitcoins are essentially the same.

我第一次关注到比特币是在 2013 年的时候。当时新闻报道比特币的价格一下子冲破了 1000 美元一枚，引起了我的关注。我自己对新鲜事物的好奇心往往比较重。比特币又涉及很多的数学问题，所以我就感兴趣地研究了起来。

Bitcoins started to catch my eye in 2013. At the time, news media reported that the price of bitcoins had exceeded US$1,000 each, attracting my attention. As I am always curious about new ideas and the concept of bitcoins involves many mathematical questions, I was intrigued so I did some research.

我仔细读了中本聪写的白皮书。这个研究让我吃了一惊，世界上居然有人能够发明这么神奇的东西。

Having close-read the bitcoin white-paper by Satoshi Nakamoto, I was startled by the research. I have never expected that human beings would be able to come up with such a novel invention.

我从小就对钱比较感兴趣，所以在我来到美国之后，曾经很仔细地研究了一下钱到底是什么。读 MBA 之后更是这样。大部分和我背景类似的华人，可能都被教育过钱是"一般等价物"。大家也大体上明白钱是如何从实物黄金，演变为银行钱庄开出来的承诺汇票，再到政府信用债券的过程。这里我就不再说了。对金融再感兴趣一点的人可能明白布雷顿森林体系。美国 1972 年放弃金本位，现代货币是法令货币 Fiat Money 这些概念。Fiat Money 是无实际价值的法定货币，通过政府规定赋予其交易价值。

I have always been interested in how money walks, so I did some research to understand the concept of money after I settled in the U.S. My MBA further aroused my interest in studying money. Most Chinese Americans who share a similar background as mine were inculcated with the belief that "Money is a universal equivalent." As we all understand how money evolved from being real gold to promissory notes issued by a financial institution and finally to a government-issued currency that derives its value from the relationship of trust between the general public and government, I will not go into detail. Those of you who are interested in finance may have knowledge of the Bretton Woods system. In 1972, the U.S. decoupled the U.S. dollar from gold and has since adopted a system of fiat money, a legal tender that does not have an inherent value. Its value is backed by the government that issued it through the law.

我对货币的兴趣比这些知识可能再古老一点，就是太平洋岛上的 RaiBlocks。那些完全搬不动的巨石如何就成为货币了，如何又退出不再是货币了。还有就是我的另外一个有争议的观点，就是中国古代辛辛苦苦烧制瓷器换来了全世界的白银。其实中国人这些努力并没有换来财富到中国，这些白银只是起到了中国货币的功能，和政府定量印点纸币没有区别。这些白银并没有给中国带来实物，所以那些人几百年的努力全是白忙活一场。

My interest in money motivated me to dig deeper into the form of money used in archaic times. I read about Rai stones used on Pacific islands and was curious how these huge immovable rocks were used as money and why they were removed from the monetary system. In addition, I also studied how ancient China obtained almost all the silver in the world by trading china. My point of view, albeit controversial, is that the hard work of ancient Chinese did not help them bring wealth to China because the silver served as legal tender in China, which was no different from currencies issued by the government. Therefore, all the silver did not bring any real wealth to the Chinese people. Their hundreds of years of hard work was all in vain.

我第一次听说世界上有电子货币这个事情，是 2001 年左右在一本介绍金融体系的书上看到的，比中本聪发明比特币要早 8 年。那本书上只是模模糊糊地说，随着互联网的普及，未来的一种电子货币可能会取代今天的货币系统。可是没有任何更多具体的信息。我遐想了一下，也想不出电子货币是啥样的。可能当时作者自己恐怕都不知道电子货币应该是什么样的。

I first heard of the idea of electronic currency from a book on financial systems in 2001, which was eight years earlier than the creation of bitcoin by Satoshi Nakamoto. The book made a general claim that with the increasing popularity of the internet, a form of digital currency will replace the existing monetary system without giving any details. I tried to imagine how a digital currency would look like but to no avail. Perhaps even the author had no idea how it would work.

懂计算机和数学的，都会明白区块链本质是一个速度极慢，效率很低的分散式数据库系统。软件上其实没有什么了不起的。但是区块链对货币系统而言绝对是革命性的。我曾经写过一篇博客，"只有比特币才是属于你的财富"。可以帮助读者理解比特币最大的革命性之处。

Those who have a background in computer science and/or mathematics will know that the technology of blockchain is based on a system of dispersed data among parties that has a very low speed and efficiency. While the relevant software is not particularly groundbreaking, its influence on our monetary system is revolutionary. I once wrote an article titled "Bitcoin Is the Only Form of Wealth That Truly Belongs to You" to help my readers understand the revolutionary changes brought by bitcoin.

比特币才是真正属于你的财富 (2017 年前后)

Bitcoin Is the Only Form of Wealth That Truly Belongs to You (written in around 2017)

by Bayfamily

曾经星云法师讲过这样一个故事。他说有个富人和他抬扛，说钱可以给他带来很多快乐。然后给星云法师看自己的存款数量，描述他有多少珠宝和首饰。

Hsing Yun, one of the most influential teachers of modern Buddhism, once told the following story. A rich man told him that money could bring the former lots of happiness, showed Hsing Yun his bank account balance, and described how much gold and jewelry he owned.

星云法师问他，你的珠宝在哪里？明天会不会被别人偷走？

Hsing Yun asked him, "Where did you store your gold and jewelry? Will they be stolen?"

他说，珠宝在银行保险箱里面，很安全。每次去拿要过三道机关。他都快十年没有去看过了。

The rich man answered, "I locked them in my safety box in the bank with a high-security level. Every time when I want to access my gold and jewelry, I need to pass three security steps, so I haven't checked on them for ten years."

星云法师说那这些财富都不是你的。存折也好，金银珠宝也好，都是银行的，无论是钱还是珠宝，你只是挂一个名字而已。星云法师的本意是说，大家不要对财富过于痴迷。我想用这个例子说，对于大部分的人来说，那些名义上你的财富其实都不是你的财富。你很难对财富拥有绝对的控制权，大部分财富只是在你这里临时挂一个名而已。

"All the wealth does not belong to you. Whether it's your bank savings, gold, diamond, and jewelry, they belong to the bank even though your name is on the safety box," said Hsing Yun. The message behind this story is that for most people, all this wealth does not truly belong to them because they cannot exercise absolute control over wealth. At best, the wealth is just held in their names.

举个例子说，你拥有房产，但是房产的财富是你的财富么？政府可以指定政策，没收充公，可以设定房产税，可以限制交易。让你的房产财富分分钟缩水，或者化为乌有。这在 1949 年的上海、排华时期的印尼、内战时期的美国都发生过。如果是太平盛世呢？你可能面临诉讼，面临索赔。比如在美国，如果你开车不幸撞了人，如果你的访客在你家不幸发生了意外，你的房子也会被索赔被迫变卖。

Let's say you own some real properties, but does all this wealth really belong to you? The government may introduce a certain policy to confiscate your real properties, impose a property tax, or limit the buying and selling in the real estate market, taking your wealth away from you. All this happened in 1949 in Shanghai, during discrimination against Chinese in Indonesia and in the American Civil War. What about during peaceful times? You may still be sued and face a compensation claim. For example, if unfortunately your car hits a pedestrian or a visitor is injured in your house, you may be forced to sell your house to pay for the compensation claim.

好吧，也许房地产不是一个好例子，那么我的股票呢？股市要是被关停了，你可能会认为我还有个公司，公司总是我的吧。如果你经历过公私合营，经历过破产清算，你就知道那些财富也可能分分钟不是你的。

You may argue that real estate is not a good example, so what about stocks? You may think that even if the stock market was closed, you would still own some interest in a company. However, if you have experienced the state's taking over private businesses or bankruptcy of a company, you will know that all the wealth may be taken away from you the next minute.

再举个例子，你手中的现金是你的么？大部分人的现金都是用实名的方式存储在银行里的。如果你犯罪了，或者被诬陷犯罪了，你银行里的钱分分钟会被充公。战争年代，你必须押对方向。如果你不幸持有了美国内战期间南方的美元、或者二战期间德国的马克、1949 年的国民党法币、1974 年的南越货币，你的现金都会化为乌有。即使在和平年代，2008 年的塞浦路斯，曾经 20 万欧元以上的存款统统被冻结。在美国，你被告了，民事官司打输了，同样你的银行账号会分分钟被冻结。

A third example is cash. Is your cash at hand really yours? Most people's cash sits in their bank accounts. If you are convicted of an offense or framed by the government, all the money in your bank account may well be confiscated. During times of war, you have to bet on the winning party. If unfortunately, you held currency issued by the southern U.S. during the American Civil War, the Deutsche Mark during the Second World War, legal tender issued by Kuomingtang in 1949 in China, or currency issued by South Vietnam in 1974, all your money would go down the drain. Even during peaceful times, there is still uncertainty. In 2008 in Cyprus, savings over €200,000 were all frozen. In the U.S., if you are sued and lose the lawsuit, your bank account may also be locked.

以上的所有财富都有个共同点，就是需要第三方确认你是财富的主人。事实上任何一笔实名的财富，就是通过某个第三方，无论是政府还是银行之类的机构认证的财富，都不是真正意义上你的财富。因为如果这些认证的机构不承认你拥有这笔财富，或者剥夺了你对财富的控制权，你的钱就会化为乌有。

A common characteristic of the above three forms of wealth is that they require a third party acknowledgment by an institution such as the bank or government that you are the owner of the wealth. Therefore, they are not technically your wealth because you are subject to the recognition and control of those middle-men. If those institutions do not acknowledge that you are the owner of the wealth or deprive you of the right to control it, all your money will vanish.

那么我物理上实际控制的财富呢？你要是觉得把钱存在银行不靠谱，放在家里总可以了吧。如果你看过"人民的名义"，看见上亿的现金怎样被查抄，你就会知道，现金放在哪里都是不安全的。

You may then ask, "How can I have actual, physical control of my wealth? If saving my money at the bank is not safe, what about at home?" If you have watched the Name of the People, China's hit TV show, in which hundreds of millions of cash stored at the home of the corrupt officials is confiscated, you will know that cash is unsafe regardless of where you store it.

那么黄金呢？我家里放着金条银洋，金条和银洋的尺寸比较小，可以藏在床底下。或者像过去的地主老财一样，院子里挖个坑埋了。黄金白银虽然千百年来，作为保值储蓄已经深入人心。尤其是在乱世，黄金一次次显示它的稳定的保值能力。但是他们携带太不方便了，而且很容易成为政府或者劫匪的袭击目标。

Some of you may also wonder, "What about gold? As gold bars and silver coins have a smaller size and are durable, can I store them under the bed? Or dig a hole in my backyard and bury them?" Gold and silver have been stores of value for hundreds, if not thousands, of years. Gold was an especially good store of value during war times. But as these precious metals are not portable, owners will easily become an attack target of the government or criminals.

比如，1949 年的国民党政府，在推行法币的时候，强制民间上交黄金白银。文革时期，上海有些人家怕抄家，不得不在半夜里把黄金白银扔到黄浦江里面。越战结束的时候，越南政府掀起大规模排华浪潮，华侨们把他们所有的财富变卖为金条，但是在海上，还是被海盗们洗劫一空。

For example, in 1949, in China, the Kuomintang government forced citizens to give their gold and silver to the government. During the Chinese Cultural

Revolution, some families in Shanghai were afraid of being persecuted, so they had no choice but to throw their gold and silver into the Huangpu River. After the Vietnam War, the Vietnamese government started a large-scale anti-Chinese movement, and the Vietnamese Chinese turned all their wealth into gold bars. But unfortunately, their wealth was robbed by the pirates.

所以从这点上讲，物理控制的财富也不靠谱。盗匪横行的时候不靠谱，即使是在安定法制社会也不靠谱。比如美国 1934 年臭名昭著的 Gold Reserve Act，规定除了少量珠宝和艺术品之外，所有的黄金必须统统上交给联邦储备局。政府按照$35 一盎司黄金的价格兑换。 任何美国人在世界上的任何地方私自买卖黄金的行为都是重罪违法。这个法令一直到 1975 年才被废止。

So trying to exert physical control over one's wealth is not reliable either, whether it is during a state of disorder or in an orderly society with a well-developed legal system. An example of the latter is the U.S. Gold Reserve Act in 1934 that stipulated that all gold, except a small number of jewelry and art pieces, had to be handed over to the Fed at $35 per ounce. Trading of gold by any American in any corner of the world was against the law. The Act was only abolished in 1975.

比特币最牛的地方就是彻底摆脱了第三方认证，回到了物理控制。物理控制又实现了大脑对财富的绝对控制。比特币无法被火烧掉，无法被物理毁灭掉。如果你不说，没有人能从你的大脑里没收你的比特币。

The genius of bitcoins is that it completely removes intermediaries from the transactions and reverts the ownership of wealth to physical control. But the form of physical control is absolute control of wealth by one's mind. Bitcoin cannot be destroyed by any fire or other physical means. And no one can seize your bitcoins from your mind unless you reveal the private key.

比特币等加密货币的私密性和便于携带使其具有无可比拟的先进性。一句行话叫作，"if you do not own private key, you do not own the coin"。比特币的持有方式就是私匙，一串数字。你拥有这串数字，你就拥有这串数字账号里面的所有比特币。 这串数字你可以写在一个小纸片上，可以存在电脑里，如果你记性好的话，还可以直接背在脑子里。 如果你记性不好的话，你还可以用 Brain wallet, 就是脑钱包。脑钱包就是一句话，一句你自己能记住的话。

The advancement brought by the strong privacy and easy portability of cryptocurrencies such as bitcoins is unparalleled. The sentence that "if you do not own private key, you do not own the coin" succinctly describes the nature of ownership of cryptocurrencies. People hold and own bitcoins through a private key, which is a secret number. As long as you have access to this number, you own all the bitcoins associated with that account. You may choose to write the number down on a piece of paper or save it on your computer. If you have a good memory, you can choose to memorize it. If you have a bad memory, you can choose to use a brain wallet, a concept of storing bitcoins in one's own mind by memorizing a seed phrase, which is essentially a sentence that you can easily remember.

脑钱包成立是因为比特币存储方式不过是一个 160 bit 的公共钥匙和一个 256 bit 的私密钥匙。由于公匙可以通过私匙计算得出，所以记住私匙就可以了。256bit 的私匙很难记住，除非写在纸条上。但是写在纸条上不安全，任何人拿手机拍走了，你的钱就丢了。最好的办法是把私匙 256 位变成一个高位的数字存储。 比如，"1011100010000000100101" 很难记住，但是转化成十进制的 30222885 就比较容易记住，进制的位数越高，字节数越短。脑钱包最常用的是 58 位进制转换。58 位用了 26 个字母大小写的绝大多数部分和 1-9 这些数字。这样避免了 0，和 O，I 和 l 这些容易手写出错的字母。由于私匙可以是任意的，所以人们先写出一段话，根据这段话来生成 256 bit 的代码。否则逆行出来的脑钱包无法记住。 脑钱包支持任何一种语言系统，因为每个字本质上也都是有一一对应的代码。

Brain wallet is a feasible idea because bitcoins are owned and stored through a 160-bit number public key and a 256-bit number private key. As the public key can be deduced from the private key, memorizing the private key will suffice. But it is very difficult to memorize a 256-bit number unless you write it down. However, writing it down on a piece of paper is unsafe because if anyone takes a picture of that paper, all your bitcoins will be gone. The best way to memorize the private key is to store the 256-bit number in a top digit format. For example, it is difficult, if not impossible, to memorize "1011100010000000100101," but it will be much easier if you convert it into a decimal number "30222885." The greater the weight of the digit, the shorter the number the 256-bit private key will be converted into. Therefore, the common base digit used in creating a brain wallet is 58. A 58-base-digit number system uses almost all the letters in the alphabet in both their letter case and uppercase forms and the numbers, except 0, O, I, and 1, which may cause confusion. As bitcoin holders can choose their own private key, people will first start with coming up with a sentence. Then, a 256-bit number will be created based on that sentence. It is impossible to memorize a brain wallet that is created in reverse order. Brain wallets support any language system because each word in whatever language will have a corresponding code.

但是注意，常用的句子千万不要用来做脑钱包。比如"To be or not to be."早就被用了。被用的结果不是你没法存钱进去了，而是存在里面的钱任何人都能使用。每天网络上有上万亿次的计算，搜索常用语和常用的句子，在破解粗心大意的新手们制作的大脑钱包。

However, an important point to note is never to choose a common saying as your brain wallet. If you use a sentence that has already been used by others, such as "to be or not to be," as your brain wallet, the consequence is not that you cannot deposit your money in the wallet but that the money in your wallet can be used by anyone. This is why countless hackers are searching for common phrases and sentences to break into brain wallets created by careless beginners.

比如，你可以记住"一切反动派都是纸老虎"，根据加密程序，这句话可以被分解成一个私匙。私匙那串漫长的数字和符号不好记，但是一句话很好记。当然像这样的"一切反动派都是纸老虎"的脑钱包很容易被破译。

比特币的脑钱包还可以通过暗语实现对财富的绝对持有。

Another example of an easily hackable brain wallet is "all reactionaries are paper tigers," a well-known saying by Mao Zedong. This passphrase can be converted into a private key after encryption. As mentioned earlier, the private key will consist of numbers and symbols that are difficult to memorize. In contrast, memorizing this sentence is much easier. However, such a common saying among Chinese will be easily cracked.

你可以改成"一切外星人的二舅妈都是喜马拉雅山上的纸老虎"。这句话容易记，如果你还不放心，可以把这句话反过来写，作为你的脑钱包。你可以在这个脑钱包里面放入任意数量的财富。可以是一分钱，也可以是100 个亿。没有人能够知道你拥有这些财富，也没有人能够偷走这笔财富，除非他知道这句暗语。

You can also use the sentence, "The aunts of all aliens are paper tigers in the Himalaya," which is easy to memorize and a much safer phrase. If you are still worried about cracking attacks, you can reverse the order of words in this sentence as your brain wallet. Then you can deposit whatever amount of wealth in this brain wallet. You can choose to deposit 1 cent or even $10 billion. No one will know you own all this wealth or steal it unless he or she also knows this passphrase.

你不用在家里藏匿任何实物财富，你不需要向任何第三方机构出示证件。你可以一切都被剥夺，赤手空拳，到地球上的任何一个角落，找到一台能上网的计算机或者手机。几分钟之后，你就可以凭这句暗语，用你的比特币购买任何东西，或者转化成当地货币。没有人能够用任何方式阻拦住你。除非你的脑袋不受你自己控制。

You do not need to store any physical wealth at your home or show proof of identity to any third party institution anymore. Even if you are deprived of everything, you can still access your wealth from any corner of the world as long as you have access to a computer (or cell phone) that is connected to the internet. All it takes for you to purchase anything using your bitcoin or to convert it into local currency are a few minutes and your passphrase. No one can stop you unless they can control your mind.

你的大脑拥有对你的财富的绝对所有权。想明白了这点，我想任何一个拥有一些财富的人，都会分散一部分财富到加密货币中。否则不知道自己的财富在哪一轮政治漩涡或者经济风暴中就被剥夺了。如果持有的是加密货币，思聪的 Daddy 也不会那么快乖乖地讨饶，表示今后只专注本土投资 (Domestic investment)。他就可以理直气壮地说，"我的钱是我的，你管我想去哪里投资。"

Your mind has absolute control over your wealth. Anyone who understands this and owns some wealth will be tempted to store some of his or her wealth in the form of cryptocurrency for fear that they may lose everything in a political coup or economic crisis. I guess if Wang Jianlin, one of the richest men in China, had stored at least some of his wealth in bitcoins, he would not have conceded to the Chinese government's requests so easily. He would be free to tell the Chinese government that "This is my money and none of your business. I should have the freedom to decide what investments I want to make."

如果你觉得自己生活在太平盛世，生活在完美的法律框架下，任何银行机构或者公共机构不会错待你自己挣的每一分钱。既不会货币超发也不会巧取豪夺。那么想想遗产吧，在现有中外法律框架下，并不支持遗产的持有者对遗产具有无可置疑的分配权。但是加密货币解决了这个问题，你想把财富给任何人，只需要告诉他而不是其他人一串数字就可以了。

What is the value of bitcoins for those who think they live in a peaceful world in which their interests are protected by the law, any financial and governmental institutions will not take away even a penny of their hard-owned money, and the government will not print too much money or rob its citizens of their wealth? Think about estate planning. Under existing laws in both the U.S. and China, the parties who are entitled to the deceased's estate do not have absolute control over the estate. But cryptocurrencies can solve this problem. If a person would like to leave his or her wealth to anyone after his or her death, all he or she needs to do is to tell that person but not other people a number.

"私人财产神圣不可侵犯"这句话奠定了现代资本主义的发展，也是当今社会财富极大丰富的一个重要原因。因为道理很简单，只有财富是安全的、不被剥夺的，人们才有动力去创造更多的财富。但是在过去的人类历史上，私人财产一次次被剥夺的事件屡见不鲜。无论是政局动荡、社会变革、还是法律误判，你的财富在暴力、强权面前只是一头养肥的猪。只有加密货币从技术层面上解决了这个问题，从数学上保证了私人财产神圣不可侵犯。仅凭这一点，对世界经济的贡献恐怕不亚于历史上的保险，证券，有限责任股份公司的发明。

That "private assets are sacred and inviolable" is the cornerstone of the development of modern capitalism and the fundamental reason why modern society enjoys immense wealth. The logic behind this is simple: Only when people feel that their wealth is safe and will not be arbitrarily taken away will they be motivated to create more wealth. However, in mankind's history, expropriation of assets is commonplace. Whether it is due to political unrest, a social revolution, or legal errors, people's wealth is an attractive prey in front of violence and arbitrary power. Cryptocurrency is the only form of wealth that solves this problem from a technical point of view. It uses mathematics to ensure that private assets are truly sacred and inviolable. Thanks to this characteristic alone, cryptocurrencies make a comparable contribution to human civilization as the creation of insurance, the stock market, and the limited company structure in mankind's history.

只有拥有比特币，才是拥有真正属于你自己的财富。

To sum up, only when a person holds bitcoins will his wealth truly belong to him.

02 比特币的价值
02 The Value of Bitcoins

是的，在比特币之前，人们从来没有发明过这样的一种财富形式，你可以做到100%的自我完全控制。你可以不需要第三方认证。没人可以用任何形式，包括法庭、军队、暴力的方式把你的财富剥夺。你永远可以对一笔财富拥有绝对的管理权，只要你保护好自己的密码。

Yes, before the advent of bitcoin, mankind never invented such a form of wealth that gives the owners 100% control through the elimination of the intermediaries. No one can use any kind of coercion, including through the court, army, and violence, to deprive you of your wealth. You can exercise absolute control over your wealth provided that you keep your private key confidential.

我小时候看各种绑匪的电影，当时意识到对于绑匪来说最困难的事情，就是如何拿到绑票索要的钱。所有的绑匪片，电影高潮部分都是赎金交付的时候。绑匪只能索取物理财富，比如小面额美元这样的散钞。可是即使是这样的，交割地也是问题，真钱还是假钱也是问题。这些永远都是各类动作片枪战电影里，最出戏的地方。无论你怎么想，都想不到一个绝对安全的财富交割方式，似乎这是个不可克服之障碍。

When I was watching action thriller films that featured kidnapping, I realized that the kidnappers' greatest difficulty was how to get their hands on the ransom money. In almost all such films, the climax is the handover of the ransom. The kidnappers could only demand physical money such as small-denomination U.S. dollars without consecutive serial numbers. Another difficulty for the kidnappers was the venue for the handover of money. They would also be concerned about whether the banknotes were authentic. These issues are often the plotholes in the movie because no one, including real kidnappers and film directors and screenwriters, can come up with an absolutely fail-proof way to receive the money, which seems to be an insurmountable obstacle.

那个时候我还不明白，这个现象的根源在于2009年之前，人世间所有的非实物财富都是需要第三方认证的，而所有的实物财富都是随时可以被暴力剥夺的。如果想不明白这个道理，我再给大家举个例子就是中国电影

《1942》。地主明明知道灾荒年来了，自己家里储存了粮食、银圆和枪以防不测。可是他完全没有办法控制这些实物财富不被别人抢走。最后事实上他家也的确被人抢光了，落到家破人亡，沿街乞讨。

At the time, I did not understand that the problem stemmed from the need for trusted intermediaries in all transactions that involve wealth does not have an inherent value. But meanwhile, "real wealth" such as gold and silver can be easily taken away any time from the owners through violence. If you are still confused, let me further explain this using a Chinese movie "Back to 1942" as an example. In the movie, the landlord knew that a famine would soon arrive, so he stored some food, silver, and guns in his house. However, he could not make sure that all this physical wealth would not be stolen. In the end, his family was robbed of everything and became beggars on the street.

比特币横空出世解决了这个问题。这是财富和货币历史上的一次革命。

The advent of bitcoins solves this problem. It is revolutionary in the history of wealth and monetary system.

我在写这本书的时候，美国刚刚刺杀了伊朗的苏莱曼尼将军，两国处于战争的边缘。网络传言伊朗打算悬赏 8000 万美元给任何能够杀死特朗普总统的人。如果这个事情想落实，就带来一个难题，伊朗如何支付这 8000 万美元呢？因为成功刺杀特朗普总统的人肯定不想暴露自己的身份。而支付这 8000 万美元又绕不开美国对美元的监管。无论是现金还是银行转账，都会被美国追踪到。刺杀特朗普总统的人也不希望把自己的身份暴露给伊朗政府。所以银行转账也转不了，他自己亲身去拿现金也不可能。

As of writing this book, the U.S. has just announced its assassination of top Iranian general Qasem Soleimani. The two countries were on the verge of starting a war. An Internet rumor has it that Iran offers a bounty of US$80 million to anyone who can kill President Trump. Hypothetically speaking, if the Iranian government wants to implement this plan, a great difficulty is how to pay the US$80 million to the killer? Firstly, the assassin would not want his or her identity revealed.

Secondly, if the Iranian government pays the bounty in US dollars, how can it and the assassin get around the U.S. government's monitoring of US dollars? Whether the payment is in cash or through bank transfer, the U.S. government will be able to trace it. Thirdly, the assassin may prefer not to disclose his or her identity to the Iranian government either. Therefore, both bank transfer and physically retrieving a bag of cash by the assassin are infeasible.

比特币的出现解决了这个问题，他可以发一个比特币账户给伊朗政府，让伊朗政府转入这笔钱。伊朗政府如果想展示他们诚意的话，伊朗政府甚至可以开出一个多重签名(multi signature)的比特币账户。这样任何人都可以看到账户里确确实实有值 8000 万美元的比特币。任何一个人刺杀了特朗普总统，伊朗政府只需要把另外一个密钥发给他就可以了。

The advent of bitcoins can also solve this problem. The killer can send a bitcoin account number to the Iranian government for it to transfer the bounty to the account. To prove its sincerity, the Iranian government can even set up a multi-signature bitcoin account to show everyone that this account has bitcoins that are worth US$80 million. When someone kills President Trump, all the Iranian government needs to do is to send him the private key.

很多人认为比特币只是一种炒作的东西，单纯击鼓传花的游戏。那些复杂的数学只是庞氏骗局的伪装。在我看来，比特币的确有很大的炒作成分，投机因素占了很高的比例。甚至你可以说目前比特币最大的需求就是投机需求。可是另外一方面比特币是有功能价值的。它的功能价值就是世界上从来没有这样一种财富形式被创造出来。这种财富形式有一定的市场刚需，特别是在政府功能崩溃，社会正常秩序丧失的地方和时候。

It is often believed that bitcoins investments are purely speculative, the success of which depends on whether there are more people who are willing to enter the market despite the high price. Opinions that the complicated mathematics behind bitcoins are a disguise for a Ponzi scheme are also common. In my opinion, the bitcoins market is indeed highly speculative. One can even say that most of the current demand for bitcoins is speculative. But meanwhile, bitcoins also have their functional value because, after all, human beings have never seen such a form of wealth before. There is a certain rigid demand for this form of wealth, especially during times when there is no society, government, or law and order.

在 2013 年的时候，你就可以听到截然相反的两种不同的声音。传统的经济学家大部分认为比特币是一个炒作。比特币本质是一个电子符号，并不值一分钱，所以它的价值是 0。另外一个声音是比特币的粉丝派，他们认为比特币可以取代黄金，可以成为世界的储存货币。

In 2003, you could hear two diametrically opposite opinions on the issue of bitcoins. On one hand, traditional economists believed that most bitcoin usages were speculation. The reason behind this is that the nature of bitcoins is an electronic symbol that is worthless, so its value is zero. On the other hand, supporters of bitcoins argued that bitcoins might soon replace gold as the world's store of value.

我当时的想法是两者之间的一个折中。比特币肯定有价值。不会一文不值。但是另外一方面它到底值多少钱这个事情实在不好说，取决于有多少人相信它，以及会不会有其他的山寨币取代比特币，那个时候大家还没发明山寨币这个词，而是叫克隆币。2013 年的时候，我也仔细研究了一下当时的第一大克隆币，莱特币。我当时不是很肯定会不会因为任何人都能克隆比特币，而让比特币变得不值钱。

At the time, I took a middle ground between these two stances. Bitcoins have an inherent value, so it is unjustified to say that they are worthless. But meanwhile, it is difficult to ascertain the real worth of bitcoins because the value depends on how many people believe in the idea and whether bitcoins will be replaced by altcoins. At the time, the term "altcoins" had not been coined yet, so people referred to alternative coins as "bitcoin clones." Back then, I was not sure whether the clonability of bitcoins meant that they would become worthless.

03 泡沫破裂

03 The Bursting of a Bubble

2013 年的时候。我只是看看和了解了一下比特币而已，我什么都没做。因为投资是一个相对需要谨慎的事情，我一直相信巴菲特的那句话 never lose money。房地产投资之所以比股票更能被普通中产阶级接受，也是因为价格的稳定性。所以在当时让我花 1000 美元去买一枚比特币，那是不可能的事情。

In 2013, I was merely trying to understand what bitcoins were, so I did not take any action. I believe that it is of utmost importance that we invest prudently. I am also a firm believer in Warren Buffett's famous saying of "never lose money." The reason why real estate investing is more popular than stocks among ordinary middle-class people is due to the stability of property prices. Therefore, at the time, I would never buy a bitcoin at US$1,000.

物极必反，就在 2013 年比特币突破 1000 美元不久。之后发生了 Mt. Gox 黑客事件。Mt.Gox 交易所丢失了 85 万枚比特币。从此比特币的价格一落千丈，从 1000 美元迅速跌回到 100 多美元。

As an old Chinese philosophical saying goes, "Things will develop in the opposite direction when they become extreme." Not long after the price of bitcoins exceeded US$1,000 each in 2013, the notorious Mt. Gox hack incident occurred. Mt. Gox, once the largest bitcoin exchange in the world, lost 850,000 bitcoins to hackers. Immediately after the report, the price of bitcoins plummeted from US$1,000 to around US$100.

我当时也是个悲观派。我阅读了黑客事件的前因后果。我的判断是这些事情和比特币本身的结构没有关系，而是交易平台出了问题。但是一个货币能值多少钱，完全取决于有多少人相信它。如果最大的交易所，也几乎是唯一的比特币交易平台都能出安全问题，可能会让很多人对比特币的安全性失去信心。所以我也不知道它的价格会跌多少。

At the time, I was holding a pessimistic view. Having read the details of the hacker incident, I concluded that the Mt. Gox incident had nothing to do with the structure and bitcoins. It was the trading platform offered by Mt. Gox that was problematic. That being said, the worth of a currency entirely depends on how many people are willing to trust it. If the largest bitcoin at the time, which was also the only trading platform, could be hacked, many people might lose their faith in the safety of bitcoins. But I had no idea how much the price would decline.

2013 年之后，比特币渐渐淡出了我的视野。我不再关注这个投资品。后来我忙着在中国和美国买房子，这件事情也就渐渐淡忘了。我只知道比特币价格跌得惨不忍睹，媒体上一大批幸灾乐祸的人群。

After 2013, bitcoins were no longer on my radar, and I stopped paying attention to it. Later, I was busy buying investment properties in China and the U.S., so bitcoins gradually fell into oblivion. The only follow-up I had was that the media were gloating over the abysmal decline in bitcoin prices.

04 会走路的钱

04 Money Walks

时间渐渐地进入了 2016 年。这一年比特币发生了减半事件。减半是比特币的一种特有的控制货币发行总量的方式。就是比特币挖矿的奖励，每隔四年要减半。我很感兴趣地研究减半事件对价格的影响。因为我经常思考的一个事情就是到底市场是否是充分效率的？或者说哪些市场是充分效率的，哪些市场是非充分效率的？

In 2016, bitcoins halved. Bitcoin halving is a way to control the total number of bitcoins issued. It happens every four years when the number of Bitcoins rewarded to miners is halved. I am interested in studying the effects of bitcoin halving on the price because the efficient market hypothesis is one of the economic theories that I often ponder upon. Do markets function efficiently? Or which markets are efficient and which are not?

如果一个市场是充分效率的，那么发生减半这样的事情，价格应该不涨，甚至减半之后反而下跌。因为减半之前，信息已经充分反映在市场预期里。所有人都知道减半要发生而且知道为何要发生。通过减半前后价格的变化，可以知道比特币的交易市场是不是足够的有效率。如果不是充分效率的，那就有通过短线买卖挣钱的机会。如果是充分效率的，那就没有什么做短线挣钱的机会。如果用我两大投资法来解释，就是在充分效率的市场，就应该用懒人投资法。在非充分效率的市场，那就应该用勤快人投资法。

If the bitcoin market is efficient, bitcoin prices will not increase at all after halving and should decrease instead. This is because before the halving, all available information should already have been fully reflected in the price, and everyone knows when the halving is going to happen. We can determine whether the bitcoin market is sufficiently efficient by looking at the changes in the price before and after the halving. If the analysis tells us that the price in a market does not fully reflect all information available, there are opportunities to make short-term profits in the market. If the market is an efficient one, there is no room for making short-term profits. Applying my investment strategies, we should use "Investment Strategies for Lazy People" in an efficient market and "Investment Strategies for Diligent People" in an inefficient market.

2016 年减半之后，比特币的价格基本平稳。只是在年初的时候有小幅上涨，之后维持在 600 美元左右。这件事情让我有些出乎意外，这样的价格变化说明有足够多的人在买卖比特币。另外市场有足够大的流动性，市场充分效率。

After the halving in 2006, bitcoin prices remained steady at around US$600 despite a slight increase at the beginning of the year. The changes in price surprised me because they showed that there was a sufficient number of buyers and sellers trading bitcoin. The market is liquid and efficient.

由于对这个事件的关注让我有机会接触一些论坛上关于比特币的讨论。我当时是想登陆这些论坛看看大家对减半事件后的价格预期是怎样的。那个时候论坛非常活跃，每天都有大量的帖子。大部分看上去都是相当年轻的

人。而且他们都很聪明，因为在讨论很多山寨币以及算法的问题上，他们对
数学和计算机都说得头头是道。

Because of my interest in bitcoins, I was also paying attention to some
discussion on bitcoins on online forums. At the time, I was trying to find out how
forum users would predict bitcoin prices to change after the halving. Back then, the
forums were an active community that had a large number of new discussion
threads every day. Most of the users were young, intelligent people. From their
discussion on altcoins and algorithms, it is easy to see that they were very
knowledgeable about mathematics and computer science.

我查了一下那些在论坛上比较活跃的人的教育和技术背景。发现他们都
是计算机行业中真正的牛人。比如当时讨论比特币的闪电网，主要的开发人
员都来自 MIT 的媒体实验室。可是这些绝顶聪明、拥有高学历、在 IT 领域工
作的人，谈及他们 N 年后比特币成为储蓄货币的梦想，却让我大跌眼镜。

I looked into the educational background and professional qualifications of the
more active forum users and realized that they were all experts in computer science.
For example, the principal developers of bitcoins' lightning network were MIT
researchers. They were intelligent, well-educated, and possessed the relevant
qualifications. However, I was shocked by their discussion on how they hoped that
bitcoins would one day become a reserve currency.

2016 年我的梦想是实现我 1000 万美元的目标。而且已经完成了大半。
可是这些论坛里的人的梦想居然只是希望发财之后能够把学生贷款还掉。没
有贷款一身轻，然后就可以攒钱买名车了。还有一些更穷的人，经常说的就
是今天拿比特币去买比萨饼。

My dream in 2016 was to accomplish my \$10-million goal, and I was already
halfway through. Therefore, I was shocked when I saw that the dream of these
talented young people was to pay off their student mortgage and buy a nice car.
Some poorer forum users were saying that they bought a pizza with their bitcoins.

会走路的钱
Money Walks

这时候，我意识到除了个别大户，他们这些比特币普通玩家都是屌丝，是一帮穷人。这帮穷人未来可能会很有钱，因为他们都受过良好的教育又绝顶聪明。这非常符合我的"会走路的钱"投资原理。让我豁然开朗，眼前一亮。

At this moment, I realized that all bitcoin investors, except a few wealthy ones, were young and broke. But these poor people might become very rich in the future because they were well-educated and smart. This is in line with my "money walks" investment strategy, so I had my eureka moment.

我曾经看过很多人讲改革开放初期到中国购买古董瓷器的故事。80 年代改革开放不久，中国百废待兴，为了积攒外汇，允许出口乾隆六十年以后的古董，想狠狠宰外国人一笔。这些古董经常就放在中国友谊商店里。几万元人民币一个的瓷器当时绝非大陆普通民众可以承受的。当时一些精明的国外古董商人，廉价买入大批的古董，把这些古董扣在手上，到了 90 年代或者2000 年以后卖出。这些古董普遍都涨了 100 多倍。因为刚刚改革开放的时候，中国人很穷。可是到了 90 年代和 2000 年之后，中国人一下子变得有钱了。这些古董自然也就贵了。

I have read many stories of people buying china antiques in the early days of China's economic reform. In the 1980s, China had just begun its economic reform, and the country's devastated economy needed much stimulation. In order to increase its foreign exchange reserves, the government allowed exporting of Qianlong antiques that were made after 1795. At the time, some savvy foreign antique dealers purchased loads of such antiques at a low price, stored them, and resold them in the 1990s or after 2000 when the price of the antiques had increased by a factor of 100. This is because Chinese people were still very poor in the early days of China's economic reform. However, after the 1990s and 2000, China's economy took off, and the Chinese became rich. This is why those antiques are so expensive now.

2016 年的比特币在我眼里，和那些 20 世纪 80 年代初的古董、猴年的邮票，明清红木家具一样。这个时候不买它，什么时候再买它呢？

The way I saw it was that investing in bitcoins in 2016 was like buying antiques in the 1980s, postage stamps in the Year of the Monkey, and rosewood furniture from the Ming and Qing Dynasty: If not now, then when?

05 涉猎

05 Adding Bitcoins to My Portfolio

但是购买一个投资品光有一番热情还不行，还要仔细分析。因为价格起伏太剧烈，一不当心就会被套在里面。于是我写了一篇博客文章，就是比特币的上限在哪里。这篇文章叫作"比特币会涨到一枚一百万美元么？"

However, in making an investment, passion is not a sufficient condition of success. Detailed analysis is crucial. Because of the drastic fluctuations in bitcoin prices, careless investors may be trapped in the market. In light of this, I wrote a blog article exploring the upper limit of bitcoin price titled "Will bitcoin price rise to US$1 million?"

比特币会涨到一枚一百万美元么？(2017 年 2 月 11 日)

Will bitcoin price rise to US$1 million? (February 11, 2017)

by Bayfamily

2016 年是比特币等加密货币(Cryptocurrency)的减半年。比特币风起云涌，得到全世界无数无政府主义者、自由经济主义者、反凯恩斯学派、极客的追捧。各种说法都有。有的人认为比特币会涨过 100 万美元一枚。我想泼一点冷水，说比特币不太可能长期稳定地涨过一百万美元一枚。是因为比特币能耗实在太大了，而且增长迅猛，对环保而言是个灾难。

The year 2016 marked the second halving of cryptocurrencies, including bitcoins. It is also the year in which bitcoins attracted the attention of the world and gained the support of countless anarchists, advocates of a free economy, anti-

Keynesians, and geeks. These people have differing views on future bitcoin prices. Some of them believe that the bitcoin price will rise to US$1 million. I hate to ruin their dreams, but I have to say it is almost impossible for the price to reach US$1 million in the long term. The main reason is that bitcoins are an environmental catastrophe because they use far too much electricity and grow too rapidly.

是的， 比特币消耗的电力在急剧增长。目前比特币挖矿的出块速度是每十分钟 12.5 个。每天挖矿的速度是 1800 枚。按照价格 5000 美元一枚的话，每天矿工的收益是 900 万美元，每年的收益是 32.8 亿美元。矿工挖矿都在电力最便宜的地方，在中国的四川贵州的小水电厂，内蒙古的煤电厂。 由于挖矿是市场充分竞争的，长期来看矿工的主要成本就是电费。由于硬件上很快就落伍，硬件的投入一般是通过比特币增值对冲掉的。所以矿工收益约等于他们的电费投入。按照保守估计，按照 0.3 元人民币一度电的情况来算，一年大约消耗了 6.57×10^{10} 度电。 目前人类一年的总耗电量是 20×10^{12} 度电，也就是如果比特币长期站在现在的价格上，那么 0.32% 地球上的电力就会被用在比特币挖矿上。

Bitcoins' energy consumption is increasing drastically. According to the current mining power, a bitcoin mining device can produce 12.5 bitcoins every 10 minutes, which means a daily output of 1,800 bitcoins. Assuming a bitcoin price of US$5,000, the daily profit of a mining device is US$9 million and the annual profit is US$3.28 billion. Miners set up their machines in places with the lowest electricity fee, for example, Suizhou and Inner Mongolia in China. As the mining market is an efficient one, the primary, long-term costs of mining are the electricity fee. Though the hardware may soon become outdated, any new hardware input will be offset by the increase in bitcoin prices. Therefore, the main profit comes from their input of electricity fees. Let's use a conservative number of an electricity fee of US$0.042 per kWh in China in our calculations. This will mean that Bitcoin mining consumes 6.57×10^{10} kWh of electricity every year. The total annual consumption of electricity of all human beings is 20×10^{12}. This means that if bitcoin price remains stable at the current level, bitcoin mining will account for 0.32% of the world's entire electricity consumption.

问题是比特币的价格还在一路暴涨，有相当一部分人认为比特币在未来 5-10 年有可能成为全球的储蓄货币。全球黄金总市值是 8 万亿美元左右。全球的美元总量是 10 万亿美元。要想成为储蓄货币，比特币的总市场规模应该达到万亿美元这个数量级，在此之前价格不会稳定下来。如果比特币能够持续过去 8 年的增长，未来的价格会在 10 万-100 万美元一枚。

The real problem is that bitcoin prices are still soaring. Some people believe that bitcoins will become the world's reserve currency in the next 5-10 years. The total value of all gold ever mined is around US$8 trillion. There is a total of about 10 trillion U.S. dollars in circulation in the world. In order to become a reserve currency, the total market value of bitcoins must be in the trillions. Bitcoin prices will continue to fluctuate before the market reaches such a scale. If bitcoin price can repeat its growth in the last eight years, the future price will be US$100,000 to US$1 million.

我们来看看那个时候的比特币电力消耗是多少？未来 10 年比特币还会经历两次减半(halving)，分别是 2020 年和 2024 年。2024 年以前的挖矿速度将会是 900 枚每天，如果按照现在的速度在 2024 年以前价格涨到 10 万美元。那么每天的矿工收益是 9 千万美元，折算到一年的电费是 328 亿美元。也就是说几年之后，地球上 3.2%电力将被用来挖掘比特币。

Let's then take a look at the future total energy consumption of bitcoins. In the next decade, bitcoins will experience two more halvings in 2020 and 2024 respectively. The mining speed will be 900 bitcoins per day before 2024. Assuming the mining speed remains unchanged and bitcoin price grows to US$100,000 before 2024, the bitcoin miner revenue will be US$90 million per day, which entails an electricity fee of US$32.8 billion. In other words, in a few years, 3.2% of the world's energy will be used for bitcoin mining.

有人推算过，地球上所有银行系统耗电功率大约是 6,000-10,000 MW，是现在比特币总功率的 5-20 倍。 未来几年如果比特币的电力消耗增长趋势不变，比特币的耗电总量将会和银行系统的耗电量持平。这样来看，比特币的电子货币革命，至少从能源角度来说，是历史的倒退。如果比特币成为全球性储蓄货币(global reserve currency), 那么能耗总量将是现有银行系统的 1-2 个数量级之上。

According to some estimates, all the banking systems in the world consume 6,000-10,000 MW of electricity, which is about 5-20 times the current energy consumption of bitcoins. If the increase in the energy consumption of bitcoin remains constant, the total energy consumption of bitcoins will be the equivalent of that of banking systems. In this sense, such a revolution of electronic money brought by bitcoins is a step backward, at least from the energy perspective. If bitcoins indeed become the global reserve currency, the total energy consumption will be double or even triple the energy consumption of existing banking systems.

如果按照那些更加大胆的预测，比如著名的防病毒软件 McAfee 的创始人 John McAfee，他坚定地认为比特币会在 2030 年之前涨到 50 万美元一枚。

There are some bolder estimates of bitcoin prices. For example, John McAfee, the founder of the well-known anti-virus software McAfee, firmly believes that the bitcoin price will increase to US$500,000 before 2030.

权且不说一百万美元了。如果比特币能够保持过去的增长趋势，8 年内涨到五十万美元一枚，那么比特币挖矿的总电力消耗是 7.3×10^{12}kWh, 7.3 万亿度电。这是一个天文数字，地球上人类一年的总耗电量是 20,000 TWh, 20×10^{12}kWh, 就是 20Trillion 度电。就是说地球上每年三分之一的电力消耗将被用在比特币挖矿上，才能够支撑比特币价格涨到这个价格。 逻辑上感觉很荒谬，别忘了中国一年的耗电量只有 5.5 万亿度。

Let's forget about the number of US$1 million per bitcoin for a moment and focus our discussion on the bitcoin price of US$500,000. If bitcoin prices can maintain its past growth rate in the next eight years, one bitcoin will be worth

US$500,000 in eight years' time, at which point the total energy consumption of bitcoin mining will be 7.3×10^{12} kWh. This is an astronomical number because the total energy consumption of all human activities is 20,000 TWh, which is equal to 20 trillion kWh. In other words, the bitcoin price of US$500,000 needs to be supported by such a scale of bitcoin mining that consumes one-third of the world's total energy. Logically speaking, this is absurd. Do not forget that China's total energy consumption is only 5.5 trillion kWh.

荒谬的事情不见得不会发生。地球上每年出产 2,500 吨黄金，产生 120Billion 美元的价值。假设金矿本身在成本中占一半的价格。那么金矿挖矿需要投入的资源大约是 60Billion 美元。这似乎和那个时候的比特币挖矿的投入在一个数量级上。这其中绝大部分的黄金从挖出来就直接放到地库里变成金块一动不动。如果有未来世界的人穿越到现在看我们动用了这么多人力物力挖黄金摆在仓库里，也是极其荒诞的事情。

But that which is absurd may happen in reality. Each year, global gold mining adds approximately 2,500 tonnes, which was worth US$120 billion, to the overall stock of gold. Assuming the cost of the gold mine occupies 50% of the total costs, the total input of resources is US$60 billion, which seems to be on par with the input required of bitcoin mining. Most of the gold mined will be directly transported to storage facilities. Perhaps if a time traveler from the future saw that we are expending so much labor work and resources on mining the gold and storing them in the warehouse, he or she would think this was ridiculous.

如果说 8 年后地球上 1/3 的电力被用来挖掘比特币是很大的遗憾，是环境和能源的灾难，但是也不是不可能。比特币的挖掘最初在个人电脑上就可以实现，现在必须大规模的公司和数据中心组成挖矿池。等到世界上很多地方都像对待黄金一样动用国家之力挖掘比特币的时候，估计比特币的电力消耗就会达到 1/3 全球电力消耗的水平了。注意这个电力消耗和硬件进步没有关系，因为矿工和矿工之间是竞争关系，电力消耗唯一的影响因素是挖矿减半 (halving)的时间。

If one-third of the world's energy is used for bitcoin mining in eight years' time, I think it will be a huge regret and environmental disaster, but this is not an impossible occurrence. In the early stage of the development of bitcoins, they could be mined from a personal computer. Now, bitcoin mining requires a special mining pool backed up by a large-scale company and data center. If all countries started bitcoin mining at the existing scale of gold mining, bitcoins would account for one-third of the world's total energy consumption. A point to note is that energy consumption is not affected by an improvement in hardware because miners are competitors to each other. The only factor that will reduce energy consumption is the timing of halving.

这样的事情会不会发生呢？会发生而且已经发生了。北朝鲜最近已经开始启动国家之力挖掘比特币，用来获取外汇收入，这样可以避开贸易禁运和封锁。如果萨达姆和曾经的那些中东独裁者今天还活着，他们也会动用国家之力，获取比特币。因为相对于存储美元而言，美国政府拿他们没有任何办法。等到伊朗这样的被贸易制裁的国家开始自己烧油发电，挖比特币换外汇的时候，你就知道地球人又开始疯了。

Will we see that governments start mining bitcoins at the scale of gold-mining? We will, and it is already happening. North Korea has recently started mobilizing government resources to mine bitcoins in order to earn foreign exchange. Bitcoins allow North Korea to get around trade sanctions and embargoes. If Saddam Hussein and other dictators in the Middle East were still alive today, they would probably also mobilize public resources to procure bitcoins because, unlike U.S. dollars, the U.S. government had no control over bitcoins. If countries that are subject to trade sanctions such as Iran begin to mine bitcoins to earn more foreign exchange by burning oil and generating more electricity, you will know that human beings have gone nuts again.

纵观历史长河，半个地球都曾经相信资本家消灭了，人类就进入共产主义了。历时千年，中国有一亿妇女痛苦地裹小脚，只为嫁个好人家。一个信仰和价值观体系一旦建立起来，被大多数人接受，所有的人，任你有多么清醒的自由思想，都会裹挟其中，动弹不得。 当大家都认为裹小脚有价值的时候，你的天足观念就会当作傻瓜。全世界都用比特币的时候，你口袋里的纸币就会一钱不值。 现在也有越来越多的人相信比特币是解决人世间一切疾苦的良方。比如著名的比特币领袖 Roger Ver，他投身比特币运动的原动力在于他相信比特币能够消灭人间的战争，因为大家都用比特币，政府就没钱打仗了。听上去似曾相识那句"一个幽灵在欧洲游荡"，理想都很美好，带来的却全是苦难。

Throughout our history, there was a point where half of our population believed that we would enter the era of communism when capitalists disappeared. In China's thousands of years' history, there was a time when close to 100 million women bound their feet for a better marriage. Once a certain belief and value system have been established and accepted by the majority in society, everyone will be bound and constrained by such values, no matter how rational and forward-thinking that person is. When everyone in society believed in foot binding, advocates of natural feet would be dismissed as fools. When everyone is using bitcoins, the paper money in your pockets will become worthless. Now, an increasing number of people believe that bitcoins are the panacea for all human misfortunes. Take Roger Ver, a famous bitcoin leader. His motivation for devoting himself to the bitcoin movement is that he believes bitcoins can eliminate wars. If everyone is using bitcoins, the government will not have the money to start a war. My response to this is that his view reminds me of the first line in the Communist Manifesto, "A specter is haunting Europe- the specter of communism." The picture is rosy, but the reality is cruel.

加密货币（Cryptocurrency）的浪潮汹涌澎湃。持有和使用过加密货币的人一般都再也不愿意转回 Fiat（法币）。因为加密货币在保值、投资、非国家化、流动性、跨境交易、隐私、持有成本等方面拥有很大的优势。就像车轮子、交流电、互联网一样，没有发明之前，人们也能正常生活。但是这些发明一旦出现，再想把它们塞回瓶子里，比登天还难。有了互联网，人们再也不愿意只看报纸了。Fiat money 流动到加密货币的这个单向阀恐怕一时半会是关不上的。再多的监管也是螳臂挡车，有点当年的"不许片板下海的味道"。Fiat 渐渐退出历史舞台，恐怕也是早晚的事情。

Cryptocurrencies have brought enormous changes to our lives. Those who own and have used cryptocurrencies are often reluctant to change back to fiat money because the former is superior in terms of retaining its value, investment returns, denationalization, mobility, cross-jurisdictional transactions, privacy, and holding costs. The advent of cryptocurrencies is similar to the inventions of wheels, alternating current, and the internet. Before their advent, people carried their lives as usual. But after their advent, they would no longer go back to their old way of life. For example, with access to the internet, people are not willing to read traditional newspapers now. I am afraid the one-way transition from fiat money to cryptocurrencies can no longer be paused. Governments that are trying to stop the trend is like a mantis that is trying to stop a moving chariot. That fiat money will be eliminated is a matter of time.

问题是比特币的挖矿只是为做数学题而做数学题，完全没有必要这样。比特币挖矿 POW(Proof of work)的本质就是你必须消耗电力资源来证明你做了工作，但是做这些数学题并不是实现去中心化交易所必需的。第二代的电子货币采用 POS(Proof of stake), 或者 proof of capacity，或者采用 Tangle 完全可以避开挖矿这个环节。可惜第二代电子货币可以实现零费用支付，实现智能合约，却似乎没有一个有潜力能够替代比特币，作为 Reserve currency 的候选人。因为 POW 是真金白银的投入，是最可靠的。让比特币改变算法从 proof of work 到 proof of stake 也是完全不可能，但是因为去中心化的特点，任何结构上的改动比登天还难。一个简单的扩容问题（Scaling problem），Segwit(隔离见证)派和 Big blocker(大区块)派已经是恶斗了四年，刚刚硬分叉(hard forking)，目前还在彼此哈希算力攻击中。

The problem with the mechanism of bitcoin mining is "applying mathematics for the sake of mathematics." It is totally unnecessary. The nature of PoW, which stands for proof of work, in bitcoin mining is that miners have to prove that they have done their job by consuming electricity. However, all these mathematics are not necessary for achieving a decentralized ledger. The mining requirement can be eliminated if the second generation of cryptocurrency uses PoS (proof of stake) or proof of capacity or Tangle. Regrettably, even though the second generation of cryptocurrency can achieve zero-fee transactions and smart contracts, none of them has the potential to replace bitcoins as a candidate for reserve currency. That being said, PoW is the most reliable option among them because it requires an input of actual money. It is not impossible for the algorithms to change from proof of work to proof of stake. But because of the characteristic of decentralization, any structural changes are almost impossible. The simple question of the "scaling problem" has divided the bitcoin community into two camps, Segwit and Big Blocker, who have had heated debate on the issue for four years. After the recent hard fork, the two camps are attacking each other on hash rate and processing power.

谁拥有廉价的能源，谁就拥有更多的比特币挖矿能力，这点上比特币本质上是能源币。国内倍受并网卖电约束所折磨的，开工不足的发电厂还没明白这点，等他们弄清楚了，就会开足马力挖比特币。

Overall, who owns cheaper energy owns more bitcoin mining capabilities. The nature of bitcoins is an energy coin. China is limited by a grid-connected photovoltaic system, and those power stations that have an excess supply have not figured this out yet. When they do, they will boost their turbo in mining bitcoins.

在可预见的未来，不论大家喜欢还是不喜欢，比特币能耗将会持续攀升。在能源结构调整和气候变化大背景下，它会成为一枚越来越不环保的货币。未来 10 年内也不可能涨到 100 万美元一枚。

In the foreseeable future, the energy consumption of bitcoins will continue to increase, whether you like it or not. Under the backdrop of an adjustment in the energy structure and climate change, bitcoins will become a more environmentally-damage currency. It is impossible for the price to increase to US$1 million in the next decade.

我的博客在投资理财论坛发表之后，没有一个人回应。投资理财平时我的文章经常上万的点击数，然而99%的人对比特币的陌生程度就像对火星人一样。很多熟悉我的人当时可能会很吃惊，我怎么会突然搞起比特币来了？

After I published this article on the forum, no one responded. My blog articles usually have tens of thousands of views on the forum. Yet 99% of people are strangers to bitcoins. Some of my friends were surprised that I was now interested in bitcoins.

每个社交媒体往往是圈住了一个固化人群。文学城的用户在一点点地衰老，年轻人越来越少，大部分人都是中年以上的人，和我的年龄相仿。我几乎是文学城成立的第一天就来访问这个网站的人，也见证了这个网站的用户变化。总的趋势是越来越老。二十年前的时候，谈情说爱的论坛最热闹。后来渐渐是子女教育、我爱我家、投资理财这样的BBS变得热闹起来。我想再过二三十年，可能是养老院、遗嘱葬礼这些话题变得热闹起来。我甚至怀疑每年文学城用户的平均年龄也是增长一岁。

Each social media platform caters to fixed demographics. The users of wenxuecity.com are getting older, and we have fewer young users. Most of the users are middle-aged or above, just like me. I have been visiting wenxuecity.com since it was created. I have witnessed the changes in user demographics. The overall trend is that users are getting older. Twenty years ago, it was the "relationships" section that was the most popular. As time went by, communities of parenting, investing and wealth management, and family BBS on wenxuecity.com grew larger. I believe that in the next 20-30 years, nursing homes and funerals will become hot topics. I even doubt that the average age of wenxuecity.com's users increases by one every year.

2017 年的时候，文学城的大部分读者都是年富力强的中年人，处于他们一生收入的最高阶段。可是竟然没人对我这样一篇博文有任何反应。所以我知道比特币还是一个非常小众的投资品，还没有引起普通投资人的关注，这个时候进场应该是很好的时机。

In 2017, most readers of wenxuecity.com were middle-aged people who are energetic and wealthy because they are in the stage of their life in which their income is the highest. However, none of them responded to my article on bitcoins. This was how I knew that bitcoins were a niche investment vehicle. As it still had not attracted the attention of ordinary, normal investors, I knew that this was the perfect timing for me to enter the market.

绝大部分的投资都是击鼓传花的游戏。关键是后面有没有人为你接棒。如果后面没有人接棒，你是最后一棒了，那你最好不要去碰这个投资品。如果你是最早接棒的几个人，后面你能看见乌泱乌泱的接棒队伍。那这可能就是一个好的投资品。

Most investments are a game of betting on whether there will be more people who are willing to enter the market after you. The key is whether someone is willing to buy your asset. If no one is willing to be the last buyer, my advice is that you should not invest in that product. But if you are among the earliest buyers in the market and can see a long queue of people waiting to enter the market, these are good signs that it is an ideal investment product.

所以很关键的一点就是你要想一下，传递到你的信息到底是从哪里来的。大部分投资决定的正确与否其实都和我们获得的信息有关。信息不会免费地平白无故地到你耳朵里来。是主动获得的信息，还是被动获得的信息，以及你在整个社会人群中获得信息的快慢程度，决定了你的投资决定是否正确。

Therefore, you must ask yourself, "where does my information come from?" The correctness of an investment decision is closely related to how the relevant information is obtained. Information will not knock on your door. In order to assess whether an investment decision is sound, ask yourself, "Did I obtain such information passively or actively?" and "Was I among the first batch of people who knew this?"

永远不要和旧钱(old money)、旧贵拼体力，要抢在新钱(New money)、新贵前面一步。New money 人群未来喜欢的东西，就是你现在要买入的投资品。无论是湾区的房子、中国古董，还是当下的比特币。

Never compete with old money. Instead, you have to be one step ahead of the new money. The things that will be highly sought after by the new money in the future are the things that you need to invest now. Such examples include properties in the Bay Area, Chinese antiques, and bitcoins.

06 筹措资金

06 Soliciting Funds

所以我决定投资比特币，但是怎么投呢，这却是一个令我伤脑筋的问题。

So, I decided to invest in bitcoins. But how should I do it? This was a headache.

肯定不能断然一股脑儿地买进，那样风险太高，因为比特币的波动性太大，随时有可能下跌。分期投入也是一个好办法，如果你看清楚它是一个长期上涨的趋势。可是即使分期投入，我也不确定是否靠谱。因为长期到底是多长比较合适呢？比特币的税务问题也比较麻烦。当时 IRS 已经明确了比特币是 Asset。买卖赚钱了，需要按照投资的方式交税。

Going all in is too risky because of the drastic fluctuations in bitcoin prices. Dividing up the total amount to be invested across several purchases is a better alternative if you can ascertain that the price will increase in the long term. But I still was not sure if this is a safe strategy. How long is the long term? Furthermore, taxes on bitcoins are complicated. IRS has already confirmed bitcoins are an asset, so taxpayers must report bitcoin transactions for tax purposes.

第十七章 从 100 到 1000 万（三）比特币
Chapter 17: From $1 million to $10 million (3): Bitcoins

此外投资比特币的钱从哪里来呢？2016 年的时候我刚刚抄完湾区的次贷危机的底，手上也是完全没有现金的状态。首先我决定用我的 Roth IRA 来投资买比特币，就是前面第四章我说的那笔钱。我用那笔钱直接购买 GBTC。

Where should I find the capital? In 2016, I had just finished my "buying the bottom" operation, so I had no cash at hand. I first decided to use my Roth IRA to invest in bitcoins, which was the sum of money that I mentioned in Chapter 4. I used this sum to buy GBTC directly.

GBTC 每年有 2%的管理费而且有很高的溢价。一枚比特币当时 GBTC 的价格整整比实际价格高 30%。但是 GBTC 的好处是比较方便，直接像股票一样购买就可以了。金额不多的话，不是什么问题。因为是 Roth IRA 账号，买卖不用交税。而且每次买卖的手续费极低。不像当时的主流比特币交易平台都是按照交易总额收取千分之一的费用的。买卖 GBTC 只需要每次交 6 美元的手续费即可。于是我用那笔钱分期分阶段买入比特币。

GBTC has a 2% annual fee and a high mark-up. At the time, holding a bitcoin through GBTC was 30% more expensive than the actual price, but the greatest advantage of GBTC is its convenience. I can buy bitcoins like stocks. GBTC did not have a high minimum capital requirement. As I was using my Roth IRA account, I did not pay tax on each transaction. Meanwhile, the transaction fee was also minimal. While other mainstream bitcoin trading platforms were charging a 0.1% transaction fee, GBTC was charging a $6 flat fee. Therefore, I used the sum to invest in bitcoins in several purchases at different stages.

但是这点投入太少，我需要动用更大的资金量。除了 Cash out（抵押套现）小黑屋的钱，我只能动用 401K 的养老金来投资比特币。401K 涨了这么多年，已经形成了比较大的规模。我打算拿出 20%的 401K 来投资比特币。这个时候，直接购买 GBTC 就不再是一个好主意了。不单单是因为 GBTC 每年要收取 2%的管理费。更关键的是持有 GBTC 违反持有比特币的三个基本原则。

413

But I felt that my investment was too small, and I needed to increase my capital. Other than cashing out on my investment property that is located alongside the railway, I decided to use my 401K money to invest in bitcoins. After growing my 401K for these years, I had a large bird nest, so I decided to take out 20% of my 401K to invest in bitcoins. At this moment, I felt that buying GBTC ceased to be a good idea not only because of the 2% annual management fee, but also holding GBTC runs contrary to the three fundamental principles of bitcoins.

这三个基本原则是我在看过大量的比特币论坛上自己总结出来的。但是这些年过去了，我觉得这三条依旧是金科玉律。这三个原则是：

I first summarized these three basic principles from reading dozens of forums online. But after all these years, I think these are the golden rules. They are:

一、不直接持有私钥的比特币就不是你的币。只有持私钥才真正是你的币；

1. If you do not directly own the private key, the bitcoins are not yours. Only when you own the private key can you truly own your bitcoins.

二、不用把比特币放在交易所里。世界上一切 Hack proof (抗黑客)的交易所只是暂时还没被攻陷；

2. Do not keep you bitcoins on an exchange. All "hack-proof" exchange platforms are currently "hack-proof." But it is just a matter of time.

三、永远不要卖出你的比特币。

3. Never sell your bitcoins.

如果你对这三个原则还不理解，可能是因为对比特币的一些背景知识的不够熟悉。限于篇幅的限制，我在这本书里不再展开说明这三个原则的重要性。就比特币本身我也可以写厚厚的一本书来讨论，那不是本书的重点。

If you still do not understand the rationale behind these three golden rules, this may mean that you are not familiar with some background knowledge of bitcoins. Because of space constraints, I will not go into detail the importance of these three rules. Discussion on bitcoins warrants another full-length book, but it is not the focus of this book.

07 比特币退休金账户

07 Bitcoin Account for Retirement

于是那个时候，我又干了一件几乎所有人都没有干过的事情。我估计全美国恐怕不超过 50 人和我做了同样的事情。我之所以这样说，因为我当时问遍了所有的银行和交易机构。所有的回复都是这件事情做不了。我直到今天也不是很清楚我办的手续是否完全合乎管理法规。所以请读者不要盲目重复。

Back then, I did something that almost no one had done before. I guess that fewer than 50 people in the U.S. have done the same thing. I base this claim on my own observation. At the time, I had contacted all the banks and financial institutions in the U.S., and they replied that my request was not feasible. Even today, I am not sure whether my requested procedures are completely within the ambit of the law, so I would like to remind my readers not to blindly follow my action plan.

2016 年我打算给自己开一个 Solo 401K 的账号。把我的 401K rollover(转账)这个账号里，然后用这笔钱去买比特币。Solo 401K 开账号这件事情并不难，网上找代理机构，每年交一定的年费就可以帮你出具好文件。

In 2016, I decided to open a solo 401K account for myself so that I could roll over my existing 401K to the new account and use the money to buy bitcoins. Opening a solo 401K account is not difficult. All you need to do is to find an agency online and pay an annual fee for the relevant documents.

问题是你有了 Solo 401K 文件，你需要去银行开一个同样名字的账号才能把钱从其他 401K 转过来。不然退休金转账(Rollover)的支票没法兑现。钱转过来之后，我还需要同时在比特币的交易所开一个同样名字的 Solo 401K 账号，这样才能把这笔钱转到交易所。然后在交易所，我还需要买好比特币之后，把比特币提取到我的私人纸钱包里面，这样才算真正的完成整个流程。

The difficulty lies in the rollover part. After I had the relevant documents for a solo 401K, I needed to go to the bank to open an account using the same name before I can roll over my money from other 401K. Otherwise, the rollover cheque could not be cleared. After rolling over the money, I also needed to open a solo 401K account at a bitcoin exchange using the same name before I could transfer the money to the exchange. After buying those bitcoins at the exchange, I had to transfer them to my personal paper wallet. The above are the steps of the whole process of how I invest in bitcoins.

我跑遍了我在的这个城市周围的所有银行，Bank of America, Union Bank, Wells Fargo，Citi Bank，US Bank 等等。每个办事人员一开始都是热情洋溢，告诉我说没有问题。不过听到我说要用 401K 的钱直接去买比特币，他们就像外星人一样的看我。不单单是他们，其实当时比特币的粉丝论坛上，也没有人提过如何直接用 401K 买比特币。当然这事我理解，因为那里都是一群穷学生。学生贷款还没还清呢。哪里来的钱买 401K。银行的人每次去后台请教一下经理该怎么办，随后就卡壳了。少则一天，多则几天，最后告诉我无法开这样的账号。

I visited all the banks in my city and neighboring areas, including Bank of America, Union Bank, Wells Fargo, CitiBank, and US Bank. At first, the staff members were all very helpful and told me that everything would be fine. But when they heard that I was trying to use my 401K money to buy bitcoins, they looked at me as if I were an alien. It was not only them who were new to the idea. Even on some bitcoin fans forums, no one mentioned how to use 401K to buy bitcoins. I could understand why this was the case. The forum users were all poor students who had not even paid off their student loans. How did they afford to buy 401K? The staff members at the bank would go to the back office to ask their managers for assistance and then asked me to wait for their response. After one or a few days, they would get back to me and say I could not open such an account.

但是越是因为办不下来，越会让我越觉得这里有投资的机会。因为道理也很简单，GBTC 比比特币现货市场的价格有 30%的溢价。这个溢价不是凭空而来的，是因为办不下来这些手续造成的。我在银行四处碰壁，就反映了30%溢价带来的困难。

The more difficult the process was, the more I felt that it would be an excellent investment opportunity. The logic behind this is simple. GBTC has a mark-up of 30% on bitcoin price. This 30% fee does not come from nowhere: It is caused by the unavailability of relevant procedures. The setbacks I encountered at banks reflected the difficulty faced by investors that justified the 30% mark-up.

不断碰壁反而坚定了我的决心。第一个吃螃蟹的人，肯定能拿到红利。当没人知道手续应该怎么办的时候，你办下来就是赢家。于是我就咨询给我开 Solo 401K 管理文件的人。问他们哪个银行可以开这样的一个账号，一个可以买比特币的账号。Solo 401K 的管理公司也不是特别清楚，但是他给我介绍了网上的一个网络银行，让我咨询一下。

But these setbacks only strengthened my determination. The early bird gets the worm. When no one knows what the relevant procedures are, you will be the winner if you can find out about them and finish the process. Therefore, I reached out to the institution that managed my solo 401K plan documents. I asked them if they knew which bank could help me open such an account that would allow me to buy bitcoins. The management company said they were not familiar with these procedures, but they recommended me to contact an online bank.

我也不是特别清楚这个网络银行是不是靠谱，网站上看起来好像还可以，不像是诈骗。所以我想从小金额开始试一试。这个流程大概是这样的，我从 Fidelity 这样的管理公司申请 rollover， 他们会开出一张我名字加上 Solo 401K 的支票，然后我把这个支票存入这个网络银行。

I was not sure if this online bank was legitimate. From its website, it did not look like a scam, so I wanted to start by investing a small amount of money through this online bank. The overall procedures were something like this: I first applied to such an investment management company as Fidelity for a rollover. They would then issue a cheque payable to me that was marked with "solo 401K" for me to deposit the cheque into this online bank.

然而下一步又卡住了，因为需要在比特币交易所开 Solo 401K 的退休账号。当时，所有比特币的交易所都不支持开设 Solo 401K 的账号。美国当时主要交易所只开设个人账户，2016 年能开设退休金账户交易所一个都没有。我打了一圈电话，碰了一鼻子灰。

I was stuck in the next step when I was trying to open a solo 401K retirement account at the bitcoin exchange. At the time, all bitcoin exchanges did not support solo 401K accounts. All common bitcoin exchanges in the U.S. allowed trading through personal accounts only. None of them offered the option of opening a retirement account. After numerous phone calls, I was still stuck.

就在几乎绝望的时候，终于找到了一个当时还是很不起眼的小交易所，他们愿意开这样的账户给我。可能是他们生意刚开张不久，所以并不拒绝每一个可能的客户。不过即使这样，他们还是严格地审查了我很久。我平时做咨询业务的往来账目都要给他看，客户电话也要给他们，生怕我是一个洗钱的。

Just when I was about to lose my hope, I found an exchange that was little known at the time. They were willing to help me set up a retirement account probably because they had just opened their business and did not want to reject any potential customers. That being said, they still strictly adhered to the procedures in checking my background by asking me to show them all of the books of my consulting business and also the phone numbers of my clients lest I was a money launderer.

这件事情来来回回折腾有三周的时间，渐渐终于我把所有的账户都开好了，路也走通了。我在办手续的每一个环节里碰到的人，都是瞪大了眼睛说，从来没有过这样的事情。我还记得当时我转第一笔钱从基金公司索要转账(rollover)支票的时候。因为我不知道那家网络银行是否靠谱，只要了

1000 美元。服务员再三和我确定这笔金额，可能是想这么点钱还瞎折腾个啥。

It took me three weeks to set up all the accounts in preparation for my bitcoin investment journey. In every step of the way when I was inquiring about the relevant procedures, the staff members were all flabbergasted and said they had never encountered such a request before. I still remember that the first time when I applied to the investment management company for a rollover, I only requested a sum of US$1,000 because I had no idea whether the online bank would be a scam. The bank teller confirmed the amount with me several times, probably wondering why I went through all the trouble just to transfer such a small amount of money.

08 免费获得比特币

08 Getting Bitcoins for Free

账户开好了，钱也转好了，新的问题又来了。如何买比特币这也是一个困难。资金小的时候，分阶段买进长期持有就好了。资金大的时候，我可不敢冒这样的风险。

After I set up my account and transferred the money, new problems arose: How to buy bitcoins? Before, I had a limited amount of capital, so all I needed to do was to invest my money over several intervals of time and hold my bitcoins for the long term. But as I had a large amount of capital, I did not dare take such risks.

我仔细研究了一下。最稳妥的方式是通过放债的方式去拥有比特币，而不是直接买。当时的比特币放贷利息非常高，因为投机活跃。就是说买比特币的人主要的任务就是投机，所以短线交易者会用杠杆买进卖出，导致贷款给他们可以获得比较高的利息。

After some research, I found out that the safest way to own bitcoins is through extending credits instead of buying them directly. The interest rates on bitcoin loans were very attractive because speculators were active in the market. In other words, most bitcoin purchasers were speculators, so short-term traders will use leverage in their buying and selling, leading to higher interest rates on loans to these people.

但是如果直接在加密货币交易市场上去放贷款，那么就面临着税务上的风险，因为贷款获得的钱你需要去交税。但是 401K 账号没有这个问题。

However, if I give out loans directly in the crypto-assets market, I will face tax issues because the profits from loans are taxable. But fortunately, 401K accounts do not have such a problem.

放贷最好的办法是买入比特币，然后到衍生品交易市场上直接放空。这样的对冲方式叫 naked sale（裸空卖）。熟悉金融衍生品交易的人可能明白我在说什么。不熟悉的可以直接跳过这些技术细节。利息的来源在于现货市场和衍生品期货市场的价格差异。用做空的方式，当时贷款的回报年利率在 10%~20% 之间。最高的时候有的时候一天就有 1% 的利率回报。因为比特币每天价格起伏很大。所以对于那些做短线买卖的人 1% 的利率不算什么，因为每天价格的震荡起伏就可以到 10%。

The best way to give out bitcoin loans is by first buying bitcoins and then shorting them in the derivative market. This way of hedging is also known as naked sales. Readers who are familiar with the trading of financial derivatives may already be familiar with the mechanism. For those of you who do not understand what I am talking about here, do not worry. Feel free to skip the technical details. The interests come from the difference in prices between the spot market and the futures market. Through short-selling, the annual return from crypto loans was around 10-20% at the time. When the market was booming, investors would see a daily interest rate of 1%. Because of the drastic fluctuations in bitcoin prices, a 1% daily interest rate was negligible for short-term traders. The daily fluctuation in bitcoin prices was often 10%.

但是这样我可以免于比特币价格起伏的风险。涨了我也赚钱，跌了我也赚钱。我觉得我不是炒短线的人，对于炒短线需要专心坐在那儿，每天凌晨开机盯着屏幕，我还有自己的事业要做，炒短线对我来说是件不可能的事情。所以我要做的事情就是把机器设置好，然后比特币就可以哗啦哗啦的进到我的钱包里来了。

This was how I managed the risks caused by fluctuating bitcoin prices. I would make a profit anyway, regardless of whether the bitcoin price increased or decreased. I did not consider myself capable of being a short-term trader because short-term traders needed to constantly monitor the changes in the market, even at midnight. I have my career, so short-term trading was almost impossible for me. Therefore, I decided to set up my machine, after which I could sit back and enjoy my life while bitcoins walked into my pocket.

我小心翼翼地把我的对冲交易结构设置好，剩下的事情就全部交给机器了。机器会每天源源不断地生产出比特币给我。每 8 个小时作为单位结算一次，一天三次。按照我的计算，一年下来，也会收获相当可观，因为 2016 年之后比特币进入快速飞涨期。

Having meticulously set up my hedging system, I left my machine in charge. My machine would generate bitcoins 24/7 for me. The settlement period was every 8 hours, three times a day. According to my calculations, the profits from my setup would be staggering because bitcoins had entered a stage of rapid growth since 2016.

一年后，我还把我的这个贷款办法写成博客分享给投资理财的朋友。虽然我知道这个市场非常小众。越多的人进来，我的利润率就越小。可是我抵挡不住与人分享挣钱方法的诱惑。独乐乐，与人乐乐，孰乐？看见因为我的分享，可以给其他人带来更多的财富与快乐，这会让我很开心。

A year later, I shared this setup with other forum users who were interested in investment and wealth management on my blog. Even though I knew that it was a niche market, which implied that the more the new market entrants, the lower my profits would be, I still could not resist the temptation of sharing how to make money with others. Happiness is much sweeter when shared with others. Nothing is sweeter than seeing that my sharing also brings other people more wealth and joy.

然而好景不长，天有不测风云，就在我把机器和程序都设置好了，每天欢快地数钱的时候，另外一个新的打击就来了。

Yet the good days did not last long before another storm hit. Not long after I set up my machine and program and could finally indulge myself in counting my money, a new obstacle popped up.

09 最赚钱的列车

09 The Most Profitable Train Ride

中国把比特币给禁了。

Bitcoins are banned in China.

历史上中国不知道多少次把比特币禁掉了，因为比特币采矿、交易一半以上的量都来自中国。所以每次中国禁止比特币,都会引起市场的恐慌，价格的下跌。

This was not the first time that China had banned bitcoins. But every time when China imposed restrictions on bitcoins sparked fears in the bitcoin market because more than half of bitcoin mining and transactions came from China. After each round of new restrictions, bitcoin prices would drop.

应该说，中国政府对比特币的看法一直是处在一种暧昧和犹豫之中。2013 年后一开始是暗中观察的阶段，只要不违反金融管制条例，基本上是睁一只眼闭一只眼，偶尔对大陆的三大交易商上各种各样的紧箍咒。2017 年初把 ICO 都禁了，用来防止非法集资。

The Chinese government's previous response to bitcoins was more elusive and hesitant. In 2013-2017, the Chinese government was merely observing the bitcoin market. As long as bitcoin investors did not contravene any financial regulations, the authorities turned a blind eye to it notwithstanding some occasional tightening of regulations against the three biggest bitcoin exchanges in China. At the beginning of 2017, the Chinese government prohibited Initial Coin Offerings in order to curb illegal fundraising.

但是 2017 年秋天的那次禁令是把所有的交易所全部封杀了。而且政府也搞不清楚什么是 utility token（功能代币），什么是 security token （证券代币）， 什么是 coin（币），什么是 cryptocurrency （加密货币）。把所有的代币和电子币通通一律禁掉。所有的挖矿和交易所统统都明令禁止。

However, the ban in the fall of 2017 killed all crypto exchanges in China. Meanwhile, the government did not bother to distinguish between utility tokens, security tokens, coins, and cryptocurrencies. It banned all altcoins and digital currencies and shut down all mining activities and exchanges.

这次国家出台的禁止令之狠是前所未有的。国家传递的信号很明显，就是和电子货币相关的任何商业行为都不要在中国出现，政府打算自己发行央行的电子货币。政策力度之狠以至于有一个非常大的比特币交易公司，宣布关闭的时候干脆把自己公司的平台代码全部公开。表明的意思是以后再不做交易平台了，交易的平台代码都拿出来了，任何人都可以一夜之间成立一个交易平台。

China had never declared such an all-out war against bitcoin and other digital currencies before. The government's message was clear: Any business activities related to digital currencies would be eradicated in China. China's central bank was looking to issue its own digital currencies. Under such a harsh ban, a top bitcoin exchange in China even published the codes of its platform, implying that it would stop trading forever. With the code published openly, anyone can now establish a new exchange platform overnight.

比特币价格一路下跌。从 7000 多美元一路跌到 3000 美元。我虽然是放债，所有本金没有任何损失。但是我的利息挣来的比特币价格却跌了一半。经验告诉我，历史上一次次出现像这样情况的时候，都是投资的最好时候，那就是当所有人都绝望和放弃的时候。这次也不例外。

The government's decision dragged the bitcoin price from US$7,000 to US$3,000. Even though I did not lose any capital as a lender, the price of bitcoins that I earned from interest income dropped by 50%. My experience tells me that in mankind's history, the best investment opportunity arose when everyone lost hope. This time was no exception.

你看好一个资产，需要侧重看它的长期发展潜力，而不被一时的大众情绪所困扰。就像 2017 年浑水公司搅局揭露美国上市的中国互联网公司财务作假一样。2017 年那个时候是买入阿里巴巴这些公司股票的最好时机。不过我从来不炒股，所以可能可以不带感情色彩，作为局外人可以清楚地看清这一点。

When we try to evaluate the investment prospect of an asset, we should focus on its long-term potential and should not be affected by the overall sentiment in the market. For example, the best timing to buy the stocks of internet titans such as Alibaba is when Muddy Waters Research exposed the alleged financial fraud of China's internet companies in 2017. However, as I rarely trade stocks, this is probably why I can separate my emotions from my thinking and see the real picture.

如果了解比特币的人就会知道，比特币从设计之初就是一个屌丝造反的工具。一个国家禁止，甚至多个国家禁止都是没有意义的。除非整个地球人齐心协力都来禁止它。比特币的整个设计和核心思想就是禁不掉的。但是大部分人此时还是猖狂逃出，我可以看到价格一轮一轮地下跌。

Anyone who is familiar with bitcoins will know that they were originally designed by young, poor people as a tool to eliminate the role of the government. It is meaningless even if one or several countries ban it unless every person on this planet does so. The original design and core values of bitcoins cannot be banned. That being said, most people still chose to escape the market, driving bitcoin prices lower and lower.

很快我就找到了一个满地捡钱的机会。中国的交易所要关闭，所以大家都在抛售，短期内形成海外市场和中国市场有 20% 的差价。中国市场买，海外市场卖。卖了再买，买了再卖。我还记得当时非常不巧在中国出差，市场崩盘的时候，我正坐在京沪高铁列车上。时不待我，一路下跌我就一路买，凭空做差价，转一圈就是 20%的利润。那次火车大约是我这辈子坐过的最赚钱的火车了。忙得我都不想下火车，感觉自己怎么一抬头就到站了。

Soon I found another highly profitable opportunity. As Chinese bitcoin exchanges were closing, everyone was selling their bitcoins. In the short term, there was a 20% price difference between the foreign market and the Chinese market, which meant a lucrative opportunity for me to buy bitcoins in the Chinese market and sell them in the overseas market. I can still remember that I was unfortunately on a business trip to China at the time. When the Chinese market crashed, I was on a high-speed train from Beijing to Shanghai. I could not afford to miss the opportunities, so I kept buying bitcoins in the Chinese market and selling them in the overseas market to make a 20% profit while I was still on the train. The train ride was probably the most profitable trip in my life. It was so enjoyable that I did not even want to get off the train. Time flies when you have fun. I did not realize that I arrived at my destination.

这是比特币交易的一个特点，它是 24 小时连续交易。当然也是因为这个原因，做短线的人会很痛苦，也会很兴奋，他们感觉每一分钟都在赚钱，每一分钟也都在输钱。因为两边市场的差价不会持续很久，只有几个小时，稍纵即逝，所以我只能是忙着在火车上捡钱。

This is a characteristic of the bitcoin market: It operates 24/7. It is also because of this reason that short-term traders are in both stress and joy at the same time. They feel that they are making money every minute but also losing money at the same time. As the market difference will only last for a few hours, I could only trade on the train.

当时同样持坚定信念的是赵长鹏，他和合伙人在中国出台全面禁止比特币，大家纷纷退出的时候，创立了 Binance。让这个名不见经传的小交易所一跃成为全球最大的比特币交易中心，让他自己的照片也登在了美国财富杂志的封面上。那年 Binance 号称赚了 10 亿美元。其实没有什么神奇的，投资永恒的真理就是不要随大流。逆流而上，特立独行才能有机会。

At the time, Zhao Changpeng was another firm believer in the potential of bitcoins. When China cracked down on bitcoins and everyone was leaving the market, Zhang Changpeng and his partners founded Binance, which became the largest bitcoin exchange in the world seven months after its establishment. Zhang's photo was also on the cover of Forbes magazine. That year, Binance claimed that it made US$1 billion in profit, which was not surprising. The eternal truth in investing is to never follow the herd. You can only win the game if you are a contrarian in the market.

2017 年比特币经历了严重的内斗，分叉为比特币、比特币现金。后来比特币现金又分叉出 Bitcoin SV。每个人都表明自己的立场。我也就写了一篇博客，说明自己为什么是见证分离派。后来看来的的确确只有见证分离派站住了脚。比特币现金等其他分叉币价格都一落千丈。

In 2007, the bitcoin community broke apart into camps of bitcoins and Bitcoin Cash, which then forked in Bitcoin SV. Everyone made their stance clear. I also wrote a blog article to explain why I am a Segwit supporter. In retrospect, only the Segwit camp won. The price of other forks such as Bitcoin Cash collapsed.

我是隔离见证派 (2017 年 12 月 5 日)
I am a Segwit supporter (December 5, 2017)
by Bayfamily

我是隔离见证派(Segwit)，俗称核心党人。虽然我不齿于核心党的很多做法，比如 reddit 上的言论管制，开发组内部排斥异己。但是从技术角度来看，我认为隔离见证派技术路线是对的。

I am a Segwit supporter, also known as "decentralists." Even though I disapprove of the behaviors of the Segwit camp, for example, speech control on

Reddit and attacking those who hold opposite opinions, I think they have chosen the right path from a technical point of view.

比特币扩容之争愈演愈烈。隔离见证派(Segwit)和大区块派（big blocker）的殊死搏斗从比特币创立之初就开始了，一直到今年 8-11 月份达到最高潮。现在虽然平淡了下去，但是恐怕两派之间的缠斗会持续几十年。 世上很多伟大运动的开始到兴盛都符合这样一个规律。

1.一个奇特新颖的想法，横空出世

2.一群狂热铁杆份子追捧

3.渐渐势力变大，生存危机过去，狂热分子因为很小的一个事件，意见不统一，分成两派或者多派

4.进入主流，外部压力消失，两派为夺权进行生死搏斗

5.短期激烈矛盾告一段落，变成长期派系斗争，渐渐腐朽没落，成为社会进步的阻力

6.又一个新的想法，横空出世

On the issue of how to increase bitcoins' block size, the community was divided into proponents of Segwit and big blockers. Their heated debate has started since the advent of bitcoins and reached its climax in August-November this year. Even though the discussion was quieter, the fight between the two camps will probably persist in the next several decades. The development of many other great movements in the world also shows the following pattern:

1. First, a novel idea appears.

2. Second, the idea is promoted by a group of die-hard fans.

3. Then, the idea survives an existential crisis after gaining more influence. However, the community of die-hard fans was divided into two or more camps because of some disagreement over a small issue.

4. The invention has become a mainstream idea. External pressure disappears. The two camps fight for power.

5. The fierce, short-term disagreement turns into a long-term factional struggle. The community becomes more corrupt and a hindrance to the progress of society.

6. Another new idea appears.

有人说，比特币的发展史可以看到伊斯兰教的影子，逊尼派和什叶派因为继承人的事情，互相仇恨千年。也有人说比特币如中国革命，一开始，为了打倒满清和军阀，诞生了国民党和共产党，随后分家。当然你可以把比特币的历史看成中国革命史。星星之火，可以燎原，但是革命胜利了，文革各派就开始撕斗了。

Some also said that the development of bitcoins reminds them of the Islam religion. The conflict on the caliph between Sunni Islam and Shia Islam has persisted for hundreds of years. Another analogy is China's revolution against the Qing Dynasty and warlords that gave birth to Kuomintang and the Chinese Communist Party. These two camps had a serious feud after defeating the Qing Dynasty and warlords. You can also read the history of bitcoins as if you were reading the history of Chinese revolutions. Just as how a single spark can light a prairie fire, a small revolutionary belief has the power of overthrowing the government, but a civil war often ensues after the defeat of the government.

先简单科普一下技术层面的事情，什么是隔离见证，什么是大区块。

Let me give you some background information on the relevant technologies, for example, what Segwit and blockchain are.

比特币在创立之初，一个 block 的大小被限定在 1MB，中本聪自己的解释说，担心区块大了，会容易被黑客利用。他认为随着交易量的增大，block 的大小应该同步放大。这点上他的讨论被大区块派反复引用，认为见证分离派违背了创始人的意愿。如果从宗教情节上看，大区块派应该属于原旨主义者。而见证分离派认为，加大区块的容量是没有意义的，即使放大十倍，仍然无法最终满足全世界的交易。必须靠侧链和闪电网来扩容。而闪电网的扩容必须依靠修改原来主链上的数字签名的存储方式。需要把数字前面，就是支付的见证部分分离到另外一个文件中。 这就是见证分离派这个名词的来源。 从宗教意义上看，见证分离派属于改良派。

In the early history of bitcoins, the size of a block was limited at 1M. The creator of bitcoins, Satoshi Nakamoto, explained that a bigger block size will increase the chance of spam transactions hijacking blockspace. He believes that as the transaction volume increases, the block size should increase correspondingly. This point of view is often cited by big blockers in arguing that Segwit is contrary to the wishes of the creator. From a religious point of view, big blockers subscribe to originalism. Meanwhile, decentralists believe that increasing the block size is meaningless because even if the size is multiplied by a factor of 10, the bitcoin system will still be incapable of handling all the transactions in the world. They will have to rely on the lightning network and sidechains to expand the capacity anyway. And the expansion of the lightning network depends on changing the original storage format of the digital signature of the main chain. They will have to separate the witness part before the numbers into another document. This is why decentralists are also called Segwit, which stands for Segregated Witness. From a religious perspective, SegWit supporters belong to reformists.

如果你把见证分离派和大区块派关在一个屋子里，他们争吵的对话内容大概是这样的。

If you lock a decentralist and a big blocker in a room, you will hear the following conversation:

核心党：“喂，老兄，咱们的队伍一天天壮大，法币(fiat)快被咱们颠覆了，庆祝一下？”

Decentralist: Hi, bro. Now our bitcoin community is growing larger every day, and we have almost overthrown all fiat money. Let's celebrate it.

大块党：“庆祝个球啊，Visa 一秒钟的交易能力是几百万，咱们是七次， 都堵成北京二环了，咱们把区块改改大吧，1MB 实在不适应人民日益增长的交易需要啦，不扩大区块大小，我怎么用比特币买咖啡啊？”

429

Big blocker: What celebration? The transactional capacity of visa is several million per second, which is sevenfold our existing capacity. The traffic in our bitcoin system is so congested now. Let's increase our block size. The original size of 1MB can no longer suit the needs of our growing transactions. If we don't expand the block size, how can I use bitcoins to buy coffee?

核心党："改改改，改你个头啊，你别忘了，比特币所有的交易都存在公共账簿(public　　ledger)上，俺家的硬盘都快爆炸了，网络的节点数越来越少，你再扩大比特币就全完了，节点要多大的硬盘啊。你没看见节点数年年在下降。"

Decentralist: Are you insane? Don't you forget that all bitcoin transactions are stored in a public ledger? Our hard disk is exploding! The number of network nodes is shrinking. The expansion will mean the death of bitcoins. All these nodes will require a gigantic hard disk. Besides, the number of nodes is decreasing every year.

大块党："你别吓唬我，摩尔定律你懂不懂，硬盘越来越便宜你知道不？就算明天咱们把区块扩大到 1 个 G，你买个 100T 的硬盘，要几十年才能填满，你有啥好担心的。"

Big blocker: What a nonsense. Haven't you heard of Moore's law? Hard disks will only get cheaper. Even if we expand our block size to 1G, we can buy a 100T hard disk that can handle several decades of storage needs. Your worry is unjustified.

核心党："那终极之战呢？你听说过中国的万里长城不？100T 的数据咋跨越长城呢？100T 的数据怎样上 TOR 呢？"

Decentralist: What about the end game? Haven't you heard of the Great Firewall in China? How can 100T of data pass through the Firewall? How can 100T of data pass through TOR?

大块党："别吓唬我，哪有啥终极之战，就算有终极之战，对付政府的最好办法是人海战术，你懂不懂，要是每个屌丝都用比特币买咖啡了，终极之战来临那天，政府不让大家买咖啡了，他们就会揭竿而起。你要是把比特币弄成一个结算网络，终极之战来临那天，谁管你啊。"

Big blocker: There is such a thing as an end game. Even if there is one, the best way to fight against the government is through crowd tactics. If every poor and broken user of bitcoins can use their bitcoins to buy coffee and the government bans bitcoins, everyone will wage a war against the government. If you turn bitcoins into a clearing system, everyone will ignore you when the end game comes.

核心党："你是不是怀有二心啊，怎么天天想加大区块大小啊，我瞅你们那帮小子都是矿工，而且用 ASIC 挖矿，是不是为了你的矿场赚钱，天天催着扩大啊。"

Decentralist: What a traitor. Why are you always thinking about increasing the block size? The only explanation is that you and other big blockers are all miners using ASIC. You are advocating an increased block size only because you want to make bigger profits.

大块党："你是不是申请了闪电网的专利啊，主链不让扩容，这样闪电网以后你就可以狠得劲的收费啊。"

Big blocker: I am sure that you have applied for a patent of the lightning network. You are against expanding the main bock so that you can charge more on the lightning network.

核心党："狠得劲收费，我，我干吗要害死比特币啊，比特币可是我一手抚养大的啊。"

Decentralist: What will I gain if I kill bitcoins by charging expensive fees on the lightning network? Bitcoins are like my children.

大块党："你小子是不是 GMBOX 那场风暴，把比特币都丢光了啊，这是堵死比特币，弄死比特币的节奏，然后趁机低价捡漏啊。"

Big blocker: Then it must be that you lost all your bitcoins during the GMBOX storm. You are trying to ruin the bitcoin system so that you can buy the dips.

核心党： "你是不是偷偷买了不少以太坊,辣条啊，弄死比特币然后发财啊。"

Decentralist: You are the only one who bought a lot of Ethers and Litecoins. You are trying to kill bitcoins so that you can make a fortune.

大块党： "血口喷人，你违背中本聪先生的训诫，算力为王。"

Big blocker: That's a dirty lie. You ignore the teachings by Satoshi Nakamoto. Hashrate is the king!

核心党： "啥算力为王，俺们要的就是算力去中心化，特别你们是躲在万里长城后面的算力，我要弄个比特金(BTG)，终结你们 ASCI 的算力。"

Decentralist: Hashrate is nonsense. We must decentralize hashrate, especially the hashrate behind the Firewall. We are going to create a Bitcoin gold (BTG) to end the hashrate of your ASCI.

大块党： "你们这是，开发中心化，也违背中本聪先生的原意，我要弄个比特现金(BCH),和你们分道扬镳。"

Big blocker: What you guys are doing is centralizing bitcoins. This is contrary to the spirit of bitcoins.

你瞧，本来的一个技术问题，渐渐变成了一个政治问题，人格问题。吵到这里，你知道这已经是不可调和的矛盾了。 我们人类解决不可调节的矛盾，经验丰富，最常用的办法就是在肉体上消灭对方。 于是有了香港协议，纽约协议，于是有了硬分叉，Bitcoin Cash, Bitcoin Gold，有了算力攻击，有了 11 月份冻僵 BTC 的技术建议。

As you can see, a technical problem has slowly turned into a political problem and personal attacks. It has become an unresolvable conflict. Mankind is no stranger to unresolvable conflicts. The most common method is to destroy our opponents physically. This is why we have the Hong Kong Agreement, New York Agreement, hard forks, Bitcoin Cash, Bitcoin Gold, hash rate attack, and technical suggestions that froze BTC in November.

第十七章 从 100 到 1000 万（三）比特币
Chapter 17: From $1 million to $10 million (3): Bitcoins

隔离见证派和大区块派的意见我看了很多。总的来说，我觉得隔离见证派占了上风。让比特币唯一能够灭亡的其实是政府，而且必须是大国的联合行动。可惜的是大部分政府现在可能还没明白过来这个问题。

I have read numerous arguments from both Segwit and Big block camps. Overall, I think decentralists are winning the race. The only thing that can eliminate bitcoins is governments, or to be more precise, large-scale cooperation between top economics. However, most governments have not realized this yet.

明白过来最快的是各种专制政府。你瞧禁止比特币的急先锋是委瑞内拉，越南，摩洛哥。因为他们知道比特币最先动摇的是这些专制政府脆弱的法币。

The countries that have already figured this out are the authoritarian governments and dictatorships. Countries such as Venezuela, Vietnam, and Morocco are among the first batch of countries to ban bitcoins because they know that bitcoins will be a huge blow to their ailing currency.

天朝还有点稀里糊涂的。其实比特币终结的是美元霸权，天朝这样的比特币矿业大国趁机可以上位。不抓住时机，反而搞起来了不许片板下海的锁国政策。和当年烧了郑和宝船的傻瓜官员们是一个路数。

China is still confused about what the bitcoin revolution entails. Bitcoins are an attempt to end the dollar's global dominance. Such a large bitcoin mining country as China should have grasped the opportunity brought by bitcoins instead of banning them in the country. Such a ban is no different from how in the Ming Dynasty, the Chinese officials burned down the most famous Chinese explorer Zheng He's ships.

巴菲特（可能是谣传）说，如果中国政府都禁不了比特币，其他国家就不要想了。我觉得他说的不一定对，世上只有一个国家可以禁掉比特币，那就是三胖领导的国家。除非人类社会重回那个时代，比特币恐怕很难根除。

It is rumored that Warren Buffett once said that if the Chinese government fails to ban bitcoins, all other countries have no hope of succeeding. I do not think this is true. If there is only one country in the world that can successfully ban bitcoins, it has to be North Korea. Unless all other human societies are governed by a similar regime, bitcoins will be here to stay.

在我看来，比特币存在的价值在于美国这样的政府无法消灭它，而不是多快被大多数人使用。这点必须从技术层面保证才可以。再多的人使用比特币，政府一句话也就没有了。俺们在天朝上国待过，知道人多这事不一定靠谱。而大区块派的确会让比特币变得更加容易被技术上消灭和禁止。

In my opinion, the value of bitcoins is that such a government as the U.S. cannot eliminate it but not how fast its user base grows. The wide circulation of bitcoins needs to be backed up by relevant technological capacities. The government may still easily eliminate bitcoins regardless of how widely circulated they are. I was born and raised in China, so I know that the popularity of a certain invention is no guarantee of its value. Big blocks will indeed render bitcoins more vulnerable to bans.

当然比特币的信徒认为从技术上美国这样的政府也无法消灭比特币，美国政府可不一定这样认为。 人世间一切战争都在于有一方误判了形势。如果胜负结果明显，战争是打不起来的。比特币如果开始全面流行和使用，最终政府会被逼到死角。因为现有的税收体系会崩溃，无论是企业税还是个人税，现有的几乎所有的金融体系基本上全部推倒重来。不但是华尔街基本要完全关门，连华盛顿都要关门。因为政府没有比特币，也无法从税收上获得比特币，除了能印没人认的美元，没有经济来源。

Of course, supporters of bitcoins believe that such a superpower as the U.S. is not capable of eliminating bitcoins, but the U.S. government may think otherwise. All wars in human history stem from a misjudgment about the enemy. If who will be the winner is crystal clear, there will be no war. If bitcoins are used by everyone in the world, the existing tax systems, including corporate tax and income tax and financial systems will collapse. The government will be backed into a corner. Not only will Wall Street shut down, so will Washington D.C. because the government cannot own bitcoins nor collect them as tax. Other than printing U.S. dollars that are no longer recognized, the government will have no income.

比特币要颠覆的不仅是金融体系，也包括现有的税收，政府体系。政府岂能善罢甘休，不殊死一搏呢？

Bitcoins are not only looking to decentralize the financial system but also the existing tax system and the government. How can the government stand such a decentralized innovation? How can the government not fight back?

像所有的货币一样，比特币的价值在于信心。未来遥远的事情，会映射到今天，影响到今天的价格。认为比特币是泡沫的人，选择不信比特币，可能是高估政府的能力。比特币的铁杆粉丝，Holder（持有者）们可能也是低估了政府可能的手段和决心。终极之战如何演绎，我后面会慢慢写来，一切还是未知数。

Similar to all other currencies, the value of bitcoins lies in trust. People's expectations of the distant future will be reflected in today's prices. Those who opine that bitcoins are a bubble and do not believe in bitcoins may have overestimated the power of the government. Meanwhile, holders and die-hard fans of bitcoins may have underestimated the government's determination and resources. I will talk about how we should interpret the end game later. The future is full of unknowns.

当人们想到终结之战的时候，一切能增加比特币胜算的，我觉得都是对比特币好的。所以仅凭这点，我就是核心党，隔离见证派。

If our main consideration is the end game, anything that can increase the chance of bitcoins winning is a good development. Therefore, I am a decentralist.

10 长期持有

10 Holding Bitcoins for the Long Term

但是我也不是神仙。赚钱的事情让人永远难忘。亏损的事情我也没有少干，应该说电子货币在一开始鱼龙混杂，各种骗子都有。

But I am in no way perfect. Even though I did have some success in trading bitcoins, losses were not uncommon in my journey. Or I should say the crypto market is full of all kinds of players, including scammers.

2017 年的时候，我自己当时错误的想法就是觉得应该分散投资。因为比特币的分叉风波，让我感到比特币来自内部的风险要大于来自外部的风险。一个方法就是分散投资一部分资产，因为我也不确定比特币是不是能够获胜。我觉得未来的趋势肯定是电子货币，因为电子货币应用的功能太强大了，不单是点对点支付，更多的应用还包括财富的管理、会计、公司管理、保险证券的点对点分散化。

In 2017, I mistakenly believed that I should diversify my risks. The controversy of bitcoin forks made me feel that most of the risks of bitcoins are internal than external. Therefore, I should diversify my portfolio because I was not sure whether bitcoins would win the competition. But I was certain that the future belonged to digital currencies because of their powerful functions. Not only do they support P2P payments, but they also facilitate the P2P diversification of wealth management, accounting, business management, insurance, and stocks.

所以我把我拥有的比特币相当一部分拿出来分散投资去购买各种山寨币。现在看来这是一个错误的做法。分散投资并没有给我带来良好的收益。因为鱼龙混杂，骗子也多。很多山寨币在 17 年之后下跌了 100 倍之多。

Therefore, I took out a certain portion of my bitcoins to diversify my risks by buying some altcoins. In retrospect, this was an erroneous move. Diversification did not bring me better returns. The crypto market is full of all kinds of players, including scammers. The prices of many altcoins declined by more than a factor of 100 after 2017.

山寨币风波之后，有一个观点我自己也不是特别肯定。那就是区块链唯一的应用可能只有比特币。除此之外，可能区块链没有其他的任何可以落地的功能。因为不管怎么说，区块链都是一个速度和效率非常低的数据库。这样一个数据库，总是不如集中式的数据库，或者不如几个集中式数据库更有效率。除了储蓄货币，其他所有的交易都可以在相对集中或者半集中的数据库中实现。比如中国和 Facebook 在研究发行的电子货币虽然也都是打着区块链的旗号，而实际上是一个集中或者半集中的数据库系统。

After the altcoin incident, I had doubts about another point of view: the only blockchain application is bitcoins. Apart from bitcoins, it seems that blockchain does not have other valuable functions because, after all, blockchain is a low-efficiency and low-speed database. Such a database cannot compete with a centralized database. It is also not as efficient as several centralized databases. Other than the function as a reserve currency, all other transactions can be completed in a centralized, or semi-centralized, database. For example, even though China and Facebook use the label of "blockchain" in developing their digital currencies, the database is, in fact, a centralized or semi-centralized system.

我在写这本书的时候，中国和 Facebook 的电子货币还没有出台。Libra 可能因为政府监管胎死腹中。但是在我看来，金融市场从传统的银行系统的垄断一直转到新的一种经营方式，新的一种货币方式恐怕是难免的。因为道理很简单，我们人类在过去 5000 多年甚至更久远的时间里，其实只用了一种货币就是黄金，我们用法币 Fiat 系统其实只是从 1972 年到今天，仅仅 50 年。

As of writing this book, the Chinese government and Facebook have not debuted their digital currencies yet. Perhaps Project Libra has been aborted because of government regulations. That being said, as the financial market evolves from a traditional bank-dominated system to a new way of operation, the advent of a new currency is inevitable. The logic is simple. In the past 5,000 years or even dating further back, mankind used one kind of currency only which is gold. The current fiat money system that has been adopted since 1972 has a short history of 50 years.

在美元黄金脱节之前，人们使用美元，本质上是使用黄金作为货币。而历史上所有的法币系统最终都失败了。去世界各地旅行的人们，无论是去西亚如伊朗、东亚如韩国、东南亚如越南、南美如阿根廷，都会注意到世界上的货币怎么那么多个零。 数数全世界各国货币上零的个数，你就知道靠政府限制货币滥发是多么不靠谱的事情。历史上所有的法币最后都变得一钱不值。从中国元代的宝钞，到今年的委内瑞拉。历史上一个又一个国家印刷的法币最后都变成废纸。我没有任何理由会相信，现在拥有的货币系统会持续200 年或 300 年的历史。

Before the decoupling of the U.S. dollar from gold, when people were using the U.S. dollar, they were essentially using gold as their currency. Yet all fiat money systems in mankind's history failed in the end. Those who have been to Western Asia such as Iran, Eastern Asia such as Korea, South-Eastern Asia such as Vietnam, or South America such as Argentina will notice that some banknotes have countless zeros on them. Counting the zeros on banknotes issued by different governments, you will know that relying on the government to exercise self-constraint in printing money is meaningless. All fiat money in mankind's history, ranging from Baochao in China's Yuan Dynasty to bolívar in modern Venezuela, became worthless in the end. In our history, all the fiat money printed by different regimes became wastepaper in the end. I have no reason to believe that the current fiat money system will last for 200-300 years.

法币除了滥发的可能性之外的另外一个问题就是，今天的法币银行系统被政府给搞死了。比如我曾经有一个印度的客户，想购买我的一点商品，但是在印度要把卢比换成外汇，那是一件非常复杂和困难的事情。再比如我们普通人在商品交易的时候，每一笔钱都需要通过银行来中转。而政府为了税收和防止洗钱，可以追踪每一笔钱的运转。这让人觉得很烦。

In addition to the over-printing of money, another problem is that today's fiat money banking system is a major source of nuisances that are a result of government's intervention. Take my personal experience as an example. I once had a customer from India who was trying to order some goods from me. As he was based in India, he needed to first convert Rupee into foreign currency, which was a highly complicated and difficult procedure for him. In daily transactions, our money needs to go through banks so that the government can trace it. This requirement is very annoying.

因为我们社会上不是所有的事情都是那么清清白白的，可以说清楚的。也不是所有的事情，政府都会给你讲道理的。因为和政府讲道理本身就要花很高的成本。就像我当时没有办法把上海的房子卖掉，把钱转到美国来投资一样，因为我惧怕这些麻烦。

Not everything is as clear as black and white. Not everything is explainable. And the government may not give you a chance to explain yourself every time. Furthermore, explaining yourself to the government involves a high cost. This is exactly why I did not choose to raise money for my U.S. investments by selling my investment property in Shanghai. I was scared of all these troubles.

也许你的交易是一些游走在法律和非法之间的灰色地带的经济活动。比如你可能是卖大麻的。还有一些是来自某地区的跨境交易，比如也许你是一个政治犯。比如像我之前写的文章里头，也可能发生了战乱，你需要逃亡，这个时候比特币是比任何一种货币都方便储存和安全携带财富的方式。或者也许你就是天然地不喜欢政府，不想让政府知道太多你财产的事情。这个时候就会选择比特币。

Perhaps your business is an economic activity that is in the gray area of the law, for example, a marijuana dealer. Perhaps your business involves a cross-border transaction. Perhaps you are a political criminal. Perhaps you need to escape from a war in your country. These are the times when bitcoins are a much safer and portable form of wealth. Perhaps you do not like the government. Or perhaps you do not want the government to have too much information about your net worth. These are the moments when you will choose bitcoins.

所以不是比特币本身太强大了，而是法币的服务太差了。政府滥用了控制法币的能力，让所有的交易都需要走金融机构。今天你可以从中国订购一个商品，走 Fedex 24 小时就可以送到，你可以实时通讯和地球上的任何人视频对话。但是今天一个跨境的汇款往往要 3-5 天的时间。

Therefore, it is not that bitcoins are too powerful. It is just that the service provided by fiat money is unsatisfactory. Governments abuse the fiat money system by requiring all transactions to go through financial institutions. Today, you can buy a product in China and receive it within the next 24 hours through FedEx. You can communicate instantaneously with the rest of the world through a video call. However, a cross-border money transfer often takes 3-5 days.

11 什么是钱

11 What is Money?

在我小的时候，大家学物理的时候都很崇拜牛顿。我的物理老师当时曾用叹息的口吻说，牛顿在做完三大力学杰出贡献之后，去英国当钱币局的局长，实在太可惜了。

When I was younger, all my classmates idolized Isaac Newton when we were studying physics. My then physics teacher sighed and said, "What a pity that Newton decided to take up the post of warden of the Royal Mint, a coinage department, after discovering the laws of motion."

然而今天看来英国金融的霸权，全靠钱币局的牛顿局长。牛顿其实只是用了一个非常简单的方法就让英国实现了金融霸权。那就是金本位。让政府来管理货币发行量是一个很恐怖的事情，这就好像是让猫来管理金鱼一样。政府有一万个理由会愿意印出更多的货币，特别是在它缺钱的时候。而政府总是缺钱，有的时候还会特别缺钱。

Yet the reason why the U.K. enjoys a financial hegemony today is all because of Isaac Newton of the Royal Mint. He used a very simple way to help Britain achieve a financial hegemony that is the gold standard. Entrusting the government with the task of issuing currency is terrifying. It is analogous to letting a cat manage a goldfish.

The government has a million incentives to print more money, especially when it ran out of money. And the government always needs more money.

投资理财到最后都不知道什么是钱，岂不是笑话。我为此专门写了一个博客，"什么是钱"。

It will be embarrassing if an investor does not know what money is. Therefore, I specifically wrote an article titled "What is Money?"

什么是钱? (2017 年 11 月 2 日)

What is Money? (November 2, 2017)

by Bayfamily

投资理财的首要任务可能也是搞明白到底什么是财富，什么是钱。这个问题不搞清楚，就贸贸然投资理财，难免会犯各种投资错误。

The first task for any investor is to understand what wealth and money are. If they make their investments before figuring out these two questions, mistakes are inevitable.

财富和钱两个词通常大家都混用。房地产，食物这些实实在在为我们提供服务的物件，很容易理解他们是财富的一部分。这个道理连猴子都明白，所以动物会为领地大打出手。

"Wealth" and "money" are often used interchangeably. And it is easy to see why the items that tangibly serve us, such as real properties and food, are also wealth. Even monkeys understand this. This is why they often fight for territory.

股票虽然能够带来红利，对于猴子而言，恐怕难以理解这是财富。事实上，股票的财富是需要借助于现代社会的基础建设(infrastructure)，能够把未来的可能的收入折现到今天。这里面包括证券市场，包括政府保证股份公司按照法律运行，按照股份比例分红。当这个社会结构不再存在的时候，股票也就灰飞烟灭不值钱了。

Even though stocks can also generate profits, it is difficult for monkeys to understand that they are a form of wealth. In fact, the stock price today represents possible future income thanks to the infrastructure of modern society. Examples of modern infrastructure include the stock market and a legal system that ensures listed companies act in accordance with the law and protects the interests of all stakeholders. When our society structure ceases to exist, stocks will also become worthless.

提到财富，人们会很自然想到黄金，白银这些东西。黄金和白银数千年来作为流通工具而渐渐变成了财富的象征。你瞧，Trump 总统都是一个黄金狂。啥东西都是金色的。

When the word "wealth" pops up, gold and silver will naturally spring to mind. After being a currency for thousands of years, gold and silver have become a symbol of wealth. For example, President Trump is a big fan. Everything in his home is covered in gold.

但是我想告诉大家，黄金，白银，宝石，艺术品，这些都不是财富。是的。我没有写错。他们不是真正意义上的财富。因为他们本质上不提供任何服务，不分红。对于猴子而言，他们一钱不值，一吨黄金都不如一个苹果。千万不要轻易觉得猴子傻，猴子恐怕觉得我们是神经病。到底谁傻，谁是神经病，恐怕很难说。我们觉得黄金是财富，有价值，是因为我们生活在幻影中，这是一个持续了几千年的幻影。这个幻影可以用一句话概况，就是

"后面会有人可能用更高的价格买入。"

However, I want to tell everyone that gold, silver, other precious metals, and art pieces are not wealth. Yes, you have read it right. Strictly speaking, they are not wealth because they do not provide any services or generate profits. To monkeys, these items are worthless. They would rather take a ton of apples than gold. While you may think that monkeys are dumb, monkeys probably think that we are nuts. It is difficult to say who are the dumb and crazy ones. The reason why human beings think that gold is wealth and valuable is that we live in an illusion that has lasted for thousands of years. The illusion is: "There will always be people who are willing to buy it at a higher price."

只要这个幻影一直持续下去，黄金白银宝石就会一直有价值下去。但是记住这只是一个幻影，一个持续千年的幻影。虽然可能还会持续几千年，但是终究是人类自欺欺人的幻影。

As long as this illusion continues, gold, silver, and other precious metals will continue to be valuable. But do remember that this is merely an illusion, albeit one that has lasted for thousands of years. Even though it may stay for the next thousands of years, we are deceived by our own illusion.

我们人类最擅长的就是编织故事，制造幻影。买卖过股票的都知道其中的道理。公司本身赚不赚钱不是特别重要，而是大家以为公司未来会不会赚钱，或者说，会不会未来有更多人觉得公司的未来会不会赚钱最重要。

Our strength is that we are good at telling stories and creating illusions. Anyone who has traded stocks will have an idea about how the stock market operates. It does not matter whether a company is profitable. The key is whether the market thinks that the company will be profitable in the future. In other words, the fundamental question is whether there will be more people who believe that the company will be profitable in the future.

拿物理学做比较，财富的多少好比位移。如果用 PE ratio 估算股价,好比是用速度估算位移。如果用预期的 PE 估计股价，那就好比是用加速度估计位移。如果用大家未来共同预期的 PE 来估价，那就是位移的四阶导数了。用四阶导数估算位移无论怎么说都是编织幻影。

An analogy to the concept of company shares as a form of wealth is the concept of displacement in physics. Using the P/E ratio to evaluate the share price is similar to using velocity to evaluate displacement. Using the projected P/E ratio to predict the share price is similar to using acceleration to predict displacement. Using the P/E predicted by everyone to evaluate the share price is similar to using the 4th order derivative to calculate displacement. The common thread: It is all an illusion.

你也许会说，黄金有首饰的功能啊，做装饰品啊。你需要明白那是因为先有这个幻影，才有黄金的装饰功能。世界上黄澄澄亮闪闪的东西很多。而且大家之所以选择黄色，不是蓝色作为财富的象征，也是因为这个幻影。黄金的真实价值，只是在工业品上做催化剂，而且需求量很小。

Perhaps you will argue that gold can be used to make ornamental objects. My response is that it is precisely because of this illusion that gold is used as ornamental objects. There are countless golden and shimmering objects in the world. Besides, why do humans choose yellow instead of blue as a symbol of wealth? It is because of that illusion. The real practical value of gold is as an industrial catalyst, but such a demand is very small.

提到黄金不得不说的是货币。黄金的这个幻影之所以成立，是因为黄金几千年前率先成为了地球上唯一的跨越人类社会和地区的全球货币。所以我们不得不说说货币到底是什么。这样才能明白到底比特币有没有价值。

Gold was a currency for thousands of years. The formation of the gold illusion is because gold became the first global currency that transcends societies and geographical locations. Therefore, the next question we need to answer is, "What is a currency?" before we can determine whether bitcoins have a value.

人们日常习惯使用美元，人民币这些货币，时间虽然不是很久远，但是已经足以让大家渐渐忘记了什么是货币了。

In our daily lives, people are accustomed to using currencies such as the U.S. dollar and the Chinese Yuan. Even though the history of these currencies is not long, people have already forgotten what currency is.

贝壳，青铜，黄金，白银，纸币的历史大家都耳熟能详，我们先看看人类历史上其他的一些货币的例子。

As most of us are already familiar with the history of bronze, gold, silver, and paper money, let us look at some other examples of currency in mankind's history.

贝壳作为钱的历史过于遥远。当时没有记录下来，到底贝壳是怎样被用于钱的，怎样控制通货膨胀，怎样生产和消失的。结绳作为货币的方法在中国和南美洲的印加文化都有被记载过，但是细节也不是特别清楚。

The first example is shell money. Its history dates back to ancient times. At the time, our ancestors did not document why shell was being used as a currency, how they controlled inflation, how they manufactured shell money, and why it disappeared. Another example is knotted cords as money. There are records of knotted cords as money in ancient Chinese text and Inca civilization in South America, but the details were missing.

曾经太平洋上的某个岛国，用巨石作为货币。这个岛国的面积很小，据说小到岛上的人真诚问前来访问的人类学家，说，"朋友，这世上真的有个地方听不到海风的声音么？"

Once upon a time in a country on a Pacific island, people there used huge stones as currency. This island is so small that it is rumored that the residents asked the visiting anthropologist, "My friend, is there really such a place in the world where you cannot hear the sound of the ocean?"

这个岛上的人以巨石为货币。巨石一开始还搬来搬去，后来这些巨石连搬大家都懒得搬了。大家都知道那块巨石是哪家的。曾经有岛上的人去隔壁岛屿搬运巨石回来。快要上岸的时候，巨石不幸落入海里。 那些落入海里的巨石也被大家承认为货币，平时只要指指说那些巨石是谁家的，就完成了交易。

People on this island used huge stones as currency. At first, the residents would move the huge stones around. Later, they gave up because it was too much work. But everyone knew who owned which stones. One time, a resident of that island was trying to move a stone from a neighboring island. When he was about to step ashore, the stone dropped into the sea. And other people also recognized that the stone that dropped into the sea was currency. In a transaction, they just needed to point to the stone and identify its ownership.

再举一个例子，是眼前的活生生的例子。在加州的监狱里面，犯人把方便面作为货币。方便面有实际的作用，而且整齐便于携带。和在战俘营里面大家把香烟作为货币有异曲同工之妙。这不是最神奇的，神奇的是有些方便面流通太久，已经过了保质期，不能再食用，但是大家还是把它们作为货币。

A fourth example is a contemporary one. In California's prisons, the inmates use instant noodles as currency. These instant noodles have a functional value and are portable. This is similar to how prisoners of war used cigarettes as currency. But the most fascinating is that people will still use expired instant noodles that are no longer edible as currency.

我举这两个例子是为了清理我们头脑中很多关于货币的不一定正确的观点。这些观点有：

I raised these examples to clarify some misconceptions about currency. They include:

货币必须要政府背书。无论是监狱，海岛，战俘营，大家选择何种物质作为货币都是自愿行为。古代选择金银铜作为货币，也完全没有政府背书。历史上政府背书的货币屡屡崩溃，远的元代的宝钞。近的是民国的金元券，魏玛共和国的马克，委内瑞拉的货币。

The currency must be backed by the government. From the above examples of different settings, we can see that what material is being used as a currency is a voluntary behavior by the people. In ancient times, gold, silver, and copper were used as currency, but they were not backed by the government either. In contrast, we can see from our history that currencies backed by the government almost always failed, such as Baochao in the Yuan Dynasty, Jinyuan Juan issued by the Kuomintang in 1948, Mark issued by Deutsches Reich, and the Venezuelan Bolívars.

货币必须有价值。沉默在海底的巨石，过期的方便面都没有价值。政府印刷出来的纸币也没有价值。电子货币从物理上也没有价值。黄金白银本质上物理功能的价值不如青铜。

The currency must have an intrinsic value. Sinking stones and expired instant noodles do not have an intrinsic value, but they are still used as currency. Both the paper money printed by the government and digital currencies do not have an intrinsic value. The intrinsic and functional values of gold and silver are lower than that of bronze.

货币必须有生产成本。货币不需要成本，成本越小越好。只要能控制住总量就可以。这点比特币比起其他的 POS 的货币没有优势。难以获得的是控制总量，而不是反过来。

The currency must have a manufacturing cost. The correct view is that a currency does not necessarily involve a manufacturing cost. But if it does, a lower manufacturing cost is more preferable as long as the total amount of currency issued is controllable. In this respect, bitcoins do not have an advantage over other proof-of-stake currencies. It should be the total amount of currency issued that is difficult to obtain, not the reverse.

货币和物理价值无关。货币的本质是记账工具。哪种记账工具最方便，最便捷，最便于携带，最有私密性，最不容易被篡改，那么那种货币就会胜出。 这点电子货币无疑是胜利方。法币一方面是被政府滥发给害了，另外一方面是法币目前渐渐变成了一个实名制的货币。

The currency has nothing to do with its physical value. The nature of currencies is that it is a tool for recording transactions. The currency that is more portable, convenient, and private and cannot be easily tampered with will win. In this regard, it is no doubt that electronic currencies are the winners. On one hand, fiat money suffers from the government's overprinting. On the other hand, fiat money is now becoming a currency that operates on a real-name basis.

447

从目前比特币投资现场情况来看，和买卖股票不同。进入电子货币的钱一般都是单向流。就是进入电子货币的钱，拥有者感受到了空前的自由。不愿意再回到法币的束缚。电子货币像一个巨大的黑洞。 各国政府为了税收，为了防恐，为了防洗钱，为了莫名其妙的外汇管控，推广法币实名制，自己害死了自己的法币。

The current bitcoin market is different from the stock market. The money that goes into digital currencies is a one-way road. The owners of digital currencies feel unprecedented freedom, so they are reluctant to be confined by fiat money again. Therefore, digital currencies are like a giant black hole. In order to manage taxation, prevent terrorist activities and money-laundering, and control foreign exchange, governments worldwide promote a real-name system of fiat money. But this move pushes fiat money to its death.

那么问题就来了，在一个市场里，会不会有混用的情况。就像艺术品和黄金同时被大家当作财富收藏起来。一个市场里，会不会有多个货币同时存在。 这是比特币和法币之争，甚至比特币和 800 多个电子货币之争的关键问题。

But the problem is whether there will be a mix of different candidates in the market. For example, people treat both gold and art pieces as wealth and collect them. Is there a coexistence of various currencies in the same market? The battle is not only one of bitcoins versus fiat money, but also bitcoins versus more than 800 other digital currencies.

目前也是大多数人持有的观点，那就是你比特币再牛，估计也就是服务一个小众市场，搞点黄赌毒。和美元会并存相当长的一个时间。所以对于大部分老百姓可以看热闹一样无忧。

The majority views are that no matter how powerful bitcoins are, they only serve a niche market of criminals and that they will co-exist with the dollar for a very long time, so most people consider themselves a spectator in the battle.

我本人觉得这个不一定对。人类生活在同样的经济圈里，货币可能具备天生的排他性。法币和比特币如何演绎，以及平民老百姓如何防范风险。下文我再慢慢道来。

But I do not agree with this point of view. Currencies in the same economic circle will have a natural tendency to exclude one another. I will talk about how we should interpret the battle between fiat money and bitcoins and how normal, ordinary people manage the risks of bitcoin investments in the following article.

我对比特币也一直保持谨慎乐观的态度。就是未来也许很乐观，但是如果投资比特币一定要谨慎。不要一股脑倾家荡产买进去。反过来谨慎来自另外一方面，如果你是富人，你可能需要稍微分散一下自己的投资，特别是你的钱比较多的时候，分散一部分在比特币里。

As for me, I hold a prudent and optimistic attitude toward bitcoins. To be more specific, I am optimistic about the future of bitcoins. But meanwhile, we have to be conservative in investing in bitcoins. We should never go all in. Especially when you are rich, you need to diversify your portfolio by owning some bitcoins.

为了这个我还专门写了一篇博客文章，叫作"如何规避比特币的风险"。

Therefore, I specifically wrote a blog article titled "How Can Normal, Ordinary People Manage the Risks of Bitcoin Investments?"

普通人如何规避比特币风险 (2017 年 11 月 28 日)

How Can Normal, Ordinary People Manage the Risks of Bitcoin Investments? (November 28, 2017)

by Bayfamily

记得微信和支付宝刚刚出现的时候，很多中老年人的态度是不学习，不了解。觉得一辈子用纸币用习惯了。只要国家法律规定纸币还能用，自己可以一直保持下去。

I still vividly remember that when Wechat and Alipay first attracted our attention, the attitude of many middle-aged to elderly people was a reluctance to learn the new technologies because they felt that they were used to fiat money and that they could keep their old habits as long as fiat money was still backed by the government.

后来的结果可想而知。只用纸币的人从一开始无法打车，无法网上消费。现在渐渐地到菜市场和售货机无法购物了。

The consequence is obvious. They cannot hail a taxi, shop online, and shop in the wet market and vending machines now.

如果你认为规避比特币最好的办法就是不学习，不了解，不买卖，捂着耳朵不看世界。认为自己反正不参与加密货币的买卖，不持有电子货币，就没有风险，那么结果可能最终就像那些几年前的老爷爷、老太太一样。

You may think that the best way to manage the risks is by not understanding, learning, or using bitcoins. If you think that you can eradicate the risks by not participating in the bitcoin market, you may fall behind just as those grannies and grampies who refused to learn how to use Wechat and Alipay.

对于大多数的投资品，比如投资房和股票，的确不参与买卖就没有风险。 但是对于刚需产品，比如自己的自住房，不买和不卖的风险是一样的高。因为最后你会不得不买。 比特币等加密货币和普通投资品不太一样，因为它试图颠覆的是长久以来大多数人财富的赖以生存的基础，法币系统。

For most investment products, for example, investment properties and stocks, it is true that you will not bear any risks if you are a non-participant. However, for financial products that have a rigid demand, for instance, a principal residence, the risks for both market participants and spectators are the same because the latter will have to buy the product at some point. Cryptocurrencies such as bitcoins are different from ordinary investment products because the former try to overthrow the fiat money system that is the basis of people's wealth.

年轻的时候，自己第一次接触进化论的时候，一个观点花了相当的时间才想明白。达尔文老爷爷说，在一个生物节点上只能有一个物种存在。可是这和我们普通人的观察不一样啊，明明鸟儿都在吃虫子，为什么有那么多种

450

飞鸟呢？ 明明虫子都在吃叶子，为什么有那么多虫子呢？地上所有的草都在干一件事，完成光合作用和释放种子，为何地上那么多种草呢？

When I first came across the Darwinian theory, I spent quite some time on figuring out the principle that there can be only one species at every biological node. But it seemed to me that this runs contrary to our daily observation. All birds eat worms, so why are there so many different species of birds? All worms eat leaves, so why are there so many different species of worms? All grasses only do two things: photosynthesis and releasing seeds, so why are there so many different species of grasses?

后来随着自己观察的深入，渐渐理解了达尔文老爷爷的观察是对的。一个生物节点上，由于充分竞争的关系，经过足够长的时间，的确只能有一个物种存活下来。就像智人出现了，尼安特人就消亡了。白人在美洲出现了，印第安人就消亡或被同化了。

Later, as I deepened my understanding of the theory, I realized that Darwin's observation is correct. Because of full competition on the same biological node, only one species can survive after a sufficiently long time. This is why Neanderthals became extinct when Homo sapiens emerged and why Indians were assimilated when white people came to America.

今天套用达尔文老爷爷的理论看待货币，你也会想明白同样的道理，经过足够长的时间，在一个特定的社会空间里，只能有一种货币存在下来。无论是监狱，还是世界上任何的主权国家，人们都很快在用什么货币这个问题上达成共识。共识以外的会被无情抛弃。贝壳和金属没有同时作为货币通用，是金属取代了贝壳。监狱里只有一种流通货币，或者是香烟或者是方便面。1949 年国人突然一夜之间选择了袁大头作为实际的交易货币，取代了国民党的金元券。

Applying the Darwinian theory to currencies will help us understand that the survival of currencies also follows the same pattern: After a sufficiently long time, only one currency will survive in a certain society, whether it be the prison or any sovereign countries in the world. People will soon reach a consensus on the issue of currency.

451

Shell money and metal were not used as currency at the same time. What happened is metal replaced shell money. There is only one type of currency in prison: either cigarettes or instant noodles. In 1949, the Chinese chose Yuan Shikai silver coins as the medium of exchange to replace Jianyuan Juan issued by Kuomintang overnight.

今天在我看来，加密货币最终取代纸币应该是一个历史趋势。只是不知道哪种加密货币最终会胜出，何时现在的法币系统会被淘汰。如果硬要加一个概率是否比特币会成为主流世界货币的话，我觉得概率大约是 10%。

I believe that cryptocurrencies will replace paper money in the future. It is just a matter of time, and we do not know which cryptocurrency will win. I will also say that there is a 10% probability that bitcoins will become the world's currency.

10%的概率足以让我们每个人警惕。因为如果这个事件发生了，你手中的所有法币都会化为乌有。无论是当下你在银行的美元存款，还是未来的美元现金流，比如养老金，社会保险，养老金(pension)，债券股息等等。

We should be alert to a probability of 10%. If this possibility materializes, all the fiat money we own will become worthless, whether it be our USD bank savings, future USD cash flow, for example, pension, social insurance, and bond interests.

我的投资策略是钱少的时候要胆大，钱多的时候需要谨慎。所以对待10%可能性的事件，还是需要认真对待的。

My investment strategy is to be bold when poor and prudent when rich. Therefore, I will treat this incident of a 10% probability seriously.

我不建议直接买入比特币。尤其是大量的买入。比特币当前的价格在我看来，20%是底层的趋势，80%是投机者疯狂。没人知道比特币应该值多少钱。那些告诉你他们能预测未来的都是在豪赌。回头像 2013 那样暴跌 90%，你哭都来不及。

I do not recommend directly buying bitcoins, especially large purchases. I think 20% of the current bitcoin price is explained by an underlying demand or trend and 80% by speculation. No one knows the worth of a bitcoin. Those who tell you that they can predict the future are gambling. If bitcoin prices plummet by 90% again, like what happened in 2013, they will be doomed.

我的投资方式深受当年美国淘金时代，那个选择卖淘金工具而不是直接去淘金的人的影响。当很多人陷入比特币疯狂的时候，我选择出借给他们资金，获取高额利息，而不是去直接买卖比特币。然后用挣来的利息获得比特币。这样我的本金没有任何风险。

My investment philosophy is influenced by those who chose to buy and sell tools instead of flocking to dig gold in the Gold Rush era. When many people were crazy about bitcoins, I chose to lend them money at high interest rates instead of buying and selling bitcoins myself. I then used my interest profits to buy bitcoins. By doing so, I eliminated the risk of losing my capital.

针对加密货币革命成功上位引发的风险，我建议的策略是这样的。

1）学习了解加密货币的机理，使用，买卖。获得更多的信息和知识总是对的。跟上时代，避免头脑僵化，对于中年人尤其如此。

2）如果比特币上位成功，你大约需要 0.1-1 个比特币就足够了。想办法获得这点币。

3）密切观察比特币发展，在法币崩溃的前夜，大举借债。法币如果崩溃了，房子还是一样值钱，股票一样的值钱，只是换了一个计价符号。所以利用房子最大限度地尽可能多的借债，是发国难财的最好办法。这些债务随着法币的崩溃而化为乌有。这点地主们深谙其道，很在行，我不用多说。

4）法币的崩溃会从最弱那些国家开始。比如津巴布韦，委内瑞拉，越南之类的。你看全面禁止比特币的国家名单就会明白为何比特币挑战的是法币，为什么这些国家会紧张。如果比特币能够颠覆 10-20 个小国家的货币，那就是美国中国这些法币崩溃的前夜了。

5）技术角度关注闪电网上线时刻表和点对点小额支付增长趋势，前夜会出现爆炸性增长。

My recommended strategy on how to manage the risks brought by the cryptocurrency revolution is as follows:

1. Understand the mechanism of cryptocurrencies. Use them, buy them, and sell them. It never hurts to acquire more information and knowledge. Keep up with the society. Do not be stubborn (this piece of advice is especially applicable to the middle-aged).

2. If bitcoins are the winner in the evolution of money, you will need 0.1-1 bitcoin. Try to get your hands on it.

3. Keep a close eye on the development of bitcoins. When fiat money is about to collapse, borrow as much money as possible. If fiat money collapses, real properties and stocks will still retain their value despite the change in unit. Therefore, use your real properties as collateral to raise as much money as possible. This is the best way to profit off the collapse of the fiat money system. All your liabilities will disappear with the collapse of the system. I guess many landlords are already familiar with this point, so I will not go into detail.

4. The collapse of the fiat money system will start from weaker countries such as Zimbabwe, Venezuela, and Vietnam. Take a look at the list of countries that have banned bitcoins. You will understand the threat posed by bitcoins to fiat money and why these countries are so anxious. If bitcoins have successfully overthrown the currencies of 10-20 small countries, this is a sign that the fiat money system in China and the U.S. will soon collapse.

5. Keep a close eye on the timestamp server and the increase in peer-to-peer transactions on the lightning network. They will grow explosively the night before the collapse of the fiat money system.

这一切都取决于你对加密货币的理解，和终极之战胜负的判断。什么是终极之战，后面我再慢慢解释。

Success depends on your understanding of bitcoins and your judgment on who will win in the end game. I will explain what the end game is in my subsequent articles.

454

给你一个这几天的简单数据。Tether 的流入量每天增长率是 2%。这是美元法币转化成美元加密代币(USTD)的增长速度。大家都明白指数增长的厉害。如果这个加速度持续下去，不用多久，所有的美元法币都会被变成加密货币。

Let me show you some data. The increase in Tether daily transaction volume is 2%. This marks the speed of how USD fiat money is being converted into USDT, a blockchain-based currency. Given the power of compound interest and exponential growth, it is not difficult to see that it will not take long before all USD fiat money is turned into cryptocurrencies.

当然，你也可以选择无视这一切，像几年前的老爷爷老奶奶们一样。马照跑，舞照跳。毕竟 90% 的概率下，什么都不会发生。

Of course, you are free to ignore all this like those grannies and grampies. You can choose to carry on your life as usual because there is a 90% chance that nothing will happen.

关于比特币的讨论我在 2016 到 2018 年之间写了很多。其他的博客文章我贴在附录里面。感兴趣的读者可以去阅读。我们生活在一个科技快速发展，社会快速变化的世界。做一个与时俱进的投资者，你需要放眼世界，知晓世界每个角落发生的各种变化，这样才能把握更多的机会。无论是技术行业、房地产行业、还是股票金融市场。机会总是有的，每隔几年就有一次。

I have dedicated most of my articles written in 2016-2018 to bitcoins. I have attached them in the Appendix for those of you who are interested. We live in a world where technology is rapidly advancing and society is undergoing drastic changes. In order to be an investor that keeps up with all the changes, we need to adopt an international mindset by looking beyond what's happening in our own culture and country. Familiarizing ourselves with what is happening in other corners of the world can help us identify more opportunities. Whether it be in the technical field, real estate, stock market, or other financial markets, opportunities will present themselves every 3-9 years.

我自己在中国读研究生的时候。我的导师在 PC 机兴起的时候坚决不使用计算机。他认为没有什么东西比书本、杂志阅读起来更方便。久而久之，最后他错过了信息革命和互联网带来的所有好处与方便。

When I was a postgraduate in China, my supervisor was reluctant to use a personal computer because he believed that nothing was more convenient than reading from physical books and magazines. As time went by, he missed all benefits brought by the information revolution and advent of the internet.

后记

Epilogue

　　一开始网友劝我写这本书的时候，我是想写一些投资理财的道理，一些初涉生活的年轻人需要掌握的基本常识。特别是供刚刚移民美国不久的中国人做参考。但是后来写着写着，变成了一本记录我和钱之间关系的自传书。

When I was first urged by my friends on the forum to write this book, my plan was to write about some principles of investing and wealth management and basic knowledge that every young adult should possess. My original target audience was new Chinese immigrants to the U.S. But as I worked on my book, it turned into an autobiography on my relationship with money.

　　历史记录不可能完全真实，虽然我会努力这么做。但我不得不说随着岁月的推移，很多细节我可能记得不是那么准确。人的大脑就像一个巨大的过滤器，过滤网就是自己坚信的那些理念。过滤网会把一些有利于自己的证据保留下来，而滤除那些不利于自己信仰系统的内容。我自己恐怕也不能免俗，虽然我力求真实。写这本书的时候我的心态是一方面给我自己有个交代，也是给我们这个时代，我们这一代"洋插队"的人一个交代。

No matter how hard I tried to tell you the real stories, there are bound to be discrepancies between what happened in reality and my recollection. And I have to say that with the passage of time, I might not be able to recall the details accurately. Our brain is like a huge filter machine, with the filter membranes being our core beliefs. These membranes will filter out the evidence that runs contrary to our interests and core beliefs. I am no exception to this, however hard I tried to show you the real picture. I dedicate this book to myself and also my generation of Chinese who studied abroad.

另外一方面，我想说的是我不是财务专家、投资专家。我从来不懂怎样帮其他人理财。"没有人比你更在意你的钱。" 这句话从我小时候失去第一个猪娃娃之后，一直是我的警语。

I would also like to point out that I am not a finance or investment expert. I have no idea how to help others manage their wealth. "No one cares your money more than you do" is a lesson I learned after losing my first piggy bank that still serves as a helpful reminder today.

读者阅读我的博客过程中，可以看到我自己渐渐成长的过程。十多年前写的博客里面的细节内容，有些是错误的，或者幼稚可笑，或者是自相矛盾的。特别是在关于比特币上，很多想法当时也是欠考虑的。这都不要紧，我不想把自己伪装成一个未卜先知的财经算命师。所以无论是今天看来是对的还是错的观点，我都不作修改贴上来。但是随着时间的推移，我自己也在慢慢地成长。观点越来越成熟，也越来越成系统。文字能力有了很大的提高，文章越写越长。文思泉涌，写起文章来如马桶水一样滔滔不绝。冲了下去，又咕咕冒出来。最终到不得不写书的地步。

When readers are reading my blog, they can see how I have grown. Some of the details that I included in my articles more than a decade ago are erroneous, naïve, or self-contradictory. Especially when I was writing about bitcoins, most of my beliefs were not well-thought-out. But this does not matter because I do not want to present myself as a financial prophet who can predict the future. Therefore, I did not correct those arguments that have been proven wrong today. I attached them verbatim in this book. With the passage of time, I have also developed into a mature thinker with my own system of thoughts and improved my writing skills. As you can see from the blog articles, they also grew in their lengths because I was able to find more inspirations as I progressed. Sometimes I felt that I had endless ideas as if they were water in toilet flushing: You push the button, and the water disappears and then new water fills the toilet again. My flowing ideas are longing to be expressed.

读这本书很重要的原则，就是不要试图复制我曾经的经历。每一代人每一个人的经历都是不可复制的，因为周围的环境也都不一样。复制他人的人生，哪怕是投资的经历，又有什么意义。读者最好把它当作一个历史故事来看，从我一个小人物看到我们这个时代的历史缩影。并借鉴里面的故事来思考自己的投资方法与原则。

An important point to note for my readers is, "Don't try to copy my experience." The experience of every generation and every individual is unique because of different surroundings. Copying others' life experiences, even investment experiences is meaningless. My advice is that this book will serve my reader well if they read it as a biography or history book.

投资理财其实不复杂，概括起来就这么几点。因为我是理工科背景，所以我用流程图的方式来说明。

Investing and wealth management are not as complicated as they seem. Because of my background in science, I will use a flowchart to summarize the major takeaways for my readers.

Start： 投资理财最重要的起步还是了解自己。知道自己是一个什么样的人，自己擅长什么，不擅长什么？如果看到不足，那就努力去改变。当你发现无法改变的时候，也要认清形势，做自己擅长的事情。最主要的是确定自己是勤快人，还是懒人？在充分效率的市场，就应该用懒人投资法。在非充分效率的市场，那就应该用勤快人投资法。

Start: The most important step is to understand yourself: who you are and what your strengths and weaknesses are. Work on your weaknesses. If you realize that you cannot change something, you should try to recognize the situation and multiply your strengths. The fundamental question is: Are you a lazy person or a diligent person? In a fully competitive market, you should use my "Investment

459

Strategies for Lazy People." Otherwise, apply my "Investment Strategies for Diligent People."

Step 1：牢记从机场接我的老中的美国五条生活指南，并付诸行动。这五条理财真经是：提高信用分数、避免超前消费、开二手车、亲自修理、不打官司多运动。

Step 1: Bear in mind the five tips by my Chinese American friend who picked me up at the airport when I first arrived in the U.S. and apply them in your life. They are:

improve your credit score,

avoid spending beyond your means,

drive second-hand cars,

repair everything yourself, and

don't get yourself involved in a lawsuit and work out more.

Step 2：勤俭是一种美德。虚荣是人性的弱点需要克服。热爱劳动的人是美的，四体不勤的人是丑陋的，树立积极向上的三观。

Step 2: Frugality is an enriching virtue. Pride is a weakness that we need to overcome. Hardworking people are attractive and lazy individuals are ugly. Always be proactive, hardworking, and optimistic.

争取做一个特立独行的人。端正自己的价值观，不要人云亦云。不要在意别人怎么说，怎么看。人们往往被心魔所累。举个例子，祥林嫂辛辛苦苦挣来的钱本来可以吃好穿好用好，但是她为什么要到庙里去花自己那么多钱，去建一个门槛呢？因为她有心魔。她不确定人死后有没有鬼，于是便来问鲁迅先生。当她依旧不知道死后，她之前的两个丈夫会不会来抢她的时候，她就会倾其所有去捐一个门槛，寻找一些心灵的安静。

Be a contrarian. Establish your own values. Resist the impulse to follow the herd. Do not attach too much emphasis on what others think of you. Human beings are trapped by their own beliefs. For example, in Zhufu (New year's sacrifice, also translated as Benediction), one of Lu Xun's most important works, the protagonist

Aunt Xianglin could have had better material life with the money she saved. Why would she donate all her money to a temple and lived a miserable life? Because she suffered from her own beliefs in oppressive feudal ethical codes. She was not sure whether there was an afterlife, so she asked Mr. Lu Xun. As she was not sure whether she would be cut into halves in hell because of her remarriage after the death of her first husband, she donated all her money to the temple in hopes of preventing such a torture in the afterlife and finding some inner peace.

今天喜欢买爱马仕 LV 的人，能把这个公司的主人买成世界上第 3 首富。本质上就是千千万万个患有心魔的人捐款捐给他导致的。不同的时代有不同的心魔，现在我们回首看看祥林嫂觉得傻得可怜。未来的人看看我们今天省吃俭用购买奢侈品的行为，也会觉得我们傻得可怜。

Thanks to fans of luxury brands such as LV, Céline, and Bvlgari, Bernard Arnault, the chairman and CEO of LVMH Moët Hennessy, is now the third richest man in the world. His wealth comes from people who suffer from their own beliefs. People from different generations have their own battle to fight. We think that Aunt Xianglin is a pitiful victim of oppressive feudal ethics. Our future generation may think that we are slaves to luxury brands.

财富是我们辛苦劳动获得的，我们应该用它去购买自己真正需要的东西。用财富获取生活的自由，而不是满足虚荣心。我自己虽然节俭，但是在我投资很紧张的时候，也无偿捐助过一个在美国的中国留学生。当时他博士学费有难处，我给了他 5000 美元，不求归还。钱需要用到真正值得用的地方上去。有了正确的三观，你就可以实现古人所说的不以物喜，不以己悲，知道自己要干什么，自己需要什么。

We work hard to accumulate our wealth, so we need to use it to purchase the things that we truly need. We should use our wealth to pursue freedom and let go of our vanity. Even though I am a frugal person, I lent a helping hand to a Chinese Ph.D. student by gifting him US$5,000. I made good use of my money. With good values and beliefs, we will be able to detach our feelings from our physical possessions, know the direction of our life, and what we need.

Step 3：你永远都是可以把三分之一的收入存下来的，因为比你收入低三分之一的人活得好好的。不要超前消费。除了房子，不要借债。投资是需要资本的。我们今天生活在资本主义的顶峰时代。靠出卖劳动力，赚取工资是永远不会财务自由的。想不明白这点可以多玩几次大富翁游戏。

Step 3: You are always capable of saving one-third of your income because those who have 2/3 of your income are still living their lives. Do not spend beyond your means. Do not borrow money, except for a mortgage. You need capital for investing. Today, we are at the peak of capitalism. You can never achieve financial freedom by selling your labor for a wage. If you do not understand this, my recommendation is to try to play the Monopoly game.

Step 4：检查自己是否完成了 Step 1，Step 2，和 Step 3。没有完成，回到 Start。

Step 4: Check if you have finished steps 1-3. If you have not, go back to "Start."

投资不要成为守财奴一样地守着现金，要勇敢地把存下来的钱投资出去。学习"会走路的钱"基本原理。找到合适你的投资机会。对于普通家庭，首先推荐住宅类建筑投资。因为那是政府给你的福利。

You must not insist on holding all your wealth in cash. You need to be brave in putting your money to good use in different investments. Learn the basic "Money Walks" principle. Find investment opportunities that suit you. For ordinary families, I recommend real estate investing because it is a government welfare for you.

学习知识，至少需要系统学习微观经济学、宏观经济学、资产管理这三门课。不能只是当评书听听，最好是有作业的那种课。

Acquire more knowledge. You need to at least study microeconomics, macroeconomics, and asset management in a systematic manner. You cannot simply receive the knowledge passively. Engage yourself with the knowledge by choosing courses that require output from you.

Step 5：如果你是懒人。请参考懒人投资法。寻找充分效率市场，做一些税法优化。End。

Step 5: If you are a lazy person, please refer to my "Investment Strategies for Lazy People." Find markets that are fully competitive. Optimize your tax. If you are a diligent person, read on.

Step 6：如果你是勤快人。请用勤快人投资法。寻找非充分效率市场，去 Step 7。

Step 6: If you are a diligent person, use "Investment Strategies for Diligent People." Look for markets that are not fully competitive. Go to step 7.

Step 7：造一个自己能够滚动起来的赚钱机器。可以通过 Timing 住宅市场实现这点。住宅市场是可以 Timing the market 的。股票市场是不可以的。保持杠杆，用银行的钱去挣钱。

Step 7: Set up a self-operating machine that will keep making money for you. You can achieve this by timing the residential real estate market. You can time the real estate market but not the stock market. Maintain your leverage. Use the bank's money to make more money for yourself.

End

你瞧，写起代码来不过 7 个步骤。那些理财产品、教育基金、养老保险都可以统统不用考虑。因为没有人会比你更在意你的钱。

You see, it consists of seven steps only. You can now forget about all the financial products, education funds, and pension insurance because no one cares about your money more than you do.

我的"普通人家十年一千万理财计划"在 2018 年画上一个完美的句号。历时 11 年半。我写完了我的故事，有时会有一种幻觉。过去的投资故事，就像在玩一个大富翁的游戏。这个游戏很多人都玩儿过。一开始的时候你一圈圈地飞奔，忙着买地，逢地就买。这很像我们年轻的时候，年轻力壮，对未来充满期待。等地都买完了，互换地契取得垄断。很快你就面临人生重大抉择，你需要盖房子了。这时候，你开始捉襟见肘。好像我们三十而立，娶妻生子，安定下来需要解决自己的自住房问题了。　再过几圈，好似人到中年。有的人居无定所，不断交房租。有的人房子越来越多，地越买越多。如果你不买房子，不盖房子，最终肯定就是一个输家。因为坐吃山空日子过得没有希望。

My "Average Family's \$10 million in 10 years Investment and Wealth Management Plan" came to a perfect ending in 2018, spanning a period of 11 years and a half. Having finished writing my story, I felt that I played a real-life Monopoly game in the last decade. I believe that many of you have played this game before. At first, everyone is busy buying land. Players will jump on every opportunity to buy a piece of land. This is similar to when we are young in real life. We are energetic and excited about our future. Back to the game, after finally obtaining a monopoly through buying the land or exchanging with other players, we will face a major decision: building houses. We face this decision in real life too. This is when we may experience some financial difficulties. People usually start their own families in their 30s when they need to solve their housing problem too. After several rounds, we enter middle-age, but some people who do not own their home need to keep paying rents. Meanwhile, some players own more houses and buy more land. If you do not purchase real properties, you are bound to be a loser because you will lose hope when every day of your life is about making ends meet.

　　如果你选择买房子盖房子，一开始很辛苦，到后来就会越来越容易，因为你不断地有收入进来。房子越多收入越多，然后你就有机会买更多的地盖更多的房子。可是等你把台面上所有的房子都吃进的时候，打败了所有的对手。最终也是游戏结束，曲终人散。

If you choose to buy or build houses, you will have a difficult time at first. But it will get easier with the passage of time because of rental income. The more houses you own, the more income you will have, which means you can then buy more land and build more houses. But when you take over all the houses in the game and beat all other players, the game ends.

回首往事。有时我这十几年的经历就像做梦一样，感觉也就像是玩了一个大富翁的游戏。因为本质上那些街上的房子，跟大富翁游戏里的红红绿绿的房子也没有什么区别。反正我也从来不去住。那些美元人民币真钱和游戏桌上的假钱又有什么区别呢？反正绝大多数时候我也不用它们。它们永远奔跑在各个银行账户之间。

In retrospect, my experience in the last 10 years or so feels surreal. I felt as though I played a real-life Monopoly game. The houses in real life are essentially the same as the red and green houses in the game. After all, I have never lived in them. Or never will I. What is the difference between Monopoly money and real money such as the Chinese Yuan and the U.S. dollar? Most of the time, we do not use them. They are always sitting in banks.

说这话可能有些消极。我只是想说大家不要在投资理财赚钱的路上迷失了自己。钱是赚不完的。我更倾向把整个赚钱的过程，当作一个旅程，在过程中看看风景，而不是终点。另外一方面，很多人对投资感到害怕。其实如果你不玩这个游戏，肯定是人生输家。如果你玩这个游戏，最多你会输掉自己存下来的那一点钱，但是如果赢的话，你就可以赢到很大一个世界。

My words here may be discouraging, but what I am trying to say is that do not lose yourself in your investment and wealth management journey. You can never earn all the money in the world. I prefer to treat the process of making money as a journey, not a destination. Meanwhile, many people are intimidated by investing. If you do not play this game, you are bound to be a loser in life. If you decide to play this game, the worst that can happen is you lose the little money you have saved. However, if you win the game, you will unlock the door to a whole new, bigger world.

完成 100 万到 1000 万美元这段人生路程。我的"迈向一亿美元的旅途"又开始了。

After concluding this stage of my life where I went from US$1 million to US$10 million, it is time to start my "Toward US$100 million Journey."

附录：历年投资总结
Annex: A Summary of My Investment Journey (By Year)

普通家庭十年一千万的理财计划-（第二年 2008 年 2 月 3 日）
An Average Family's $10 million in 10 years Wealth Management Plan- Year 1 Summary and Plans for 2008 (February 2, 2008)

by Bayfamily

　　去年春节写了个未来十年的理财计划。有道是好事不出门，坏事传千里。写了这文章，害得我骂名远扬，挨了一年的砖头。砖头多的都够我再盖栋房子的了。

　　I formulated my investment and wealth management plan for the next 10 years of my life last Chinese New Year. Because of its controversial title and content, it traveled fast. Other forum users had a heated debate on my article. I received numerous criticisms in the previous year, the number of which were sufficient for me to build a house if they were bricks throw at me.

　　坛子上还有几位背功极好的朋友，拿出当年学习毛爷爷老三篇的毅力。现在已做到倒背如流，句句是典故，随手就能引用文章中的原话来讥讽我。在下实在是佩服。

　　There are several netizens who have excellent memory. They studied my investment plan as if they were studying for the SAT. They are so familiar with my plan that they can memorize the direct quote from the article and use them to mock me all the time. I was amazed.

　　既然是十年计划，就要不折不扣地执行。不然就成了政府领导，计划计划，墙上挂挂，领导一句话。一年过去了，写个猪年的总结与大家分享。

467

As I have already said that this is my goal for the next decade of my life, I have to treat it seriously. Otherwise, I would become no different from government officials: all their great ambitious slogans are empty words.

先学老地主，翻出地契、房契、股票、现金，先来算算净资产。

The first step I took was to calculate my net worth by looking at all my land deeds, stocks, and cash.

去年一年是个激动人心的一年。中国，美国，股市，房市震荡起伏，好不精彩。房市方面，美国全面下滑。湾区虽然总体情况比全国稍好，但中等学区和新开发区的房子下跌也很明显。旧金山和南湾个别好学区的房子目前还能岿然不动，甚至小幅上扬。个人投资虽在好学区，保守起见，以下跌10%计算。

The year 2007 has been an exciting one. China and the U.S. saw fluctuations in their real estate market and the stock market. Regarding the U.S. real estate market, there is an overall decrease. The property prices in the Bay Area performed slightly better than the national average, but districts with average schools and newly-developed neighbors saw an obvious decline. Property prices in San Francisco and Los Angeles, however, remained strong. They even saw a slight increase. Though my investment properties are located in good school districts, I will adopt a prudent number of a decrease of 10%.

401k 的投资回报丰厚。去年年底的年终回报达到 17%。今年开始一路下滑。但比起去年春节写十年理财计划的时候，大约增长了 8%。中国房市的投资回报丰厚，房价全面翻翻，由于财富杠杆的原因，总体回报率更高。国内的房产投资，因为鞭长莫及的原因，错过很多好的机会，不然表现会更好一些。不过现在风险控制得不错，总体实现了 even cash flow （现金流平衡）. 去年在 IPO 市场还发了点小财，回报率很高，到目前为止涨了 80%，但总量很小。

On the other hand, my returns from 401K are handsome. My annual return in 2007 was 17%. Despite decreasing stock prices since the beginning of 2008, my 401K has grown 8% since I last wrote about my 10-year investment and wealth management plan. My investment returns from my investment properties in China are lucrative. The property prices in China doubled or even tripled. Thanks to my leverage, the actual return rate is even higher. However, as I am based in the U.S., I missed many good opportunities in China's real estate market. Otherwise, the investment return would have been even better. That said, I am grateful that I have managed my risks well and achieved even cash flow. Furthermore, I made quite a handsome profit in the IPO market last year. The return from this investment, albeit small, is 80% so far.

总体投资，此消彼长，鼠年来临之际，除去各项债务，家庭总净资产达到 135 万。 算完变天账，再来合计合计鼠年的好日子。

Overall, after deducting all liabilities, the current net worth of my household is US$1.35 million. Now that I have got a clear picture of my current situation, it is time to plan ahead.

美国房市短期前景很难预料。个人感觉旧金山的房子也许和纽约一样，是国际市场决定的，有欧洲和亚洲投资热钱涌入的可能。个人财务上，坚决执行一年前写的，十年一千万计划里面，三年不买房的计划。目前的首要任务是积累现金，等待房市的复苏。401K 上面，除了公司的匹配(match)以外，停止一切新的 contribution(养老金储蓄)，因为目前的 401K 总量三十年后已经够满足退休的基本生活了，多存实属无益。401k 是退休用的，不能指望它发财。 总的来看，第一年的理财计划总体执行情况良好。房市股市的走向和自己一年前计划的情况基本相符。净资产的增长率和预测的相符，因为盘子大了，净资产总体回报率持续下降，从早期的 50%，30%，一路降到现在的 12%。 未来随着现金流的改善，回报率有望重新提升到 30%。总结写好了，送各位打油诗一首。

人生有命语荒唐，贫富不可赖爹娘。

若是身为无能辈，坐拥金山也败光！

有钱难买少年穷，匹夫志气非寻常。

待到风云来际会，百姓亦变千万郎！

金银富贵本无种，身是男儿当自强！

It is difficult, if not impossible, to predict the short-term price changes in the U.S. real estate market. My belief is that California's real estate market, like New York's, will be predominantly influenced by the international market because of the possibility of hot money from European and Asian investors. In relation to my personal finance, I will stick to "not buying investment properties in the next three years," which was also listed in my $10-million-in-10-year plan. My top priority for the coming year is to accumulate as much cash as possible to prepare for a recovery of the real estate market.

As for my 401K, other than company match, I will stop all contributions because my current account balance is already sufficient to support my retirement life, assuming that I will retire 30 years from now. Making additional contributions will only be counterproductive. After all, 401K is to prepare oneself for his or her retirement. It is not a tool to create massive wealth.

Overall, my performance in the first year of executing my $10-million-in-10-year plan is pretty good. The trends in the stock market and real estate market are in line with my predictions. So is the growth of my net worth. As my portfolio has now grown larger, the overall return rate has gradually decreased from 50% to 30%, and from 30% to 12% now. In the future, I expect that the return rate will climb back to 30% because of an improved cash flow. The above is my summary of the first year of my journey to US$10 million. I would like to conclude it with a poem:

Our life is in our own hands,

and never should we reprimand

our parents for not giving us a wealth wonderland.

If a person is incompetent,

no amount of inheritance

can maintain his extravagance.

A difficult childhood will teach a person

many valuable lessons

and make him a gentleperson.

Time is the best friend

of the man who never unbends

until his dreams impend.

Our life is in our own hands,

and a great man never misunderstands

this command.

人生如白驹过隙，财富如过眼云烟，生不带来，死不带走。金钱总量毫无意义，乐在游戏过程。大家鼠年玩好。

Time flies and wealth is temporary. We did not bring our money with us when we first arrived in this world, and neither can we bring it to our afterlife. The amount of money that we end up with is meaningless. The fun is in the journey.

普通家庭十年一千万的理财计划-（第三年 2009 年 1 月 5 日）
An Average Family's $10 million in 10 years Wealth Management Plan- Year 2 Summary and Plans for 2009 (January 5, 2009)

By Bayfamily

年年写理财计划，最后还是计划不如变化快。2008 就是个风云突变的年头。

Life does not always go according to plan. 2008 is a year of great, unexpected changes.

房地产、股票持续下跌。危机的总爆发在雷曼兄弟倒闭之后。大约算了一下，因为这场危机各种直接、间接的总损失在 30 万左右。一个不当心，差点一夜回到解放前。先学各位坛子里面的老地主，翻出地契、房契、股票、现金，来算算净资产。

Both the stock market and the real estate market are declining. The climax of the crisis is when Lehman Brothers filed for bankruptcy. My estimated loss was around US$300,000.

401K 遭受重创。到 2008 年的最后一个交易日，总共比年初跌了 31.8%。幸亏过去两年没有存 401K，不然会更惨。公司 IPO 的股票，unrealized gain (未套现收益) 基本归零。原本打算今年靠股票混个买菜钱，全部落空了。湾区的房地产持续下跌。虽然在好学区，但是至少下滑 10%。市场价值很难估算，因为最近成交量很小。

My 401K suffered a huge blow. On the last trading day of 2008, it lost around 31.8% compared to a year ago. Fortunately, I did not make any contribution to my 401K in the last two years. Otherwise, my loss would be even greater. The unrealized gain on my IPO shares is now close to zero. My original plan to use my profits from stocks to cover some of my daily expenses is now impossible. The property prices in the Bay Area are also declining. Even though my investment properties are in good school districts, they also decreased by at least 10%. It is difficult to estimate their market value now because of the small number of closing transactions lately.

投资的亮点还是有的。年中的时候，在最高点上，成功将上海的房子抛出。

However, there are also some highlights of my investment journey this year. In the middle of the year, I successfully sold my investment property at the highest point of the real estate market.

因为积极的存现金政策，现金情况明显改善，银行总存款 12 月底的时候达到 26 万。总体投资，此消彼长，牛年来临之际，除去各项债务，按照当前的市场价格，家庭总净资产达到 128 万，比去年下跌 7 万。个人感觉，在史无前例的房市危机面前，投资股市还是比房市要来得悲惨。普通投资人，买房子还是比较稳妥的。

Because of my aggressive saving policy, my cash flow situation has greatly improved. At the end of December, my household's total savings amounted to

US$260,000. Overall, my current net worth is US$1.28 million, a US$70,000 decrease from last year. My takeaway this year is that in an unprecedented economic crisis, it is preferable to invest in real properties than in the stock market. It is much safer for an ordinary investor to buy real properties.

回顾一下，从积极意义上来看，第二年的理财计划总体执行情况没有犯什么错误。风暴来临前，能做的事情，全做了。没有什么可以后悔的。

In retrospect, I did not make many mistakes in the second year of executing my plan. I have done everything I can prior to the financial storm, so I have no regrets.

倒完了苦水，来合计合计来年的日子。

After the complaints, it is time to plan for the coming year.

美国房市还会下行，未来一年的重灾区应该是好学区。对于湾区而言，坏学区的房子已经没有什么可跌的了。好学区的房子开始松动。

The U.S. real estate market will continue to decline. In the coming year, good school districts in the Bay Area will see the biggest drop in prices. In the Bay Area, houses in bad school districts did not have room for a further decrease in prices. There will be more listings of houses in good school districts.

密切注意房市动态，随时准备抄底入市。今年年底是三年不买房政策的最后期限。年底，在适合的时候，开始考虑逐步进货。

I need to keep a close eye on the price trend in the real estate market to prepare myself for "buying the bottom" operation. This year marks the last year of my "not buying investment properties in three years" policy. I am going to buy them at appropriate times at the end of the coming year.

从来不炒股票，股市行情难以预料。个人感觉还会有一个起伏，不可能就这样一路复苏过去了。继续少买 401K。

Do not buy stocks. It is difficult to predict the stock market. I believe that there will be more fluctuations in the stock market and that we are still far away from a recovery. My plan is to keep minimizing my 401K contributions.

投资和庖丁解牛一样，要因势利导 顺应天时。不可以为之的事情，不用
硬上。贝多芬说他要扼住命运的咽喉，我看最终是他扼住了自己的咽喉。
2009 年乌云滚滚，风暴还没有退去。与其当乔潮儿，不如在家拿着望远镜，
观潮、赏景。

Investing is like dismembering an ox.[15] A dexterous investor/butcher makes good use of the market trend and timing. They do not go against the wave. When Beethoven said that he would take fate by the throat, I guess many were taking themselves by the throat. The financial storm will not subside in 2009. Instead of going against the wave in the market, I would rather sit back and relax at home.

祝大家看到美丽的风景，玩得开心。

I wish all of you the best of luck and fun in your investment journey.

普通家庭十年一千万投资计划 （第四年 2010）

An Average Family's $10 million in 10 years Wealth Management Plan- Year 3 Summary and Plans for 2010 (written in 2010)

by Bayfamily

时光过得真快了。一下子从写文章到现在已经是 3 年了。这三年发生了
多少变故啊。美国地产泡沫的崩溃，金融机构的崩盘，中国人财富的迅速膨
胀。按照惯例，每年写一个投资总结。

Time flies. It has been three years since I wrote about my $10-million-in-10-year investment plan. A lot has happened in these three years: the bursting of the real estate bubble in the U.S., the collapse of financial institutions, and the strong wealth creation and growth in China. This is a summary of the third year of my investment journey.

今年最大的变化就是间接地受金融危机的影响。不幸失业。失业是不幸
的，对人心理的打击比较大。但是马克思说过，无产阶级失去的只是锁链，

---

[15] "The Dexterous Butcher" is a famous philosophical story from Chuang Tzu's "The Basic Writings." The dexterous butcher carefully studied the spaces between the joints before cutting up the ox. That is why after cutting up thousands of oxen, the blade of his knife is still as good as when it first came from the grindstone.

得到的是整个世界。稍稍想过，决定放弃寻找新的工作，做一个自由的人，走上了创业的道路。和朋友一起成立公司。

The biggest change in my life in 2009 is that, unfortunately, I lost my job because of the financial crisis. It was a mental blow to me, but as Marx exclaimed, "The proletarians have nothing to lose but their chains." After some consideration, I decided to end my job hunt and embrace freedom. I started my own business with some friends of mine.

与其买股票，不如自己制造股票。你看看我买了这么多年的 401K 股票，买到了什么下场。送进去的现金比现在市价资产都多。完全是无偿奉献给华尔街发奖金了。

Rather than buying shares, why don't I create shares? The contributions I made to my 401K in all these years far exceeded the account balance. All the money went into the pockets of bankers on Wall Street.

公司成立之后，新的投资人入股价格已经比原始成立的价格涨了一倍。也许是投资人对我们的产品和服务的看好。也许是我们忽悠有功。当然了，一切都是纸上富贵。今年股市表现不错，把 2008 年崩溃掉了的 401K 和其他退休计划补偿了一些回来。继续坚持以前的观点，再也不买 401K。

After founding our own company, the asking price of the company shares has doubled the original price at the time of its founding. Perhaps this is because investors have confidence in our company's products and services. Or it may also be that we have done an excellent job convincing them this is the case. Of course, all my wealth is numbers on the books. Last year, the stock market started to recover, and I was able to recoup some of the losses I incurred in my 401K and other pension funds. That being said, I will stick to my plan that I am not going to make more contributions to my 401K.

美国房市持续低迷。好学区的房子 2009 一直处于持续阴跌中。价格大约下降 10%。2010 年前景看不清，坏学区也许已经触底，但是好学区的房子随着持续的失业率，一定是应该继续处于阴跌的下降通道中。三年不买房政策已经到期。2010 年，好学区的房子也许可以适当寻找机会。

The real estate market in the U.S. remains sluggish. The property prices in good school districts are still slowly declining in 2009, with a 10% drop. I am not sure about the market trend in 2010, but my guess is that the property prices in poor school districts have already hit the bottom and that property prices in good school districts will continue to decrease because of the increasing unemployment rate. The year 2010 also marks the end of my "not buying investment properties in three years" plan. In 2010, I will try to look for good opportunities in good school districts.

中国房子的行情火爆。房价迅速飙升。2008 年底的时候,严重看空上海楼市。几乎犯下严重错误。忘了自己在 2006 年对上海长期行情的分析。看来老文章需要经常回去看看,保持头脑清醒。好在 2009 年初的时候,及时调整航向,及时入市,好在自己也有自由的时间来分配。要是工作缠身的话,估计是赶不上这波了。还是石头同志说的对。要发财,赶紧辞职。M 大说,投资不能有穷人心态,不能只看着工资小钱。

China's real estate market has been booming. Property prices are soaring. At the end of 2008, I almost made a fatal mistake because of my bearish views on Shanghai's real estate market. I have almost forgotten about my own analysis of the long-term trend in the real estate market that I made in 2006. Therefore, I made a mental note to myself that I need to revisit my previous blog articles to keep a cool head. Fortunately, at the beginning of 2009, I adjusted the course of my investments and entered the market in time. I am also grateful that I can freely allocate my time as a self-employed person. If I were still working a busy office job, I would probably never have been able to grasp the opportunities. Comrade *Shitou* has made a point that the first step toward the path to wealth is quitting one's job. Forum user *M-da* also reminded me that investors cannot have a poor mindset and that they should not focus too much on earning wages.

每年投资的结果都是此消彼长。股票和中国房价上涨。美国房价回落。到了年底,噼噼啪啪一算,扣除一切债务,纸上的富贵一共是 190 万美元。比去年上升 40%左右。2010 年的展望。希望股价能继续翻倍。希望我买的一切资产都能迅速飙升。呵呵。梦想而已。1000 万的投资路需要慢慢走。明年收盘的时候，希望继续此消彼长，就是长的比消的多。突破 200 万的关口。

At the end of every year, there are bound to be some investments that are winners and some that are losers. While China's stock market and real estate market are booming, property prices in the U.S. decline. After deducting all my debts, my net worth is US$1.9 million, a 40% increase from last year. I hope that stock prices will continue to soar and that all my investments will grow rapidly in 2010. Of course, these are my wishes. After all, the path toward US$10 million is a long journey. I expect that some of my investments will grow and that some of them will decline in value. I hope that the overall gain will outweigh my loss. My realistic goal for 2010 is that my year-end net worth can exceed US$2 million.

普通人家十年一千万理财计划（第五年 2011 年 1 月 21 日）

An Average Family's $10 million in 10 years Wealth Management Plan- Summary of Year 4 and Plans for 2011 (January 21, 2011)

By Bayfamily

马克思说，无产阶级失去的只是锁链，得到是整个世界。这是理财到了第四年感受之一。通常人们只能看见自己拥有的。但是看不见自己未能拥有的。

As Marx said, "The proletarians have nothing to lose but their chains." This is one of my reflections in the fourth year of my investment journey. Usually, people can only see what they own but fail to see what they do not own.

这就是为什么很多人，总是觉得自己住的地方最好，不愿意动。住在加州的认为加州最好，住在纽约的，认为自己在宇宙的中心。住在 DC 的认为，自己这里的潜力最好，政府在膨胀，机会多多。住在 IOWA 的认为自己最安逸，用不着为房价烦恼。连住在明尼苏达的，都觉着自己生活在美国最好的州。

会走路的钱
Money Walks

This is why so many people think that their place of residence is the best and why they are reluctant to move elsewhere. Californian residents think that California is the best. New Yorkers believe that they are in the center of the universe. Those who live in D.C. opine that the area has the best potential because of the opportunities created by an expanding government. IOWA residents feel that their life is the most relaxing and stable as they do not have to worry about exorbitant property prices. Even Minnesota residents think that they live in the best state in America.

这让我想起一件事情，"为什么爱斯基摩人在北极"。发现新大陆的，大家都在往南走，水草丰美。为啥有人会留在北极？因为人都有惰性。害怕失去手中拥有的，看不见自己未能得到的。爱斯基摩人看见手中的海豹，无法判断远方草原上是否有野牛。即使有人传话过来，告诉他们有野牛，多得满地捡。他们第一未必信，第二觉着自己的日子蛮好的，老婆孩子热炕头，有吃有喝，小康生活，何必去搞攀比，野牛再多，也吃不完啊。自己虽然是冰屋子，可是空气新鲜啊，东西又不会坏。草原上泥巴多，尘土大，每天疲于奔命，有啥好的。

This reminds me of the story of "Why Eskimo live in the North Pole." Our ancestors kept migrating to the south for more fertile land there, so why do some human beings choose to stay in the North Pole? Because human beings are lazy. We are afraid of losing what we already have and fail to see what we have yet to possess. When Eskimos focus on the seals they have in the North Pole, they fail to judge whether there will be oxen on a far-away land. Even if someone tells them that there are herds of oxen there, they may not believe his or her words. Besides, they may already be content with their existing lifestyle. In the North Pole, they have a family, food, and water. Even though the North Pole is freezing, the air is fresh, and food does not go bad. Grassland is full of mud and dust. They will have a much busier life living on grassland.

这点对于工程师尤其严重，特别是高学历，高技能的工程师们。英文叫 technology myopia （技术性短视）。拥有了一项手艺，过上小康生活，就不舍得放弃。如同最好的剃头师傅一样，只能做重复性的工作，不能开连锁店。马云不会写程序，却能指挥写程序的。不是马云手下的程序员不如马云聪明。而是因为一旦拥有一项技能，就不舍得放弃。

Engineers, especially those with an excellent educational background and skills, are the Eskimo. They suffer from technology myopia. When they possess a certain skill and are living a middle-class life, they are reluctant to give up their current lifestyle. This is similar to how the best hairdresser keeps doing repetitive work and does not choose to open his own business. Even though Jack Ma has no coding knowledge, he gives instructions to those who can code. This is not because the engineers at Alibaba are not as intelligent as Jack Ma. The reason is that once a person possesses a certain skill, he or she is reluctant to give it up.

当大家努力让自己的孩子爬藤校，当医生，当工程师，拥有一技之长，金字招牌在社会谋生的时候。别忘了，这些技能同时对他也是有害的。因为，舍得，舍得，有舍，才有得。技能越多，越无法放弃。

Many parents are busy with paving a path to an Ivy League for their children and hope that their children can become a professional, such as a doctor or engineer. But they should also bear in mind that these professional skills may also be harmful to the children. Professionals are more reluctant to explore new opportunities in life because of the high opportunity cost they have already incurred in obtaining those qualifications.

春节到了，说说今年的理财成果。今年继续过着无业游民的漂泊日子。说起无业，当然是自嘲。主要是时间继续完全由自己控制。何时工作，做什么工作，在哪里工作，都是自己定。这样的日子一旦习惯了，很难回到坐办公室打瞌睡的日子。投资方面嘛。和我原先预测的 infiltrating（渗滤）理论一样。湾区好学区的房价开始放量下行。俺家美国的房子基本上过去 10 年的升值全部归零，从哪里来，到哪里去。俺在美国的确混得够惨的，要工作没工作，过去 10 年投资升值几乎都归零。

It is Chinese New Year again, so it is time to summarize my investment performance in the last year. I am still a jobless person. Of course, this is a self-deprecating joke. As I now run my own business, I can have total control of my time. I can decide when I want to work, where I want to work, and what projects to work on. Once a person gets used to this kind of freedom, it will be very difficult for him to go back to the life of an office worker. Regarding my investments, my infiltrating theories have come to reality. Property prices in good school districts in the Bay Area are starting to decline. The appreciation value in my real estate investments in the U.S. in the last decade is now back to zero. My life in the U.S. is quite miserable: I do not have a job, and my 10-year investment return is now close to zero.

中国的房子房价继续飙升。加上人民币升值，所以账面上很好看。以前存的 401K 去年也涨了不少。自己的公司被投资人追捧，市值涨了几倍。去年的现金流情况全面好转，乱七八糟挣了不少，到年底的时候，手上的现金有 30 万美元。去年一年没有买房子。噼噼啪啪算了一下。此消彼长，把套现和未套现的都算在一起。扣除全部债务，总资产一共是 280 万美元。当然这里面有很多经常在变化的价格，有些价格不好评估。保守算，大约是 260 万，往高里算，应该在 300 万左右。

Property prices in China keep soaring. Thanks to an appreciation of the Chinse Yuan, the book value of my investments in China looks good. In addition, my 401K balance has drastically increased too. The market cap of my own company has more than tripled because of its popularity among investors. My cash flow has also significantly improved. With the profits I made here and there, I have US$300,000 of cash at the end of 2010. As I did not buy any investment properties in 2010, my net worth is now US$2.8 million. As my investments involve changing prices, a more conservative number of my net worth is US$2.6 million. And a more aggressive estimate will be US$3 million.

账面上虽然不错。但是这里面有很多问题。一个问题就是中国占的比重太高。因为美国的房地产升值几乎全部被 wipe out（抹平）。财富稀里糊涂地一下子都集中在中国。另外一个问题，就是财富的不确定性更高。因为资产价格变动很大，特别是公司股票。真正立刻可以变现的，估计在 150 万到 200 万之间。明年的计划是加强在美国的投入。特别是现金流比较好的房子的投入。不知不觉中，中国的一个房子卖了，就可以购买美国 10 个正现金流的房子。所以今年计划开始动手，先期购房 2-3 间。争取到了明年这个时候，资产水平保持在 300 万左右，做到中美进一步平衡。

Despite a high book value, I have identified several problems in my portfolio. Firstly, my portfolio has tilted too much toward Chinese investments. As the appreciation gain in my U.S. real estate investments have almost been wiped out, all my wealth has been concentrated in Chinese investments now. Secondly, because of the greater fluctuations in asset prices, especially the stock price of my company, there are more uncertainties involved in my investments. The assets that I can cash out are worth around US$1.5-2 million. My plan for 2011 is that I will increase my investments in the U.S., especially by buying real properties that have good cash flow. As time goes by, selling one investment property in China now means that I can buy ten properties that have positive cash flow in the U.S. Therefore, my plan is to take action in 2011 by first buying 2-3 investment properties. My goals are to keep my net worth at US$3 million one year from now and strike a better balance between my investments in China and the U.S.

去年也有投资失败的例子。一个小项目上，公司破产，投入的几万块钱基本是血本无归。当然教训学了不少。明年再接再厉吧。 去年著书一本，不知道今年销量如何，无论怎样，也算是对人类精神文明有所贡献吧。

In 2010, I did stumble. I invested more than thirty grand in a small project. The company later bankrupted, and I lost all my investment. Of course, I have learned from this experience. I also wrote a book in 2011, but I am not sure about its sales. Anyway, it is my attempt to make contributions to the progress of human civilization.

普通人家十年一千万理财计划 （第六年 2012）

An Average Family's $10 million in 10 years Wealth Management Plan- Summary of Year 5 and Plans for 2012 (written at the beginning of 2012)

会走路的钱
Money Walks

by Bayfamily

六年前开始写这个系列，一年发一篇。每到春节来临的时候总结一下。在这个坛子上久的人可能还会记得，坛子上新来的人恐怕都不知道是怎么回事了。

Six years ago, I started the habit of writing a yearly review of my investment journey toward US$10 million during the Chinese New Year. Those who are experienced forum users may still remember this series, but new forum users probably have no idea about my past investment performance.

在过去六年里，如果说最让我自豪和骄傲的事情，那就是这个坛子，通过介绍经验和方法，给一大批人带来财富和信心。大家不再傻乎乎只存401K 和 529，给华尔街送血汗钱。 这些朋友大部分都是和我一样，十几年前来到美国，现在有了一定的积累，进入财富快速积累阶段。有时我会收到坛子里读者的短信和感谢，这是对写文章的人最好的慰劳了。

In the last six years, one of my proudest achievements is my blog on this forum. I have helped countless people gain much confidence in managing their own wealth and create wealth. Now, this little community of forum users no longer give away their hard-earned money to Wall Street through making contributions to 401K and 529. The netizens here have become my friends. Just like me, they arrived in the U.S. more than 10 years ago and have now accumulated their wealth. We are now in the stage of rapidly accumulating our wealth. Sometimes I receive thank you messages from readers. This is the greatest motivation for me to keep building my blog.

坛子成立之初，当年和我一起写文章的故友大部分已经离去，有的已经发财了，在沙滩上每天晒太阳数钞票。有的发财发到看破红尘，遁入空门，一边数钱，一边开始追求终极真理。

Most comrades who also wrote their blog on this forum in the early days when this forum was first founded have left this forum. Some of them have already made their fortune and are now enjoying their wealth, and some are now seeking the meaning of life.

482

我的资金有限，能力也有限，所以还在这里可怜巴巴地年复一年总结自己的投资体会。我坚持写下来也是想看看当初一个疯狂的想法，经过十年的实践到底会变成啥样。

I have limited capital and abilities, so I am still here writing my blog article, reflecting on my investment performance. Another reason why I continue this reflection practice is that I want to keep track of how a crazy idea will come true after 10 years of hard work.

2012 年，按照 6 年前的方案继续我的投资计划。市场的确如 6 年前预测的那样，也和加州过去经历过的 4 次房地产循环一样，先是大幅下跌，然后攀升和恢复到新的最高点。外部条件满足了当初的方案，但是我的投资脚步总是比计划的差一步。应了那句话，理想和现实总是有差距的。

My plan for 2012 is that I will stick to the investment plan that I made six years ago. In 2011, just as how I predicted it six years ago, California's real estate market did repeat its last four cycles: it first plummets and then recovers, and finally reaches a new historical high. The external conditions satisfied my original plan, but my actual investment performance was different from what my plan predicted.

今年最大的教训是不能书生气用事，不能靠数学模型指导投资。

The biggest takeaway this year is that I cannot simply rely on my calculations to guide my investment decisions.

举个例子，同样是买投资房，如果投资 A 的 IRR 回报是 12%，投资 B 的 IRR 回报是 15%。你买哪个？

For example, assuming that you are now buying an investment property. The IRR return from a house A will be 12%, and house B 15%. Which one will you buy?

如果其他条件都一样，任何一个学过数学的人都会毫不犹豫地回答 B。

Assuming all other conditions are the same, anyone who has studied mathematics will, without a doubt, choose House B.

在 2012 年，数次的经验和教训告诉我，上面答案的错误的。

However, the year 2012 taught me that B is the wrong answer.

如果你的资金很多的话，正确答案是 A 和 B。把他们都买了。因为他们都远远高于存款利率。

If you have much capital, the correct answer is to buy both because the return is much higher than the interest you can earn from bank savings.

如果你的资金有限，只能购买一个的话，答案往往也是 A，而不是 B。因为对于 B，你会面临更多的竞争，最后导致的结果是拿不到这个 Deal，最后 A 和 B 都没拿到，竹篮打水一场空。对于 A，你面临的竞争比较少，你有更多的机会拿到。

If you have limited capital and can only buy one of them, the answer is A, not B because you will face more competition in buying B. The outcome is often that you cannot get the deal, so you fail to buy any investment property. If you try to buy house A, you will face less competition, which means it is more likely for you to get it.

这就是书本和现实的区别。另外一方面，人的精力是有限的。不可能在比较数个 Deal 的最后，选择你认为最佳的方案。

This is the difference between theories and reality. On the other hand, we have limited energy and time. It is impossible for us to choose the best option after comparing several deals.

2012 年的湾区房市回到疯抢的阶段。2012 年下半年的上海和北京，一天一个价。在疯抢的阶段，抢到篮子就是菜。是否抢到是王道，抢到的是什么不重要。

The real estate market in the Bay Area in 2012 went back to the stage of fierce competition among buyers. In the second half of 2012, both Shanghai and Beijing's real estate market are booming. Under such fierce competition, the key is whether you managed to buy a house. The house that you bought does not really matter.

这让我回想起 2000 年的时候中国的房市，关键不是你买了什么，而是你买了还是没有买。

This reminds me of China's real estate market in 2000. The key is not what you bought but whether you bought any.

484

过去一年，中国的房市渐渐回暖，未来应该可以看到上海和北京的房价如脱缰之马继续狂飙。道理很简单，温同学不懂经济。任何一个正常智商的人都知道，如果想让猪肉价格下来，应该做的事情是鼓励养猪户多养猪。可惜温同学过去几年一直认为，打击开发商，让他们日子不好过，甚至破产，房价会下跌。这样的政策后果就是房屋供应极度短缺，供求矛盾在 2013 年会集中爆发。

In the past year, China's real estate market is recovering. In the future, the property prices in Shanghai and Beijing will skyrocket. The logic is simple, but Mr. Wen does not know about economics. Anyone who has a normal IQ will know that the only way to lower pork prices is to encourage pig farms to increase the scale of their operation. However, in the last several years, Mr. Wen believed that discouraging property developers, for example, by forcing them into bankruptcy, would lower property prices. The outcome of such a policy is that there will be a serious shortage of residential properties. The shortage will reach its peak in 2013.

国家大事我们管不了，到了年底，算盘珠子噼里啪啦算算变天账。房子涨，股票涨，乱七八糟加在一起，终于总净资产过了 3 粒米（millions）。啥都涨，不是俺聪明，是因为票子发的太多。中国发得多，美国也发得多。回想过去，从身无分文到第一粒米，用了 6 年的时间，从一粒米到三粒米用了另外 6 年的时间。这样看来，10 粒米的梦想在未来 4 年里面实现的希望的确不大。未来四年争取再长两粒米，就阿弥陀佛了。等到 10 年到期的时候，比较靠谱的估计大约是 4-5 粒米左右。

Anyway, we have little say over how the Chinese government formulates its policies, but I do have control over my own investments. It is time to calculate my net worth. After adding all my assets and deducting the liabilities, my net worth has finally exceeded US$3 million. The reason why almost every investment of mine has grown is not that I am clever but that both the Chinese government and the U.S. government have printed too much money. It took me six years to go from not having a single penny to my first million and another 6 years to grow my US$1 million into US$3 million. It will seem that it is impossible to achieve my dream of US$10 million in the next four years, so my adjusted goal is to make US$2 million in the next four years. A more realistic estimate of my net worth at the end of my 10-year plan is around US$4-5 million.

在美国衡量一个人的财富其实挺简单，通过他的税表厚度就知道。刚到美国的时候，是 1040EZ，简单的两张纸。后来是 10 页，再后来是 20 几页，今年已经达到 50 几页了。所以吧，要致富，多填税表，后面自然钱也会随之而来。以后办相亲节目，不用数男生有多少房子，多高职位，问问税表厚度就知道对方家底了。哪位同学有机会可以把这个建议给"非诚勿扰"。

An easy way to guess how much wealth an American has is to look at his or her tax documents. When I first arrived in the U.S., I only needed to fill in a 1040EZ form. It is a simple document of two pages. Later, I filled in 10 pages of tax documents, then 20 pages. This year, I was filling in more than 50 pages of tax documents. Therefore, if you want to be rich, fill in more tax papers. The money will come. I have an idea. In speed dating, women do not need to ask how many real properties the guy owns and how senior his position is. They can simply ask the men about how many tax documents the latter need to file.

过去的几年里，其实大约有两三次的机会，如果能够正确把握住，现在就已经过 5 粒米了。可惜每次都是失之交臂。这些机会的共同特点是，当他们在你眼前的时候，你是那么浑然不觉，同时需要的资本投入又让你有些胆战心惊。于是机会就稍纵即逝。我说的不是豪赌股票和期货，只是房产投资，经历过的人，可能有同感。未来 4 年，希望自己能吸取教训，把握住这样的机会。

In the last several years, I had 2-3 good investment opportunities. If I had grabbed them, my net worth would have been more than US$5 million now. However, I just missed these opportunities. The common thread in these stories is that: when a good opportunity presented itself, I could not even notice it. Meanwhile, I was kind of scared to put in my money. This is why good investment opportunities are fleeting. I am not referring to big bets on stocks or futures. I am talking about real estate investing.

Anyone who has a similar experience will echo with me on this. In the next four years, I hope that I can remember this lesson and jump on good investment opportunities.

展望 2013 年，超额发钞带来的资产泡沫会越来越大。抢到大额长期低息贷款的人，就是最终胜利的人。指望人民币升值的人，可以渐渐打消念头了。人民币未来贬值的压力会越来越大，中国在走韩国的老路。天佑天朝，希望通货膨胀的猛兽不要让政权崩溃。当然崩溃了也挺好的，投资人就喜欢泡沫和崩溃，不然哪有机会。

Looking ahead into 2013, the asset bubble caused by over-printing of money will grow even bigger. Those who successfully apply for long-term low-interest loans are the ultimate winners. Meanwhile, those who expect that the Chinese Yuan will appreciate can forget about it. The pressure for the Chinese Yuan to depreciate will mount even greater. China is following the path of South Korea. God bless China. I hope that the government party does not collapse in the face of the inflation monster. Of course, collapse is not a bad thing. Investors like bubbles and collapses because crises also imply opportunities.

展望未来，身体是革命的本钱，身体是最好的投资。生锈的机器已经开始常常出问题，过去 6 年，2011 年是投资最失败的一年，这也和身体状态不佳有关。

Another takeaway is that our health is our most precious asset. The best investment we can make is on our health. I had the worst investment performance in 2011 because of my deteriorating health.

投资是体力活，经历过的人都知道。请大家投入时间锻炼身体吧，留得青山在，不怕没柴烧，生命足够长，机会总会有，这是才是投资中的投资。

Any experienced investors will know that investing consumes energy and time, so I urge everyone here to invest more time in their health. I say, "Where there is health, there is hope." There will be more good opportunities in our life if we can live long. Health is the best investment we can ever make.

普通人家十年一千万理财计划（第七年 2013）

An Average Family's $10 million in 10 years Wealth Management Plan-Summary of Year 6 and Plans for 2013 (written in 2013)

by Bayfamily

今年湾区的天热，樱桃已经开花了，春节要到了，又是写年终总结的时候了，这是第七年写这个系列。

The weather in the Bay Area this year is warmer than usual. Cherry blossoms are already blooming. It is Chinese New Year again, which means time for me to write a summary of my investment performance in the last 12 months. This is the seventh year since I started this series.

在过去的 12 个月里面，股票涨，房子涨，美国的房子涨价，中国的房子涨价。坛子的各位大财主们都赚翻了天。我也是小小地搭上顺风车，各方面的业绩也不错。

In the past 12 months, the stock market and real estate market boomed. Property prices in both China and the States increased. Investors on this forum have made handsome profits. I have also benefitted from this market trend. The return from all my investments is pretty good this year.

今年让我很有体会的是两件事情，一个是人对经济和市场预期的正确判断到底从哪里来？一个是应该怎样做到可持续发展？

I have learned two important lessons this year. The first is on how a person can derive his or her correct judgment about the market. The second is on how we can grow our portfolio persistently.

先说第一件事情，如果要在投资理财上获得成功，必须对大的市场有个正确的判断，但是这个判断往往事后容易，事先很难。

My first takeaway is that our success as an investor depends on whether we have a correct judgment about the big market. However, it is difficult to make such a judgment in advance. A correct analysis of the situation is often made in hindsight.

每天我们都能看到很多大牛，名人对市场未来的判断。有的是著名基金
的经理，有的是著名学者。和很多人一样，我一开始也被他们的名头糊弄的
不清，但是后来市场血淋淋的现实告诉我们。他们做的预测往往极其不靠
谱，甚至根本就是南辕北辙。 就那诺贝尔奖的新科状元 Robert J. Shiller 来说
吧，因为 2008 年前判断楼市崩盘而出名，但是在房市回暖的时候，他依旧不
断地认为新的 bubble 在形成，让很多投资者错失这次探底的良机。

Every day, we can read about all sorts of market predictions made by experts.
Some of these people are famous fund managers, and some of them are distinguished
scholars. Just like many other people, I blindly trusted their analysis because of their
impressive job titles. However, the reality taught me that the predictions made by these
experts are unreliable, or even a complete opposite to the reality. Take Robert J. Shiller,
a Nobel laureate in economics. He is famous for correctly predicting the collapse of the
real estate market in 2008. However, when the real estate market began to recover after
the crisis, he still believed that a new bubble was forming, discouraging many investors
from buying the bottom.

大家可否还记得 2012 年底的时候，媒体和报纸也是充斥了 Foreclosure
second wave(第二波法拍屋浪潮) 的说法？ 我随便翻出来一个。今天看着是否
觉得可笑？

http://www.washingtonpost.com/wp-
dyn/content/article/2010/03/11/AR2010031104866.html

http://www.zerohedge.com/news/second-foreclosure-tsunami-coming-and-about-
kill-any-hopes-housing-bottom

Furthermore, do you still remember that at the end of 2012, articles that said there
would be a second wave of foreclosure were all over mainstream media? The following

are two examples among many. Now reading them, don't you feel that the content is ridiculous?

http://www.washingtonpost.com/wp-
dyn/content/article/2010/03/11/AR2010031104866.html

http://www.zerohedge.com/news/second-foreclosure-tsunami-coming-and-about-
kill-any-hopes-housing-bottom

两年前这个时候，我写过一篇文章，告诫大家不要去投资黄金。

Two years ago, I wrote an article to recommend against investing in gold.

当时是黄金的顶峰，没有人听，反而被嘲笑了一番。

At the time, the price of gold reached its peak, so no one listened to my advice. Instead, I was mocked.

加州大学的心理学家 Philip Tetlock 做了大量的统计数据，他发现越是在媒体上频繁出现的人，越是对自己的判断无比自信的人，做出的判断往往和市场的结果偏差越大。越是能够质疑自己的人，说出话带着犹豫和动摇的人，不断否定自己的人，预测的结果恐怕越正确。可惜这样的人在媒体上不出彩，没人看。普通投资人往往不明白其中的道理，往往是自己有了一套现成的 belief (信念)，然后通过电视媒体报纸去寻找这个结论的支持，迷信名人和专家，于是在错误的道上越走越远。

Philip Tetlock, a former psychologist at the University of California, Berkeley, and now a professor at the University of Pennsylvania is a researcher in expert judgment and the science of prediction. His research found out that the predictions made by experts who appear more frequently on mainstream media and are more confident about their own judgments stray further away from what has actually happened. In contrast, the predictions made by people who speak with hesitation and doubt their own analysis are more accurate. However, the latter are not popular interviewees on mainstream media. Normal, ordinary investors often do not understand this logic, so they form their own set of beliefs and then try to validate these beliefs by cherry-picking news reports that prove their points. They also blindly trust those famous people and experts. This is how they stray further away from the path of truth.

我自己也犯过同样的错误，在过去这些年里最失败的一次投资，也是在一个无人商量和挑战我的判断的情况下做出的。如果把各种机会成本的损失加起来，大约导致半粒米(millions)打水漂了。

I once fell victim to the same mistake. I made the decision to invest in a project that turned out to be the most terrible investment in these years without any discussion with others or challenging my own analysis. Adding all the opportunity costs and losses, I lost about half a million.

如果总结第一件事情的话，就是对投资的判断千万不要被主流媒体所左右，也不要迷信任何著名人士的判断，虽然他们口若悬河，振振有词，但是实际上他们往往和你我一样无知。

My conclusion on my first takeaway is that do not be swayed by the mainstream media when making investment decisions. Do not blindly trust the analysis by experts. Even though they may sound smart, they are, in fact, as ignorant as you and me.

再说说第二件事情吧。就是如何做到可持续发展，如何做到保证持续的增长，特别是自己的规模到达一定数量之后。

Moving on to my second takeaway on how to achieve persistent growth, especially when your portfolio is quite large.

世间万事，不怕慢，就怕停。我发现投资也是，一次撞大运的投资容易，是否能够重复就变得很重要。以万达为例，其实模式很简单，就是在城市的边缘建设综合体。建一个赚一个，于是再去建下一个。

The biggest enemy to achieving progress is not slow improvements but a pause. The same is also true of investments. It is easy to bump into a profitable investment project one time, but what's more important is whether you will be able to repeat this success. Take Wanda Group, a Chinese multinational conglomerate based in Beijing. Its business strategy is simple: build an entertainment complex in the outskirts of cities, and then build another with the profits from the first one, and so on.

我们投资房地产也是这样。过去这些年里，在中国我的确找到一个可以简单复制的办法，这里和大家分享一下。

I also use a similar strategy in my real estate investing. In the past years, I found an easily replicable strategy in China. The details are as follows.

以上海为例，最简单的办法就是在地铁通车 1-2 年前，在地铁沿线偏远的地方购入房产。等到地铁通车，房价一般都会上扬 50% 到 100%。这个简单的规律屡试不爽。大约 20 年前，地铁一号线通车的时候，莘庄房价一年攀升一倍。2013 年夏天，我告诉大家应该去临港买房子，2013 年底，地铁 16 号线通车，如果你 2013 年中购入惠南到临港的任何一个小区的话，现在也差不多是涨一倍。这个规律和大盘的规律无关，几次经济的大起大落，都保持不变。过去 11 号线，10 号线通车，每次都是这样。这是个傻瓜都能发财的办法。如果你过去 20 年里一直利用这个规律，买进卖出的话，会变得很有规模。上海北京的地铁还要修很多年，大家还有机会。

Take Shanghai. The simplest way is to buy real properties that were located in remote areas along metro lines 1-2 years before the opening of a new metro station nearby. After the opening, property prices will increase by about 50-100%. I made handsome profits every time I used this strategy. About 20 years ago, when Metro line 1 was opened, property prices in Xinzhuang doubled in a year. In the summer of 2013, I told everyone that they should buy real properties in Lingang. At the end of 2013, Metro line 16 was opened. If a person listened to my advice and bought a real property in Huinan or Lingang area, his or her investment would double now. This pattern is not affected by the market. This strategy holds true in several cycles of ups and downs in the economy. When Metro lines 11 and 10 were opened, the property prices in nearby areas also doubled. This is a fail-proof strategy. If a person has been following this pattern for the last 20 years in his real estate investing, his or her portfolio will be quite impressive now. There will still be further extensions of the metro system in Shanghai and Beijing, so we will still have great investment opportunities in the future.

在美国，作为可持续发展，我只想出来了一个 16 年退休的懒人投资法。

As part of my quest to seek sustainable growth in the U.S., I was only able to come up with "Investment Strategies for Lazy People," which will take 16 years.

现在离写这篇文章的时候，已经过去了近 7 年，如果有人用我的懒人投资法的话，估计离胜利的终点已经过半了。不过懒人投资法看似容易，需要极其懒的人才行。懒得酱油瓶倒了都懒得扶才行，否则前功尽弃。

It has been seven years since I published my article on "Investment Strategies for Lazy People." If someone has followed the principles, he or she will be almost halfway through. Even though the strategies may seem easy, investors need to be extremely lazy if they want to be successful. Anyone who uses these strategies should be as lazy as they can.

我自己是勤快人，无法用懒人投资法，作为勤快人，就使用勤快人投资法，我自己依旧在探索可持续发展的办法，如果只是靠工资积累去投资，一方面很辛苦，一方面还要时常有市场大环境的风险。希望今年能摸索出一些新路子。

I am a diligent person, so "Investment Strategies for Lazy People" will not work for me. As a diligent person, he or she must apply "Investment Strategies for Diligent People." I am still exploring more ways to keep a portfolio growing. If we are merely financing our investments using our salaries, we face two problems. Firstly, it will be a tough journey. Secondly, we sometimes need to face the risks inherent in the overall market. Therefore, I am hoping to explore some new strategies this year.

啰啰嗦嗦写了这么多，到了数钱的时候。坛子里有钱人很多，我这里也不是为了和大家比阔。自己是湾区普通家庭，在过去几年里，还经常处于失业状态，身体也不好，错失很多投资机会。

Alrighty, it's time to count my money. I know that there are many rich people on this forum. My purpose is not to show off my wealth and compare myself to them. My household is an average family in the Bay Area. Besides, in the last couple of years, I was unemployed and had a health condition, so I missed many investment opportunities.

2006 年，我第一次写普通家庭十年一千万理财计划的时候。当时我认为加州会重复以前四次房地产周期循环一样的模式，在下调之后，价格重新抬升。当时也是基于这样的判断，写了我的 10 年一千万的理财计划。有兴趣的读者可以回去翻翻看我过去的博客。理论增长和实际增长总是有很大的差距，很遗憾市场底部的时候，因为健康和工作调整错过一些机会，不然的确可以做的更好。噼里啪啦算了一下，已经到了 X 粒米(millions)，十年 10 粒米看来是无望了，估计需要 15 年左右吧。

In 2006 when I first wrote about my "An Average Family's $10-million-in-10-year Investment Plan," I believed that California's real estate market would repeat its last four cycles: prices recovered after a downward adjustment. Because of such a judgment, I wrote my $10-million-in-10-year investment plan. Those of you who are interested can glance through my past blog articles. However, there are always discrepancies between theories and reality. Unfortunately, when the market hit its bottom, I missed some opportunities because of my health and a change in my job. Otherwise, I could have done better. Now, my net worth is US$X million. It seems impossible for me to reach my goal of $10 million according to the plan. I guess it will take a total of 15 years now.

普通人家十年一千万理财计划（第八年 **2014**）

**An Average Family's $10 million in 10 years Wealth Management Plan-
Summary of Year 7 and Plans for 2014 (written in 2014)**

by Bayfamily

人生苦短。想到未来 10 年是那么的漫长，可是回首往事 10 年就在弹指一挥间。每年总是春节开始写总结，今年春节晚，提前写了。

Life is short. When we think about the next decade of my life, everything seems distant. However, in retrospect, the things that happened in the past decade fleeted away. I usually write my summary at the beginning of Chinese New Year, but I cannot wait until this year's Chinese New Year, which is on 31 January, to start writing my summary.

今年房价涨，股市涨。美国股市涨，中国股市涨。工资涨，外快涨。这些都没什么，最关键的是房租涨。今年湾区房租涨到连自己都不敢要价的地步，一个广告来了50多封邮件。你开什么样的房租，马上有人立刻接盘。什么都涨，唯有体重没有涨，微降数磅。人生还有什么能够再幸福的呢。

In 2013, property prices and stock prices rose. The stock markets in the U.S. and China were also booming. People's salaries also increased. The most important trend is that rents also went up. This year, I was even embarrassed to make an offer to my tenants. One single advertisement for rent attracted more than 50 emails. No matter what price I asked, there would be someone who was willing to take it. Everything is increasing, except for my weight. In fact, I lost some weight. My life cannot get happier.

言归正传，说说投资。投资讲究的是信息优势。当任何一个项目，你不具备信息优势的时候，最好不要去碰。比如投资油井，投资黄金，比如你不了解行业股票。每次你获得某种投资信息的时候，需要思考一下，这个信息是怎样进入我的视野的，然后再做出投资判断。

Anyway, let's go back to investing. The key to success is an information advantage. If you don't possess an information advantage in a project, don't even touch it, whether it be an oil well, gold, or stocks. Every time when we obtain some investment information, we have to first ask ourselves, "How does such information come into my life?" before we make an investment decision.

老中在美国到底有什么样的信息优势呢？今年我的感受是，我们的视野比大多数的美国人更加宽阔。大部分美国人沉醉在美国的体育和娱乐新闻里，由于不关心，而不了解世界。不知道这个世界正在和已经发生了哪些变革。2012 年，我在买投资房的时候，一个老美中介带我看房。她感到非常惊讶，她说这个地区突然冒出来的投资者都是 Asian (亚裔)，她好奇怎么亚裔突然开始买这个地区的房子呢。我没有好意思和她仔细讲，因为她不知道我们能够感受到的 IT 行业复苏，她也不知道成千上万的中国家庭正在把他们的孩子送往美国中学的路上，她也不知道华人蜂拥而至的温哥华、悉尼曾经经历过怎样翻天覆地的房价变化。

What kind of information advantage do Chinese Americans possess? My takeaway this year is that we enjoy a broader horizon than most Americans who spend much of their time on sports and entertainment news. As they neither care about nor understand global affairs, they don't know about the changes in the world. In 2012, when I was buying an investment property, an American real estate agent told me that she was surprised to see the investors in the region were all Asians. She was also curious why Asians were now interested in that neighborhood. I did not know how to explain to her that Asians could feel that the IT industry was recovering. The real estate agent had no idea that tens of thousands of Chinese families were sending their children to high schools in the U.S. Neither did she know that cities such as Vancouver and Sydney that Chinese families flocked to have witnessed drastic changes in their property prices.

在美国的老中因为受到比较好的教育，和全世界华人同呼吸共命运，又能够在欧洲、亚洲和美国到处走走，所以视野可能更加开阔一点。

Most Chinese Americans have a broader horizon because they are often well-educated, identify themselves as Chinese, and often travel to different cities in Europe, Asia, and America.

赚钱其实是个简单的事情。往往是个偶然的机会，发现了某种投资机会。然后就是不断复制，一遍遍的重复。比如大富豪万达的王健林，无非就是把同样的万达广场一遍遍地重新建设。过去 5 年里，买银行拍卖屋的也是一样。一旦熟悉和了解法院的拍卖程序，一遍遍地复制。一次次 20-100%的收益，累计起来就很多。

Making money is less difficult than we imagined. In fact, it's quite easy. There is a replicable pattern. First, someone finds out about an investment opportunity by chance. Then, he or she grabs this opportunity, which turns out to be a success. All he or she needs to do now is to repeat the previous success story. Take Wang Jianlin, a Chinese billionaire and chairman of Wanda Group. All he has been doing is to renovate Wanda plazas. The same is also true of buying foreclosures. Once you understand the procedures, you can copy your actions and reap a 20-100% profit every time again and again.

这些投资机会肯定不是报纸媒体铺天盖地宣传的。铺天盖地宣传的 401K 是因为背后有利益团体金融公司在做广告。没人宣传的投资机会，才是有价值的机会。过去这些年，我靠的也是自己摸索出来的两个可复制的投资规律。可以反复复制。简单说一下。

No one will advertise these opportunities. All the advertisements on 401K are funded by financial institutions who make their money from it. Therefore, only those investment opportunities that are not in the ads are valuable ones. In the past years, I have found out two replicable investment patterns.

一个是国内的房地产投资。只要跟着城市的基础建设开发，在北京和上海这样的城市，一般不会错。就是在地铁规划好，还没建成通车的时候，买下离地铁站非常近的楼盘。等到地铁开通，房价一般都会有 50%的增幅。投资周期一般是 1 年左右。

The first is on how to invest in real properties in China. Following infrastructure projects in cities such as Beijing and Shanghai seldom goes wrong. Before the construction of a metro line or opening of a station, buy real properties that are in proximity to the planned station. After the opening, the property prices in the neighborhood will often increase by 50%. This investment takes about a year.

二是美国的房地产投资。其他州我不了解。加州过去四次房地产周期的循环特征非常像。和股票不同，房产周期的变化是可以预测，又有非常大的滞后性，也是可以捕捉的。每次复苏之后都是租金的狂飙，本来打平的房子立刻变成财源滚滚的正现金流。按照这个周期一遍遍地去复制就是了。

The second is on how to invest in real properties in California. I am not familiar with the real estate market in other states. However, California's real estate market has shown four similar cycles in the past. Unlike the stock market, you can predict and catch the changes in the real estate market because the real estate market often lags behind the real economy. After each economic recovery, rents soar. Investment properties that have an even cash flow before the recovery will now have positive cash flow. Therefore, all we need to do as investors is to copy this successful strategy according to the cyclical changes.

说说未来，我觉得对未来的美国会持续繁荣一阵子，至少有 5-10 年的成长空间。说出来也许你不信，但是我觉得未来 5-10 年里，湾区的房价会再有 50-100%的升幅。低价位的房子增值潜力更大。如果投资，稳妥地买正现金流的房子，会有很多机会。 喜欢海边的同学们，经过了这么多年，夏威夷的房子终于开始有投资价值。变得负担得起(affordable). 感兴趣的同学可以去关注一下。

Looking ahead, I think the U.S. economy will continue to prosper in the next 5-10 years. Perhaps you won't believe this, but I think that property prices in the Bay Area will witness a 50-100% increase in the next 5-10 years. Properties with a low price now have greater potential in the future. Investment opportunities abound for investors who are looking to buy investment properties with positive cash flow. Those of you who like the beach can consider buying investment properties in Hawaii, which have now become affordable.

中国的近期经济形势看不清。文革背景下长大的同志。搞经济不行，整人都是一把好手。我个人估计，不出意外的话，中国未来几年里会爆发大的危机。根据经济学原理，几乎所有的交易都是好的，都是创造价值的。大家看到的是贪官拿了几千万，但是输送几千万的商人，项目能够批下来，产生的社会效益就是几个亿。腐败是过去这台破机器破体制还能运作下去的润滑油。当商人不上项目，官员天天喝茶看报搞清廉的时候，反腐会让这台经济的列车在缺少润滑油的情况下戛然而止。

However, I am not sure about the recent economic development of China because government officials who grew up during the Chinese Revolution are bad at formulating effective economic policies but good at seizing power. I guess that China will experience a big crisis in the next few years. According to economics theories, almost all transactions are good because they create value for society. We can often come across news articles on corruption in China reporting that corrupted officials embezzled tens of millions of Chinese Yuan or received bribes from businesses. These transactions also create value for society. In fact, corruption is how the broken economic machine in China can still operate. When businesses cannot get their projects approved by the authorities and officials spend all their time and energy cracking down on corruption, the economic machine in China will stop running.

经济和政治的风险很多，即使是北京上海同样存在风险。但是用我说的投资地铁沿线的办法过去 20 年里证明无论什么样的大的经济环境，都是适用的。北京的地铁已经是世界上里程最长的了，　总共 500 多公里。可是到了 2020 年，　这个数字还会翻一翻，达到 1000 公里。这是什么规模？相当于未来 5 年，新建一个完整的纽约地铁网络。如此巨大的地铁网络，会对市中心房价产生巨大压力，　同时也是投资远郊地铁房的好机会。南边大兴在修新机场，会出现新的望京，北边在修往张家口的高铁，会出现新的雾霾移民。多看看规划，多看看地图，满眼都是财富。

Furthermore, there are many economic and political risks in China, even in cities such as Beijing and Shanghai. However, my strategies of investing in real properties located along metro lines have proved effective in the last 20 years regardless of the macroeconomic conditions. Beijing already has the biggest rapid transit railway system in the world, with a total route length of more than 500 km. However, in 2020, this number will double and reach 1000 km. This means that Beijing builds a new, complete New York City subway system every five years. Such a massive railway system will exert great pressure on property prices in city centers. Meanwhile, it also implies that buying real properties in the more remote areas of the city will be good investments. There is a new airport under construction in Daxing, the southern part of Beijing, which is expected to be the new Wangjing subdistrict. The northern part of the city is home to a high-speed railway station that can take citizens all the way to Zhangjiakou, a city in Hebei. There will soon be people who emigrate because of air pollution in China.

Therefore, we should all learn more about the urban planning of a city. When we read the map, we can see that there are investment opportunities everywhere.

中国远期的经济形势非常好。未来 10-20 年里，不出意外的话，中国的人均 GDP 会达到台湾相当的水平。中国没有任何道理比台湾更穷。上海北京这些中心地区的人均 GDP 会超过美国，达到香港新加坡的水平。上海和北京按照现在的成长速度，最终的人口会突破 4000 万的规模。如果你投资的时候，心中有这样的远景，就会明白，如果中国爆发大的政治经济危机，就几乎是此生最好的投资机会了。现在的当务之急是准备现金，等待那个激动人心的时刻。

China's long-term economic prospect is promising. In the next 10-20 years, if nothing goes wrong, China's GDP per capita will be equal to Taiwan's. There is no reason that China is poorer than Taiwan. The GDP per capita of central cities such as Beijing and Shanghai will exceed that of the U.S. as a whole, catching up with Singapore and Hong Kong. The population of Shanghai and Beijing will each exceed 40 million. If we bear these predictions in mind when making investment decisions, we will understand that if there is a huge political or economic crisis in China, it will be the best investment opportunity in our lives. What we should do now is to prepare our cash and wait for that exciting moment.

年底噼噼啪啪算账，第 10 年的时候，完成原来预定任务的一半没有任何问题，因为现在已经很接近了。坛子里和我几乎同时起步的人，有些人已经或者很接近一千万了。自己没有实现一千万的目标的原因有这么几个。

It's time to calculate my net worth. I guess that my net worth can easily reach US$5 million in my 10th year because I am now already very close to it. However, those forum users who started their investment plans at the same time as I did are already very close to hitting US$10 million. I reflected on this and identified several reasons why I lagged behind.

1. 没有把投资赚钱作为生活的第一优先。没有打算做专业的房地产投资人。所以不搞商业地产，不搞开发。人生有很多其他的考虑，也有很多更加有趣的事情，比如自己的事业和爱好。很多时候没有为金钱做出牺牲。如果专业做投资，更加专注一点，成绩会再好一点。

Firstly, I did not prioritize making money. As I did not plan to become a professional real estate investor, I ruled out commercial properties from my portfolio. Neither was I interested in developing land. There are many other considerations and fun things in life, for example, my own career and hobbies. Sometimes, I did not make sacrifices for money. If I had been a more professional and focused investor, my performance would have been better.

2. 没有承担更多的风险。小富则安心理严重。觉得自己孩子上大学的钱够了，自己养老的钱也够了，自己又不是那么喜欢奢侈浪费的人，不需要那么急吼吼地实现目标。2012 年正确的做法是卖掉中国的一部分房产，拿到美国来投资，现在应该再多 1-2 粒米。年纪大了，渐渐开始懒得折腾。

Secondly, I don't want to bear more risks. I will be content with a small fortune that will help me support my children through college and take care of my life after retirement. Besides, I do not have an extravagant lifestyle, so I took my time to achieve my goal. In 2012, if I had sold some of my investment properties in China and used the money to invest in the U.S., I would have had $1-2 million more now. But as I am now older, I am getting lazier.

3. 懒惰。有时明明看着是正确的房产投资。但是因买卖房屋手续复杂，涉及税财务等等一系列事情，放弃。还是那句老话，投资房地产，需要勤快人。投资股票需要懒人。

Thirdly, I am lazy. Sometimes, I knew that I should buy that investment property, but I gave up because of the complicated procedures. It's the old saying again, "Real estate investors need to be diligent, and stock investors need to be lazy."

4. 的确是普通人家。一没股票，二无高工资。平均收入在湾区贫困线以下的以下。预祝各位新春愉快。实现一千万的同学们，别忘了出来吼几嗓子。

Fourthly, after all, my household is an average family in the Bay Area. We don't own IPO shares in tech companies or earn a high income. My household income is, in fact, below the low-income limits in the Bay Area. Finally, I wish all of you a happy Chinese New Year. If any of you have already achieved $10 million, don't forget to share your happiness with us on this forum.

普通家庭十年一千万投资理财计划（第九年 2015）

An Average Family's $10 million in 10 years Wealth Management Plan-Summary of Year 8 and Plans for 2015 (written in 2015)

by Bayfamily

又是春节了。日子一年年地过去了，年年汇报。这是第九个年头来汇报我的十年计划了。

It's Chinese New Year again. This is my eighth annual investment summary.

这一年觉得过得格外的快。不对，应该说过去的九年里，自己觉得写汇报的间隔一次比一次短了。此时和百年孤独里面的乌苏拉有同感，她觉得人老了，就会发现孩子们一代比一代长得快。自己的儿子需要漫长的时间才能长大，等到重孙子的时候，觉得一眨眼孩子就长大成人了。

Time flies. Or I should say in the last nine years, I felt that the time between writing each investment summary ticked away faster. I can echo with how Amaranta Úrsula's feelings, a character in One Hundred Years of Solitude. She said that as she aged, it seemed that the faster the children grew up. It felt centuries for her own son to grow up, but the blink of an eye for her great-grandchildren to become an adult.

9 年过去了，昔日坛子里的战友只剩寥寥无几了，人换了一茬又一茬。当年他们各自的理想和目标，除了网友 va_landlord, 不知道实现的怎样了。

It's been nine years since I announced my US$10-million-in-10-year plan. Many of my old comrades left this forum, which has welcomed new forum users. I haven't heard of any updates on the progress of achieving their goals from my old comrades except for user *va-landlord*.

拿老朽的话来说，人生就像坐火车，旅程一站又一站。只是发现后来站与站之间的间距越来越短。当然，这对投资理财其实是好事，就是发现自己的财富越长越快。头一个一百万是那么地漫长。后面的一百万转眼即过。如果人生再有重来的话，似乎我更喜欢最开始的那个一百万。人生若只如初见。呵呵。

To borrow a saying from forum user *Laoxiu*, "Life is like a train ride that stops at different stations, but we will realize in the second half of the journey that the distance between stations is getting shorter." Of course, this is a good thing for investors because they will find that their wealth grows more rapidly in the life journey. The first million often feels centuries, and the millions in the second half of the journey are in the blink of an eye. But if we can relive our memories, I enjoy my first million the most. If only life was as beautiful as it seemed at first sight.

今年基本什么都没有做，只是看自己的钱在生钱。因为以后不打算一个个买房子了，套句时髦的话，正在酝酿经济转型。常言道，有苗不愁长。房子也是，房子在手，剩下的事情就是静等市场推波助澜。一天天的涨上去就是了。

I basically did nothing in 2014 (Year 8). All I did was watching how my money grows more money for me. I am planning to undergo an "economic transformation," as I have decided not to buy individual residential properties anymore. As the old saying goes, "Once your seeds start to sprout, you don't have to worry about their growth." The same is also true for real estate investing. Once you have bought your investment properties, all you need to do next is to wait for the market to boom and prices to rise.

中国一线城市的房子在涨，湾区的房子也在涨。所以自己年底噼里啪啦一算，的确是原来的十年目标完成一半了。看来原定的目标十年内难以实现。大约需要 15 年左右的时间。

The property prices in tier-1 cities in China are surging, and so are those in the Bay Area. After some calculations, I realized that I have finished 50% of my $10-million goal. I guess that it will be difficult, if not impossible, for me to achieve this goal in 10 years. I will probably need 15 years in total.

影响目标实现的最大原因，应该是第 4 年金融危机的时候，悟出来的一个重要教条——"剩者为王"。投资有 20% 左右的成长，就不要追求再高的目标了。因为游戏能够一直进行下去，比游戏玩得更好更加重要。所以即使面临再好的投资机会，也要抱着谨慎稳妥的方式。在过去 9 年里，我从来还没有用投资挣的钱再去投资，也没有放大杠杆比例，也没有做全职投资的人。不然改变一下的话，也许已经实现目标，但也许也会一败涂地。毕竟，人生除了挣钱，还有那么多其他的重要事情要去做。

The greatest hindrance is that in the fourth year of my investment journey when the financial crisis beset the economy, it dawned on me that a rule of thumb in real estate investing is "the remainer takes all." When one has an investment return of about 20%, he or she should not set a higher goal. What's more important than the growth rate is how to remain in the game. Therefore, even if this investor may face better investment opportunities with a higher return rate, he or she needs to be prudent first and foremost. In the last nine years, I haven't reinvested the profits from my investments, obtained more leverage, or become a full-time investor. If I had done any of these, I would have achieved my goal already. Meanwhile, I might also lose everything. After all, life is not only about making money.

顺便说说这一年的投资感悟吧。最大的感悟就是发现原来说的，房地产就是"Location, Location, Location." 这话不完全对。如果只从表面意义上理解 Location，那么投资的回报不会特别理想。

Let me talk about the lessons I learned. My biggest takeaway is that the mantra of "location, location, location" is not necessarily correct. If one only understands the literal meaning of location, his or her investment returns will not be ideal.

正确的说法应该是 future location, future location, future location。就是说应该投资到因为各种原因，地区会变好的地方。比如东湾著名的 West Oakland。是一个犯罪率高，人人不敢涉足的地方，我的中介过去也屡次劝我到那边买房，我因为害怕流弹，从来都懒得去看。但是随着 gentrification， 事实上过去几年 West Oakland 是东湾房价增长最快的地方。特别是在地铁站附近，到旧金山只有一站地，其实那边很安全。

The more accurate saying should be "future location, future location, future location." This means that we should buy investment properties in areas that will become better in the future. Take West Oakland, East Bay. The area is notorious for its high crime rate. Everyone was scared to go there. In the past, my real estate agent had recommended that I buy investment properties there. But I didn't bother to go to the area because I was afraid of being hit by stray bullets. However, the property prices in West Oakland, especially areas that are in proximity to subway stations, saw the greatest increase in the East Bay thanks to gentrification. West Oakland is one subway station away from San Francisco. Contrary to common beliefs, West Oakland is actually a safe place.

同样的道理适合在中国。中国投资房地产不是买在市中心就好。而是要看市政府的轨道交通规划。就拿北京来说，金融街的房价目前是 15-20 万一平米左右。而未来几年马上要竣工的新机场快线，从南六环到金融街只有两站，耗时 20 分钟。而南六环的房价目前只有两万。可以想象，当过几年机场快线通车之际。机场快线各站附近的房价翻翻是很容易的事情。上海的虹桥商务中心，同样的道理，你打开地图和规划看看，到处都是翻翻挣钱的机会。这一切其实和宏观的经济环境没有太大的关系。

The same also applies to real estate investing in China. Real properties situated in city centers are not necessarily the best investments. Instead, we need to look at the metro-plan of the city. Take Beijing. The property prices in the Financial Street area is around CN¥150,000-200,000 (approximately US$24193-32,258) per square meter. In the next few years, the Airport Express will soon open, which means that Financial Street is two metro stations or 20-minute away from the South Sixth Ring area. Right now, the property prices in the South Sixth Ring area is only CN¥20,000 (about US$3,225) per square meter. When the Air Express opens in a few years, the property prices along it will double or even triple. Another potential area is the Hongqiao Commercial Center in Shanghai. The same strategy is applicable. Just look at maps and urban planning and you will find good investment opportunities are everywhere. And none of this is much affected by macroeconomic conditions.

房地产的投资和股票不一样。有这样消息的公司股票，一夜之间就会涨价到位。根本不给投资人什么机会。房地产价格的变动非常有黏性(sticky). 就是眼瞅着利好，价格需要好长一段时间才能上去。因为买房不是点点鼠标那么容易，需要走流程办手续。还是那句话，勤快人买房子，懒人买股票。

Real estate investing is different from buying stocks. The stock of any company with such good news will increase to the corresponding level overnight, leaving little room for investors. In contrast, the changes in property prices are very sticky, which means that it takes a long time for the prices to rise to the corresponding level in response to the good news. This is because buying a house is not as easy as clicking your mouse. Real estate investors need to go through all sorts of procedures. It's the old saying: Diligent people should invest in real estate and lazy people stocks.

说到懒人买股票。如果用我 9 年前公布的 16 年懒人投资法。现在应该进程过半了，赚得盆满钵满，收获颇丰了。可是我知道大部分人只是看看，落实的人基本不会有。因为人改变自己的习性实在太难了。懒人变勤快人不可能，勤快人变懒人更难。所以投资看来还是需要认清自己的习性。

Speaking of stocks and lazy people, if a person has been applying my "Investment Strategies for Lazy People" published nine years ago, he or she will now be more than halfway through the goal and have made big profits. But I also know that most of my readers are spectators. They rarely take action. After all, it's difficult for human beings to change their old habits. It's almost impossible for lazy people to become more hardworking and diligent people lazier. In conclusion, before we start our investment journey, we have to first understand our own personality.

再说说宏观经济形势吧。去年预测的中国经济下滑正在愈演愈烈。但是一线城市的房价还是像打了鸡血一样，尤其是深圳。持币观望的还需要继续持币观望。不过今年要稍微说点反话，可能中国正在经历经济最糟糕的底部，并且在不知不觉中就会过去了。一般底部的底部就是一些极端事件 (dramatic events). 比如破产，群众事件，大规模下岗之类的，我觉得未来几年可能就会有。大家看戏的时候，别忘了抄底。

Let's talk about macroeconomics. The prediction that the Chinese economy will go downwards that I made last year seems to have materialized. However, property prices in tier-one cities, especially Shenzhen, are still surging. Anyone of you who is holding onto your cash should continue to adopt a prudent attitude. That being said, I must say that China is probably experiencing the bottom of its economy, which will soon pass. The bottom of an economy or market is characterized by dramatic events, for example, bankruptcies, public events, and large-scale layoffs, which I think may well happen in the next few years. Don't forget to buy the bottom.

好了，明年是 10 年计划的最后一年。到时候做个最终总结，能够和大家交流一些自己的心得体会，希望能够最终完成原计划的 60%。

Alrighty, 2015 marks the final year of my 10-year investment plan. I will do a final summary next year to share my takeaways with you. I hope that I will be able to reach 60% of my goal.

普通家庭十年一千万理财计划 （第十年完 2016）

An Average Family's $10 million in 10 years Wealth Management Plan- Summary of Year 10 and Future Plans (written in 2016)

By Bayfamily

这是这个十年序列的最后一篇文章。此刻的投资理财论坛已经物是人非。十年前的大侠们所剩无几，剩下的，当然有赚的盆满钵满，早已过了一千万的，当然也有人看尽了热闹，耍够了嘴皮，最后两手空空。能坚持写十年的理财故事，能有几人？

This is the last article in my 10-year series. A lot has changed on this forum. Few of the users who started using this forum since its early days have stayed. Some of those who have stayed have a net worth of much more than US$10 million now, and some of them are just a spectator who earned nothing. I am probably the only one who has persevered with sharing my 10-year investment and wealth management journey.

先说成绩，再说道理。到了第十年写这篇文章，很遗憾，一千万的目标没有实现。打开账本噼里啪啦算了一下，共有双位数的房子和一些股票。接着国内房价去年的高歌猛进，总共净资产是七粒米不到一点。如果不出意外的话，按照最近几年的财富增长情况，应该在第 13 年到第 15 年实现一千万的目标。

Let's talk about my performance first and takeaways next. Unfortunately, I have not achieved my goal of US$10 million in the tenth year of my investment journey. After some calculations, my net worth is south of US$7 million. According to my investment returns in the last several years, I estimate that I can achieve my goal of US$10 million in 13-15 years in total.

没有实现目标的主要原因是自己没有去做更高风险的事情。比如，从来没有做过二次投资，就是用投资赚的钱再去投资。从来没有买过地，从来没有做过开发项目，从来没有碰过商业地产，从来没有大额在中国美国换汇。我做的都是力所能及，不用担惊受怕的事情。因为游戏的时间还长着呢，没必要为早两年实现目标去冒那么多的风险，让自己寝食难安。国内资产和美国资产正好各占 50%。所以汇率发生什么变化都完全和我无关。

The main reason why I have not yet achieved my goal is that I have never tried to bear more risks. For example, I have never reinvested my profits, bought a piece of land, or developed property projects. Commercial properties were out of my radar in the last 10 years. Never have I ever made a large sum of CN¥-US$ foreign exchange investments. All of my investments in the last decade were within my capabilities, and I have never made risky investments. I know that it's not worth it to bear extra risks in an attempt to realize my goal two years earlier because investing is a long game. Since 50% of my investment portfolio is Chinese assets and 50% U.S. assets, I don't have to worry about fluctuating exchange rates.

还有一个原因是人算不如天算吧。过去 10 年里，有一个阶段身体不是很好。没有把握住几个机会。

The second reason is that life is full of uncertainties that cannot be prepared for in advance. In the last 10 years, there was a stage in which I had a health condition, so I failed to jump on a few investment opportunities.

最后一个原因就是投资一直不是生活的主旋律。投资其实是很容易的事情，也是很无聊的事情。人生是否快乐和钱的关系也不大。过去十年里做了两个公司，一个失败关门，一个奋斗了 8 年，终于可以活下来了，未来十年打算再做一个初创公司(startup)。人生和玩游戏一样，游戏是输赢本身其实不重要，能够让自己快乐地把各种游戏玩下去才是快乐所在。算算自己离退休还有 20 多年，还可以捡几个有趣的游戏玩玩。投资理财只是其中的一个。

The final reason is that I have not prioritized making investments. Investing is a piece of cake, but it is also boring. There is little correlation between happiness and money. In the past 10 years, I worked in two companies. One of them failed, and another survived after eight years of hard work. In the next 10 years, my plan is to start a startup. Life is like a game. Whether you win or lose does not matter. The key is whether we enjoy the process. There are more than two decades left before I retire, so I have room to pick a few more interesting games. Investing and wealth management is one of them.

在过去 10 年里，我的家庭现金收入情况不是很好。在湾区应该算是中下阶层。十年前的年总收入不超过 15 万，现在不到 20 万。从来没有过公司分配的原始股，没有发过大的横财。我们也不是特别勤劳的人，每周的工作时间也从来没有超过 40 个小时。每年也没耽误出国度假。

In the last decade, my household income was not very ideal. My family probably belongs to the lower middle class in the Bay Area. A decade ago, my annual household income was below US$150,000, and it now stands at short of US$200,000. My family has never received stock options from companies or other unexpected money. My wife and I are not particularly hardworking people. We have never worked more than 40 hours every week, and we take a vacation every year.

但是我的投资经历完完整整地呈现给大家。供后人参考。每年的记录，从来没有一丝的夸张，也没有一丝的掩饰。

I have shared every detail of my investment journey with you. These articles are also a reference point for future generations. I have not concealed or exaggerated anything in documenting my investment journey.

过去十年，我只是按照自己 2006 年的计划，在中国和湾区买了一些房子，仅此而已。想看我何时何地买了房子的，可以 Google 一下过去这个系列的每年年终汇报。

In the last ten years, I bought some investment properties in China and the Bay Area according to the plan I formulated in 2006. This is all I did. For those of you who would like to know when I bought these properties, feel free to Google my annual summary of my investment performance.

要说要总结什么不成熟的经验的话，有如下几个：

I have identified several areas that have room for improvement.

1）对宏观大趋势需要有正确的判断。2006 年的时候，当时湾区的房价还在高歌猛进，我第一次提出 10 年一千万的理想。我的预测是未来 10 年，加州房地产会像之前四次的循环一样，经历下跌，恢复，再高涨的过程。所有的投资准备也都是按照这个预测做出的。虽然我没有办法预测到准确的时间，但是心里对大趋势需要有一个明确的概念。老实说，我自己也不知道正确的判断从哪里来。记得 2010 年的时候，国内房价大涨。当时正值美国房市破裂。在湾区跟一群人聊天，每个人都说国内房价很快就会崩盘。众人围着桌子举手表决，没有一个人认为中国房价会涨上去。我没好意思和大家抬杠，只说我不置可否。

1) Making judgments about macroeconomic trends. We need to have correct judgments about macroeconomic trends. In 2006, when property prices in the Bay Area were soaring, I mentioned my goal of US$10 million in 10 years. My then prediction was that in the next 10 years, California's real estate market would repeat its previous four cycles: a decline, then recovery, and finally a boom. I prepared all of my investment

plans based on this prediction. Even though we cannot predict the exact timing, we must have a correct understanding of major market trends. To be honest, I have no idea where to find a correct judgment about the market. I still remember that in 2010, when China's property prices were surging, the U.S. real estate market was collapsing. At the time, I had a conversation with a bunch of people in the Bay Area. They all said that China's property prices would soon collapse too. They even had a vote by raising their hand. The vote showed that no one believed China's property prices would continue to increase, so I did not dare disagree with the group and said that I had not formed a view yet.

我不知道很多人为什么对房价的未来形势总是看不清。我自己觉得市场很多时候是明明白白。再比如，2011 年湾区房价大涨。我觉得这一轮的上涨会持续 3-5 年，所以一路果断买进。但是还是有很多人看到涨了 20%就犹犹豫豫不再跟进。老实说，我不知道他们在犹豫什么。是什么影响了大家正确的判断。

I am confused about why many people always fail to see the future trend of property prices clearly. In my opinion, the market trends are obvious. For example, in 2011, when property prices in the Bay Area surged, I believed that this round of price increase would last for 3-5 years, so I did not hesitate to buy some investment properties. Meanwhile, many other people were hesitating after seeing a 20% price increase. To be honest, I had no idea why they were so indecisive and what affected their ability to make correct judgments.

2）不要停留在空谈。空谈误国。我也认识一些人，对形势的判断基本正确，但是停留在空谈。喜欢给自己找借口和理由不去做投资。投资股票最简单。点点鼠标就行了。房地产投资却是一个力气活。需要有坚韧不拔的态度和克服困难的决心。一个人不想做什么事情，可以找出一万个理由出来。一个人想做什么事情，上帝都会来帮忙。

2) Taking action. Don't content yourself with empty talk. Empty talk holds you back. Some acquaintances of mine stopped at the empty talk stage though they have a correct judgment about the market. These people like to find excuses not to take action.

Investing in stocks is easier. All it takes is just a few clicks. On the other hand, real estate investing is time-consuming and requires determination. When a person does not want to actually achieve something, he or she has a million excuses. But when a person wants something, all the universe conspires in helping him or her achieve it.

3）不能傲慢。傲慢和偏见害死人。当然，每个深陷其中的人是不知道自己带着傲慢和偏见的。这点我也很困惑，时时照镜子问自己，是否自己也带着傲慢和偏见看投资。投资房地产最常见的傲慢和偏见就是对地段的态度。涨幅最大的永远是城市的边缘非核心地段。是 Future　　　Location,　　　不是Location。但是有地域歧视的人往往戴着有色眼镜看世界。 这点在美国可以看到，在中国上海和北京也可以看到。我承认我自己对黄金和艺术品投资有很强的歧视偏见。尽管我自己有一堆的理由支持我的论证。

3) Pride. Never let your pride and prejudice affect your judgments. Of course, a person that is proud and prejudiced will never know that this is the case. This is why I often look at the mirror and ask myself whether pride and prejudice have affected my investment decisions. The most common type of proud and prejudiced thinking in real estate investing is our attitude toward the location. The areas that will witness the greatest price increase are almost always city outskirts. Remember, the rule is future location, not location. However, some people cannot control their proud and prejudiced thinking. Such people exist in the U.S., Beijing, and Shanghai. Well, I have to admit that I am prejudiced against investing in gold and art pieces, despite the valid reasons I raised in support of my stance.

4）利用现有资源，做可重复的事。中国首富王健林的秘密就是找到一个成功的模式，一遍遍的复制。所以全国的万达广场看起来都一样。投资也是一样，找到一个自己可以复制的模式很重要。我自己 10 年前找到了这个适合自己模式，所以敢给自己树立一千万的目标。各位读者需要结合自己的实际情况，找到自己的模式。每个人的模式都不一样，不要只看着他人样子模仿，或者因为无法模仿而叹息。比如中部的人看着湾区和纽约的高房价觉得自己没有机会投资房地产。湾区和纽约的人看着中部的好现金流，觉得自己生活错了地方。同样的事情发生在中国，上海北京人面对已经是天价的房子和限购政策望洋兴叹。投资机会天天有，钻石就在自己后院。只是你没有找到它。你每做一个投资的决定，需要想一想，这个行为是否未来可复制，如何有可能，那还是去做吧。比如投资度假屋，很难 copy and paste. 所以还是看看就好，算了吧。

4) Make good use of existing resources and repeat successful strategies. The secret of success of the richest man in China is that he repeats a single successful business strategy. This is why all Wanda Plazas in China look identical. The same applies to the game of investing: finding a replicable, successful strategy is crucial. I set a US$10 million goal for myself because I found such a strategy that suits ten years ago. My advice to readers is that find a strategy that suits your particular situation. Everyone needs a different strategy, so don't blindly follow the footsteps of other successful investors. Equally, don't lose your hope when you find that others' success is not replicable. For example, looking at the exorbitant property prices in the Bay Area and New York, those who live in middle states in America lament that they have no chances to invest in real estate properties. Meanwhile, looking at positive cash flow properties everywhere in the Middle West, those who live in the Bay Area or New York think that they live in the wrong place. The same phenomenon is also happening in China. Shanghainese and Beijingers sigh at expensive property prices and limited purchase policy. Investment opportunities are everywhere. In fact, the diamond is buried right in your backyard. It's just that you haven't found it yet. Think thoroughly about every investment decision. If it can be repeated in the future, go ahead. For example, as it's difficult to copy and paste investing in vacation homes, we'd better be a spectator, not an actor.

5）房地产市场是粘性很大的市场。就是人人都觉得市场要涨了，还需要3-6个月左右时间才能飞涨起来。比如2016年的上海和北京，比如2011年的湾区。因为买房子不是股票，不是简单鼠标点点就可以的。所以房地产投资赚钱的道理特别简单，就是不涨不买，一涨立刻买。你只需要比其他人速度快几个月就可以了。当市场前景不明朗的时候，比如现在的湾区和中国，持币观望就可以了。

5) The real estate market is sticky. This means that even when everyone thinks property prices will rise, the actual increase won't materialize until another 3-6 months. Examples include the 2016 Shanghai real estate market and Beijing real estate market and the 2011 Bay Area real estate market. This is because, unlike buying stocks, buying houses cannot be finished within a few clicks. Therefore, making profits in real estate is easy: Don't buy it unless the prices are rising. Once the property prices start to increase, enter the market. All you need to do is to be a few months ahead of other buyers. When there are uncertainties of the market, for example, the current situation in the Bay Area and China, hold onto your cash and wait patiently.

既然说到未来的形势，不妨展望一下未来吧。

Speaking of future trends, here are some of my predictions.

1）先说个大胆的预测。预测需要逐步调整。但是大方向需要正确。我有种感觉中国未来 10 年到 20 年可能会变得非常的富裕。 人均 GDP 会达到甚至超过美国的平均水平。一线城市高学历白领的收入会比美国高 2-3 倍。 中间的道理可以说很久也说不完。 最重要的原因是人口的规模和单一民族，其次是体制和商业环境。当然这不是一路平坦的，中国会遇到很多问题很多危机。能否在这些危机中把握机会，就看诸位各自的本事了。当国内发生大的危机的时候，对未来要有信心。曾几何时，也就是 20 年前，中国很穷的时候，多少美国华人想着将来老了回国养老，有用不完的钱。当时的人们有想到今天么？

1) A bold prediction of mine is that China will become extremely rich in the next 10-20 years (It's okay to make predictions that need adjustments along the way, but the overall direction needs to be correct). Its GDP per capita may even exceed that of the U.S. The income of well-educated white-collar workers in tier-1 cities in China may even be a double or triple of that of their counterparts in the U.S. There are many reasons behind this prediction. The most important ones are China's population base and

mono-ethnicity. Secondary causes are its commercial environment and economic system. However, this is going to be a bumpy road in which China will experience a myriad of problems of crises. Whether you can grab these chances depends on your own skills and abilities. When big crises erupt in China, we need to have faith in the future. Don't forget that China was still a poor country and that many Chinese Americans were hoping to go back to China for their retirement to enjoy unlimited money just about 20 years ago. How many of them had correctly predicted today's China's economic capabilities?

2）中国一线城市，美国湾区房地产在未来 1-2 年里会短暂平静。应该是逐步建仓的好机会。中国限购政策是筑坝蓄水，添水止沸。湾区面临加息政策，未来价格应该相对平稳。

2) The real estate market in the Bay Area and tier-1 cities in China will be quiet in the next 1-2 years, which means good chances for investors to build their portfolio. The limited purchase policy in China will only make houses less affordable. As the Bay Area faces the risk of increasing interest rates, property prices will remain stable in the future.

3）中国变化之快让人有些跟不上趟。以上海北京为例，未来会发生的事情是城市空心化。就是城市中心没有人了，商业凋零，没有新兴产业支撑。如果你想继续投资这些城市，要避开传统市中心和环线概念。北京可以买大兴，昌平，通州。上海可以买虹桥，青浦。要是你再有长远计划，可以买上海东站。

3) China will change even rapidly. Take Beijing and Shanghai. They will experience a "hollowing out of the city center." This means that businesses will shrink and that people will move out of the city center. There will be no more new industries to support the economic growth of the cities. If you are still interested in these two cities, remember to avoid central areas and Ring areas. In Beijing, you can still buy properties located in Daxing, Changping, and Tongzhou. The Hongqiao area and Qingpu area in Shanghai are also good options. If you have a long-term horizon, the Shanghaidong Railway Station area has potential.

4）湾区变化也是非常快的。湾区的年均 GDP 成长是 7%-8%的样子，一点都不输给中国。房地产未来大家也是基本可想而知。

4) The Bay Area will also change drastically. The annual growth of its GDP is around 7-8%, which is on par with that of China. The real estate market will have a bright future.

说了很多。车轱辘话也说了十年了。所有发财的道理我觉得已经说尽了。爱听的也听烦了，不爱听的早已逃之夭夭。自己不知不觉随着年龄的成长爱唠叨，一开始是和身边的人说，后来不过瘾在网上写博客对更多的人说。最后是写书对全世界说。过去十年我写了两本书，过去十年，"普通人家十年一千万理财计划"和其他理财博客一共有 100 万左右人次的阅读量。基本满足我的唠叨欲望，当然我也从大家的回复中受益良多。

I have been sharing my investment strategies with you for ten years. I think that I have touched upon all the tips on becoming rich that are within my knowledge. Long-time supporters of this blog may already be bored with my repeated messages. And those who are not convinced by my words have already fled. I think I have become chattier as I age. At first, I was only sharing my investment strategies with those around me, then I couldn't help sharing them with more people by writing a blog. Now, here I am: writing a book to share my ideas with the whole world. In the last decade, I wrote two books. My blogs have accumulated 1 million views. I have thoroughly enjoyed my time sharing my ideas and also benefitted from my interactions with netizens.

最后祝大家新年快乐, 送上我体会的房地产投资四原则：

1）"Future Location, Future Location, Future Location"

2）不涨不买

3）正现金流

4）保持 leverage

Finally, I wish all of you a happy Chinese New Year. My four principles of real estate investing are my gifts for you:

1) "Future location, future location, future location"

2)   Don't buy investment properties unless the prices are rising

3)   Positive cash flow

4)   Maintain leverage

普通家庭十年一千万理财计划（第十一年 2017）

An Average Family's $10 million in 10 years Wealth Management Plan-Summary of Year 11 and Plans for 2017 (written in 2017)

by Bayfamily

微信公众号：WXC-Bayfamily

Wechat Fanpage: WXC-Bayfamily

每年春节我都喜欢总结一下自己一年的投资。连续十一年没有变化。今年依旧是各种资产全面增长的一年。总体资产稳中有升。

I like to summarize my investment performance during the Chinese New Year. This is a habit that I have been maintaining for 11 years. The eleventh year of my investment journey is one in which different types of assets have appreciated. Overall, my portfolio has grown steadily.

有这样一句名言。"喊空的人只能做三天新闻头条的红人，终将一无所有。看多的人，才是默默每天捡钱的"。毕竟无论股市还是房市，价格增长的时段比例，远远超过价格暴跌的时候。只是默默地增长，上不了头条，博不来大家的关注。

As the famous saying goes, "A short, or bearish investor will be a celebrity in the mainstream media for 3 days and end up with nothing. A long, or bullish investor will be making money every day without others knowing it." Whether it be the stock market or real estate market, the number of trading days that see a rise in price is far greater than the days when prices plummet. However, a steady growth rate will not attract eyeballs.

总结一下，过去 11 年自己主要是把握住了三次机会。一个是 2000-2010 的中国京沪房地产。一个是 2010 以后的湾区房地产。一个是 2016-

2018 年的加密货币。另外加上 401K 在过去 11 年持续的增长，所以最终获得了一个不错的积累。

In summary, in the last 11 years, I was able to jump on three major opportunities:-

1. Shanghai and Beijing's booming real estate market in 2000-2010,
2. the Bay Area's real estate market after 2010, and
3. bitcoins in 2016-2018.

Adding my continuously growing 401K to all the above, I have accumulated impressive gains.

我们家庭的收入一直不是很高，按照前一阵子投资理财坛子里面列的家庭收入，在湾区属于贫下中农。我想每个常年细心经营自己财务的人都会意识到，工资收入对财富的影响其实不是很大。真正有影响的是能否在关键的时间点，抓住关键的机会。而这些机会往往 2-3 年就会出现一次。

My family does not have a high household income. According to a previous discussion thread on household income on this forum, I belong to the lower middle class only. But I think that anyone who is an experienced investor and manages his or her wealth well will realize that a high salary income is not the most crucial factor in getting rich. The key is whether an investor can grab good investment opportunities at the right timing. These opportunities often only present themselves every 2-3 years.

如果想总结如何抓住这些机会的话。我想就是如何提前把握未来可能出现的共识。建议大家不要跟着新闻和富人去拼财力。你需要到天涯海角，那些还未引人注意的地方，用你独特的眼睛发现那些机会。

Personally, the way to grasp these chances is to make a correct judgment about future consensus. But remember not to compete with old money or follow the advice by the mainstream media. Instead, you have to explore new opportunities in areas that have received less public attention. Use your unique perspectives to find these opportunities.

财富的本质上是"共识"。就是大家都觉得这个值钱，这个东西就会值钱。而人们在不同的时代，不同的空间达成不同的共识。比如，现在大家达成共识觉得房子很值钱。曾经大家觉得猴年邮票很值钱。远一点，大家觉三代贫农很值钱。再远一点，大家曾经觉得妇女小脚很值钱。很多共识，你仔细想一下其实没有什么道理，都是跟风起哄，都是想象出来的刚需，大部分时候都是为了面子。比如今天的日本，大家不再觉得必须拥有房子。年轻人对买房子没什么兴趣。而我天朝上国的年轻人，奇葩地形成了一个没房子不能结婚的共识。

The nature of wealth is "consensus." When everyone believes that a certain thing is worth a lot of money, it will be so. Human beings reach different consensus depending on the timing and geographical location. For example, in contemporary society, we all agree that real properties are valued. People used to believe that postage stamps in the Year of the Monkey were worth a lot of money. When we further examine China's modern history, we will find that the Chinese used to think that family background of three generations of peasants was a great asset. Going further back in history, we will see that people went after bound feet. All this consensus does not make much sense when examined closely. It's just a phenomenon of following the herd. The demands are purely based on a herd mentality that comes from imagination. In Chinese culture, we have a concept of face (mianzi) that represents a person's reputation and feelings of prestige within multiple spheres, including displaying wealth. While young Chinese people form a bizarre view that they will not get married without a wedding house, their Japanese counterparts are not interested in owning a real property.

有钱人达成共识的东西就会很值钱，比如最近 20 年中国的古董字画。同样的这些古董字画 20 年前很便宜，因为当时达成共识的人很穷。换句话说，我小时候小朋友达成共识觉得香烟壳子很珍贵。可是香烟壳子不值钱，因为我们小朋友当时口袋没有钱。投资人的任务就是成功地捕捉到这些共识在人群中的变化。

When rich people believe that a certain thing is or will be worth a lot of money, its price will go up. Take price changes in Chinese antiques and paintings in the past twenty years. Two decades ago, these antiques and paintings were very cheap because the people who reach a consensus were poor. In other words, when I was a child, my companions and I also reached a consensus that cigarette boxes were valuable. However, cigarette boxes were still cheap because children did not have any money. The job of investors is to find out the consensus among the public and how it is changing.

我举几个例子。

Let me give you a few more examples.

首先说说我最熟悉的房地产的例子。在上海过去十几年买房子的人都会发现，增值幅度最大的不是市中心的传统好区，既不是徐家汇，也不是黄浦区静安区。当然这些地方的房价也很贵。如果算起百分比增长的话，涨幅最高的是上海的张江。

My first example is real estate, with which I am the most familiar. Anyone who has bought a real property in Shanghai in the last decade or so will realize that the neighborhoods that have seen the greatest appreciation are not traditional hot spots such as Xujiahui, Huangpu, and Jingan, that are the city centers. Of course, the property prices in these communities are exorbitant too. But if we are talking about the percentage increase in prices, Zhangjiang is the winner.

为什么是这样的呢，因为上海的高校每年毕业的高才生们，他们集中去的地方是张江高新区。这些年轻人很聪明，未来事业发展前途无量。可是在他们刚刚毕业的时候，他们很穷，所以你的钱和他们去竞争，非常占便宜。当然很快随着他们的事业起步，薪资增加，他们会把他们工作和生活的地方的价格抬升上去。这些智力超群的年轻人也硬生生靠着他们强大的基因，让他们的孩子把张江变成了浦东最好的学区。

Why is this so? Because talented university graduates settle in Zhangjiang after their graduation. These young people are smart and have a bright future. However, when they are fresh out of college, they are poor. Competing with these people gives investors an advantage. As these young people develop their careers, the property prices in the areas where they live and work will also go up. Besides, these young people's intelligence will also be passed down to their children, who make Zhangjiang the best school district in Pudong.

同样的现象发生在北京，北京每年高校高才生们，他们集中去的地方是中关村，上地，五道口这些地方。 这些地方房价的升值比例也超过了市中心三环里面。

The same phenomenon also occurs in Beijing. Bright university graduates settle in communities such as Zhongguancun, Shangdi, and Wudaokou, driving the property prices in these areas higher than those in the city center.

如果你要投资，你需要跟着年轻人走，跟着未来走。跟着他们未来可能形成的共识，不要和 old money 去拼体力。

When it comes to investing, we need to follow the young, who are the future of our society. Try to follow any future consensus reached by these young people. Don't compete with old money.

回首往事，我第一次意识到需要在上海买房子的时候，是在 1998 年，那个时候我刚到美国不久。但我意识到中美的收入巨大差距不会一成不变。你在美国挣的钱，和当地人比起来是没有什么竞争力的，但是和尚处于贫困和低收入的中国，实在是比较合算的买卖。 当然，行动永远都会比自己的想法和计划差一点，我也是错过了很多京沪投资的机会，不过好歹总算是抓住了大头。

In retrospect, the first time I realized that I should buy investment properties in Shanghai was in 1998, when I had just settled in the U.S. At the time, it dawned on me that the huge income discrepancy between China and the U.S. would not remain unchanged. I did not have a big competitive advantage over other American investors because of my average salary income. However, when compared to people in China, many of whom were still living under the poverty line, I had an edge. Of course, plans never go as planned. I still missed many good investment opportunities in Beijing and Shanghai, but I managed to get on the bus.

美国投资房地产也有同样类似的规律。大家跟着 Hipsters（赶时髦的人）买房子。哪里 Hipsters 最集中，未来房价爆发的可能性最大。这个 Hipsters 用现在流行的中文就是屌丝。文化程度高，屌丝集中的地方，就是一个城市的未来。 所以有一个专门的研究发现，追踪屌丝最好的办法就是跟着星巴克。星巴克在那里开张，你就买附近的房子。 星巴克开每一个店都会仔细计算周围的屌丝人群。像成功而有钱中年大叔大婶是很少去星巴克的。

Real estate investing in the U.S. also shows a similar pattern. Real estate investors should follow the hipsters. The areas where hipsters are concentrated will probably see the greatest increase in property prices. Follow hipsters with a good educational background. They will be the future of the city. A research study shows that the best way to follow these well-educated hipsters is to follow the opening of new Starbucks stores. Buy an investment property in the community where a new Starbucks store will soon open. Starbucks' expansion strategy is to calculate the number of hipsters in that community because successful, rich, middle-aged people rarely go to Starbucks.

湾区就是这样一个屌丝汇集的地方。每年无数世界各地来的受过高等教育的屌丝，带着他们的聪明和勤奋，到这里成就他们的梦想。可是在他们梦想实现之前，他们还很穷。这和纽约很不一样，曼哈顿虽然是寸土寸金。但是你需要和华尔街的 old money 去竞争。而你的钱不占优势。

The Bay Area is a place full of hipsters. Every year, highly educated hipsters from around the world come to the Bay Area with their talents and diligence to achieve their dreams. However, before they succeed, they are poor. Therefore, the Bay Area is different from New York. Even though Manhattan's property prices are exorbitant, your competitors are old money from Wall Street. You don't have any competitive advantages over them with the little money you've got.

时间一晃就到了 2016 年，我开始关注加密货币。我最终决定重仓加密货币主要的原因是我发现买卖加密货币的主流人群都很穷。我去研究比特币到底是怎么回事，发现玩家居然经常提起的梦想就是 pay off student loan（付清学生贷款），挖矿挣几个币吃顿免费批萨。虽然他们都是受的高等教育，名校云集。可惜他们或者是学生，或者是博士，或者刚刚毕业，还没有挣到钱。我的钱以一当十。虽然你在 MIT，未来前途无量，但是在你变成富人达成共识之前，我的钱还是很值钱的。

In 2016, I started paying attention to cryptocurrencies. The reason why I decided to make a big investment in cryptocurrencies is that I realized most bitcoin traders were poor people. When I was researching bitcoins, the dreams of the users were to pay off student loans and buy pizzas with bitcoins. Even though they were highly educated and studied at prestigious universities, they were poor because they were still students or just graduated. Therefore, my money was worth even more when I tried to compete with them. Even though these young people might come from MIT and have a bright future, I had more purchasing power before they became rich.

展望未来，我自己的投资趋向保守。我觉得湾区和上海北京的房子，按照现在的价格都不再有暴利的机会了。中国未来几年的经济和政策方向看不清。美国利率在提高。所以我打算停止房地产的投资，安心等待后面的机会。加密货币的投资也是不再增加仓位，保持长期持有。Ethereum 有一次core programmers 开会，据说环顾四周，大家发现没有一个人不是千万富翁。我在文学城第一次写帖子介绍 Ethereum 的时候，价格是 10 美元。现在虽然历经暴跌，价格是 800 美元。

Looking ahead, I will continue to adopt a more conservative investment approach. I think that there is less room for making handsome profits in the real estate markets in the Bay Area, Shanghai, and Beijing. I am not sure about China's future economic developments. In addition, interest rates in the U.S. are increasing, so I have decided to pause my real estate investing and wait patiently for other opportunities in the future. Regarding my bitcoin investments, I will not add my position and will continue to long hold. Cryptocurrencies have created much wealth for many people. It was rumored that core programmers of Ethereum are now all millionaires. When I first wrote about Ethereum on wenxuecity.com, its price was US$10. Despite significant decreases, the current price is US$800.

如果你实在忍不住想要投资的话，看看每年硅谷来的年轻人都住在哪里。不要跟谷歌和苹果的那些富豪们去成熟好区拼体力。远离 old money.

If you really want to make an investment, try to find out where young people from Silicon Valley live in. Don't compete with billionaires and millionaires from Google and Apple in traditional real estate hot spots. Stay away from old money.

过去 11 年我笔耕不断，经常把自己的心得写出来和大家分享。BBS 上人多口杂，风凉话不断。如果感兴趣，大家可以翻翻 10 年前的帖子。我提出十年一千万的时候，冷嘲热讽远超过今天的加密货币。这些冷嘲热讽，负面作用就是常年非常打击我的写作积极性。中间很长一段时间几乎我都不写了。最近发现公众号挺有趣的，才重新捡起笔来。

In the last 11 years, I have been a diligent writer who is eager to share his tips and takeaways with readers. There are some haters on this forum who laughed at my $10-million-in-10-year goal. If you are interested, feel free to read my blog posts that were written 10 years ago. The mocking discouraged me from updating my blog for a very long time. It's only when I have recently discovered that managing a WeChat official account on investing is quite fascinating that I have started writing articles again.

2017 我对加密货币的介绍，尤其争议颇多。好像我在搞传销一样。很多次我会想，也许算了，不写也罢。现在反思一下，这么多年能够坚持下来，其实原因只有一个。孟子见梁惠王，曰："独乐乐，与人乐乐，孰乐乎？"曰"独乐乐不如众乐乐。"这是中学背诵的课文。年轻时候被教育洗脑了，无法改变。

My introduction to cryptocurrencies in 2017 was quite controversial. It seemed that I was hard-selling cryptocurrencies. There have been times that I wanted to give up writing this blog. The reason why I persevered is that I was inspired by the saying that "Happiness is only real when shared." I studied an ancient Chinese text that taught me this lesson, which has been deeply rooted in my mind.

自己一个人闷头发财是个挺没意思的事情，最多只能说明你运气好，不能证明你水平高，可复制。换成一句土老冒的话，"一个人富不算本事，带着全村富才是共同富裕。"我想也许这就是我能写下去，能够身体力行实践下去的动力吧。

The best we can say of a person who gets rich but is reluctant to share his or her tips with others is that he or she is lucky. It is difficult to say that such a person is a skilled investor who has developed a replicable investment strategy. As the old Chinese saying goes, "The only person who gets rich in his or her village quietly has achieved nothing. A great person will bring the whole village on the path of wealth." This also motivates me to keep writing my blog and helping others get rich.

迈向一亿美元的旅程 （2018）

Embarking on My Journey Toward US$100 million

By Bayfamily

微信公众号：WXC-Bayfamily

过完年了，大家都有这样的体会。人如果没有目标，很容易被日常的琐事所左右。最后忙碌了一年，回头一想觉得自己一年什么都没有做。时间也就稀里糊涂消失了。而有目标的人，也许平时也不显得更忙，但是最后总有成果。

After the Chinese New Year, I realized that if a person does not have a goal, he or she will be easily distracted by trivial matters in life and achieve nothing despite a busy life. They lose their precious time. In contrast, the life of individuals with goals is not as busy, but they often accomplish much every year.

投资也是一样，有目标和没有目标，几个月的时间里面，没有什么区别。日子久了就可以显示出差别来了。

The same also applies to investing. There may not be much difference between the performance of a person who has no goal and that of an individual who sets his or her eyes on a certain goal in the short term. However, as time goes by, the difference will be stark.

我自己也是，需要不断给自己设定目标点，给自己打气。如果一个人真的想做成什么，上帝都会跑来帮忙。如果一个人不想做什么事，很多理由会特别体贴地自动跑上门来，让你顺水推舟，借坡下驴。

That's why I have been setting goals to motivate myself. When you want something, all the universe conspires in helping you achieve it. If a person does not want anything, he or she will keep finding excuses for his or her inaction.

应该说，我自己都为自己十年新目标吓了一跳。我开车走神的时候想到这个数字，差点闯了一个红灯。

That being said, I was also startled by my new 10-year goal. I was distracted by this staggering number that I almost ran a red light while driving.

一亿美元还是很多钱的。美国大约一千万的个人拥有$1 million to $5 million 的财富。1.3 million 个人拥有$5 million to $25 million 的财富。大约15 万个家庭拥有$25 million 以上的财富。但是只有 5000 个家庭拥有超过一亿美元的财富。

US$100 million is a lot of money. In the U.S, about 10 million individuals have a net worth of $1-5 million; 1.3 million individuals have a net worth of $5-25 million, and around 150,000 families have a net worth of $25 million or above. However, only 5,000 households have a net worth of over $100 million.

美国有 50 个州。如果你拥有一亿美元。对于大多数中等规模的州而言，平均下来，你可以是州里最有钱的 100 个家庭。

There are 50 states in America. If your household net worth is US$100 million, your family may be one of the richest 100 households in the most average states.

这可不是闹着玩的，不是简单拥有几个豪宅就可以做到的。所以我为自己的狂想也吓了一跳。

This goal of US$100 million is no joke. It will take much more than owning a few luxury properties. I was again startled by my own ambition.

世上无难事，只怕肯攀登。

When there's a will, there's a way.

那么来看看现实情况，对于我而言有没有可能呢？

That being said, it is crucial to assess the realistic possibility of me achieving this goal.

如果买房子，考虑通货膨胀等因素，按照湾区 100 万美元一套投资房子计算。你需要管理 100-200 套房子。才能净资产达到 1 亿美元。这理论上，可以做到。当然很难，这么多房子有很多不可控的风险。

If I want to achieve this goal by relying on real estate investments, I will have to manage 100-200 properties, taking into account factors such as inflation and assuming that each of my investment properties in the Bay Area costs US$1 million. This is theoretically feasible. However, it is fraught with challenges because managing such a large number of investment properties involves many uncontrollable risks.

如果在上海北京买房子，按照 1000 万人民币一套。你大约需要 60 套房子付清贷款。中国买房子是个体力活。买 60 套房子，先不说限购，就是跑这么多房子，哪怕雇了全职的经纪人也会把你累死。

What about buying investment properties in Shanghai and Beijing? Assuming that each investment property costs CN¥10 million (approximately US$1.5 million), I will need to manage sixty such investment properties and achieve my goal when the mortgages of all these sixty properties are paid off. Buying investment properties in China is exhausting. Even putting the issue of getting around the limited purchase policy aside, I will probably exhaust myself to death even if I hire a full-time manager.

常言道：

泥瓦匠，住草房；卖盐的，喝淡汤。种田的，吃米糠；做奶妈，卖儿郎。

As the famous Chinese nursery rhyme goes, "Bricklayers live in houses made of grasses; Salt merchants cook with tasteless condiments; Rice growers eat rice brans, and nannies ever get to take care of their own babies."

会走路的钱
Money Walks

钱是为人服务的。我也不想为了一个亿把自己累得半死。管钱变成全职工作，每天和淘粪的各种烦恼打交道。今年过节照镜子，发现鬓角第一根白发。人生苦短，还是及时行乐为好。

Money is here to serve us, so I don't want to exhaust myself to death in return for US$100 million. When managing my money becomes my full-time job, all sorts of troubles will also come, for example, I will need to be a gong farmer every day. During this Chinese New Year, I looked at the mirror one day and found my first grey hair. Life is short, and I should seize the day.

股票市场从一千万成长到一个亿会轻松很多。但是需要时间。股票是不可能 time market 的。所以按照 8% 的成长率，你需要大约 20-30 年时间。

It's quite easy to grow $1 million to $100 million in the stock market. All it takes is time. As it is impossible to time the stock market, I will need about 20-30 years to grow $1 million into US$100 million by relying on stock investments, assuming an annual growth rate of 8%.

所以一个亿不是小数字。也是美国只有 5000 个家庭能做到的原因。如果是房地产的积累，大部分人止步于 2000 万这个数量级。做到一亿美元只有通过公司和股票。

Therefore, US$100 million is quite an astronomical number. It's no wonder that only 5,000 families in the U.S. have managed to achieve this. If we merely rely on real estate investing, most people's portfolios will stop at US$20 million. The only way to achieve US$100 million is through companies and stocks.

苹果、谷歌、股票市值不到一万亿美元。如果你想拥有一亿美元，大约需要持有万分之一这些公司的股票。

The market capitalizations of Apple and Google are about US$1 trillion each. In other words, if you want to have a net worth of US$100 million, you need to own 1/10000 of such a company's shares.

对于我而言，我现在唯一能看到的渠道是加密货币。我觉得这也很难。但是至少是可能的。因为我觉得有一种很大的可能，整个金融业在未来 10-20 年，会被加密货币颠覆掉。

Personally, the only feasible way I can achieve my goal is through cryptocurrencies. I know that this will be difficult, but at least it is a possibility. I feel that there is a huge possibility that the finance industry will be disrupted by cryptocurrencies in the next 10-20 years.

为了更好地理解加密货币，我先来说说过去 20 年的互联网发展历史。这段历史对加密货币的发展非常有借鉴意义。

In order to better understand what cryptocurrencies are, let me first go through a brief history of the development of the internet in the last two decades, which will serve as a useful reference point for us to estimate how far cryptocurrencies will go.

整理一下思路，如果我没有记错的话。最近一些年，记忆力有时不好使。

This is also my attempt to organize my thoughts. In recent years, my memory seems to have deteriorated.

在我看来，互联网的发展，大约有这么三个阶段：

If I am not mistaken, there are three stages of the development of the internet.

1990-1995 年之间，大约互联网的"发现"阶段。就是大家都觉得这个是能够改变世界的东西。但是还不确定。互联网还很难用，最常见的用途是大家通过互联网传播黄色图片。我记得自己用过 telenet, gopher, ACT, 这些现在看来像石器时代一样的东西。和加密货币一样，那个时候，只有高校的年轻人玩互联网。我记得最搞笑的一次经验。一个国内的同学给我写信，居然把我给他的 email 地址写在信封上。他以为那是邮递员用的地址。

The "discovery" stage of the internet is 1990-1995. During this period, everyone thought that the internet could change the world, even though they were not so sure about how. It was difficult to use the internet. The most common use was people spreading pornographic pictures through the internet. At the time, I used networks such as Telnet, gopher, and ACT, which now seemed to be as ancient as the Stone Age. Just like cryptocurrencies, the internet was something that only college students were interested in back then. I have a funny anecdote to share with you. One time, a classmate of mine who was in China wrote a letter to me. He wrote my email address on the envelope because he thought that was a special address used by the post office.

这个阶段结束的标志性事件，我觉得是 Netscape 横空出世。互联网开始在大众中普及。可是那个时候大家除了看看黄色图片，还是不知道有啥用。一个著名的诺奖经济学奖获得者总结说，互联网没啥了不起，就是一个大的 Fax machine。

The advent of Netscape, which made the internet accessible to the general public, marked the end of this stage. However, people still had no idea about the uses of the internet, other than for porn. A famous Nobel Prize laureate in Economics once concluded that there was nothing special about the internet and that it was probably just an enormous fax machine.

1996-2000 年之间，这是互联网的"基础设施"建设阶段。这是互联网的第一次高潮。2001 年，Dotcom 泡沫破裂，是这个阶段的结束。我觉得应该叫基础设施阶段，那个时候报纸天天叫喊的是如何解决最后一公里的问题。就是如何让千家万户通上宽带。那个时候如日中天的公司是美国在线 AOL，YAHOO。　但是每个互联网公司都没解决自己的盈利模式。不知道怎样才能赚钱。

The "infrastructure" stage of the internet is 1996-2000. This is also the first climax in the development. In 2001, the dot-com bubble burst, marking the end of this stage. The reason why I name this period the "infrastructure" stage is that the mainstream media was talking about how to solve the "last kilometer problem," namely, how to connect thousands of households to the internet. At the time, companies such as AOL and YAHOO were booming. However, all these internet companies had not solved the profit problem yet. They were clueless about how to make money.

2001-2010 年，我觉得是互联网的"应用"阶段。这个阶段才是真正的庞然大物出现时候。在 Dotcom 的废墟上，出现了一批人们今天广泛使用，并且盈利的公司。比如 Google, Amazon, Facebook,腾讯，阿里巴巴。

I think that 2001-2010 is the "deployment" stage of the internet. Gigantic companies emerged against the backdrop of the ruins of the dot-com bubble. These companies, such as Google, Amazon, Facebook, Tencent, and Alibaba, have now become an indispensable part of our daily lives and made staggering profits.

如果你做类似的对比，你看加密货币的发展就很清晰了。应该也是类似的三个阶段。我觉得所有的变革性的技术都是这样三个阶段。加密货币现在处于 1998 左右的互联网阶段，即"基础设施"建设的中期。

If we make a comparison, we will have a much clearer picture of the development of cryptocurrencies, which will also entail similar stages. In fact, I believe that any revolutionary technological changes will all undergo these three stages. Cryptocurrencies are now in the middle of the "infrastructure stage," similar to how the internet was developing in around 1998.

2009-2015. 这是加密货币的"发现"阶段。就是一些年轻人，极客，发明了比特币这样神奇的东西，然后他们互相玩得很开心。比特币用了 8 年时间证明这个东西有生命力，很多人意识到区块链，加密货币会颠覆性改变人类的生产和合作方式，甚至颠覆掉整个人类的金融系统。但是怎样实现完全不知道。比特币和当年的互联网一样，主要任务是洗钱，涉及黄赌毒的买卖和交易，以及 Wikileak 这样的反政府机构。

2009-2015 is the "discovery stage" of cryptocurrencies. Some young people and geeks invented such a fascinating technological invention as bitcoins, and they were having fun. The proponents of bitcoins used eight years to prove that bitcoins are a vital development. Many people have started to realize that blockchains and cryptocurrencies will completely change the way we collaborate and how the economy operates. They will even overthrow the entire financial system, even though we don't know the "how?" The main usage of bitcoins was money-laundering. The main users of bitcoins are antigovernment organizations such as WikiLeaks and parties in transactional sex, gambling, and drug dealing.

2016-2019 我觉得是加密货币的基础"设施"阶段。以太坊横空出世。ICO 解决了加密货币可以有什么用途的问题。一下子所有的主要区块链网络发生拥塞。大家比的是哪个加密货币速度快，容量大。哪个平台可以承载更多的交易。每天研究争吵的是扩容问题(scaling problem). 不过你别忘了，要想解决 scaling problem，你需要先有 scaling problem 扩容问题斗争最激烈的就是比特币，整个 2017 几乎全部就是比特币扩容之争年。

I think that 2016-2019 will be the "infrastructure" stage of cryptocurrencies. The advent of Ethereum ICO has solved the problem of "What other uses do cryptocurrencies have?" All of a sudden, the major blockchain networks are congested. People are comparing the speed and storage of these cryptocurrencies and which platform can handle more transactions. They are also debating the scaling problem. Let's not forget that in order to solve a scaling problem, we have to first have such a problem. The most heated debate is on the scaling problem of bitcoins. The entire year of 2017 is the peak of such a debate.

如果不出意外的话。随着比特币闪电网上线，EOS 的纵横扩容，ETH 的 sharding, plasma 上线，而大量的后起之秀第三代加密货币，如 IOTA，Nano 等，扩容问题会在 2018 年末，2019 年初渐渐解决。

2019 年以后，我觉得是加密货币的"Deployment (应用)"真正开始出现的时候。那个时候会有 killer app 出来。Killer app 我觉得至少会有如下这些应用。

I believe that the "deployment" stage of cryptocurrencies will only arrive after 2019. At the time, we will have killer apps, which will at least have the following applications:

首当其冲的是华尔街的债券市场。债券市场是最容易用智能合约实现的。智能合约下的债券市场比现在的效率高出不知道多少倍。省去了大量中间商的费用。

1. Efficient bond transactions. The wave of change will first hit Wall Street's bond market because it is the easiest to adopt smart contracts in the bond market. Smart contracts will drastically improve the efficiency of the bond market and save a significant amount of transaction costs incurred by the need for middlemen.

其次是股票市场。股票市场会被 tokenize, 或者叫作 ethereumized。24 小时连续交易，没有交易费用的股票平台，会渐渐成为主流平台。STO，或者监管下的 ICO，会取代风投和 ICO。

2. Efficient stock transactions. The stock market will be tokenized or ethereumized. Trading platforms that trade 24/7 and do not charge transaction fees will become the mainstream. STO, or supervised ICO, will replace venture capital and ICO.

然后是点对点的支付 killer app。类似现在的微信支付宝的手机支付，但是去中心化手机支付会渐渐取代 Visa。Visa 5%的收费在加密货币面前毫无竞争力。大家支付的还是美元或者人民币，但是底层的交易支持全部是加密货币。其他的应用场景很多。比如房地产，房地产的交易模式，贷款方式和 Title 的保存方式都会被改变。2018 已经有四个 ICO 涉及这个领域。不展开写了。

3. Efficient P2P payments on killer apps. They will be similar to the mobile payment methods offered by WeChat and Alipay. However, decentralized mobile payment methods will gradually replace Visa. The 5% Visa fees will be easily defeated by cryptocurrencies. People will still be paying in the U.S. dollar or the Chinese Yuan, but the most basic transactions will be in cryptocurrencies. There are many other applications of P2P payments, for example, real estate. Real estate transactions, loans, and methods to keep legal titles will all change. In 2018, there have already been four Initial Coin Offerings (ICO) in real estate, and I will not go into detail.

最后我觉得才是，Reserve currency。就是让加密货币取代法币成为真正的全球储蓄货币。我觉得这是最后一步，也是最难的一步，牵涉到的税务，政治文化因素太多。希望比特币能完成这个光荣的使命，不过一切尚且未知。

4. Reserve currency. Cryptocurrencies replacing fiat money to become a global reserve currency is the last step in this stage. This is also the most difficult step because it involves tax issues, political and cultural factors. I hope that bitcoins can achieve this glorious mission, but everything remains uncertain.

未来的事情太远了看不清。历史会重演，但是一般不会简单重复。

To be honest, the future is distant, and I cannot see clearly the picture ahead. That being said, history doesn't repeat itself, but it does rhyme.

如果历史有什么可以借鉴的话，我觉得会在完成加密货币基础设施建设，到 Deployment 阶段之间有一次大的泡沫崩溃。这个时间节点应该在 2018 年末到 2020 年初某个时候。需要等到整个华尔街都 fear of missing out（恐慌错过上车）的时候。

Applying the lessons that I learned from the history of technology, I believe that there will be a collapse caused by a bubble between the infrastructure stage and the deployment stage. The timing will be the end of 2018 or the beginning of 2020 when Wall Street falls victim to FOMO (fear of missing out).

如果这个时间节点有什么历史案例可循的话，就是当年的 AOL 吞并了时代华纳。在我看来，当年的时代华纳是处于极度的恐惧才被 AOL 用很低廉的价格合并掉的。时代华纳是做传媒的，而当时的互联网的架势是能够把所有的传媒一网打尽。

A similar historical story is how AOL acquired Time Warner. In my opinion, the reason why Time Warner was acquired by AOL at a very low price was that the former was in deep fear. Time Warner was a media company, and the booming internet industry was like a tiger catching its prey, the media industry.

能让华尔街感到恐惧的时候，就是华尔街意识到加密货币会把传统金融一网打尽的时候。那个时候会出现大规模的兼并重组。人人都想逃离传统的金融模式。我想那个时候，应该是泡沫吹到最大的时候。

When Wall Street realizes that cryptocurrencies will disrupt, or even destroy, the traditional finance industry, it will be in deep fear. Large-scale mergers and acquisitions and restructuring may take place. That everyone is trying to escape the traditional financial model signals the peak of the bubble.

在这个大的泡沫崩溃的前夜，如果我能顺利高点逃出，并且用逃出的资金成功抓到下一个加密货币 Deployment 阶段的 Google，下一个 Facebook，拥有它们的万分之一。那么我可能可以走上 5000 万到一亿美元这个台阶。而且我需要做的事情很少很少。只需要点点鼠标卖出和买入各一次即可。一点也不累。有大把的时间享受人生。只是这个时机的判断我自己也不知道能否把握好。

On the night before this gigantic bubble bursts, if I can successfully exit the market by selling at the highest point and then use the capital to invest in the next "Google" in the cryptocurrency market in its deployment stage, I will then progress to the next milestone in my investment journey, which is $50-100 million. I only need to own 1/10000 of the company's shares. There is not much work involved. I only need to click my mouse two times: "sell" and then "buy." There is nothing tiring, and I will have plenty of time to enjoy my life. However, I am not sure if I can make a correct judgment about the timing.

这很难，不但需要头脑清晰，还需要命好。因为如意算盘你可以随便打，事情发展也许完全和你想的不一样。也是只能走一步看一步。

Successfully executing this plan is very difficult. Not only will I need to approach the stock market and cryptocurrency market with a clear mind, but I will also need some luck. No matter how detailed our plans are, they often don't go as planned. I can only execute my plans step-by-step while constantly making adjustments.

虽然很难很难，但是不是不可能。

Even though I said that it will be difficult, it is still doable.

不过，即使失败也没啥，继续收租子当老地主。

Anyway, it won't hurt even if I fail. I may as well go back to my old life of being a landlord.

计划写完了，加州阳光这么好，掸掸灰尘迎接春天。

That's the end of my investment plan. The weather in California is lovely, and I am embracing Spring.

Disclaimer (友情提醒)：本人非专业财经人士，所有言论只供娱乐和酒后吹牛使用，没有任何财经参考价值。千万不要轻易模仿和跟随投资。加密货币投资风险极高极高，随时会暴跌 90%-100%。因为不受政府监管，所以市场价格操纵现象严重，市场充斥大量非法集资与传销。比特币等加密货币源代码公开，任何人都可以 copy-paste 滥发。历史上 90%的加密货币最终都已死掉和清零，未来也会如此。加密货币技术非常不成熟。Coinbase 每天平均有六个客户被盗。几乎每月都有大型 coin exchange(币交易所)被黑客攻陷。因为本人持有加密货币，你的每笔买进都是直接间接在帮我抬轿子。

Disclaimer: I am not a professional finance worker. All content is for entertainment and discussion purposes only. They are not financial advice or recommendations. Please do not follow the content in your investments without exercising your own judgment. The risks of cryptocurrency investments are extremely high. They may plummet by 90-100% anytime. As cryptocurrency markets are not subject to government regulation, price-fixing is rampant. Meanwhile, the markets are full of illegal fundraising and multi-level marketing campaigns. In addition, the source codes of cryptocurrencies such as bitcoins are public, so anyone can copy and paste them. 90% of bitcoins have hitherto died or been eliminated. This will happen in the future too. Meanwhile, the technologies of cryptocurrencies are still developing. On average, there are six cases of thefts on Coinbase every day, and a large-scale coin exchange platform is hacked almost every month. You should also note that as I own cryptocurrencies, an increase in buying, including your activity, will benefit me either directly or indirectly.

比特币政策风险很高，随时会被各国政府取缔而清零。加密货币涉嫌大量的黄、赌、毒、洗钱等非法交易。你的币来源可能涉嫌非法活动，所以随时会被执法人员抄没，被 FBI 破门而入，被 CIA 跟踪调查，被银监会或

IRS 查封银行账户，被支付宝删除账号，被朝阳区吃瓜群众暴力扭送司法机关。

The policy risks associated with bitcoins are also high because governments worldwide may ban them anytime. Cryptocurrencies involve a large amount of illegal trading, such as transactional sex, gambling, drug dealing, and money-laundering. Therefore, your bitcoins may come from illegal activities and be confiscated by law enforcement anytime. The FBI may suddenly break into your house; you may be followed and investigated by the CIA; your bank accounts may be seized by banking regulatory commissions or IRS; your Alipay accounts may be deleted, and you may be arrested by violent citizens.

比特币等加密货币被 5000 年历史悠久的东方巨龙级文明古国明文严令取缔，被历史更悠久的金字塔国埃及认定违反神圣教义，被风景优美的湄公河国越南定为非法，被风景更优美的珠穆朗玛峰尼泊尔国定为违规，被风景最最优美的美女之国委内瑞拉禁止，被同志加兄弟的朝鲜国认定为帝国主义阴谋，被亡我之心不死的樱花国日本认定为合法货币支付手段。希望自觉遵守当地法律，保持和世界五大洲各国真理局统帅部思想始终高度一致。

Cryptocurrencies such as bitcoins are strictly banned by such an ancient Eastern civilization that has 5000 years of history as China; deemed contrary to religious beliefs by a more ancient civilization famous for its pyramids, Egypt; illegalized by a country that is located along the Mekong River and enjoys beautiful sceneries, Vietnam; declared illegal by a country that enjoys an even more breathtaking view because of Mt. Everest, Nepal; banned by the country with the most captivating view in the world, Venezuela, the country of gorgeous women; and considered an imperial conspiracy by North Korea. Meanwhile, Japan, an ambitious country of Sakura, officially recognized cryptocurrencies as a legal medium of exchange. Please abide by local laws and align your views with the governing regimes worldwide.

加密货币投资和毒品一样极其容易上瘾，和邪教传销模式一样让人无法自拔，倾家荡产。加密货币制幻作用强烈，让人无法分清什么是真假，什么是钱什么是数字，什么是虚拟什么是现实。故名虚拟货币，魔幻现实。

Cryptocurrencies are as addictive as drugs and multi-level marketing campaigns. Players or users may easily lose every single penny. Cryptocurrencies have the ability to confuse the users so that they cannot tell nature from imagination, money from numbers, reality from the virtual world. This is why the Chinese translation of cryptocurrencies is "Virtual Currencies." They are magical and surreal.

总之，请勿在现在和将来买进、持有任何一种加密货币。远离毒品，远离虚拟货币。

To sum up, please do not buy or own any kind of cryptocurrencies in the present or in the future. Stay away from drugs and stay away from cryptocurrencies.

微信公众号：WXC-Bayfamily
官网主页：https://bayfamily.us
微信号：key-east
邮箱：Bayfamily2020@gmail.com

WeChat Official Account: WXC-Bayfamily
Homepage: https://bayfamily.us
WeChat Contact: key-east
Email: bayfamily2020@gmail.com

Made in the USA
Las Vegas, NV
30 April 2024

89347189R00302